# Charles W. Kegley, Jr. / Eugene R. Wittkopf
University of South Carolina              Louisiana State University

# WORLD

# POLITICS

## TREND AND TRANSFORMATION

### Fifth Edition

St. Martin's Press
New York

*For Linda and Barbara*

*Executive editor:* Don Reisman
*Manager, publishing services:* Emily Berleth
*Editor, publishing services:* Doug Bell
*Project management:* Till & Till, Inc.
*Production supervisor:* Joe Ford
*Text design:* Patrice Fodero
*Graphics:* TCSystems, Inc.
*Maps:* Maryland CartoGraphics, Inc.
*Cover photo:* Copyright © COMSTOCK, INC./Mike and Carol Werner

Library of Congress Catalog Card Number: 94-65227
Manufactured in the United States of America.
98765
fedcba

For information, write:
St. Martin's Press, Inc.
175 Fifth Avenue
New York, NY 10010

ISBN: 0-312-10658-0

Published and distributed outside North America by
THE MACMILLAN PRESS LTD
Houndmills, Basingstoke, Hampshire RG21 2XS and London
Companies and representatives throughout the world.

ISBN 0-333-63760-7

A catalogue record for this book is available from the British Library.

## ACKNOWLEDGMENTS

Acknowledgments and copyrights are continued at the back of the book on page 612, which constitute an extension of the copyright page.

# PREFACE

. . .

Since publication of the fourth edition of this book in 1993, the world has continued to witness dramatic changes. The end of the Cold War, the third great-power conflict of the twentieth century, is propelling a transformation of world politics whose scope and dimensions continue to unfold daily. The end of East–West competition has marked the end of bipolarity, the disintegration of the Soviet external empire and the Soviet Union itself, the emergence of powerful economic rivals to the United States (from China, Japan, and Germany to the European Union), and the triumph of liberalism and democratic capitalism over competing ideologies. Yet in this emerging new system, nuclear weapons—so dominant a part of world politics since World War II—have not receded in importance, despite the Strategic Arms Reduction Treaty (START) and other monumental disarmament agreements. The threat of new nuclear powers remains, and this could undermine the fragile nonproliferation regime. At the same time, economic power increasingly rivals military power as an instrument of statecraft, and embryonic trade blocs in Europe and Asia portend the emergence of a multipolar world. In addition, war and other forms of violence inspired by ethnic and nationalist animosities long suppressed by the Cold War have erupted with increasing frequency and ferocity; bullets and bloodshed still cast their shadow over the late twentieth century.

Understanding the rapid changes unleashed in the wake of the Cold War poses an enormous challenge to scholars and policymakers alike. There no longer exists a principal axis in world affairs, and no agreement exists about the dimensions of world politics that will be most important in the twenty-first century. This uncertainty requires that we confront not only the evidence of change but also of continuities in world politics. It makes it imperative that we also probe the theoretical underpinnings of our knowledge and ask not only what is new but also how we know what we know about the forces of change and continuity in the world around us.

*World Politics: Trend and Transformation* is a comprehensive treatment of the theory and evidence that inform our understanding of the pattern of relations among global actors, the historical developments that underlie them, and how they have been affected by the pace of change of today's world.

The book is divided into five parts. Part I explains the macro, or holistic, view of world politics that frames the book's analyses. It focuses on the contending analytic perspectives that scholars and policymakers have developed to comprehend the kaleidoscopic trends and transformations occurring in world politics. We draw on these theoretical traditions throughout the remainder of the book, using them to enhance an understanding of contemporary world politics.

Part II examines the principal actors on the world stage. Nation-states necessarily command particular attention, and we examine the nature of their decision-making processes, world views, national capabilities, and position in the international hierarchy, all of which propel their efforts to adapt policies to changes in their external environments. Great-power rivalries, as played out in the three global conflicts of the twentieth century and the North–South conflict between the world's rich and poor countries since World War II, are given prominent attention. We also examine the role of international institutions and other nonstate actors, with particular emphasis on international organizations and nongovernmental organizations (such as the United Nations and multinational corporations) and on nonstate entities such as recently resurgent ethnonational movements. This treatment explores the capacity of each of these actors to shape contemporary world politics, and the ways in which the international environment, in turn, shapes their character.

Parts III and IV probe the nature of transnational policy issues. Issues comprising material well-being and countries' efforts to provide for their citizens' general welfare are examined in Part III. Here we explore the nature of the world political economy, the forces promoting conflict and cooperation within the new global marketplace, and developments in demography, the environment, and resources. Although these issues have long been important on the global agenda, many analysts now believe that increasingly they will figure more prominently in the currency of world politics.

In Part IV we examine peace and security and the factors underlying preparations for national defense, the nature of power and influence, the role of military force, and the causes and control of war and other forms of violence in world politics. These, of course, are concerns that have traditionally received the most attention in discussions of world politics, and, as noted, while the end of the Cold War may have changed their character, it has not diminished the compelling need to understand military power and the causes and consequences of changes in its distribution.

We conclude *World Politics: Trend and Transformation* in Part V, where we explore how the underlying trajectories in world politics might influence future trends. Our concern here is how today's world will affect tomorrow's world as well as the policy problems recent developments create for the twenty-first century on the horizon.

# NEW TO THIS EDITION

Readers familiar with the previous edition of the book, published in 1993, will quickly recognize that its structure and organization remain intact, but the global changes that have occurred since have caused us to revisit and refine every passage in the book. We also seized this opportunity simultaneously to expand the book's theoretical coverage and to enhance its pedagogical effectiveness. The result is a thoroughly revised text.

In short, the fifth edition captures and explains all the major changes that have occurred since publication of the fourth edition in 1993. The revised text describes a transformed international system that no longer includes a Soviet empire, a Soviet Union run by a Soviet Communist Party, a Warsaw Pact, a Yugoslavia, a Czechoslovakia, a South Africa firmly based in apartheid and run by Afrikaners who still had Nelson Mandela imprisoned and who gave no sign of ever being willing to substantially change their ways, and governments and institutions in a host of other places—Japan and NATO to name but two—whose previous political composition and familiar policy purposes seemed all but permanently installed to us. The world has been turned upside down, and the fifth edition of *World Politics* explains the meaning of these transformations—and others—for the twenty-first century.

Several examples illustrate how thoroughly this edition has been revised:

- The survey of theories has been reorganized to (1) emphasize more the role of perceptions and images, (2) introduce feminist theories and the feminist critique of realism, (3) bring rival theories to the realist perspective up to date, (4) introduce the postmodern critique better and more thoroughly, and (5) reposition regime and hegemonic stability theory to more accurately show how they lie at the intersection of realism and liberalism.

- Neoliberalism is elaborated as a newly popular theoretical umbrella that gives meaning to the European Union, democratization, free trade, international law, international organizations, and other dimensions of global change and cooperation.

- Hegemonic stability theory and the contribution of classical and structural realism, or neorealism, to understanding of the forces that inhibit international cooperation are given revised treatment. Both theoretical thrusts are used to explain the importance of the relative position of U.S. power, in comparison with ascending great powers like China and Japan, and how these changes relate to the world political economy and the emergent multipolar international political system.

- The regionalization of the world political economy, as manifested in transnational capital flows and the emergence of regional monetary and trade blocs, is covered more thoroughly.

- The treatment of the global marketplace has been expanded and updated, so as to cover the recently approved and enlarged North American Free Trade Agreement (NAFTA), the General Agreement on Tariffs and Trade (GATT), and other trade agreements, as well as neomercantilist attempts to impose new protective barriers to trade.

- The treatment of nonstate actors is refined and updated to better picture the place and performance of intergovernmental international organizations (IGOs), nongovernmental organizations (NGOs), and ethnonational movements in the global arena.

- The coverage of the global refugee problem, migration, and expatriates is expanded, along with a better historical description of the origins of this growing problem.

- New sections deal with ethnicity in international politics and in particular the causes of ethnonationalism and its consequences as a source of international conflict.

- The cultural dimensions of world politics are treated more heavily, with particular attention given to the thesis that a "clash of civilizations and/or cultures" will replace the East–West conflict as the globe's primary axis.

- Greater attention is explicitly given to the moral and ethical dimensions of many of the problems discussed (war, refugees, gender issues, political repression, income disparities, minority persecution, etc.).

- The chapter on great-power relations has been totally reorganized (1) to compare three global wars in the twentieth century, (2) to account for the probability that two rivals (the United States and the USSR) will be replaced by at least five (the United States, Russia, China, Japan, and Germany), and (3) to look to the future of a twenty-first-century multipolar system.

- The chapter on national security has been revised and expanded to provide a comparison of the evolving national security strategies of the United States, Russia, China, Japan, and Germany, as well as to treat the rise of regional powers in a shifting strategic environment.

- The shifting strategic/military balance is assessed in terms of disarmament agreements such as START and the Chemical Weapons Convention, but more pointedly in terms of the continuing arms trade and threat of new nuclear weapon states that could undermine the prospects for renewal of the Nuclear Nonproliferation Treaty in 1995.

- The analysis of changes in warfare captures the rise of separatist revolts and changes in the incidence of interstate wars since the Cold War and accommodates recent thinking about the roots of violence.

- The institutional characteristics of the European Union and its changing character as a nonstate actor are brought up to date, along with an enlarged North Atlantic Treaty Organization (NATO) and changes in its membership, geographical scope, and strategic doctrine.

- In the wake of the Cold War and the Persian Gulf War, the prospects for multilateral cooperation and collective security as a substitute for the balance-of-power mechanism in the management of future international conflict are examined, and treatment of UN peacekeeping and peacemaking operations and the reconfigured NATO is expanded.

- Just war theory is updated in light of recent developments in international law.

- Trends toward democratization of the world, and the countertrends away from that liberalization and their consequences, are freshly examined.

- New maps and cartograms have been added, all designed to enhance the clarity of the text and contribute to readers' geographic literacy.

- The glossary has been amended to facilitate the book's accessibility by providing definitions of key terms and esoteric concepts.

The list of those to whom we are indebted for their contributions of time and insight to this book continues to grow. In addition to those who have helped so generously in the past, we are especially pleased to acknowledge the contributions to this edition made by Arthur G. Atkins, Shannon Lindsey Blanton, Mark N. Crislip, Michael Gubser, Pamela R. Howard, Pavel Kaźmierczyk, John N. Kinnas, Dunbar Lockwood, Jeffrey Morton, Christina Payne, Gregory A. Raymond, Joseph Reap, Linda S. Schwartz, and Franke Wilmer. We would also like to thank our colleagues who reviewed the manuscript for St. Martin's Press and offered many helpful comments and suggestions: Eileen M. Crumm, University of Southern California; Patrick J. Haney, Miami University; and D. Michael Shafer, Rutgers University. The many professional staff members at St. Martin's Press contributed importantly to the final production of the book. Mary Hugh Lester, our charming and responsive editor, eased the strains of final production measurably, and Don Reisman, our editor and friend, was unfailing in his support and encouragement throughout a project that exceeded our wildest time and effort estimates. Finally, we are appreciative of the professional assistance provided by Suzanne Mieso and Russell Till for the book's production.

Charles W. Kegley Jr.<br>
Eugene R. Wittkopf

## Note to Instructors

We would like to note the availability of an Instructor's Manual, authored by Gregory A. Raymond of Boise State University. This manual closely follows the major themes of *World Politics* and has been extensively class tested. Featured in the manual are chapter outlines, thematic summaries, learning objectives, key terms, teaching suggestions, and—for each chapter—approximately five essay and twenty-five multiple-choice questions—the latter of which are graded for degree of difficulty. Additionally, the manual contains enlarged versions of the major maps and line art that appear in the text, for use as transparency masters. The manual is available in both print form and in formats for IBM-compatible and Macintosh computers. For more information, please write or call St. Martin's Press, College Desk, 175 Fifth Avenue, New York, NY 10010 **(1-800-446-8923)** or Fax (212) 780-0115; or contact your local St. Martin's Press sales representative.

# About the Authors

CHARLES W. KEGLEY JR. received his doctorate from Syracuse University. Currently, he is Pearce Professor of International Relations at the University of South Carolina. President of the International Studies Association (1993–1994), Kegley has held appointments at Georgetown University, the University of Texas, Rutgers University, and the People's University of China. He is the editor of *Controversies in International Relations Theory: Realism and the Neoliberal Challenge* (St. Martin's Press, 1995) and *The Long Postwar Peace* (HarperCollins, 1991). With Gregory A. Raymond, Kegley is the coauthor of *A Multipolar Peace? Great-Power Politics in the Twenty-First Century* (St. Martin's Press, 1994) and *When Trust Breaks Down: Alliance Norms and World Politics* (University of South Carolina Press, 1990).

EUGENE R. WITTKOPF received his doctorate from Syracuse University. Currently R. Downs Poindexter Professor of Political Science at Louisiana State University, Wittkopf is a past president of the Florida Political Science Association and of the International Studies Association/South. He has also held appointments at the University of Florida and the University of North Carolina at Chapel Hill. Wittkopf is the author of *Faces of Internationalism: Public Opinion and American Foreign Policy* (Duke University Press, 1990) and the editor of the second editions of *The Future of American Foreign Policy* (St. Martin's Press, 1994) and *The Domestic Sources of American Foreign Policy* (St. Martin's Press, 1994).

Together, Kegley and Wittkopf have coauthored and edited several texts and readers for St. Martin's Press, including *American Foreign Policy: Pattern and Process*, fourth edition (1991); *The Future of American Foreign Policy* (1992); *The Nuclear Reader: Strategy, Weapons, War*, second edition (1989); and *The Domestic Sources of American Foreign Policy* (1988). They are also the coeditors of *The Global Agenda: Issues and Perspectives*, fourth edition (McGraw-Hill, 1995).

# Summary Table of Contents

• • •

# CONTENTS

• • •

# MAPS

• • •

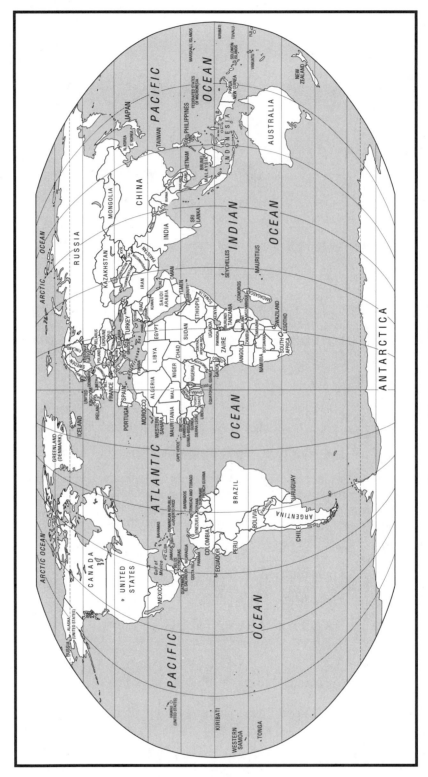

POLITICAL MAP OF THE WORLD

# Change and Transformation in World Politics

. . .

# CHAPTER 1

. . .

# INTRODUCING TREND AND TRANSFORMATION IN WORLD POLITICS: THEMES

. . .

*Historic changes since 1989 have profoundly destabilized the previously existing order without replacing it with any recognizable or legitimate system. New vacuums are setting off new conflicts. Old problems are being solved, begetting new ones.*

Chester A. Crocker,
Former U.S. Secretary of State, 1993

*Today, a generation raised in the shadows of the Cold War assumes new responsibilities in a world warmed by the sunshine of freedom but threatened by ancient hatreds and new plagues. . . . Profound and powerful forces are shaking and remaking our world, and the urgent question of our time is whether we can make change our friend and not our enemy.*

Bill Clinton,
U.S. President, 1993

The spinning sphere we call earth is a planet in space approximately 8,000 miles in diameter and 25,000 miles in circumference. It is at least 4.5 billion years old; however, only in the last 3 billion years of its existence can we speak of the earth as possessing a biosphere (a system of life and living organisms). And a sociosphere—a system of interacting human beings—is, since the planet's origins, a relatively recent development. A cosmic calendar would tell us that the drama of human history commenced only in the last 340,000 years (Childe, 1962). Humankind has habitated the earth's biosphere for merely $\frac{1}{1000}$ of its existence, and only for the past 5,000 years or so can we speak of a record of human history.

Ever since Homo sapiens first began to roam the 200 million square miles of the earth's surface, human behavior has transformed the earth's terrestrial habitat. In the earth's ecosphere, the natural environment in which humans live, the quality of life has been influenced by the ways that humans have organized themselves politically for making decisions and managing disputes, how they have extracted resources from the earth to sustain and enhance life, and how they have exchanged and transferred

. . .

3

those resources. And the technologies they have developed to make weapons have affected their capacity to defend themselves from attack and to destroy others.

Although human behaviors that change global conditions are relentlessly varied, they are not random. Since antiquity, *patterns* of political, economic, and social behaviors are discernible. These regularities make it meaningful to talk about characteristic ways in which people act toward one another. To understand contemporary world politics, therefore, we must look for commonalities in past patterns of human and national interaction.

Today the world stands on the threshold of a new era. Since the Cold War ended, the globe has witnessed an enormous tide of change—so overwhelming, in fact, that the historical continuities are sometimes obscured. The conflict between the United States and the Soviet Union that colored virtually every dimension of political, economic, and social life in world politics for fifty years is over. So, too, is the division of the world between East and West. Now the Berlin Wall is history, the Soviet Union has disintegrated, communism has collapsed, Germany is united, and the European Union has expanded its membership and geographical reach. Moreover, Israel and the Palestinian Liberation Organization have reached a historic peace accord, democracy has spread throughout much of the world, and hopes have risen that peace will come to Bosnia, Somalia, and other regions where strife remains rampant.

How can we best understand the political convulsions in the world that engulf us almost daily? How can we anticipate their significance for the future? To begin, we must heed philosopher George Santayana's warning that "Those who cannot remember the past are condemned to repeat it." As former British Prime Minister Winston Churchill once remarked, "The farther backward you look, the farther forward you are likely to see." We must judge today's dramatic changes from a long-term perspective that brings into view both the extent of change and the force of continuity, both the hopes for lasting order and the entrenched pressures that threaten to disrupt it.

To explore world politics, then, we must examine the ways in which the contemporary international system has changed and the ways in which its fundamental characteristics have resisted change. What do recurrent historical practices, and deviations from them, tell us about the current state of world politics? What are the implications of the dramatic recent changes that have sent shock waves throughout the world? Are these revolutionary changes symbolic of an earthquake in world affairs, setting the stage for a truly new world order? Or will these dramatic developments prove temporary, mere spikes on the seismograph of history without lasting impact? These are among the principal questions we address in *World Politics: Trend and Transformation*.

## CONTINUITY AND CHANGE IN WORLD POLITICS . . . . . . . . . . . . . . . . . .

Every historical period is marked to some extent by change, but today the pace of change has seemed more rapid and the consequences more profound than ever before. Indeed, the cascade of recent events suggests that a revolutionary restructuring of world politics has occurred. Restructuring is suggested by many integrative trends. The nations of the world are drawing more closely together in communications, ideas, trade, and even peace and security. Similarly, restructuring is also suggested by many disintegrative trends that may presage disorder, such as environmental deterioration, weapons proliferation, the end of bipolar stability, and the resurgence of nationalism and ethnic conflict. Together, the countervailing forces of integration and disintegration (see Gaddis, 1991b) point toward a transformation in world politics that matches in extensiveness and importance the system-disrupting convulsions that swept the world following World War II. The present period is comparable to the late 1940s, when a new era colored by the Cold War commenced. At that time, states sought to find new policies and institutions to deal with the new conditions. The search for redefined national interests in a still-changing post–Cold War world is now once again much in evidence. To most observers, it appears that world politics is entering a new phase.

In the past several decades, scholars energetically examined the nature of transformation in history in order to isolate the "turning points in international politics" (Oren, 1984). Differentiating meaningful transformations or true historical watersheds from ephemeral changes or those that occur with the passage of time is difficult. New phases and turning points do not fall neatly into easily defined periods, signaling that one system has truly ended and a new one has commenced.[1]

Throughout history, important turning points have been perceived at the end of major wars, which have disrupted or destroyed preexisting international arrangements. World Wars I and II symbolized fundamental breaks with the past because each set in motion major transformations in world politics. Similarly, the end of the Cold War is a historical breakpoint of no less epic significance. The conclusion of the ideological conflict between communism and capitalism at the root of the so-called East–West dispute gives states "the luxury of some genuine choices for the first time since 1945" (Hyland, 1990). It appears we are now at the threshold of a new era in world politics, having just experienced, as U.S. President George Bush in 1992 put it, changes "of biblical proportions."

Yet, despite all in world politics that is radically different, there is much that remains the same. Indeed, "history usually makes a mockery of our hopes and expectations. . . . We are entering a new world . . . and many well-established generalizations about world politics may no longer hold." Thus we must "question . . . the ways and areas in which the future is likely to resemble the past" (Jervis, 1991–1992). Some continuities doubtlessly will persist.

How, then, can we recognize the beginning of a new international system? Political scientist Stanley Hoffmann (1961) argues that we have a new international system when we have a new answer to any of three questions (see also Zinnes, 1980; Thompson, 1988). First, what are the system's basic units (for example, nation-states instead of city-states)? Second, what are the predominant foreign policy goals that the units

---

[1] The disagreement among analysts about the dates of previous transformations in world politics testifies to the problems. See Kaplan (1957) and Rosecrance (1963) for alternative ways to distinguish periods in world politics and discussions of the analytic principles on which distinctions are made.

seek with respect to each other (for example, deterrence rather than the coercion of others)? And third, what can the units do to each other with their military and economic capabilities?

Using these criteria would indicate that today a new system *has* emerged. First, the quest for new economic unions in Europe, North America, and the Pacific Rim has accelerated. Moreover, some international organizations such as the United Nations have begun to flex their political muscle. The Soviet Union, however, once the largest territorial unit in the world and a powerful actor on the world stage for more than seventy years, has fragmented into smaller, often fractious political entities searching for national identity. And other national units could also disintegrate, either peacefully as the former Czechoslovakia did or violently as the former Yugoslavia did.

Second, territorial conquest is no longer the predominant goal of nations' foreign policies. There is evidence, furthermore, that nations have shifted their emphasis from traditional military methods of exercising influence to economic means (Luttwak, 1990). At the same time, ideological contests, like that between democratic capitalism and Marxism–Leninism which animated the Cold War contest between the United States and the Soviet Union, no longer exist as cleavages to define the primary threat with which national security policies must deal.

Third, advances in weapons technology and its proliferation represent a sea change in the boundaries of what states can do to each other. Great powers alone no longer control the world's most lethal weapons. Their economic well-being, however, is sometimes dependent on those with an increasing capacity to destroy.

The profound changes in units, goals, and capabilities witnessed in recent years have dramatically altered the rank of particular nations in the pecking orders that define the structure of international politics. Still, the hierarchies themselves endure. The *economic* hierarchy that divides the rich from the poor, the *political* hierarchy that separates the rulers from the ruled, the *resource* hierarchy that makes some suppliers and others dependents, and the *military* asymmetries that pit the strong against the weak—all still shape the relations among nations, as they have in the past. Similarly, the perpetuation of international anarchy and insecurity continue to encourage preparations for war and the use of force without international mandate. Thus change and continuity coexist to define the shape of contemporary world politics.

The interaction of constancy and change makes it difficult to determine unambiguously that the new post–Cold War era is an altogether new international system. What is clear is that constancy and change will determine the structure of relations among global actors in the late 1990s. Their interactions prevent extreme deviations from the general course of world politics and can pull conditions back to the patterns characteristic of an earlier period. This is why the impression is sometimes conveyed that in world politics "the more things change the more they stay the same." Trends in world politics rarely unfold in a constant, linear direction. Historical trends sometimes exhaust themselves; others stabilize or even reverse themselves as natural barriers interrupt their evolutionary progression. Indeed, persistence forecasting (pointing to automatic eventual transformation) usually fails because the conditions that coalesce to produce a development almost never continue indefinitely. As conditions change, they breed obstacles to their continuation. The historically minded observer may encounter a sense of *déjà vu* because the new international system that has just emerged could share many characteristics with those that existed in earlier periods.

## PREDICTING THE PROBLEMATIC FUTURE . . . . . . . . . . . . . . . . . . . . . .

Change and continuity in world politics do not allow us to know with confidence what is in store for the world's political future. As we will elaborate throughout *World Politics: Trend and Transformation*, some analysts see political authority fragmenting into even smaller parcels. Others see authority consolidating into large, competitive military or trade blocs as the number of rival centers of power expand. Some perceive science and technology propelling the world into abundance and affluence; others see it breeding chaos and environmental destruction. And some project the spread of democracy worldwide, whereas others foresee a resurgence of hypernationalism and cultural clashes between civilizations (Huntington, 1993) and a rekindling of support for strong (and, potentially, war-waging) autocratic rulers.

To predict which forces will dominate the future, we must think in multicausal terms. No trend or trouble stands alone; all interact simultaneously. The path toward the future is influenced by multiple determinants. Each causal force is connected to the rest in a complex web of linkages. Collectively, these may produce stability by inhibiting the impact of any single disruptive force. On the other hand, if interacting forces converge, their combined effects could accelerate the pace of change in world politics, moving it in directions not possible without such a symbiosis.

In *World Politics: Trend and Transformation* we look at international relations as a system, with patterns of interaction among parts. We direct attention to underlying causes and the ways they interact to shape the system. We assume the need to be sensitive to the impact of the past on the present. We picture the world as it might appear if it were viewed from outer space. Such a macroscopic perspective provides a bird's-eye view and sacrifices detail (in contrast to a microperspective that yields a worm's-eye view of the world). A macro approach prevents dwelling on particular events, particular nations' foreign policies, particular individuals, or other transitory phenomena whose long-term significance is likely to diminish. It helps identify behaviors that cohere into general global patterns—trends and transformations that will measurably affect the human political habitat as we enter the twenty-first century.

The macropolitical orientation of *World Politics: Trend and Transformation* is not meant to denigrate the importance of examining political processes peculiar to individual nations and their impact on the larger context of world politics.[2] However, a concern for the larger picture necessarily implies a greater focus on the general rather than the particular, on the recurrent rather than the ephemeral. Thus we explore the nature of international relations from a perspective that places general patterns into

---

[2] Our previous work on American foreign policy and policy-making processes (Kegley and Wittkopf, 1991) demonstrates our commitment to understanding international politics from the viewpoint of individual actors as well as from the macropolitical perspective that underlies this book.

a larger, lasting theoretical context, providing the conceptual tools and theories that will enable us to interpret subsequent developments.

## ORGANIZING INQUIRY: A FRAMEWORK FOR ANALYSIS

The chapters that follow provide a framework for investigating the forces driving contemporary world politics. We begin in Chapter 2 with a review of contending theories used by scholars and policymakers to make sense of world politics. This theoretical overview shows, among other things, how events in the world shape our views of the world and how prevailing theories of international politics change in accordance with changes in the real world of diplomatic practices and dramatic events that disrupt those practices.

The next thirteen chapters are divided into four parts. In Part II we focus on the actors in world politics. Nation-states are a primary concern here, with attention given to the way in which they make decisions to cope with the international environment (Chapter 3) and to the conflicts that characterize rivalries among great powers (Chapter 4) and between them and the less economically developed states in the Third World (Chapter 5). This part concludes (Chapter 6) with an examination of the nonstate actors that play important roles in world politics and sometimes challenge nation-states' preeminence.

Parts III and IV examine transnational policy issues. Part III addresses the increasing importance of issues surrounding material well-being. Here questions relating to the world political economy and the impact of national and international behavior on the global commons are examined. In Part IV the emphasis shifts to issues of war and peace, those geostrategic matters that are the essence of the traditional concerns of scholars and diplomats seeking to find paths to international security.

We conclude in Part V by returning briefly to themes examined in greater detail in previous chapters. Here we ask how the underlying tendencies in contemporary world politics enable us to anticipate future trends. Our attention is directed here at the probable shape of tomorrow's world politics and the questions that prevailing developments raise about the human prospect on the eve of the twenty-first century.

Understanding today's complex world requires a willingness to understand complexity. The challenge is difficult. A true but complicated idea always has less chance of succeeding than does a simple but false one, the French political sociologist Alexis de Tocqueville (1969 [1835]) warned over 160 years ago. But the rewards warrant the effort. Humankind's ability to free the future from the paralyzing grip of the past is contingent on its ability to entertain complex ideas for a complicated world and to develop a questioning attitude about rival perspectives on international realities.

## SUGGESTED READINGS

Cleveland, Harlan. *Birth of a New World.* San Francisco: Jossey-Bass Publishers, 1993.
Czempiel, Ernst-Otto, and James N. Rosenau, eds. *Global Changes and Theoretical Challenges: Approaches to World Politics for the 1990s.* Lexington, Mass.: Lexington Books, 1989.

Doran, Charles F. *Systems in Crisis: New Imperatives of High Politics at Century's End.* Cambridge: Cambridge University Press, 1991.

Holsti, Ole R., Randolph M. Siverson, and Alexander L. George, eds. *Change in the International System.* Boulder, Colo.: Westview Press, 1980.

Kegley, Charles W., Jr., and Eugene R. Wittkopf, eds. *The Global Agenda: Issues and Perspectives*, 4th ed. New York: McGraw-Hill, 1995.

Kennedy, Paul. *Preparing for the Twenty-First Century.* New York: Random House, 1993.

McWilliams, Wayne C., and Harry Piotrowski. *The World Since 1945: A History of International Relations*, 3rd ed. Boulder, Colo.: Lynne Rienner, 1993.

Morse, Edward L. *Modernization and the Transformation of International Relations.* New York: Free Press, 1976.

Rosenau, James N. *Turbulence in World Politics: A Theory of Change and Continuity.* Princeton, N.J.: Princeton University Press, 1990.

Ruggie, John Gerard. "Continuity and Transformation in the World Polity," *World Politics* 35 (January 1983): 261–285.

Singer, Max, and Aaron Wildavsky. *The Real World Order: Zones of Peace/Zones of Turmoil.* Chatham, N.J.: Chatham House, 1993.

Vasquez, John A., and Richard W. Mansbach. "The Issue Cycle: Conceptualizing Long-Term Global Change," *International Organization* 37 (Spring 1983): 257–280.

• • •

# CHAPTER 2

# THE STUDY OF WORLD POLITICS: RIVAL PERSPECTIVES IN CHANGING CONTEXTS

• • •

*It's important that we take a hard, clear look . . . not at some simple world, either of universal goodwill or of universal hostility, but the complex, changing and sometimes dangerous world that really exists.*

Jimmy Carter,
U.S. President, 1980

*Seek truth through facts.*

Mao Zedong, President,
People's Republic of China, 1966

We live in a world defined by our expectations and images. No one really "knows" what that world is like; we infer its nature from how we perceive it. Because we cannot "see" international relations directly, many of our images of the world's political realities may be built on illusions and misconceptions. Even if our images are not inaccurate, they are likely to become obsolete, as adjustments in the way we think about world politics often follow changes in international conditions.

The shape of the world's future will be determined not only by changes in the "objective" facts of world politics but also by the meanings that people ascribe to those facts, the assumptions on which their interpretations are based, and the actions that flow from these assumptions and interpretations. Because the way we act is shaped by what we perceive, we must continually question the validity of our images of world politics and ask if they are accurate views of reality or misperceptions.

Our purpose in this chapter is to describe the major analytical perspectives through which scholars and policymakers have interpreted international relations. The perceived "realities" of the international phenomena these perspectives seek to describe and explain understandably influence their content. We will therefore relate the perspectives to the underlying political climate in which they emerged. We will also use them to identify the intellectual heritage informing *World Politics: Trend and Transformation*.

We begin with a discussion of individuals' perceptions of their social and political environments, the factors that shape them, and their importance for understanding world politics.

## IMAGE AND REALITY IN WORLD POLITICS . . . . . . . . . . . . . . . . . . . . . .

We all have some kind of "mental model" of world politics. It may be explicit or implicit, conscious or subconscious. But whatever our level of awareness, the mental models we carry with us necessarily simplify "reality" by exaggerating some features of the real world and ignoring others. The pictures we form in our heads—our perceptions—are all distortions of sorts, inasmuch as they cannot fully capture the complexity and configurations that even physical objects possess.

To illustrate, consider the four world maps, Maps 2.1 to 2.4. All were designed to depict the distribution of the earth's land surfaces, but the image portrayed by each is different. They are all artificial representations of the way the globe "looks" because it appears different if viewed from different locations or vantage points. Moreover, the maps arrange the globe's appearance so it can be visualized, but each arrangement produces a different image. We call these *projections* to sensitize ourselves to the fact that the globe will look very different if its proportions are charted differently (as they must be). All maps are thus poor replications of reality—the earth is round, but the maps are flat. (The difficulty cartographers face can be appreciated by trying to flatten the peeling of an orange.)

Map 2.1 is a conventional orthographic projection of the globe made popular by the cartographer Richard Edes Harrison. The map centers on the mid-Atlantic, and it conveys some sense of the curvature of the earth by using rounded edges. The relationships among sizes and shapes are inevitably inaccurate in some places, but the distortions caused by depicting the globe's spherical shape (instead of making it look like a flat surface) are less than in many other representations. In suggesting how the globe might appear if viewed from outer space, this projection views the world as a whole and pictures the relationships of its land masses in ways that other projections miss altogether.

Map 2.2 is a Mercator projection, created in the sixteenth century by the Flemish cartographer Gerardus Mercator. Here the distortions in sizes and shapes are egregious. Greenland looks as though it is larger than China, even though China covers nearly four times as much land surface, and Europe appears larger than South America, which is twice Europe's size. Moreover, two-thirds of the map is used to represent the northern half of the world and only one-third the southern half. The Mercator projection is a classic Eurocentric view of the world.

Map 2.3 illustrates a quite different geographic world view. Here each land mass is spread on a flat or plane surface to pull attention away from the two-dimensional image that most people maintain of the earth and to escape the illusion that directions such as "North" or "East" have meaning. Known as a circular projection, the map illuminates well the connections of regions to each other but condenses and masks distances within regions.

Finally, Map 2.4 uses a polar projection of the world. It was popular during the height of the Cold War because it highlights the principal political and military

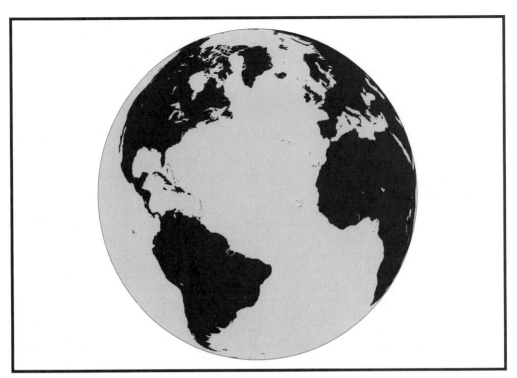

**Map 2.1** Orthographic Projection of the World

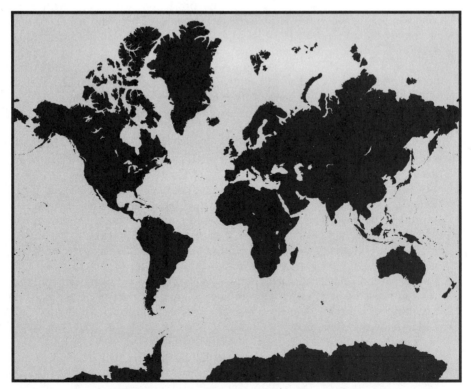

**Map 2.2** Mercator Projection of the World

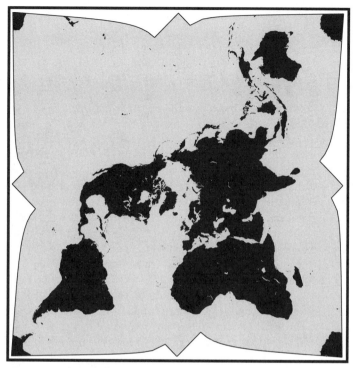

**Map 2.3**  Circular Projection of the World

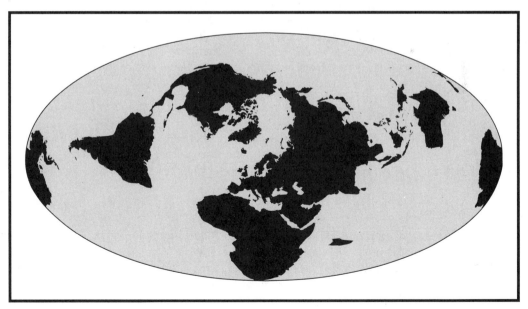

**Map 2.4**  Polar Projection of the World

alignments that existed when the countries of the world joined counterpoised coalitions or blocs (see Chapter 4). The perspective thus served military planners' needs in viewing the relationships of the adversaries: If intercontinental war between the United States and the former Soviet Union had broken out, and if the antagonists had resorted to ballistic missiles to fight it, the polar icecap, which here is the center of the world, would have become a major pathway to destruction.

There is nothing pernicious about simplifying our views of the world. Just as cartographers create simplifications of a complex geophysical space so we can better understand the world around us, each of us must create mental maps of the world to make sense out of a confusing abundance of information. Mental maps are actually conceptual models, since concepts are abstractions that organize perceptions.[1] They are neither inherently right nor wrong. They derive their importance from our human tendency to "respond [not] to the 'objective' facts of the situation . . . but to [our] 'image' of the situation. It is what we think the world is like, not what it is really like, that determines our behavior. . . . We act according to the way the world appears to us, not necessarily according to the way it 'is'" (Boulding, 1959). Even political leaders are captives of this tendency. As political scientist Richard Ned Lebow (1981) warns, "Policy-makers are prone to distort reality in accord with their needs even in situations that appear . . . relatively unambiguous."

## Images of Reality

Scholars interested in the psychological dimensions of international relations stress the importance of understanding the sources of individuals' images of reality. Political psychology is important to the study of international relations because (among other reasons) people differ in their perceptions of and reactions to conflicting or discrepant information.

### The Sources of Images

Social cognition theory demonstrates that one's perception of the world is not a passive act. The mind learns to select, screen, and filter what it perceives. The factors that influence individuals' perceptions of politics include the following:

- psychological needs, drives, and dispositions (for example, trust or mistrust) ingrained in personalities as a result of early childhood experiences
- what we are socialized into thinking about international relations as children (for example, tolerance of cultural diversity or the fear of it) by parents, teachers,

---

[1] We use the word *map* to indicate the extent to which mental models are necessarily imperfect replicas of the global realities they are intended to portray. We are referring not only to the kind of world geography that people carry in their heads regarding distance, size, and topography but also to how resources, military capabilities, power, diplomatic influence, and populations, as well as their political meaning, are distributed. Having described mental models in these terms, it is perhaps axiomatic that many such maps may bear little relationship to the realities of a fast-changing, interdependent planet (see Sprout and Sprout, 1971).

and peer groups, as these thoughts are influenced by the values embedded in our cultural system

- our images of world history as shaped by our teachers and the kinds of history books to which we are exposed
- opinions about world affairs articulated by those with whom we routinely associate, such as our close friends
- attitudes expressed by policymakers and other respected experts
- the positions we occupy and the roles we perform (What we see depends on where we sit: child, student, bureaucrat, policymaker, diplomat, and so forth.)

Tolerance of ambiguity and receptivity to new ways of organizing thinking vary among individuals and personality types. Some are more "open" and less rigid than others and therefore more accepting of diversity and more able to revise perceptual habits to accommodate new realities. Nevertheless, all of us are to some extent prisoners of the perceptual predispositions to which we are conditioned.

## The Nature of Images

Most people are prone to look for information that reinforces preexisting beliefs, to assimilate new data into familiar images, and to distort cognitions and to deny information that fails to conform to previous expectations. Individuals process information using schematic reasoning, which causes them to interpret new information according to existing schemata (a kind of psychological diagram) (Conover and Feldman, 1984). They use information shortcuts to make political judgments and to relate their preferences toward specific policy issues to their general beliefs.

Individuals organize information about the world because it helps them to simplify the world. The process applies to international politics, as individuals attempt "to cope with an extraordinarily confusing world by structuring views about specific foreign policies according to their more general and abstract beliefs" (Hurwitz and Peffley, 1987). Preexisting values and beliefs also encourage individuals to accept some cognitions but to exclude others from their consciousness that may be discrepant or "dissonant" (Festinger, 1957). This means that what we "see" about world politics depends not just on what happens in the world but also on how we interpret and internalize those events. Thus mental maps inescapably play a central role in shaping individuals' dispositions toward world politics.

## The Role of Images in International Politics

We must be careful not to assume automatically that what applies to individuals applies to entire nations. Still, leaders' images of historical circumstances often predispose them to behave in particular ways toward others, regardless of the "objective" facts of the situation. For example, the loss of 26 million Soviet soldiers and citizens in the "Great Patriotic War" (as the Russians refer to World War II) created an exaggerated fear of foreign invasion. This caused a generation of Soviet policymakers to perceive defensive moves made by the United States with considerable suspicion and often alarm. Another example of perceptual bias was the U.S. image of European power politics as "dirty," which reinforced not only its isolationist impulse—its disposition to withdraw from world affairs—but also its counter impulse—a determination to reform the world in its own image. The latter gave rise to the globalist foreign policy the United States pursued following World War II. That others might regard that policy orientation as ill advised and sometimes threatening is not easily understood by Americans. (As former U.S. President Jimmy Carter once lamented, "The hardest thing for Americans to understand is that they are not better than other people.")

Because individuals (and, by extension, leaders and citizens of nations) are prone either to ignore or reinterpret information that runs counter to their beliefs and values, mutual misperceptions often fuel discord in world politics, especially when relations between nations are hostile. For example, distrust and suspicion between conflicting parties may arise because each sees the other as the other sees it. That is, *mirror images* emerge. This syndrome is especially clear in the images the leaders in Moscow and Washington held of each other during the Cold War, and it applies to many other antagonistic relationships as well. When mirror images develop, self-righteousness often leads parties entrapped in conflict to view their own actions as constructive, but to view their adversary's responses as negative and hostile. When this occurs, resolution of the conflict is extraordinarily difficult, as the recurrent wars in the Middle East since 1945 illustrate. Thus fostering peace is not simply a matter of expanding trade and other forms of transnational contact, or even of bringing political leaders together in international summits. Rather, it is a matter of changing deeply entrenched beliefs.[2]

## Sources of Image Change

Although individuals' mental maps of world politics are resistant to change, change is possible. It occurs when people experience punishment or discomfort as a result of clinging to false assumptions. (As Benjamin Franklin once observed, "The things that hurt, instruct.") Dramatic events also can alter international images, sometimes drastically (see Deutsch and Merritt, 1965; also Wittkopf, 1990). The use of atomic bombs against Japan in 1945, the Korean and Vietnam conflicts, and the Cuban missile crisis in 1962 were learning experiences for many Americans, causing them to adjust their previous images of international politics.

---

[2] The classic empirical examination of the impact of images on foreign policy making is Ole R. Holsti's (1962) study of John Foster Dulles, U.S. secretary of state in the Eisenhower administration. Demonstrating that Dulles operated within the framework of an "inherent bad faith" model of the Soviet Union, Holsti's findings "suggest the fallacy of thinking that peaceful settlement of outstanding international issues is simply a problem of devising 'good plans.' Clearly as long as decision-makers on either side of the Cold War [adhered] to rigid images of the other party, there [was] little likelihood that even genuine 'bids' to decrease tensions [would] have the desired effect."

Similarly, the surprising collapse of communist rule in the Soviet Union and Eastern Europe exerted pressure on the world views of policymakers and political commentators alike, provoking them to reexamine their assumptions about foreign policy priorities in a new system without the Cold War. Often such jolting experiences encourage the creation of new mental maps, new perceptual filters, and new criteria through which later events may be interpreted and situations defined.

## UNDERSTANDING WORLD POLITICS: THE ELUSIVE QUEST FOR THEORY . . . . . . . . . . . . . . . . . . . . . . . . . . . . . . . . . . .

Like the mental maps individuals use to make sense of a complex and often confusing world, social scientists devise different models to think about world politics to help make it more comprehensible. Like cartographers, they develop analytical models that highlight some features of reality but distort others. And, like the geographic world views maps with different purposes convey in different times, the models (sometimes called theories or *paradigms*)[3] that scholars fashion change as new problems cry out for new understanding and solution. Thus the analytical perspectives dominant in the thinking of both scholars and policymakers in different historical circumstances tell us much about world politics itself. New paradigms arise during changing international climates when changes in values occur as a result of the persuasiveness of their proponents' messages and as a result of the ability of an advocated new paradigm to explain the developments then unfolding in world affairs (Ferguson and Mansbach, 1988).[4]

Major wars involving the preponderant (hegemonic) powers in particular historical epochs have often been significant turning points in world history.

These periodic conflicts have reordered the international system and propelled history in new and uncharted directions. They resolve the question of which state will govern the system, as well as what ideas and values will predominate, thereby determining the ethos

---

[3] The word *paradigm* is commonly used to describe the dominant way of looking at a subject of inquiry, such as international relations. It was popularized by Thomas Kuhn's (1970) influential book *The Structure of Scientific Revolutions*. Unfortunately, the term has been used in a variety of overlapping ways. But the general idea underlying the term is that thoughts about a particular area of inquiry tend to be structured by the acceptance of particular aspects of the subject's characteristics as more important than others and by agreement about the puzzles to be solved and the criteria that should govern their investigation. The concept is helpful to understanding how images of world politics are shaped by sociological forces operating within the intellectual community of scholars as it seeks to assess the nature and meaning of global political developments.

[4] There have always been scholars outside the intellectual paradigm dominant during any particular time, challenging it, questioning its relevance to world politics, and proposing alternative conceptions of reality and what knowledge about it should entail. Often those outside the paradigm have come from countries other than those dominant in world politics itself. Marxist thinking clearly was dominant in the scholarly work of those living in socialist societies during the Cold War, for example. However, the ability of marxist interpretations of reality to attain dominance worldwide was constrained by the inability of communism as defined by Karl Marx (that is, a classless, stateless society) to become the world's preferred form of political and social organization.

of succeeding ages. The outcomes of these wars affect the economic, social, and ideological structures of individual societies as well as the structure of the larger international system. (Gilpin, 1981: 203)

The twentieth century has been dominated by three such conflicts: World War I, World War II, and the Cold War. Each stimulated a search for the causes of war and the foundations of peace; each reshaped policymakers' images about the principles that organize world politics and the policy programs that could best preserve world order; each caused the dominant world view to be jettisoned and encouraged the search for new theoretical orientations. As the historian Arthur Schlesinger (1986) mused, "Every war . . . has been followed in due course by skeptical reassessments of supposedly sacred assumptions."

The theoretical perspectives fashioned during this century demonstrate the impact of these wars on the study of world politics. We will discuss six of them: (1) current history, (2) political idealism, (3) political realism, (4) behavioralism, (5) neorealism, and (6) neoliberalism. We will conclude by identifying five additional schools of thought advocated by their proponents to address particular aspects of world politics and foreign policy.

## Current History

International relations as a distinct field of intellectual inquiry is largely a phenomenon of the twentieth century. The historical roots of the discipline lie in diplomatic history, an approach to understanding international relations that focuses on the description of historical events, not theoretical explanation. For convenience, we call this the *current history* approach to the study of international relations.

The environment at the dawn of the twentieth century when the formal study of international relations began was filled with optimism. Many believed that peace and prosperity had taken root and would persist. International law had recently been strengthened, and The Hague peace conferences in 1899 and 1907 inspired hope that arms would be controlled and Europe would be spared another series of wars like those experienced between 1848 and 1870. Moreover, many people, including the American industrialist and philanthropist Andrew Carnegie who gave much of his fortune to the cause of world peace, assumed that as industrialization progressed and the costs and risks of war increased, the chance of protracted war among the great powers would decline dramatically (see also Angell, 1910).

In those halcyon times, students of international relations studied history to provide insightful commentary on the events of the day. The study of international relations at the turn of the century was largely the study of personalities and events, past and present. Rarely did scholars seek to generalize theoretically about the "lessons" of history or about the principles or "laws" that could account for the characteristic responses of states to similar stimuli or influences.[5]

---

[5] Sir Halford Mackinder (1919) and Alfred Thayer Mahan (1890) are exceptions to this broad generalization. Both sought to generate theoretical propositions pertaining to the influence of geographic factors on national power and international politics. Their efforts laid the foundations for the study of political geography that survives today as an important approach to world politics.

The large-scale death and destruction exacted by World War I destroyed the security that had made current history a comfortable approach to international politics. That catastrophic global war, begun in 1914, was a painful learning experience that stimulated the search for knowledge that could address contemporary policy problems—notably war—in a theoretical context. However interesting descriptions of past wars and the individuals who waged them might be, they were of dubious utility to a world in search of peace and of ways to prevent wars of mass destruction. For those purposes, policymakers and scholars needed a *theory* that could reliably predict the outbreak of war and instruct leaders on the policies that could best prevent it.

## Political Idealism

World War I opened the door to a paradigmatic revolution in the study of world politics in which several perspectives on international relations competed for attention in the period of intellectual ferment that followed. Current history as an approach continued to claim some adherents. Marxist-Leninist thought also became an increasingly influential paradigm in the waning days of World War I following the Bolshevik Revolution in Russia, when its critique of capitalism's creation of inequality, class conflict, and imperialistic war gained a following. Later, with the rise of Adolf Hitler and the Nazis in Germany, national socialism (or fascism) also challenged conventional European thinking about international politics. Nazism, the German variant of national socialism, was particularly provocative. Not only did Nazism glorify the role of the state (as opposed to that of the individual) in political life, it also advanced a political philosophy that rationalized war as an instrument of national policy. Emerging as dominant, however, was a perspective known as *political idealism*.

### The Idealist World View

Idealists held divergent views of world politics.[6] What joined them was their shared assumptions about reality and the homogeneity of their conclusions. Collectively, idealists embraced a world view based on the following beliefs:

---

[6] Scholars and publicists leading this intellectual movement and introducing its vocabulary in international discourse included G. Lowes Dickinson, Alfred Zimmern, Norman Angell, James T. Shotwell, and, especially, Woodrow Wilson. In many respects, idealism in its post–World War I formulation was not new. Idealism was derivative of the much larger and longer philosophical tradition known as *liberalism*. This philosophy dates to antiquity and has been interpreted divergently in different periods. At the core of liberalism is emphasis on the importance, equality, and liberty of the individual as a human agent and the need to protect people from excessive regulation by the state. From this comes a conceptualization of the individual as the seat of moral value and virtue and the belief that human beings should be treated as ends rather than means. Liberalism emphasizes principle over the pursuit of power and regards capitalism, free trade, and republican or democratic rule as an antidote to authoritarian and dictatorial governance and to the absence of world order. Liberalism's proponents in the modern period include such thinkers as Immanuel Kant, Thomas Jefferson, John Stuart Mill, Montesquieu, John Locke, David Hume, and Adam Smith. For reviews and summaries of the liberal legacy as a perspective on world politics, see Doyle (1995), Howard (1978), and Zacher and Matthew (1995).

1. Human nature is essentially "good" or altruistic and people are therefore capable of mutual aid and collaboration.[7]

2. The fundamental human concern for the welfare of others makes progress possible (that is, the Enlightenment's faith in the possibility of improving civilization was reaffirmed).

3. Bad human behavior is the product not of evil people but of evil institutions and structural arrangements that motivate people to act selfishly and to harm others—including making war.

4. War is not inevitable and its frequency can be reduced by eradicating the institutional arrangements that encourage it.

5. War is an international problem that requires collective or multilateral rather than national efforts to control it.

6. International society must reorganize itself to eliminate the institutions that make war likely.

To be sure, not all advocates of political idealism subscribed to each of these tenets derived from the liberal heritage of international relations theorizing with equal conviction. Many political idealists would probably disagree with some of them or be uncomfortable with their simplistic wording. Nevertheless, these tenets describe the basic assumptions articulated in one way or another by the leaders and theorists whose orientation toward international relations captivated the discussion of world politics in the period between the two world wars. Overtones of moralism, optimism, and universalism laced the discussion.

## The Idealist Reform Program

Although important differences existed in the idealists' prescriptions for reforming the international system (see Herz, 1951), they tended to fall into three groups. One group called for the creation of international institutions to replace the anarchical and war-prone balance-of-power system that had precipitated World War I. That system was characterized by independent states who formed coalitions (in the form of shifting alliances) to wage war or defend a weaker coalition partner from attack. Idealists sought to create in its place a new system based on the principle of collective security. It dealt with the problem of war by making aggression by any one state an aggression against all who, acting in concert, would thwart the ambitions of the dominance-seeking actor. The League of Nations was the embodiment of the collective security principle. It reflected simultaneously the emphasis that idealists placed on international institutions as a mechanism for coping with the problem of war (and,

---

[7] The role of human nature in theories of politics is controversial. See Nelson (1974), Lewontin, Rose, and Kamin (1984), and Wilson (1993) for reviews and critical discussion.

secondarily, social injustice) and the possibility of international cooperation as a mechanism of global problem-solving.

A second group of idealist prescriptions emphasized the legal control of war. It called for the use of legal processes, such as mediation and arbitration, to settle disputes and inhibit recourse to war. Creation of the Permanent Court of International Justice to litigate interstate conflicts and ratification of the Kellogg-Briand Pact of 1928, which "outlawed" war as an instrument of national policy, illustrated this facet of the idealists' policy prescriptions.

A third group of prescriptions followed the biblical injunction that nations should beat their swords into plowshares. The efforts during the 1920s (the Washington and London naval conferences, for instance) to secure arms control and disarmament agreements exemplified this orientation.

Several corollary ideas gave definition to the emphasis that idealists placed on international organization, law, and disarmament. Among them were the need to substitute attitudes that stressed the unity of humankind for those that stressed parochial national loyalties to independent sovereign states; using the power of ideas through education to arouse world public opinion against warfare; the promotion of free international trade in place of economic nationalism; the replacement of secret diplomacy by a system of "open covenants, openly arrived at"; and, above all, the termination of interlocking bilateral alliances and the power balances they sought to achieve. Some idealists saw in the principle of self-determination a chance to redraw the world's political geography to make national borders conform to ethnic groupings, under the conviction that a world so arranged would be a more peaceful world. Related to this was the call for democratic domestic institutions. "Making the world safe for democracy," idealists believed, would also make it secure and free from war. Woodrow Wilson's celebrated Fourteen Points speech (delivered by the U.S. president before Congress in 1918), which proposed the creation of the League of Nations and, with it, the pursuit of other idealists' aims, expressed the sentiments of the idealist world view and program perhaps better than did any other statement.

Although idealism dominated policy rhetoric and academic discussions during the interwar period, much of the idealist program for reform was never tried, and even less of it was ever achieved. When the winds of international change again shifted and the world confronted the German, Italian, and Japanese pursuit of hegemony and world conquest, idealism as a world view receded.

## Political Realism

The drive for world conquest that led to World War II provoked strong criticism of the idealist paradigm. Critics blamed the outbreak of war on what they believed to be the idealists' naive legalistic and moralistic assumptions about progress through human aspiration and the possibility of peace. They alleged that idealists neglected the "realities" of power politics (see Carr, 1939). The "lessons" the critics drew from the interwar period gave shape to a new set of perceptions and beliefs.

Advocates of the new, ascendant paradigm, known as *political realism,* coalesced to frame an intellectual movement.[8] Their message reads like the antithesis of idealism. Because it was compelling—and because it remains so today—it deserves careful scrutiny.

## *The Realist World View*

As a political theory, realism can trace its intellectual roots to the ancient Greek historian Thucydides and his account of the Peleponnesian War between Athens and Sparta (431–404 B.C.E.). Elements of realist thought can also be found in the writings of Kautilya, minister to the Maurya emperor of India more than 2,000 years ago. Recent realist thinking derives especially from the political philosophies of the Italian theorist Niccoló Machiavelli (1469–1527) and the English theoretician Thomas Hobbes (1588–1679). They emphasized in their treatises *The Prince* and *The Leviathan,* respectively, a political calculus based on interest, prudence, power, and expediency above all other considerations, such as morality. Thus political realism is synonymous with realpolitik, as moral crusades are anathema to realist thinking.

As applied to twentieth-century world politics, realism views nation-states as the principal actors in world politics, for they answer to no higher political authority. Moreover, conflicts of interests among them are assumed to be inevitable. Realism also emphasizes the way the (perceived) realities of international politics dictate the choices that foreign policy makers, as rational problem solvers, must make. States are the superordinate actors on the world's stage. The purpose of statecraft is national survival in a hostile environment. No means is more important to that end than the acquisition of *power.* And no principle is more important than *self-help*—the ultimate dependence of the state on its own resources to promote its interests and protect itself. State *sovereignty,* a cornerstone of international law, enshrines this perspective, giving heads of state the freedom—and responsibility—to do whatever is necessary to advance the state's interests and survival. Respect for moral principles is a wasteful and dangerous interference in the rational pursuit of national power. To the realist, therefore, questions about the relative virtues of the values within this or that *ism* (ideological system) cannot be allowed to interfere with sound policy making. The ideological preferences of states are neither good nor bad—what matters is whether one's self-interest is served. Accordingly, the game of international politics revolves around the pursuit of power: acquiring it, increasing it, projecting it, and using it to bend others to one's will.

---

[8] Among the principal prophets of this new world view were E. H. Carr (1939), Hans J. Morgenthau (1948), Kenneth W. Thompson (1960), Reinhold Niebuhr (1947), George F. Kennan (1951, 1954), and, later, Henry A. Kissinger (1964). For critical reviews of the realist paradigm, see Brown (1994), Holsti (1989b), Rosenthal (1991), Smith (1986), and Vasquez (1993).

At the risk of oversimplification, realism's message can be summarized in the form of ten assumptions and related propositions:

1. A reading of history teaches that people are by nature sinful and wicked.

2. Of all of people's evil ways, no sins are more prevalent, inexorable, or dangerous than are their instinctive lust for power and their desire to dominate others.

3. The possibility of eradicating the instinct for power is a utopian aspiration.

4. Under such conditions international politics is, as the English philosopher Thomas Hobbes (1588–1679) put it, a struggle for power, "a war of all against all."

5. The primary obligation of every state in this environment—the goal to which all other national objectives should be subordinated—is to promote the "national interest," defined as the acquisition of power.

6. The nature of the international system necessitates the acquisition of military capabilities sufficient to deter attack by potential enemies.

7. Economics is less relevant to national security than military might and is important primarily as a means to acquiring national power and prestige.

8. Allies might increase the ability of a state to defend itself, but their loyalty and reliability should not be assumed.

9. Never entrust the task of self-protection to international organizations or to international law.

10. If all states seek to maximize power, stability will result from maintaining a **balance of power,** lubricated by fluid alliance systems.

### Realism in the Nuclear Age

The realist thinking that came to dominate actual policy making as well as academic discourse in the 1940s and 1950s (often described as **classical realism**) fit the needs of a pessimistic age. World War II, the onset of rivalry between the United States and the Soviet Union, the expansion of the Cold War confrontation between the emergent superpowers into a global struggle between East and West, the stockpiling of nuclear weapons, the periodic crises that threatened to erupt into global violence—all confirmed the realists' image of world politics.

The realists' belief that the structure of the international system and humankind's lust for power determined the behavior of all nations appeared particularly persuasive considering these developments. States and their incessant competition were the defining elements of global reality. All other aspects of world politics became secondary. Simultaneously, the view that a threatening international environment demanded that foreign policy take precedence over domestic problems and policies also appeared cogent. As the historical imperatives of "power politics" required unceasing attention to the politics of peace in the global arena, the logic of realpolitik asserted that the "high politics" of military security *was* world politics.

## The Limitations of Realism

Persuasive though the realists' arguments about the essential properties of international politics may have been, the consistency of their arguments and the conclusions they drew were frequently at odds and even contradictory.

> Critics . . . noted a lack of precision and even contradiction in the way classical realists use such concepts as "power," "national interest," and "balance of power." They also see possible contradictions between the central descriptive and prescriptive elements of classical realism. On the one hand, nations and their leaders "think and act in terms of interests defined as power," but, on the other, statesmen are urged to exercise prudence and restraint, as well as to recognize the legitimate national interests of other nations. Power plays a central role in classical realism, but the correlation between the relative power balance and political outcomes is often less than compelling, suggesting the need to enrich analyses with other variables. (Holsti, 1989b: 19)

Thus, once analysis moved beyond the pithy notion that people are wicked and beyond the rhetoric requiring that foreign policy serve the national interest, important questions remained. What policies best serve the national interest? Do alliances encourage peace or instability? Do arms promote national security or provoke costly arms races and war? Are states more prone to act aggressively when they are strong or weak? Are the interests of nations served only through competition with one another, never through cooperation? If humankind is unchanging, then how do we explain the observable changes in the evolution and transformation of the international system? Indeed, how do we explain the growth of collaborative multinational institutions and states' willingness to abide by ethical principles?

Such questions are empirical and need real-world evidence and corresponding means of analyzing them to find satisfactory answers. In these respects, political realism failed. Realism presented a distinctive perspective on international affairs, but it lacked a methodology for resolving competing claims. It had no criteria to determine what data were significant and what rules to follow to interpret the information perceived to be relevant. Even the policy recommendations that purportedly flowed from the logic of realpolitik were often divergent. Realists themselves, for example, were sharply divided about whether U.S. intervention in Vietnam served American national interests and whether nuclear weapons contributed to international security.

A growing number of critics also pointed out that political realism did not account for significant new developments in world politics. It could not explain the forces behind the new institutions that began to be constructed in Western Europe in the 1950s and 1960s, for example, where the cooperative pursuit of mutual advantage rather than narrow self-interest seemed to dominate (at least in economic if not always in military affairs). Other critics began to worry about realism's disregard for ethical principles and the material and social costs that some of its policy prescriptions seemed to impose, such as retarded economic growth as a result of unrestrained military expenditures.

Thus, by the end of the 1960s, (classical) realism, which had emerged as the dominant paradigm in international relations following World War II, found itself bombarded by criticism. Some found its logical consistency flawed, others found its empirical content dubious, and still others found its policy recommendations confusing and its worship of power to the neglect of ethical principles disquieting.

### Realism's Continuing Relevance

Despite the shortcomings of classical realism, its shadow is still visible. Much of the world continues to think about international politics in its terms. Indeed, realism enjoyed a resurgence in the early 1980s, as the embittered Cold War competition between the United States and the Soviet Union entered a new phase and the role of military power in world politics received renewed emphasis. Even without that resurgent emphasis, however, realism provides important insight into the drive for national security that continues to motivate states' foreign policy behavior.

The continuing relevance of classical realism also finds expression in its recent reformulation, known as **neorealism** or *structural realism*. This variant on classical realism continues to recognize the anarchical nature of world politics and the dominance of the nation-state in world politics, but it severs the link classical realists postulated between human nature and the behavior of states in world politics. Instead, the structure of the system, rather than the unceasing lust for power, dictates exclusively the foreign policy choices of national leaders. Thus neorealism speaks directly to the importance of the recent transformation in the structure of world power, in which a bipolar configuration of power has been replaced by one variously described as unipolar or multipolar. We will therefore return below to a consideration of neorealist theory. First, however, we will briefly address the methodological debate that dissatisfaction with classical realism provoked.

## The Behavioral Approach

Among its other contributions, classical realism prepared the way for serious theoretical thinking about global conditions and empirical (verifiable) linkages among them. Nonetheless, as dissatisfaction with its shortcomings mounted, a counterreaction, cast largely in terms of language and method, gained momentum in the 1960s and early 1970s. Because the **behavioral** approach to the study of international relations, as it came to be known, was defined largely by its approach to theory and the logic and method of its inquiry, it is better described as a methodology than as a theoretical perspective.

### Science versus Traditionalism

Behavioralism in international relations was part of a larger movement spreading across the social sciences in general. Often called the *scientific* approach, behavioralism challenged preexisting modes of studying human behavior and the basis on which previous theorists, now called *traditionalists*, derived their truth-claims. An often-heated debate between the behavioralists and traditionalists about the principles and procedures most appropriate for investigating international phenomena resulted. The debate centered on the meaning of theory, on the requirements for adequate theory, and on the methods best suited to testing theoretical propositions. Indeed, "theorizing about theory" (Singer, 1960) rather than theorizing about international relations often typified it. The literature of this period attests to the extent to which methodological issues, and not substantive ones, commanded the attention of professional analysts.[9] This perhaps reflected the uncertainty and immaturity of a "new" science in its incipient stages of development, one unsure about itself and its goals.

## *A Science of International Politics?*

A number of shared assumptions and analytic prescriptions were at the core of the behavioral movement. Behavioralism sought ***nomothetic*** or lawlike generalizations, that is, statements about patterns and regularities about international phenomena presumed to hold across time and place. Science, the behavioralists claimed, is foremost a generalizing activity. The purpose of scientific inquiry, therefore, is to discover recurrent patterns of interstate behavior and their causes. From this perspective (a view incidentally consistent with that of many "traditional" realists and idealists), a ***theory*** of international relations should contain a statement of the relationship between two or more variables, specify the conditions under which the relationship(s) holds, and explain why the relationship(s) should hold. To uncover such theories, behavioralists leaned to comparative cross-national analyses rather than to case studies of particular countries at particular times (as is characteristic of the current history approach). Behavioralists also stressed the need to gather data about the characteristics of nations and how they behaved toward one another. Hence, the behavioral movement spawned and encouraged the comparative and quantitative study of international relations (see, for example, Rosenau, 1980; Singer, 1968).

What made behavioralism innovative was not so much its reliance on controlled comparative techniques and quantitative analyses as its temperament toward inquiry. Behavioralists sought greater rigor and precision in analysis. They tried to replace subjective belief with verifiable knowledge, to supplant impressionism and intuition with testable evidence, and to substitute data and reproducible information for mere opinion. In this sense, they embraced liberal idealism's "high regard for modern science" and its "attacks against superstition and authority" (Hall, 1993). In place of appeals to the allegedly "expert" opinion of authorities, behavioral scientists sought to acquire knowledge and build on it cumulatively by suspending judgment in claims about truth until sufficient evidence could support them. They aspired to conduct objective or value-free research (while recognizing the obstacles to that goal). They sought to replace ambiguous verbal definitions of concepts (such as *power*) with so-called "operational" ones built on indicators on which empirical tests could be conducted and whose meaning was easily communicated from one analyst to the next.

---

[9] For examples of the debate and illustrations of the tone of dialogue, see Hoffmann (1960), Kaplan (1968), Knorr and Rosenau (1969), Knorr and Verba (1961), Tanter and Ullman (1972), and Wright (1955). See also Lijphart (1974) for a review of the issues that this debate encompassed.

They also sought to avoid the tendency of previous scholarship to select facts and cases to make them fit preexisting hunches. Instead, *all* available data, those not supportive of as well as those consistent with existing theoretical hypotheses, were to be examined. Knowledge, they argued, would advance best if a cautious, skeptical attitude toward any empirical statement were assumed. "Let the data, not the armchair theorist, speak." "Seek evidence, but distrust it." These slogans represented the behavioral posture toward the acquisition of knowledge.

The advocates of behavioralism were understandably enthusiastic about their approach. They came armed with new tools for analyzing international relations, with newly generated data for testing competing hypotheses voiced over decades of traditional speculation, and with sometimes generous research support from governments and private foundations. An entire generation of scholars was trained to study international relations with powerful new conceptual and methodological tools. In the process, some behavioralists addressed empirical questions at the core of competing ideas about the social and political organization of national societies, including not just propositions grounded in realism, but also marxist and other ideas about the causes and consequences of the inequalities within and between states.

## *Postbehavioralism*

Cumulating verifiable knowledge is a difficult, even tedious, task, requiring dedication and patience. The early enthusiasm and optimism of the effort thus began to wane, as the labors invested failed to produce prompt results. Even within the behavioral movement itself, voices began to ask sometimes embarrassing questions about the approach and its suitability. One of the early proponents of behavioralism, David Easton (1969), asked if the field was not moving into a *postbehavioral* period.

At the heart of this self-scrutiny was a common set of criticisms: (1) that some devotees of behavioralism had become preoccupied with method to the exclusion of real-world problems; (2) that they had focused on testing interesting (and often the most accessible) hypotheses but ones that were largely trivial and meaningless to the policymakers responsible for protecting their nations and making the world a better place in which to live; and (3) that the methodology of behavioralism, which sought to ground theories in hard data, relied on past patterns of human experience that sometimes did not relate to a rapidly changing world or the future. Hence the findings might be historically accurate but largely irrelevant to today's world or tomorrow's.

Although some behavioral research spoke directly to the moral issues central to the differences between realism and idealism, its relative neglect of many of the ethical questions raised in a world of poverty, hunger, violence, and other forms of malaise was also criticized. Hence the postbehavioral critique called for a new research agenda that would focus on new types of issues and reexamine their underlying philosophical implications from a multidisciplinary perspective. Interestingly, however, the advocates of new approaches to the study of international relations rarely recommended discarding scientific methods. More commonly they urged the application of such methods to new kinds of questions or to the reconstruction of theories grounded in the realist (and idealist) tradition (for example, Wayman and Diehl, 1995; Cusack and Stoll, 1990).

## Postmodernism

The most recent critique of behavioralism, **postmodernism,** is representative of what is often described as a "postpositivist" reaction. Positivism is a philosophical tradition underlying the scientific method concerned with positive facts and phenomena, to the exclusion of speculation about ultimate causes or origins. Thus behavioralists and those committed to the scientific method as a way of understanding the social and political world are typically described as positivists. Postmodernists are postpositivistic because they call for a reexamination of the philosophical foundations of international relations theory.

As with the earlier debate between traditionalists and behavioralists, postmodernism is part of a broader movement in the humanities variously known as **critical social theory, poststructuralism,** or **deconstructionism.** Postmodern theorists of these related approaches take the inherently subjective nature of images of world politics and the "social construction of reality" as their point of departure.[10] A common feature of their critical introspection into the foundations of scientific methods of inquiry in general and international relations theory in particular is a questioning posture toward the possibility of truly understanding reality. Postmodernists believe that there is no objective international reality that we can discover—it is inherently intangible. The purpose of inquiry therefore is to expose the fallacy of those who pretentiously contend that they understand it. For this goal, postmodernists refuse to study international relations. Instead, they study the texts, "subtexts" (hidden meanings), and discourse in the writings, speeches, and arguments of those policymakers and analysts who interpret world affairs. Revealing the distortions and misrepresentations through the deconstruction of their words and texts and thereby identifying the coexisting "multiple realities" and the fictional basis within their "stories" is their primary aim. As such, this mode of literary criticism is better suited to exposing the limits of others' analyses (deconstructing their logic) than to constructing theories that might identify ways of better explaining and improving world affairs.

## Extending Realism: The Neorealist Structural Approach

As noted, classical political realism remains an important theoretical perspective underlying contemporary analyses of national security affairs. More recently, it has gained popularity in reconstructed form as a general theory of international politics. This reformulated perspective is known as **neorealism** or *structural realism.*[11]

---

[10] For a discussion as it applies to world politics, see the special issue of *International Studies Quarterly* on "Speaking the Language of Exile: Dissident Thought in International Studies," coedited by Richard K. Ashley and R. B. J. Walker (1990), Der Derian and Shapiro (1989), Onuf (1989), Sjolander and Cox (1994), Wendt (1992), and Walker (1993); for a critique of the postmodern critique, see Rosenau (1992).
[11] For a discussion, see the "Symposium on the New Realism" in *International Organization* 38 (Spring 1984), with special attention to the essays by Richard K. Ashley (1984) and by Robert Gilpin (1984). In addition, *Neorealism and Its Critics* (Keohane, 1986a) and R. B. J. Walker (1987) provide overviews.

## A Systems Theory of International Politics

The pioneer of the "new" realism, Kenneth N. Waltz, set out in his influential book *Theory of International Politics* (1979) to convert the loose and disjointed body of classical realist *thought* into a formal *theory* (Waltz, 1995). "To systematize political realism into a rigorous, deductive systemic theory of international politics" (Keohane, 1986b), neorealism distinguished between explanations of international politics cast at the national level of states, commonly known as foreign policy, from explanations cast at the level of the international system, which are systems or systemic theories.

> The new realism, in contrast to the old, begins by proposing a solution to the problem of distinguishing factors internal to international political systems from those that are external. Theory isolates one realm from others in order to deal with it intellectually. By depicting an international-political system as a whole, with structural and unit levels at once distinct and connected, neorealism establishes the autonomy of international politics. . . . Neorealism develops the concept of a system's structure which at once bounds the domain that students of international politics deal with and enables them to see how the structure of the system, and variations in it, affect the interacting units and the outcomes they produce. (Waltz, 1995:74)

As Waltz (1991) elaborated, "international structure emerges from the interaction of states and then constrains them from taking certain actions while propelling them toward others." As in classical realism, anarchy and the absence of central institutions (a government) characterize the structure of the system. States remain the primary actors. They act according to the principle of self-help, and all seek to ensure their survival. Thus, according to structural realism, states do not differ in the tasks they face, only in their capabilities. Capabilities define the position of states in the system, and the distribution of capabilities defines the structure of the system. Similarly, changes in the distribution of capabilities stimulate changes in the structure of the system, as from a unipolar to a bipolar power configuration, or from a bipolar to a multipolar one.

Power also remains a central concept in structural realism. However, the quest for power is no longer considered an end in itself, as in classical realism; nor does it derive from human nature. Instead, states pursue power as an instrument of survival. As Waltz (1979) explains, "states . . . try in more or less sensible ways to use the means available in order to achieve the ends in view. Those means fall into two categories: internal efforts (moves to increase economic capability, to increase military strength, to develop clever strategies) and external efforts (moves to strengthen and enlarge one's own alliance or to weaken and shrink an opposing one)." A balance of power emerges more or less automatically from the instinct for survival. "Balances of power tend to form whether some or all states consciously aim to establish and maintain a balance, or whether some or all states aim for universal domination" (Waltz, 1979). Once the international system is formed, it "becomes a force that the units may not be able to control; it constrains their behavior and interposes itself between their intentions and the outcomes of their actions" (Ruggie, 1983).

## *Implications of Systemic Constraints*

The conclusion that balances of power must form is a central element in neorealism. This deduction reinforces the notion that the structure of the system determines outcomes, not the characteristics of the units that make up the system. Neorealists recognize that states pursue many goals that sometimes "fluctuate with the changing currents of domestic politics, are prey to the vagaries of a shifting cast of political leaders, and are influenced by the outcomes of bureaucratic struggles." But they contend that such factors as whether governments are democracies or dictatorships tell little about the process whereby states come to pursue the goal of balancing power with power. Instead, "structural constraints explain why the [same] methods are repeatedly used despite differences in the persons and states who use them" (Waltz, 1979).

Neorealist theory also helps to explain why the prospects for international cooperation and change often appear so dim. Fear is endemic to the international system. As long as states wish to survive, they must be wary of the threat posed by others and protect themselves against others. Hence, they must be sensitive to their *relative position* in the distribution of power.

> When faced with the possibility of cooperating for mutual gain, states that feel insecure must ask how the gain will be divided. They are compelled to ask not "Will both of us gain?" but "Who will gain more?" If an expected gain is to be divided, say, in the ratio of two to one, one state may use its disproportionate gain to implement a policy intended to damage or destroy the other. Even the prospect of large absolute gains for both parties does not elicit their cooperation so long as each fears how the other will use its increased capabilities. (Waltz, 1979: 105; see also Snidal, 1993)

The impediments to cooperation thus inhere not in the intentions of the parties to potential collaborative endeavors, but rather result from the insecurity bred by the anarchical system. "The condition of insecurity—at the least, the uncertainty of each about the other's future intentions and actions—works against their cooperation" (Waltz, 1979).

Waltz argues there is a second reason why states shy away from international cooperation, namely, fear that they may become too dependent on others for their own well-being. Dependence can take the form of a superior-subordinate relation, a one-way street, or it can take the form of interdependence, a two-way street. Both kinds of relationships exist in world politics, and, according to the logic of structural realism, both may be perceived as threatening. "Like other organizations, states seek to control what they depend on or to lessen the extent of their dependency. This simple thought explains quite a bit of the behavior of states: their imperial thrusts to widen the scope of their control and their autarchic strivings toward greater self-sufficiency" (Waltz, 1979).

Not everyone agrees that increased interdependence will diminish the prospects for international cooperation. Conflict among states has been endemic throughout much of world history, but so has international cooperation; there are compelling reasons to expect that patterns can change and that increased interdependence can lead to still even higher levels of cooperation. It is this expectation that lies behind the so-called "neoliberal" (Baldwin, 1993; Kegley, 1995; Nye, 1988) challenge to realism and neorealism that has recently arisen.


## Neoliberalism

As the Cold War ended, dissatisfaction with realism and neorealism began to rise. Arguing that "it is time for a new, more rigorous idealist alternative to realism" (Kober, 1990), critics point to several shortcomings: (1) power-politics perspectives failed to predict the peaceful end of the Cold War and international social change in general (Scholte, 1993); (2) realism and neorealism were scientifically inaccurate; research findings suggest that their "underlying theory of war and peace [was] flawed" (Vasquez, 1993) because realists "oversimplified the concept of power and misunderstood the lessons of history" (Kober, 1990); and (3) realism's approach would "not be an adequate guide for the future of international politics" (Jervis, 1992) because the broadened post–Cold War global agenda includes many questions and problems "which realist theory cannot reach" (Scholte, 1993). The problems of AIDS, ecological deterioration, economic underdevelopment, and global warming are among those for which realism is seen deficient.

Asking "Is realism finished?" (Zakaria, 1992–1993), these critics contend that there exists the need to "rethink neorealism" (Buzan, Jones, and Little, 1993) since they perceive structural realism to be "a research enterprise in crisis" (James, 1993). But they go beyond this prescription by advocating that "the recovery of liberalism" (Little, 1993) be treated as a theoretical goal in international relations. As Francis Fukuyama (1992b) put it, "there are good reasons for examining aspects of the liberal international legacy once again." In response, a new or *neoliberal* approach emerged in the early 1990s.

This analytic departure goes by several labels. Sometimes called "neoliberal institutionalism" (Grieco, 1995), "neoidealism" (Kegley, 1993), or "neo-Wilsonian idealism" (Fukuyama, 1992a), neoliberalism seeks to build theories of international relations by giving the basic tenets of classical liberalism and post–World War I idealism a fresh examination. Emphasizing the prospects for peace, prosperity, and progress, it explores the mechanisms by which such cooperation and change might be fostered. In particular, neoliberalism focuses on the contribution that influences such as democratic governance, public opinion, mass education, free trade, liberal capitalism, international law and organization, arms control and disarmament, collective security and multilateral diplomacy, and ethically inspired statecraft could make to improvement of life on our planet. Because they perceive global conditions to have changed, neoliberal theorists maintain that the ideas and ideals of the liberal legacy can today describe, explain, predict, and prescribe international conduct in ways that they could not during the conflict-ridden Cold War.

Part of the reason why the new idealists and liberal theorists harbor this hope springs from the findings of regional integration studies that began to flourish in the

1950s and 1960s. At that time, scholars sought to understand the processes whereby the political unification of sovereign states might be achieved. Efforts to create new institutions in Western Europe, historically one of the most war-prone of all world regions, commanded the most attention, as expanding transaction flows in trade, communication, and immigrant labor propelled Europeans to sacrifice portions of their sovereign independence in an effort to create new political units out of previously separate ones. The integrative achievements unfolding in Europe also inspired interest in their applicability to other world regions, such as Central America and East Africa (see Nye, 1971). As a consequence, these investigations pointed to developments outside of realism's world view and suggested that a theory grounded in the liberal tradition was needed to explain them.

In addition, the rapid growth of international economic transactions, especially since the 1960s, further undermined the cogency of the state-centric perspective of political realism and made greater attention to transnational collaboration imperative. A growing number of economically powerful transnational actors, particularly multinational corporations, pushed theoretical inquiry away from its conventional focus on nation-states and toward the threats that nonstate actors posed to state sovereignty. As the costs and benefits of growing interdependence affected politics within states, not just between them, the ascribed importance of nonmilitary issues, such as environmental protection and trade protectionism, on national political agendas increased sharply. And for this realm of behavior, the liberal tradition provided a compelling account.

As the density of interdependent transnational linkages multiplied in the 1970s and 1980s, the perceived utility of military power as an instrument of political influence, so central in realist theory, also began to wane. The balance of military power seemed to lose instrumental value compared with the balance of economic power, as the United States and other Western industrialized nations realized when the world's oil-producing countries restricted supplies and drove up prices during the 1970s and early 1980s.

Historical precedents, unfolding trends, and dramatic transformations together exerted pressure for a refashioned liberal theory. We witness the result in neoliberal theoretical activity today. But in considering this recent theorizing, the divergent strands within it must be recognized (see Zacher and Matthew, 1995, for an overview). Like realism and neorealism, neoliberalism does not represent a cohesive intellectual movement or school of thought. Neoliberals operate from different assumptions, and they examine different aspects of the processes through which international change and cooperation might be promoted. Some, like neorealists, embrace a structural theory that examines the characteristics of the international system. Other neoliberals concentrate on the characteristics of the units and subunits that comprise it, such as the types of governments (democracies or dictatorships) and leaders who govern states. And still other neoliberals give primary attention to the influence of international institutions like the United Nations and nonstate actors like multinational corporations. All neoliberals, however, share an interest in probing the conditions under which cooperation may be promoted as a result of the convergent and overlapping interests among otherwise sovereign political entities.

To illuminate these similarities and differences among neoliberals, we will examine three theoretical perspectives of neoliberalism that encapsulate its orientation: complex interdependence, international regimes, and feminism.

## Complex Interdependence as a World View

As an explicit analytical perspective, *complex interdependence* first arose in the 1970s to challenge the key assumptions of its rival theoretical frameworks, particularly classical realism. First, it challenged the prevailing assumption that nation-states are the only important actors in world politics by treating other actors, such as multinational corporations and transnational banks, as "important not only because of their activities in pursuit of their own interests, but also because they act as transmission belts, making government policies in various countries more sensitive to one another" (Keohane and Nye, 1988). In this sense complex interdependence is a "holistic," systemic conception that pictures world politics as the sum of its many interacting parts in a "global society" (see Holsti, 1989b).

Second, complex interdependence questioned whether national security issues dominate nation-states' decision-making agendas. Under conditions of interdependence, foreign policy agendas become "larger and more diverse" because a broader range of "governments' policies, even those previously considered merely domestic, impinge on one another" (Keohane and Nye, 1988).

Third, this perspective disputed the popular notion that military force is the only, even dominant, means of exercising influence in international politics, particularly among the industrial and democratic societies in Europe and North America. "Intense relationships of mutual influence exist between these countries, but in most of them force is irrelevant or unimportant as an instrument of policy" (Keohane and Nye, 1988).

Advocates of the complex interdependence perspective extended many of these insights to the range of issues relating to international economic interdependence that came to the fore in the 1970s (Puchala, 1988) and, later, to environmental protection. International institutions commanded a central place in many of these analyses, as demonstrated in Robert O. Keohane and Joseph S. Nye's (1977, 1989) *Power and Interdependence*, which remains the classic statement on the complex interdependence extension of classical idealism.

However, a careful reading of *Power and Interdependence* shows that complex interdependence does not altogether reject realism. Instead, the initial concern of many of those dedicated to the perspective was "the conditions under which assumptions of Realism were sufficient or needed to be supplemented by a more complex model of change" (Nye, 1987; see also Keohane, 1983). Keohane and Nye in particular sought to devise structural models of international *regime* change. The regime concept derived from, and extended, international legal studies. It eventually became a central component of the neoliberal perspective and has been widely used in analyses of international politics that seek to understand cooperation under conditions of anarchy.

## International Regimes

Although the international system continues to be characterized by anarchy, its nature is more properly conceptualized as an ordered anarchy, and the system as a whole as an "anarchical society" (Bull, 1977), because cooperation, not conflict, is often the observable outcome of relations among states.

Given this reality, the question arises: How can institutionalized procedures and rules for the collective management of global policy problems—*international regimes* based on coordinated cooperation—be established and preserved? Interest in that question derives from two goals that motivate many neoliberal analysts. One is "a desire to understand the extent to which mutually accepted constraints affect states' behaviors" (Zacher, 1987). The other is an interest in devising strategies for creating a less disorderly "world order."

As the study of regimes or rules for the management of global problems developed in the 1980s, Stephen Krasner's definition of a regime emerged dominant:

> Regimes can be defined as sets of implicit or explicit principles, norms, rules, and decision-making procedures around which actors' expectations converge in a given area of international relations. Principles are beliefs or fact, causation, and rectitude. Norms are standards of behavior defined in terms of rights and obligations. Rules are specific prescriptions or proscriptions for action. Decision-making procedures are prevailing practices for making and implementing collective choice.[12] (Krasner, 1982: 186)

According to this definition, regimes are institutionalized systems of cooperation in a given issue-area. As Krasner (1982) explains, "It is the infusion of behavior with principles and norms that distinguishes regime-governed activity in the international system from more conventional activity, guided exclusively by narrow calculations of interest." Thus an essential property of a regime is that it constitutes "a system of injunctions about international behavior" (Smith, 1987). Because the international regime perspective directs attention to institutions and to the influence of norms on patterns of state behavior,[13] as opposed simply to the pursuit of national interests, it is in some ways best viewed as an attempt to reconcile the idealist and realist perspectives on world politics (Haggard and Simmons, 1987).

The global monetary and trade systems created during and after World War II are vivid expressions of international regimes. And both, as well as particular sectors within the trade system, have been the focus of considerable inquiry from the regime perspective.[14] Together the monetary and trade regimes defined a *Liberal International Economic Order* (LIEO) that limited government intervention in the world political economy and otherwise facilitated the free flow of capital and goods across

---

[12] For reviews of the regime concept and this and other definitions that have been offered, see Haggard and Simmons (1987), Kratochwil and Ruggie (1986), Rittberger (1993), Strange (1982), and Young (1986).
[13] International institutions figure prominently as the bridge linking these orientations, although it should be understood that the term *regime* was construed to cover more than just organizations. As Oran Young (1986) explains, "Institutions are practices composed of recognized roles coupled with sets of rules or conventions governing relations among the occupants of these roles. Organizations are physical entities possessing offices, personnel, equipment, budgets, and so forth."
[14] The literature on international regimes is large and growing. The best single introduction remains the special issue of *International Organization* edited by Stephen D. Krasner (1983), which was published in book form by Cornell University Press in 1983. The journal *International Organization* publishes many analyses of issues related to regime dynamics.

national boundaries. The *International Monetary Fund* (IMF) and the *General Agreement on Tariffs and Trade* (GATT) played important institutional roles in the LIEO and reconfirmed the importance of international institutions in fostering transnational cooperation (see Chapter 7 for elaboration).

Most illustrations of the regime perspective appear in the world political economy arena. Relatively few "security regimes" (Jervis, 1982) have emerged in the defense issue-area to provoke examination. Exceptions are the nuclear nonproliferation regime and the regime used by the former superpowers to manage crises (see George, 1986; Tarr, 1991). With the end of the Cold War, the pressures of interdependence may propel creation of regimes in widening areas of international conduct to facilitate states' control over their common fates (Zacher, 1991). This is likely to accelerate efforts to grapple theoretically with the causes and consequences of multilateralism (see Caporaso, 1992).

### Liberal Feminist Theory

*Feminist theory* arose in the 1960s in response to the pronounced disregard of females in discourse about public and international affairs and the injustice and inequity that this bias caused. The mainstream literature on world politics underestimated or ignored altogether the contributions of women and treated differences in men's and women's status, beliefs, and behaviors as unimportant. Gender roles were also ignored, along with the evidence that sexism is a pillar of the war system (Reardon, 1985) and that a corrective of this problem might be to give women the prominence and power in policy making that traditionally they have been denied (Peterson and Runyan, 1993).

As feminist theory crystallized, it began to direct its criticism at realism. In particular, it was alleged that realism, formulated and dominated by males, ignored the human roots of global conditions and promoted an essentially masculine interpretation of relations between states that was inattentive to human rights and rife with rationales for aggression.

Derived in part from liberal precepts supportive of fair play, justice, and philosophical acceptance of love over power, feminist theory went beyond this initial critique of realism's bias to chart an independent theoretical "standpoint" (Keohane, 1989). That perspective has opened windows to aspects of international affairs heretofore hidden from view. These include a focus on the performance of women as leaders of government and as members of infantry combat units and an examination of the differences gender makes (Grant and Newland, 1991); also representative is feminist theory's exploration of females as a subject of study in the dynamics of population growth. Perhaps the greatest impact of feminist theory in the field has been its consideration of alternatives to realism in developing strategies for world security (see Tickner, 1992). In this sense, feminist theory, like neoliberalism generally, is motivated by the quest for discovering the paths to greater international cooperation.

## INTERNATIONAL POLITICS IN A WORLD OF CHANGE . . . . . . . . . . . . . . . . .

To understand today's changing world and make reasonable prognoses about tomorrow's, we must first arm ourselves with an array of knowledge and conceptual tools, entertain rival interpretations of the alternative ways to map world politics, and question the assumptions on which these contending world views rest. As we have demonstrated (see Table 2.1 for a brief summary), there are several alternative, sometimes incompatible ways of organizing theoretical perspectives about world politics. The reason is clear: The *global problematique* is one of vast proportions and complexity—a challenge to insight and understanding—that cannot be reduced to a single, simple, yet compelling account.

## Rival Theories and Evidence

Although the theoretical perspectives discussed in this chapter begin to equip us for the challenge of understanding the changing world, from time to time we will also find it useful to draw on still other theoretical foci. Five that are elaborated in greater detail in later chapters are briefly identified here: hegemonic stability theory, long-cycle theory, world-system theory, dependency theory, and comparative foreign policy.

### *Hegemonic Stability Theory*

To understand the relationship between national power and international order, **hegemonic stability theory** examines what happens when a clearly predominant state, a **hegemon,** exercises leadership and control of the international system. "A hybrid of liberal/neorealist theory" (Gill, 1993b), this perspective maintains that "hegemony is a necessary, but not a sufficient, condition for the creation of an open economic order." If it is willing and able to lead, the hegemon can set and enforce the rules governing international trade, finance, and investment (and other issues, such as environmental regulation). In this way, when hegemony is achieved it is believed to contribute to peaceful and cooperative interstate relations, providing, of course, the preeminent state does not ruthlessly exploit its power through domination and imperialism. The theory argues that hegemons, such as Great Britain after World War I and the United States after World War II, will seldom engage in this abuse. Instead, when they obtain top-dog status, hegemons promote regimes that benefit not only themselves but also others. Why? Because it is in the hegemon's enlightened self-interest to seek global stability. Peace, accordingly, will result from a leading state's capacity to manage world order (Gilpin, 1981; Keohane and Nye, 1989; Levy, 1991; for critiques, see Haggard and Simmons, 1987; Snidal, 1985).

This theory also advances predictions about the consequences that will result if and when a hegemon declines. When this kind of structural transformation occurs and the system is left without an unchallenged leader, instability follows. To the extent that U.S. power and position have begun to recede,[15] hegemonic stability theory predicts that the post–World War II global order will eventually collapse and

---

[15] For discussions of this thesis, see Burman (1991), Dietrich (1992), Fry, Taylor, and Wood (1994), and Kennedy (1987); for rebuttals, see Nau (1990) and Nye (1990).

### TABLE 2.1 THE QUEST FOR THEORY: FOUR PERSPECTIVES

| Model | Idealism | Realism | Behavioralism | Neoliberalism |
|---|---|---|---|---|
| Core Concern | Institutionalizing peace | War and security | Discovering through science "laws" about the causes and consequences of interstate interaction | Fostering interstate cooperation on the globe's shared economic, social, and ecological problems |
| Submodel(s) | International law; international organization; democratization | Neorealism; structural realism | Comparative study of foreign policy, quantitative analysis | Complex interdependence; regimes; feminist theory |
| Outlook on Global Prospects | Optimistic/ Progress | Pessimistic/ Stability | Progress through reason | Expectation of cooperation and creation of a global community |
| Key Units | Institutions transcending nations | Independent nation-states | Individuals, states, and the international system | Individuals; "penetrated" nations and nonstate transnational actors |
| Motives of Actors | Collaboration; mutual aid; meeting human needs | National interests; zero-sum competition; security; power | Rational choice, as modified by environmental opportunities and constraints | National interests; justice; peace and prosperity; liberty; morality |
| Central Concepts | Collective security; world order; law; integration; international organization | Structural anarchy; power; national interests; balance of power; polarity | Theory building and hypothesis testing against reproducible evidence and deductive modeling | Transnational relations; law; free markets; interdependence; integration; liberal republican rule; human rights; gender |
| Prescriptions | Institutional reform | Increase national power; resist reduction of national autonomy | Ground policy advice on verifiable knowledge | Develop regimes and promote democracy and international institutions to coordinate collective responses to diverse global problems |

a new period of conflict and disorder will commence. The theory thus speaks directly to the potential dangers of a post–Cold War future.

## Long-Cycle Theory

**Long-cycle theory** seeks to explain the historical ebb and flow of world politics, global leadership, and systemwide war (Goldstein, 1988; Modelski and Thompson, 1994). The rise and fall of the great powers and empires is a central concern. An important assumption is the belief that many features of international politics—especially the patterns of great-power rivalry—cannot be understood adequately without a long-term perspective focused on recurrent historical patterns and on the economic, political, and military forces that underlie these evolutionary processes.

## World-System Theory

**World-system theory** also looks at system dynamics from a long-term, structural perspective, with emphasis on its economic underpinnings. It arose in part in response to the theories of political development and nation building prevalent in comparative politics in the 1950s and 1960s and seeks to explain the rise to dominance of the capitalist societies of the Western world and the lack of economic development in many other geographic areas. Contending variants of world-system theory stress different factors. The best known is Immanuel Wallerstein's (1980) macrosociological theory of economic change in the world capitalist system, which examines the forces driving the formation and disintegration of world empires (see Chapter 5).

## Dependency Theory

The primary concern of **dependency theory** is the pattern of dominance and dependence that characterizes the unequal relationship between the world's rich and poor nations (Packenham, 1992). Its intellectual father is Dr. Raúl Prebisch, an Argentinean economist who directed the United Nations Economic Commission for Latin America in the 1950s. Initially looking at the unfavorable terms of trade alleged to have led to economic stagnation and foreign control of Third World economies, dependency theorists have expanded their analysis to account for other phenomena, such as "dependent development," that is, economic growth where previously it was thought impossible. They are also concerned with such paradoxes as the tendency of Third World economic growth to exacerbate social inequalities and class cleavages.

## Comparative Foreign Policy

Most of the perspectives described in this chapter focus on the so-called international system level of analysis. Structural realism does so unabashedly. It argues that differences in the characteristics of the international actors and their decision processes are irrelevant to an understanding of recurrent behavior in international politics. As explained by Robert O. Keohane (1983), "The key distinguishing characteristic of a systemic theory is that *the internal attributes of actors are given by assumption rather than treated as variables.* Changes in actor behavior, and system outcomes, are explained not on the basis of variation in these actor characteristics, but on the basis of changes in attributes of the system itself."

Other scholars are critical of this perspective. Those working in the neoliberal tradition, for example, place considerable emphasis on the potential role that the type of government and domestic politics may play in shaping the responses of different foreign policymakers to the challenge of interdependence. Still, accounts that trace countries' international behavior to the combined force of both domestic political pressures and of systemic constraints and opportunities are rare (Bueno de Mesquita and Lalman, 1992, represents a recent beginning).

Advocates of the comparative study of foreign policy seek to pursue this analytic goal by probing the similarities and differences in states' international circumstances and in their national attributes and capabilities, foreign policy decision-making processes, and individual policymakers. Their focus is cogent in the post–Cold War system in which, as U.S. President Bill Clinton put it in 1993, "there is no longer division between what is foreign and domestic." To explain and predict how countries act, comparativists contend that both the international and internal factors that shape their conduct should be examined. The comparative study of foreign policy commands considerable analytical attention. We will therefore devote an entire chapter (Chapter 3) to that single perspective.

## Levels of Analysis

The comparative study of foreign policy focuses analytical attention primarily on the nation-state. Other theories and perspectives discussed in this chapter direct attention to other *levels of analysis.* Thus the psychological approach to images emphasizes the role of individuals in world politics, while the neorealist perspective directs attention exclusively to the international system as a whole. What we learn about world politics, then, depends in part on the analytical perspective we choose and on the analytical level it emphasizes.

The levels-of-analysis issue in the study of world politics (see Singer, 1961; also Waltz, 1954) underscores the need to trace changes in world politics to different groups of actors, their attributes, and their activities and interactions. Levels are commonly determined by the relative size and scope of their composition. Three are distinctly identifiable and theoretically important.

At the smallest (narrowest) level is the so-called idiosyncratic or *individual level* of analysis. It refers to the personal characteristics of each human being, from the average citizen to those who make the important decisions on behalf of both state and nonstate actors in world politics. At the second or *national level* are the authoritative decision-making units that govern nation-states' foreign policy processes and the attributes of those states, such as their size, location, and power, that shape and constrain the foreign policy choices of those who govern. And at a third level are the conditions that result from the interactions of nations and nonstate actors with one another around the globe. This international or *system level* of analysis is also used to refer to those macro properties that simultaneously influence the entire global environment, such as its international legal rules, distribution of power, or the number of cross-cutting alliances in existence and amount of war under way.

The differentiation of levels of analysis is important because it emphasizes that transformations in world politics cannot be attributed to a single source but must consider the influence of many causes. Common sense suggests that there are interrelationships across all levels and that trends and transformations in world politics are linked simultaneously to forces operating at each level. The behavior of any one nation, for instance, will likely be affected by the dispositions of its leaders, its domestic political and economic circumstances and type of government, and changes in the conditions beyond its borders. Similarly, changes in international tension tomorrow will be governed in part by how actors at each level choose to act toward one another today. For this reason, we must examine trends and transformations in world politics by reference to a variety of causal factors flowing from all three levels of analysis. It is an analytical task that permeates the remaining chapters of this book.

## WORLD POLITICS: THE ANALYTICAL CHALLENGE

Armed with the tools and theories described in preceding sections, and being sensitive to the dimensions of world affairs which each highlights or obscures, we can begin to address difficult and often disturbing questions. Will the world's complex metamorphoses outrun its ability to devise new mechanisms of political and social control? Will the world be flexible enough to adjust its perceptions to changing global realities? Which theories will best guide such adjustments? Can we adapt conventional mental habits to comprehend unconventional circumstances? The challenge is ours to meet.

## SUGGESTED READINGS

Baldwin, David A., ed. *Neorealism and Neoliberalism: The Contemporary Debate*. New York: Columbia University Press, 1993.

Dougherty, James E., and Robert L. Pfaltzgraff Jr. *Contending Theories of International Relations*, 3rd ed. New York: Harper & Row, 1990.

Ferguson, Yale H., and Richard W. Mansbach. *The Elusive Quest: Theory and International Politics*. Columbia: University of South Carolina Press, 1988.

Gabriel, Jürg Martin. *Worldviews and Theories of International Relations*. New York: St. Martin's Press, 1994.

Holsti, K. J. *The Dividing Discipline: Hegemony and Diversity in International Theory*. Boston: Allen & Unwin, 1985.

Kegley, Charles W., Jr., ed. *Controversies in International Relations Theory: Realism and the Neoliberal Challenge*. New York: St. Martin's Press, 1995.

Keohane, Robert O., and Joseph S. Nye Jr. *Power and Interdependence: World Politics in Transition*, 2nd ed. Glenview, Ill.: Scott, Foresman/Little, Brown, 1989.

Rothstein, Robert L., ed. *The Evolution of Theory in International Relations*. Columbia: University of South Carolina Press, 1991.

Sjolander, Claire Turenne, and Wayne S. Cox, eds. *Beyond Positivism: Critical Reflections on International Relations*. Boulder, Colo.: Lynne Rienner, 1994.

Sylvester, Christine, *Feminist Theory and International Relations in a Postmodern Era*. Cambridge: Cambridge University Press, 1994.

Viotti, Paul, and Mark V. Kauppi. *International Relations Theory: Realism, Pluralism, Globalism*, 2nd ed. New York: Macmillan, 1993.

Wight, Martin. *International Theory: The Three Traditions*. New York: Holmes and Meier, 1992.

# Part II

# Relations among Global Actors

. . .

# CHAPTER 3

• • •

# FOREIGN POLICY DECISION MAKING: COPING WITH INTERNATIONAL CIRCUMSTANCES

• • •

*Foreign policy is the system of activities evolved by communities for changing the behavior of other states and for adjusting their own activities to the international environment.*

George Modelski,
Political Scientist, 1962

*We can no longer afford a [policy making] process that results in duplication or programs that work at cross purposes. . . . Simply put, if we are not clear about where we want to go and about our options for getting there, we will not fare well in the post–Cold War era.*

U.S. Department of State,
Management Task Force, 1993

People who study world politics typically use the term *actor* to refer to entities that are its primary performers. The image portrayed is that of a stage on which those most capable of capturing the drama of world politics act out the roles assigned to them. The leading actors dominate the center of the stage, and others cast in supporting roles are less evident as they move along the periphery. Moreover, they play their roles under constraints not readily visible to the casual observer, much as the actors in a community playhouse production follow their scripts under the guiding hand of the director.

Today the actors on the world stage are many and varied. They include countries, properly called nation-states (like the United States and Japan), international organizations (the United Nations), multinational corporations (General Motors), nonstate nations (the Kurds in Iran and Iraq), and terrorist groups (the Irish Republican Army). We will discuss each of these types of actors in later chapters. Here we focus on nation-states, in particular on the processes they use to make foreign policy decisions designed to cope with challenges from abroad. Nation-states demand attention because they remain the principal repositories of economic and military capabilities in world affairs, and they alone assert the legal right to use force.

The term "nation-state" is often used interchangeably with state and nation, but technically the three are different. A **state** is a legal entity that enjoys a permanent population, a well-defined territory, and a government capable of exercising sovereignty (that is, supreme authority over its inhabitants and freedom from interference by others). A **nation** is a collection of people who, on the basis of ethnic, linguistic, or cultural affinity, perceive themselves to be members of the same group. Thus **nation-state** refers to a polity controlled by members of some nationality recognizing no higher authority. It implies a convergence between territorial states and the psychological identification of people within them.[1]

When we speak generically about *foreign policy* and the decision-making processes that produce it, we refer to the goals that the officials representing nation-states seek abroad, the values that underlie those goals, and the means or instruments used to pursue them. We begin our inquiry of how states make foreign policy choices by studying the model of rational decision making. Following this, we will consider two alternative frameworks: the bureaucratic politics and the hero-in-history models. We conclude by examining how states' national attributes influence their foreign policy behavior.

## The Unitary Actor and Rational Decision Making . . . . . . . . . . . . . . .

According to the theory of political realism, discussed in Chapter 2, the primary goal of nation-states' foreign policies is to ensure their survival. That is, states seek to preserve their independence or sovereignty in a hostile environment. From this viewpoint, strategic calculations about national security are the primary determinants of policymakers' choices. Domestic politics and the process of policy making itself are of secondary concern.

## States as Unitary Actors

Political realism in both its classical and neorealist forms emphasizes that the international environment determines state action. It assumes that foreign policy making consists primarily of adjusting the nation-state to the pressures of an anarchical world system whose essential properties do not vary. Accordingly, it assumes that all states and the individuals responsible for their foreign policies confront the problem of national survival in similar ways. Thus all decision makers are essentially alike in their approach to foreign policy making.

---

[1] Many states are made up of multiple nations, not just one, and some nations are not states. These nonstate nations are ethnic groups, such as Native American tribes in the United States, Sikhs in India, or the Basques in Spain, composed of people without sovereign power over the territory they occupy. Some seek national (ethnic) independence and/or merger with another state with which they feel greater solidarity. See Chapter 6 for a discussion of nonstate nations and ethnonational independence movements active throughout the world.

If they follow the [decision] rules, we need know nothing more about them. In essence, if the decision-maker behaves rationally, the observer, knowing the rules of rationality, can rehearse the decisional process in his own mind, and, if he knows the decision-maker's goals, can both predict the decision and understand why that particular decision was made. (Verba, 1969: 225)

Because the goals and corresponding decision calculus of states are the same, the foreign policy decision-making processes of each can be studied as though it were a *unitary actor.* One way to picture this assumption is to think of states as billiard balls and the table on which they interact as the state system. The metaphor compares world politics to a game in which the billiard balls (states) continuously clash and collide with one another. The actions of each are determined by their interactions with the others, not by what occurs within them. According to this "mental map," the leaders who make foreign policy, the types of governments they head, the characteristics of their societies, and the internal economic and political conditions of the states they lead are unimportant.

## Policy Making as Rational Choice

The decision processes of unitary actors that determine definitions of national interests are typically described as *rational.* What is rationality? And how do decision makers go about making foreign policy rationally?

For our purposes, we can define rationality as purposeful, goal-directed behavior exhibited when "the individual responding to an international event . . . uses the best information available and chooses from the universe of possible responses that alternative most likely to maximize his goals" (Verba, 1969). By way of elaboration, scholars who study decision making and advise policymakers on ways to improve their policy-making skills describe rationality as a sequence of decision-making activities involving the following intellectual steps:

1. *Problem recognition and definition.* The need to decide begins when policymakers perceive an external problem with which they must deal and attempt to define its distinguishing characteristics objectively. Objectivity requires full information about the actions, motivations, and capabilities of other actors as well as the character of the international environment and trends within it. The search for information must be exhaustive, and all the facts relevant to the problem must be gathered.

2. *Goal selection.* Next, those responsible for making foreign policy choices must determine what they want to accomplish. This disarmingly simple requirement is often difficult. It requires the identification and ranking of *all* values (such as security, democracy, and economic well-being) in a hierarchy from most to least preferred.

3. *Identification of alternatives.* Rationality also requires the compilation of an

exhaustive list of *all* available policy options and an estimation of the costs associated with each alternative course of action.

4. *Choice*. Finally, rationality requires selecting from competing options the single alternative with the best chance of achieving the desired goal(s). For this purpose, policymakers must conduct a rigorous means–ends, cost–benefit analysis, one guided by an accurate prediction of the probable success of each option.[2]

The requirements of perfect rationality are stringent. Nonetheless, policymakers often describe their own behavior as resulting from a rational decision-making process designed to reach the "best" decision possible. Moreover, some past foreign policy decisions reveal elements of this idealized process.

The 1962 Cuban missile crisis, for example, illustrates several ways the deliberations of the key U.S. policymakers conformed to a rational process (Allison, 1971; for reassessments, see Blight and Welch, 1989; also Nathan, 1992). Once Washington discovered the presence of Soviet missiles in Cuba, President John F. Kennedy charged the crisis decision-making group he formed to "set aside all other tasks to make a prompt and intensive survey of the dangers and all possible courses of action." Six options were ultimately identified: Do nothing; exert diplomatic pressure; make a secret approach to the Cuban leader Fidel Castro; invade Cuba; launch a surgical air strike against the missiles; and blockade Cuba. Goals had to be prioritized before a choice could be made among these six. Was removal of the Soviet missiles, retaliation against Castro, or maintenance of the balance of power the objective? Or did the missiles pose little threat to the vital interests of the United States? Until the missiles were determined to pose a serious threat to U.S. security, "do nothing" could not be eliminated as an option.

Once the advisers agreed that removing the missiles was the goal, their discussion turned to evaluating the surgical air strike and blockade options. The latter was eventually chosen because of its presumed advantages. Among them was the demonstration of firmness it permitted the United States and the flexibility about further choices it allowed both parties.

The decision of U.S. President George Bush to send a military force to the Middle East following Iraq's invasion of Kuwait on August 2, 1990, is another example of crisis decision making that conforms in part to the model of rational choice. As in the Cuban case, the "do nothing" option was quickly dismissed by the president and his advisers. Instead, "much of the initial debate among senior government officials on August 2 and 3 focused on diplomatic and economic retaliation against Iraq, and possible covert action to destabilize and topple Saddam Hussein" (Woodward and

---

[2] As we will note in more detail below, the concept of "rationality" has been defined in different ways. For our purposes, we at this point employ a "procedural" definition of rationality. Later we will contrast it to the "instrumentalist" definition used in *rational choice* theory, which is more suited to individuals than to the policy-making process whereby organizations make foreign policy choices and which is often derived from mathematical cost–benefit analyses (see Bueno de Mesquita, 1981; Bueno de Mesquita and Lalman, 1992; Levy, 1990–1991; Nicholson, 1992; and Zagare, 1990).

Atkinson, 1990). By August 4, Bush decided to mount a military response. Two days later, after vowing that Iraq's invasion of Kuwait "will not stand," he ordered the dispatch of U.S. troops in pursuit of three missions: to deter further Iraqi aggression, to defend Saudi Arabia, and to "improve the overall defense capabilities of the Saudi peninsula" (Woodward and Atkinson, 1990). Eventually, those defensive missions gave way to an offensive one designed to force Iraq out of Kuwait.

## Impediments to Rational Choice

Despite the apparent application of rationality in these important crises, the rational decision-making model is often more an idealized standard by which to evaluate preferences than an accurate description of real-world behavior. Theodore Sorensen, himself a participant in the Cuban missile deliberations, has written not only about the steps policymakers in the Kennedy administration followed as they sought to emulate the process of rational choice[3] but also of how actual decision making often departed from it:

> Each step cannot be taken in order. The facts may be in doubt or dispute. Several policies, all good, may conflict. Several means, all bad, may be all that are open. Value judgments may differ. Stated goals may be imprecise. There may be many interpretations of what is right, what is possible, and what is in the national interest. (Sorensen, 1963: 19–20)

Despite the virtues promised by rational choice, then, the impediments to its realization are substantial. Some are human. They derive from deficiencies in the intelligence, capability, and psychological needs and aspirations of those who make foreign policy decisions under conditions of uncertainty. Others are organizational. Individuals meeting in groups make most policy decisions. As a result, most decisions require group agreement about the national interest and the wisest course of action to pursue. Reaching agreement is not easy, however, as reasonable people with different values understandably often disagree about goals or preferences and the probable results of alternative options. Thus the impediments to sound (rational) policy making are substantial.

Scrutiny of the actual process of decision making reveals more impediments. Problem recognition is often delayed, for example. Information sufficient to define emergent problems accurately is frequently lacking, resulting in decisions that are made on the basis of incomplete information. In fact, rationality is usually "bounded" (Simon, 1982), not "comprehensive," as policymakers must deal not with perfect information but only with approximations of it and must absorb the costs of acquiring and analyzing it. Moreover, the available information is often inaccurate because the

---

[3] Sorensen (1963) described an eight-step process for policy making that the Kennedy administration sought to follow that is consistent with the model we have described: (1) agreement on the facts; (2) agreement on the overall policy objective; (3) precise definition of the problems; (4) canvassing of all possible solutions; (5) listing of the possible consequences flowing from each solution; (6) recommendation of one option; (7) communication of the option selected; (8) provisions for its execution.

bureaucratic organizations on which political leaders depend for advice screen, sort, and rearrange it.

In addition, ascertaining what goals best serve the national interest is difficult, and decision makers' inability to gather and digest large quantities of information rapidly constrains their capacity to make informed choices about goals. "Decision making often takes place within an atmosphere marked by value-complexity and uncertainty. The existence of competing values about a single issue forces value trade-offs; uncertainty refers to the absence of complete and well-organized information on which to base a confident policy choice" (Walker, 1991).

Furthermore, because policymakers work constantly with overloaded agendas and short deadlines, the search for policy options is seldom exhaustive. "There is little time for leaders to reflect," observes former U.S. Secretary of State Henry Kissinger (1979). "They are locked in an endless battle in which the urgent constantly gains on the important. The public life of every political figure is a continual struggle to rescue an element of choice from the pressure of circumstance." In the choice phase, then, decision makers rarely make value-maximizing choices. Instead of selecting the one option or set of options with the best chance of success, they typically terminate their evaluation as soon as an alternative appears that seems superior to those already considered. Herbert Simon (1957) describes this as *satisficing* behavior. Rather than *optimizing* by seeking the best alternative, decision makers are routinely content to choose the first option that meets minimally acceptable standards. Because they frequently face "unresolvable" choices that preclude satisfaction across competing preferences, often only "admissible" ones appear available (see Levi, 1990). As *prospect theory* tells us, those making decisions are inclined to choose by comparing the options with a recalled "reference point." Fearing losses more than they crave gains, they then select the option that looks preferable to the past reference point rather than a riskier one with better prospects for gains (Levy, 1992; also Stein and Pauly, 1993). In a phrase, foreign policy makers are more *risk averse* than they are *risk acceptant*.

The assumption that states are unitary actors explains in part the discrepancy between the theory and practice of rational decision making. As suggested above, states consist of individuals with different beliefs, values, preferences, and psychological needs. These differences generate disagreements about goals and alternatives that are seldom resolved through tidy, orderly, rational processes. As one former U.S. policymaker put it, "Rather than through grand decisions or grand alternatives, policy changes seem to come through a series of slight modifications of existing policy, with new policy emerging slowly and haltingly by small and usually tentative steps, a process of trial and error in which policy zigs and zags, reverses itself, and then moves forward" (Hilsman, 1967).

Thus, despite the image that policymakers seek to project, the actual practice of foreign policy decision making is an exercise that lends itself to miscalculations, errors, and fiascoes. Policymakers tend "to avoid new interpretations of the environment, to select and act upon traditional goals, to limit the search for alternatives to a small number of moderate ones, and finally to take risks which involve low costs" (Coplin, 1971). Thus, although policymakers sometimes can quickly absorb new information under great pressure and take calculated risks through deliberate planning, more often

## TABLE 3.1 FOREIGN POLICY DECISION MAKING IN THEORY AND PRACTICE

| Ideal Rational Process | Common Actual Practice |
| --- | --- |
| Accurate, comprehensive information | Distorted, incomplete information |
| Clear definition of national interests and goals | Personal motivations and organizational interests bias national goals |
| Exhaustive analysis of all options | Limited number of options considered, none thoroughly analyzed |
| Selection of optimal course of action most capable of producing desired results | Selection of course of action by political bargaining and compromise |
| Effective statement of decision and its rationale to mobilize domestic support | Confusing and contradictory statements of decision often framed for media consumption |
| Careful monitoring of implementation of decision by foreign affairs bureaucracies | Neglect of tedious task of managing implementation of decision by foreign affairs bureaucracies |
| Instantaneous evaluation of consequences followed by correction of errors | Superficial policy evaluation, uncertain responsibility, poor follow-through, and delayed correction |

the degree of rationality "bears little relationship to the world in which officials conduct their deliberations" (Rosenau, 1980; see Table 3.1.)

Although rational foreign policy making is more an ideal than a description of reality, we can still profit from the assumption that policymakers aspire to rational decision-making behavior, which they may occasionally approximate. Indeed, as a working proposition, it is useful to accept rationality as a picture of how the decision process should work and as a description of key elements of how it does work:

> Officials have some notion, conscious or unconscious, of a priority of values; . . . they possess some conceptions, elegant or crude, of the means available and their potential effectiveness; they engage in some effort, extensive or brief, to relate means to ends; and . . . therefore, at some point they select some alternative, clear-cut or confused, as the course of action that seems most likely to cope with the immediate situation. (Rosenau, 1980: 304–305)

## THE BUREAUCRATIC POLITICS OF FOREIGN POLICY DECISION MAKING . . . . .

Picture yourself as a head of state charged with managing your nation's relations with the rest of the world. To make the right choices, you must seek information and advice, and you must see that the actions generated by your decisions are carried out properly. To whom can you turn to aid you in these tasks? Out of necessity, you must turn to those with the expertise you lack.

In today's world, the extensive political, military, and economic relations of states require dependence on large-scale organizations. Leaders turn to them for aid as they face critical foreign policy choices. This is more true of major powers than of small states. But even those without large budgets and complex foreign policy bureaucracies make most of their decisions in an organizational context (Korany, 1986). The reasons are found in the vital services organizations perform, services that enhance the state's capacity to cope with changing global circumstances.

## Foreign-Policy-Making Organizations

Not only has bureaucracy become a necessary component of modern government but making and executing a state's foreign policy usually involves many different organizations. In the United States, for example, the State Department, the Defense Department, and the Central Intelligence Agency are key elements of the foreign policy machinery. They are joined by other agencies that bear responsibility for specialized aspects of U.S. foreign relations, such as the Treasury, Commerce, and Agriculture departments. Multiple agencies with similar responsibilities characterize the foreign affairs machinery of most other major powers, whose governments face many of the same foreign policy management problems as the United States.

## Bureaucracy, Efficiency, and Rationality

Bureaucratic management of foreign relations is not new. It was in evidence long ago in Confucian China. But with the internationalization of domestic politics in this century, the growth of large-scale organizations to manage foreign relations has been ubiquitous throughout the globe. Bureaucratic procedures are commonplace mainly because they are perceived to enhance rational decision making and efficient administration. The source of those ideas is the theoretical work on bureaucracies by the German social scientist Max Weber, who argued a century ago that bureaucratic organizations could produce effective administration and enhance rational choice.

Bureaucracies increase efficiency and rationality by assigning responsibility for different tasks to different people, defining rules and standard operating procedures that specify how tasks are to be performed, relying on systems of records to gather and store information, and dividing authority among different organizations to avoid duplication of effort. They also permit some specialists the luxury of engaging in forward planning designed to determine long-term needs and the means to attain them. Unlike heads of state, whose roles require attention to the crisis of the moment, bureaucracies can consider the future as well as the present.

Even the existence of many organizations may be a virtue. Ideally, when foreign policy choices and alternatives with which to meet them are required, the presence of several organizations may result in "multiple advocacy" (George, 1972) and, with it, improve the chance that all possible policy options are considered.

### The Limits of Bureaucratic Organization

What emerges from this description of bureaucracy is another idealized picture of the policy-making process. Before jumping to the conclusion that bureaucratic decision making is a modern blessing, we should emphasize that the foregoing propositions tell us how, according to organization theory, bureaucratic decision making *should* occur; they do not tell us how it *does* occur. The actual practice and the foreign policy choices that result depict a reality of burdens and not just benefits.

THE CUBAN MISSILE CRISIS    Consider again the 1962 Cuban missile crisis, probably the single most threatening crisis in the post–World War II era. The method U.S. policymakers used in orchestrating a response to the surreptitious deployment of offensive Soviet missiles to Cuba is often viewed as having nearly approximated the ideal of rational choice. From another decision-making perspective, however, often described as the ***bureaucratic politics model***,[4] the missile crisis reveals how decision making by and within organizational contexts sometimes compromises rather than facilitates rational choice.

As described by Harvard political scientist Graham Allison (1971) in his well-known book on the missile crisis, *Essence of Decision*, there are really two elements in the bureaucratic politics model. One, which Allison (now a deputy secretary of defense in the Clinton administration) calls *organizational process*, reflects the constraints that organizations place on decision makers' choices. The other, which he calls *governmental politics*, draws attention to the "pulling and hauling" that occurs among the key participants in the decision process.

How do large-scale bureaucratic organizations contribute to the policy-making process? As noted, one way is by devising ***standard operating procedures*** (SOPs) for coping with policy problems when they arise. For example, once the Kennedy administration opted for a naval quarantine of Cuba during the missile crisis to prevent further shipments of Soviet missiles, the U.S. Navy could carry out the president's decision according to previously devised procedures. However, these routines or SOPs effectively limit the range of viable policy choices from which policymakers might select options. Rather than expanding the number of policy alternatives in a manner consistent with the logic of rational decision making, what organizations are prepared to do shapes what is and is not considered possible. In the Cuban crisis, a surgical air strike designed to destroy the Soviet missiles then under construction was seen as a leading alternative to the blockade, but when the U.S. Air Force confessed it could not guarantee 100 percent success in taking out the missiles, the alternative

---

[4] The characteristics of the bureaucratic politics model of foreign policy decision making are elaborated and evaluated in Allison (1971), Art (1973), Bendor and Hammond (1992), Caldwell (1977), C. Hermann (1988), Krasner (1972), and Welch (1992).

was dropped. Thus organizational capabilities profoundly shaped the means from which the Kennedy administration could choose to realize its goal of removing all Soviet missiles from Cuban soil.

Governmental politics, the second element in the bureaucratic politics model, is related to the organizational character of foreign policy making in complex societies. Not surprisingly, the many participants in the deliberations that lead to policy choices often define issues and favor policy alternatives that reflect their organizational affiliations. "Where you stand depends on where you sit" is a favorite aphorism reflecting these bureaucratic imperatives. Thus professional diplomats typically favor diplomatic approaches to policy problems, while military officers routinely favor military solutions.

Because the players in the game of governmental politics are responsible for protecting the nation's security, they are "obliged to fight for what they are convinced is right." The consequence is that "different groups pulling in different directions produce a result, or better a resultant—a mixture of conflicting preferences and unequal power of various individuals—distinct from what any person or group intended" (Allison, 1971). Rather than being a value-maximizing choice, then, the process of policy making is itself intensely political. Thus, one explanation of why states make the choices they do lies not in their behavior vis-à-vis one another but within their own governments. And rather than presupposing the existence of a unitary actor, "it is necessary to identify the games and players, to display the coalitions, bargains, and compromises, and to convey some feel for the confusion" (Allison, 1971). From this perspective, the decision to blockade Cuba was as much a product of *who* favored the choice as of any inherent logic that may have commended it. Once Robert Kennedy (the president's brother and the attorney general), Theodore Sorensen (the president's special counsel and "alter ego"), and Secretary of Defense Robert McNamara united behind the blockade, a coalition of the president's most trusted advisers and those with whom he was personally most compatible had formed (Allison, 1971). How could the president have chosen otherwise?

**THE CRISIS OVER THE INVASION OF KUWAIT**  Who favored what also colored President Bush's decision in 1991 to dispatch U.S. troops to Saudi Arabia. Key Pentagon officials might have been expected to be hawkish. But some—specifically Dick Cheney, secretary of defense, and Colin Powell, the four-star general who was chairman of the Joint Chiefs of Staff—were reluctant supporters of the military option. Instead, it was members of the president's White House staff, notably Brent Scowcroft, the president's national security adviser (and a retired air force lieutenant general), and the president himself (a former navy World War II pilot) who were the principal advocates of a military response (Woodward, 1991). Scowcroft continued to push a reluctant military as the crisis evolved into the fall, when the strategic plan changed from defense to offense.

The disastrous Vietnam War, which the professional military regarded as a debacle in part because it lacked public support at home and a clear political objective abroad, helps to explain the nonaggressiveness of the Pentagon on the military option. General Powell, who served President Reagan as national security adviser, believed in the axiom that "There is no legitimate use of military force without a political objective." And he apparently gave so much political advice during the early days of the crisis over Kuwait that "Cheney firmly suggested that the president would be better served if Powell offered more military advice" (Woodward and Atkinson, 1990).

Beyond the pulling and hauling at the top levels of government, in some sense what the military could offer constrained the Bush administration in much the same way that Kennedy was in the Cuban situation. For many years the Pentagon had been preparing for "low-intensity" conflicts in jungle or forested terrain. Thus, its standard operating procedures were ill suited to the conduct of mechanized warfare in the kind of flat, open, and featureless desert terrain that became the theatre of activity in the Middle East. Those plans did not prepare the United States for the military situation it faced when Iraq invaded Kuwait.

The logistical obstacles that the Pentagon confronted as it contemplated fulfilling a mission in a distant region where the United States had no military bases were daunting, and the gut response of Powell and others during the early hours of the crisis was despair about the absence of preparations (Woodward and Atkinson, 1990). How, then, to proceed? As in Cuba, the choice was shaped by previous decisions. The United States relied on Operations Plan 90-1002, first devised in the early 1980s. Calling for a massive air- and sealift of U.S. military personnel and equipment and ground deployment of heavy armor and antitank weapons (Woodward and Atkinson, 1990), it became the basis for Operation Desert Shield. Once the president ordered troops to the Persian Gulf region, it was an alternative the professional military could support and execute. It became their standard for operations.

### Attributes of Bureaucratic Behavior

Besides the influence that bureaucratic organizations exert on the policy choices of political leaders, they possess several other characteristics that affect the decision-making environment.

One characteristic derives from the proposition that bureaucratic agencies are parochial. According to this argument, every administrative unit within a state's foreign policy-making bureaucracy seeks to promote its own purposes and power. Organizational needs come before the state's needs; this sometimes encourages the sacrifice of national interests to bureaucratic interests.

As a corollary, bureaucratic parochialism breeds competition among the agencies charged with foreign policy responsibilities. Far from being neutral or impartial managers desiring only to carry out orders from the head of state, bureaucratic organizations frequently take policy positions designed to increase their own influence relative to that of other agencies. Characteristically they are driven to enlarge their prerogatives and expand the conception of their mission; they seek to take on the responsibilities of other units and to gain the powers that go with those responsibilities. Thus organizations driven by the need to enhance their own importance, not always the national interest, often determine states' foreign policies.

To protect their interests, bureaucratic organizations attempt to reduce interference from and penetration by political leaders to whom they report as well as other agencies within the government. Because knowledge is power, a common device for promoting organizational exclusivity is to hide inner workings and policy activities from others. The "invisible government" operating within the U.S. National Security Council during the Reagan administration illustrates this syndrome. Lieutenant Colonel Oliver North used his authority as a staff member of the council to orchestrate a secret arms-for-hostages deal with the Iranian government, part of what became popularly known as the Iran-*contra* affair.

The natural proclivity of professionals who work in large organizations is to adapt their outlook and beliefs to those prevailing where they work. This reinforces the tendency of bureaucracies to act as entities unto themselves. Every bureaucracy develops a shared "mind-set" or dominant way of looking at reality akin to the **groupthink** characteristic of the cohesiveness and solidarity that small groups often develop (Janis, 1982). An institutional mind-set discourages creativity, dissent, and independent thinking; it encourages reliance on standard operating procedures and deference to precedent rather than the exploration of new options to meet new challenges.

## The Consequences of Bureaucratic Policy Making

A corollary of the notion that bureaucracies are often self-serving and guardians of the status quo finds expression in their willingness to defy directives by the political authorities they are supposed to serve. Bureaucratic unresponsiveness and inaction sometimes manifest themselves as lethargy. At other times bureaucratic sabotage is direct and immediate, as vividly illustrated again by the U.S. experience in the 1962 Cuban missile crisis. While President Kennedy sought to orchestrate U.S. action and bargaining, his bureaucracy in general, and the navy in particular, were in fact controlling events by doing as they wished.

> [The bureaucracy chose] to obey the orders it liked and ignore or stretch others. Thus, after a tense argument with the Navy, Kennedy ordered the blockade line moved closer to Cuba so that the Russians might have more time to draw back. Having lost the argument with the President, the Navy simply ignored his order. Unbeknownst to Kennedy, the Navy was also at work forcing Soviet submarines to surface long before Kennedy authorized any contact with Soviet ships. And despite the President's order to halt all provocative intelligence, an American U-2 plane entered Soviet airspace at the height of the crisis. When Kennedy began to realize that he was not in full control, he asked his Secretary of Defense to see if he could find out just what the Navy was doing. McNamara then made his first visit to the Navy command post in the Pentagon. In a heated exchange, the Chief of Naval Operations suggested that McNamara return to his office and let the Navy run the blockade. (Gelb and Halperin, 1973: 256)[5]

Bureaucratic recalcitrance is a recurrent annoyance to world leaders in dictatorial and democratic political systems alike. Bureaucratic resistance to change is one of the

---

[5] Although this anecdote illustrates graphically the potential ability of bureaucratic agencies to defy political leaders, its historical accuracy has been questioned. For an examination of the events surrounding the account, see Caldwell (1978).

major problems that reformers in the Soviet Union and the other centralized communist countries of Eastern Europe encountered, which impaired their efforts to chart new policy directions and to remain in power. The foreign policy process in China, also a centralized communist regime, operates similarly. It is "subject to the same vicissitudes of subjective perception, organizational conflict, bureaucratic politics, and factional infighting that bedevil other governments, perhaps more so given its size" (Whiting, 1985). And in the United States nearly all chief executives have complained at some time about how the bureaucracy ostensibly designed to serve them has undercut their policies (see Box 3.1). The implementation of foreign policy innovations thus poses a major challenge to most leaders (see Smith and Clarke, 1985).

## Box 3.1
### BUREAUCRATIC OBSTACLES TO DECISIVE FOREIGN POLICY MAKING: ACCOUNTS BY U.S. LEADERS

• • •

"You should go through the experience of trying to get any changes in the thinking, policy, and action of the career diplomats and then you'd know what a real problem was. But the Treasury and the State Department put together are nothing as compared with the Navy. . . . To change anything in the Navy is like punching a feather bed. You punch it with your right and you punch it with your left until you are exhausted, and then you find the damn bed as it was before you started punching."
—Franklin D. Roosevelt

"I sit here all day trying to persuade people to do the things they ought to have sense enough to do without me persuading them."
—Harry S Truman

"There is nothing more frustrating for a President than to issue an order to a Cabinet officer, and then find that, when the order gets out in the field, it is totally mutilated. I have had that happen to me, and I am sure every other President has had it happen."
—Gerald Ford

"You know, one of the hardest things in a government this size is to know that down there, underneath, is the permanent structure that's resisting everything you're doing."
—Ronald Reagan

"The federal government is now organized in a way that requires all the decision-making to be handled by a centralized authority. But we don't have time to let information wend its way slowly up the hierarchy, through layer after layer of middle managers. . . . For too long, government has been an obstacle to change."
—Al Gore

Bureaucratic obstinance is not the only inertial force promoting status quo foreign policies and preventing change. The dynamics of governmental politics, which reduce policy choices to the outcome of a political tug of war, also retard the prospects for change. From the perspective of the participants, decision making is a political game with high stakes in which differences are often settled at the minimum common denominator instead of by rational, cost–benefit calculations. As former U.S. Secretary of State Henry A. Kissinger described the process:

> Each of the contending factions within the bureaucracy has a maximum incentive to state its case in its most extreme form because the ultimate outcome depends, to a considerable extent, on a bargaining process. The premium placed on advocacy turns decision making into a series of adjustments among special interests—a process more suited to domestic than to foreign policy. This procedure neglects the long-range because the future has no administrative constituency and is, therefore, without representation in the adversary proceedings. Problems tend to be slighted until some agency or department is made responsible for them. . . . The outcome usually depends more on the pressure or the persuasiveness of the contending advocates than on a concept of over-all purpose. (Kissinger, 1969: 268)

Thus it is not surprising that bureaucracies throughout the world are frequently the object of criticism by both the political leaders they ostensibly serve and the citizens they so often touch.

## The Role of Leaders in Foreign Policy Decision Making  . . . . . . . . . .

The decisions of political elites determine the course of history. Leaders—and the kind of leadership they exert—shape the way that foreign policies are made and the consequent behavior of nation-states in world politics. These simple propositions describe a popular image: that the world's political elites control their nations' foreign policies. "There is properly no history, only biography" is the way Ralph Waldo Emerson encapsulated the view that individual leaders move history.

## Leaders as Makers and Movers of World History

This *hero-in-history model* equates national action with the preferences and initiatives of the highest officials in national governments. Leaders are expected to lead, and new leaders are assumed to make a difference. We reinforce this image when we routinely attach the names of leaders to policies as though the leaders were synonymous with the nation itself and when we attribute most successes and failures in foreign affairs to the leaders in charge at the time they occur. The equation of U.S. policy with the Nixon Doctrine in the 1970s and the Reagan Doctrine in the 1980s are examples of this tendency.

Citizens are not alone in thinking that leaders are the decisive determinants of states' foreign policies and, by extension, world history. Leaders themselves seek to inculcate impressions of their own self-importance while attributing extraordinary powers to other leaders. The assumptions they make about the personalities of their counterparts, consciously or unconsciously, in turn influence their own behavior toward them (Wendzel, 1980).[6]

One of the dilemmas that leader-driven explanations of foreign policy behavior pose is that the movers and shakers of history often pursue decidedly irrational policies. The classic example is Adolph Hitler, whose determination to seek military conquest of the entire European continent proved disastrous for Germany. How do we square this kind of behavior with the logic of political realism, which says that survival is the paramount goal of all states and that all leaders engage in rational decision making designed to maximize the benefits to their nation and minimize the costs? If the realists are indeed correct, even defects in states' foreign policy processes cannot easily explain such wide divergences between what leaders sometimes do and what is expected of them.

We can explain this divergence in part by distinguishing between **_procedural rationality_** and **_instrumental rationality_** (Zagare, 1990). Procedural rationality underlies the billiard ball view of world politics, which sees all states acting similarly because all decision makers engage in the same "cool and clearheaded ends–means calculation" (Verba, 1969) based on perfect information and a careful weighing of all possible alternative courses of action. Instrumental rationality, on the other hand, is a more limited view of rationality. It says simply that individuals have preferences, and when faced with two (or more) alternatives, they will choose the one that they believe will yield the preferred outcome.

> In contrast to the proceduralist [definition of rationality], the instrumentalist [definition] does not presume to offer normative evaluations of an actors' preferences, however bizarre, reprehensible, or ill-founded they may be. For instance, consider a leader who prefers systematic genocide to the benign neglect of a minority population. If his actions are consistent (or are perceived by the actor to be consistent) with this obviously repugnant order [of preferences], he is rational by [the instrumentalist definition of rationality] . . . . How best to understand Hitler's behavior? Simply by understanding his goals. (Zagare, 1990: 242)

The implications of these seemingly semantic differences are important. They demonstrate that rationality does not "connote superhuman calculating ability, omniscience, or an Olympian view of the world," as is often assumed when the rational actor model described above is applied to real-world situations. They also suggest that individuals may act rationally (in the instrumentalist sense) at the same time that the process of decision making and its product appear decidedly irrational (Zagare, 1990). Why did Libya's leader, the mercurial Muammar Qaddafi, repeatedly challenge the United States, almost goading President Ronald Reagan into a military strike against the North African desert country in 1986? Because, we can postulate, Qaddafi's

---

[6] This interpretation stresses that leaders' images shape their actions (see Kelman, 1965, 1970). It is because perceptions indisputably shape foreign policy decisions that political psychology is so important to an understanding of international relations. The journal *Political Psychology* publishes interpretations of international affairs informed especially by psychoanalytic approaches to leaders and their personalities, beliefs, and behavior.

actions were consistent with his preferences, regardless of how "irrational" it was for a fourth-rate military power to take on the world's preeminent superpower.

## Factors Affecting Leaders' Capacity to Lead

Despite the popularity of the hero-in-history model, we must be wary of ascribing too much importance to individual leaders. Their influence is likely to be much more subtle than popular impressions would have us believe. Henry Kissinger, himself a highly successful U.S. diplomatic negotiator once described as "the most powerful individual in the world in the 1970s" (Isaak, 1975), in 1985 urged against placing too much reliance on personalities:

> [There is] a profound American temptation to believe that foreign policy is a subdivision of psychiatry and that relations among nations are like relations among people. But the problem [of easing protracted conflicts between states] is not so simple. Tensions . . . must have some objective causes, and unless we can remove these causes, no personal relationship can possibly deal with them. We are [not] doing . . . ourselves a favor by reducing the issues to a contest of personalities.

Most leaders operate under a variety of political, psychological, and circumstantial constraints that limit what they can accomplish and reduce their control over events. In this context, Emmet John Hughes, an adviser to President Dwight D. Eisenhower, concluded that "all of [America's past presidents] from the most venturesome to the most reticent have shared one disconcerting experience: the discovery of the limits and restraints—decreed by law, by history, and by circumstances—that sometimes can blur their clearest designs or dull their sharpest purposes." "I have not controlled events, events have controlled me" was the way Abraham Lincoln summarized his presidential experience.

The question at issue is not whether political elites lead. Nor is it whether they can make a difference. They clearly do both. But leaders are not in complete control, and their influence is severely circumscribed. Thus personality and personal political preferences do not determine foreign policy directly. The relevant question, then, is not whether leaders' personal characteristics make a difference but, instead, under what conditions their characteristics are influential.[7]

In general, the impact of a leader's personal characteristics on his or her state's foreign policy increases when the leader's authority and legitimacy are widely accepted by citizens or, in authoritarian or totalitarian regimes, when leaders are protected from

---

[7] As Margaret G. Hermann has observed, the impact of leaders is modified by at least six factors:

(1) what their world view is, (2) what their political style is like, (3) what motivates them to have the position they do, (4) whether they are interested in and have any training in foreign affairs, (5) what the foreign policy climate was like when the leader was starting out his or her political career, and (6) how the leader was socialized into his or her present position. World view, political style, and motivation tell us something about the leader's personality; the other characteristics give information about the leader's previous experiences and background. (Hermann, 1988: 268)

broad public criticism. Moreover, certain kinds of circumstances enhance individuals' potential impact. Among them are new situations that free leaders from conventional approaches to defining the situation; complex situations involving a large number of different factors; and situations devoid of social sanctions that permit freedom of choice because norms delineating the range of permissible options are unclear (DiRenzo, 1974).

A leader's self-image—that person's belief in his or her own ability to control events politically (known as political efficacy)—will also influence the degree to which personal values and psychological needs govern decision making (DeRivera, 1968). Conversely, when a sense of self-importance or efficacy is absent, self-doubt will undermine a leader's capacity to lead and to initiate policy changes. This linkage is not direct, however. The citizenry's desire for strong leadership will also affect it. When public opinion coalesces to produce a strong preference for a powerful leader and when the head of state has an exceptional need for admiration, for example, foreign policy will more likely reflect that leader's inner needs. Thus Kaiser Wilhelm II's narcissistic personality allegedly met the German people's desire for a symbolically powerful leader, and German public preferences in turn influenced the foreign policy that Germany pursued during Wilhelm's reign, which ended with the disaster of World War I (see Baron and Pletsch, 1985).

Other factors undoubtedly also influence how much leaders can shape their state's choices. For instance, when leaders believe that their own interests and welfare are at stake in a situation, they tend to respond in terms of their private needs and psychological drives, as suggested by the highly personalized policy reactions of the Shah of Iran and Ferdinand Marcos of the Philippines when they felt themselves personally threatened by internal insurrections that led to their regimes' overthrow. However, when circumstances are stable and when leaders' egos are not entangled with policy outcomes, the impact of their personal characteristics is less obtrusive.

The amount of information available about particular situations is also important. Without pertinent information, policy is likely to be based on leaders' gut likes or dislikes. Conversely, "the more information an individual has about international affairs, the less likely is it that his behavior will be based upon non-logical influences" (Verba, 1969).

Similarly, the timing of a leader's assumption of power is important. When an individual first assumes a leadership position, the formal requirements of that role are least likely to circumscribe what he or she can do. That is especially true during the "honeymoon" period routinely given to new heads of state, during which time they are relatively free of criticism and excessive pressure. Moreover, when a leader assumes office following a dramatic event (a landslide election, for example, or the assassination of a predecessor), he or she can institute policies almost with a free hand, as "constituency criticism is held in abeyance during this time" (Hermann, 1976).

A national crisis is an especially potent circumstance that increases a leader's control over foreign policy making. Decision making during crises, which are ambiguous but threatening situations, is typically centralized and handled exclusively by the top leadership. Crucial information is often unavailable, and leaders see themselves as responsible for outcomes. Not surprisingly, therefore, great leaders in history, like Napoleon Bonaparte, Winston Churchill, and Franklin D. Roosevelt, customarily arise during periods of extreme tumult. Leaders are heroes capable of determining events. The moment may make the person, rather than the person the moment, in the sense that a crisis can liberate a leader from the constraints that normally would inhibit his or her capacity to control events or engineer foreign policy change.

History abounds with examples of the seminal importance of political leaders who arise in different times and places and under different circumstances to play critical roles in shaping the contours of world history. Mikhail Gorbachev is a dramatic recent illustration of an individual's capacity to change the course of history. Many experts believe that the Cold War could not have been brought to an end, nor Communist Party rule in Moscow terminated and the Soviet state set on a path toward democracy and free enterprise, had it not been for Gorbachev's vision, courage, and commitment to engineering these revolutionary, system-transforming changes (see Bundy, 1990). Ironically, those reforms led to his loss of power when the Soviet Union imploded in 1991.

## Limits to the Hero-in-History Model

Having said that the hero-in-history model may be compelling, we must be cautious and remember that leaders are not all-powerful determinants of states' foreign policy behavior. Rather, their personal impact varies with the context, and often the context is more influential than the leader.

Thus, the utility of the hero-in-history model of foreign policy is questionable. The "great person" versus "zeitgeist" debate is pertinent here. At the core of this timeless controversy is the perhaps unanswerable question of whether the times must be conducive to the emergence of great leaders or whether, instead, great people would have become famous leaders regardless of when and where they lived (see Greenstein, 1987). At the very least, the hero-in-history model appears much too simple an explanation of how states react to challenges from abroad. Most world leaders follow the rules of the "game" of international politics, which suggests that how states cope with their external environments is often influenced less strongly by the types of people heading them than by other factors. Put differently, states respond to international circumstances in often similar ways, regardless of the predispositions of those who lead them. This may account for the striking uniformities in state practices in a world of diverse leaders, different political systems, and turbulent change. In this sense, political realists' postulates about nations' foreign policy goals, which are hypothesized to derive from the rational calculation of opportunities and constraints and stress survival above all else, are not without foundation.

## OTHER DETERMINANTS OF FOREIGN POLICY BEHAVIOR . . . . . . . . . . . . . .

The three models of how states make foreign policy decisions—the rational actor model, the bureaucratic politics model, and the hero-in-history model—described above apply to all countries to some degree. But none applies to every country under every circumstance. It is useful, therefore, to consider other factors in the international system and within states themselves that influence the foreign policy choices that different countries make.

History, culture, geostrategic location, military might, economic prowess, resource endowments, system of government, and position in the international pecking order—all are mediating variables that affect foreign policy choice. Still, it is difficult to generalize about these factors because of the diversity that characterizes the actors that make up the contemporary state system.

To help determine the relative impact of these factors under different circumstances, we can first distinguish usefully between the international and domestic sources of, or influences on, national choice. The international or "external" influences on foreign policy refer to all activities occurring beyond a country's borders that structure the choices made by its officials (that is, to the conditioning impact of the international system).[8] Here, ideological opposition, the content of international law, the cohesiveness of military alliances, and the levels of trade ties with others illustrate factors that sometimes profoundly affect the choices of decision makers.

Domestic influences, on the other hand, are those that exist at the level of the state, not the system. Here attention focuses on variations in *national attributes*—such as military capabilities, level of economic development, and type of government—insofar as they may influence different states' foreign policy behavior. Examples of both orientations follow.

## Geopolitics

One of the most important influences on states' foreign policy behavior is their location on the global terrain. The presence of natural frontiers, for example, may profoundly shape the mental maps that guide policymakers' choices. Consider the United States, which has prospered under a fortuitous set of circumstances because vast oceans separate it from Europe and Asia. This, combined with the absence of militarily powerful neighbors, permitted the United States to develop into an industrial giant and to practice safely an isolationist foreign policy without any immediate security threat for more than 150 years. Or consider mountainous Switzerland. Its topography and geostrategic position have made the practice of neutrality a compelling foreign policy posture.

In much the same vein, maintaining autonomy from continental politics has been an enduring theme in the foreign policy of Great Britain, an island country whose physical separation from continental Europe served historically as a buffer separating it from major-power machinations on the continent itself. Preserving this protective

---

[8] In classifying the determinants not only of the foreign policies of states but also of trends in world politics generally, it is important to recall the *level of analysis* concept introduced in Chapter 2. Nation-states and the international system comprise two distinct levels, the "national" level encompassing domestic characteristics and the "systemic" or international level encompassing interstate relations and temporal changes in them. The possibility that these two traditionally discrete realms have become increasingly fused in what has become known as *intermestic* politics to highlight the integration of domestic and foreign policy should not be ignored. As the U.S. Department of State (1993b: 79) observes, today "the assertion that 'all foreign policy is ultimately local' is closer to the mark than many in government admit."

shield has been a priority for Britain and helps explain why the British government in the early 1990s resisted greater integration of its economy into the European Union.

Most countries are not insular, however; they have many states on their borders, and this situation denies them the option of noninvolvement in world affairs. Germany, which sits in the very heartland of Europe, historically has found its domestic political system and foreign policy preferences profoundly affected by its geostrategic position. Even before the unification of East and West Germany, in this century alone Germany has "undergone five radical changes in political personality—from Wilhelm II's empire to the Weimar Republic, from Hitler's *Reich* of the Thousand Years to its two postwar successors, the Federal Republic of Germany . . . and the German Democratic Republic" (Joffe, 1985). Significantly, these changes have been tied directly to the geopolitical aspects of war, the five noted above by lethal ones and the sixth, unification, by a Cold War whose conclusion made possible the peaceful absorption of communist East Germany into West Germany's capitalistic democracy.

Similar to Germany, extended frontiers with the former Soviet Union shaped the foreign policies of China and Finland. For Finland, neutrality in the Cold War contest between the United States and the Soviet Union helped ensure Finnish survival in the face of a powerful and threatening neighbor. China, on the other hand, has long regarded its relationship with the (now defunct) Soviet Union and its Czarist predecessor as unequal, and in the late 1960s the two communist giants clashed militarily as the Chinese sought to rectify past injustices. The "unequal treaties" between China and outside powers, in part a product of its location, which seemed to fate its penetration by the great powers who carved China into spheres of influence with relative ease in previous centuries, encapsulate these perceived injustices.

China's fate is similar to that of Latin American countries in the sense that they have found themselves geographically proximate to a much stronger power (whose capabilities are in part a function of geophysical resource endowments). Latin America has long been the object of studied interest and frequent intervention by the giant to the north. Given their economic dependence on the United States, it is understandable that concern for Yankee imperialism has been a continuing theme in many Latin American states' foreign policies. In this sense the countries of Latin America share a concern with other states in world politics that find themselves unable to compete on an equal footing with the world's more advantaged states.

History is replete with many other examples of the influence of geography on states' foreign policy goals. The underlying principle is axiomatic: Leaders' perceptions of available foreign policy options are influenced by the geopolitical circumstances that define their countries' place on the world stage.[9]

---

[9] The "geopolitics" school of realist thought and ***political geography*** generally stress the influence of geographic factors on national power and international conduct. Illustrative of the early geopolitical thinking is Alfred Thayer Mahan's (1890) *The Influence of Sea Power in History*, which maintained that national power was shaped by control of the seas. Thus states with extensive coastlines and ports purportedly enjoyed a competitive advantage in the race for hegemony. Later geopoliticians, such as Sir Halford Mackinder (1919) and Nicholas Spykman (1944), stressed that not only location but topography, size (territory and population), climate, and distance between states are powerful determinants of the foreign policies of individual countries.

Geopolitics is only one aspect of the external environment that may influence states' foreign policies. In the chapters that follow we will examine more thoroughly other external factors and how they intertwine to shape states' foreign policy behavior.[10] We also will examine in greater detail how characteristics of states themselves and their relative position in the structure of the international system affect their behavior abroad. Here, by way of illustration, we will comment briefly on three national attributes: military capabilities, economic development, and type of government.

## Military Capabilities

The proposition that states' internal capabilities shape their foreign policy priorities is captured by the demonstrable fact that countries' preparations for war strongly influence their later use of force (see Levy, 1989a; Vasquez, 1993). Thus all states may seek similar goals, but their ability to realize them will vary depending on their military capabilities.

Because military capabilities limit a state's range of prudent policy choices, they act as a mediating factor on leaders' national security decisions. Consider two recent examples. Libyan leader Muammar Qaddafi, as noted earlier, repeatedly provoked the United States through anti-American and anti-Israeli rhetoric and by supporting various terrorist activities. Qaddafi played out the "hero-in-history" model because of the failure of bureaucratic organizations or a mobilized public to constrain his personal whims and militaristic foreign policy preferences. However, Qaddafi was doubtlessly more highly constrained by the outside world than were the leaders in the more militarily capable countries toward whom his anger was directed. Limited military muscle compared with the United States precluded the kinds of bellicose behaviors he threatened to practice. Conversely, Saddam Hussein, the Iraqi dictator, made strenuous efforts to build Iraq's military might, which by 1990 (partly with the help of U.S. arms sales) made his army the fourth largest in the world. The invasion of Kuwait became a feasible foreign policy option as a result. In the end, however, even Iraq's impressive military power proved ineffective against a vastly superior coalition of military forces, headed by the United States, which forced Saddam Hussein's capitulation and withdrawal from his conquered territory.

## Economic Development

The level of economic and industrial development enjoyed by a state affects the foreign policy goals it can pursue. As a general proposition, the more developed a

---

[10] See Macridis (1989) for essays that explore ideas related to the historical, strategic, and cultural conditions that affect countries' foreign policy behavior.

state is economically, the more likely it is to play an activist role in the world political economy. Rich nations have interests that extend far beyond their borders and typically command the means necessary to pursue and protect them. Not coincidentally, countries that enjoy industrial capabilities and extensive involvement in international trade also tend to be militarily powerful, in part because military might is a function of economic capabilities. Historically, only the world's most scientifically sophisticated industrial economies have produced nuclear weapons, for example, which many regard as the ultimate expression of military prowess. In this sense nuclear weapons are the *result* of being powerful, not its cause.

For four decades after World War II, the United States and the Soviet Union stood out as superpowers precisely because they benefited from that combination of economic and military capabilities, including extensive arsenals of nuclear weapons and the means to deliver them anywhere, that enabled both to practice unrestrained globalism. Their "imperial reach" and interventionist behavior were seemingly unconstrained by limited wealth or resources. In fact, major powers (rich states) have been involved in foreign conflict more frequently than minor powers (poor states). For this reason gross national product (GNP) is often used in combination with other factors to distinguish great powers from middle-ranked or minor powers and by itself is an important national attribute predicting the extensiveness of states' global interests and involvements.

Although economically advanced states are more active globally, this does not mean that their privileged circumstances dictate adventuresome policies. Rich states are often "satisfied" ones that have much to lose from the onset of revolutionary change or global instability. For this reason, they usually perceive preservation of the status quo as serving their interests best (Wolfers, 1962), and they often forge international economic policies to protect and expand their envied position at the pinnacle of the global hierarchy.

Levels of productivity and prosperity also affect the foreign policies of the poor states at the bottom of the hierarchy. Some respond to their economic weakness by complying subserviently with the wishes of the rich on whom they depend. Others rebel defiantly, and they sometimes succeed (despite their disadvantaged bargaining position) in resisting major-power efforts to control their international behavior.

Hence efforts to generalize about the economic foundations of states' international political behavior often prove unrewarding. Levels of economic development vary widely among states in the international system, but they do not by themselves determine foreign policies. Instead, the opportunities and constraints that leaders perceive in their nations' attributes may be the determining source of states' international conduct, rather than the actual level of development.

## Type of Government

Besides levels of military capability and economic development, a third important national attribute that affects states' international behavior is the nature of their political system. Although structural realism would predict otherwise, type of government demonstrably constrains important choices, including whether the use of force is threatened and whether the threat is carried out (Nincic, 1992). Here the important distinction is between constitutional democracy (representative government) on one end of the spectrum and autocratic (authoritarian or totalitarian) rule on the other.

In neither democratic (sometimes called "open") nor autocratic ("closed") political systems can political leaders long survive without the support of organized domestic political interests (and sometimes the mass citizenry). But in the former those interests are likely to be potent politically, dispersed beyond the government itself, and active in their pressure on the government to make policy choices from which they benefit. Public opinion, interest groups, and the mass media are more visibly a part of the political process in democratic systems, and the public participates openly in an effort to penetrate and influence government structures in ways actively prevented in closed political systems. Similarly, the electoral process in democratic societies typically frames choices and produces results about who will lead more meaningfully than in authoritarian regimes, where the real choices are made by a few elites behind closed doors. In short, in a democracy public opinions and preferences matter, and therefore differences in who is allowed to participate and how much they exercise their right to participate are critical determinants of foreign policy choice (see Hermann and Hermann, 1989).

Contrast, for example, the foreign policy of Saudi Arabia, which is controlled by a king and royal family, with that of Switzerland, which is governed by a multiparty democratic process. In the former, foreign policy decisions have sometimes been bold and unexpected, as illustrated by the revolutionary policies of the Saudi family when it authorized the dispatch of U.S. military forces during the 1991 Persian Gulf War to its territory in contravention of long-standing Arab policies designed to prevent Western encroachments against Muslim lands. In the latter, the policy of neutrality has been pursued without deviation since Switzerland's last war in 1815.

Public preferences help shape democratic societies' foreign policies. However, this does not deny that *elitism* operates in them, too, for it clearly does (Mills, 1956). Often, but especially when international crises erupt, decisions are made even in democratic governments by a small ruling elite, and opposition is usually silenced. The military-industrial complexes, obtrusively evident in many countries, are examples of elite groups sometimes believed to exercise disproportionate control over defense policy making, in both turbulent and calm times (see Hooks, 1991). But the rival model, known as *pluralism,* which sees policy making as an upward-flowing process in which competitive domestic groups pressure the government for policies responsive to their interests and needs, is a peculiarly democratic phenomenon whose pervasiveness is widespread even if its effects are sometimes difficult to pinpoint.

## Democracies' Foreign Policy Performance

The proposition that domestic stimuli and not simply international events are a source of foreign policy is not novel. In ancient Greece, for instance, Thucydides observed that what happened within the Greek city-states often did more to shape their external behavior than what each did toward the others. He added that Greek leaders frequently behaved in ways designed not to influence relations with the targets of their action but, instead, the political climate within their own polities. Similarly, leaders today sometimes make foreign policy decisions for domestic political purposes, as, for example, when bold or aggressive acts abroad are intended to influence election outcomes or to divert public attention from economic woes.[11]

In the eyes of some observers, the intrusion of domestic politics into foreign policy making in democratic political systems is a disadvantage that undermines their ability to deal decisively with foreign policy crises or to bargain effectively with less democratic adversaries and allies. As the French political sociologist Alexis de Tocqueville (1835) put it more than a century ago, in the management of foreign relations democracies are "decidedly inferior" to centralized governments because they are prone to "impulse rather than prudence." Democracies, so this reasoning goes, are slow to respond to external dangers but, once they are recognized, to overreact to them (see Box 3.2). "There are two things that a democratic people will always find difficult," de Tocqueville mused, "to start a war and to end it." In contrast, authoritarian regimes can "make decisions more rapidly, ensure domestic compliance with their decisions,

---

### Box 3.2
### DEMOCRACIES IN FOREIGN AFFAIRS:
### A U.S. POLICYMAKER'S CHARACTERIZATION

• • •

I sometimes wonder whether a democracy is not uncomfortably similar to one of those prehistoric monsters with a body as long as this room and a brain the size of a pin: he lies there in his comfortable primeval mud and pays little attention to his environment; he is slow to wrath—in fact, you practically have to whack his tail off to make him aware that his interests are being disturbed; but, once he grasps this, he lays about him with such blind determination that he not only destroys his adversary but largely wrecks his native habitat. You wonder whether it would not have been wiser for him to have taken a little more interest in what was going on at an earlier date and to have seen whether he could not have prevented some of these situations from arising instead of proceeding from an undiscriminating indifference to a holy wrath equally undiscriminating.

*Source: George F. Kennan (1951: 59).*

---

[11] Of interest here is the "scapegoat" phenomenon, according to which even democratic leaders provoke war and crises abroad to distract their populations from economic and political problems at home. For an examination of the scapegoat phenomenon and "the diversionary theory of war," see Levy (1989b).

and perhaps be more consistent in their foreign policy" (Jensen, 1982). But there is a cost: "Authoritarian regimes often are less effective in developing an innovative foreign policy because of subordinates' pervasive fear of raising questions." In short, the concentration of power and the suppression of public opposition can be dangerous as well as advantageous.

### Consequences of the Spread of Democracy

The impact of regime type on foreign policy is not a mere abstract theoretical question. It has real-world consequences whose effects are likely to take on added significance in the post–Cold War world as democracies have sprung up where they have never before existed—in Russia and many other countries across the globe. Between 1974 and 1980, more than thirty countries converted their governments from dictatorial to democratic rule (Huntington, 1991b). This pace accelerated since the 1980s, as the percentage of countries that were not free fell from 44 percent in 1974 to 25 percent in 1993 (see Figure 3.1). By 1992, more than half the world's governments

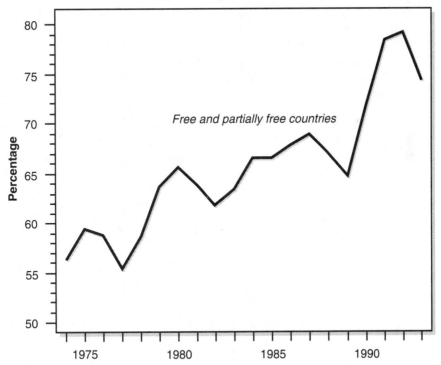

**Figure 3.1**    Expanding the Zone of Freedom: The Growth in the Number of Democratic States, 1974–1993.

*Source:* Classifications of "free," "partly free," and "not free" countries based on Freedom House inventories, as compiled by Harvey Starr and Michael Gubser; graphics prepared by Mark Crislip.

were, for the first time ever, democratic (*Wall Street Journal*, December 31, 1991: A6). Although a modest reversal was evident in 1993, the long-term trend toward democratization is entrenched.

As the tide of freedom spread, speculation arose as to its long-term impact. Francis Fukuyama (1989), a high-level official in the U.S. State Department, predicted that "we may be witnessing . . . the end of mankind's ideological evolution and the universalization of Western liberal democracy as the final form of government." The contagious proliferation of democratic states could end, of course, because many of these fledgling new democracies are fragile. If they survive, however, and if still new democratic governments take root elsewhere, a transformation of the international system of the twenty-first-century could occur.

Because changes in domestic political regimes often precede changes in foreign policy behavior (see Hagan, 1993), the recent growth of democracy has provoked neoliberals to predict that a world increasingly dominated by democratic governments will be a more peaceful world. Their reasons for this prophecy vary (see Zacher and Matthew, 1995; Onuf and Johnson, 1995). Yet most revert to the logic that Immanuel Kant used centuries ago in his 1795 treatise *Perpetual Peace*. In this pioneering liberal theoretical statement, Kant posited that democracies are inherently less warlike than autocracies because under republican rule leaders are accountable to the public, which restrains them from waging war. Because ordinary citizens would have to supply the soldiers and bear the human and financial costs of imperial policies, he contended, liberal democracies are "natural" forces for peace.

The political idealist paradigm (recall Chapter 2) provides theoretical support for this prediction, and empirical evidence buttresses it. Whereas democracies experience just as many wars as nondemocratic polities because they may be the targets of dictatorships' aggression (Small and Singer, 1976), they almost never initiate wars against one another (Doyle, 1995; Ray, 1995; Russett, 1993). In addition, democracies are prone to mediate their disputes (Raymond, 1994) and to seek each other as alliance partners (Siverson and Emmons, 1991)—a communitarian effect evident since World War II that arguably has contributed to the claim that "we have not had a real war between democracies in over a century and a half, from 1816 to 1980" (Rummel, 1983: 48). Hence, if democracy continues to spread, this trend may be critically important to the future preservation of international peace.[12]

---

[12] We must be careful not to assume that the historically tight linkage between democracy and peace will necessarily hold in the future (see Ray, 1995; Russett, 1993). As Samuel Huntington (1989) warns, "The 'democratic zone of peace' argument is valid as far as it goes, but may not go all that far." Democracies are prone to aggression during times of economic and domestic crisis (Morgan and Campbell, 1991), and important exceptions to the propensity of democratic regimes to be less bellicose exist (Wright, 1942). In addition, the record of democratic states' active participation in colonial wars undermines liberalism's expectation that democratic rule is an antidote to imperialism (see Chan, 1984). So, too, does democratic states' frequent practice of intervention short of war (Stedman, 1993). Indeed, critics note that the longest surviving democracy, the United States, initiated or supported military or paramilitary actions against elected governments in Vietnam, Grenada, and Nicaragua, and that Hitler came to power through the ballot, only to wage the most destructive war in history. Hence we must suspend judgment on the question of whether a world of democracies will, as neoliberal theorists argue, be a more peaceful world.

These observations about the ways states' attributes relate to their foreign policy-making processes highlight the extent to which internal conditions, not just those external ones captured in the billiard ball model, influence the foreign policy choices of even great powers (see Snyder, 1991). Contrary to political realism's structural model, which presumes only the existence of unitary actors, type of government, domestic pressures on politicians, grass-roots movements, and whether leaders are answerable to the public can make a decisive difference in the goals states pursue abroad. Thus the degree of freedom that citizens enjoy constrains their leaders' choices, shapes the manner in which policy decisions are implemented by their governments, and influences the pattern of international interactions (see Russett, 1990 and 1993). Many developments in world politics examined in later chapters will draw further attention to the internal roots of external behavior.

## CONSTRAINTS ON FOREIGN POLICY MAKING IN A TRANSFORMING WORLD: PROBLEMS AND PROSPECTS . . . . . . . . . . . . . . . . . . . . . . . .

Can states respond to the demands that external challenges and internal politics simultaneously place on their leaders? For many reasons, that capability is increasingly strained.

Foreign policy choice occurs in an environment of uncertainty and multiple, competing interests. On occasion, it is also made in situations that threaten national values, when policymakers are caught by surprise and a quick decision is needed. The stress these conditions produce impairs leaders' cognitive abilities and may cause them, preoccupied with sunk costs, short-run results, and postdecisional rationalization, to react emotionally rather than as analytical thinkers.

Although a variety of impediments stand in the way of wise foreign policy choice, it fortunately is possible to design and manage policy-making machinery to reduce their impact. Multiple advocacy, subgrouping, formal options systems, second-chance meetings, and the use of devil's advocates are among the procedural tools often recommended for this purpose (Janis, 1982). None, however, can transform foreign policy making into a neat, orderly system. Policy making is a turbulent political process, one that involves complex problems, a chronic lack of information, and a multiplicity of conflicting actors. As President Kennedy summarized it, there will always be "the dark and tangled stretches in the . . . process—mysterious even to those who may be most intimately involved."

The trends and transformations currently unfolding in world politics are the product of countless decisions taken daily in diverse national settings throughout the world. Some decisions are more consequential than others, and some actors making them are more important than others. Throughout history, great powers like the United States have at times stood at the center of the world political stage, possessing the combination of natural resources, military might, and the means to project power worldwide that earned them great-power status. How such major powers have responded to one another has had profound consequences for the entire drama of world politics. To better understand that, we turn our attention in the next chapter to the dynamics of great-power rivalry on the world stage.

## SUGGESTED READINGS

Bendor, Jonathan, and Thomas H. Hammond. "Rethinking Allison's Models," *American Political Science Review* 86 (June 1992): 301–322.

George, Alexander L. *Bridging the Gap: Theory and Practice in Foreign Policy.* Washington, D.C.: United States Institute of Peace, 1993.

Hagan, Joe D. *Political Opposition and Foreign Policy in Comparative Perspective.* Boulder, Colo.: Lynne Rienner, 1993.

Hermann, Charles F., Charles W. Kegley Jr., and James N. Rosenau, eds. *New Directions in the Study of Foreign Policy.* Boston: Allen & Unwin, 1987.

Hermann, Margaret G., and Charles F. Hermann. "Who Makes Foreign Policy Decisions and How: An Empirical Inquiry," *International Studies Quarterly* 33 (December 1989): 316–388.

Hilsman, Roger. *The Politics of Policy Making in Defense and Foreign Affairs: Conceptual Models and Bureaucratic Politics,* 2nd ed. Englewood Cliffs, N.J.: Prentice-Hall, 1990.

Janis, Irving L. *Crucial Decisions: Leadership in Policymaking and Crisis Management.* New York: Free Press, 1989.

Jensen, Lloyd. *Explaining Foreign Policy.* Englewood Cliffs, N.J.: Prentice-Hall, 1982.

Korany, Bahgat. *How Foreign Policy Decisions Are Made in the Third World.* Boulder, Colo.: Westview Press, 1986.

Ray, James Lee. *Democracies and International Conflict.* Columbia: University of South Carolina Press, 1995.

Roberts, Jonathan M. *Decision-Making During International Crises.* New York: St. Martin's Press, 1988.

Vertzberger, Yaacov Y. I. *The World in Their Minds: Information Processing, Cognition, and Perception in Foreign Policy Decisionmaking.* Stanford, Calif.: Stanford University Press, 1990.

CHAPTER 4

· · ·

# GREAT-POWER POLITICS: PAST, PRESENT, AND FUTURE

· · ·

*In an international system characterized by perhaps five or six major powers . . . order will have to emerge much as it did in past centuries: from a reconciliation and balancing of competing national interests.*

Henry A. Kissinger,
Former U.S. Secretary of State, 1994

*The old geopolitical order is passing from the scene and a new order is being born. That order is likely to bear little resemblance to the familiar world of the last half of the twentieth century. In the next millennium, humanity's fate will be shaped by a new set of winners and losers.*

Jacques Attali,
President, European Bank for Reconstruction
and Development, 1991

Change is endemic to world politics. But one constant stands out: great-power rivalry for position in the hierarchy of states. British historian Arnold J. Toynbee (1954) underscores the centrality of this fact in his famous theory on the cycles of history. "The most emphatic punctuation in a uniform series of events recurring in one repetitive cycle after another," he writes, "is the outbreak of a great war in which one Power that has forged ahead of all its rivals makes so formidable a bid for world domination that it evokes an opposing coalition of all the other powers."

That conclusion lies at the center of political realism. The starting point for understanding world politics, argues Hans J. Morgenthau (1985), the leading post–World War II realist theorist, is to recognize that "All history shows that nations active in international politics are continuously preparing for, actively involved in, or recovering from organized violence in the form of war."

Cycles of war and peace have dominated twentieth-century world politics. As U.S. Secretary of State James A. Baker observed in late 1991, "For the third time this century, we have ended a war—this time a cold one—between the Great Powers." In this chapter we explore the causes and consequences of these great-power rivalries

· · ·

73

that led to total war. Two of them, World Wars I and II, which began in Europe and then spread to engulf the entire world, were fought by fire and blood. The third, the Cold War, which pitted the United States against the Soviet Union, was fought by different means but was no less intensive for that reason. Each of these three global wars set in motion the transformations in world politics that are only now becoming apparent. By examining their origins and impact, we will be able to better comprehend the future character of great-power relations in the twenty-first century.

## THE QUEST FOR GREAT-POWER HEGEMONY

Great-power war is not unique to this century. Indeed, the thrust of Toynbee's cyclical theory of history is that great-power war is a recurrent phenomenon. Changes in the balance of power over the past five hundred years have regularly been followed by the outbreak of a great-power war. For this reason the relationship between the rise and fall of the great powers and global instability is a core concern in theories of world politics.

*Long-cycle theory* seeks to explain the rhythmic transformations between periods of war and peace associated with shifts in the relative power of the major states (see Goldstein, 1988; Levy, 1995; Modelski and Thompson, 1989 and 1995; Rapkin, 1990). That each global war witnesses the emergence of a victorious *hegemon,* a dominant military and economic leader, is the primary assertion of long-cycle theory. With its acquisition of unrivaled power, the hegemon reshapes the existing system by creating and enforcing rules to preserve not only the existing world order but also the hegemon's own power.

Hegemony characteristically imposes an extraordinary tax on the world leader. The costs of maintaining economic and political order and preserving an empire eventually weaken the hegemon. In time, as the weight of global responsibilities take their toll, new rivals ascend to challenge the increasingly vulnerable world leader. Historically, this diffusion of power has set the stage for another global war, the demise of one hegemon, and the rise of another.

Long-cycle theory also draws attention to the fact that "world politics has rarely been reordered without a major war" (Jervis, 1991–1992). Often such attempts to reorganize international society have centered on the task of war prevention, as in the case of the Peace of Westphalia (1648) following the Thirty Years' War, the Congress of Vienna (1815) following the Napoleonic wars, the League of Nations (1919) following World War I, and the United Nations (1945) following World War II. "Only after such a total breakdown has the international situation been sufficiently fluid to induce leaders and supporting publics of dominant nations to join seriously in the task of reorganizing international society to avoid a repetition of the terrible events just experienced" (Falk, 1970). Table 4.1 summarizes the cyclical rise and fall of great powers and the political transitions associated with them over the past five hundred years.

Long-cycle theory is disarmingly simple, and for this reason it is not without critics. Must great powers rise and fall as if to conform to the law of gravity—that

TABLE 4.1 THE EVOLUTION OF GREAT-POWER RIVALRY FOR WORLD LEADERSHIP SINCE 1495

| Preponderant State(s) Seeking Hegemony | Other Powers Resisting Domination | Global War | New Order after Global War |
|---|---|---|---|
| Portugal | Spain, Valois France, Burgundy, England, Venice | Wars of Italy and the Indian Ocean, 1494–1517 | Treaty of Tordesillas, 1517 |
| Spain | The Netherlands, France, England | Spanish-Dutch Wars, 1580–1608 | Truce of 1609; Evangelical Union and the Catholic League formed |
| Holy Roman Empire (Habsburg Spain and Austria-Hungary) | Shifting ad hoc coalitions of mostly Protestant states (Sweden, Holland) and German principalities as well as Catholic France against remnants of rule by the papacy | Thirty Years' War, 1618–1648 | Peace of Westphalia, 1648 |
| France (Louis XIV) | The United Provinces, England, the Habsburg Empire, Spain, major German states, Russia | Wars of the Grand Alliance, 1688–1713 | Treaty of Utrecht, 1713 |
| France (Napoleon) | Great Britain, Prussia, Austria, Russia | Napoleonic Wars, 1792–1815 | Congress of Vienna and Concert of Europe, 1815 |
| Germany, Austria-Hungary, Turkey | Great Britain, France, Russia, United States | World War I, 1914–1918 | Treaty of Versailles creating League of Nations, 1919 |
| Germany, Japan, Italy | Great Britain, France, Soviet Union, United States | World War II, 1939–1945 | Bretton Woods, 1944; United Nations, 1945 |

what goes up must come down? There is something disturbingly deterministic in that proposition, which implies that global destiny is beyond policymakers' control.[1] Still, long-cycle theory provides important insight into a fundamental continuity in world politics and provokes questions about whether this entrenched cycle can be broken in the new post–Cold War system. Thus it usefully orients us to a consideration

---

[1] Fundamental hypotheses drawn from long-cycle theory are difficult to confirm, for example. Long-cycle theorists differ about whether economic, military, or domestic factors produce these cycles and about their comparative influence. They also fall short in accounting for differences in processes in different historical epochs.

of the three great-power wars of the twentieth century and the lessons they suggest. We now turn to that comparative assessment.

## THE FIRST WORLD WAR . . . . . . . . . . . . . . . . . . . . . . . . . . . . . . . . . . .

World War I tumbled onto the world stage when a Serbian nationalist seeking to free Slavs from Austrian rule assassinated Archduke Ferdinand, heir to the throne of Austria-Hungary, at Sarajevo in June 1914. In the two months that followed, this singular event sparked a series of moves and countermoves by nations and empires uncertain about each other's intentions.

Two hostile alliances had formed before Sarajevo. They pitted Germany, Austria-Hungary, and the Ottoman Empire on the one hand, against France, Britain, and Russia, on the other. The strategic choices of the two alliances culminated in the cataclysm that involved all of the most powerful nations in the world in what became the longest European war in a century. By the time it ended, nearly ten million people had died, empires had crumbled, new states were born, and the world's geopolitical map was redrawn.

## The Causes of World War I

How is such a catastrophic war explained? The answers are numerous, but many converge around *structural* explanations. Their theme holds that World War I was an **inadvertent war,** not the result of anyone's master plan. Instead, it was a war bred by uncertainty and circumstances beyond the control of those involved, but one that none either wanted or expected.

### *Structuralism*

Many historians find the structural interpretation convincing because the European great powers were aligned against one another on the eve of World War I in a way that made a military struggle to resolve their rivalry irresistible. The viewpoint takes for granted that "the sort of military system that existed in Europe at the time—a system of interlocking mobilizations and of war plans that placed a great emphasis on rapid offensive action—directly led to a conflict that might otherwise have been avoided" (Trachtenberg, 1990–1991). Thus, historians and neorealist political scientists see the anarchical international system creating a climate—that is, a "structure"—conducive to a great-power struggle.

Proponents of this interpretation emphasize the great powers' prior rearmament efforts and their alliances and counteralliances. The Triple Alliance of Germany, Austria-Hungary, and Italy, initiated in 1882 and renewed in 1902, and the Entente Cordiale between Britain and France forged in 1904 were among them. These, historians argue, created a momentum that along with "the pull of military schedules" dragged European statesmen toward war (Tuchman, 1962). In short, the mutually reinforcing alliances in what had become a polarized balance-of-power system dictated the great powers' reactions to the 1914 Austrian succession crisis.

A related element in the structuralist explanation directs attention to the period prior to the outbreak of hostilities. Britain dominated world politics in the nineteenth century. An island country isolated by temperament, tradition, and geography from European affairs, Britain's sea power gave it command of the world's shipping lanes and control of a vast empire stretching from the Mediterranean to Southeast Asia. As such, the British Empire was a world leader without rival. However, a challenge to British power would arise from Germany.

Although Germany did not become a unified country until 1871, it prospered and used its growing wealth to create a formidable army and navy. With strength came ambition and resentment of British preeminence. As the predominant military and industrial power on the European continent, Germany sought to compete for international position and status. As Kaiser William II put it in 1898, Germany had "great tasks . . . outside the narrow boundaries of old Europe." With Germany ascendant, the balance of power shifted, as its rising power and global aspirations altered the European geopolitical landscape.

Germany was not the only newly emergent power at the turn of the century. Russia was also expanding at the time, and therefore threatened Germany. The decline in power of the Austro-Hungarian Empire, Germany's only ally, heightened Germany's fear of Russia. Hence Germany reacted strongly to Archduke Ferdinand's assassination. It became convinced that a short, localized, and victorious war was possible. It feared an unfavorable shift in the balance of power in the event of a long war. Accordingly, while the advantages seemed clear-cut, Germany gave Austria-Hungary a "blank check" to crush Serbia. Its unconditional support proved to be a serious miscalculation.

To Germany's imperial rulers, the risk involved in the blank check made sense from the viewpoint of preserving the Austro-Hungarian Empire. The disintegration of the empire would have left Germany isolated without an ally. Unfortunately for Germany, however, its guarantee provoked an unexpected reaction. France and Russia, the two powers on Germany's eastern and western borders, combined forces to defend the Slavs. Britain then abandoned its traditional "splendid isolation" and joined France and Russia in opposing Germany. The immediate objective was to defend Belgian neutrality. The war later expanded across the ocean when in April 1917 the United States, reacting to German submarine warfare, entered the conflict. For the first time ever, war became truly global in scope.

This chain reaction and the rapidity of escalation that led to World War I fit the interpretation that it was an "inadvertent war." Simply put, European leaders were not in full control of their own fate. Still, historians ask why they miscalculated so badly. Did they simply fail to recognize their primary interest in successfully managing the crisis? If so, was this because the alliances in which they were partners gave them a false sense of assurance, blinding them to danger and dragging them into a conflict that was not a part of anyone's design?

## Rational Choice

*Rational choice* theory provides an alternate interpretation of World War I. From this perspective, the war's outbreak is properly viewed as a result of German elites' preference for a war with France and Russia in order to consolidate Germany's position on the Continent, to confirm its status as a world power, and to deflect domestic attention from Germany's internal troubles (see Fischer, 1967; Kaiser, 1990).

If the rational choice interpretation is correct, then World War I is best seen as another instance of the quest for power that political realists believe is an "iron law of history." In this light, Germany's challenge to British dominance was driven by its desire to become a leading state and to prevent it from being surpassed by lesser challengers, who were also growing in strength (Gilpin, 1981). From this perspective, World War I can be interpreted as "an attempt by Germany to secure its position before an increasingly powerful Russia had achieved a position of equality with Germany (which the latter expected to happen by 1917)" (Levy, 1995).

As these alternative interpretations suggest, the causes of War World I remain in dispute. Questions about motives and causes—the decisive forces behind historic events—are difficult to resolve. Structural explanations that emphasize the distribution of power and others that direct attention to the calculations and (mis)perceptions of individual leaders undoubtedly help us understand the sequences that produced the world's first truly global war. We must, however, also consider other factors that, in association with these underlying causes, led to the guns of August.

## Other Explanations

Some historians see the growth of nationalism (especially in southeastern Europe) and long-suppressed ethnic and national hatreds as exerting a strong cultural influence on the inability of European statesmen to avoid war.[2] Domestic unrest inflamed these passions, as did the pressure for war fostered by munitions makers who played on nationalistic sentiments (Blainey, 1988). The reaction of the Austro-Hungarian Empire to the assassination crisis, although based in part on misperceptions, suggests the potency of national passions. Nationalism and ethnic hatred fed Austria-Hungary's diabolic image of the enemy, its hypersensitivity about the preservation of the empire, and its overconfidence in its military capabilities.

Austria-Hungary was not the only player governed by nationalistic passions. The Germans and Russians were also driven by the ethnocentric assumption of their special importance and superiority, which caused them to make serious miscalculations. In particular, Germany's lack of empathy prevented it from understanding "the strength of the Russians' pride, their fear of humiliation if they allowed the Germans and Austrians to destroy their little protégé, Serbia, and the intensity of Russian anger at the tricky, deceptive way the Germans and Austrians went about their aggression" (White, 1990).

---

[2] As discussed in Chapters 6 and 12, nationalism is widely regarded as a cause of war. Nationalism is "a state of mind, permeating the large majority of a people and claiming to permeate all its members," which "recognizes the nation-state as the ideal form of political organization and the nationality as the source of creative cultural energy and of economic well-being" (Kohn, 1944).

Still, as powerful as these national passions may have been, the inertia produced by the evolving diplomatic relationships clearly structured the context in which such psychological forces became influential. World War I is unlikely to have unfolded without Anglo-German commercial rivalry, the Franco-Russian alliance, the blank check given to Austria-Hungary by Germany, and, most important perhaps, the formation of two entangling alliances. "One cannot conceive of the onset of World War I without the presence of the Triple Entente, which existed as an alliance of ideologically dissimilar governments" uniting Britain, France, and Russia (Midlarsky, 1988). Hence, the bifurcation of the multipolar balance-of-power system that drew the growing number of great-power contenders into two opposing coalitions—and the absence of a hegemon to maintain order—may have made war inevitable.

Thus a world war began, even though "political leaders in each of the great powers . . . preferred a peaceful settlement" of their differences.

> The primary explanation for the outbreak of the world war, which none of the leading decision-makers of the European great powers wanted, expected, or deliberately sought, lies in the irreconcilable interests defined by state officials, the structure of international power and alliances that created intractable strategic dilemmas, the particular plans for mobilization and war that were generated by these strategic constraints, [and] decision-makers' critical assumptions regarding the likely behavior of their adversaries and the consequences of their own actions. (Levy, 1990–1991: 184)

## The Consequences of World War I

World War I was tragic in its human, social, economic, and political costs. It destroyed life and property, and changed the face of Europe (see Map 4.1). Three empires, the Austro-Hungarian, Russian, and Ottoman (Turkish), crumbled. In their place emerged the independent nations of Poland, Czechoslovakia, and Yugoslavia. Finland, Estonia, Latvia, and Lithuania were also born. In addition, the war contributed to the overthrow of the Russian czar in 1917. The destruction of the monarchy by the Bolsheviks, under the leadership of Vladimir I. Lenin, produced a change in government and ideology that would have far-reaching consequences.

Despite its costs, the coalition consisting of Britain, France, Russia, and (later) the United States and Italy did succeed in meeting the threat of domination posed by the Central Powers (Germany, Austria-Hungary, and Turkey and their allies). Moreover, the war set the stage for a determined effort to build a new international system that would deal with the causes of war and prevent its recurrence.

> For most Europeans, the Great War had been a source of disillusionment. . . . When it was all over, few remained to be convinced that such a war must never happen again. Among vast populations there was a strong conviction that this time the parties had to plan a peace that could not just terminate a war, but a peace that could change attitudes and build a new type of international order. . . .
>
> For the first time in history, broad publics and the peacemakers shared a conviction that war was a central problem in international relations. Previously, hegemony, the

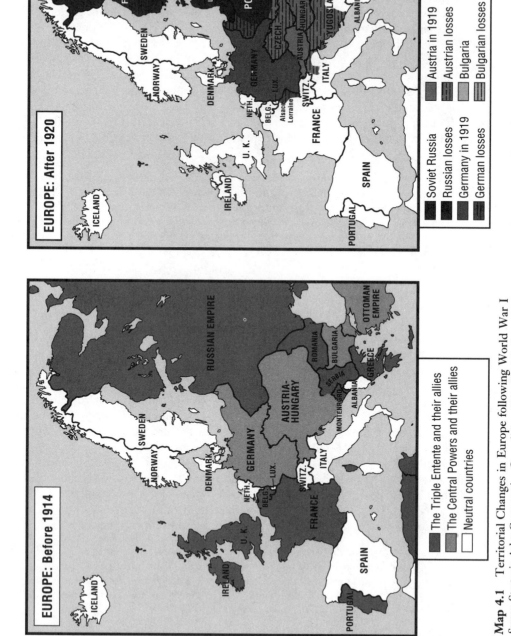

**Map 4.1** Territorial Changes in Europe following World War I

*Source:* Strategic Atlas Comparative Geopolitics of the World's Powers, 3rd Edition by Gérard Chaliand and Jean-Pierre Rageau. Copyright © 1993 by Gérard Chaliand and Jean-Pierre Rageau. Reprinted by permission of HarperCollins Publishers, Inc.

aggressive activities of a particular state, or revolution had been the problem. In 1648, 1713, and 1815, the peacemakers had tried to resolve issues of the past and to construct orders that would preclude their reappearance. But in 1919 expectations ran higher. The sources of war were less important than the war itself. There was a necessity to look more to the future than to the past. The problem was not just to build a peace, but to construct a peaceful international order that would successfully manage all international conflicts of the future. (Holsti, 1991: 175–176; 208–209)

Thus World War I evoked revulsion of war and the logic of realpolitik that rationalized great-power rivalry, arm races, secret alliances, and balance-of-power politics. The experience led the policymakers gathered at the Paris peace talks at the Versailles Palace to reevaluate assumptions about the rules of statecraft and to search for substitute principles for building a new world order. Their deliberations crystallized in policies rooted in the idealism of liberal international relations theory.

The two decades following World War I were the high point of political idealism. Woodrow Wilson's ideas about world order, expressed in his "Fourteen Points" speech, gave voice to the tenets of idealism. As noted in Chapter 2, his reform program included a diplomacy of "open covenants, openly arrived at"; "making the world safe for democracy" by making leaders accountable to public opinion; creating the first universal international organization (the League of Nations) to mediate disputes and safeguard peace; and the substitution of collective security for interlocking alliances and the balance-of-power system they create.

Idealists also advocated bringing state sovereignty under the jurisdiction of international law; permitting national independence movements to determine their own fate according to the principle of self-determination (as seen in the creation of Poland, Czechoslovakia, and Yugoslavia); and promoting global prosperity through free trade. The Washington Naval Conference, which sought to maintain the arms balance, and the Kellogg-Briand Pact (or Pact of Paris) in 1928, which outlawed war as part of a design to substitute peaceful methods of dispute settlement for war, were symptomatic of the reforms the idealist vision inspired. But the idealists' proposals failed to deter the resumption of great-power rivalry. Another system-transforming global war was on the horizon.

# THE SECOND WORLD WAR

Germany defeated Russia in World War I and was then itself defeated by a coalition of Western states. However, Germany's defeat did not extinguish its hopes for global status and influence. On the contrary, it intensified them. Thus conditions were ripe for the second great-power war of the twentieth century, as Germany again pursued an aggressive course.

World War II was a struggle for power cast in the image of realism. Global in scope, it pitted a fascist coalition striving for world supremacy—Germany, Japan, and Italy—against an unlikely "grand alliance" of great powers who united to prevent this hegemonic goal despite the fact that the Allies espoused incompatible ideologies—communism in the case of the Soviet Union and democratic capitalism in the case of Britain, France, and the United States.

The world's fate hinged on the outcome of this massive effort to meet the Axis threat of world conquest and restore the balance of power. Success was achieved, but at a terrible cost over a six-year ordeal: Each day 23,000 lives were lost, as World War II resulted in the death of nearly 17 million soldiers and 34 million civilians.[3]

## The Causes of World War II

Several factors propelled renewal of Germany's hegemonic ambitions. Domestically, German nationalism inflamed latent *irredentism* (forceful recovery of lost territory) and rationalized the expansion of German borders to regain provinces ceded to others and to absorb Germans living in Austria, Czechoslovakia, and Poland. The rise of fascism animated this renewed imperialistic push. That ideology glorified the "collective will" of the nation and preached the most extreme version of realism, *machtpolitik* (power politics), to justify the forceful expansion of the German state.

German aggression was fueled further by resentment of the punitive terms imposed at the 1919 Paris peace conference by the victorious World War I powers (France, Great Britain, Italy, Japan, and the United States). Bending to French pressure, the Peace of Paris (the Versailles treaty) insisted on the destruction of Germany's armed forces, the loss of territory (such as Alsace-Lorraine, absorbed by Germany following the Franco-Prussia war of 1870), and the imposition of heavy reparations to compensate the Allies for the damage that German militarism had exacted. The Austro-Hungarian Empire was also divided.

Not only was the Peace of Paris punitive; more significantly and painfully, it prevented Germany's reentry into the international system as a coequal member. (Symbolically, Germany was denied membership in the League of Nations until 1926.) As a result of its exclusion, Germany, propelled by nationalistic sentiments and the rise of fascism, sought to recover it rightful status as a great power by force of arms.

### Proximate Causes

Why did the other great powers permit German rearmament? A key reason was the failure of the British hope for Anglo-American collaboration to maintain world order. That hope vanished when the United States, in a fit of anger, repudiated the Versailles peace treaty and retreated to isolationism. In this circumstance, Britain and France fought for advantage in the treatment of Germany. France wanted to deter Germany's reentry into the system and prevent its revival. Britain, in contrast, preferred to preserve the new balance of power by encouraging German rearmament and recovery as a counterweight against the chance that France or the Soviet Union might dominate continental Europe. Thus Britain's belief (and U.S. indifference) that a revitalized

---

[3] For accounts of the campaigns that finally led to victory, see Churchill (1948–1953).

Germany would help preserve the balance of power led to British neglect of the threat posed by growing German power and the fascists' goals of aggrandizement.

Unfortunately, acquiescence to German rearmament and other militaristic maneuvers led to ***appeasement.*** Adolf Hitler, the German dictator who by this time controlled Germany's fate, pledged not to expand German territory by force. He betrayed that promise when in March 1938 he forced Austria into union with Germany (the *Anschluss*). Shortly thereafter he demanded the annexation of the German-populated area of Sudetenland in Czechoslovakia (see Map 4.2 on page 86). The fears that German actions provoked led to the September 1938 Munich Conference attended by Hitler, British Prime Minister Neville Chamberlain, and leaders from France and Italy (Czechoslovakia was not invited). Under the erroneous conviction that appeasement would halt further German expansionism and lead to "peace in our time," Chamberlain and the others agreed to Hitler's demands.

Instead of satisfying Germany, appeasement whetted its appetite and that of the newly formed fascist coalition consisting of Germany, Italy, and Japan, whose goal was the overthrow of the international status quo.

Japan was disillusioned with Western liberalism and the Paris settlements, and suffered economically from the effects of the Great Depression of the 1930s. To end dependency and subordination, and to create a Greater East Asian Co-Prosperity Sphere under its influence, Japan embraced militarism. In the might-makes-right climate that Germany's imperialistic quest for national aggrandizement helped to create, Japanese imperialism and colonialism seemed justifiable. Japan invaded Manchuria in 1931 and China proper in 1937. This accelerated the momentum for still more aggression. Italy absorbed Abyssinia in 1935 and Albania in 1939. Germany and Italy also intervened in the 1936–1939 Spanish civil war on the side of the fascists, headed by General Francisco Franco, while the Soviet Union supported antifascist forces.

Despite these aggressive actions elsewhere, appeasement of Germany was the catalyst that paved the way for the century's second global war. Germany occupied the rest of Czechoslovakia in March 1939. Belatedly, Britain and France reacted by joining in an alliance to protect the next likely victim, Poland. They also opened negotiations in Moscow in hopes of enticing the Soviet Union to join the alliance, but they failed. Then, on August 23, 1939, Hitler, a fascist, and Joseph Stalin, a communist and the Soviet dictator, stunned the world with the news that they had signed a nonaggression pact. Now certain that Britain and France would not intervene, Hitler promptly invaded Poland on September 1, 1939. Britain and France, honoring their pledge to defend the Poles, declared war on Germany two days later. World War II had begun.

The war expanded rapidly as Hitler turned his forces to the Balkans, to North Africa, and westward. The powerful, mechanized German troops invaded Norway and marched through Denmark, Belgium, Luxembourg, and the Netherlands. They swept around France's defensive barrier, the Maginot Line, and forced the British to evacuate a sizable expeditionary force from the French beaches at Dunkirk. Paris itself fell in June 1940. In the months that followed, the German air force, the Luftwaffe, pounded Britain in an attempt to force it into submission. Instead of invading Britain, however, the Nazi troops now turned against Hitler's former ally, attacking the Soviet Union in June 1941. Japan launched a surprise assault on the United States at Pearl Harbor on December 7. Almost immediately, Germany declared war on the United States. The unprovoked Japanese assault and the German challenge pushed U.S. aloofness and isolationism aside, enabling President Franklin Roosevelt to forge a coalition with Britain and the Soviet Union to oppose the fascists.

## Underlying Causes

Many historians regard the reemergence of a multipolar power distribution as a key factor in the onset and expansion of World War II. The post–World War I system was placed "at risk when the sovereign states, which were its components, became too numerous and unequal in power and resources, particularly when (as happened after 1919) the Great Powers were reduced in number and new, lesser states proliferated" (Calvocoressi, Wint, and Pritchard, 1989). "By 1921 the League of Nations had 41 members, whereas in 1914 the European central states had only 22 members." When combined with resentment over Versailles, the Russian Revolution, and the rise of fascism, the growth in the number of nation-states and the resurgence of nationalistic revolts and crises made "the interwar years the most violent period in international relations since the Thirty Years' War and the wars of the French Revolution and Napoleon" (Holsti, 1991).

The collapse of the international economic system during the 1930s was also a major contributor to the war. Great Britain found itself unable to perform the leadership and regulatory roles in the world political economy, as it had before World War I. The United States was the logical successor to Britain as world economic leader, but its refusal to exercise leadership hastened the war. "The Depression of 1929–1931 was followed in 1933 by a world Monetary and Economic Conference whose failures—engineered by the United States—deepened the gloom, accelerated nationalist protectionism and promoted revolution" (Calvocoressi, Wint, and Pritchard, 1989). In this depressed global environment exacerbated by deteriorating economic circumstances at home, Germany and Japan sought solutions through imperialism abroad.

The failure of the League of Nations to mount a collective response to the German, Japanese, and Italian acts of aggression symbolized the weak institutional barriers to war. So, too, did the preceding collapse of the Disarmament Conference in 1934. When Germany withdrew from the League of Nations in 1933, as did Italy in 1937, war clouds gathered which the League was powerless to dispel.

The Soviet Union's invasion of neutral Finland in 1939 provoked public indignation and united the League of Nations. In a final act of retaliation, it expelled the Soviet Union. Yet, characteristically, defense fell on the shoulders of the victim. Ninety thousand fiercely independent Finns gave their lives in the "Winter War" to defend their country while the rest of the astonished world watched and cheered but did little to help.

Other psychological forces that led to World War II include "the domination of civilian discourse by military propaganda that primed the world for war," the "great wave of hyper-nationalism [that] swept over Europe" as "each state taught itself a mythical history while denigrating that of others," and the demise of democratic governance (Van Evera, 1990–1991).

In the final analysis, however, the war would not have been possible without Adolph Hitler and his plans to conquer the world by force. Hence "German responsibility for the Second World War is in a class of its own" (Calvocoressi, Wint, and Pritchard, 1989). Under the mythical claim of German racial superiority as a "master race" and virulent anti-Semitism and anticommunism, Hitler waged war to create an empire that would settle the historic competition and precarious coexistence of the great powers in Europe by eliminating Germany's rivals.

> The broad vision of the Thousand-Year Reich was . . . of a vastly expanded—and continually expanding—German core, extending deep into Russia, with a number of vassal states and regions, including France, the Low Countries, Scandinavia, central Europe and the Balkans, that would provide resources and labor for the core. There was to be no civilizing mission in German imperialism. On the contrary, the lesser peoples were to be taught only to do menial labor or, as Hitler once joked, educated sufficiently to read the road signs so they wouldn't get run over by German automobile traffic. The lowest of the low, the Poles and Jews, were to be exterminated. . . .
>
> To Hitler . . . the purpose of policy was to destroy the system and to reconstitute it on racial lines, with a vastly expanded Germany running a distinctly hierarchical and exploitative order. Vestiges of sovereignty might remain, but they would be fig leaves covering a monolithic order. German occupation policies during the war, whereby conquered nations were reduced to satellites, satrapies, and reservoirs of slave labor, were the practical application of Hitler's conception of the new world order. They were not improvised or planned for reasons of military necessity. (Holsti, 1991: 224–225)

## The Consequences of World War II

By May 1945 the Thousand-Year Reich lay in ruins. By August, Japan was devastated, as the atomic bombs the United States dropped on Hiroshima and Nagasaki destroyed Japan's receding hope of carrying on its war of conquest. The Allied victory over the Axis redistributed power and reordered borders, and a new geopolitical terrain emerged. The Soviet Union absorbed nearly 600,000 square meters of territory in the west from the Baltic states of Estonia, Latvia, and Lithuania, and from Finland, Czechoslovakia, Poland, and Romania.[4] Poland, a victim of Soviet expansionism, was compensated with land taken from Germany. Germany itself was divided into occupation zones that eventually provided the basis for its partition into East and West Germany. And pro-Soviet regimes assumed power throughout Eastern Europe (see Map 4.2). In the Far East, the Soviet Union also took the four Kurile Islands, or the "Northern Territories" as Japan calls them, from Japan, and Korea was divided into Soviet and U.S. occupation zones at the thirty-eighth parallel.

---

[4] These territorial changes enabled the Soviet Union to recover what Russia had lost in the 1918 Treaty of Brest-Litovsk after World War I.

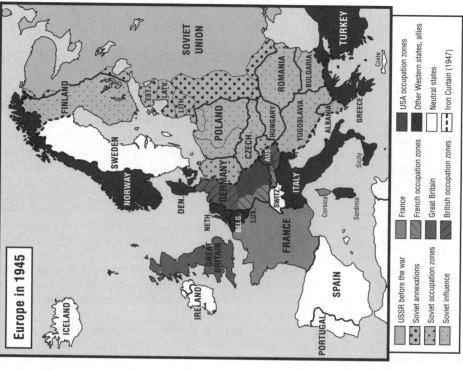

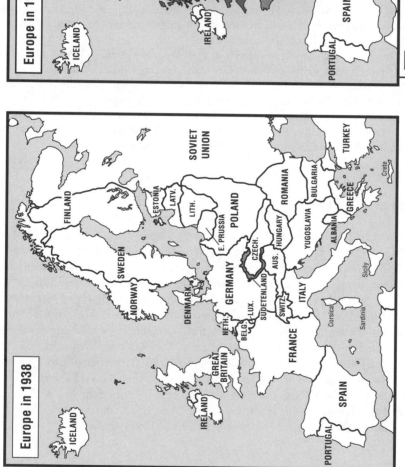

**Map 4.2**   Territorial Changes in Europe following World War II

*Sources:* Europe 1938 is based on Map 5.3 from Charles W. Kegley Jr. and Gregory A. Raymond (1994a: 118); Europe 1945 is from Gérard Chaliand and Jean-Pierre Rageau (1992: 49).

The end of World War II also generated uncertainty and mistrust. The agreements governing goals, strategy, and obligations that guided the collective Allied effort to defeat the common enemy began to erode even as victory neared. Victory only magnified the growing distrust that each great power harbored about the others' intentions in an environment of ill-defined borders, altered allegiances, power vacuums, and economic ruin.

The "Big Three" leaders—Winston Churchill, Franklin Roosevelt, and Joseph Stalin—met at Yalta in the Crimea in February 1945 to design a new world order, but the vague compromises reached concealed the differences percolating below the surface. Following the death of Roosevelt in April and Germany's unconditional surrender in May, the Big Three, with the United States now represented by Harry Truman, met again at Potsdam in July 1945. The meeting ended without agreement, and the façade of Allied unity began to fade.

Perhaps the most certain feature of this otherwise uncertain environment was the ascendancy of the United States and the Soviet Union as its dominant powers. The other major-power "victors," Great Britain and France, had exhausted themselves during the war and fell from the apex of the world-power hierarchy. Germany and Japan, defeated in war, also fell from the ranks of the great powers. Germany, which lay in ruins, was partitioned into four occupation zones that the victorious powers later used as the basis for creating the Federal Republic of Germany (West Germany) and the German Democratic Republic (East Germany). This followed a simple principle of realpolitik: divide and rule (the victors loved Germany so much, some noted, that they created two of them). Japan, too, was removed from the game of great-power politics, having been devastated by atomic bombs and then occupied by the United States. Thus, as the French political sociologist Alexis de Tocqueville had foreseen in 1835, the Americans and Russians now held in their hands the destinies of half of mankind. In comparison, all other states were dwarfs.

Despite the emergent differences between the United States and the Soviet Union, World War II, like all previous great-power wars, paved the way for a new world order. Planning by the Allies for a new postwar structure of peace had begun even as the war raged. As early as 1943 the Four Power Declaration advanced principles for allied collaboration in "the period following the end of hostilities." The product of the Allies' determination to create a new international organization to manage the postwar international order—the United Nations—was conceived in this and other wartime agreements. Consistent with the expectation that the great powers would cooperate to manage world affairs, China was promised a seat on the United Nations Security Council along with France and the Big Three. The purpose was to guarantee that all of the dominant states would share responsibility for keeping the peace.

In practice, the United States and the Soviet Union mattered most. And they used the fledgling United Nations not to keep the peace, but to pursue their competition with one another. That competition eventually became known as the Cold War. As the most recent great-power war of the twentieth century, it still casts its shadow over the post–Cold War geostrategic landscape.

## THE COLD WAR AS HISTORY . . . . . . . . . . . . . . . . . . . . . . . . . . . . . . . .

As World War II drew to a close in 1945, it became increasingly apparent that a new era of international politics was dawning. Unparalleled in scope and unprecedented in destructiveness, the second great war of the twentieth century brought into being a transformed system dominated by two superstates, the United States and the Soviet Union, whose combined power and resources far surpassed those of all the rest of the world. It also speeded the disintegration of the great colonial empires assembled by imperialist nations in previous centuries, thereby hastening the emancipation of many peoples from foreign rule. Unlike earlier international systems, the emergent one featured a distribution of power consisting of a large number of sovereign states outside the European core area that were dominated by the two most powerful ones. The advent of nuclear weapons also added novelty to this system, for they radically changed the role that threats of warfare would henceforth play in world politics. Out of these circumstances grew the competition between the United States and the Soviet Union for hegemonic leadership that became the East–West conflict known as the Cold War.

## The Causes of the Cold War

Determining the origins of the twentieth century's third hegemonic fight for domination is difficult because the historical evidence is amenable to different interpretations (see Gaddis, 1972; Schlesinger, 1986; Melanson, 1983). Despite this, an evaluation of its postulated causes is instructive. It can help us to understand the sources of great-power rivalries and to explain why this one, unlike its other twentieth-century counterparts, ended without recourse to war.

### *A Conflict of Interests*

Realism provides one structural theory of the Cold War's determinants: The preeminent status of the United States and the Soviet Union at the top of the international hierarchy made each naturally suspicious of the other and their rivalry inescapable.

> The principal cause of the Cold War was the essential duopoly of power left by World War II, a duopoly that quite naturally resulted in the filling of a vacuum (Europe) that had once been the center of the international system and the control of which would have conferred great, and perhaps decisive, power advantage to its possessor. . . . The root cause of the conflict was to be found in the structural circumstances that characterized the international system at the close of World War II. (Tucker, 1990: 94)

These circumstances thus gave each superpower reasons to fear and to combat the other's potential global leadership.

But was the competition truly necessary? The United States and the Soviet Union both had demonstrated an ability to subordinate their ideological differences and competition for power to larger purposes during World War II (Gaddis, 1983). Neither had sought unilateral advantage relentlessly. Both had practiced accommodation to protect their mutual interest in remaining alliance partners. Their success at this suggests that Cold War rivalry was not predetermined, that continued collaboration was possible.

In fact, both superpowers expressed their hope that cooperation would continue (Gaddis, 1972) and reached agreements for that purpose. President Roosevelt, for example, advocated preserving accommodation through mutual respect for their informal accord to let each enjoy dominant influence in its own *sphere of influence* or specified area of the globe (Morgenthau, 1969; Schlesinger, 1967). The shift "to a practice of separate, regional responsibility," noted in January 1945 by U.S. presidential policy adviser John Foster Dulles, was also indicative of the two powers' efforts to negotiate a formula for avoiding disputes. Rules that were written into the United Nations Charter, which obligated the United States and the Soviet Union to share (through the United Nations Security Council) responsibility for preserving world peace, further symbolized their expectation of continued cooperation.

If such were the superpowers' hopes and aspirations when World War II ended, why did they fail to achieve them? To answer that question, we must go beyond the logic of realpolitik and probe other explanations of the origins of the Cold War.

### Ideological Incompatibilities

Another interpretation holds that the Cold War was simply an extension of the superpowers' mutual disdain for the other's political system and way of life. U.S. Secretary of State James F. Byrnes embraced this thesis at the conclusion of World War II, arguing that "there is too much difference in the ideologies of the U.S. and Russia to work out a long-term program of cooperation." To the extent that such assumptions were widely held in both Washington and Moscow, as they undoubtedly were, ideological differences contributed to political disputes. Thus the Cold War was a conflict "not only between two powerful states, but also between two different social systems" (Jervis, 1991).

U.S. animosity was stimulated by the 1917 Bolshevik revolution, which brought to power a government that embraced the marxist critique of capitalistic imperialism—and in a country that Karl Marx himself felt was infertile soil for a communist experiment. Whether real or imagined, U.S. fears of marxism stimulated the emergence of *anticommunism* as a U.S. counterideology (Commager, 1983; Morgenthau, 1983). Accordingly, the United States embarked on a missionary crusade of its own, dedicated to containing and expunging the despised atheistic communist menace from the face of the earth (see Gardner, 1970; Parenti, 1969).

U.S. policy was fueled by the fear that communism's appeal to the world's less fortunate nations and peoples would make its continued spread likely. This prophecy was popularized in the 1960s as the *domino theory* to dramatize the perceived danger that the fall to communism in one country would cause the fall of its neighbors, and still others in turn. Like a row of falling dominoes, a chain reaction would bring the entire world under communist domination unless checked by U.S. power.

Similarly, Soviet policy was fueled by the belief that capitalism could not coexist in the long run with communism since the two systems were incompatible. Each was destined to struggle with the other. It was the purpose of Soviet policy, therefore, to pursue this struggle by pushing the pace of the historical process in which communism would eventually prevail. But they did not believe that this historical outcome would automatically occur. Soviet planners felt the capitalist states, led by the United States, sought to encircle the Soviet Union and smother communism in its cradle, and it was the Soviet obligation to resist. Hence, ideological incompatibility ruled out compromise as an option.[5]

This interpretation of the Cold War as a battle between diametrically opposed systems of beliefs contrasts sharply with the view that the superpowers' differences stemmed from discordant interests. Although the adversaries may have viewed "ideology more as a justification for action than as a guide to action," once the interests that they shared disappeared, "ideology did become the chief means which differentiated friend from foe" (Gaddis, 1983).

## Misperceptions

A third explanation describes the Cold War as rooted in psychological factors, particularly the superpowers' *misperceptions* of each other's motives. Their conflicting interests and ideologies were secondary.

Mistrustful actors are prone to see in their own actions only virtue and in those of their adversaries only malice. When such **mirror images** and "we-they," "we're OK, you're not" outlooks exist, hostility is inevitable (Bronfenbrenner, 1971). Moreover, when perceptions of an adversary's evil intentions become accepted as dogma, prophecies often become self-fulfilling.[6] Mirror images and self-fulfilling prophecies contributed heavily to the onset of the Cold War.

The two countries' leaders operated from very different images. They imposed on events different definitions of reality and became captives of those visions.[7] Expectations shaped how they interpreted developments: what they saw is what they got. George F. Kennan, the American ambassador to the Soviet Union in 1952, noted that misread signals were common to both sides:

---

[5] A conflict driven by ideology "excludes the idea of co-existence. How can [one] compromise or co-exist with evil? It holds out no prospect but opposition with all might, war to the death. It summons the true believer to a *jihad*, a crusade of extermination against the infidel" (Schlesinger, 1983). Lenin described the predicament—prophetically, it turned out—this way: "As long as capitalism and socialism exist, we cannot live in peace; in the end, either one or the other will triumph—a funeral dirge will be sung either over the Soviet Republic or over world capitalism."

[6] Prophecies are sometimes self-fulfilling because the future can be affected by the way it is anticipated. The tendency is illustrated by arms races: Mistakenly anticipating that a rival is preparing for an offensive war, a potential victim then arms in defense, thereby provoking the rival to fulfill the prophecy by arming out of fear.

[7] See the fourth edition of *World Politics: Trend and Transformation* (Kegley and Wittkopf, 1991: 88–90) for a description of the Soviet and American images of each other's actions and the way they were misperceived.

The Marshall Plan, the preparations for the setting up of a West German government, and the first moves toward the establishment of NATO were taken in Moscow as the beginnings of a campaign to deprive the Soviet Union of the fruits of its victory over Germany. The Soviet crackdown on Czechoslovakia (1948) and the mounting of the Berlin blockade, both essentially defensive . . . reactions to these Western moves, were then similarly misread on the Western side. Shortly thereafter there came the crisis of the Korean War, where the Soviet attempt to employ a satellite military force in civil combat to its own advantage, by way of reaction to the American decision to establish a permanent military presence in Japan, was read in Washington as the beginning of the final Soviet push for world conquest; whereas the active American military response, provoked by this move, appeared in Moscow . . . as a threat to the Soviet position in both Manchuria and in eastern Siberia. (Kennan, 1976: 683–684)

Hence, in the Cold War's formative stage U.S. leaders and their allies in the West saw the many crises that erupted as part of a Soviet plan to take over the world. The Soviets saw these same crises altogether differently—as tests of their resolve and as Western efforts to encircle and destroy their socialist experiment. Both states operated from the same "inherent bad faith" image of the rival's intentions. In this respect, their images were the same. Mistrust led to misperceptions, which bred conflict.

If the Cold War originated in divergent images and each power's insensitivity to the impact of its actions on the other's fears, it is difficult to assign blame for the deterioration of Soviet–American relations. Both superpowers were responsible because both were victims of their misperceptions. The Cold War was not simply a U.S. response to communist aggression—the orthodox American view. Nor was it simply a product of postwar U.S. assertiveness—the revisionist historians' position (see Schlesinger, 1986). Both of the great powers felt threatened. And each had legitimate reasons to regard the other with suspicion. Thus, we can view the Cold War as a conflict over reciprocal anxieties bred by the way policymakers on both sides interpreted the other's actions.

Other factors beyond those rooted in divergent interests, ideologies, and images undoubtedly combined to produce this explosive Soviet–American hegemonic rivalry. Scholars have yet to sort out their relative causal influence. But to grasp more completely the dynamics of this great-power rivalry in particular (and others in general), it is useful to move beyond its causes and examine its character.

## The Cold War's Characteristics

The Cold War lasted more than four decades. As it evolved, it changed in character, in part because of the two rivals' policies and in part because global circumstances changed. Several conspicuous patterns are observable, however, amidst continual change. The history of the two rivals' Cold War interactions reveals six primary principles or characteristics:

- Until its closing phases, the Cold War was characterized by a high level of superpower conflict.

- Periods of intense conflict alternated rhythmically with periods of relative cooperation.

- Reciprocal, action–reaction exchanges were evident: Periods when the United States directed friendly initiatives toward the Soviets were also periods when the Soviets acted with friendliness toward the United States; similarly, periods of U.S. belligerence were periods of Soviet belligerence.

- Throughout the Cold War contest, both rivals consistently made avoidance of all-out war their highest priority.

- Both actors displayed a willingness to act in violation of their respective professed ideologies whenever their perceived national interests rationalized such inconsistencies; for example, they both backed allies with political systems antithetical to their own when the necessities of power politics seemed to justify it.

- Through a gradual learning process involving push and shove, restraint and reward, tough bargaining and calm negotiation, the superpowers created rules for the peaceful management of their disputes and trust in their mutual willingness to abide by the norms of this *security regime*.

These characteristics become visible when briefly inspecting the evolution of the superpowers' relationship. For this, we divide the Cold War into three chronological phases, as depicted in Figure 4.1.

## Confrontation, 1945–1962

A brief period of wary Soviet–American friendship soon gave way to mutual antagonism when the Cold War began and the United States reigned preeminent militarily. In this short **unipolar** period, the United States alone possessed the capacity to devastate its adversaries with the atomic bomb, and this doubtlessly played heavily in Soviet calculations.

Yet despite this restraining factor, all pretense of superpower collaboration rapidly vanished as their vital security interests collided in confrontations over crises in countries outside the superpowers' clearly defined respective spheres of influence. At this critical juncture George F. Kennan, then a diplomat in the American embassy in Moscow, sent to Washington his famous "long telegram" assessing the sources of Soviet conduct. Kennan's conclusions were ominous: "In summary, we have here a political force committed fanatically to the belief that with [the] U.S. there can be no permanent modus vivendi, that it is desirable and necessary that the internal harmony of our society be disrupted, our traditional way of life be destroyed, the international authority of our state be broken, if Soviet power is to be secure."

Kennan's ideas were circulated widely when, in 1947, the influential journal *Foreign Affairs* published his ideas in an article he signed "X" instead of disclosing himself as the author. In it, Kennan argued that Soviet leaders would forever feel insecure about their political ability to maintain power against forces both within Soviet society itself and in the outside world. Their insecurity would lead to an

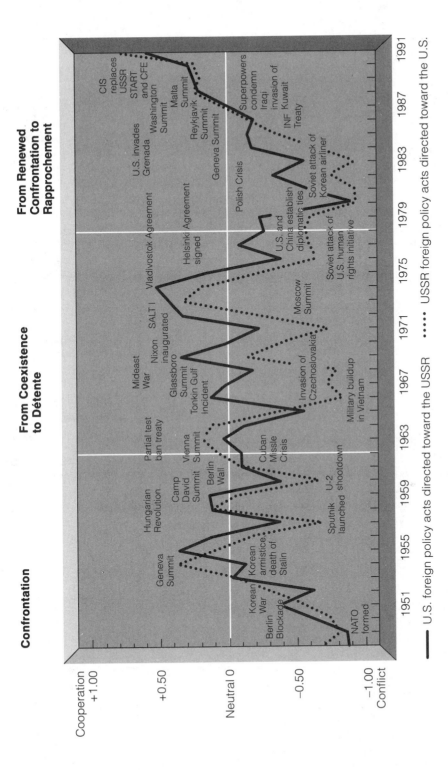

**Figure 4.1**  U.S.–Soviet Relations during the Cold War, 1948–1991*

*Source:* Adapted from Edward E. Azar's Conflict and Peace Data Bank (COPDAB), with data based on Edward E. Azar and Thomas J. Sloan (1973). Data for 1966–1991 are derived from the World Event Interaction Survey (WEIS), as compiled and scaled by Professor Rodney G. Tomlinson.

* The net conflict index is the sum of the proportion of cooperative acts and conflictual acts.

activist—and perhaps aggressive—Soviet foreign policy. Yet it was within the power of the United States to increase the strains under which the Soviet leadership would have to operate, which eventually could lead to a gradual mellowing or final end of Soviet power. Hence, Kennan concluded: "In these circumstances it is clear that the main element of any United States policy toward the Soviet Union must be that of a long-term, patient but firm and vigilant *containment* of Russian expansive tendencies" (Kennan, 1947, emphasis added).

Not long thereafter, Harry S Truman made Kennan's assessment the cornerstone of American postwar policy. Provoked in part by violence in Turkey and Greece, which he and others believed to be communist inspired, Truman declared, "I believe that it must be the policy of the United States to support free peoples who are resisting attempted subjugation by armed minorities or by outside pressures." Eventually known as the **Truman Doctrine,** this statement defined the *containment* strategy, which the United States would pursue for the next forty years to deter the Soviet Union's perceived hegemonic ambitions.[8] U.S. recruitment of allies for support in pursuing this strategy soon followed.

Soon followed a seemingly unending eruption of new Cold War confrontations and crises. They included the Soviet refusal to withdraw troops from Iran in 1946, the communist coup d'état in Czechoslovakia in 1948, the Soviet blockade of West Berlin in June of that year, the communist acquisition of power on the Chinese mainland in 1949, the outbreak of the Korean War in 1950, the Chinese invasion of Tibet in 1950, and the on-again, off-again Taiwan Straits crises that followed. Hence the "war" was not simply "cold"; it became an embittered worldwide quarrel that threatened to escalate into open warfare.

Nonetheless, superpower relations began to improve in the 1950s. Shifts in the balance of power prompted the accommodative shift away from confrontation. After the Soviets broke the U.S. atomic monopoly in 1949, military ratios increasingly shaped the superpowers' political interactions. The risks of massive destruction necessitated restraint and changed the means of the struggle. In particular, both superpowers began to expend considerable resources recruiting allies. The global power configuration quickly became **bipolar:** The United States and its allies were one pole and the Soviet Union and its allies the other.

---

[8] Whether the policy of containment was appropriate, even at the time of its initial promulgation, remains controversial. Kennan himself criticized the way he thought U.S. leaders misinterpreted his celebrated statement. He wrote:

I . . . went to great lengths to disclaim the view, imputed to me by implication . . . that containment was a matter of stationing military forces around the Soviet borders and preventing any outbreak of Soviet military aggressiveness. I protested . . . against the implication that the Russians were aspiring to invade other areas and that the task of American policy was to prevent them from doing so. "The Russians don't want," I insisted, "to invade anyone. It is not in their tradition. They tried it once in Finland and got their fingers burned. They don't want war of any kind. Above all, they don't want the open responsibility that official invasion brings with it." (Kennan, 1967: 361)

As Kennan lamented, "the image of a Stalinist Russia poised and yearning to attack the West, and deterred only by [U.S.] possession of atomic weapons, was largely a creation of the Western imagination." Cautioning against "demonizing the adversary, overestimating enemy strength and overmilitarizing the Western response" (Talbott, 1990), Kennan recommended a political rather than a military containment approach.

Europe, where the Cold War first erupted, was the focal point of their jockeying for influence. The principal European allies of the superpowers divided into the North Atlantic Treaty Organization (NATO) and the Warsaw Treaty Organization (WTO). Both alliances became the cornerstones of the superpowers' external policies, as the European members of the Eastern and Western alliances willingly acceded to the leadership of their superpower patrons.

To a lesser extent, alliance formation outside of Europe also enveloped other states in the two titans' contest. The United States in particular sought to contain Soviet (and Chinese) influence on the Eurasian landmass by building a ring of pro-U.S. allies on the very borders of the communist world. In return, the United States promised to protect its growing number of clients from external attack (known as *extended deterrence*). Thus the Cold War expanded across the entire globe.

In the rigid two-bloc system of the 1950s, the superpowers sometimes talked as if war was imminent. But in deeds (especially after the Korean War), both acted cautiously. President Eisenhower and his secretary of state, John Foster Dulles, promised a "rollback" of the iron curtain and the "liberation" of the "captive nations" of Eastern Europe. They pledged to respond to aggression with "massive retaliation." And they criticized the allegedly "soft" and "restrained" Truman Doctrine, claiming to reject containment in favor of an ambitious "winning" strategy that would finally end the confrontation with godless communism. But containment was not replaced by a more assertive strategy. Despite their threatening language, U.S. leaders promised more than they delivered. In 1956, for example, the United States failed to respond to the call for assistance from the Hungarians who had revolted against Soviet control.

For its part, the Soviet Union remained strategically inferior compared with the United States. For this reason, Nikita Khrushchev, who assumed the top Soviet leadership position following Joseph Stalin's death in 1953, claimed to accept "peaceful coexistence" with capitalism. (Communist China protested, accusing Khrushchev of "revisionism" and challenging the Soviet claim to leadership of the international communist movement.) But the Soviet Union sometimes cautiously sought to increase Soviet power in places where opportunities appeared to exist. The period following Stalin's death saw many Cold War confrontations. Hungary, Cuba, Egypt, and Berlin became the flash points. In 1960, there was even a crisis resulting from the downing of an American U-2 spy plane deep over Soviet territory.

Yet despite the intensity and regularity of the superpowers' confrontations, none of these threats to peace resulted in open warfare. Both superpowers took accommodative steps toward improving relations. For example, in 1956 the Soviets dissolved the Cominform (Communist Information Bureau to coordinate the work of communist parties), and the 1955 Geneva summit provided an important forum for the antagonists' meaningful communication about world problems. These set precedents that would later become commonplace.

### From Coexistence to Détente, 1963–1978

Despite the Geneva precedent, a dark shadow loomed over hopes for a superpower rapprochement. As the arms race accelerated, the threats to peace multiplied. The surreptitious placement of Soviet missiles in Cuba in 1962 set the stage for the greatest test of the superpowers' capacity to manage their disputes, as the Cuban missile crisis that followed became the Cold War's most serious challenge to peace. The superpowers stood eyeball to eyeball. Fortunately, one blinked. This "catalytic" learning experience not only transformed thinking about how the Cold War could be waged but expanded awareness of the suicidal consequences of a nuclear war.

COEXISTENCE  The growing threat of mutual destruction in conjunction with the growing parity of American and Soviet military capabilities made coexistence or nonexistence appear to be the only alternatives. Given this equation, finding ways to coexist became compelling.

At The American University commencement exercises in 1963, U.S. President John F. Kennedy explained why tension reduction had become imperative and war could not be risked:

> Among the many traits the people of [the United States and the Soviet Union] have in common, none is stronger than our mutual abhorrence of war. Almost unique among the major world powers, we have never been at war with each other. . . .
>
> Today, should total war ever break out again—no matter how—our two countries would become the primary targets. It is an ironical but accurate fact that the two strongest powers are the two in the most danger of devastation. . . . We are both caught up in a vicious and dangerous cycle in which suspicion on one side breeds suspicion on the other and new weapons beget counterweapons.
>
> In short, both the United States and its allies, and the Soviet Union and its allies, have a mutually deep interest in a just and genuine peace and in halting the arms race. . . .
>
> So let us not be blind to our differences, but let us also direct attention to our common interests and to the means by which those differences can be resolved. And if we cannot end now our differences, at least we can help make the world safe for diversity.

Kennedy signaled a shift in how the United States hoped hereafter to bargain with its adversary, and the Soviet Union reciprocally expressed its interest in more cooperative relations. Installation of the "hot line" in 1963 linking the White House and the Kremlin with a direct communication system followed. So, too, did the 1967 Glassboro summit and several negotiated agreements, including the 1963 Partial Test Ban Treaty, the 1967 Outer Space Treaty, and the 1968 Nuclear Nonproliferation Treaty. In addition, the superpowers signaled their acceptance of the permanence of European borders, including tacitly those that divided Germany. Thus, in style and tone the superpowers began to depart from the confrontational tactics of the past. This laid the foundation for "détente."

DÉTENTE  Soviet–American relations took a dramatic turn with Richard Nixon's election. Coached by his national security adviser, Henry A. Kissinger, Nixon initiated a new approach to Soviet relations that in 1969 he officially labeled *détente*. The Soviets also adopted the term to describe their policies toward the United States.

In Kissinger's words, détente sought to create "a vested interest in cooperation and restraint," "an environment in which competitors can regulate and restrain their differences and ultimately move from competition to cooperation." To engineer the relaxation of superpower tensions, Nixon and Kissinger pursued a ***linkage strategy*** to bind the two rivals in a common fate by making superpower relations dependent on the continuation of mutually rewarding exchanges (such as trade concessions). Furthermore, linkage made cooperation in one policy area contingent on acceptable conduct in other areas.

The shifts in policy produced results. Relations between the Soviets and Americans "normalized." As shown in Figure 4.1, cooperative interaction became more common-place than hostile relations. Visits, cultural exchanges, trade agreements, and joint technological ventures replaced threats, warnings, and confrontations.

Arms control stood at the center of the dialogue surrounding détente. The ***Strategic Arms Limitation Treaty*** talks (SALT), initiated in 1969, sought to restrain the threatening, expensive, and spiraling arms race. They produced two agreements, the first in 1972 (SALT I) and the second in 1979 (SALT II), but the SALT II agreement was signed but never ratified by the United States. This failure underscored the substantial differences that still separated the superpowers.

### From Renewed Confrontation to Rapprochement, 1979–1991

Despite the careful nurturing of détente, its spirit did not endure. In many respects, the Soviet invasion of Afghanistan in 1979 was the catalyst to the demise of détente. As U.S. President Jimmy Carter viewed it, "Soviet aggression in Afghanistan—unless checked—confronts all the world with the most serious strategic challenge since the Cold War began." In retaliation, he enunciated the ***Carter Doctrine*** declaring U.S. willingness to use military force to protect its interests in the Persian Gulf. In addition, he attempted to organize a worldwide boycott of the 1980 Moscow Olympics and suspended U.S. grain exports to the Soviet Union.

**RENEWED CONFRONTATION** Relations deteriorated dramatically thereafter. President Ronald Reagan and his Soviet counterparts (first Yuri Andropov and then Konstantin Chernenko) delivered a barrage of confrontational rhetoric. Reagan asserted that the Soviet Union "underlies all the unrest that is going on" and described the Soviet Union as "the focus of evil in the modern world." The atmosphere was punctuated by Reagan policy adviser Richard Pipes's bold challenge in 1981 that the Soviets would have to choose either "peacefully changing their Communist system . . . or going to war." Soviet rhetoric was no less restrained or alarmist.

As talk of war increased, preparations for it escalated as well. The arms race resumed feverishly, and the contestants put weapons above all other priorities, at the expense of addressing domestic economic problems. The opponents also extended the confrontation to new territory, such as Central America, and renewed their public diplomacy (propaganda) efforts to extoll the ascribed virtues of their respective systems throughout the world.

Pernicious events punctuated the renewal of conflict. The Soviets destroyed Korean Airlines flight 007 in 1983; the United States invaded Grenada soon thereafter. Arms control talks then ruptured, the Soviets boycotted the 1984 Olympic Games in Los Angeles, and the **_Reagan Doctrine_** pledged U.S. support of anticommunist insurgents in Afghanistan, Angola, and Nicaragua who sought to overthrow Soviet-supported governments. In addition, U.S. leaders spoke loosely about the "winnabil-ity" of a nuclear war through a "prevailing" military strategy that included the threat of a "first use" of nuclear weapons in the event of the outbreak of a conventional war. Relations deteriorated as the compound impact of these moves and countermoves took their toll. The new Soviet leader, Mikhail Gorbachev, summarized the alarming state of superpower relations by fretting in 1985 that "The situation is very complex, very tense. I would even go so far as to say it is explosive."

**RAPPROCHEMENT** But the situation did not explode. Instead, prospects for a more constructive phase improved greatly following Gorbachev's assumption of power in 1985. Gorbachev felt that it was imperative that the Soviet Union practice "new thinking" in order to reconcile its differences with the capitalist West if his country was to have any chance of halting the deterioration of its economy and international position. In his words, these goals dictated "the need for a fundamental break with many customary approaches to foreign policy." Shortly thereafter, he embarked on domestic reforms to promote democratization and the transition to a market economy.

Acknowledging that Soviet economic growth had ceased and its global power had eroded, Gorbachev proclaimed his desire to end the Cold War contest. "We realize that we are divided by profound historical, ideological, socioeconomic and cultural differences," Gorbachev noted during his first visit to the United States in 1987. "But the wisdom of politics today lies in not using those differences as a pretext for confrontation, enmity and the arms race." Soviet spokesperson Georgi Arbatov went as far as to tell the United States that "we are going to do a terrible thing to you—we are going to deprive you of an enemy."

Surprisingly, the Soviets did what they promised. They began to act like an ally instead of an enemy. Building on the momentum created by the **_Intermediate-range Nuclear Forces (INF) agreement_** signed in 1987, the Soviet Union agreed to end its aid and support for Cuba, withdrew from Afghanistan and Eastern Europe, and announced unilateral reductions in military spending. Gorbachev also agreed to a new disarmament agreement, **_START (Strategic Arms Reduction Talks),_** for deep cuts in strategic arsenals and to the **_Conventional Forces in Europe (CFE)_** treaty to reduce the Soviet presence in Europe. In addition, the Soviet Union liberalized its emigration policies and permitted greater religious freedom. As these seismic changes shook the world, the Soviet Union then sped its reforms to introduce democracy and a market economy, eagerly seeking (and receiving) economic assistance from the West.

The pace of steps to rapprochement—the establishment of cordial relations—then accelerated, and the normalization of Soviet–American relations moved rapidly. The Cold War—which began in Europe and had centered on Europe for 45 years—ended there. All the communist governments in the Soviet "bloc" in Eastern Europe, includ-ing even hardline Albania, permitted democratic elections in which Communist Party candidates routinely lost. Capitalist free market principles replaced socialism. To the astonishment of nearly everyone, the Soviet Union acquiesced in these revolutionary changes. Without resistance, the Berlin Wall came down, Germany reunited, and the Warsaw Pact dissolved.

The failed conservative coup against Gorbachev in August 1991 put the nail in the coffin of Communist Party control in Moscow, the very heartland of the international communist movement. As communism was repudiated, a new age began. Communism was in retreat everywhere (even China and Cuba). The face of world politics was transformed.

The abrupt end of the Cold War suggested some lessons quite different from those of World War I and World War II. The latter implied that great-power rivalries are doomed to end in armed conflict. The Cold War was different; it came to an end peacefully. This suggests that great powers have it within their capacity to settle their struggles and disputes without bloodshed. Reconciliation and rapprochement *are* possible; differences and disputes can be resolved.

The Cold War concluded in a way and at a time when the prospects for its end appeared remote. The friction and confrontation that had characterized most periods of the Soviet–American contest for supremacy could easily have escalated to a hot war. But the two rivals' respect for the rules to which they mutually agreed—such as the prohibition against the first use of nuclear weapons—served their shared interests. So, too, did their willingness to reciprocate initiatives in tension reduction and to reduce insecurities by cutting their strategic weapons stockpiles. These concessions brought about a true transformation that could have a lasting impact on great-power relations in the future.

## The Cold War's Consequences

The end of the Cold War has already altered the face of world affairs in profound and diverse ways. Two consequences warrant particular attention. First, what does the ***power transition*** caused by the changes in Russia's domestic system and its decline in power bode for the future? Second, what inferences about the causes of the Cold War's end can be drawn, and what principles do these derived lessons suggest for managing future great-power rivalries?

### *The Problematic Russian Future*

The reform policies of ***glasnost*** (openness) and ***perestroika*** (restructuring) unleashed forces *within* the Soviet Union that were not a part of Gorbachev's plan. In December 1991 these forces led to the disintegration of the Soviet Union itself. Gorbachev had sought to introduce gradually some measure of democracy and a free market spirit into a society in which liberty and growth had been crushed by communist rule. He never intended to commit political suicide by starting a revolution that would leave him without a country to lead. Yet that is precisely what happened. As George Bush lamented in November 1991, "The collapse of communism has thrown open a Pandora's Box of ancient ethnic hatreds, resentment, even revenge." Shortly thereafter, nationalism and frustration with failed economic reforms and the uncertain political future culminated in the unanticipated disintegration of the former union into fifteen separate republics. In place of the Soviet Union, a new and highly fragile creature, the Commonwealth of Independent States (CIS), emerged. The CIS, created on December 21, 1991, to replace institutionally the former Soviet Union, soon fragmented.

In what is left of the CIS, Russia, as principal heir to the vast Soviet strategic arsenal, remains a military threat despite its retreat from external involvements. Some argue that Russia is no longer vulnerable to "adventurous leaders who might try to resolve the economic crisis by resuming the imperialistic strategies of the past" (Barnet, 1992). While that may not be true,[9] another outcome is possible: that Russia's long-neglected domestic problems will compel the search for more collaborative relations with the United States and the other great powers. Russian President Boris Yeltsin signaled his preference in 1992 when he announced that Russia would stop targeting U.S. cities and military sites with nuclear weapons and proclaimed that Russia would "no longer consider the United States our potential adversary." This policy was reaffirmed in the 1992 Camp David Declaration on New Relations, in which Yeltsin and Bush stated that "from now on the relationship [between Russia and the United States] will be characterized by friendship and partnership, founded on mutual trust."

In the long term, if Russia's long-neglected domestic problems are overcome, Russia could again emerge as a superpower on the world stage. It lies in the heartland of Eurasia, a bridge between Europe and the Pacific Rim, with China and India to the south. And Russia still stands tall—even if it is a military power ringed by emerging great-power rivals (see Map 4.3). However, the immediate consequence of the Cold War is a transformed global hierarchy in which the former Soviet Union is no longer a challenger to U.S. leadership. In the Soviet acceptance of the devolution of its external empire, the most dramatic peaceful retreat from power in history has occurred. The United States now sits alone at the apex of the international hierarchy.

### Lessons from the Cold War's End

Opinions differ on why the third hegemonic war of the twentieth century ended without mass destruction. The conclusions reached do matter, for the inferences

---

[9] Noteworthy is that Russian imperialism long predated the heavy hand of the former communist regime. Russia's democratic experiment is no guarantee that its imperial ambitions are dead. As Mikhail Gorbachev warned on December 26, 1991, the day he resigned as leader of the now defunct Soviet Union, "Watch out for Russia." Germany is a possible parallel. "One recalls that after the First World War, Germany became a democratic nation free of its imperial burden. During its first four years, to be sure, the new Weimar Republic had a troubled time. . . . During the following five years, however, Germany enjoyed stable democratic government, vigorous economic growth, minimal unemployment, friendly relations with all its neighbors, and a burst of extraordinary cultural creativity. Europe and the world seemed at peace. Suddenly, the Great Depression and its wave of massive unemployment tilted the political forces in Germany (and Japan as well) in favor of an ideology of violence and expansion" (Iklé, 1991–1992). If history is a guide, then, Russia could repeat this pattern. Boris Yeltsin's response to domestic violence in October 1993—unleashing controlled violence against his political foes to prevent another Bolshevik revolution—suggests how ripe Russia's situation is for a return to centrist rule and militarism. Russian expansionism could reassert itself.

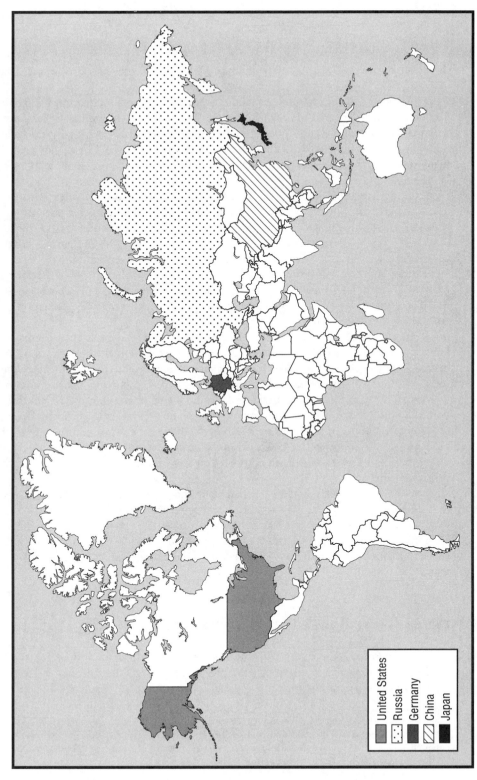

**Map 4.3**  Emerging Centers of Power in a New Multipolar System

United States
Russia
Germany
China
Japan

drawn are certain to affect leaders' thinking about how to manage great-power rivalries in the future.

To some observers, the policies recommended by George Kennan in his famous "X" article now appear prophetic. Recall that his version of nonmilitary *containment* anticipated that this would "promote tendencies which must eventually find their outlet in either the breakup of or the gradual mellowing of Soviet power." As many believe, this was precisely what *did* happen, albeit more than forty years later!

Structural realists, in contrast, emphasize the contribution of nuclear weapons, essential parity of military power, rigid bipolarity, and extended deterrence through alliances. And liberal and neoliberals cite still other influences. These include especially the superpowers' crisis management capabilities and arms control agreements, as well as the promotive part played by international law and institutions and by grass-roots peace movements. The liberal school stresses in particular the internal and interpersonal sources of the changes. A consensus has not materialized about the ways these factors individually or in combination put an end to the Cold War.[10]

A fundamental question sits at the center of this postmortem speculation, however. Did *militant* containment force the Soviet Union into submission? Or, instead, as Kennan urged, did Soviet leaders succumb to the inherent *political* weaknesses of communism, which caused an internal economic malaise that left them unable to conduct an imperial policy abroad or retain communist control at home? In other words, was the end of Communist Party rule accepted because of the intimidation of U.S. military strength and political pressure? Or was the outcome produced by other political and economic influences within the Soviet Union? The ideas recorded in Box 4.1 frame alternative viewpoints in this continuing debate.

The answers remain unclear. Sorting out the contribution of different causes that ended the Cold War will doubtless intrigue historians for decades to come, just as determining the causes for its onset has done. As noted, the lessons derived are important nonetheless, as they will long shape thinking about the most effective strategies for maintaining great-power cooperation in the post–Cold War world.

## The Future of Great-Power Politics after the Cold War . . . . . . . .

With the end of the Cold War both superpowers found themselves liberated from a rivalry that had extracted enormous resources and reduced their economic strength relative to other ascending great powers such as Germany and Japan (see Lebow and

---

[10] For discussions and comparisons of rival explanations of why peace resulted and the Cold War died without warfare, see Cox (1991), Deudney and Ikenberry (1992), Gaddis (1992), Kegley (1991 and 1994), Lebow and Stein (1994), and the special issue of *The National Interest* (No. 31, Spring 1993) devoted entirely to "The Strange Death of Soviet Communism."

## Box 4.1
### RIVAL THEORIES OF THE COLD WAR'S END

• • •

### THE PERSPECTIVE OF U.S. REALISTS

"The political and economic reconstruction attempted by the Soviet Union followed in part from external causes. . . . Gorbachev realized that the Soviet Union could no longer support a first-rate military establishment on the basis of a third-rate economy. Economic reorganization, and the reduction of imperial burdens, became an externally imposed necessity, which in turn required internal reforms."

—Kenneth N. Waltz, Political Scientist, 1993

"There are few lessons so clear in history than this: only the combination of conventional and nuclear forces have ensured this long peace in Europe.

—President George Bush, 1990

"Those who argued for nuclear deterrence and serious military capabilities contributed mightily to the position of strength that eventually led the Soviet leadership to choose a less bellicose, less menacing approach to international politics. . . . We're witnessing the rewards of the Reagan policy of firmness."

—Presidential adviser Richard Perle, 1991

### THE PERSPECTIVE OF RUSSIAN POLICYMAKERS

"The version that President Reagan's 'tough' policy and intensified arms race being the most important source of perestroika—that it persuaded communists to 'give up'—is sheer nonsense. Quite to the contrary, this policy made the life for reformers, for all who yearned for democratic changes in their life, much more difficult. . . . In such tense international situations the conservatives and reactionaries were given predominant influence. That is why . . . Reagan made it practically impossible to start reforms after Brezhnev's death (Andropov had such plans) and made things more difficult for Gorbachev to cut military expenditures."

—Georgi Arbatov, Director,
Institute for the USA and Canada Studies, 1991

"The Cold War ended because it was no longer feasible. The United States and the USSR had exhausted their capacity to carry on their global confrontation, which had engendered repeated and disastrous military interventions and extraordinarily expensive new weapons systems. These commitments had overburdened the socioeconomic and political bases for the East/West conflict."

—Peter Gladkov, Policy Analyst,
Institute for the USA and Canada Studies, 1994

*(continued on next page)*

## NEOLIBERAL PERSPECTIVES

"Many of the demonstrators . . . who sought to reject communist rule looked to the American system for inspiration. But the source of that inspiration was America's reputation as a haven for the values of limited government, not Washington's $300-billion-a-year military budget and its network of global military bases."
—Ted Galen Carpenter, Political Analyst, 1991

"There are ironies for Americans in the victory of democracy over Soviet communism. During the years of the Cold War . . . Washington consistently undervalued the attraction of people elsewhere of the American system of constitutional government and individual rights."
—Anthony Lewis, Political Journalist, 1991

"Some conservatives argue that the Reagan defense buildup forced Gorbachev to change his policies. . . . But it seems likely that internal pressures played as much, if not more, of a role in convincing the Soviet leader to agree to measures that cut his country's firepower more than they cut U.S. strength."
—Carl P. Leubsdorf, Political Journalist, 1991

Stein, 1994). Caught breathless, each superpower faced unfamiliar circumstances. No longer was there "a clear and present danger to delineate the purpose of power, and this basic shift . . . invalidated the framework for much of the thought and action about international affairs in East and West since World War II" (Oberdorfer, 1991).

## Post–Cold War Scenarios

The peaceful end of the Cold War does not ensure a peaceful future. On the contrary, the insights of long-cycle theory predict pessimistically that prevailing trends in the diffusion of economic power will lead to renewed competition, conflict, and even perhaps warfare among the great powers and that the range of new problems and potential threats will multiply (see Box 4.2). As political scientist Robert Jervis explains,

Cyclical thinking suggests that, freed from the constraints of the Cold War, world politics will return to earlier patterns. Many of the basic generalizations of international politics remain unaltered: it is still anarchic in the sense that there is no international sovereign that can make and enforce laws and agreements. The security dilemma remains as well, with the problems it creates for states who would like to cooperate but whose security requirements do not mesh. Many specific causes of conflict also remain, including desires for greater prestige, economic rivalries, hostile nationalisms, divergent perspectives on and

## Box 4.2
## POST–COLD WAR PERILS?

• • •

"[The Western victory in the Cold War was] so complete that it threatens to destabilize many habitual relationships [at the very time] the United States itself manifests too many characteristics of national decline for comfort."
—David Calleo (1994: 175, 179)

"Rather than the end of history, the post–Cold War world is witnessing a return of history in the diversity of sources of international conflict."
—Joseph S. Nye Jr. (1994: 51)

"Far from ushering in a period of 'kinder, gentler,' and more purely cooperative relations among the industrial democracies, the end of the Cold War is likely to mark the dawning of the era of tougher bargaining and greater self-assertion."
—Aaron L. Friedberg (1992: 102)

"The near-term prospects for a stable Russian democracy are not very promising. . . . Regrettably, the imperial impulse remains strong and even appears to be strengthening."
—Zbigniew Brzezinski (1994: 72)

"The prospect of major crises, even wars, in Europe is likely to increase dramatically now that the Cold War is receding into history."
—John J. Mearsheimer (1992: 158–159)

incompatible standards of legitimacy, religious animosities, and territorial ambitions. To put it more generally, both aggression and spirals of insecurity and tension can still disturb the peace. (Jervis, 1991–1992: 46)

To political realists, great-power rivalry for power and position is likely to resume inasmuch as the international anarchy that promotes this continues to shape states' conduct in world politics. Moreover, realists foresee probable instability resulting from the changes unfolding in the international system's structure. The hegemonic preponderance of the United States is unlikely to continue. As rivals rise to challenge its leadership, a new multipolar structure will emerge.

## A Twenty-First-Century Multipolar World

The distribution of power in the Cold War system was bipolar. The post–Cold War world promises to be very different. The demise of Russia was a dramatic *power transition* that produced a new unipolar structure, ephemeral though it may be. In early 1991 when it victoriously fought the Persian Gulf War, the United States basked in a "unipolar moment." Then it was the "one first-rate power [with] no prospect in the immediate future of any power to rival it. . . . [It was] the only country with the military, diplomatic, political and economic assets to be a decisive player in any conflict in whatever part of the world it [chose] to involve itself" (Krauthammer, 1991b).

This condition is not likely to last into the next millennium, however. As Figure 4.2 shows, the long-term trajectories of history unmistakably point to the advent of a world in which two or more great powers will rise to challenge the financial prominence and political clout of the United States, even if its military supremacy remains unchallenged. One does not have to be a "declinist" to recognize that China, Japan, and Germany are ascending in economic power relative to the United States (Kennedy, 1993; Thurow, 1992; Fry, Taylor and Wood, 1994).

We call such a future world *multipolar* in order to contrast it with situations where either one (unipolar) or two (bipolar) countries possess overwhelming power.

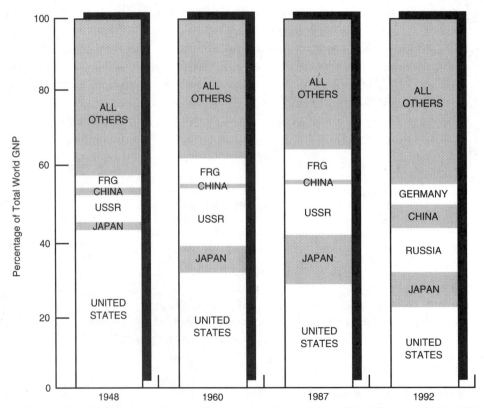

**Figure 4.2**   The Rise and Fall of the Great Powers' Share of Gross World Product, 1948–1992
*Source: The Economist* (May 15, 1993, p. 83); Ruth Sivard (1991: 51–52); Stephen Van Evera (1992: 110).
*Note:* Data are not available for China in 1948; its share is based on conventional estimates.

## The Challenge of Multipolarity

The character of a new multipolar structure could be very different from the stability that characterized the unipolar and bipolar phases of international politics since World War II. In part this is because a dispersed distribution of power will introduce greater complexity and uncertainty about allegiances and alignments and because "international security issues will exhibit themselves in all their variety once again—issues of markets, resources, technology, ethnic animosities, political philosophy, and different conceptions of world order, as well as armies and nuclear weapons" (Carter, 1990–1991). The multipolar global agenda will encompass continuing concerns with military security—the focus of political realism—alongside mounting concerns about the great powers' economic relations—the topic on which liberal international relations theory concentrates.

Many theorists point out the dangers inherent in multipolar distributions of power. Their warnings are inspired by memories of the historical record, which suggest that if we look to the past to anticipate the future we have many reasons to fear the reemergence of this kind of system. Today's hopes for great-power cooperation in the wake of the Cold War have many precedents. The end of every previous great-power war was followed by an initial hopeful burst of collaborative institution building to forge a stable new order among the victorious powers. But each of these great-power designs, constructed at the conclusion of a multipolar period's war, ultimately proved ephemeral. Recall the Peace of Westphalia (1648), the Treaty of Utrecht (1713), the Concert of Europe (1815), the League of Nations (1919), and the United Nations (1945). In each case, as the new multipolar distribution of power underwent changes in the great powers' relative strength, collaboration gave way to competition. Sooner or later, every previous multipolar system collapsed, as one or more of the major powers expressed dissatisfaction with the existing hierarchy, rejected the rules on which they had agreed to manage their relations, and endeavored by force to overturn the status quo. Rivalry routinely culminated in a hegemonic struggle for supremacy that ended in a new catastrophic general war, each of which was more destructive than the one that preceded it.

Multipolar politics also looks menacing when one takes into account the interplay of military and economic factors in the perceived rankings of the great powers.[11] In a new multipolar environment without the stark simplicities and the self-evident symmetries of a bipolar system, any effort to maintain partnerships will prove problematic. For in such a system, differentiating friend from foe is likely to be exceedingly difficult—and exacerbated by the fact that allies in the realm of military security are

---

[11] Consider one description:

A profound disparity already has defined itself between the strategic rank-order of the major powers and their economic rank-order. The strategic hierarchy for a six-power central balance would still read: the United States, Russia . . . , the European [Union], China, India, and Japan. The economic hierarchy would read: the European [Union] (which by mid-decade may be at least 30 percent larger than the United States), the United States, Japan (by then about 70 percent the size of the U.S.), then possibly China, with India and [Russia] bringing up the rear. (Bell, 1990–1991: 38)

likely to be rivals in trade relationships (Hart, 1992). Symptomatic was the U.S.–Japan discussion in 1993 about developing and deploying a joint antimissile system at the very time they were arguing about "fair trade."

The diffusion of wealth presages the likely intensification of great-power political competition. Throughout history changes in comparative *economic* advantage have preceded changes in comparative *political* advantage. As economic rivals have struggled to protect their wealth and compete for economic position, political and even military conflicts have often resulted. Economic conflict often generates military conflict when multipolarity exists. As power disperses to an expanding number of powerful actors, warfare is more likely.

> Strategies of security through expansion make more sense in multipolar situations than in bipolar ones. In multipolarity, an expansionist power may be able to defeat its opponents piecemeal if they fail to unite because they cannot agree on who should bear the costs of resistance. At the same time, great powers in multipolarity may have strong incentives to expand to achieve autarky, since they are less likely to be self-sufficient in the resources needed for national security than are bipolar powers. (J. Snyder, 1991: 26)

In Lester Thurow's (1992) apt phrase, the United States, Europe, and Japan are likely to go "head to head" on the economic battlefield. To this arena for conflict we can expect China and perhaps a re-ascendant Russia and India to join the fray.

Table 4.2 presents a projection of the kind of cross-cutting bilateral relationships that could develop among the great powers by the century's end. It estimates the probability of military cooperation and of economic conflict between any pair of the five major powers. The potential for economic conflict is given in the upper-right-hand portion of the diagonal and the potential for military cooperation through alliances in the lower-left portion.

Table 4.2 forecasts quite different and inconsistent types of great-power relations in the economic and military spheres. The probability of economic rivalry and conflict is generally high, whereas the likelihood of security cooperation for many of these same relationships is also high. For example, the United States, Japan, and China

TABLE 4.2 THE NEW GREAT-POWER CHESSBOARD: ECONOMIC RIVALRY AND MILITARY ALLIANCE POSSIBILITIES

|  | United States | Japan | Germany | Russia | China |
|---|---|---|---|---|---|
| United States | — | H | H | L | H |
| Japan | H | — | H | M | M |
| Germany | M | L | — | M | L |
| Russia | M | L | L | — | H |
| China | M | M | L | M | — |

*Source:* Adapted from Kegley and Raymond (1994a: 197).
*Note:* Lower-left matrix classifies the probability of military alignments, whereas upper-right matrix pictures the probability of economic conflict, with the symbols H = high, M = medium, and L = low signifying the likely character of the bilateral relationships that may develop in the new millennium.

are predicted to exhibit conflict in their commercial relations but also to cooperate in their security relations.

Awareness of this problem may have been behind the warning that U.S. Secretary of State Lawrence Eagleburger expressed in 1989: "We are . . . returning to a more traditional and complicated time of multipolarity, with a growing number of countries increasingly able to affect the course of events despite the wishes of the superpowers. . . . The issue . . . is how well the United States accomplishes the transition from overwhelming predominance to a position more akin to a 'first among equals' status, and how well America's partners—Japan and Western Europe—adapt to their new-found importance. The change will not be easy for any of the players, as such shifts in power relationships have never been easy."

Few observers see advantages for the United States to the fact that, as former U.S. Secretary of State Henry A. Kissinger declared in 1993, "for diplomatic purposes there are no longer two superpowers, but five or six more or less equal power centers. . . . The United States is militarily the strongest, but the circumstances in which its military power is relevant are diminishing." This, Kissinger astutely summarized, poses a serious challenge because "the United States has very little experience with a world that consists of many powers and which it can neither dominate nor from which it can simply withdraw in isolation."

Yet, we have no way of knowing if the future will resemble the gloomy past history of multipolar systems. Patterns and practices can change, and it is possible that policymakers can learn from previous mistakes and avoid repeating them.

## Responding to Multipolarity's Challenge

What, then, can the great powers do to prevent the resumption of their unbridled rivalry? What security policies should they pursue in order to avoid the twin dangers of shared power and of rapid transitions in their position and strength in the great-power hierarchy?

The answers are highly uncertain. As we will discuss in Part IV of *World Politics: Trend and Transformation*, debate about the *methods* by which international security can be guaranteed in Washington, Moscow, Berlin, Beijing, and Tokyo today revolves around four basic options. Each is actively under consideration. And each will become more or less practical, prudent, or problematic for each great power depending on the circumstances that materialize in tomorrow's multipolar world.

A *unilateral* conception of a great-power's role represents one possible option. Acting alone is especially attractive for a self-confident great power assured of its independent strength. With sufficient power, a potential hegemon can be self-reliant. Unilateralism can entail isolationism, an attempt to exert hegemonic leadership, or an effort to play the role of a "balancer" who skillfully backs one side or another in a great-power dispute, but only when necessary to maintain a military equilibrium between the disputants.

Cultivation of a *specialized relationship* with another great power, similar to the kind built between Great Britain and the United States in this century, is illustrative of a second approach some great powers may choose to pursue. The kind of "condominium" partnership between the United States and Russia advocated by former U.S. Deputy Secretary of Defense Fred Charles Iklé (1991–1992) suggests the kind of relationship that could develop. There are several variants of this strategy, ranging from informal understandings to cooperations (sometimes termed *ententes*) to formal alliances concretized by treaties.

A third strategy under consideration is construction of a great-power *concert* designed to manage the international system jointly and prevent disputes among the leading states from escalating to war (see Rosecrance, 1992). The Concert of Europe, at its apex between 1815 and 1822, is the epitome of previous great-power efforts to pursue this path to peace.

Finally, some policymakers recommend that today's great powers unite with the lesser powers in constructing a true system of *collective security*. The principles rationalizing the formation of the League of Nations in 1919 exemplify this multilateral approach to peace under conditions of multipolarity.

Whichever combination of approaches receives the most emphasis in the strategies forged to prevent great-power rivalries from escalating to war in a multipolar future, the ultimate outcome will not depend on the great powers alone. The policy response of other, less powerful actors is likely to be increasingly important in shaping world politics, and their role in the system must also be examined. We begin in Chapter 5 with a consideration of the history and characteristics of those at the bottom of the international system's hierarchy, the Third World, and of the foreign policy interests and goals that motivate their behavior.

## SUGGESTED READINGS

Bueno de Mesquita, Bruce, and David Lalman. *War and Reason: Domestic and International Imperatives*. New Haven, Conn.: Yale University Press, 1992.

Doran, Charles F. *Systems in Crisis: New Imperatives of High Politics at Century's End*. Cambridge: Cambridge University Press, 1992.

Joseph, Paul. *Peace Politics: The United States Between the Old and New World Orders*. Philadelphia: Temple University Press, 1993.

Kegley, Charles W., Jr., and Gregory A. Raymond. *A Multipolar Peace? Great-Power Politics in the Twenty-First Century*. New York: St. Martin's Press, 1994.

Kennedy, Paul. *The Rise and Fall of the Great Powers*. New York: Random House, 1987.

Kissinger, Henry. *Diplomacy*. New York: Simon & Schuster, 1994.

Layne, Christopher. "The Unipolar Illusion: Why New Great Powers Will Rise," *International Security* 17 (Spring 1993): 5–51.

Lebow, Richard Ned, and Janice Gross Stein. *We All Lost the Cold War*. Princeton, N.J.: Princeton University Press, 1994.

Midlarsky, Manus I., John A. Vasquez, and Peter V. Gladkov, eds. *From Rivalry to Cooperation: Russian and American Perspectives on the Post–Cold War Era*. New York: HarperCollins, 1994.

Modelski, George, and William R. Thompson. *Leading Sectors and World Powers*. Columbia: University of South Carolina Press, 1995.

Rock, Stephen R. *Why Peace Breaks Out: Great Power Rapprochement in Historical Perspective*. Chapel Hill: The University of North Carolina Press, 1989.

Wittkopf, Eugene R., ed. *The Future of American Foreign Policy*, 2nd ed. New York: St. Martin's Press, 1994.

# CHAPTER 5

• • •

# THE NORTH–SOUTH CONFLICT: ROOTS AND CONSEQUENCES OF GLOBAL INEQUALITIES

• • •

*The world is still hopelessly split into areas of wealth and poverty, with little prospect of narrowing the gap. The politics of international economic affairs in our lifetimes must therefore be a politics of inequality, inherently a politics of mutual suspicion and struggle.*

> Robert Heilbroner,
> Norman Thomas Professor of Economics, 1991

*Fundamentally, . . . the Third World is a state of mind. . . . In the circumstances, we should not be too surprised if the term "Third World" is widely used even in a post–Cold War world.*

> James O. C. Jonah,
> Under-Secretary General of the United Nations, 1991

The end of colonialism is one of the most remarkable developments in world politics. As U.S. Secretary of State George Shultz observed in 1983, "Since the Second World War, the world has undergone a vast transformation as more than one hundred new nations have come into being. An international system that had been centered on Europe for centuries, and that regarded all non-European areas as peripheral or as objects of rivalry, has become in an amazingly short span of time a truly global arena of sovereign states."

Despite their legal status as sovereign entities, the new states born since World War II were thrust into an international system they had no voice in shaping but whose organization and operation they view as a barrier to overcoming the overwhelming political, economic, and social problems that beset them at home. The system seems structured to prevent their rise above their underdog status. Herein lies the source of the North–South conflict, a struggle by states at the bottom of the international hierarchy to improve their position in the global pecking order. The debate between the wealthy North and the poor South has stressed economic and related welfare issues, but the conflict is "inherently a politics of mutual suspicion and struggle" (Heilbroner, 1991).

• • •

The countries that make up the ***Third World*** include the world's poorer, economically less developed states, which not only tend to share a colonial heritage but also are located primarily below the equator in the Southern Hemisphere (hence the designation "the South"). The South contains more than three-fourths of the world's population but accounts for less than a fifth of the goods and services produced in the world (as measured by gross national product [GNP]). There are so many Third World nations that it takes less space to describe those nations that are developed than those that are not. The Third World includes all of Asia, the Middle East, and Oceania except Australia, Israel, Japan, New Zealand, and Turkey; all of Africa except South Africa; and all of the Western Hemisphere except Canada and the United States.

In contrast, the industrialized countries of the North, otherwise known as the ***First World***,[1] account for most global production and enjoy a high standard of living. The First World includes the wealthy countries of North America and Western Europe, Japan, Australia, Israel, Malta, New Zealand, South Africa, and the resource-rich countries of the former Soviet bloc. These states exhibit a preference for democratic political institutions and free market economic principles and, with the exception of Japan, share a common cultural heritage. Reflecting their common economic characteristics, they are known in the idiom of international diplomacy as *developed market economies.*

Our purpose in this chapter is to explore the divisions between North and South and the consequences they portend for world politics. We will find that the term *Third World* often masks important differences among the world's less developed (or developing) countries. Indeed, some analysts have seized on their growing diversity in combination with the end of the Cold War to pronounce the end of "third worldism." We will consider the reasons for that viewpoint in the concluding section of the chapter. First, however, we will examine the reasons underlying the "Third World" idea and inquire into its analytical utility.[2] We begin with an examination of colonialism and imperialism, historical experiences shared by most developing nations and ones that have shaped their contemporary world views in distinctive ways.

## THE RISE AND FALL OF EUROPEAN EMPIRES  . . . . . . . . . . . . . . . . . . . . . .

As noted, the emergence of the less developed world is primarily a post–World War II phenomenon. Although most Latin American nations were independent before

[1] During the Cold War it was common to distinguish the First World in the "West" from the ***Second World***, which consisted of the state-owned and state-managed *centrally planned economies* in the "East" or Soviet bloc ideologically committed to the eventual victory of socialism over capitalism. Today, with the collapse of communism and acceptance of a market economy in the former Soviet Union and its previous satellites in Eastern and Central Europe, the Second World label is an anachronism. Few centrally planned economies remain. (Even during the Cold War era the Second World largely disassociated itself from the North–South conflict, making it a North/West–South dispute.) Hence the term *Second World* has disappeared from diplomatic discourse and has only historical meaning.
[2] See Leslie Wolf-Phillips (1987) and James Mittelman (1993) for discussions of the derivation of the term *Third World* and how it came to be accepted in the development literature.

that time, having gained their freedom from Spain and Portugal early in the nineteenth century, it was not until 1946 that the floodgates of decolonization were first opened. In the next four decades a profusion of new states joined the international community as sovereign entities. Nearly all of the new nations were carved from the former British, French, Belgian, Spanish, and Portuguese empires (see Figure 5.1). Often the areas granted independence had been colonized only since the late 1800s, when a wave of new imperialism swept the world. In other cases, the dependent relationships had existed for hundreds of years. Today, few colonies remain. A dozen or so remaining dependent territories may yet someday become independent members of the world community, but most of them have populations of less than 100,000. In short, *decolonization*—the independence of peoples formerly under imperial rule—is a distinctly contemporary phenomenon, but as a political process is now complete.

But the vestiges of colonialism remain, with important consequences for the shape of contemporary world politics, as the needs, circumstances, and objectives of Third World countries are often quite dissimilar from those of the older and more established states. For a variety of reasons these dissimilarities stem from the "gap"—the immense disparity in income and wealth between the world's rich and poor nations, between those that have advanced economically and those that have remained underdeveloped or only recently have begun to develop.

Differing perceptions of the causes of the gap and correspondingly different prescriptions for its cure lie at the heart of a major controversy in contemporary world politics. As viewed through the nationalistic eyes of Third World leaders, the disparity between the rich North and the poor South is the consequence of ***neocolonialism*** or ***neoimperialism.*** Unequal exchanges, they contend, permit the advantaged to exploit the disadvantaged through the international economic processes institutionalized by the rich. This victimization, and the South's malaise, they complain, are products of the oppressive colonial heritage of the Third World and of the commercial domination that the affluent today exert over the impoverished.

## The Emergence of the Modern State System

As a network of relationships among independent units (and hence the term *international* relations), the *state system* was born with the Peace of Westphalia in 1648, which ended the Thirty Years' War in Europe. Thereafter European potentates refused to recognize the temporal authority of the papacy (the Roman Catholic church). A system of geographically and politically distinct states that recognized no authority above them replaced the previous quasi-world government. The newly independent states were all given the same legal rights: territorial inviolability, the ability to conduct foreign relations and negotiate treaties with other states as they saw fit, and the authority to establish whatever form of government they thought best and to rule their own population. The concept ***sovereignty*** captures these legal rights.

Although the new European states were assumed to be equal in law, they were not equal in military and economic capabilities. In fact, the international law that

## Bottom table

| Year | Country | Belgium | Britain | France | Spain | Italy | Netherlands | USA |
|------|---------|---------|---------|--------|-------|-------|-------------|-----|
| 1945 | Vietnam | | | • | | | | |
| 1946 | Jordan | | • | | | | | |
| | Syria | | | • | | | | |
| | Philippines | | | | | | | • |
| 1947 | Bhutan | | • | | | | | |
| | India | | • | | | | | |
| | Pakistan | | • | | | | | |
| 1948 | Brunei | | • | | | | | |
| | Ceylon (Sri Lanka) | | • | | | | | |
| | Myanmar (Burma) | | • | | | | | |
| | Palestine (Israel) | | • | | | | | |
| 1949 | Indonesia | | | | | | • | |
| | Laos | | | • | | | | |
| 1951 | Libya | | | | | • | | |
| 1954 | Cambodia | | | • | | | | |
| | Laos | | | • | | | | |
| | North Vietnam | | | • | | | | |
| | South Vietnam | | | • | | | | |
| 1956 | Morocco | | | • | • | | | |
| | Sudan | | • | | | | | |
| | Tunisia | | | • | | | | |
| 1957 | Ghana | | • | | | | | |
| | Malaysia | | • | | | | | |
| 1958 | Guinea | | | • | | | | |
| 1960 | Benin | | | • | | | | |
| | Bukina | | | • | | | | |

## Top table

| Year | Country | South Africa | Britain | France/Italy (■) | Spain | Portugal | Netherlands | USA |
|------|---------|--------------|---------|------------------|-------|----------|-------------|-----|
| | Singapore | | • | | | | | |
| | Zanzibar (part of Tanzania) | | • | | | | | |
| 1964 | Malawi | | • | | | | | |
| | Malta | | • | | | | | |
| | Zambia | | • | | | | | |
| 1965 | Gambia | | • | | | | | |
| | Maldives | | • | | | | | |
| | Singapore | | • | | | | | |
| 1966 | Barbados | | • | | | | | |
| | Botswana | | • | | | | | |
| | Guyana | | • | | | | | |
| | Lesotho | | • | | | | | |
| 1967 | Southern Yemen | | • | | | | | |
| 1968 | Equatorial Guinea | | | | • | | | |
| | Mauritius | | • | | | | | |
| | Nauru | | • | | | | | |
| | Swaziland | | • | | | | | |
| 1969 | Sidi Fini | | • | | | | | |
| 1970 | Fiji | | • | | | | | |
| | Tonga | | • | | | | | |
| 1971 | Bahrain | | • | | | | | |
| | Qatar | | • | | | | | |
| | Sierra Leone | | • | | | | | |
| | United Arab Emirates | | • | | | | | |
| 1973 | Bahamas | | • | | | | | |

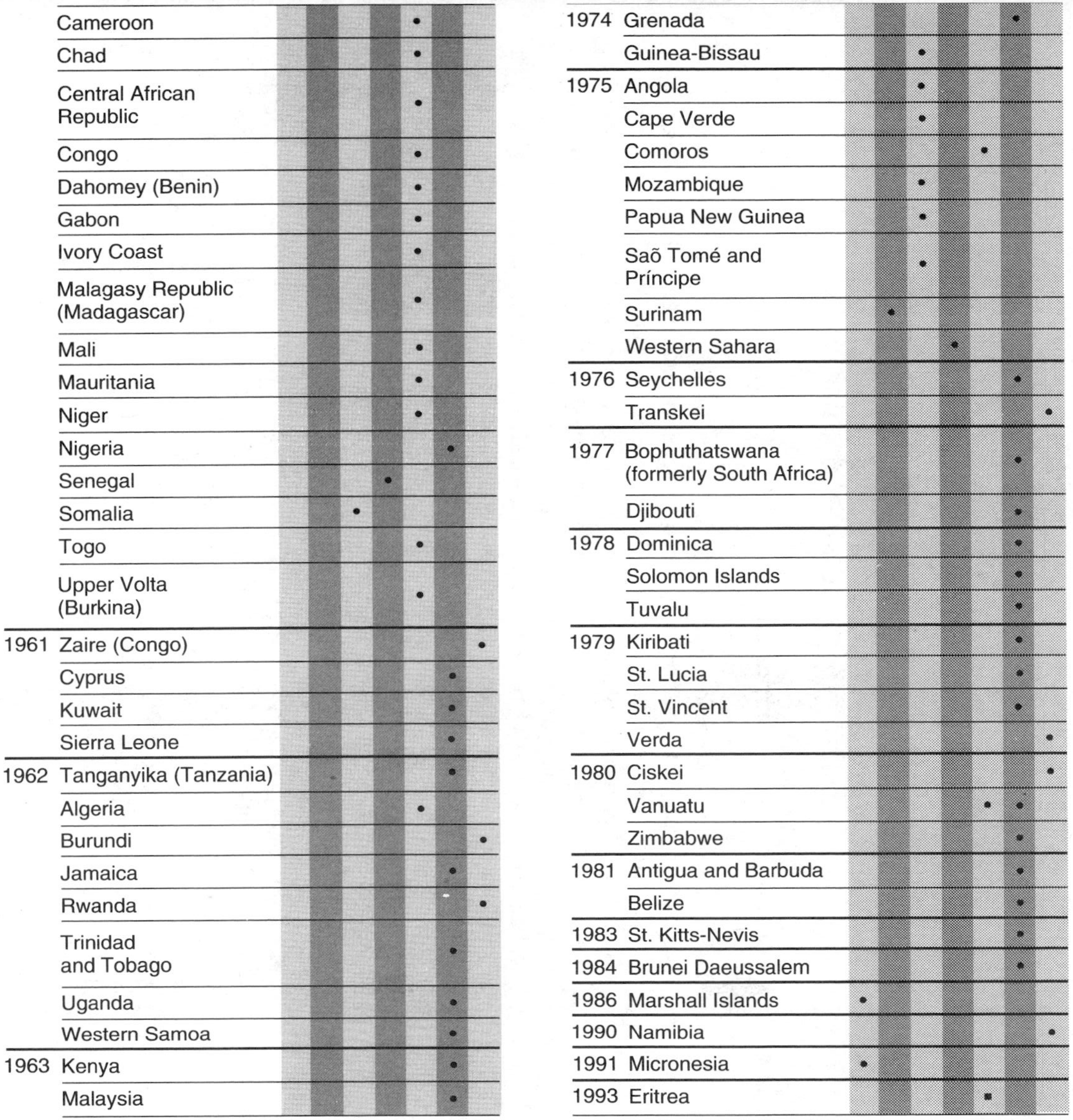

1974 Grenada
1975 Guinea-Bissau
     Angola
     Cape Verde
     Comoros
     Mozambique
     Papua New Guinea
     Saõ Tomé and Principe
     Surinam
     Western Sahara
1976 Seychelles
     Transkei
1977 Bophuthatswana (formerly South Africa)
     Djibouti
1978 Dominica
     Solomon Islands
     Tuvalu
1979 Kiribati
     St. Lucia
     St. Vincent
     Verda
1980 Ciskei
     Vanuatu
     Zimbabwe
1981 Antigua and Barbuda
     Belize
1983 St. Kitts-Nevis
1984 Brunei Daeussalem
1986 Marshall Islands
1990 Namibia
1991 Micronesia
1993 Eritrea

Cameroon
Chad
Central African Republic
Congo
Dahomey (Benin)
Gabon
Ivory Coast
Malagasy Republic (Madagascar)
Mali
Mauritania
Niger
Nigeria
Senegal
Somalia
Togo
Upper Volta (Burkina)
1961 Zaire (Congo)
     Cyprus
     Kuwait
     Sierra Leone
1962 Tanganyika (Tanzania)
     Algeria
     Burundi
     Jamaica
     Rwanda
     Trinidad and Tobago
     Uganda
     Western Samoa
1963 Kenya
     Malaysia

**Figure 5.1**  A Decolonization Chronology
*Source:* Revised and updated adaptation from Peter J. Taylor (1990: 16–17), with data from U.S. CIA (1992b).

emerged in the post-Westphalia state system legalized the drive for power and created rules by which states could compete with one another for position in the international hierarchy. Some became great powers, such as Austria-Hungary, England, France, Prussia, and Russia. Others remained minor powers, such as the various principalities in Germany and the Italian peninsula. And still others, such as the Netherlands, Portugal, and Spain, who once enjoyed great-power status but whose capabilities and influence had diminished noticeably by the time the state system emerged in 1648, were reduced to a secondary rank. Collectively, the major and secondary powers carried their competition for territorial control beyond the European arena, thereby transforming the European state system into a global one. Europeans controlled a third of the globe by 1800, two-thirds by 1878, and over four-fifths by 1914 (Field-house, 1973: 3).

## The First Wave of European Imperialism

The first wave of European empire building began during the fifteenth century, as the Dutch, English, French, Portuguese, and Spanish used their military power to achieve commercial advantage overseas. Innovations in a variety of sciences made the adventures of European explorers possible. Merchants followed in their wake, "quickly seizing upon opportunities to increase their business and profits. In turn, Europe's governments perceived the possibilities for increasing their own power and wealth. Commercial companies were chartered and financed, with military and naval expeditions frequently sent out after them to ensure political control of overseas territories" (Cohen, 1973).

The economic strategy underlying the relationship between colonies and colonizers during this era of classical imperialism was known as *mercantilism:* "the philosophy and practice of governmental regulation of economic life to increase state power and security" (Cohen, 1973). European rulers believed that state power flowed from the possession of national wealth measured in terms of gold and silver. Maintaining a favorable balance of trade (exporting more than is imported) was one way to accumulate the desired bullion. "Colonies were desirable in this respect because they afforded an opportunity to shut out commercial competition; they guaranteed exclusive access to untapped markets and sources of cheap materials (as well as, in some instances, direct sources of the precious metals themselves). Each state was determined to monopolize as many of these overseas mercantile opportunities as possible" (Cohen, 1973). To maximize the power and wealth of the state, the acquisition of territory by conquest was seen as a natural complement to active government management of the economy.

By the end of the eighteenth century, the European powers had spread themselves, although thinly, throughout virtually the entire world. But the colonial empires they had built had by that time already begun to erode. Britain's thirteen North American colonies declared their independence in 1776, and most of Spain's possessions in South America achieved independence early in the nineteenth century. Between 1775 and 1825, ninety-five colonial relationships were terminated (Bergesen and Schoenberg, 1980: 236).

Concurrent with the breakup of colonial empires was the waning of the mercantilist philosophy that had sustained classical imperialism. As argued by Adam Smith in his 1776 treatise *The Wealth of Nations*, national wealth grew not through the accumulation of precious metals but, rather, from the capital and goods they could buy. A system of free international trade consistent with the precepts of laissez-faire economics (minimal governmental interference in the market) became the accepted philosophy governing international economic relations. European powers continued to hold numerous colonies, but the prevailing sentiment was now more anti- than pro-imperial.

## The Second Wave of European Imperialism

Beginning in the 1870s and extending until the outbreak of World War I, a new wave of imperialism washed over the world as Europe (joined later by the United States and Japan) colonized new territories at a rate nearly four times faster than during the first wave of colonial expansion (Bergesen and Schoenberg, 1980). By 1914, nearly all of Africa was under the control of only seven European powers (Belgium, Britain, France, Germany, Italy, Portugal, and Spain). In all of the Far East and the Pacific, only China, Japan, and Siam (Thailand) remained outside the direct control of Europe or the United States. Even China, however, was divided into spheres of influence by foreign powers, and Japan itself practiced imperialism by occupying Korea and Formosa (Taiwan). Elsewhere, the United States expanded across its continent, acquired Puerto Rico from Spain, extended its colonial reach westward to Hawaii and the Philippines, leased the Panama Canal Zone "in perpetuity" from the new state of Panama (an American creation), and exercised considerable political leverage over several Caribbean lands, notably Cuba. The British Empire, built by the preeminent imperial power of the era, symbolized the imperial wave that in a single generation engulfed the entire world. By 1900 it covered a fifth of the earth's land area and comprised perhaps a quarter of its population (Cohen, 1973: 30). As British imperialists were proud to proclaim, it was an empire on which the sun never set. The result of this imperial conquest and control is that the history of most of the globe includes a colonial past, as nearly every country was at one time a former colony of one or more of the European imperial powers (see Map 5.1).

In contrast with classical imperialism, extraordinary competition among the imperial powers marked the new imperialism of the late nineteenth century. Expansionism to build overseas empires was energetically practiced in order to occupy and militarily subjugate colonies, which became important symbols of national power and prestige. In the process, local inhabitants of the conquered lands were often ruthlessly suppressed. As Benjamin Cohen explains in his book *The Question of Imperialism*:

> The imperial powers typically pursued their various interests overseas in a blatantly aggressive fashion. Bloody, one-sided wars with local inhabitants of contested territories were

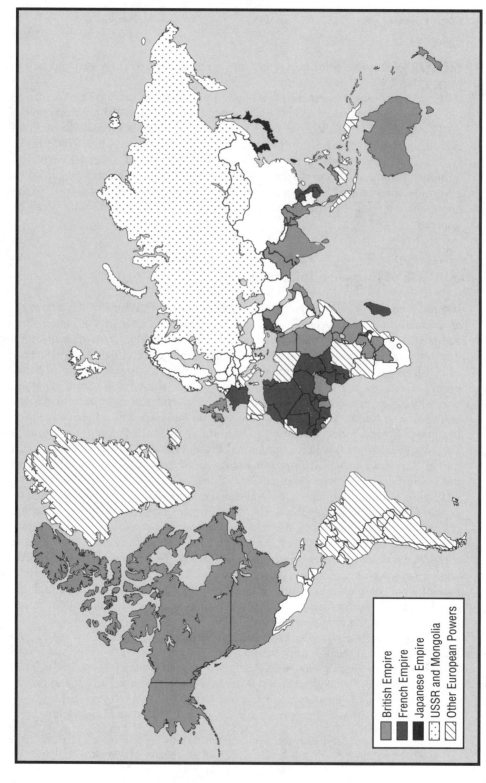

**Map 5.1**   The Legacy of Imperialism:  The Major Empires and Former Colonies of Previous Hegemonic Powers

commonplace; "sporting wars," [Prussian ruler Otto von] Bismarck once called them. The powers themselves rarely came into direct military conflict, but competition among them was keen, and they were perpetually involved in various diplomatic crises. In contrast to the preceding years of comparative political calm, the period after 1870 was one of unaccustomed hostility and tension. (Cohen, 1973: 30)

## Economic Explanations of the New Imperialism

Several explanations of the causes of the new imperialism exist. Marxists see imperialistic competition and aggression resulting from capitalism's need for profitable overseas outlets for surplus or "finance" capital. Thus V. I. Lenin argued in his famous monograph *Imperialism, The Highest Stage of Capitalism* that military expansion abroad was produced by the "monopoly stage of capitalism." From the marxist perspective, the only way to end imperialism was to abolish capitalism. Classical or liberal economists, on the other hand, regarded the new imperialism "not [as] a product of capitalism as such, but rather [as] a response to certain maladjustments within the contemporary capitalist system which, given the proper will, could be corrected" (Cohen, 1973). What the two shared was the belief that economics explained the new imperialism. "The fundamental problem was in the presumed material needs of advanced capitalist societies—the need for cheap raw materials to feed their growing industrial complexes, for additional markets to consume their rising levels of production, and for investment outlets to absorb their rapidly accumulating capital. The rush for colonies was supposed to be the response of these capitalist societies to one or another of these material needs" (Cohen, 1973)

World-system analysts also embrace an economic explanation of the new imperialism. They begin by noting that a single capitalist world-economy emerged during the "long sixteenth century" between 1450 and 1640 (Wallerstein, 1988). During this time a world division of labor developed that demarcated "core" (industrial) political entities from those in the world's (nonindustrial) "periphery." Northwest Europe first emerged as the core. As the industrial revolution proceeded, the core states exchanged manufactured goods for agricultural and mineral products produced in the colonial territories at the periphery. From this perspective, colonization became a mechanism of imperial control that "was the principal political form of incorporating external areas into the capitalist world-economy" (Boswell, 1989). Imperialism expanded during periods of economic contraction in the core areas and contracted during periods of economic prosperity.

Despite the common world-system emphasis on economics, even its advocates recognize that the new imperialism of the late eighteenth century differed from the previous colonial period in important ways. "The earliest colonies were usually coastal trading posts for merchants involved in long-distance preciosity exchange with the contact periphery, such as the spice trade. Following rivers upstream, these were later superseded by settler colonies involved in the production of necessities, primarily mining and cash-crop agriculture using coerced labor. After 1870, 'occupation' colonies became common where a small number of European sojourners coerced an indigenous population into production for the world-economy" (Boswell, 1989).

## Political Explanations of the New Imperialism

Political factors also explain the new imperialism. As the pioneering student of this thesis, J. A. Hobson, argued in his influential 1902 book *Imperialism: A Study*, the jockeying for power and prestige between competitive empires was historically characteristic of traditional European balance-of-power politics. Imperialism through military expansion overseas was simply an extension of the European powers' competition for hegemony that they had pursued among themselves since the sixteenth century.

By the 1800s Britain emerged as Europe's hegemonic core state. As the new leader in politics and economics, it became the chief promoter of free international trade (which, incidentally, promoted disproportionate economic growth in the core relative to the periphery) (McGowan, 1981). By 1870, however, Britain's superiority was on the wane. Germany emerged on the European continent as a powerful industrial nation, as did the United States in the Western Hemisphere. Accordingly, Britain endeavored to keep its privileged position in the international division of labor in the face of growing competition from Germany and the United States, the newly emerging core states. British efforts to maintain the hierarchical status quo helps to explain the second wave of imperial expansion, especially in Africa.

As Africa's partition illustrates, the European powers competed for power not in Europe itself, but in the peripheral areas of the capitalist world-system. Competition for political preeminence led to economic domination and exploitation.[3]

> As in the days of mercantilism, colonies were integrated into an international economic system designed to serve the economic interest of the metropole [colonial power]. The political victors controlled investment and trade, regulated currency and production, and manipulated labor, thus establishing structures of economic dependency in their colonies which would endure far longer than their actual political authority. (Spero, 1990: 6–7)

Until the outbreak of World War I, the British-sponsored laissez-faire system of free international trade promoted rapid economic growth in many colonial territories. Even so, Western Europe, North America, Australia, and New Zealand were able to complete their industrial revolutions during this period and to advance as industrial societies. Thus the gap between the world's rich and poor nations began to take shape. After World War I the economies of the North and the South alike stagnated as worldwide depression engulfed both, but there was an important difference between them. In most of the countries of the North, income levels remained comparatively high, for already by the time of the Great Depression in the 1930s it was evident

---

[3] Within Europe itself, the disintegration of political units into smaller ones was more prevalent than their integration into larger ones. (The unification of Germany and Italy are the principal exceptions.) Europe consisted of about fifteen sovereign states in 1871, twenty-five by the outbreak of World War I, and over thirty by the 1930s. The increase was due partly to the independence movements created by rising nationalistic aspirations and was fueled by the goal of national self-determination emulated worldwide after World War II.

The number of independent European states remained relatively constant from the late 1940s onward. In the post–Cold War environment, however, the breakup into separate states of Yugoslavia and Czechoslovakia and the successor to the Soviet Union, the Commonwealth of Independent States, has again accelerated the trend toward larger numbers of European states.

that Western Europe, North America, and the southern Pacific were rich and that the rest of the world was poor (Higgins and Higgins, 1979).

## Colonialism and Self-Determination in the Interwar Period

There was little movement toward the breakup of the colonial empires amassed in previous centuries between World War I and World War II. The Versailles peace settlement, which ended the First World War, incorporated the principle of national *self-determination,* which U.S. President Woodrow Wilson had espoused in justifying American participation in the war. Self-determination meant that nationalities would have the right to determine which authority would represent and rule them. Freedom of choice would lead to the creation of nations and governments content with their territorial boundaries and therefore less inclined to make war. In practice, however, the principle was applied almost exclusively to war-torn Europe, where six new states were created from the territory of the former Austro-Hungarian Empire (Austria, Czechoslovakia, Hungary, Poland, Romania, and Yugoslavia). Most territorial adjustments elsewhere in Europe, many guided by the outcome of popular plebiscites, were also made, but the proposition that self-determination ought to be extended to Europe's overseas empires enjoyed little serious support.

However, the colonial territories of the powers defeated in World War I were not simply parceled out among the victorious allies. Instead, following the insistence of President Wilson, the territories controlled by Germany and the Ottoman Empire were transferred under League of Nations auspices to countries that would govern them as mandates pending their eventual self-rule. In the Middle East, France assumed the mandate for Syria and Britain assumed it for Iraq, Transjordan, and Palestine. In Africa, most of the German colony of Tanganyika went to Britain; the West African colonies of Cameroon and Togoland were divided between Britain and France; and the Union of South Africa gained responsibility for the mandate governing German South-West Africa. In the Pacific area, Australia, New Zealand, and Japan acquired jurisdiction over the former German colonies.

Many of these territorial decisions shaped political conflicts during the next half-century or more. The decisions relating to the Middle East and Africa were especially crucial, as the League of Nations called for the eventual creation of a Jewish national homeland in Palestine and arranged for the transfer of control over South-West Africa (now called Namibia) to what would become the white minority regime of South Africa.

The principle implicit in the mandate system gave birth to the idea that "colonies were a trust rather than simply a property to be exploited and treated as if its peoples had no right of their own" (Easton, 1964). None of Germany's former colonies or provinces was annexed outright following World War I. This set an important precedent for the negotiations after World War II, when territories placed under the trusteeship system of the United Nations were not absorbed by others but were promised eventual self-rule.

## The End of Empire

Imperialism threatened the world again in the 1930s and early 1940s as Germany, Japan, and Italy sought to expand their political control in Europe, Asia, and Africa. With the defeat of the fascist powers, the threat of regional empire building receded and support for self-determination gained momentum. As noted earlier, in the space of a few short decades, more than a hundred new nations, representing about three-quarters of humanity, gained their freedom in a political emancipation unprecedented in recorded history.

The decolonization movement accelerated in 1947, when the British relinquished political control of the Indian subcontinent and India and Pakistan joined the international community as sovereign members. War eventually erupted between the new states as each sought to gain control over disputed territory in Kashmir; it ignited twice more, in 1965 and again in 1971, when East Pakistan broke away from West Pakistan to form the new state of Bangladesh. Violence also broke out in Indochina and Algeria in the 1950s and early 1960s as the French sought to reaffirm political control over colonial territories they had held before World War II. Similarly, bloodshed followed closely on the heels of independence in the Congo (later Zaire) when the Belgians granted their African colony independence in 1960, and it dogged the efforts of Portugal to battle—unsuccessfully—the winds of decolonization that swept over Africa as the 1960s wore on.

For the most part, however, decolonization was not only extraordinarily rapid but also remarkably peaceful. Arguably, this is explained by the fact that World War II sapped the economic and military vitality of many of the colonial powers. As world-system analysts contend, a growing appreciation of the costs of empire also eroded support for colonial empires (Strang, 1990, 1991). Regardless of the underlying cause, colonialism became less acceptable in a world increasingly dominated by rivalry between East and West. The Cold War competition for political allies and the fear of large-scale warfare militated against efforts to suppress revolutions in overseas empires. Decolonization "triumphed," political scientist Inis Claude (1967) has written, "largely because the West [gave] priority to the containment of Communism over the perpetuation of colonialism."

The United Nations also played a role in the "collective delegitimization" of colonialism (Claude, 1967). With colonialism already in retreat, Third World nations took advantage of their growing numbers in the UN General Assembly to secure passage in 1960 of the historic Declaration on the Granting of Independence to Colonial Countries and Peoples.

The General Assembly proclaimed that the subjection of any people to alien domination was a denial of fundamental human rights, contrary to the UN Charter, and an impediment to world peace and that all subject peoples had a right to immediate and complete independence. No country cast a vote against this anticolonial manifesto. . . . It was an ideological triumph. The old order had not merely been challenged and defeated in the field—its adherents were no longer willing to be counted in its defense. (Riggs and Plano, 1994: 195)

As the old order crumbled—and as Third World leaders found that political freedom did not translate automatically into political autonomy, economic independence, and domestic well-being—the North–South conflict between the rich nations of the First World and the newly emancipated nations of the Third World took shape.

## PROFILES AND PROJECTIONS: GLOBAL DISPARITIES IN INCOME AND WEALTH

The unequal distribution of the world's wealth and its people both reflects and explains the poverty of the South. As noted earlier, the more than three-quarters of humanity who live in the South account for only about one-fifth of the world's total economic product, whereas those in the North, making up less than a quarter of the population, account for nearly 80 percent of it. On a per-capita basis, this means (using 1990 data) that the average annual income for the Third World as a whole is $2,170 compared with $14,440 for the First World—a ratio of nearly seven to one between the world's rich and poor (UNDP, 1993: 202). Figure 5.2 lucidly illustrates how lopsided the world is, with its largest mass of people in the South and its greatest concentration of wealth in the North. Although based on 1988 data, this distribution remains accurate today as the proportions are about the same (see *World Development Report 1993; The Economist* 330, January 8, 1994: 102). The discrepancies in wealth are even more stark when particular countries are compared.[4]

## Third World Diversity

Table 5.1 records differences in population and wealth for various countries and groups of countries. We have already commented on the overall differences between the First and Third Worlds. Below we consider some groups within the Third World itself to show just how great these disparities sometimes are (see also Box 5.1).

### Least Developed Countries

It is estimated that 1 billion people worldwide live on less than $1 per day (*Harper's* 288, April 1994: 17). Most of these people reside in the South, or, more specifically,

---

[4] Consider, for example, the following comparison:

A child born in the United States will consume thirty to fifty times as many goods in his or her lifetime as one born in the highlands of Bolivia. . . . Rich is what we are when we are consuming thirty times as much as someone else—and that someone is managing to stay alive. Add a grain of salt to the statistics—add enough salt to take care of any quibbles about differing life expectancies or faulty measuring techniques—and say that our wealth exceeds that of the average Bolivian peasant by a ratio of twenty to one. (*New Yorker*, May 16, 1983: 32)

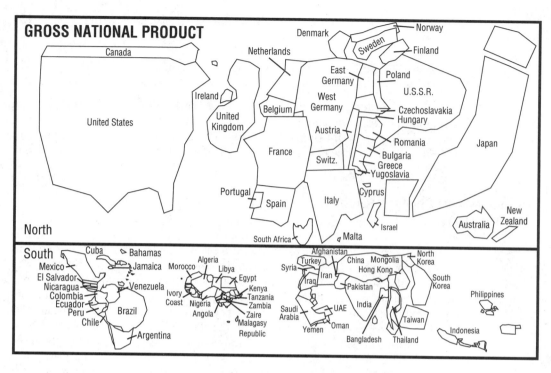

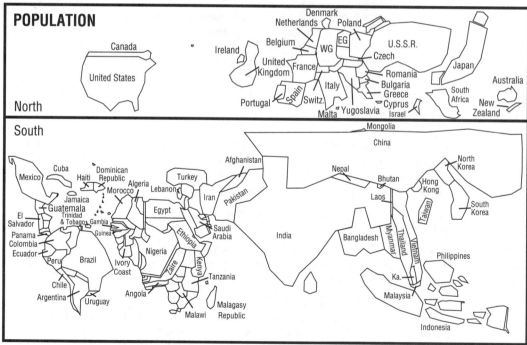

**Figure 5.2** Disparities in Prosperity and Population, North and South

**TABLE 5.1 The Distribution of World Population and Gross National Product Per Capita, by Selected Countries and Country Groups, 1991**

| Country or Group | Per-capita GNP (U.S.$) | Population (millions) |
|---|---|---|
| **Country Data** | | |
| Switzerland | 33,610 | 6.8 |
| Japan | 26,930 | 123.9 |
| Germany | 23,650 | 80.1 |
| United States | 22,240 | 252.7 |
| France | 20,380 | 57.0 |
| Saudi Arabia | 7,820 | 15.4 |
| Russian Federation | 3,220 | 148.7 |
| Brazil | 2,940 | 151.4 |
| Thailand | 1,570 | 57.2 |
| Zimbabwe | 650 | 10.1 |
| China | 370 | 1,149.5 |
| India | 330 | 866.5 |
| Burundi | 210 | 5.7 |
| Mozambique | 80 | 16.1 |
| **Group Averages**[a] | | |
| World (entire) | 4,010 | 5,351.0 |
| First World (High income) | 16,920 | 822.0 |
| Third World (Low income) | 1,097 | 3,127.0 |
| Severely indebted countries | 2,350 | 486.2 |
| Fuel exporters | 1,990 | 262.8 |
| Organization of Petroleum Exporting Countries (OPEC) | 6,186 | 35.6 |
| Newly Industrialized Countries (NICs)[b] | 7,316 | 351.3 |
| Asian Newly Industrialized Countries[c] | 10,352 | 73.1 |

*Source: World Development Report 1993* (New York: Oxford University Press, 1993: 199, 238–239); U.S. CIA (1992a: 18–20).
[a] Group averages are based on statistics for 127 countries for which the World Bank has data.
[b] The U.S. CIA (1992a: 18) identifies NICs for 1991 as Argentina, Brazil, Hong Kong, Mexico, Singapore, South Korea, and Taiwan.
[c] Asian NICs are Taiwan, Hong Kong, Singapore, and South Korea.

in a subset of the developing countries. Included among the nearly 170 independent countries and dependent territories that make up the Third World is a group of forty-one regarded by the United Nations Conference on Trade and Development (UNCTAD) as the "least developed" of the less-developed countries (LLDCs). Nearly two-thirds are in Africa; most of the rest are in Asia. For all of 1990 the average per-capita income of the LLDCs as a group was a miniscule $240 (UNDP, 1993: 171).[5]

---

[5] We must exercise caution when interpreting per-capita income figures. They can understate the value of goods and services actually produced and consumed in poorer societies. It is absurd, for example, to

## Box 5.1
## TWO WORLDS OF THIRD WORLD DEVELOPMENT

• • •

Nothing better illustrates the growing differences among developing countries than the fact that in the 1960s, South Korea had a per capita GNP exactly the same as Ghana's ($230) whereas today it is ten to twelve times more prosperous. Both possessed a predominantly agrarian economy and had endured a half century or more of colonial rule. Upon independence, each faced innumerable handicaps in trying to "catch up" with the West, and although Korea possessed a greater historico-cultural coherence, its chances may have seemed less promising, since it had few natural resources (apart from tungsten) and suffered heavily during the 1950–53 fighting. Decades later, however, West African states remain among the most poverty-stricken countries in the world—the per capita GNPs of Niger, Sierra Leone, and Chad today, for example, are less than $500—while Korea is entering the ranks of the high-income economies. Already the world's thirteenth-largest trading nation, Korea is planning to become one of the richest countries of all in the twenty-first century, whereas the nations of West Africa face a future, at least in the near term, of chronic poverty, malnutrition, poor health, and underdevelopment. Finally, while Korea's rising prosperity is attended by a decrease in population growth, most African countries still face a demographic explosion that erodes any gains in national output.

*Source: Paul Kennedy (1993: 193).*

Other characteristics accompanying this stark reality set the least developed countries apart from most others: agriculture (rather than manufacturing or services) is the dominant form of productive activity; two-fifths of the adult population is illiterate; life expectancy at birth is only fifty years; and infant mortality rates are among the highest in the world (see *World Development Report 1993*). Their present condition is desperate, and their future is bleak.

---

think that a Burundian could actually live on an income of only $210 a year. Part of the problem is that the GNP measures only those goods and services that enter a society's monetary sector. Yet in many developing societies where barter trading is common, much activity occurs outside the exchange economy, particularly in the agricultural sector. The problem of comparing purchasing power for different countries is compounded by the fact that gross national products valued in domestic currencies are typically converted for international comparative purposes to a single currency unit, such as the U.S. dollar, using fixed rates of exchange (the rate at which one currency can be exchanged for another). Because exchange rates do not account for differences in a currency's purchasing power in different countries, cross-national comparisons of income probably overstate the magnitude of the difference between the world's rich and poor, and an index based on **purchasing-power parity** also should be consulted, such as the one recently constructed by the International Monetary Fund.

## Oil-Exporting Countries

The poverty of the LLDCs contrasts starkly with many of the world's oil-exporting countries, whose oil price increases during the 1970s compounded the problems of other developing economies. Although it fell in 1991 by one-sixth from 1990, the average per-capita income of the thirteen major oil-exporting countries in OPEC (Organization of Petroleum Exporting Countries) was $6,186 (U.S. CIA, 1992a: 20)—twenty-two times larger than the average of a person living in the least developed countries.

There are wide disparities in income even among the oil exporters, however.[6] Indonesia and Nigeria are at one end of the spectrum, with 1991 per-capita incomes of $600 and $210, respectively, and United Arab Emirates and Kuwait are at the other end, with 1991 per-capita incomes of $14,000 and $11,000, respectively. These incomes approximate the incomes of many of the world's most advanced societies.

In part the differences within OPEC reflect not only the high concentration of rich oil deposits in the Middle East but also the much larger populations of Indonesia and Nigeria compared with Middle Eastern oil producers. For all the oil exporters, however, perhaps what is most notable is not how high their incomes are compared with other Third World countries but how far they have plunged since worldwide oil prices nose-dived in the mid-1980s. OPEC's share of the world market dropped from 63 percent in 1972 to 38 percent in 1985, and its revenue dropped proportionately (Stanislaw and Yergin, 1993: 83). For particular members, such as Kuwait, the plunge in oil-based wealth was even more dramatic. And the downward spiral continued largely uninterrupted until the Iraqi invasion of Kuwait in 1990. Since then oil demand has increased and "could be 15 to 20 percent higher a decade from now," as economic advancement in the Pacific Rim and the other major emerging economies is pushing the expansion of oil consumption to support new economic growth (Stanislaw and Yergin, 1993). These changes are certain to disrupt further the past pattern of income differentials among developing countries.

## Newly Industrialized Countries

Countries that have realized very rapid growth in their manufacturing sectors and have become important exporters of manufactures comprise a third important group among the developing nations, known as the *Newly Industrialized Countries* (NICs) or *Newly Industrialized Economies* (NIEs). The composition of the group varies somewhat depending on the criteria used to define it. The calculations in Table 5.1 follow the U.S. CIA (1992a: 18) classification of Argentina, Brazil, Mexico, Singapore, South Korea, Taiwan, and the British crown colony of Hong Kong as the major Third World exporters of manufactured products, which describes the NICs. The Newly Industrialized Countries are essentially upper-middle-income countries, with

---

[6] OPEC consists of Algeria, Ecuador, Gabon, Indonesia, Iran, Iraq, Kuwait, Libya, Nigeria, Qatar, Saudi Arabia, United Arab Emirates, and Venezuela. The other major oil exporters include Angola, Bahrain, Brunei Darussalem, the Congo, Oman, the Russian Federation, Syria, and Trinidad and Tobago. The differences in income among them are even more pronounced.

annual per-capita incomes in 1991 ranging from \$2,300 (Brazil) to \$14,250 (Singapore). Moreover, some—particularly the four Asian NICs known both as the "Asian Tigers" or "Asian Dragons" (Hong Kong, Singapore, South Korea, and Taiwan)—experienced rates of economic growth during the 1980s far greater than those of the more advanced industrial societies of the First World.[7] As a result, they have become not only important exporters of manufactured goods (such as consumer electronics and automobiles) but also important markets for the major industrial countries that export capital goods. Those facts increasingly have made the Asian Tigers major players in the world political economy (Fallows, 1994; see also Chapter 7).

The comparatively higher growth rates of the Asian NICs relative to the industrial societies of the First World reflect in part the fact that they began from a smaller base. It also means that their economies grew more rapidly than their populations, which is crucial. If developing nations are to advance economically and to provide a standard of living for their people that approximates the standard enjoyed in the Newly Industrialized Economies, their much higher population growth rates must be reduced (see Chapter 9).

Although developed and developing nations alike have experienced unprecedented economic growth since World War II, the developing nations as a whole have experienced higher growth rates, again in part as a result of the lower bases from which they began. Despite this, the gap between the poor developing countries and the rich developed countries has continued to widen (UNDP, 1994).

The widening absolute gap between rich and poor has become most apparent since World War II. One estimate (Brown, 1972: 42) put the ratio between incomes in the industrializing societies of Western Europe and the rest of the world in 1850 at roughly two to one and estimated that by 1950 the gap had opened to ten to one, and by 1960 to nearly fifteen to one. It predicted that if prevailing trends continued, the ratio could reach thirty to one by the year 2000. This estimate underscores the fact that since 1950 the developed countries nearly tripled their incomes, whereas the per-capita incomes of those at the periphery of the world political economy have remained largely unchanged. As a consequence, the gap in 1991 remained large, at an approximate ratio of eighteen to one (UNDP, 1993: 171).

Narrowing the economic gap between the rich and poor countries requires that the poor continue to grow more rapidly than the rich. Yet only twenty-two developing nations fit this requirement on the basis of their performance from 1960 to 1975. Even if their relative growth rates remained constant, only a small proportion of this handful of countries are likely to close the gap—China, India, Russia, Brazil, and

---

[7] East Asia's dramatic success is illustrated by the Asian Tigers' extraordinary improvement in their citizens' living standards:

> A Taiwanese child born in 1988 could expect to live seventy-four years, only a year less than an American or West German, and fifteen years longer than a Taiwanese born in 1952; a South Korean born in 1988 could expect seventy years on earth, up from fifty-eight in 1965. In 1988 the Taiwanese took in 50 percent more calories each day than they had done thirty-five years earlier. They had two hundred times as many televisions, telephones and cars per household; in Korea the rise in the possession of these goods was even higher. (Kennedy, 1993: 200)

Mexico, the "five of the world's twelve largest economies [which are] developing countries" (*The Economist* 330, January 8, 1994: 102). For most of the others, the development process will likely take literally hundreds or even thousands of years, obviously not a realistic economic or political goal.

## Measuring Economic Development and Standards of Living

Gross national product, per-capita GNP, and growth rates are the measures traditionally used to assess the progress of economic development. It is clear, however, that they offer too narrow a description of development. Even though developing countries as a whole have realized substantial gains in income since World War II, traditional measures fail to show that not everyone has enjoyed the fruits of progress because they cannot tell how evenly or unevenly income is spread.[8] Other factors must therefore be considered in weighing progress toward the reduction of poverty, such as reducing the highly unequal distribution of income within societies, increasing employment for everyone, and fulfilling basic human needs, including access to food, water, housing, health and health care, and education (see Box 5.2 for a personal perspective on the human dimensions of poverty).

The desirability of alternative measures to assess Third World living standards became especially apparent in the 1970s, when development economists and foreign aid donors shifted their attention from promoting economic growth toward meeting basic human needs. To this end, the United Nations Development Programme (UNDP) has sought to measure *human development* using a combination of economic and noneconomic measures, under the conviction that "the real purpose of development should be to enlarge people's choices."[9] For this, the concern is not with how much a nation is producing but instead with how its people are faring. The UNDP accordingly has continued "to refine the methodology" by which the well-being of people's lives in different countries might best be estimated (UNDP, 1993: 10–11).

Recognizing that some distance separates the *concept* of human development from its *measurement*, the UNDP devised a **Human Development Index** (HDI) that uses such indicators as life expectancy and literacy to measure well-being and standards of living. It also adds the average number of years of schooling attained within

---

[8] Widespread poverty within countries tends to be associated with extremely high concentrations of wealth in the hands of a few. Samir Amin (1987: 1132) estimates that only 10 percent of the population in developing countries disposes of 25 percent of total income, compared with 50 percent of the population in developed countries, and that only a third of the population in developing countries disposes of half of total income, compared with 75 percent of the population in developed countries. For supporting data on the pervasive imbalance of income distribution in selected countries, see UNDP (1994).

[9] For an alternative evaluation of countries' relative capacity to meet the basic human needs of its citizens, see the Physical Quality of Life Index (PQLI) developed by the Washington-based Overseas Development Council (ODC). It traces variations in life expectancy, infant mortality, and literacy rates to assess progress in improving the welfare of citizens. See Black (1991) and Sklair (1991) for critical evaluations of the PQLI and other indices of human welfare.

# Box 5.2
## An American Student Discovers the Meaning of the Third World

• • •

I spent the first 24 years of my life in South Carolina. When I left . . . for Colombia [South America], I fully expected Bogota to be like any large U.S. city, only with citizens who spoke Spanish. When I arrived there I found my expectations were wrong. I was not in the U.S., I was on Mars! I was a victim of culture shock. As a personal experience this shock was occasionally funny and sometimes sad. But after all the laughing and the crying were over, it forced me to reevaluate both my life and the society in which I live.

Colombia is a poor country by American standards. It has a per capita GNP of $550 and a very unequal distribution of income. These were the facts that I knew before I left.

But to 'know' these things intellectually is much different from experiencing first-hand how they affect people's lives. It is one thing to lecture in air conditioned class-rooms about the problems of world poverty. It is quite another to see four-year-old children begging or sleeping in the streets.

It tore me apart emotionally to see the reality of what I had studied for so long: "low per capita GNP and maldistribution of income." What this means in human terms is children with dirty faces who beg for bread money or turn into pickpockets because the principle of private property gets blurred by empty stomachs.

It means other children whose minds and bodies will never develop fully because they were malnourished as infants. It means cripples who can't even turn to thievery and must beg to stay alive. It means street vendors who sell candy and cigarettes 14 hours a day in order to feed their families.

It also means well-dressed businessmen and petty bureaucrats who indifferently pass this poverty every day as they seek asylum in their fortified houses to the north of the city.

It means rich people who prefer not to see the poor, except for their maids and security guards.

It means foreigners like me who have come to Colombia and spend more in one month than the average Colombian earns in a year.

It means politicians across the ideological spectrum who are so full of abstract solutions or personal greed that they forget that it is real people they are dealing with.

Somewhere within the polemics of the politicians and the "objectivity" of the social scientists, the human being has been lost.

*Source: Brian Wallace, excerpted from "True Grit South of the Border," OSCEOLA, January 13, 1978, pp. 15–16.*

societies, which helps to differentiate among countries at the top stratum on the human development scale. And it specifically incorporates income (using a strategy that measures its diminishing utility as countries become richer). Including income rests on the conviction that "a realistic view [of development] is that growth in income and an expansion of economic opportunities are necessary preconditions of human development. . . . Although growth is not the end of development, the absence of growth often is" (UNDP, 1991).

Table 5.2 records the HDI for sixteen countries, which fall into three different income groups. It also includes the HDI rank of each of the countries among some 173 independent polities based on 1990 per-capita GNP data.

A comparison of the countries' human development performance shows remarkably wide discrepancies in how people live in different countries. The quality of life and the standard of living vary tremendously. But this variation is not determined exclusively by variations in countries' income levels. The evidence shows that

*There is no automatic link between income and human development.* Several countries—such as

### TABLE 5.2 LEVEL OF HUMAN DEVELOPMENT, SELECTED COUNTRIES

| HDI Category | HDI Rank[a] | HDI Value | GNP Per-capita Rank | Income Group[b] |
|---|---|---|---|---|
| **Low Human Development** (HDI value less than .50) | | | | |
| Guinea-Bissau | 164 | .090 | 165 | Low |
| Yemen | 143 | .233 | 124 | Middle |
| India | 134 | .309 | 146 | Low |
| Zimbabwe | 121 | .398 | 117 | Middle |
| **Medium Human Development** (HDI value .50 to .799) | | | | |
| Gabon | 109 | .503 | 44 | Middle |
| Philippines | 92 | .603 | 114 | Middle |
| China | 101 | .566 | 142 | Low |
| Sri Lanka | 86 | .663 | 130 | Low |
| Cuba | 75 | .711 | 101 | Middle |
| Brazil | 70 | .730 | 53 | Middle |
| **High Human Development** (HDI value .80 or above) | | | | |
| Hong Kong | 24 | .913 | 15 | High |
| South Korea | 33 | .872 | 103 | Middle |
| Poland | 48 | .831 | 48 | Middle |
| United States | 6 | .976 | 10 | High |
| Switzerland | 4 | .978 | 1 | High |
| Japan | 1 | .983 | 3 | High |

*Source:* United Nations Development Programme (UNDP) (1993: 170–171, 202–203, 227).
[a] Rank among 173 independent countries included in the UNDP inventory.
[b] The income categories are based on the following criteria: *Low income* (Low), a per-capita income of less than $500; *Middle income* (Middle), $501–$6,000; *High income* (High), $6,000 or above.

Chile, China, Colombia, Costa Rica, Madagascar, Sri Lanka, Tanzania and Uruguay—have done well in translating their income into the lives of their people: Their human development rank is way ahead of their per capita income rank. Other societies—such as Algeria, Angola, Gabon, Guinea, Namibia, Saudi Arabia, Senegal, South Africa and United Arab Emirates—have income ranks far below their human development rank, showing their enormous potential for improving the lives of their people. . . . Income alone is obviously a poor indicator of human development. (UNDP, 1993: 11, 14)

There thus is no one-to-one correspondence between income and nonincome measures of development.

Overall, however, a correlation between wealth and well-being is evident. The pattern is unmistakable that, in general, the highest living standards occur in the North, where per-capita incomes are also generally high. Conversely, generally lower standards of living occur in the South, where per-capita incomes are measurably lower. Many, in fact, live in unimaginable poverty. This is especially true in Sub-Saharan Africa and in South and Southeast Asia. Still, the quality of life varies across Third World countries. For some rapidly emerging economies the distance between their citizens' living conditions with those in the North is narrowing, whereas for most others the gap continues to widen. (The only promising trend consistent across the Third World is that average life expectancy is beginning to move closer to that in the North; see UNDP, 1993).

Consider what this assessment reveals about the deprivation that people in the Third World experience (UNDP, 1993: 12):

- Of the 300 million people above the age of sixty, only 70% have any form of income security.

- About 17 million people die each year from infectious and parasitic diseases [and] more than 80% of the 12–17 million HIV-infected people are in the developing world.

- Some 800 million people still do not get enough food [and] almost one-third of the total population, or 1.3 billion people, are in absolute poverty.

- Nearly one billion people—35% of the adult population—are still illiterate [and] two-thirds of illiterates are women.

It is no wonder that poverty, desperation, and despair are regarded as synonymous with living conditions for all but the wealthy few in the Third World. And for particular segments of these societies—especially women and children—the circumstances are even more deplorable. Gender discrimination and oppression govern the lives of these poor and largely powerless unfortunates, who suffer from exploitive practices that are extreme:

In 1980, the United Nations summed up the burden of inequality: Women, half the world's population, did two thirds of the world's work, earned one tenth of the world's income and owned one hundredth of the world's property. Fourteen years later, despite the fall of repressive regimes, a decade of high growth, the spread of market economies, and the rise of female prime ministers and CEOs [chief executive officers], women remain victims of abuse and discrimination just about everywhere. (MacFarquhar, 1994: 42, 44)

Do political variables determine Third World countries' weak economic and welfare performance? Liberal theorists have long argued that human development rests on political formulations. That perspective maintains that market economies thrive in a political atmosphere that minimizes governmental interference in the economic laws of supply and demand. A corollary is that individual initiative in the marketplace is more likely to occur in an atmosphere of political freedom. The rejection of socialist planned economies in Eastern Europe and the Soviet Union (in which, during the Cold War, governments sought to replace the market as the determinant of supply and demand and otherwise ruled with an iron hand) was inspired in part by liberal theory's premise that laissez-faire economics and political freedom go hand in hand.

This philosophy also predicts that "triumphant liberalism" (Fukuyama, 1992a) will promote human development elsewhere as it spreads. Accordingly, China's conversion to a free market economy is predicted to be followed eventually by democratic reforms that will overcome the pronounced resistance to democratization now evident (Brauchli, 1994), if, as anticipated, prosperity breeds pluralistic pressure groups and mass participation in domestic politics. The same process is believed possible elsewhere throughout the Third World, where democratization could become the engine for growth in alleviating the deprivation currently so ubiquitous there.

The United Nations Development Programme sought to address this proposition in its 1991 report. It based its inquiry on the premise that for development to occur, people "must enjoy freedom—cultural, social, economic and political." Measuring freedom throughout the world is exceedingly difficult, but the UNDP (1991) concluded after a preliminary examination of the relationship between its human development index and the performance of (a limited number of) countries on some forty different indicators of freedom that "there seems to be a high correlation between human development and human freedom" (see also Pourgerami, 1991; Moon and Dixon, 1985). This inferred association thus lends support to liberal theory's expectation that prosperity and liberty are tightly linked. Beyond this now widespread belief, however, remain questions about the ways poor Third World states can overcome the structural barriers to their economic development.

## Impediments to Growth in a Typical Developing Country

The preceding discussion hints at the complexity of the development process. The improvement of economic and social well-being is influenced by the simultaneous interaction of political, social, economic, and cultural factors—the level of resource endowment, the extent of industrialization, prevailing cultural norms about family size, and the ability and willingness of governments to make often politically costly development decisions. Also involved is the degree of penetration of rich countries in the economies of poor countries.

We can better understand the political dispute between the North and South if we isolate the primary factors underlying the persistent underdevelopment that is today the plight of so many nations. Hans Singer and Javed Ansari (1988) identify high rates of population growth, low levels of income, underemployment, technological dependence, and, as a result, "dualism" as especially important determinants of the widening gap between rich countries and poor.

- Higher birthrates mean that developing nations have a far larger proportion of young people in their societies than do developed nations; thus, they "have to devote much more of their resources to the task of raising a new generation of producers, besides providing services of a given standard to an enlarged and rapidly urbanizing population."

- Low income levels exacerbate the challenge because they prevent poorer countries from generating enough economic surplus to make sizable investments in their future economic growth. "New sectors of modern economic growth thus remain very small, especially in terms of employment, and are often foreign-controlled. The national economy at large remains deprived of new capital infusion."

- "About three-quarters of the total population of a poor country is engaged in the agricultural sector." Many in fact are underemployed, and some perhaps are better classified as unemployed. This means that labor is underutilized. Underutilization is not confined to agriculture, however. Many people in the Third World, and especially women, are deprived of meaningful employment opportunities or, more commonly, are engaged in unproductive labor, and this is "both the cause and effect of a distortion of the consumption and investment patterns and of high and rising inequalities of income distribution." The result is an inadequate investment in education, health, transportation facilities, credit facilities, and other socioeconomic infrastructure. Without this investment the poor remain poor, and the gap between them and the rich widens.

- Developing countries have not been able to evolve an indigenous technology appropriate to their own resource endowments. Instead, they depend critically on powerful multinational corporations (MNCs) spawned in the North to transfer technical know-how from the world's rich to its poor. But counterproductively, "Almost all world expenditures on science and technology take place inside the richer countries, and research and development are therefore quite naturally directed towards solving *their* problems by methods suited to *their* circumstances and resource endowments." Consequently, the needs of the poorer countries are seldom met by technological advances.

When the interaction among these four obstacles to development is considered, we can begin to see why a fifth obstacle, ***dualism,*** characterizes the social and economic structures of developing societies and inhibits their growth. In the Third World the existence of two separate sectors is common. Dual societies have a rural, impoverished, and neglected sector operating alongside an urban, developing, or modernizing sector. Typically, however, there is little interaction between the two:

> Most [developing countries] have a large, stagnant, agricultural sector which is linked to the small, modern, large-scale, industrial sector mainly through the supply of resources, both labour and capital, from the former to the latter. The growth of the industrial sector neither initiates a corresponding growth process in the rural sector nor generates sufficient employment to prevent a growing population in the stagnant sectors. (Singer and Ansari, 1988: 45–46)

Hence, dualism poses a high barrier to development.

The reasons for dualism in the developing countries' economic structures are lodged in their colonial past, when the metropolitan powers regarded themselves as the best producers of manufactured goods and their colonies as the best suppliers of basic foodstuffs and raw materials. This resulted in few "spread effects" in the colonial economies' secondary and tertiary sectors. Eventually, rapid population growth overwhelmed the ability of the colonies' rising incomes to generate continued economic growth (Higgins and Higgins, 1979). Meanwhile, the hope for a better life in the urban areas led to a flood of migrants from farm to city, resulting in decrepit urban slums with massive numbers of unemployed seeking work in the small industrial sector. Because the advanced technology of the industrialized societies is almost always more capital intensive than labor intensive (that is, requiring money more than people), it tends to exacerbate rather than alleviate the plight of the jobless.

Historically, in the industrial world urbanization and industrialization were associated with declining, not rising, rates of population growth. One reason that developing societies do not mirror this pattern is that their death rates have fallen more precipitously than those in the industrialized world. The difference is caused more by newly available technologies to reduce death rates, such as improved medicines, than by the changes in attitudes toward family size associated with urbanization and industrialization in the North. In addition, the industrialization experienced by colonial economies occurred mainly in the areas of basic foodstuffs and raw materials and therefore did not substantially alter the traditional societal patterns established under colonialism. "Hence the checks on family size enforced by the urban industrialization of Europe and the New World operated less effectively in the underdeveloped countries" (Higgins and Higgins, 1979).

The persistence of economic dualism in the developing societies portends that even in countries with incipient industrial sectors, the local population will not share widely in the benefits. In fact, "the industrial sector of the poor countries is really a periphery of the metropolitan industrial economies, critically dependent on them for the technology it uses" (Singer and Ansari, 1988). Accordingly, benefits are likely to be confined only to those groups in developing societies that are able to link themselves to the rich countries:

> These will become oases of growth surrounded by a desert of stagnation, thus reinforcing other elements of dualism already present in the poorer countries. The way leads to polarization within the poor country, clashing with the objectives of national planning and national integration. This polarization expresses itself in widening internal income disparities, larger numbers exposed to extreme poverty, and rising unemployment. (Singer and Ansari, 1988: 28)

The problems faced by developing countries thus resemble a series of vicious circles, none of which seem capable of being broken because they are so closely intertwined with so many other difficult problems.

## Dominance and Dependence in International Economic Relations

The discussion to this point leads logically to the conclusion that a combination of factors indigenous to Third World countries and inherent in their relationships with the First World causes the widening gap between the North and the South. Many theorists would not agree with that simple statement, however. In their attempt to explain the persistent underdevelopment of developing economies, some direct attention primarily toward what happens within Third World nations, while others focus on the position of developing nations in the world political economy. We identify and briefly discuss three variants on these viewpoints: the liberal theory of economic development, dependency theory, and world-system theory.

### Liberal Economic Development Theory

Liberal theories of economic development first emerged in the early post–World War II era and soon became dominant or "conventional." These Western-oriented "modernization" interpretations emphasized the internal attributes of Third World countries as impediments to their development and sought to devise ways of overcoming them. Based on the assumption that growth meant increasing increments of per-capita GNP (rather than, say, meeting basic human needs), development theorists attempted to identify the major obstacles to growth. They also recommended overcoming these barriers through the use of the wealthy countries' supply of various "missing components," such as investment capital (through foreign aid or private sources) (Todaro, 1989).

Once capital was accumulated sufficiently to promote economic growth, liberal theorists predicted that its benefits would eventually "trickle down" to other segments of society. In this way, everyone, not simply a privileged few, would enjoy the benefits of rising affluence. Walt W. Rostow, an economic historian and U.S. policymaker, wrote an influential book entitled *The Stages of Economic Growth* (1960), in which he formalized this theory. He predicted that traditional societies entering the development path would inevitably pass through various stages by means of the operation of the free market and eventually would become similar to the mass-consumption societies of the West. That prognosis proved wrong, of course, as did other liberal ideas about the route to economic development. Dependency and world-system theorists purport to explain why those ideas failed.

### Dependency Theory

Dependency theory builds on Lenin's theory of imperialism identified in the introduction to this chapter, but it goes beyond Lenin "by specifying the nature of imperialism more completely and by accounting for changes that have occurred since Lenin wrote [his treatise] at the beginning of the century" (Shannon, 1989).

A central proposition in dependency theory is that the relationship between the advanced capitalist societies and those at the periphery of the world political economy is exploitative.[10] From this viewpoint, underdevelopment "is not a stalled stage of linear development, a question of pre-capitalism, retarded or backward development, but rather a structural position in a hierarchical world division of labor" (Shannon, 1989). "The very term *dependency* highlights the extent to which the movement of economics and politics in poor countries is conditioned by a global economy dominated by others" (Evans, 1993: 232). Hence, dependency theorists aver that we need only to look "to contemporary relations with other societies to explain underdevelopment" (Bergesen, 1980).

This viewpoint denies that development is merely a diffusion process automatically passing through various stages, such as from the traditional society to the mass-consumption society, as Rostow had argued. Instead, it views Third World poverty as rooted in past colonial ties and their contemporary external linkages, and therefore the provision of technological resources "from advanced industrial countries would not cause poor industrializing countries to replicate the developmental trajectories of Western Europe or the United States" (Evans, 1993). The developed countries could not serve as a model because, as Andre Gunder Frank (1969), a leading dependency theorist, explained, "The now developed countries were never underdeveloped, though they may have been undeveloped."

In contrast with the "stages of growth" theory that developing states would attain autonomous self-sustaining growth as they mature, Frank attributed "the development of underdevelopment" to the historical expansion of the capitalist system that "effectively and entirely penetrated even the apparently most isolated sectors of the underdeveloped world." *Dependentistas*, as they were frequently called, viewed the penetration process as fueled by capitalism's need for external sources of demand and profitable investment outlets. The overseas branches of the giant multinational corporations (MNCs), whose headquarters are in the North, were the agents of penetration. Foreign investment, whether made as private investments by MNCs or in the form of foreign economic and military aid by other governments, was also considered an instrument of penetration. Technological dependence and "cultural imperialism," which were perpetrated through ideas alien to the indigenous cultures of Third World societies, were among the consequences. Ultimately, the MNCs' role was to transfer profits from the penetrated societies to the penetrators, as it is the profit motive that leads to the penetration of peripheral societies in the first place.

---

[10] For a sampling of some of the extensive dependency theory literature, see Amin (1974), Baran (1968), Emmanuel (1972), Frank (1969), and the special issue of *International Organization* on dependence and dependency in the global system edited by James A. Caporaso (1978). Todaro (1989) reviews the basic tenets of neo-marxist views of dependency; Smith (1979, 1981) provides insightful critiques of dependency theory; and Caporaso (1980) and Packenham (1992) discuss the theoretical controversies surrounding the perspective.

Once those that are underdeveloped have been penetrated by the advanced capitalist states, continues the dependency argument, the inherently exploitative linkages that bind them together are sustained by the local elites within the penetrated societies. The fortune of these privileged aristocrats is tied to the dominant powers; therefore, they are co-opted by their desire to maintain their privileged positions in their own societies. Third World local elites perpetuate their countries' domination and dependence by acting domestically in ways that favor their international connections. They put personal welfare over that of their country. "Thus, it is not the sheer economic might of the outside that dictates the dependent status of the South, but the sociological consequences of this power. . . . A symbiotic relationship has grown up over time in which the system [of dominance and dependence] has created its servants whose needs dictate that its survival be ensured, whatever the short-term conflicts of interests may be" (Smith, 1979). Implicit here is the thesis that Third World leaders practice political repression (often with foreign support) to protect their own privileges. Inconsistently, these rulers complain about their countries' oppression by wealthy states at the same time that they oppress their own populations.

Finally, dependency theorists also reject dualism as a description of Third World countries' economic and social systems. Instead of a division into "modern" and "traditional" sectors, they maintain that in fact there is only a single international capitalist economy that determines social, economic, and political outcomes throughout the global economy.

> The persistence of marginal groups of poor workers and peasants in developing countries reflects a consciously planned system, designed to protect profits by keeping peasant incomes and wages down and reserving for capitalists of advanced countries production requiring advanced technology. (Higgins and Higgins, 1979: 100)

## World-System Theory

World-system theorists, such as the French historian Fernand Braudel (1981, 1982, 1984), share with dependency theorists the assumption that the world is divided into a core (the advanced capitalist states) and a periphery (the developing states). World-system theorists, however, take a longer-term perspective on the emergence of disparities between the core and periphery and the forces that determine where states are positioned in the globe's hierarchic class system. They treat as potent the influences of market conditions as shaped by an integrated single capitalist world-system. Moreover, although world-system analysts concern themselves with the interaction of state power and economic resources, they treat the actors in world politics in terms of classes, much as Karl Marx regarded class as the basic unit of social analysis. Immanuel Wallerstein (1974a, 1974b, 1980, 1988), widely regarded as the intellectual father of world-system theory as it developed in North America, rejects the charge that it is fundamentally a marxist theory, but the label "neo-marxist" is nonetheless often used to describe his perspective on the ways the capitalist world-system produces and institutionalizes inequalities.

For world-system theorists, a critical issue is how states fit into the international division of labor.

> By claiming that there is a single division of labor, world-system theorists [reject] the more conventional approach, which [views] the world-economy as composed of isolated and independent national economies that just happen to trade with one another. . . . Economic activities in each part of a true world-economy depend on and make possible the activities of the other parts. . . . The result is an economic system that includes a number of cultural areas, states, or societies but constitutes a single economy based on a complex division of labor. Each part or area has acquired a specialized role producing goods that it trades to others to obtain what it needs. Thus, the world-economy is tied together by a complex network of global economic exchanges. (Shannon, 1989: 21)

It is here that the core–periphery concept becomes important. "Within the world division of labor, core states specialize in the production of the most 'advanced' goods, which involves the use of the most sophisticated technologies and highly mechanized methods of production ('capital-intensive' production). At least until recently, this meant that core states specialized in the production of sophisticated manufactured goods" (Shannon, 1989). Core states, limited historically to Western Europe but joined in this century by the United States and, later, Japan, are also the most powerful militarily and the best organized administratively.

The periphery, of course, consists of those geographic areas that now make up the Third World. "Economic activities in the periphery are relatively less technologically sophisticated and more 'labor intensive' than those in the core. . . . For most of the modern era, production for export was concentrated on raw materials and agricultural commodities" (Shannon, 1989). Those on the periphery have historically been militarily inferior to core states and less well organized administratively, which limited their ability to compete with the capitalist states.

World-system theorists have found it difficult to explain the industrialization now taking place in the periphery. To account for that, they have introduced the *semiperiphery* to accommodate geographic areas or countries, such as the Newly Industrialized Economies (NIEs), that do not fall neatly into either the core or the periphery in the current international division of labor. Yet, dependency theorists also have difficulty rationalizing these countries' growth. To explain the anomaly, they use the term **dependent development** to describe the industrialization of peripheral areas in a system of First World hegemony. As the term suggests, the possibility of development (at least industrialization) is acknowledged, but not outside the confines of the dominance–dependence relationship between North and South.

Each of the perspectives described above illuminates in important ways the nature of underdevelopment and development and prescribes methods of moving from the former to the latter. None, however, is entirely persuasive or able adequately to account for the current dire circumstances in which so many of the world's developing countries find themselves. Debates about theories and facts and about beliefs and perceptions therefore animate much of the North–South conflict. They also inform the motives underlying the foreign policy goals of Third World countries, to which we now turn.

## BEYOND DEPENDENCE: THE FOREIGN POLICY GOALS OF THIRD WORLD NATIONS . . . . . . . . . . . . . . . . . . . . . . . . . . . . .

The preceding discussion identifies many elements in the often contentious relations between the rich countries of the North and the poorer countries of the South, which range over many different issues such as trade, aid, and transnational pricing mechanisms. Together, many controversies in the North–South conflict have spurred the Third World to adopt foreign policy strategies designed to move them beyond dependence and poverty. The effort has focused on five major pursuits, as we will discuss.

### A New International Economic Order

Developing countries believe that the present structure of international economic relations is responsible for their plight. They therefore want to change the regimes that shape the international movement of goods, services, capital, labor, and technology. The widely shared belief among Third World elites in the premises of dependency theory facilitates this effort. During the 1970s and early 1980s in particular, it galvanized the developing countries into a collective drive toward goals they were too weak to realize by traditional bilateral means (Krasner, 1981, 1985). Their collective demands culminated in a vociferous call for a *New International Economic Order* (NIEO).

The New International Economic Order sought by developing countries would be profoundly different from the *Liberal International Economic Order* (LIEO) created under the aegis of U.S. hegemony after World War II, which many Third World leaders viewed as an instrument of their continued oppression. Their goal was to be equal to the more advanced countries in fact, not just in law. Thus Third World countries saw the NIEO as an alternative to the prevailing exploitative system. Speaking for the Third World before the United Nations General Assembly in 1979, Cuba's Fidel Castro expressed this view in words commonly used to depict the Third World spirit. He demanded the creation of a "new world order based on justice, on equity, on peace" to replace "the unjust world system that exists today." Under the current system, he said, "wealth is still concentrated in the hands of a few powers" who profit from "exploitation" of the Third World.

The historical roots of the NIEO were grounded in the 1950s and 1960s, when the Third World, with support from the Soviet bloc, formed a united front to deal with the industrialized West on international economic issues. These efforts resulted in the first *United Nations Conference on Trade and Development* (UNCTAD), held in Geneva in 1964. The meeting became the forerunner of several later conferences that focused on various aspects of the relations between the world's rich and poor nations.

During the 1964 conference, the *Group of 77* (known in diplomatic circles as simply G-77) was formed as a coalition of the world's poor countries to press for concessions from the world's rich. Now numbering over 120 developing countries, the G-77 continues to act in that caucusing capacity today. UNCTAD is also now a permanent organization in the United Nations' family of organizations. Building on the intellectual guidance and aggressive leadership of its first secretary general, Dr. Raúl Prebisch, it became a staunch advocate for the world's less fortunate countries.

The issues addressed in the UNCTAD forum (and in other international bodies) have changed over time in response to changing international circumstances. Among the changes of the post–World War II period has been the ascendance of three independent centers of industrial power in the North: the United States, the European Union, and Japan. Because each industrial center has different needs and interests, each has responded differently to the Third World's interests and demands. The United States is a continental power less heavily dependent on the rest of the world than most countries. The European Community (the forerunner to what is now known as the European Union) had strong historical ties and cultural bonds with many Third World countries. And Japan, an island nation, is critically dependent on raw-material imports. Conversely, among Third World countries vastly different levels of development, degrees of economic and political affiliation with the North, colonial experiences,[11] and perceptions of national interests have all affected both the stakes in and the positions of individual countries in the outcome of the North–South dialogue. The situation compelled the members within the movement to concentrate on bilateral and regional negotiations. Nonetheless, a common goal of developing countries was the search for agreement from the rich states to abide by new rules and system-restructuring reforms that could be favorable to Third World interests. "Almost none of the NIEO goals have been achieved, although some proposals are still being pursued. . . . In short, the NIEO is a classic illustration of failed international reform" (Rothstein, 1993).

## Equal Rights

Third World criticism of the existing international order does not focus on the exclusivity of the global system as much as on the manner in which the dispossessed are excluded from rank, status, and a fair share of global well-being. This ambivalence finds expression in developing countries' attitudes toward international law. Law cannot give them the status and rewards possessed by others, but it does help to ensure their survival in a threatening international environment, where the power of others could easily overwhelm them. Most Third World countries are therefore vigorous supporters of the principles of self-determination and the inadmissibility of

---

[11] Craig Murphy (1983) notes in his discussion of the history of Third World demands for a New International Economic Order that in the early 1970s the relative immediacy of the colonial experience helped split the South into "moderate" and "radical" camps, with the latter believing that the North owed the South restitution for past colonialism. "The radical camp included mostly Asian and African nations, nonaligned states, states that were recently independent, and other states that supported the restitution ethic. The moderate camp tended to be Latin American, aligned with the West, and included some states that had been independent longer, where people were relatively better off and whose governments rarely talked about the need for restitution for colonialism."

the acquisition of territory by force: One justifies their existence, and the other sustains it (Waldheim, 1984).

Still, the Third World drive for equality of influence extends their interests beyond preservation of the status quo. As explained by a former U.S. ambassador to Sri Lanka, many Third World leaders "are hostile to the notion that the state system should be organized in its present sharply hierarchical fashion, in which a few with wealth, industrial and technological strength, and the capability to apply force regularly make decisions that so profoundly affect the conditions and well-being of even distant states" (Wriggins, 1978). For them, equality can be achieved only through revision of the rules of international law.

## Political Autonomy

In addition to equality of influence, autonomy or independence is also sought. "Each state, it is held, should be able to manage its own political and economic affairs without interference from outside: each should be in a position to decide for itself how its resources should be utilized, what policies industrial and agricultural enterprises operating within its borders should follow, and such economic matters as interest rates for loans, rates of exchange, and export subsidies" (Wriggins, 1978). Transforming the rules of existing regimes through collective action is perceived to be necessary for this purpose, however. The developing countries recognize that individually they cannot change the environment that denies them freedom and independence; collaborative efforts are needed to reform the rules that interfere with their capacity for autonomous action. Hence, many have banded together to assert their independence. "Impatient with what many consider a haughty, domineering West," the leaders of the rapidly emerging Third World economies, finding they can flourish without the West, have become defiant and assertive (see Brauchli, 1994).

## Nonalignment

In the same way that Third World countries have sought to erase the vestiges of dependent relationships implied by the terms *neocolonialism* and *neoimperialism,* most were determined during the Cold War to avoid choosing between East and West because of fear that one form of domination might simply be replaced by another. Hence, they espoused a policy of *nonalignment.*

The nonalignment movement began in 1955, when twenty-nine Asian and African countries met in Bandung, Indonesia, to devise a strategy to combat colonialism. Shortly thereafter, in 1961, leaders of mostly former colonies met in Belgrade, Yugoslavia, and created a permanent organization, the *Nonaligned Movement* (NAM). Its membership later expanded to more than one hundred countries. Meetings have convened approximately every three years, with the tenth summit held in Jakarta in 1992.

During its early years many leading world political figures served as spokespersons for the Nonaligned Movement's push to reduce East–West tensions, nuclear arsenals, and Third World poverty. Over time, however, the NAM coalition lost much of its unity and its corresponding political muscle as the diversity among Third World countries undermined its cohesiveness.

Diversity found expression in the various foreign policy roles that Third World nations adopted as they pursued their political goals, even while they remained committed to the principle of nonalignment. Some, such as China, Algeria, and Cuba, adopted the role of *revolutionary liberator*. The task of the revolutionary liberator is "to liberate others or to act as the 'bastion' of revolutionary movements, that is, to provide an area which foreign revolutionary leaders can regard as a source of physical and moral support, as well as an ideological inspirer" (Holsti, 1970). Others, such as Burma (now Myanmar), pursued a policy of *isolation*. Instead of trying to reform the global structure, isolationism preaches withdrawal from world affairs.

*Ally* is a third orientation that some adopted. The incentives for association with a superpower patron during the Cold War were sometimes compelling. Ties to them produced not only an enhanced sense of national security but also sometimes the foreign aid needed for internal development and perhaps the arms to deal with enemies at home and abroad. Hence, some Third World leaders were willing to suffer a partial loss of freedom in return for the political and material compensations a close relationship gave them. Vietnam's one-time embrace of the Soviet Union as a shield from both China and the West is illustrative.

Few Third World states chose to take on the role of ally in an open and formal way, however. This was understandable, as it ran directly counter to the avowed principles of the Nonaligned Movement. Nonetheless, many from time to time so openly supported one or the other of the superpowers that their nonaligned status became suspect. India and Cuba stood out on the Soviet side, while Pakistan, the Philippines, Thailand, the Republic of China (Taiwan), South Korea, and many Latin American states stood out on the U.S. side. Various Middle Eastern countries that were original members of the Nonaligned Movement, such as Egypt, Iran, Jordan, and Saudi Arabia, also aligned at one time or another with one of the superpowers. The reasons for this support were rooted in the aligned states' vulnerabilities. As noted, the superpowers provided the economic and military aid their clients desperately needed and often granted them implicit or explicit security guarantees. In return they received the political support of their clients and sometimes more tangible benefits, such as military base rights.

It can be argued that the Nonaligned Movement succeeded in its primary goal of ending the Cold War and encouraging disarmament. Ironically, the end of the Cold War means the end of nonalignment. There no longer exists a superpower rivalry to fear or a bipolar division to remain nonaligned against. As a result, the coalition's focus has shifted to emphasis on economic problems, securing First World support for foreign aid, environmental protection, and the control of the regional violence that collectively confronts the movement's members.

The challenge will remain great. The history of the Nonaligned Movement's achievements during the Cold War does not inspire confidence. During that period nonalignment reflected more myth than reality, as the movement's claims of unity of purpose and principle became blurred in the face of growing Third World diversity. That condition prevails today. Differing interpretations of Third World countries' national interests continue to grow from the sharply divergent foreign and domestic situations developing countries face. Varying degrees of industrialization and economic development are among them. Different cultures and traditions and varying threats of internal instability arising from religious and ethnic differences also encourage divergent foreign policy pursuits. For some, the principal threat is internal—a lack of identity with the nation, separatism, or insurgency and disintegration under the pressure of poverty, population growth, and lawlessness (Kaplan, 1994). For others, the primary threat is external—a powerful and obtrusive neighbor or one that might become so. No single interpretation of nonalignment can accommodate such diversity. Thus, nonalignment is not likely to amount to more than a political slogan devoid of practical meaning.

## Military Might

The Cold War is now history, but the Third World drive for autonomy and security is not. That is nowhere more clear than in the developing countries' determination to arm themselves. "In the Third World, where one child in ten dies before the age of five, there are six times as many soldiers as physicians" (Sivard, 1993: 6). For the purpose of projecting military might, the Third World has energetically sought to acquire the most sophisticated military weapons available anywhere. The passing of the Cold War has already encouraged greater militarization among Third World countries, as many previously dependent on the military strength of a superpower patron have accelerated their production and purchase of arms to deal with the diverse internal and external security threats they face. As these threats continue after the Cold War, the effort to control them with military might continues as well (Ball, 1994).

Figure 5.3 shows the value of arms imported into the Third World during the 1980s. Not surprisingly, the Middle East was the major importing region. In fact, Egypt, Iraq, Saudi Arabia, and Syria were among the world's twelve largest arms importers in the latter half of the 1980s. All Third World regions have joined the race to arm, however. Nearly half of the thirty largest arms importers are found in the Third World (Kidron and Smith, 1991: 68–69).

The Third World quest for national security is examined in greater detail in Chapter 11. Here it is sufficient to highlight that treatment with three points.

- Third World nations increasingly produce arms themselves. Imports from more advanced industrial powers remain important. But now Argentina, Egypt, India, North Korea, Pakistan, South Korea, and especially Brazil and China have developed arms industries of their own that produce efficient weapons at accessible prices. And the weapons are for sale with few strings attached. China's sale of ballistic missiles to Pakistan in 1993 is illustrative.

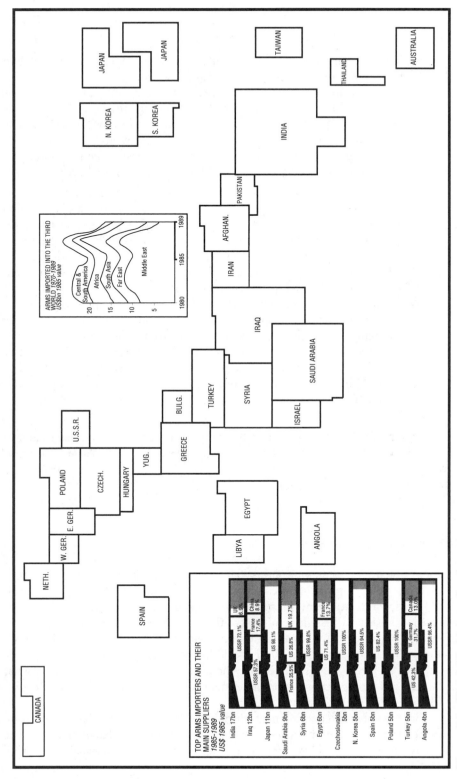

**Figure 5.3**  Third World Arms Purchases
*Source*: Michael Kidron and Dan Smith *The New State of War and Peace: An International Atlas* (1991: 68–69).

- The weaponry and technology available to Third World nations in the global marketplace are the most sophisticated in the world, "some of which are equal to the best in the arsenals of the great powers. . . . Approximately a dozen Third World countries have or are attempting to develop nuclear weapons. . . . As many as twenty-four countries (most in the Third World) either have or are actively seeking to acquire chemical weapons. All of the Third World countries that have or are developing nuclear, chemical, and biological weapons also either have or are developing ballistic missiles" (David, 1994).

- Despite the relative poverty in which most developing countries find themselves, Third World countries spend tremendous sums of money on military acquisitions, and it "appears that the arms trade [there] is on the verge of a new expansionary cycle, similar to those of the mid-1970s and the early 1980s" (Klare, 1994). Third World countries largely ignore "the trade-off between military spending and development" (Ball, 1994). The defense burden, the percentage of its GNP that a country spends on the military, is often highest among those least able to bear it (see Chapter 11). The opportunity cost (what is given up) of military spending impedes economic and social development. The actual resort to arms is even more costly, to say nothing of the lives lost in the "some 250 wars and conflicts in the Third World since the end of World War II . . . responsible for some 40 million deaths" (Ball, 1994: 217, 216). In the Third World "internal conflicts afflict some 60 countries, and about 35 million people are refugees or internally displaced" (UNDP, 1993: 12).

Despite the costs of war and preparations for it, both will continue as long as the reasons underlying the resort to arms persist. Among Third World nations, where desperation and dictatorship are often found alongside ethnic and tribal conflict, preparations for war are legion.

## THE END OF THIRD WORLDISM?

As we noted at the beginning of this chapter, some analysts have seized on the growing diversity of developing countries and the end of the Cold War to pronounce the death of "third worldism." "The Third World, as a political movement, has disintegrated," concludes Richard Bissell, an official at the U.S. Agency for International Development. "No vote was taken in an international body to disband the Third World. Rather," he continues, "the Third World lost its adherents [as] events disproved the value of its ideology. . . . In effect, the developing countries discovered what can be achieved through cooperation rather than confrontation with the rest of the world" (Bissell, 1990; see also Harris, 1987).

Several important developments during the 1980s in the Third World itself sustain that conclusion. Domestic economic policy reform, greater reliance on market mechanisms, and increased political freedom are among them. Internationally, the stridency of Third World demands so dominant in the 1970s gave way to greater pragmatism, and greater cooperation on North–South issues of mutual interest followed.

Unfortunately from the Third World viewpoint, the end of the Cold War threatens to suspend further North–South cooperation and progress on development and related issues, because it removes industrialized countries' incentives to compete for favors among the developing countries. According to this argument, the end of the Cold War signaled "the end of the postcolonial era as well. For with no Cold War, there can be no 'Third World,' or rather, no 'Third Worldism.' And with no alignment—no sharp bipolarity within the international system—there can be no nonalignment either" (Falcoff, 1990).

> Of course, there will be some sort of relationship between the former Third World and the erstwhile First . . . , but it will be very different from the past. First, because the fundamental centers of power will be more concerned with devising methods of cooperation than competing for dubious foreign clients, the capacity of peripheral societies to disrupt the system as a whole will be greatly diminished. . . . Second, these countries will find it increasingly difficult to extract concessions and resources from Western governments. Now that political influence in the former Third World is no longer a commodity worth bidding for, it will be possible to admit publicly something economists have known all along—that the majority of developing countries . . . are not developing at all and never have been. (Falcoff, 1990: 13)

The relationships between the world's more developed and less developed countries will doubtlessly continue to change in the waning days of the twentieth century. Exactly how remains uncertain, however. Some policymakers in industrial societies see in the end of the Cold War an opportunity to practice a more isolationist foreign policy posture, one that would direct limited resources to domestic problems at the expense of those faced by Third World countries. Should this happen, a posture of benign neglect of the Third World is probable. Others sense that "bipolarity's demise will allow the long-dormant seed of North–South cooperation to germinate as previously stymied North–South alliances emerge to forge solutions to common problems" (Feinberg and Boylan, 1991). From this perspective, the North will be required either to cultivate actively a closer relationship with the South or to risk "commercial, environmental, and security setbacks" (Feinberg and Boylan, 1992).

The differences between these viewpoints stem largely from differing perceptions of the importance of the South to the North. For some, security is paramount. For others, material well-being is more salient. The differences in viewpoints mirror the assumptions underlying the realist and neoliberal perspectives on world politics, as elaborated in Chapter 2.

As realists and neoliberals compete for prominence in decision-making circles, it is useful to remember the historical forces underlying the Third World as an analytical as well as a political concept. Those who learned to regard themselves as members of the Third World shared important characteristics and experiences. Most were colonized by people of another race. They experienced varying degrees of poverty and hunger, and lost hope. They felt powerless in a world system dominated by the affluent countries that once—and perhaps still—controlled them.

"Third worldism" is a post–World War II philosophy that emerged in response to the growing disparities between the North and South—and the gap grows steadily wider. It is a "state of mind" (Jonah, 1991) that will persist as a force in world politics as long as the divisions between North and South remain.

## SUGGESTED READINGS

Black, Jan Knippers. *Development in Theory and Practice: Bridging the Gap.* Boulder, Colo.: Westview, 1991.

Cammack, Paul, David Pool, and William Tordoff. *Third World Politics,* 2nd ed. Baltimore: Johns Hopkins University Press, 1993.

David, Steven R. "Why the Third World Still Matters," *International Security* 17 (Winter 1992–1993): 127–159.

Elsenhans, Hartmut. *Development and Underdevelopment: The History, Economics, and Politics of North-South Relations.* New Delhi: Sage Publications, 1991.

Fallows, James. *Looking at the Sun: The Rise of the New East Asian Economic and Political System.* New York: Pantheon, 1994.

Packenham, Robert A. *The Dependency Movement: Scholarship and Politics in Dependency Studies.* Cambridge, Mass.: Harvard University Press, 1992.

Semmel, Bernard. *The Liberal Ideal and the Demons of Empire: Theories of Imperialism from Adam Smith to Lenin.* Baltimore: Johns Hopkins University Press, 1993.

Sklair, Leslie. *Sociology of the Global System.* Baltimore: Johns Hopkins University Press, 1991.

Slater, Robert O., Barry M. Schultz, and Steven R. Dorr, eds. *Global Transformation and the Third World.* Boulder, Colo.: Lynne Rienner, 1992.

Todaro, Michael P. *Economic Development in the Third World,* 4th revised ed. New York: Longman, 1994.

United Nations Development Programme. *Human Development Report 1994.* New York: Oxford University Press, 1994.

Weiss, Thomas, G., and Meryl A. Kessler, eds. *Third World Security in the Post–Cold War Era.* Boulder, Colo.: Lynne Rienner, 1991.

• • •

# CHAPTER 6

# NONSTATE ACTORS IN WORLD POLITICS: INTERNATIONAL ORGANIZATIONS, MULTINATIONAL CORPORATIONS, AND ETHNONATIONAL MOVEMENTS

• • •

*The protection of the nation against destruction from without and disruption from within is the over-riding concern of all citizens. . . . Nothing can be tolerated that might threaten the coherence of the nation.*

Hans J. Morgenthau,
Political Realist Scholar, 1967

*Will nation-states fade away? I don't think so. Will state sovereignty fade? My answer is yes.*

François Heisbourg, Director,
International Institute for Strategic Studies, 1990

The history of world politics for the past three centuries has largely been a history of interactions among nation-states. Since 1648 the power and authority of this sovereign political unit have expanded. And today nation-states remain the dominant form of political organization in the world. Their interests, capabilities, and goals significantly shape the contours of world politics.

However, the supremacy of the nation-state is not unchallenged. Increasingly, world affairs are being influenced less by state governments and more by nonstate actors. Diverse in scope and purpose, these actors perform independent roles and exert a global impact. They include international governmental and nongovernmental organizations (like the United Nations and the International Olympic Committee), multinational corporations (like Exxon and IBM), transnational political parties (like the Social Democrats in Western Europe), and religious institutions (like the Roman Catholic Church). And they include internationally active ethnic groups within two or more countries (such as the Kurds in Iran, Iraq, and Turkey) who, from below the state and across state borders, influence and undermine the state's authority.

• • •

Despite the obvious diversity among these groups, all share a common trait: They think of themselves as *extraterritorial*—beyond the jurisdiction of the territorial state. They are dedicated to their own interests rather than those of any particular country.

This chapter examines the growth and impact of these transnational and subnational nonstate actors. Specifically, it will explore three types: international organizations, multinational corporations, and transnational ethnonational movements. The purpose is not just to describe their existence. More broadly, we will evaluate how their activities undermine the continuing autonomy of the nation-state. Our survey will focus throughout on the question of whether national governments are capable of managing global change (see Box 6.1). It will take as its point of departure the thesis U.S. President Bill Clinton articulated in his September 1993 address to the United Nations. "Twin forces," Mr. Clinton argued, offer a push-pull challenge to nations because "economic and technological forces all over the globe are compelling the world toward integration while ethnic and religious tensions tear nations apart."

## INTERNATIONAL ORGANIZATIONS

There are two principal types of international organizations, intergovernmental and nongovernmental. Governments are members of the first type, and private individuals and groups are members of the second. The Central Commission for the Navigation of the Rhine, established by the Congress of Vienna in 1815, is the first modern international *intergovernmental organization* (IGO), and the Rosicrucian Order, established in 1694, fits contemporary definitions of international *nongovernmental organizations* (NGOs).

Neither type is peculiar to the twentieth century, but both are now more pervasive

---

### Box 6.1
### EMERGING SUPRANATIONAL AND SUBNATIONAL ORGANIZATIONS: SUBSTITUTES FOR THE NATION-STATE?

• • •

Global changes . . . call into question the usefulness of the nation-state itself. The key autonomous actor in political and international affairs for the past few centuries appears not just to be losing its control and integrity, but to be the *wrong sort* of unit to handle the new circumstances. For some problems, it is too large to operate effectively; for others, it is too small. In consequence, there are pressures for a "relocation of authority" both upward and downward, creating structures that might respond better to today's and tomorrow's forces for change.

*Source: Paul Kennedy (1993: 131)*

than ever. The number of both types of organizations increased sharply during the latter part of the nineteenth century as international commerce and communications grew alongside industrialization. On the eve of World War I, in 1909, 37 IGOs and 176 NGOs were in existence. Thereafter, the pace of their growth quickened (see Figure 6.1). By 1960 there were 154 intergovernmental and 1,255 nongovernmental organizations. By 1993 these numbers had surged to 272 and 4,830, respectively (*Yearbook of International Organizations, 1993/94*: 1699).[1]

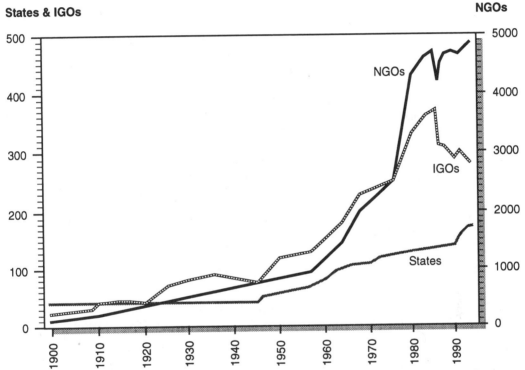

**States & IGOs**                                                                 **NGOs**

**Figure 6.1**   The Number of States, Intergovernmental Organizations (IGOs), and Nongovernmental Organizations (NGOs) since 1900
*Note:* Figures for states are based on the Correlates of War (COW) project at the University of Michigan under the direction of J. David Singer.
*Source: Yearbook of International Organizations, 1993/94* (1993: 1699), and moving averages from selected prior volumes.

---

[1] These figures imply that it is easier to identify international organizations than is in fact the case. In principle, IGOs are defined by their structure and permanence; they meet at relatively regular intervals, have specified procedures for making decisions, and have a permanent secretariat or headquarters staff (Jacobson, 1984: 8). If these criteria were relaxed, the number of IGOs would far surpass the nearly three hundred "conventionally defined" organizations just cited, as would the number of NGOs. An additional 1,464 international bodies would qualify for inclusion as IGOs, as would more than 7,929 other nongovernmental entities that share some characteristics with NGOs (see *Yearbook of International Organizations, 1993/94*, Vol. 1, 1993: 1698).

This growth has created a complex network of overlapping national memberships in transnational associations. In 1991, for example, the United States participated in more than 2,100 international organizations, over twice the number it participated in only two decades earlier. On a global scale, the national representations of some two hundred countries and territories in 4,917 international organizations numbered more than 118,000 (*Yearbook of International Organizations, 1991/92*, Vol. 2, 1991: 1171–1669). These are "networks of interdependence" (Jacobson, 1984) whose cooperative activities span the entire panoply of issues confronting international society: trade, defense, disarmament, economic development, agriculture, health, culture, human rights, the arts, illicit drugs, tourism, labor, education, debt, the environment, humanitarian aid, telecommunications, science, immigration, and refugees, to name just a few.

Even though more than 95 percent of the international organizations now in operation are nongovernmental, the remaining 5 percent are more important because their members are nation-states. The IGOs governments create and join will remain preeminent as long as the preeminence of nation-states themselves persists. Political scientist Harold K. Jacobson explains:

> Authoritative policies are more frequently made in and applied by governmental than by nongovernmental institutions; consequently in most political systems the former are more important than the latter. But the global system accords even greater importance to governmental institutions than is usually the case. States are the primary focal points of political activity in the modern world, and IGOs presently derive their importance from their character as associations of states. (Jacobson, 1984: 7)

Intergovernmental organizations share in common the fact that they are composed of states. But they vary widely in their purposes and breadth of membership. One study found that only eighteen qualify as general-purpose organizations, and of these only the United Nations approximated universal membership. All of the rest, making up more than 97 percent of the total, were limited in their membership and purposes (Jacobson, 1984: 48).

Table 6.1 illustrates these differences among IGOs. The variation among the organizations in each category is great, particularly with single-purpose, limited-membership types. The North Atlantic Treaty Organization (NATO), for example, is primarily a military alliance, while others, such as the Organization of American States (OAS), promote both military security and economic development. The latter therefore might be regarded as "political" IGOs.

Still, most IGOs engage in a comparatively narrow range of activities. The purposes are usually economic and social, such as the management of trade, transportation, and other types of functional cooperation. In this sense IGOs are agents as well as reflections of global social and economic interdependence.

In comparison, NGOs are also very dissimilar. Because of their number and diversity, NGOs are even more difficult than IGOs to characterize and classify. The Union of International Associations (itself an NGO) maintains comprehensive, up-to-date information about NGOs. It categorizes 9 percent of some 4,830 NGOs as universal membership organizations, with most of the remaining 91 percent classified

TABLE 6.1 A SIMPLE CLASSIFICATION OF INTERNATIONAL INTERGOVERNMENTAL ORGANIZATIONS

| Geographic Scope of Membership | Range of Stated Purpose | |
|---|---|---|
| | Multiple Purpose | Single Purpose |
| Global | United Nations | World Health Organization<br>International Labor Organization |
| Interregional, regional, subregional | European Union<br>Organization of American States<br>Organization of African Unity<br>League of Arab States<br>Association of Southeast Asian Nations | Conference on Security and Cooperation in Europe<br>Nordic Council<br>North Atlantic Treaty Organization<br>International Olive Oil Council<br>International North Pacific Fisheries Commission |

as intercontinental or regionally oriented membership organizations (*Yearbook of International Organizations, 1993/94*, Vol. 1, 1993: 1698). Functionally, the organizations span virtually every facet of modern political, social, and economic life, ranging from earth sciences to health care, from language, history, culture, and theology to law, ethics, security, and defense.

It is useful to think of NGOs as intersocietal organizations that help promote agreements among nation-states on issues of international public policy. Many NGOs interact formally with the IGOs that operate as servants of the state. For instance, many NGOs hold consultative status with various agencies of the extensive United Nations system, and they maintain offices scattered in more than a hundred cities throughout the world. The partnership between the two types of entities enables them to work (and lobby) together in pursuit of common policies and programs.

The United Nations also often relies heavily on the many nongovernmental organizations it helps to fund that are not under its formal authority. This involvement blurs the line between governmental and nongovernmental functions. Examples include the United Nations Children's Fund (UNICEF), the United Nations Fund for Population Activities (UNFPA), and the United Nations University, which fulfill their missions in part through nongovernmental entities.

Although widespread geographically, NGOs' impact is greater in the advanced industrial states than in the developing world. "This is so because open political systems, ones in which there is societal pluralism, are more likely to allow their citizens to participate in nongovernmental organizations, and such systems are highly correlated with relatively high levels of economic development" (Jacobson, 1984). The composition of NGOs' membership therefore also tilts in the direction of the North rather than the South.

Because of their importance, three prominent and representative IGOs will be described: the United Nations, the European Union, and regional organizations.

## The United Nations

The United Nations (UN) is the best-known international organization. It also has special characteristics that distinguish it from most others. First, its membership approximates universality. The end of the Cold War helped realize that goal. In 1991, Latvia, Lithuania, Estonia, North Korea, and South Korea, long denied a place in the UN, finally gained admission, and the breakup of the USSR also enabled the newly independent republics of the former Soviet Union (i.e., the "successor states") to join in 1992. By 1994 the organization's membership climbed to 184 countries.

Second, partly because nearly all states are members, the United Nations is a multiple-purpose organization. As stated in Article 1 of the United Nations Charter, the purposes of the organization are:

- to maintain international peace and security;
- to develop friendly relations among nations based on respect for the principle of equal rights and self-determination of peoples;
- to achieve international cooperation in solving international problems of an economic, social, cultural, or humanitarian character, and in promoting and encouraging respect for human rights and for fundamental freedoms for all;
- to be a center for harmonizing the actions of nations in the attainment of these common ends.

These ideals have carried the United Nations into nearly every corner of the complex network of relations among states. Its conference machinery has become permanent; the organization has provided a mechanism for the management of international conflict; and it has become involved in a broad range of global welfare issues.

Peace and security figured prominently in the thinking of those responsible for creating the United Nations and its predecessor, the League of Nations. Following the onset of each of the world wars, world leaders mounted concerted efforts to cope with future threats to the peace. A conviction at the core of political idealism—that war is not inevitable but can be eradicated by reforming the anarchial structures that encourage it—inspired both efforts. The first, the League of Nations, sought to prevent a recurrence of the catastrophe of 1914–1918 by replacing the balance-of-power system with one based on the principle of collective security. According to that principle, aggression by any one state is an aggression against all others, who are then obliged to unite in collective action against the aggressor. When collective security failed to restrain Japan and Italy from waging war unilaterally during the 1930s, the League foundered. By the end of the decade, global warfare broke out again.

With the restoration of peace nearing in 1945, the victors once more turned to an international organization—the new United Nations—to maintain the peace. However, in the same way that the League of Nations proved incapable of stemming fascist aggression, the ability of the United Nations to maintain international security quickly eroded. It soon became paralyzed by two unforeseen developments: the Cold War conflict between the United States and the Soviet Union and the North–South dispute between the world's rich and poor countries. The five major powers allied during World War II against Germany and Japan—the United States, the Soviet Union, Britain, France, and China—became permanent members of the Security Council and reserved the right to veto its actions. This formula reflected the assumption that the major powers would act in concert to support the principle of collective security perceived necessary to maintain the postwar peace. Hence, unanimity among the permanent members was essential, for unless all five permanent members were in agreement, the council would be deadlocked and no action could occur. As it turned out, that unanimous agreement infrequently materialized.

## False Start: The United Nations during the Cold War

The Security Council rapidly fell victim to the Cold War. Between 1945 and 1955, the Soviet Union, unable to mobilize a majority on its side, exercised its veto power 77 times to prevent action on matters with which it disagreed and accounted for three-fourths of the 149 vetoes cast in the first three decades of the United Nations' existence (Riggs and Plano, 1994: 58). But obstruction did not come from the Soviet Union alone. The United States did not cast a veto until 1970—on the issue of white minority control in Rhodesia (now Zimbabwe) and the extension of economic sanctions to South Africa[2]—but after that its veto activity increased greatly. In all, by 1992 the United States had exercised its veto power 72 times, twice as often since 1966 as all other permanent council members combined (Riggs and Plano, 1994: 58). The Security Council was often paralyzed as a result, as vetoes severely restricted the ability of the United Nations to undertake collective action.

This impotence was aggravated by two financial crises, in the mid-1960s and again in the late 1980s, when both superpowers refused to pay their mandated fees and fell into serious arrears. By 1993 the United States remained the largest UN debtor, with $1 billion unpaid dues and peacekeeping bills. There was great irony in the fact that the United Nations was on the brink of insolvency at the very time the world community began to entrust the organization with new and unprecedented responsibilities, and U.S. President Clinton had campaigned for office on the platform, in part, that "there exists an opportunity to reinvent the institutions of collective security." (In October 1993, Clinton promised to pay the U.S. debt and asked that the United Nations specify clear criteria for the performance of its expanding mission.) Together,

---

[2] During the UN's formative period, the United States did not have to veto Security Council actions it opposed because it possessed a "hidden veto," an ability to persuade a sufficient majority of other council members to vote negatively so as to avoid the stigma of having to cast the single blocking vote (Stoessinger, 1977). This ability derived from the composition of the Security Council, among whose nine (later fifteen) members the United States could easily depend to provide a pro-Western majority.

the East–West conflict and the political and financial problems it wrought destroyed the UN's capacity to operate during the Cold War as its creators had hoped.

The changing composition of the UN's membership also reduced its capacity for concerted action. As its size increased, the membership of the organization became less homogeneous. This process began with the Fifteenth General Assembly in 1960 when seventeen new states joined the United Nations, nearly all of them African. Thereafter the Third World increasingly dominated the United Nations. By 1994 well over half of the organization's 184 members came from Africa and Asia. In 1945 less than a quarter of them came from these two regions (see Figure 6.2). Disagreement and disunity were the by-products of increased size, as large groups have more problems acting together than do small ones. Consequently, between 1960 and 1990 it was difficult for the United Nations to function like a truly united body, and this disunity was a great obstacle to UN action.

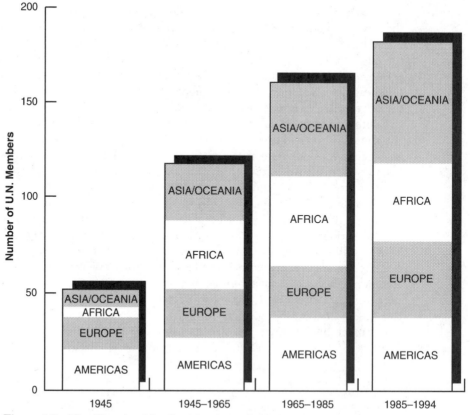

**Figure 6.2** The Changing Membership of the United Nations, 1945–1994
*Source:* United Nations, using classifications of regions of the U.S. Department of State (1985: 18).

## *Fresh Start: The United Nations after the Cold War*

The three barriers to the UN's performance posed by great-power rivalry, insufficient funds, and disunity generally have been somewhat alleviated by the Cold War's collapse. The great powers on the Security Council then began to behave in a manner consistent with what the framers of the United Nations Charter contemplated when they adopted the unanimity principle, namely, that agreement among the major powers would naturally occur to maintain international peace. How far the United States and the then Soviet Union had progressed became strikingly clear in 1990 when they joined forces in the United Nations to organize a collective UN effort to turn back Iraq's aggression in Kuwait. With Russia's repudiation of communism, collaborative crisis-management activities increased exponentially. Other postures indicative of the new cooperative attitude included the two powers' mutual advocacy of "consensus" decision making in the Security Council (that is, without voting) and their push to revitalize the moribund Military Staff Committee. So, like the end of World War I and World War II, the end of the Cold War has witnessed renewed efforts to empower the United Nations to preserve world order and promote global prosperity.

The end of the Cold War holds out the promise that continued major-power cooperation will remove the single most important obstacle to an enhanced UN role in world affairs. The Security Council in particular "has shown that it has the capacity to initiate collective measures essential for the maintenance of peace in a new world order" (Russett and Sutterlin, 1991). The Clinton administration made it clear that it shared this hope by repeatedly endorsing what U.N. Ambassador Madeleine Albright termed "assertive multilateralism." The prospects for this approach will be heavily influenced by how the United Nations is organized for its ambitious and wide-ranging purposes.

## *Organizing the United Nations: System and Structure*

The Security Council is but one of six principal organs established by the United Nations Charter. The others are the General Assembly, the Economic and Social Council, the Trusteeship Council, the Secretariat, and the International Court of Justice. Among these, the General Assembly is the only body representing all the member states. Decision making there follows the principle of majority rule, with no state given a veto.

Unlike the Security Council, which is empowered by the UN Charter to initiate actions, including the use of force, the General Assembly can only make recommendations. Unforeseen by the founders of the United Nations, however, that limited mandate enabled the General Assembly to become a partner with the Security Council in managing security. It is also now the primary body for addressing social and economic problems.

The latter issues have grown in number and importance. In response, the United Nations has evolved into an extraordinarily complex set of political institutions. The United Nations today is not one organization but a conglomerate of countless committees, bureaus, boards, commissions, centers, institutes, offices, and agencies.

The General Assembly, as the only principal UN organ representing all member states, now occupies the central role in the overall structure of the United Nations (see Figure 6.3).

The proliferation of United Nations bodies and activities parallels the growth of international interdependence and cross-cutting linkages since World War II. It also parallels the expanding uses to which states have put the United Nations to accomplish their own aims. Third World countries, seizing advantage of their growing numbers under the one-state, one-vote rules of the General Assembly, now guide UN involvement in directions of particular concern to them. The United Nations, which began as a Western-dominated political organization, later evolved into one in which the Third World became the dominant voice. This balance is reflected in the growing diversity of its affiliated agencies, which speak to the full panoply of the world's problems and needs (see Figure 6.4).

Most Third World countries have used the UN forum to espouse aims and interests directly related to decolonization and economic development. This contrasted with the U.S. view of the United Nations as a platform to pursue Cold War strategies vis-á-vis the Soviet Union. In 1971 the United States suffered a major defeat on a long-standing Cold War issue when the General Assembly voted to seat Communist China in the world body. Over the next decade it suffered other defeats. In 1974 the United States was in a distinct minority in opposing the extension by the General Assembly of permanent observer status to the Palestine Liberation Organization. In 1975 it lost an important battle when the General Assembly went on record branding Zionism "a form of racism and racial discrimination." And in 1983 the United States was the target of a resolution, approved overwhelmingly, that deplored its invasion of Grenada.

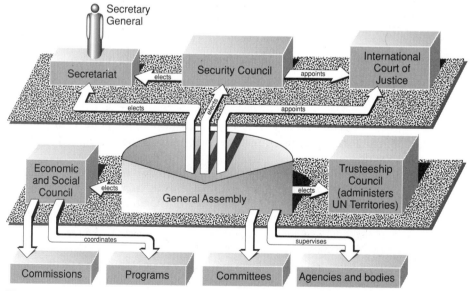

**Figure 6.3** The United Nations Overall Structure
*Source:* Peter J. Taylor (1990: 40).

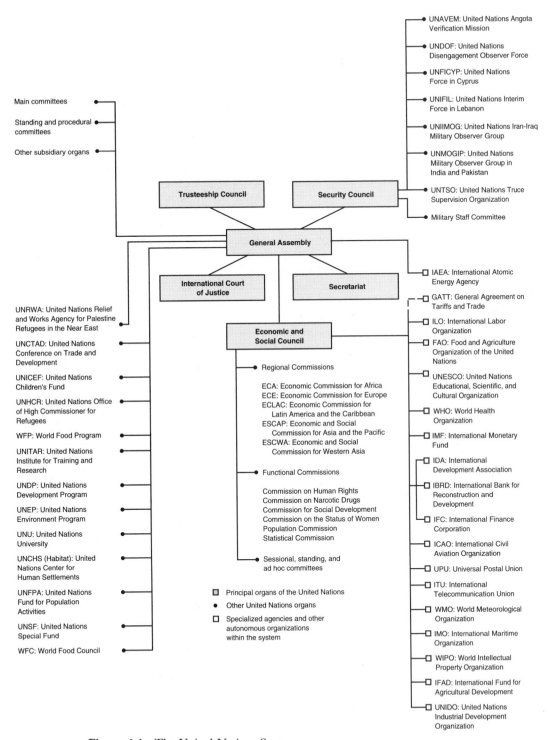

Main committees

Standing and procedural committees

Other subsidiary organs

UNAVEM: United Nations Angola Verification Mission

UNDOF: United Nations Disengagement Observer Force

UNFICYP: United Nations Force in Cyprus

UNIFIL: United Nations Interim Force in Lebanon

UNIIMOG: United Nations Iran-Iraq Military Observer Group

UNMOGIP: United Nations Military Observer Group in India and Pakistan

UNTSO: United Nations Truce Supervision Organization

Military Staff Committee

**Trusteeship Council**

**Security Council**

**General Assembly**

**International Court of Justice**

**Secretariat**

IAEA: International Atomic Energy Agency

GATT: General Agreement on Tariffs and Trade

ILO: International Labor Organization

**Economic and Social Council**

FAO: Food and Agriculture Organization of the United Nations

UNRWA: United Nations Relief and Works Agency for Palestine Refugees in the Near East

UNCTAD: United Nations Conference on Trade and Development

UNICEF: United Nations Children's Fund

UNHCR: United Nations Office of High Commissioner for Refugees

WFP: World Food Program

UNITAR: United Nations Institute for Training and Research

UNDP: United Nations Development Program

UNEP: United Nations Environment Program

UNU: United Nations University

UNCHS (Habitat): United Nations Center for Human Settlements

UNFPA: United Nations Fund for Population Activities

UNSF: United Nations Special Fund

WFC: World Food Council

Regional Commissions

ECA: Economic Commission for Africa
ECE: Economic Commission for Europe
ECLAC: Economic Commission for Latin America and the Caribbean
ESCAP: Economic and Social Commission for Asia and the Pacific
ESCWA: Economic and Social Commission for Western Asia

Functional Commissions

Commission on Human Rights
Commission on Narcotic Drugs
Commission for Social Development
Commission on the Status of Women
Population Commission
Statistical Commission

Sessional, standing, and ad hoc committees

☐ Principal organs of the United Nations
● Other United Nations organs
☐ Specialized agencies and other autonomous organizations within the system

UNESCO: United Nations Educational, Scientific, and Cultural Organization

WHO: World Health Organization

IMF: International Monetary Fund

IDA: International Development Association

IBRD: International Bank for Reconstruction and Development

IFC: International Finance Corporation

ICAO: International Civil Aviation Organization

UPU: Universal Postal Union

ITU: International Telecommunication Union

WMO: World Meteorological Organization

IMO: International Maritime Organization

WIPO: World Intellectual Property Organization

IFAD: International Fund for Agricultural Development

UNIDO: United Nations Industrial Development Organization

**Figure 6.4** The United Nations System
*Source: The UN Chronicle*, as reprinted in U.S. CIA (1993: 386).

But this era of struggle between the Third World and the United States has shifted with the Cold War's collapse. No more do control of UN peacekeeping operations and financial support of UN operations pose the same problem as they routinely did when the United States (and the Soviet Union) had a singular military agenda in mind and the Third World members had a quite different social, economic, and environmental one.

Yet North–South differences over perceived priorities have not disappeared. They are exhibited in their current form in the continuing debate over the UN's budget. The UN Charter states that "expenses of the Organization shall be borne by the members as apportioned by the General Assembly."[3] When the General Assembly apportions expenses, it does so according to majority rule. The problem is that those with the most votes—the less developed countries—do not have the money, and those that do—the more developed countries—do not have the votes. Figure 6.5 illustrates these wide disparities. It shows that the eight largest contributors to the United Nations commanded only eight votes, though they paid more than 71 percent of its costs. At the other end of the spectrum, the poorest 172 members, who collectively paid only 29 percent of the organization's costs, commanded 172 votes. Thus financial disputes reflect the "tension between the principle of sovereign equality of member states, permitting the more numerous developing countries to wield considerable influence over the kinds of issues on which the UN's attention and resources are focused, and the need to set priorities and manage more effectively the UN's limited monies and manpower, an increasing concern of the developed countries" ("Financing the United Nations," n.d.).

At issue, of course, is not simply money—which remains, with a 1993 total assessment at $1.07 billion, a comparatively paltry sum—but differences in images of what's important and in political influence. Most states that do not have money argue that needs should determine expenditure levels, rather than the other way around. The major contributors, sensitive to the amounts asked of them and the purposes for the funds, are hesitant to pay for programs they oppose (Lister, 1986).[4]

---

[3] The UN budget consists of three distinct elements: the regular budget (which includes the expenditures of the fifteen specialized agencies of the United Nations, each of which has its own budgetary procedures), the peacekeeping budget, and the budget for voluntary programs. States contribute to the voluntary programs and some of the peacekeeping activities as they see fit. The regular program and some of the peacekeeping activities are subject to assessments.

The precise mechanism by which assessments are determined is complicated (see Lister, 1986), but generally assessments are designed to reflect states' capacity to pay. Thus the United States, which has the greatest capacity to pay, contributes 25 percent of the regular budget of the United Nations, whereas several dozen poor nations pay the minimum, which is 0.01 percent of the regular budget. The United States is also a prime contributor to UN peacekeeping and voluntary programs.

[4] The United States found another way to register its dissatisfaction with what it saw as the anti-Western drift of many UN bodies: It ended its membership in them. In the 1970s, for example, the Carter administration withdrew for a time from the International Labor Organization in an attempt to influence the direction of its policies. The United States also at that time withheld payment of its UNESCO (United Nations Educational, Scientific and Cultural Organization) dues to protest an Arab-led effort to oust Israel from the organization. Later, during the Reagan administration, the United States withdrew from the 159-member UNESCO in response to what it regarded as the politicization of UNESCO and its hostility toward Western values, including in particular freedom of communication, thereby depriving UNESCO of a quarter of its budget.

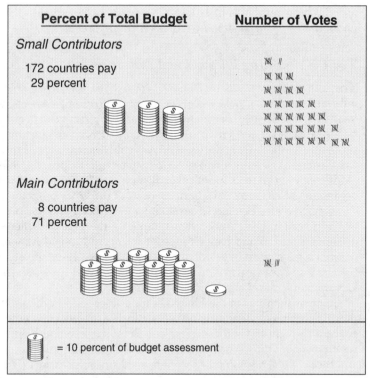

**Figure 6.5** Budgets and Influence: Disparities in UN Budget Assessments and Voting Strength in the General Assembly
*Source:* Based on UN scale of assessments in January 1993, as calculated by Robert E. Riggs and Jack C. Plano (1994: 39).

Often, the Third World supports the purposes for the funds but fails to generate broad political support for them among other important UN groups.[5]

It is against the background of endemic cash-flow problems that other disputes among the UN's members usually arise. This is exhibited visibly in the politics within the UN's affiliated agencies. The end of the Cold War and the positive contribution the United Nations made in repelling Iraq's aggression, in securing the release of American and European hostages held captive in Lebanon, in bringing the combatants in Cambodia together, and in ending the stalemate over Namibia all helped to increase the willingness of the great powers to assist the UN financially to manage its expanded

---

[5] Interestingly, however, many of the poor states have also fallen behind in their assessed payments. By 1992 80 percent of the UN members were in arrears (Schoettle, 1992: 15), and "the near collapse of the Russian economy made its assessment (9.42 percent in 1992, reduced to 6.71 for 1993) difficult to honor, especially since it had to be paid in 'hard' or 'convertible' currency" (Riggs and Plano, 1994: 38).

peacekeeping responsibilities (see Chapter 14). Nonetheless, the distance between political and financial support remained troublesome.

## The UN's Shifting Purposes and Priorities

The rich countries and the Third World have each used the United Nations to influence the foreign policy goals of the other. In some respects, however, the Third World historically has been comparatively more effective than either the United States or the other great powers in using the United Nations' institutional structures and procedures, especially in the General Assembly, to advance its interests. For example, the General Assembly's one-state, one-vote rule helped the Third World to focus global attention on the issue of colonialism and to "delegitimize" it as a form of political organization (see Chapter 5). Other aspects of the UN's programs and priorities reveal the same success. Economic development has been another principal Third World aim advanced in UN forums, for example. In the 1950s the then numerically smaller group of Third World nations pressed for organizational responses to its needs and realized some modest (if less than hoped for) results. Illustratively, the United Nations Special Fund was a partial response to Third World pressure for large amounts of UN economic development aid.

As their numbers in the United Nations increased in the 1960s, the Third World pressed even more vigorously on economic development and other issues of particular concern to them beyond the great-power military competition that preoccupied the superpowers. Third World interests found expression in a host of world conferences and special General Assembly sessions held since the early 1970s. However, because these conferences frequently became forums for vituperative exchanges between North and South, their contribution to solving—not just bemoaning—global problems was rather limited.

The range of subjects addressed nonetheless speaks to the agenda of issues especially important to the Third World that they have pursued. Included, among others, have been conferences on the human environment (1972), law of the sea (1973), population (1974 and 1984), food (1974), women (1975, 1980, and 1985), human settlements (1976), basic human needs (1976), water (1977), desertification (1977), disarmament (1978 and 1982), racism and racial discrimination (1978), technical cooperation among developing countries (1978), agrarian reform and rural development (1979), science and technology for development (1979), new and renewable sources of energy (1981), least-developed countries (1981), aging (1982), the peaceful uses of outer space (1982), Palestine (1982), the peaceful uses of nuclear energy (1983), the prevention of crime and the treatment of offenders (1985), drug abuse and illicit trafficking in drugs (1987 and 1992), the protection of children (1990), the environment and economic development (1992), transnational corporations (1992), indigenous people (1994), and social development (1995). The subjects covered in the world conferences during the past two decades are in effect a list of "the most vital issues of present world conditions," whereas the conferences themselves "represent a beginning in a long and evolving process of keeping within manageable proportions the major problems of humanity" (Bennett, 1988). In this the United Nations, spurred on by the Third World, can take some credit.

At another level, however, the conference technique represents an approach to global decision making marked with pitfalls. Developing countries prefer broadly based institutional settings, such as the global ad hoc conference forum, in which the one-state, one-vote principle gives them an advantage. In this way institutional procedures promote Third World interests. In contrast, First World countries prefer small, functionally specific forums, usually outside the General Assembly, which, they believe, "are more likely to involve those states that have a real stake in the outcome of the deliberations." According to this viewpoint, "large, general-purpose bodies only encourage ill-informed participation by states uninvolved in the issue at hand and thus increase the likelihood of irresponsibly politicizing the agenda" (Gregg, 1977). Nonetheless, the conference strategy has become an accepted mechanism for pursuing a North–South dialogue on issues of particular interest to the Third World, whose effect has been "to change attitudes, to stimulate political will, and to raise the level of national and global interest in the subject. . . . The industrialized states, although reluctantly, in general continue the dialogue in their own enlightened self-interest" (Feld and Jordan, 1994).

With the end of the Cold War, the United Nations has rediscovered its muscle and begun to play an active role in *both* the area of security, uppermost in the thinking of the great powers, and in the area of social and economic enhancement, of special concern to Third World countries. As we will examine (Chapter 14), the prospect for UN peacekeeping is promising. There exists renewed hope that the globe's most powerful IGO, the United Nations, will make a more meaningful impact in the latter category of global issues.

## The European Union

The political tug-of-war between various states and groups of states within the United Nations over how the organization might best serve their national interests is suggestive of an underlying principle—that IGOs are products of the interests of the nation-states that make them up. This severely circumscribes the ability of IGOs to rise above global conflicts and to independently pursue their own purposes. In the words of political scientist Inis Claude (1967), "The United Nations has no purposes—and can have none—of its own." That holds even more true of other IGOs. Hence, IGOs are better viewed as instruments of states' foreign policies and as arenas within which to debate issues than as independent actors. In short, because the United Nations and other IGOs cannot act autonomously, they lack the legitimacy and capability for independent, "competent global governance" (Alger, 1990).

When states dominate international organizations, as they do the United Nations, the prospects for international cooperation decline because states typically resist any organizational actions that could compromise their interests. Thus, as political realists emphasize, there are severe limits on the capacity of international organizations for collective action to engineer global change.

A rival hypothesis emerges from neoliberal theorizing. This perspective, described in Chapter 2, maintains that cooperation among powerful states is possible and that international organizations help produce it. That viewpoint is especially pertinent to the *European Union* (EU) (known prior to November 1993 as the European Community [EC]).

At its inception, the European Community consisted of three communities: the European Coal and Steel Community (ECSC, created in 1951), the European Atomic Energy Community (Euratom, 1957), and the European Economic Community (EEC, 1957). Since 1968, the three have shared common organizational structures. The members of the EU are Belgium, France, Germany, Italy, Luxembourg, and the Netherlands (who were the original "Six"), Denmark, Ireland, and the United Kingdom (who joined in 1973), Greece (1981), and Portugal and Spain (1986). In March 1994, the EU reached agreement with Austria, Finland, Norway, and Sweden on the terms for membership beginning in 1995. Each of these countries must hold a national referendum on EU membership in order to join it (see Box 6.2 on page 166).

### Organizational Components and Decision-making Procedures

A quadripartite institutional system consisting of an Executive Commission, a Council of Ministers, a European Parliament, and a Court of Justice governs the European Union (see Figure 6.6).

The Council of Ministers is the system's central component. As the name implies, it consists of cabinet ministers drawn from the European Union's member states. The foreign ministers participate in the council when the most important decisions are made. In this respect the European Union is an association of nation-states that differs little from the United Nations. But the EU is more than an association of states. That is clear in part from an examination of its other elements and decision-making procedures.

Central among the other elements is the Commission, which consists of seventeen members (two each from Britain, France, Germany, Italy, and Spain, and one each from the remaining member states). A "Eurocracy" (professional staff) of more than 25,000 civil-service "Eurocrats," who in principle owe loyalty to the European Union, not to its national constituents, assists the Commission. The Commission proposes legislation, implements EU policies, and represents the European Union in international trade negotiations. It also manages the EU's budget, which, in contrast with most international organizations, derives part of its revenues from sources not under the control of member states.

The European Parliament is chosen by direct election of the citizenry of the EU's member states. Its 518 delegates debate issues in the same way that national legislative bodies do, but its legislative powers are less pervasive than in a typical domestic political system. Still, it, too, is distinctive in that most international organizations' legislative bodies represent states (as in the UN General Assembly), not individual citizens or transnational political parties.

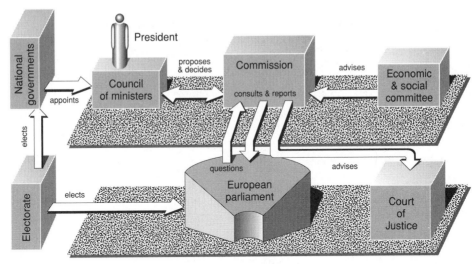

**Figure 6.6** The Organization of the European Union
*Source:* As presented for the EC by Peter J. Taylor (1990: 112).

The Court of Justice is also distinctive in this respect. Comprising thirteen judges, the court interprets EU law for national courts and rules on legal questions raised by the institutions of the EU, by member states, or, in an important deviation from traditional patterns, by individuals. Its decisions are binding, which also distinguishes the European Court of Justice from most other international tribunals.

Figure 6.7 illustrates decision-making processes in the EU. As the figure shows, there are two procedures for the adoption of directives and regulations, a consultation procedure and a cooperation procedure. The procedure actually followed depends on the nature of the proposal, and a principal difference is that the European Parliament plays a greater role in the cooperative than in the consultative process. In both, however, the central role of the Commission in the EU's legislative process is evident; indeed, the Commission has been the driving force behind European integration (Ludlow, 1991). It was under the imaginative leadership of Jacques Delors, president of the Commission, that the European Community in 1987 adopted the Single European Act, a major amendment to the 1957 Treaty of Rome that created the European Economic Community (popularly known for many years as the European Common Market). The Single European Act eliminated members' veto power for most issues to create, in principle, a true European "single" market on January 1, 1993. The goal promised a free flow of goods, services, people, and money—a market free of internal borders similar to the way the United States is free of internal restraints. Although there was much progress in 1994 toward the ideal, the dream remains unfulfilled. Many European markets remain protected, and key elements of the Maastricht blueprint—such as a uniform corporate tax—have not yet been approved. And the biggest

# Box 6.2
## CHRONOLOGY OF EVENTS LEADING TO THE EUROPEAN UNION

• • •

### 1950

**May 9** French Foreign Minister Robert Schuman proposes placing Europe's coal and steel under a common European authority.

### 1951

**April 18** Treaty creating the European Coal and Steel Community (ECSC) is signed in Paris by the Benelux countries, France, Germany, and Italy.

### 1957

**March 25** Treaties creating the European Economic Community (EEC) and the European Atomic Energy Community (Euratom) are signed in Rome.

### 1965

**April 8** Signature of the treaty merging the institutions of the three European Communities.

### 1968

**July 1** Customs union is completed 18 months early. Remaining industrial tariffs between the Six are abolished. Common external tariff enters into force.

### 1973

**January 1** Denmark, Ireland, and the United Kingdom join the Community. Free trade agreements with European Free Trade Association (EFTA) countries begin to take effect.

### 1975

**February 28** First Lomé Convention with African, Caribbean, and Pacific countries is signed.

### 1979

**March 13** European Monetary System (EMS) becomes operative.

**June 7–10** First direct elections to the European Parliament. Direct elections are held every five years.

### 1981

**January 1** Greece joins the Community.

### 1985

**June 29** EC Heads of State and Government endorse a "White Paper" outlining a strategy for creating a true common market by 1992.

### 1986

**January 1** Spain and Portugal join the Community.

### 1987

**July 1** The Single European Act, amending treaties, enters into force.

### 1989

**May 21** President George Bush renews the U.S. commitment to a "strong united Europe" in a speech at Boston University.

**June 26–27** The Heads of State and Government meeting in Madrid endorse a plan for Economic and Monetary Union.

**July 14–16** Western Economic Summit in Paris asks the EC Commission to coordinate Western assistance to Poland and Hungary.

**December 17** A new political partnership between the Community and the United States is outlined by Secretary of State James Baker in Berlin.

### 1990

**October 3** The five Laender of the former German Democratic Republic enter the Community as part of a united Germany. **November 20** The Community and the United States adopt a Transatlantic Declaration. **December 13–14** Opening of Intergovernmental Conferences of Economic and Monetary Union (EMU) and Political Union.

## 1991

**October 21** The European Community and the European Free Trade Association (EFTA) agree to form the European Economic Area (EEA), a single market of 19 countries. **December 9–11** The European Council meeting in Maastricht agrees to treaties providing for economic and monetary union and closer political union. **December 16** Poland, Hungary, and Czechoslovakia sign far-reaching trade and cooperation agreements with the European Community.

## 1992

**February 7** Treaty of Union and Final Act signed in Maastricht.

## 1993

**November** European Community formally changes its name to the European Union (EU) with the adoption of the Maastricht Treaty. **December 12** EU members agree to goal of a full overhaul of its structure by 1996.

## 1994

**January** Austria, Finland, Norway, and Sweden proceed with negotiations to join the European Union. **February** EU splits over voting rules that would be followed in a future, larger EU institution. **March** EU reaches agreement with Austria, Finland, Norway, and Sweden on terms for membership to begin on January 1, 1995. Each candidate must hold a national referendum to join the European Union. **March 8** EU agrees to enhance its foreign-policy ties with six countries that already enjoy "Association" pacts with the EU—Poland, Hungary, the Czech Republic, Slovakia, Bulgaria, and Roma-

nia. Communique endorses a plan to convene regular meetings and to invite the six countries to "align themselves jointly" with EU declarations and activities. **March 17** Poland announces its intention to apply for EU membership. **March 23** Ukraine leads the way for Russia and other non-Baltic former Soviet republics by reaching a "partnership" agreement with the EU that gives it access to EU deliberations but not right to eventual full EU membership. **April 1** Hungary applies for EU membership. **April 12** Russian Prime Minister Viktor Chernomyrdin announces that Russia plans to file for EU membership. **April 19** The Czech Republic and Slovakia announce their intention to apply for EU membership. **April–July** Old debate on whether to "deepen" the Union's institutions or to "widen" its membership resurfaces as the EU quarrels about its future direction. **June 11** Austrian voters approve joining the EU

*Source:* The European Community in the Nineties *(1992), with an update of subsequent events.*

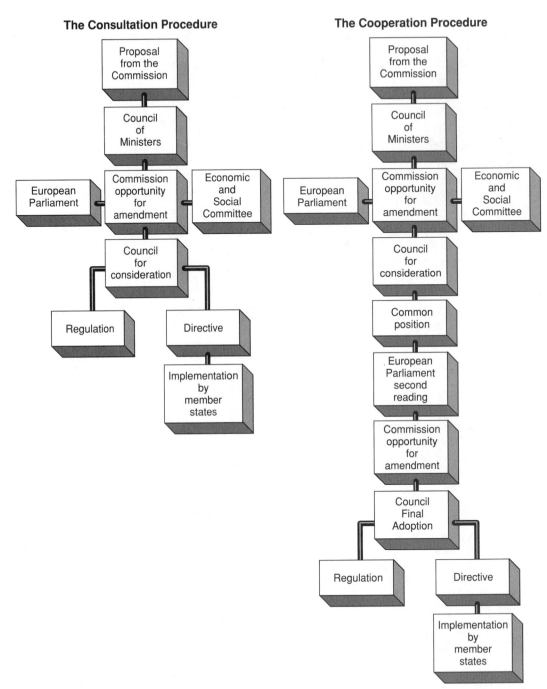

**The Consultation Procedure**

Proposal from the Commission

Council of Ministers

European Parliament — Commission opportunity for amendment — Economic and Social Committee

Council for consideration

Regulation

Directive

Implementation by member states

**The Cooperation Procedure**

Proposal from the Commission

Council of Ministers

European Parliament — Commission opportunity for amendment — Economic and Social Committee

Council for consideration

Common position

European Parliament second reading

Commission opportunity for amendment

Council Final Adoption

Regulation

Directive

Implementation by member states

**Figure 6.7** The European Union Legislative Process: Consultation and Cooperation Procedures
*Source:* Janet S. Zagorin (1990: 11).

part of the package—a single currency—remains the farthest out of reach. Although the ratified Maastricht Treaty makes monetary union and a single currency possible as early as 1997, the conditions EU countries must meet to qualify for it (low budget deficits, low inflation, minimal debt obligations, and the like) make implementation of the single currency unlikely in the near future.

### Supranationalism or Pooled Sovereignty?

How, then, is the European Union, a nonstate actor, best characterized? That is, how are its structures and decision-making procedures best described, in comparison with the United Nations and the panoply of other international organizations that now dot the global terrain?

The EU has the power to make some decisions binding on its national members without being subject to their individual approval. In this sense it is a *supranational* entity. That is, it is not an organization of or between states—an international organization—but one that goes beyond them toward creation of a new political entity that supersedes the individual countries that make it up—a supranational organization. This characterization mirrors the visionary hopes of the founding fathers of the various European institutions that make up the EU. They saw on the horizon a "United States of Europe" that would ameliorate the bitter antagonisms, particularly between France and Germany, that had periodically plunged Europe into destructive wars.

Although the EU incorporates some supranational elements, the term *pooled sovereignty* (Keohane and Hoffmann, 1991) better captures its essence, because states remain paramount in its institutional structures and decision-making procedures. Pooled sovereignty encapsulates a central property of the European Union as now configured. No transfer of authority to a central body has occurred. Instead, critical decisions are still made in the Council of Ministers, where states dominate, and most decisions of the EU still depend on national governments for implementation. Sovereignty is nonetheless shared, in the sense that decision-making responsibility is now spread among governments and between them and the EU's institutions.

Awareness of the fact that on some issues the EU members now decide by majority rule is critical to an understanding of pooled sovereignty. A major obstacle to effective decision making in the past was that most substantive proposals required unanimous approval. That rule (also used in other international institutions, such as the UN Security Council) enabled member states to protect their national interests as they alone defined them. France took advantage of this provision to thwart Community action in the late 1960s by simply refusing to send a minister to its meetings. The resulting impasse, called the "empty chair" crisis, spurred the development of new decision-making procedures.

Today, in a radical departure from past practices, and despite recurrent fears that a minority will block the will of the majority, the European Union requires only a qualified voting majority on most internal market decisions. Thus "unlike [typical] international organizations, the European [Union] as a whole has gained some share of states' sovereignty: The member states no longer have supremacy over all other authorities within their traditional territory, nor are they independent of outside authorities. Its institutions have some of the authority normally associated with institutions of sovereign governments: On certain issues individual states can no longer veto proposals before the Council [of Ministers]; members of the Commission are independent figures rather than instructed agents" (Keohane and Hoffmann, 1991).

The EU's essence is also described by its functions. On the one hand, it is so distinctly different from traditional international organizations as to be virtually in a class by itself. On the other, however, it is self-evidently not (yet) a rival of the nation-state as the dominant form of political organization, even in Europe. The principle of sovereignty as a defining legal attribute holds that the state alone has dominion over its internal and external affairs. In the EU's case, its authority in external affairs is greatest in matters of international trade and related welfare issues, is seriously circumscribed in political affairs, and has yet to fully develop in military affairs. That was nowhere more clear than during the 1991 Persian Gulf and 1992–1994 Bosnian wars, which demonstrated that the collectivity was both unwilling and ill-equipped to act quickly and decisively to protect the region's economic and security interests that were at stake. Its unresponsiveness during the Gulf crisis led Belgium's Foreign Minister Mark Eyskens to conclude that Europe "is an economic giant, a political dwarf, and a military worm."

### Europe: An Economic Giant

The historical development of the European Union is replete with evidence that military security was uppermost in the minds of those who sought to forge a new Europe out of the ashes of World War II. Still, it is on the economic front that the EU has scored its most dramatic successes. Today, if the new candidate members Austria, Finland, Norway, and Sweden join, the European Union will aggregate a combined gross national product of more than $6 trillion and a combined population of 375 million. This will make the European Union the largest, richest single consumer market in the world. Its total gross domestic product (GDP) (and population) exceed those of the members of the recently created North American Free Trade Agreement, its closest economic rival.

As noted above (see Box 6.2), an even larger EU is highly probable. This expansion builds on the precedents formerly established. The seven members of the European Free Trade Association (EFTA, created in 1960 as a counterpoint to the European Economic Community) in 1991 concluded a treaty with the EU, whose purpose was to create the world's largest trading area. The agreement anticipated a single European "common market" embracing nineteen countries and more than 385 million people. Although the treaty did not allow the EFTA countries (Austria, Finland, Iceland, Liechtenstein, Norway, Sweden, and Switzerland) power in setting EU trade policies, it set the stage for their participation in the benefits of the single market, which eliminates barriers to the movement of money, products, and workers within the

EU. In addition, the treaty eased the way for individual EFTA members to join the EU as full partners.

In March 1994, Austria, Finland, Norway, and Sweden (all members of EFTA) agreed to terms that will permit their membership to the EU in January 1995. This could easily presage a dramatic further enlargement of the European Union's membership and geographical boundaries. Not including the political fragments of the former Yugoslavia, as many as fifteen countries have positioned themselves as candidates for EU membership:

- Cyprus, Malta, Switzerland, and Turkey have applied to join.
- The Czech Republic, Hungary, Poland, and Slovakia have announced their intention to apply for membership.
- The Baltic states (Estonia, Latvia, and Lithuania) and Albania, Bulgaria, Romania, and Slovenia have declared that full EU membership beyond "Association" agreements is a goal by the year 2000 at the latest.

In addition, Russia and the other former members of the Soviet Union have voiced an interest in joining the EU. Thus a dramatically larger European Union may be in place by the turn of the century, especially if the intergovernmental conference scheduled for 1996 to reform the EU's institutions so they can accommodate the East Europeans' accession prove successful.[6]

However, the disintegrative forces of nationalism could prevent this progress toward an enlarged European Union. Expectations about the future became much less optimistic than they were in early 1993, when unanimous approval of the Maastricht Treaty was widely anticipated. Continuing resistance to the spirit and timetable of the accord has dispelled much of this optimism about achieving a true common market soon. Instead, the search has turned to finding a compromise agreement acceptable to all the members, whose enthusiasm has been reduced by a mid-1990s recession and by the continuing differences between its more industrialized northern members and those in southern Europe.

The reforms associated with the slogan "Europe 1992" promised to move the EU from a customs union, in which customs duties are eliminated, and from the free movement of workers, which the former EC also enjoyed, to a genuine common market, in which the frontiers between member states are completely abolished. A genuine common market would require the removal of countless inhibitions long apparent in Europe, including exchange controls and restraints on the free movement

---

[6] The EU is also linked to sixty-nine African, Caribbean, and Pacific (ACP) countries through the Lomé Convention, first signed in 1975 and renewed at periodic intervals since, most recently in 1989 for a ten-year period. The Lomé Convention provides the ACP countries' exports with duty-free access to the EU without the necessity of reciprocal concessions for EU exports to their economies (see also Chapter 8). It also sets up a commodity price stabilization scheme and provides a framework for the allocation of EU foreign aid to these countries. In addition to the ACP countries, the EU has agreements with several other countries throughout the Third World and has signed a cooperative agreement with ASEAN (the Association of South East Asian Nations) covering trade, economic, and development issues.

of goods (many of which are nontariff barriers to trade, discussed in Chapter 7). It also would require the harmonization of product standards (for example, uniform socket sizes for electrical appliances), variations in rules governing taxation and capital movements, regulations on transport standards (such as rules governing truckers' driving hours, rest periods, and the makeup of teams of drivers), and the like. Such inhibitions safeguard national interests and autonomy. By inference, their elimination would abjure ancient nationalistic rivalries and promote the further pooling of sovereignty between the EU's national members and the Union's institutions. It is in this context that the commitment to majority rule in the Council of Ministers rather than the previous common practice of consensus decision making takes on added meaning. Majority rule, reaffirmed in the Single European Act, restricts the ability of individual member states to veto key decisions with which they disagree.

Yet, as noted, nationalistic resistance has not abated. More than a few skeptics predict that the EU's ambitious plans will fail, despite the fact, however, that dramatic strides toward the economic objectives of Europe 1992 have been realized. National governments did successfully implement scores of directives issued by the Commission in social, environmental, economic, and monetary policy. But the hope that these steps could lead to the eventual political union of Europe has not been fulfilled.

The Single European Act formalized procedures for cooperation in foreign policy that had been operational for some time but never institutionalized, in the hope of creating a common political identity for the twelve countries that then held EC membership. At issue is whether that more ambitious goal is attainable.

## Europe: A Political Dwarf and a Military Worm?

Members of the European Union have sought since 1970 to coordinate their efforts in hopes of devising a common position on foreign policy issues (see Knudsen, 1984). The practice, known as European Political Cooperation (EPC), emerged on the sidelines of the regularized procedures of the European Union and in full recognition that the institutions of the EU would not enjoy the same powers in the domain of security as they did in the economic arena.

The amorphous character of EPC is acknowledged in the following description:

> In practical terms, the EPC essentially comes down to systematic and regular consultation and coordination among the people responsible for the definition, formulation, and implementation of national foreign policy, from the heads of governments to those responsible for regional departments in ministries of foreign affairs. This consultation process allows for defining common positions and organizing joint action as well as establishing a dialogue with other countries. The strength of the exercise derives from its synergistic development with the European . . . Community, since, if a country wants to stay in the Community, it must accept the consultation process of EPC and, on the other hand, no country in Europe can be part of EPC if it is not first a member of the . . . Community. (De Ruyt, 1989: 11)

The European Union enjoyed some success in framing community-wide positions on emergent foreign policy problems. Its efforts will doubtless intensify in the future, as the disappearance of the Soviet security threat, the need to rebuild Eastern Europe, and the growing threat of ethnic conflict increasingly push the EU to new levels of collaboration on political and security problems. The task will not be easy, however, as the foreign policy interests of the EU's member states seldom converge. Noteworthy in this respect is that Germany is now the undisputed European giant—a new geopolitical fact certain to produce occasions in which Germany's aims and interests will diverge from those of the other members of the Union. Moreover, Britain, which has long enjoyed a "special relationship" with the United States, traditionally has been unenthusiastic about releasing control to the continental European states. In 1993, however, British Prime Minister John Major pledged full support of the Maastricht Treaty, but domestic opposition to full EU policy coordination persists.

The then-EC's timid response to Iraq's invasion of Kuwait and the subsequent Persian Gulf War illustrated the obstacles to forging a common European foreign policy posture.

> The Gulf War illuminated, like a conflagration, every crack and fissure between the Community's members on foreign policy matters. On one side of a fault line that runs along the Rhine are countries who see themselves as playing a world, or a least an Atlantic, role, however diminished by their relative economic decline that role may be. On the other side are those who have eschewed military action other than for their own defense and who feel uneasy about heroic political postures. The different response of a France, a Britain, an Italy, and a Germany to the Gulf War suggest that political cooperation on foreign policy will be very hard to realize and that the convergence of interests between the members states has a long way to go before it will be feasible. (Williams, 1991: 174–175)

Commission President Jacques Delors lamented in March 1991 that the Gulf war revealed "the limitations of the European Community." Another example of those limitations occurred with its response to the civil war that erupted in Yugoslavia in 1991, an area of primary interest to the EU and the very tinderbox in which the First World War ignited. More than in any previous conflict, the Community played a central role in monitoring ceasefires and mediating between the central Yugoslav government and the Croates and Slovenes. Nonetheless, divisiveness not only between contending Croate, Serbian, and Muslim forces within the former Yugoslavia but also among members themselves postponed a concerted, effectual European response to the conflict. It was not until February 1994 that a military effort to stop the bloodletting was initiated. Instructively, that occurred through NATO and the United Nations, not the EU.

Complex issues also surround a future European security structure. For more than forty years the NATO alliance, under the leadership of the United States, provided Western Europe with protection from a possible Soviet invasion. At the same time, the members of the Atlantic alliance were consistently reluctant to involve NATO in "out of area" disputes, such as the one in the Persian Gulf. Without a Soviet security threat and the Cold War to consolidate the diverse members of the Union, the very existence of NATO became a subject of debate.

Yet, members of NATO have reaffirmed their commitment to the alliance. In 1993 they agreed, under U.S. pressure, to the general principle of participation in peacekeeping operations outside NATO's traditional sphere of influence. Recognizing that ethnic wars in the Balkans, southern and eastern Europe, and Russia could drag the neighboring members of NATO into a wider European war, NATO began in 1993 to prepare for defense against this source of future threat (at a time of great uncertainty in Russia). This was welcomed by Poland, Hungary, and the Czech Republic, which sought entry to NATO. Januscz Onyskiewicz, the Polish defense minister, summarized the aspiration in 1992 by noting, "NATO is seen by central European countries as a pillar of stability which can cast a shadow of stability on the East." Pleading for NATO's eastern expansion, Russian President Boris Yeltsin requested in 1993 that Russia also be placed on a fast track to join the Atlantic alliance, whose primary historical purpose ironically was to deter a massive Soviet invasion of Western Europe.

In a dramatic move in response to the changing European geostrategic land-scape, the NATO defense ministers endorsed a U.S. plan at the October 1993 summit in Travemuende, Germany that NATO offer limited military "partnerships" to virtually any European country that was interested, including Russia and the former Warsaw Pact states. U.S. Secretary of Defense Les Aspin described the partnership proposal as a first step toward possible—not automatic—NATO membership for the old Soviet-bloc states. The NATO defense ministers accepted this position, but stopped short of offering NATO's former East bloc full membership. The new partners will participate in NATO peacekeeping missions and crisis-management operations, but the plan does not guarantee the security of the new partners' bor-ders—a privilege NATO's existing members enjoy. This decision to restructure NATO thus redirects NATO in a fundamental way and shifts East–West security relationships in a fundamentally new direction (the Russian government joined NATO's Partnership for Peace program in April 1994). But the ultimate consequences of the Partnership for Peace for European security are uncertain. Initiated at a time when NATO is redefining its role on a continent in political transition, the new plan raises fears among its opponents that it could disrupt and disintegrate the alliance itself.

The nine-country European military pact known as the Western European Union (WEU) is another symbol of the EU's resolve to act in unity on defense problems. The WEU could eventually emerge as the military arm of the European Union and reduce European dependence on U.S. military might. Yet, while NATO exists, there is little urgency to develop closer military cooperation among the EU members.

Closer cooperation on foreign and national security policy is a prerequisite to the United States of Europe that the European Union's visionary founders once sought. National differences continue to make a unified EU foreign and defense policy an elusive goal. Even the form of a potential European government for a common Euro-pean citizenship remains a divisive, unresolved issue. Still, a single Europe remains a compelling idea for many Europeans. Consolidation could be in Europe's future. But so could disintegration and the resurrection of intra-European discord and even war (see Mearsheimer, 1990).

## Other Regional Organizations

In the decades following Europe's initiatives toward economic and political integration, a dozen or so regional economic schemes were created in various other parts of the world, notably among Third World states. Most sought to stimulate regional economic growth. Exemplary of the major Third World regional organizations are the following:

- Latin American Integration Association (LAIA), also known as Asociación Latinoamericana de Integración (ALADI), established in 1981 to promote freer regional trade. Its members are Argentina, Bolivia, Brazil, Chile, Colombia, Ecuador, Mexico, Paraguay, Peru, Uruguay, and Venezuela.

- Association of South East Asian Nations (ASEAN), established in 1967 to promote regional economic, social, and cultural cooperation. Its members are Brunei, Indonesia, Malaysia, the Philippines, Singapore, and Thailand; Papua New Guinea has observer status.

- Caribbean Community and Common Market (CARICOM), established in 1973 to promote economic development and integration. Its members are Antigua and Barbuda, the Bahamas, Barbados, Belize, Dominica, Grenada, Guyana, Jamaica, Montserrat, St. Kitts and Nevis, St. Lucia, St. Vincent and the Grenadines, and Trinidad and Tobago.

- Council of Arab Economic Unity (CAEU), established in 1964 from a 1957 accord to promote economic integration among Arab nations. Its members are Egypt, Iraq, Jordan, Kuwait, Libya, Mauritania, Palestine, Somalia, Sudan, Syria, United Arab Emirates, and Yemen.

- Economic Community of West African States (ECOWAS), established in 1975 to promote regional economic cooperation. Its members include Benin, Burkina, Cape Verde, the Gambia, Ghana, Guinea, Guinea-Bissau, Ivory Coast, Liberia, Mali, Mauritania, Niger, Nigeria, Senegal, Sierra Leone, and Togo.

- Southern African Development Coordination Conference (SADCC), established in 1980 to promote regional economic development and reduce dependence on South Africa. Its members are Angola, Botswana, Lesotho, Malawi, Mozambique, Namibia, Swaziland, Tanzania, Zambia, and Zimbabwe.

- South Asian Association for Regional Cooperation (SAARC), established in 1985 to promote economic, social, and cultural cooperation. Its members are Bangladesh, Bhutan, India, Maldives, Nepal, Pakistan, and Sri Lanka.

It is hazardous to generalize about organizations as widely divergent in membership and sometimes in purpose as this brief list suggests (for comparisons with other regional IGOs, see U.S. CIA, 1993: 392–418). None has achieved anything approaching the same level of economic integration and supranational institution building as accomplished in Western Europe. The particular reasons underlying the modest success of the attempts vary, of course (see Chapter 14), but they share a common denominator: the reluctance of national political leaders to make the kinds of choices that would undermine their governments' sovereignty. Still, these attempts at regional cooperation demonstrate states' belief that they are unable to resolve individually the problems that confront them collectively.

In this sense, the nation-state seems ill suited for both managing transnational policy problems and serving as an agent of organized cooperative efforts to do so. The effect of the collective problem-solving institutions on world politics is therefore problematic. That viewpoint is reinforced by another transnational manifestation of the transformation of world politics, the multinational corporation, to which we now turn.

## MULTINATIONAL CORPORATIONS . . . . . . . . . . . . . . . . . . . . . . . . . . .

Since World War II the role of the *multinational corporation* (MNC) has grown dramatically in scope and influence alongside the expansion of the world political economy. As a result, MNCs have provoked considerable discussion and often much animosity: Richard J. Barnet and Ronald E. Müller (1974) refer warily to the "global reach" of MNCs; George W. Ball (1971) coined the term *cosmocorp* to dramatize their increasing power; Robert Gilpin (1975) attributes U.S. power to them; Robert S. Walters and David H. Blake (1992) ask the often-posed question whether MNCs are a source of growth or underdevelopment for host countries; Robert Reich (1990) asserts that MNCs have lost their national identities; and the U.S. Office of Technology issued a 1993 report to Congress entitled "Multinationals and the National Interest: Playing By Different Rules," which warned that MNCs, "both domestic and foreign-based, increasingly [take actions that] diverge from" U.S. interests.

The proliferation and tremendous size of MNCs (or, alternatively, transnational corporations [TNCs]) add to the controversy surrounding their role and impact. In the early 1990s it was estimated that about 37,000 MNCs worldwide controlled assets in two or more countries and that these corporations were responsible for marketing roughly 90 percent of the developed countries' trade. By 1993 it was possible to identify the host-country location of some 170,000 affiliates. (*Host country* refers to the country where a corporation headquartered in another country conducts its business activities.) As the tentacles of the MNCs spread, their combined share of the world's gross domestic product has increased proportionately (UN Programme on Transnational Corporations, 1993: 99–100).

The MNCs' expansion could not have occurred on such a massive scale without the financial contribution of the world's international banks. Indeed, the transnational bank (TNB) has itself also become a major force in the world political economy. At the start of 1991 the combined equity and reserves of the world's forty largest banks exceeded $338 billion. Reflecting trends within the world political economy, two-fifths of the twenty-five largest TNBs were headquartered in Japan (*The Economist*, 1992: 52–53).

As MNCs have grown in scope and power, concern has understandably been raised about whether they undermine the ability of ostensibly sovereign nation-states to control their own economies and therefore their own fates. Is it possible that MNCs are shaking the very foundations of the present international system? Or is this question perhaps based on exaggerated expectations of the MNCs' influence and therefore unwarranted?

The benefits and costs ascribed to MNCs as they emerged to a position of prominence since World War II, summarized in Box 6.3, have been many and complex. Here we focus on four major issues: their global reach, their impact on host and home countries, their involvement in politics, and the question of their long-run impact on world politics.

## The Multinational Corporation's Global Reach and Economic Power

What is a multinational corporation? It is, typically, internationally involved, organized hierarchically, and centrally directed. Beyond this, definitions differ. Nonetheless, they all agree that it is a business enterprise organized in one society with activities in another growing out of direct investment abroad (as opposed to portfolio investment through shareholding). "A distinctive characteristic of the [multinational corporation] is its broader-than-national perspective with respect to the pursuit of highly specialized objectives through a central optimizing strategy across national boundaries" (Huntington, 1973). The modern MNC characteristically maintains an elaborate overseas network of affiliates to coordinate manufacturing and marketing globally.

The creation of the European Economic Community (EEC) in 1957 gave impetus to this form of business organization and the internationalization of production that it fostered. Because the original six EEC members hoped to create a common external tariff wall around their common market, it made economic sense for U.S. firms to build production facilities in Europe. In this way they could remain competitive by selling their wares as domestic rather than foreign products, with their additional tariff costs.[7] Ultimately, of course, "the primary drive behind the overseas expansion of today's giant corporations is maximization of corporate growth and the suppression of foreign as well as domestic competition" (Gilpin, 1975).[8]

---

[7] The reasons for direct investments overseas are more complex than this simplified explanation suggests. The *product-cycle theory* is one example. According to it, overseas expansion is essentially a defensive maneuver designed to forestall foreign competitors and hence to maintain the global competitiveness of domestically based industries. The theory views MNCs as having an edge in the initial stages of developing and producing a new product and then having to go abroad to protect export markets from the foreign competitors that naturally arise as the relevant technology becomes diffused or imitated. In the final phase of the product cycle, "production has become sufficiently routinized so that the comparative advantage shifts to relatively low-skilled, low-wage, and labor-intensive economies. This is now the case, for example, in textiles, electronic components, and footwear" (Gilpin, 1975; see also Vernon, 1971).

[8] As the world political economy has become more competitive, MNCs have had to adapt old investment strategies and develop new ones. As described by the UN's Centre on Transnational Corporations (1991), two sets of forces are operative. One includes those factors that are converging across national borders, the other those diffusing through the world political economy. The convergent forces—the regionalization of developed market economies, the convergence of discrete technologies, and the convergence of consumer tastes—mean "that transnational corporations now face larger, more homogenous markets and that the economic distance between countries, particularly developed countries, is narrowing. That implies new opportunities for the integration of international activities, along with greater returns stemming from those activities." On the other hand, the divergent forces—the diffusion of innovative activity and standardized technologies, the proliferation of production locations, and the diffusion of competition from domestic to international levels—mean "that the internationalization of activities is increasingly becoming a strategic imperative in a growing number of industries, rather than a profitable option open only to a handful of large firms" (Centre on Transnational Corporations, 1991).

## Box 6.3
### The Multinational Corporation in World Politics:
### A Balance Sheet of Claims and Criticisms

• • •

| Positive | Negative |
|---|---|
| • Increase the volume of world trade. | • Give rise to oligopolistic conglomerations that reduce competition and free enterprise. |
| • Assist the aggregation of investment capital that can fund development. | • Raise capital in host countries (thereby depriving local industries of investment capital) but export profits to home countries. |
| • Finance loans and service international debt. | • Breed debtors and make the poor dependent on those providing loans. |
| • Lobby for free trade and the removal of barriers to trade, such as tariffs. | • Limit the availability of commodities by monopolizing their production and controlling their distribution in the world marketplace. |
| • Underwrite research and development that allows technological innovation. | • Export technology ill suited to underdeveloped economies. |
| • Introduce and dispense advanced technology to less-developed countries. | • Inhibit the growth of infant industries and local technological expertise in less-developed countries while making Third World countries dependent on First World technology. |
| • Reduce the costs of goods by encouraging their production according to the principle of comparative advantage. | • Collude to create cartels that contribute to inflation. |
| • Generate employment. | • Curtail employment by driving labor competition from the market. |
| • Encourage the training of workers. | • Limit wages offered to workers. |

| POSITIVE | NEGATIVE |
|---|---|
| • Produce new goods and expand opportunities for their purchase through the internationalization of production. | • Limit the supply of raw materials available on international markets. |
| • Disseminate marketing expertise and mass-advertising methods worldwide. | • Erode traditional cultures and national differences, leaving in their place a homogenized world culture dominated by consumer-oriented values. |
| • Promote national revenue and economic growth; facilitate modernization of the less-developed countries. | • Widen the gap between the rich and poor countries. |
| • Generate income and wealth. | • Increase the wealth of local elites at the expense of the poor. |
| • Advocate peaceful relations between and among states in order to preserve an orderly environment conducive to trade and profits. | • Support and rationalize repressive regimes in the name of stability and order. |
| • Break down national barriers and accelerate the globalization of the international economy and culture and the rules that govern international commerce. | • Challenge national sovereignty and jeopardize the autonomy of the nation-state. |

Since the impetus given them by the EEC, the world's giant producing, trading, and servicing corporations have become the agents of the internationalization of production. Their economic and perhaps political importance in world politics is illustrated in Table 6.2, which ranks firms and countries by the size of their gross domestic product (GDP). The profile shows that 40 percent of the world's top one hundred economic entities are multinational corporations. Among the top fifty entries, multinationals account for only eleven, but in the next fifty, they account for thirty. Their financial clout thus rivals or exceeds that of many countries.

## Patterns of Foreign Direct Investment

Although the growth of multinational firms is a global phenomenon, the developed areas making up the First World are the location for more than 90 percent of transnational business enterprises (UN Programme on Transnational Corporations; 1993: 101). Historically, the United States has been the home country for the

### TABLE 6.2 COUNTRIES AND CORPORATIONS: A RANKING BY SIZE OF ANNUAL PRODUCT, 1990

| Rank | Country/Corporation | GDP/Sales ($ billions)[a] | Rank | Country/Corporation | GDP/Sales ($ billions) |
|---|---|---|---|---|---|
| 1 | United States | 5,446 | 51 | Venezuela | 51 |
| 2 | Japan | 3,141 | 52 | HITACHI (Japan) | 50.7 |
| 3 | Germany | 1,486 | 53 | Czechoslovakia | 49 |
| 4 | Soviet Union/Russia | 1,466 | 54 | FIAT (Italy) | 47.8 |
| 5 | France | 1,110 | 55 | SAMSUNG (South Korea) | 45 |
| 6 | Italy | 971 | 56 | PHILIP MORRIS (U.S.) | 44.3 |
| 7 | United Kingdom | 924 | 57 | Philippines | 44 |
| 8 | Canada | 543 | 58 | VOLKSWAGEN (Germany) | 43.7 |
| 9 | Spain | 429 | 59 | MATSUSHITA (Japan) | 43.5 |
| 10 | China | 416 | 60 | New Zealand | 43 |
| 11 | Brazil | 403 | 61 | Pakistan | 43 |
| 12 | India | 295 | 62 | Malaysia | 42 |
| 13 | Australia | 291 | 63 | ENI (Italy) | 41.8 |
| 14 | Netherlands | 259 | 64 | TEXACO (U.S.) | 41.2 |
| 15 | South Korea | 231 | 65 | Colombia | 41 |
| 16 | Switzerland | 219 | 66 | NISSAN MOTOR (Japan) | 40.2 |
| 17 | Mexico | 215 | 67 | UNILEVER (U.K., Netherlands) | 40 |
| 18 | Sweden | 202 | 68 | E.I. DU PONT DE NEMOURS (U.S.) | 39.9 |
| 19 | Taiwan | 157 | 69 | CHEVRON (U.S.) | 39.2 |
| 20 | Belgium | 155 | 70 | SIEMENS (Germany) | 39.2 |
| 21 | Austria | 147 | 71 | Sudan | 39 |
| 22 | Iran | 139 | 72 | Romania | 38 |
| 23 | Finland | 130 | | | |

| Rank | Name | Value | | Rank | Name | Value |
|---|---|---|---|---|---|---|
| 24 | **GENERAL MOTORS** (U.S.) | 125.1 | | 73 | Cuba | 34 |
| 25 | Denmark | 114 | | 74 | Singapore | 34 |
| 26 | **ROYAL DUTCH/SHELL** (U.K., Netherlands) | 107.2 | | 75 | **NESTLÉ** (Switzerland) | 33.3 |
| | | | | 76 | Ireland | 33 |
| 27 | **EXXON** (U.S.) | 105.9 | | 77 | **ELF AQUITAINE** (France) | 32.9 |
| 28 | Indonesia | 101 | | 78 | United Arab Emirates | 32 |
| 29 | **FORD MOTOR** (U.S.) | 98.3 | | 79 | Egypt | 31 |
| 30 | Norway | 98 | | 80 | Nigeria | 31 |
| 31 | Saudi Arabia | 92 | | 81 | **CHRYSLER** (U.S.) | 30.9 |
| 32 | Turkey | 92 | | 82 | **PHILIPS** (Netherlands) | 30.9 |
| 33 | South Africa | 90 | | 83 | **TOSHIBA** (Japan) | 30.1 |
| 34 | Thailand | 79 | | 84 | **RENAULT** (France) | 30 |
| 35 | Argentina | 76 | | 85 | Hungary | 30 |
| 36 | Yugoslavia | 73 | | 86 | **PEUGEOT** (France) | 29.3 |
| 37 | **IBM** (U.S.) | 69.0 | | 87 | **BASF** (Germany) | 29.3 |
| 38 | Hong Kong | 67 | | 88 | Libya | 29 |
| 39 | **TOYOTA MOTOR** (Japan) | 64.5 | | 89 | **AMOCO** (U.S.) | 28.3 |
| 40 | Poland | 64 | | 90 | **HOECHST** (Germany) | 27.8 |
| 41 | **IRI** (Italy) | 61.4 | | 91 | **ASEA BROWN BOVERI** (Switzerland) | 27.7 |
| 42 | Greece | 60 | | 92 | **BOEING** (U.S.) | 27.6 |
| 43 | **BRITISH PETROLEUM** (U.K.) | 59.6 | | 93 | **HONDA MOTOR** (Japan) | 27.1 |
| 44 | **MOBIL** (U.S.) | 58.7 | | 94 | **ALCATEL ALSTHOM** (France) | 26.5 |
| 45 | **GENERAL ELECTRIC** (U.S.) | 58.4 | | 95 | **BAYER** (Germany) | 26.1 |
| 46 | Iraq | 55 | | 96 | Chile | 26 |
| 47 | **DAIMLER-BENZ** (Germany) | 54.2 | | 97 | Peru | 25 |
| 48 | Algeria | 52 | | 98 | **NEC** (Japan) | 24.4 |
| 49 | Israel | 51 | | 99 | **PROCTER AND GAMBLE** (U.S.) | 26.5 |
| 50 | Portugal | 51 | | 100 | Kuwait | 24 |

*Source: The Economist* (1992: 22, 53).

[a] Figures for countries are based on gross domestic product (GDP); figures for corporations are based on annual sales.

largest proportion of parent companies, followed by Britain and Germany. This concentration is suggested by one measure that estimates that "nineteen of the world's largest corporations are U.S. MNCs, and these nineteen account for 45 percent of total sales and 62 percent of the total net income in the U.S." (Kefalas, 1992: 29). Hence, the pattern of foreign direct investment looks "bipolar" in nature, with the United States as one pole and a handful of European countries (acting independently) as the other.

By the end of the 1980s Japan also emerged as a significant participant in the global investment picture. By then, Japan, the United States, and an increasingly integrated European Community accounted for 80 percent of world investment (compared with 50 percent of world trade) (Centre on Transnational Corporations, 1991: 32). The developing countries' share of foreign direct investment grew in the 1970s, plummeted during the debt crisis of the 1980s (see Chapter 8), but rose again in the early 1990s. The First World is still the overwhelmingly dominant center of global investment activity, however, as it is the source of 97 percent of all investment outflows and the recipient of 25 percent of investment inflows (Mitchell, 1993: 168). (Foreign direct investment is measured in terms of stocks—investments already in place—and flows—investments that move across national boundaries.)

**A TRIPOLAR INVESTMENT WORLD**   The emergence in the 1980s of a "tripolar" investment world is one of the global economy's most significant investment developments (see Box 6.4). Wholly unexpected at the beginning of the decade, it grew out of the convergence of three important interrelated trends: the rapid integration of Europe, which made it possible to treat the EU as a single investment entity; the growing importance of Japan as a source of foreign direct investment; and the declining role of the United States as a source of investments and its corresponding rise as a host country.[9] By the early 1990s Europe was on a par with the United States in terms of the stock of foreign direct investment, while Japan had surpassed the United States as a major source of foreign investment in terms of flows, with much of its outward investment directed to the United States itself (Centre on Transnational Corporations, 1991).

Not only does the U.S.–Japan–EU triad dominate world investment patterns but, as the Japanese preference for the United States as an investment market suggests, the rate of growth of foreign direct investments within the triad itself has outpaced the growth of investments elsewhere. The patterns emerge from a corporate strategy in which each partner to the investment triad has sought to consolidate its own market hold and to gain a foothold in the other two regions. The preference pattern within

[9] Much of the foreign direct investment in the United States has taken the form of acquisitions by European and Canadian firms that already had some presence in the U.S. market and the building of new production facilities by Japan (a trade-replacing form of foreign direct investment) in an effort to establish itself in a market in which it had little presence before 1970. Japanese investments in banking and real estate, such as hotels and office buildings, have also been substantial. The rapid growth of foreign investments has been controversial, as many U.S. policymakers worry that the "selling of America" will make the United States unduly vulnerable to foreign influence (for an alternative viewpoint, see Kapstein, 1991–1992).

## Box 6.4
### Transnational Investment Highlights of the 1980s

• • •

- World foreign investment triples. Total global investment in stocks is now about $1.5 trillion. It was $550 billion in 1980.

- The United States emerges as the most important host country.

- The European Community emerges as the most important home region.

- Japan expands overseas investment sixfold during the decade.

- Developing countries' share in global flows declines. In spite of a near doubling of average annual flows to developing countries, their share fell from 25 percent to 17 percent.

- Latin America accounts for 80 percent of the declining share of developing countries' inflows. Some 40 percent of the inflows of large debtors was through debt-equity swaps.

- The Asian Newly Industrialized Countries emerge as increasingly important foreign investors.

- The least developed countries, including much of Africa, are marginal to global trends, now as before, in spite of sizable policy reforms.

*Source:* Transnationals *3 (March 1991: 2).*

the triad shows that the United States and the European Union prefer to invest with each other over Japan and that Japan prefers to invest in the United States compared with Europe (see Figure 6.8). The result is the development of a serious imbalance between Japan and its other First World partners, with the outward flow of stocks much greater than the inward flow. This imbalance parallels Japan's trade imbalance with other nations, notably the United States (see Chapter 7). Out of such imbalances, tougher competition among the three economic blocs as well as political struggle can be expected (Thurow, 1992).

**A Regionalized Investment World** As the market strategies of major corporations in the United States, Europe, and Japan pursued control of their existing markets and expansion in new regional markets, they also adopted strategies that sought "to build up regionally-integrated core networks of affiliates, clustered around their home country" (Centre on Transnational Corporations, 1991). Figure 6.9, which depicts the automobile operations of Toyota Motor Company in four ASEAN coun-

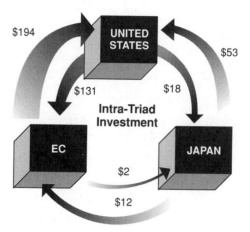

**Figure 6.8** The Magnitude and Pattern of Investments among Japan, the European Community, and the United States (1988 stocks in billions)
*Source: Transnationals* 3 (March 1991: 3).

tries, illustrates the kind of regionalized network in one industry that this plan has produced in many others.

As a result of this clustering strategy, foreign direct investment is now increasingly regional. Each of the principal host countries in Eastern Europe and the Third World receives the bulk of its funds from a single member of the investment triad, typically the one most proximate to it geographically. Countries in Central and South America tend to cluster around the United States; those in Eastern Europe tend to cluster around the EU; and those in East and Southeast Asia around Japan (see Figure 6.10). The effect is to reinforce—perhaps cause—the growing regionalization of the world political economy across a range of dimensions not only in investment but also in production and trade (see especially Chapter 7).

## Impact on Home and Host Nations

In addition to its global reach, the domestic impact of the MNC on both home and host countries is a matter of widespread concern.

The MNCs allegedly exercise their power at great cost to their home or parent countries. Charges against them include shifting productive facilities abroad to avoid labor unions' demands for higher wages. According to this view, because capital is more mobile than labor, the practice of exporting production from industrially advanced countries to industrially backward countries, where labor is cheap and unions weak or nonexistent, is the cause of structural unemployment in the advanced countries. In contrast, others contend that MNCs help reduce balance-of-payments deficits, create new employment opportunities, and promote competition in both domestic and foreign markets.

If home countries have incurred both costs and benefits, have host countries

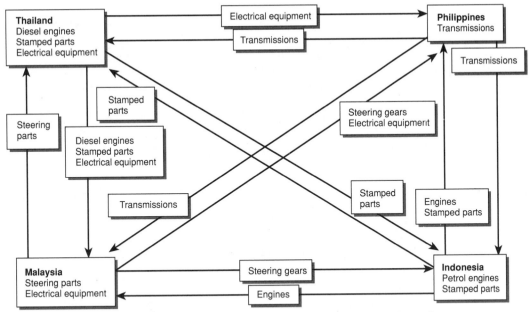

**Figure 6.9**  Automobile Operations of Toyota in Four ASEAN Countries
*Source:* Centre on Transnational Corporations (1991: 62).

shared similar experiences? "As privileged organizations," David E. Apter and Louis W. Goodman (1976) note, MNCs "hold a unique position among growth-inducing institutions able to affect the direction of development." This implies that MNCs may promote development as much as they impede it. It is nonetheless true that Third World countries have historically viewed multinationals with considerable and often emotionally charged suspicion. Although this viewpoint has changed noticeably in recent years—Third World countries now compete with one another to attract foreign direct investment—MNCs are comparatively more important to the developing countries' overall GNP and to their most advanced economic sectors than they are to the developed states' economies. We will therefore return in Chapter 8 to consider further the role of MNCs as viewed by developing countries. Here it is sufficient simply to note that the question of what weight to assign to the costs and benefits of MNCs has yielded different answers in different times and places, but none that are conclusive.

## Politics and Multinational Corporations

Another controversy about the role of MNCs as nonstate actors concerns their involvement in the domestic political affairs of the local or host countries. Increasingly, this concern has extended to MNCs' involvement in the domestic politics of their home countries, where they actively lobby home governments for policies that will enhance

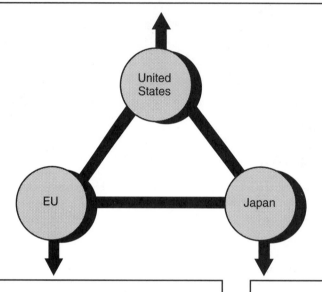

| Latin America | | Asia and the Pacific | Africa and West Asia |
|---|---|---|---|
| Argentina | El Salvador | Bangladesh | Ghana |
| Bolivia | Honduras | India | Nigeria |
| Chile | Mexico | Pakistan | Saudi Arabia |
| Colombia | Panama | Philippines | |
| Dominican Republic | Peru | Taiwan Province of China | |
| Ecuador | Venezuela | Papua New Guinea | |

| Central and Eastern Europe | Africa and West Asia | Asia and the Pacific |
|---|---|---|
| Russian Federation | Ghana | Hong Kong |
| Czechoslovakia | Kenya | Malaysia |
| Hungary | Morocco | Republic of Korea |
| Poland | Nigeria | Singapore |
| Slovenia | Tunisia | Sri Lanka |
| Yugoslavia | Zambia | Taiwan Province of China |
| | Jordan | Thailand |
| | | Fiji |

| Latin America | Asia and the Pacific |
|---|---|
| Brazil | Bangladesh |
| Paraguay | India |
| Uruguay | Sri Lanka |

**Figure 6.10**  Foreign Investment Clusters of Triad Members (Japan, the European Union, and the United States)
*Source:* UNCTAD (1993), as reported in United Nations Programme on Transnational Corporations (1993: 119).

the profitability of their business activities abroad. And both host and home governments in turn have sometimes used MNCs as instruments in their foreign policies.

Perhaps the most notorious instance of an MNC's intervention in the politics of a host state occurred in Chile in the early 1970s. There, International Telephone and Telegraph (ITT) tried to protect its interests in the profitable Chiltelco telephone company by seeking to prevent the election of marxist-oriented Salvador Allende as president and by seeking his later overthrow. ITT's efforts to undermine Allende included giving monetary support to his political opponents and, once elected, pressuring the U.S. government to disrupt the Chilean economy. The result was Allende's overthrow by a military dictatorship.

There are other instances in which MNCs have engaged in practices embarrassing to home countries—as when the West German government found that a German firm had sold mustard-gas manufacturing equipment to Libya—or that seemed to defy them—as when the French subsidiary of Dresser Industries of Dallas, Texas, exported energy technology to the Soviet Union in defiance of an effort by the U.S. government to thwart it.

MNCs also often lobby their home governments for policies that back the MNCs in disputes with host governments, though they are not always successful in these endeavors (see Spiegel, 1985). The U.S. stipulation made in the early 1970s that foreign aid would be cut off from any country that nationalized U.S. overseas investments without just compensation is exemplary of the tendency for home-state governments to support their own MNCs' overseas activities.

More broadly, MNCs have assisted in promoting the post–World War II Liberal International Economic Order (LIEO) and have helped to shape the specific U.S. policies regarding trade and taxation that contributed to the free-trade regime's effectiveness. In this sense, MNCs have been active participants in the process by which governments reach agreements on rules governing transactions in the global marketplace.

However, at another level MNCs headquartered in one country have sometimes worked at cross-purposes with the parent government by serving the wishes of the host government. During the oil crisis of 1973–1974, for example, the governments of the Organization of Petroleum Exporting Countries (OPEC) effectively used the multinational oil companies to achieve OPEC's goal of using oil as a political weapon against the West. The corporations reaped huge profits even though their home countries suffered greatly.

The political role of the MNC in home and host countries remains ambiguous. Perhaps the conclusion that best characterizes its impact is one that pictures the MNC as "a stimulant to the further extension of state power in the economic realm" (Gilpin, 1985) rather than as a potential successor to the sovereign nation-state.

Only the state can defend corporate interests in international negotiations over trade, investment, and market access. Agreements over such things as airline routes, the opening of banking establishments, and the right to sell insurance are not decided by corporate actors who gather around a table; they are determined by diplomats and bureaucrats.

Corporations must turn to governments when they have interests to protect or advance. (Kapstein, 1991–1992: 56; see also Huntington, 1973; Waltz, 1970)

Still, the blurring of the boundaries between internal and external affairs adds potency to the political role that MNCs unavoidably play as actors at the intersection of foreign and domestic policy.

## Controlling Multinational Corporations

Multinationals often make many kinds of decisions over which national political leaders have little control. Thus, a fourth significant question is whether MNCs' influence will lead to the erosion of the international system's major structural foundation—the principle that the nation-state alone is sovereign.

The question of control is especially pertinent to Third World countries, but it is not confined to them. As one senior U.S. foreign policy official declared at the time of the Dresser Industries controversy, "Basically we're in an impossible situation. You don't want to get rid of the advantages of this international economic system, but if you try to exercise control for foreign policy reasons, you cut across sovereign frontiers."

Bemoaning the suspicion that multinationals "steal" U.S. technology and fail to "generate or retain wealth and quality jobs within [U.S.] borders," the U.S. Office of Technology Assessment in 1993 called for new rules that "balance interests . . . between nations and firms" (Dentzer, 1993). The MNCs' complex patterns of ownership and licensing arrangements make the problem intractable because it is often difficult to equate the MNCs' interests with particular national jurisdictions (see Reich, 1990). General Electric, for example, one of the most "American" of all U.S. MNCs, has granted licenses for the production of energy-related equipment to Nuovo Pignone of Italy, Mitsubishi and Hitachi of Japan, Mannessmann and AEG Telefunken of West Germany, John Brown Engineering of Great Britain, and Thomassen Holland of the Netherlands (U.S. Office of Technology Assessment, 1981). Controlling such a complex pattern of interrelationships, joint ventures, and shared ownership for any particular national purpose is nearly impossible. "The internationalization of the economy—which the U.S. spearheaded—has rendered obsolete old ideas of economic warfare," Richard J. Barnet, coauthor of *Global Reach*, observed in 1982. "You can't find targets any more, and if you aim at a target you often find it's yourself."

The multinationals' potential long-run influence in the borderless international market is depicted in *Global Reach:*

The global corporation is the most powerful human organization yet devised for colonizing the future. By scanning the entire planet for opportunities, by shifting its resources from industry to industry and country to country, and by keeping its overriding goal simple—worldwide profit maximization—it has become an institution of unique power. The World Managers are the first to have developed a plausible model for the future that is global. . . . In making business decisions today they are creating a politics for the next generation. (Barnet and Müller, 1974: 363)

Whether the corporate visionaries who manage the MNCs will help create a more prosperous, peaceful, and just world—as free-trade liberal theorists hope, and others, whose interests are threatened by a new world political economy, fear—is questionable. "For some, the global corporation holds the promise of lifting mankind out of poverty and bringing the good life to everyone. For others, these corporations have become a law unto themselves; they are miniempires which exploit all for the benefit of a few" (Gilpin, 1975).

Speculation about the impact of multinational corporations on world politics has today receded in political elites' rhetoric from the high level that prevailed during the 1960s and 1970s when the MNCs' growing power was first discovered. The existence of multinational corporations "has become a fact of life. They are now permanent—and influential—players in the international arena" (Spero, 1990). Still, the challenge they pose to the existing international system of nation-states should not be taken lightly. The United Nations Commission on Transnational Corporations forcefully poses the issue:

> Over the past decade [the 1980s], a growing number of international norms has produced a body of international soft law on transnational corporations; it is, however, limited in scope and does not adequately match the globalization of business activity. In an era of globalization, it is increasingly difficult to distinguish between national and international issues of governance. The capacity of governments to manage their economies and achieve national objectives in areas ranging from fiscal policy to environmental control is being strained by the growing importance of transnational corporations in the international economy. Many issues related to corporate responsibility cannot be resolved satisfactorily in the context of a single national legal regime. . . . The effective and stable governance of international economic relations requires not only the unleashing of market forces and private enterprise, but also effective international instruments to deal with the broad range of issues related to the globalization of business activity—problems that are beyond the capacity of national regimes of governance. (Commission on Transnational Corporations, 1991: 33)

To complete the profile of nonstate actors in world affairs, we need to consider a third type, which, alongside international organizations and multinational corporations, also is becoming increasingly active on the world stage: ethnonational movements. These, too, challenge the supremacy and sovereignty of the nation-state.

## ETHNONATIONAL MOVEMENTS

As we have seen, the image of the omnipotent nation-state and its corollary concept—that of governments as sovereign and autonomous rulers of united nations—is not very satisfactory. It exaggerates the extent to which the state resembles a unitary actor, as realists often ask us to picture it. In truth, the "billard ball" metaphor is very misleading, perhaps inaccurate. The shell of this imaginary unit is highly penetrated by what other international actors do. Moreover, the shell implies a capacity to perform that in practice is not always evident. There are many reasons to question the nation-states' ability to provide "for the common defense and the general welfare" that governments proclaim as their purpose. "The nation-state," sociologist Daniel Bell (1987) bemoans, "is becoming too small for the big problems of life, and too big for the small problems of life."

## Nationalism and Nationality

Several aspects of today's changing world serve to undermine confidence in the usefulness and potency of the nation-state, which nonetheless certainly remains the most powerful actor in world affairs. Noteworthy among these is the recent rediscovery of the salience of nationalism and nationality as potent cultural factors in international relations. Many people do not pledge their primary allegiance to the state and government that rules them. Rather, they think of themselves primarily as members of their nationality and the civilization and cultural tradition it represents. They believe themselves to be members of their nationality first and of their state only secondarily. Many nationalists are not patriotic worshipers of the territorial state that governs their homeland; their primary loyalty and identification are with their own ethnonational group.

For today's world, acknowledgment of the importance of *ethnic nationalism* as a force on the world's stage correspondingly reduces the significance of the nation-state. States are divided, not united; divisions exist in the cultural, religious, ethnic, and linguistic communities within almost all of today's nearly 190 independent countries (relatively homogeneous Japan is a conspicuous exception). These divisions reduce the state's cohesion, unity, and capacity for collective action abroad. The lack of solidarity within states renders dubious the appropriateness of thinking of states as independent, singular actors in world affairs.

### The Fourth World

The pervasiveness of ethnic nations alongside nation-states is so prevalent that many feel the indigenous voice of the people behind the ethnonationalist movements they lead must be given its due account (Wilmer, 1993). Their shout is now loud, and aroused nationalists are fighting back across the globe in rebellion against the injustice, misery, and prejudice they perceive the nation-state to have perpetuated against them. This segment of global society is conventionally referred to as the *Fourth World* to heighten awareness of many "native" or "tribal" indigenous peoples within most countries, the poverty and deprivation that confronts them, the state's occupation of the land from which they originate, and the methods these indigenous national movements are pursuing.

Fourth World activities and liberation movements are present in many countries throughout the globe (see Table 6.3). Every nationality, it appears, craves a state of its own. In part, this quest is inspired by and a reaction to the evidence that between 1960 and 1983, the state was responsible for the deaths of more than four million indigenous people (Ryser, 1985: 307). In other areas, cold wars below the threshold of overt armed violence between the state and its ethnonational groups are heated and

| TABLE 6.3 STATES AND INDIGENOUS NATIONS AT WAR | |
|---|---|
| **States** | **Indigenous Nations** |
| Nicaragua and Honduras | Miskito, Sumo, and Rama |
| El Salvador | Pipil |
| Guatemala and Mexico | Mayan, Zapotec, and Mixe |
| Indonesia | Timorese, Papuans, and Moluccans |
| Philippines | Kalinga, Bontoc, Morazan, and Sabah |
| India | Naga, Sikhs, Misoram, and Kachins |
| Sri Lanka | Tamil |
| Brazil | Yananomu |
| Malaysia | Sarawak and Sabah |
| Lebanon | Maronites, Palestinians |
| South Africa | Ovimbundu, Harrah (Namibia), and Bantu |
| Syria, Iraq, Iran, Turkey, and Russia | Kurds |
| Spain | Basques |
| Italy | Corsicans and Sardinians |
| Israel | Palestinians |
| Iran and Pakistan | Baluchis |
| Turkey | Armenians |
| Afganistan and Pakistan | Pathans |
| Afganistan and Russia | Pathans, Tadziks, and Turkmen |
| Burma and Thailand | Karens |
| Ethiopia | Erirtrea, Tigre, Somalis, Hara, and Wollo |
| Morocco and Mauritania | POLISARIO, a political movement (West Sahara) |

*Source:* Rudolph Ryser (1985: 307).

appear to be growing. Examples of protracted conflicts between states and indigenous peoples are the continuing confrontations between the U.S. government and the Quinalt, Hope, Lakota, Iroquois, Inuit, and Aleute; China and the Tibetians and Taiwanese; Chile and the Mapuche; and Nigeria and the Yoruba, Iho, and Ibibo (Ryser, 1985). Table 6.3 shows where active hostilities between indigenous nations and the state are occurring. These "Fourth World Wars" are spread among every region of the globe.

## Ethnonational Challengers to the State

The multifarious ethnonational challengers to the state defy characterization. They are too diverse, as the distinctions between indigenous peoples and ethnic minorities are hard to draw. This makes counting their numbers difficult. However, a rough estimate can be provided by observing linguistic similarity. And in this respect, the number of ethnolinguistic divisions that separate cultures is huge. "Measured by spoken languages, the single best indicator of a distinct culture, all the world's people belong to 6,000 cultures; 4,000–5,000 of these are indigenous ones. Of the 5.5 billion humans on the planet, some 190 to 625 million are indigenous people" (Durning, 1993: 81).

Still, this indicator may not be telling, since the belief systems and backgrounds that animate the people in ethnonational movements are varied and often overlapping. Beyond language, these movements are based on myriad combinations of cultural, racial, and religious orientations. Hence it is extremely difficult to classify and count the numerous variety of national movements or *nonstate nations* (Bertelsen, 1977) struggling for independence and statehood against the states that dominate them. These "quasi-states" are relentlessly different (Jackson, 1990).

One characteristic is not ambiguous: Ethnonational movements transcend the existing borders that separate the nearly 190 sovereign states recognized as independent under the rules of international law. They are spread not only within these existing boundaries but across them. World or transnational cultures recognize no international borders (see Map 6.1).

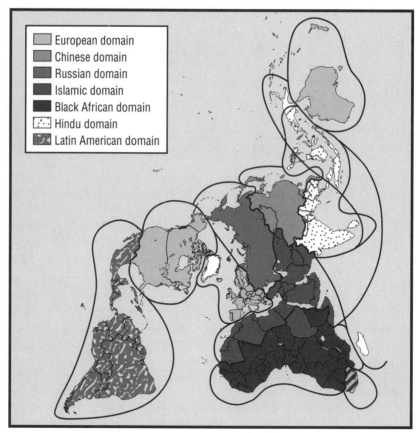

**Map 6.1**  The World's Great Cultural Domains and Divisions
*Source: Gérard Challiard and Jean-Pierre Rageau (1992:37).*

## Cultural Clash, National Disintegration, and Global Instability

Several consequences of mobilized ethnonational movements for world affairs are evident. First, the existence of these cultural identities threaten the preservation of existing states. The simultaneous presence of uniting and disuniting states promises to change the ways the earth's territorial boundaries are drawn by future cartographers. When people identify with the culture of their nationality more intensely than they do with their country, separatist revolts by peoples struggling for self-determination can be expected. Sometimes this can culminate in the peaceful separation of formerly united states, as happened in the so-called "velvet divorce" when, following a referendum at the stroke of midnight on December 31, 1992, Czechoslovakia split into the independent states of the Czech Republic and the Slovak Republic. Or, perhaps more frequently, aroused nationalism can lead to the violent effort to separate nationalities into independent countries. The bloody ethnic warfare that has wracked the former Yugoslavia since June 1991 is symptomatic of this consequence, which tragically included by both the Serbs and Croates atrocities and "ethnic cleansing"—the use of terror, destruction, and murder to force out the rival nationality. The tribal warfare in Somalia and Rwanda also epitomize the horror that results when ancient hatreds spill into warfare.

These divisions of states into separate fragments along ethnic, cultural, or religious lines are different from the political partitions that resulted in the division of Korea, Vietnam, Germany, and China into separate states. States, in short, are inherently fragile because nearly all are weak coalitions of multiple nationalities that can easily fragment (see Chatterjee, 1993). Consider the share of indigenous populations of selected countries: Bolivia, 70 percent; Peru, 40 percent; Mexico, 12 percent; the Philippines, 9 percent; Canada, 4 percent (Durning, 1993: 83). Cultural diversity is also captured by the number of distinct languages spoken in "megadiversity" countries, of which Indonesia's 670, Nigeria's 410, India's 380, Australia's 250, and Brazil's 210 are exceptional examples (Durning, 1993: 86). To speak of these states as "united" is thus to write pure fiction.

This ethnonational source of weakness of multicultural states constitutes a potential long-term threat to the state's survival should long-standing antagonisms within them escalate to intolerance and separatist revolts. The aspiration of ethnonational groups to a national homeland can only be fulfilled through the fragmentation of the territorial integrity of existing states. If these movements get their way, the balkanizing of the world will result.

The long-term conflict between the Palestine Liberation Organization (PLO) and the state of Israel illustrates the potential for two kinds of processes to produce new states. For four decades the PLO nation sought by every means available, including terrorism and war, to create a state from the territories claimed and controlled by Israel. That search destroyed life but failed to create independence. Then, through dialogue and negotiation, another process was pursued. It produced a comprehensive peace accord in September 1993. Israel and Jordan agreed to permit the Palestinians to form a government and create a new state in the West Bank and Gaza territory returned to them by Israel. The accord symbolizes the possiblity for nationalities to become independent states through discussion and compromise rather than force. This conceivably could serve as a model for other ethnonational independence movements to emulate.

There exists another consequence that could result from the existence of many cultural divisions within and transcendant across the countries of the world. It bodes disruption, too, even if a more conciliatory outcome could unfold. This is the possibility that the future will be darkened by the outbreak of clashes between world civilizations or transnational cultures every bit as destabilizing and destructive as was the East–West ideological clash during the Cold War (Huntington, 1993). According to this proposition, ethnonational conflicts between cultures that transcend state borders pose an insurmountable fissure in world affairs. Cultural hatred, fed by implicit racism and religious intolerance, could spawn a new era of conflict comparable to the Crusades, when Western Christianity and Islam engaged in a war to extinguish the influence of the other. Without the Cold War stalemate to hold such cultural conflicts in check, so this grim scenario holds, states will be powerless to suppress these ancient rivalries and animosities. The ethnic wars in 1993 between Armenian Christians and Muslim Azerbaijans, which pulled Russia, Turkey, and Iran perilously close to combat, and the separatist revolt in Georgia to create an independent Muslim state of Abkazia could be portents of future ethnic turmoil crossing borders in many other places.

## Ethnocentrism and Global Instability

Cultural conflict stems from the inherent *ethnocentrism* underlying nationalism: the belief that one's nationality is special and superior and that others are secondary and inferior. Ethnocentrism breeds intercultural conflict. Nationalists easily condone the marginalization and oppression of "outside" nationalities. Ethnocentric peoples are prone to reject conciliation and compromise with—indeed, tolerance of—national differences. This barrier to cooperation, and its conflict-generating consequences, were highly evident in the crumbling peace talks and escalating warfare in Bosnia in 1993, as concessions among the Serb, Croat, and Muslim populations proved impossible to negotiate among these ethnocentric groups.

If ethnonationalist values spread and intensify throughout the globe, cultural conflict will too. The forces of disunion and disintegration could overwhelm the power of the state, which previously has bound diverse nationalities into a common purpose. To the extent that cultural conflict within and between ethnically disunited and divided states becomes the primary axis on which post–Cold War world politics revolves, the power and independence of the state can be expected to decline exponentially.

The drive of ethnonationalism, by reinvigorating ancient cultural and ethnic animosities within the state and between existing states, could presage a new era of global instability for which the traditional nation-state is unprepared. The perils should not be underestimated. As Russian Foreign Minister Andrei V. Kozyrev warned in September 1993 in an address before the United Nations, the threat of ethnic violence today is "no less serious than the threat of nuclear war was yesterday."

The existence of between 3,000 and 5,000 active national separatist movements in the world (Nietschmann, 1991) punctuates the potential peril.

Fueled by the rising global interdependence that at the same time makes "national borders porous from without" (Barber, 1992), the era in which the state reigned supreme in world politics could slowly be coming to an end. On the horizon is a system in which new units, such as ethnocultural groups, could assume relatively greater importance.

## NONSTATE ACTORS AND THE TRANSFORMATION OF WORLD POLITICS . . . . . . . . . . . . . . . . . . . . . . . . . . . . . .

Because international organizations, multinational corporations, and ethnonational movements challenge the nation-state's authority, they also challenge the very pillars on which the contemporary state system has been built.

States will not disappear quickly, however. In the meantime, the rise and the prodigious growth of different types of nonstate actors call into question the traditional realist state-centric theory of international politics, which holds that nation-states are the primary actors on the world stage. Because the state has "purposes and power," according to this view, it "is the basic unit of action; its main agents are the diplomat and soldier. The interplay of governmental politics yields the pattern of behavior that students of international politics attempt to understand and that practitioners attempt to adjust or to control" (Nye and Keohane, 1971).

Clearly such a view no longer adequately depicts the complexity of world politics. The nonstate actors discussed in this chapter—IGOs, NGOs, MNCs, and ethnonational groups—are often the key participants in the conduct of contemporary international relations regularly occurring in such diverse areas as the law of the sea, the global monetary and trade systems, the global food system, and nationalities' resistance to state regulation.

Moving from the level of cooperative international interactions to the level of foreign policy making within nation-states, an adequate conceptualization of contemporary world politics must acknowledge the influence of nonstate actors on governments' ability to formulate public policy and on the ties among them. Nonstate actors help build and broaden the foreign policy agendas of national decision makers by serving as transmission belts through which one country's policies become sensitive to another's (Keohane and Nye, 1975, 1989). At the same time, some nonstate actors are capable of pursuing their interests largely outside the direct control of nation-states while simultaneously involving governments in particular problems as a result of their activities (Nye and Keohane, 1971; Keohane and Nye, 1989).

These reflections invite this conclusion:

> There has developed on the global level an interconnected and intensified . . . complex of relationships . . . in which demands are articulated and processed through formal as well as informal channels, governmental as well as non-governmental organizations, national as well as international and supranational institutions. These processes of interaction are interdependent . . . and they perform a variety of functions, most prominently those of

welfare and security. They are the structures through which governments perform a variety of functions; they are the way in which state and society seek to arrange their domestic and foreign environment. (Hanrieder, 1978: 1278)

The transformation of world politics manifests itself in these complex, interdependent relationships among diverse national, transnational, and subnational actors. This by no means indicates that the nation-state is dead, however. Governments still retain the capacity to influence, indeed to shape, transnational interactions. It is not accidental that matters of national security are confined largely to government-to-government interactions.

Thus it is important not to exaggerate the impact of nonstate actors on world politics. Nation-states retain a (near) monopoly on the use of coercive force in the international system, and they retain an enormous capacity to shape global and state welfare. The nation-state cannot be lightly dismissed, therefore; it still molds the activities of nonstate actors more than its behavior is molded by them. Moreover, it "may be anachronistic, but we have yet to develop an alternative form of societal organization that is able to provide its members with both wealth and power" (Kapstein, 1991–1992). Hence it would be premature to abandon the focus on the nation-state in international politics, just as it would be inadequate to regard the state as the only relevant actor or the sole determinant of its fate.

## SUGGESTED READINGS

Barnet, Richard J., and Ronald E. Müller. *Global Reach: The Power of the Multinational Corporations.* New York: Simon & Schuster, 1974.

Connor, Walker. *Ethnonationalism: The Quest for Understanding.* Princeton, N.J.: Princeton University Press, 1994.

Feld, Werner J., Robert S. Jordan, with Leon Hurwitz. *International Organizations: A Comparative Approach,* 3rd ed. Westport, Conn.: Greenwood, 1994.

Gurr, Ted Robert, and Barbara Harff. *Ethnic Conflict in World Politics.* Boulder, Colo.: Westview Press, 1994.

Huntington, Samuel P. "The Clash of Civilization," *Foreign Affairs* 72 (Summer 1993): 22–49.

Palan, Rowan, and Barry Gills. *Transcending the State–Global Divide: The Neostructuralist Agenda in International Relations.* Boulder, Colo: Lynne Rienner, 1994.

Riggs, Robert E., and Jack C. Plano. *The United Nations: International Organization and World Politics,* 2nd ed. Belmont, Calif.: Wadsworth, 1994.

Rochester, J. Martin. *Waiting for the Millennium: The United Nations and the Future of World Order.* Columbia: University of South Carolina Press, 1993.

Taylor, Paul. *International Organization in the Modern World: The Regional and Global Process.* London: Pinter Publishers, 1993.

Treverton, Gregory F., ed. *The Shape of the New Europe.* New York: The Council on Foreign Relations Press, 1992.

UNCTAD Programme on Transnational Corporations. *World Investment Report 1993: Transnational Corporations and Integrated International Production.* New York: United Nations, 1993.

Wilmer, Franke. *The Indigenous Voice in World Politics.* Newbury Park, Calif.: Sage, 1993.

# Part III

# Promoting the General Welfare

· · ·

# CHAPTER 7

• • •

# THE INTERNATIONAL POLITICAL ECONOMY: THE RICH COUNTRIES' PURSUIT OF PROSPERITY

• • •

*[The United States must] reach out and break down the barriers of trade, because we know a rich country can only create jobs through increasing the volume of trade.*

Bill Clinton,
U.S. President, 1993

*[By endorsing the GATT trade liberalization pact] the world has chosen openess and cooperation instead of uncertainty and conflict. I am convinced that today will be seen as a defining moment in modern economic and political history.*

Peter Sutherland,
GATT Director-General, 1993

"To provide for the common defense [and] to promote the general welfare." These words in the Preamble to the U.S. Constitution speak to universal pursuits. They define the basic goals of all states. Every country defines defense from aggression abroad (and from within—as noted by the words in the U.S. Constitution to "insure domestic tranquility") as a basic purpose. All governments also declare that their goal is to enhance the welfare of their populations.

Until recently, the first goal usually was placed above the second. The reason was not hard to find. Looking at the past history of international relations, leaders had powerful reasons to put national defense ahead of national wealth. That history reminded them of the dangers they face both from aggression abroad and at home. Because of national insecurities, promoting for the general welfare was often pursued *after* preparations for defense were believed sufficient.

Many analysts now believe that economic competition will replace power politics as the dominant concern in post–Cold War international politics and that this will catapult "promoting for the general welfare" to the top in the preoccupations of governments. "Except in those unfortunate parts of the world where armed confrontations or civil strife persist for purely regional or internal reasons," observes strategic

• • •

analyst Edward N. Luttwak (1990), in the wake of the Cold War "everyone, it appears, now agrees that the methods of commerce are displacing military methods—with disposable capital in lieu of firepower, civilian innovation in lieu of military-technical advancement, and market penetration in lieu of garrisons and bases." The economic foundations of national security thus are now receiving primary emphasis (see Sandholtz et al., 1992) as trade and economic policy are taking precedence over security and foreign policy (Judis, 1993b).

However, although popular, Luttwak continues, this new consensus about priorities ignores how inextricably linked politics and economics are. "The international scene is still primarily occupied by states and blocs of states that extract revenues, regulate economic as well as other activities for various purposes, pay out benefits, offer services, provide infrastructures, and—of increasing importance—finance or otherwise sponsor the development of new technologies and new products." Thus politics—the exercise of power—determines economics—the distribution of material values.

The term *political economy* highlights the intersection of politics and economics and its prolonged influence on world politics. A combination of political and economic considerations gave rise to the nation-state more than three centuries ago and has helped to shape the patterns of dominance and dependence that have characterized relations between rich and poor states ever since. The relevance of the term today is captured in the extensive interdependent relationships between states that knit national and global welfare into a single tapestry.

Interdependence has doubtless produced benefits, but it has not been without costs. For example, as realist advocates of mercantilist strategies to promote national strength through aggressively competitive economic practices warn, free trade can reduce as well as increase the number of available jobs. Moreover, because policymakers' domestic success is highly dependent on their foreign economic achievements, more than ever they must play "two-level games" simultaneously, one at the domestic level, the other at the international (Putnam, 1988). This necessity was underscored by President Bill Clinton in 1993 when he proclaimed that "to renew America, we must meet challenges abroad as well as at home. There is no longer a division between what is foreign and domestic."

Two-level games are dictated by the fact that **interdependence** creates a condition of **mutual sensitivity** and **mutual vulnerability** (Keohane and Nye, 1988) with which policymakers must try to deal. The challenge is great. Even the United States, the principal player in the post–World War II trading system, continues to face powerful domestic opposition to liberal economic precepts, such as free trade, that were the centerpiece of its foreign economic policy since the 1940s. Similar challenges to the rules for international commerce since that time have regularly been mounted elsewhere. Their breadth and intensity explain why such international economic policy issues as trade protectionism now figure so prominently on the global political agenda.

Our purpose in Part III is to examine the cluster of issues and policy dilemmas that governments face in promoting their citizens' general welfare. In this chapter and the next, we will explore the problems that now confront the world political economy. We begin with an overview of the ways individual countries and their domestic welfare are linked to the new global marketplace, including a consideration of how the international system's anarchical character affects international economic relations. Next, we examine the international monetary and trade regimes that the rich countries of the North have built, the ways they are changing, and the political economy controversies that as a result of these changes increasingly dominate their policies at home and abroad. Then, in Chapter 8, we will examine the economic relationships between the more developed countries of the North and the less developed countries of the South, and the political economy issues that arise from them. This will set the stage for consideration, in Chapters 9 and 10, respectively, of the ways that ecological issues and resource politics enter into the equation through which the welfare of the globe's 5.6 billion people is determined.

## NATIONAL ECONOMIES IN THE WORLD POLITICAL ECONOMY . . . . . . . . . . .

World exports now exceed $3.5 trillion annually and account for roughly 15 percent of world economic output. The dramatic increases in world trade since World War II that these numbers reflect have fueled the unprecedented growth in global welfare the world has experienced since then; indeed, one could not have occurred without the other.

Both increases are the product of the victorious World War II Allies' success in avoiding a repetition of the economic disaster that followed World War I. The lessons the Allies drew from the Great Depression of the 1930s inspired their wartime planning to create rules and institutions to govern post–World War II international relations. Led by the United States, the result in the economic sphere was the *Liberal International Economic Order* (LIEO). It progressively reduced barriers to the free flow of trade and capital, thereby promoting today's interdependent world political economy.

The postwar Liberal International Economic Order rested on three political bases: "the concentration of power in a small number of states, the existence of a cluster of important interests shared by those states, and the presence of a dominant power willing and able to assume a leadership role" (Spero, 1990).

Power was concentrated in the rich countries of Western Europe and North America. Neither Japan nor the Third World then posed an effective challenge to Western dominance, and the participation of the then-communist states of Eastern Europe and the Soviet Union in the global marketplace was limited. The concentration of power thus restricted the number of states whose agreement was necessary to make the system operate effectively.

The shared interests of these states facilitated the system's operation. They included a preference for an open economic system combined with a commitment to limited government intervention, if this proved necessary. The onset of the Cold War also helped cement Western unity on economic issues. Faced with a common external enemy, the Western industrial countries perceived economic cooperation as necessary not only for prosperity but also for security. That perception promoted a willingness to share economic burdens. It was also an important catalyst for the assumption of leadership by only one state—the United States—and for the acceptance of that leadership role by others.

The open (liberal) economic order created after World War II promises benefits to everyone. The unfettered flow of trade and investment between countries is essential to economic growth and higher standards of living. But states still seek through unilateral action to enhance their individual welfare, sometimes at the expense of others, rather than cooperating with one another so all can benefit. Such behavior flows naturally from governments' desire to increase the beneficial domestic effects of international economic transactions and to lessen their adverse consequences. The tactics they will use in pursuit of these goals will be shaped by domestic factors, the organization of their national economies, and by external factors, particularly their position relative to other states.

## Open versus Closed Economies

States' responses to the economic challenges they face depend in part on how they organize their domestic economies. Some have *open economic systems.* These allow the "invisible hand" of the marketplace to determine the flow of economic transactions within and across the state's borders. Such countries are commonly known as *market* economies.

*Closed economic systems* are at the opposite end of this spectrum. Because they rely on government intervention to regulate and manage the economy, closed systems are also called *centrally planned* or *command* economies. Policymakers in closed systems heavily use taxes, wage and price controls, monetary regulations, tariffs, and other policy instruments to prevent competitive market forces from determining economic transactions.

For many states, trade is their most important international economic transaction. A deficit in their *balance of trade* results from an imbalance between imports and exports, that is, when they buy more abroad than they sell. The *balance of payments* is a more inclusive summary statement of a state's financial transactions with the rest of the world. In addition to imports and exports, the balance of payments includes such items as foreign aid transfers and the income of citizens employed abroad who send their paychecks home. If more money flows out of the country than comes in, then it will suffer a balance-of-payments deficit. When this happens, some kind of corrective action is required. Policies that modify either the level of imports or the value of one's currency (relative to others') are possible options, but neither is without costs.

Where a country falls along the open–closed continuum helps to shape the options that policymakers perceive as viable as they seek to adjust imbalances in their country's economic transactions with the rest of the world.[1] For countries with closed economies,

---

[1] "Open" and "closed" are useful conventions for classifying differences between economic systems, but they are relative terms. No economy is completely open or closed, as every government practices some level of regulation. There exists no system of perfect, free market competition. The models are hypothetical extremes. The balance between unrestrained free market competition and government regulation that is most conducive to growth and welfare is the subject of much controversy (see Lindblom, 1977; Olson, 1982; Reich, 1983).

adjusting international income to international expenses is comparatively easy. The government can simply mandate an increase or decrease in the importation of certain commodities, for example.

Countries with comparatively open economic systems can use similar devices to restrict imports or capital flows to balance their international payments, but such measures would make their economies less open and policymakers therefore usually avoid them. More often, countries committed to maintaining an open economy cope with balance-of-payments problems by trying to modify their economic activity at home or to adjust their currency's exchange rates.

States can finance balance-of-payments deficits if they have access to financial assets in the form of foreign currency reserves or loans from multilateral agencies or other countries. The International Monetary Fund (IMF), a specialized agency of the United Nations, is an important source of funds for states experiencing temporary balance-of-payments shortfalls. Often, however, the IMF will provide assistance only if the borrowing state promises to undertake domestic reforms to correct the economic problems that may have caused the deficits. Such reforms are usually difficult to institute politically because they typically require domestic sacrifices that adversely affect employment opportunities and the standard of living. Indeed, whether a state's economic system is open or closed, adjustments in international economic transactions produce important domestic consequences. For this reason, all states are sensitive to the organization and conduct of their commercial relations with others.

## Realism, Relative Gains, and International Cooperation

Rules governing international commerce—like those governing international politics—often evolve according to the wishes of the stronger players. Historically, these have been the advanced capitalist societies of the Western industrialized world, particularly Britain in the nineteenth century and the United States in the twentieth century. Both used their military superiority and economic advantage to create international economic regimes in which market forces played a powerful role and enjoyed more legitimacy than state intervention and control. The economic order created following World War II is described as an "open" or "liberal" international regime because it minimized government interference in its operation.

How states respond to economic challenges is dependent not only on how they organize their domestic structures but also on their position in the international pecking order. Concern for their international rank helps to explain why states sometimes pursue goals that appear counterproductively to undermine the prospects for international cooperation, and hence the long-term benefits that cooperation with others might bring. In other words, states' competitive pursuit of narrow self-interest helps us to understand why achieving mutual gains through international cooperation is so difficult.

The theory of political realism, described in Chapter 2, explains why states often shun cooperation. The anarchical character of the international system is largely responsible. Anarchy creates fear. Because states fear one another, they are wary of others' exploitative motives. Moreover, because the international system is a self-help system, states alone are responsible for their survival and well-being. Thus, fear and uncertainty encourage each state to spend "a portion of its effort, not forwarding its own good, but in providing the means of protecting itself against others" (Waltz, 1979).

The insecurity that breeds competition and militates against cooperation is especially evident in military affairs. But it also applies to trade relations and explains why even here cooperation may fall victim to selfish calculations of short-term benefit. "Even if nation-states do not fear for their physical survival, they worry that a decrease in their power capabilities relative to those of other nation-states will compromise their political autonomy, expose them to the influence attempts of others, or lessen their ability to prevail in political disputes with allies and adversaries" (Mastanduno, 1991). Thus states seek not only *absolute gains* in their material well-being but also position in comparison with others, their *relative gains.*

Concern for relative gains explains why states seek not only to increase their own power but also to prevent others from advancing ahead of them in the international hierarchy (Grieco, 1995). Thus their international economic policies often look parochial and protective as states, more interested in relative rather than absolute gains, compete for economic rank and advantage, even in an interdependent world. In an anarchical society rich states thus are tempted to recoil from cooperation as they seek to promote and protect their particular country's position in the rankings of states. It is this motive that makes "national competitiveness" play so strongly in the calculations that underlie the rich countries' trade relationships.

## Hegemony and Hegemonic Stability

Without the regulatory authority of a government, nation-states must rely on self-help measures to protect their interests. Still, they routinely engage in various forms of cooperation, notably economic transactions, and they can do so because, paradoxically, order and predictability characterize the anarchical international system.

*Hegemonic stability theory,* a fusion of neorealist and liberal structural theories (see Chapter 2), provides an account of this observable paradox. Instead of focusing on the balance of power among contending states, this theory focuses on how the preponderance of one dominant power, a hegemon, serves as the stabilizer of the system. In particular, the theory captures the special role and responsibilities of the major economic power in a commercial order based on market forces.

### Hegemon's Roles, Responsibilities, and Benefits

*Hegemony* refers to a condition in which power and influence become concentrated in the possession of a single dominant state. As applied to the world political economy, it describes a "preponderance of material resources," of which four sets are especially important. "Hegemonic powers must have control over raw materials, control over sources of capital, control over markets, and competitive advantages in the production of highly valued goods" (Keohane, 1984).

From its vantage point as a preponderant power, a hegemon is able to promote rules for the system as a whole that protect its own interests. Capitalist hegemons, like Britain and the United States, prefer open systems because their comparatively greater control of technology, capital, and raw materials gives them more opportunities to profit from a system free of nonmarket restraints. More broadly, the "ideology [of capitalism] is cosmopolitan. Capitalism in just one state would undoubtedly be an impossibility" (Gilpin, 1987).

Capitalist states also have special responsibilities. They must ensure countries facing balance-of-payments deficits will find the credits necessary to finance their deficits. If the most powerful states cannot do this, they are likely to move toward more closed domestic economies, which may undermine the open international system otherwise advantageous to them (Block, 1977). Generally, hegemonic powers must "be willing and able to furnish an outlet for distress goods, maintain the flow of capital to would-be borrowers, serve as a lender of last resort in financial crises, maintain a structure of exchange rates, and coordinate macroeconomic politics" (Isaak, 1991). In short, the state most able to influence the system also has the greatest responsibility for its effective operation.

As a hegemon exercises its responsibilities it confers benefits known as public or collective goods.[2] National security is a public or **collective good** that all governments seek to provide for their citizens' common defense, regardless of the resources that individuals contribute through taxation. In world politics, "international security, monetary stability and an open international economy, with relatively free and predictable ability to move goods, services and capital are all seen as desirable public goods. . . . More generally, international economic order is to be preferred to disorder" (Gill and Law, 1988).

Those who enjoy the benefits of collective goods but pay little or nothing for them are *free riders.* A hegemon typically tolerates free riders, partly because the benefits that the hegemon provides encourage other states to accept its dictates.

Analysts regard the international economist Charles Kindleberger (1973) as the father of hegemonic stability theory because he was the first to theorize about the order and stability that a preponderant power provides. In his effort to explain the Great Depression of the 1930s, Kindleberger concluded that "the international economic and monetary system needs leadership, a country which is prepared, consciously or unconsciously, . . . to set standards of conduct for other countries, and to seek to get others to follow them, to take on an undue share of the burdens of the system." Britain played this role from the Congress of Vienna in 1815 until the outbreak of World War I in 1914, and the United States assumed the British mantle

---

[2] It is sometimes useful to distinguish between public and collective goods. Here we treat them synonymously. Both may be defined as goods that are jointly supplied and from which it is not possible to exclude beneficiaries on a selective basis.

in the decades immediately following World War II. In the interwar years, however, Britain was unable to play its previous role as leader, and the United States, although capable of leadership, was unwilling to exercise it. The "width and depth" of the Great Depression, Kindleberger concluded, was caused by "the absence of a leading power willing and able to bear a disproportionate share of the costs to discharge the responsibilities of a stabilizer" (Isaak, 1991).

As argued by Kindleberger, the leadership Britain and the United States provided was positive and their hegemony "benign." Other theorists take a different view. Indeed, the term *hegemony* itself often has negative connotations, suggesting an oppressive, exploitative, and sometimes coercive relationship between a leader and those it leads (see Gill, 1993b).

Those who subscribe to the "malign" view of hegemony (for example, Gilpin, 1981) argue that, even though hegemons provide order (a public good) that benefits subordinate states, they do so through coercive rather than benevolent leadership. That is, a hegemon enforces rules with positive and negative sanctions. By providing assistance but also extracting financial payments in return for its aid after World War II, the United States, for example, allegedly acted internationally as "a quasi-government by providing public goods *and* taxing other states to pay for them" (Snidal, 1985). Subordinate states may have been reluctant to be taxed, but U.S. preponderant power forced them into submission. "The focus of the theory [of hegemonic stability from this viewpoint] thus shifts from the ability to provide a public good to the ability to coerce other states" (Snidal, 1985). In this sense hegemony has a dual character. On the one hand, a hegemon contributes to stability and order; on the other, a hegemon is a dominance-seeking state that victimizes others to enhance its own power.

## International Stability and Hegemonic Decline

What happens when the power of a preponderant hegemon declines? According to the theory of hegemonic stability, "international conflict may rise" (Gill, 1993b), and instability and disorder will result. In the extreme, global war may follow, much as the hegemonic decline of Britain and absence of U.S. leadership may have precipitated the two world wars of the twentieth century.

The United States assumed the leadership mantle following World War II, of course, and it was clearly preponderant from then until the mid-1970s (see Kennedy, 1987). Hegemonic stability theory predicts that this, then, should have been an orderly period, and for the most part it was. Since the 1970s, however, instability and disorder have racked the world political economy, while simultaneously the relative power position of the United States has declined measurably.

An array of evidence points to the declining position of the United States in the world political economy. Most salient is the U.S. share of world product, which has fallen in the post–World War II period (recall Figure 4.2). In 1947, the United States accounted for nearly 50 percent of the combined gross world product. It was also the world's preeminent manufacturing center and leading exporter, and its monopoly on the atomic bomb gave it military superiority. By 1960, however, the U.S. share of gross world product had slipped to 28 percent, by 1970 to 25 percent, and by 1980 to 23 percent. Since then the proportion has ranged between 22–26 percent.

But this macro indicator does not tell the whole story. Since the late 1970s, the average annual GNP growth rate of Japan and Europe, as well as China alongside the Newly Industrialized Countries, exceeded that of the United States. Several indicators speak to the longer-term trend:

- The U.S. share of both "old manufactures," such as steel and automobiles, and "new manufactures," such as microelectronics and computers, has declined.
- Foreign ownership of U.S. manufacturing industries doubled between 1977 and 1986; between 1980 and 1991, foreign investment in the United States increased sixfold.
- Labor productivity was often greater in other industrial countries, which also exhibited personal saving rates that far surpassed those in the United States.
- The U.S. share of world financial reserves has declined precipitously. Between 1980 and 1990, the United States went from a net-creditor to the greatest net-debtor in the world.
- U.S. dependence on foreign energy sources, first evident in the early 1970s, continued unabated into the 1990s.

Thus in all the areas essential to hegemony—control over raw materials, capital, investment position and markets, and competitive advantages in the production of valued goods—U.S. preponderance has waned (U.S. CIA, 1992a; Foundation for Teaching Economics and the United Nations Association of the USA, 1992: 56).

Despite this and other evidence of U.S. decline relative to other advanced industrial states (notably Germany and Japan, which are regarded as the principal economic competitors of the United States), controversy rages over the meaning of the evidence and the probable impact of the apparent decline of the United States on its national security and foreign economic policies. Not all agree that American supremacy is vulnerable and America is "vincible" (Fry, Taylor, and Wood, 1994; compare Nye, 1992, and Dietrich, 1992). Yet not in dispute is that the United States no longer controls international outcomes in the way that it once did. This is especially so in the world political economy. Economic policy coordination and a sharing of leadership among multiple centers of power have become necessary and normal. No economic power can now unilaterally isolate its economy from trade competition from others and expect its economy to grow; even the largest national economies are highly dependent on trade for their own prominence and expansion.

Nevertheless, as this shift has occurred, cooperation for the maintenance of the LIEO has often been strained. The divergent interests of the rich economic rivals to the United States have often led them to pursue neomercantilist policies that often run counter to the (classical) liberal conviction that free markets and free trade will produce global economic prosperity.

The role of the United States in the world political economy relates intimately to the relative gains problem and to the calculus that leads states to cooperate or not to cooperate in pursuit of material welfare under conditions of anarchy. An undisputed hegemonic power typically can afford to be less concerned about its relative power position than others. Thus it is unlikely to competitively attempt to maximize its share of the global market, in contrast to aspiring hegemons or other economic powers undergoing a decline in their relative power position. As a hegemon's preponderance erodes, however, its behavior on trade issues can be expected to change.

> As [the hegemon's] relative economic power declines, it will feel that it is less able to afford, and thus less likely to tolerate, "free riding" by its allies that works to its relative economic disadvantage. Furthermore, as commonly perceived military threats diminish [as has happened with the end of the Cold War], the hegemonic state will be less inclined, in economic disputes with its allies, to subordinate its national economic interests to the pursuit of political harmony or solidarity within the alliance. In short, the transformation of international economic and security structures should inspire a dominant state to act more as an "ordinary country," and strive for relative economic advantage in relations with its allies. (Mastanduno, 1991: 81–82)

In this new context, the order and stability that the United States once provided alone are now often attributed to the rising influence of ***international regimes***. Most of the international regimes that today govern the world political economy were created during the era of U.S. preponderance, but they have continued to flourish as the world has grown more interdependent. Their existence and impact may explain why the magnitude and extent of disruptions predicted by the relative decline of U.S. power have not (yet?) materialized.[3] Nonetheless, many developments in the world political economy are potentially disruptive. It is to these, and to the historical context in which they emerged, that we now turn, beginning with changes in the international monetary regime.

## THE TRANSFORMATION OF THE INTERNATIONAL MONETARY REGIME . . . . . .

The international and domestic economies are different because countries do not use the same currencies. In the absence of an international government, there is no common currency all states can use to carry on their financial transactions and settle their international accounts. If countries are to trade or engage in other financial transactions with one another, they must devise a mechanism to determine the relative value of their currencies. The monetary system establishes such a common framework for commercial interactions among a multitude of individual, national currencies.

Currency rates of exchange express the value of one currency (say, the German mark) in relation to another (such as the U.S. dollar). A combination of governmental and market forces typically determines a currency's rate of exchange.

Because currency rates are somewhat under the control of governments (more so in closed economies than in open ones), changes in them become potential adjustment

---

[3] The contribution that international institutions make to order and stability under conditions of anarchy is a hotly debated issue among neorealists and neoliberals. For examples of contending interpretations, see Axelrod and Keohane (1985), Keohane (1984), Mastanduno (1991), Mastanduno, Lake, and Ikenberry (1989), Snidal (1991a, 1991b), and the essays in Baldwin (1993) and Kegley (1995).

mechanisms to deal with other economic problems. Changes will affect the relative attractiveness of a country's exports to foreign buyers and of its imports to domestic consumers. A currency *devaluation*, for example, will make exports cheaper and imports more expensive. As with a reduction in imports of goods or capital, a currency devaluation will not change the market, but it can change the quality of social life. If a country has a balance-of-payments deficit, for instance, lowering either the level of economic activity (deflation) or the exchange rate (devaluation) will reduce its international expenditures while increasing its revenues. Both adjustment techniques work by lowering the level of employment and the level of income in the deficit country.

Devising mechanisms to determine the value of countries' currencies in relation to one another was among the tasks that the World War II Allies faced as they began planning for the postwar world. In the international economic sphere the rules, institutions, and decision-making procedures devised by the Allies became known as the Bretton Woods system. The name comes from the New Hampshire conference site where, in 1944, agreements were negotiated to create a postwar international monetary regime characterized by stability, predictability, and orderly growth. The agreements assigned governments primary responsibility for enforcing the rules and otherwise making the system work effectively. They also anticipated that the International Monetary Fund (IMF), created at Bretton Woods, would serve as a formal mechanism to help states deal with such matters as maintaining equilibrium in their balance of payments and stability in their exchange rates with one another. The International Bank for Reconstruction and Development (IBRD), now commonly known as the World Bank, was also created to facilitate recovery from the war. The IMF continues to perform the functions expected at the time of Bretton Woods, but the primary purpose of the World Bank has since shifted to promoting Third World economic development (see Box 7.1).

## The U.S. Role in the Bretton Woods Regime

Although the International Monetary Fund and the World Bank have become important instruments for the effective operation of the international economic system, in the immediate post–World War II period they possessed too little authority and insufficient financial resources to cope with the enormous devastation that the war had caused. For these reasons they proved incapable of managing postwar economic recovery. The United States stepped into the breach.

### Unchallenged Hegemony

The U.S. dollar became the key to the role that the United States assumed as manager of the international monetary system. Backed by a vigorous and healthy economy, a fixed relationship between gold and the dollar (that is, $35 per ounce of gold), and a commitment by the U.S. government to exchange gold for dollars at any time (known as **dollar convertibility**), the dollar became "as good as gold." In fact, the

## Box 7.1
### THE BRETTON WOODS CONFERENCE AND ITS TWIN INSTITUTIONS

• • •

The International Monetary and Financial Conference of the United and Associated Nations was convened in Bretton Woods, New Hampshire, on July 1, 1944. By the time the conference ended on July 22, 1944, based on substantial preparatory work, it had defined the outlines of the postwar international economic system. The conference also resulted in the creation of the International Monetary Fund (IMF) and the International Bank for Reconstruction and Development (IBRD, or the World Bank)—the Bretton Woods twins.

The World Bank was to assist in reconstruction and development by facilitating the flow and investment of capital for productive purposes. The International Monetary Fund was to facilitate the expansion and balanced growth of international trade and to contribute thereby to the promotion and maintenance of high levels of employment and real income. Also discussed at Bretton Woods were plans for an International Trade Organization (ITO). This institution did not materialize, but some of its proposed functions are performed by the General Agreement on Tariffs and Trade (GATT), which was established in 1947.

The discussion at Bretton Woods took place with the experience of the interwar period as background. In the 1930s every major country sought ways to defend itself against deflationary pressures from abroad—some by exchange depreciation, some by introducing flexible exchange rates or multiple rates, some by direct controls over imports and other international transactions. The disastrous consequences of such policies—economic depression with very high unemployment—are well known. The participants in the Bretton Woods conference were determined to design an international economic system where "beggar-thy-neighbor" policies, which characterized the international economic community when World War II began, did not recur. There was also a widespread fear that the end of World War II would be followed by a slump, as had the end of World War I.

Thus the central elements of the system outlined at Bretton Woods were the establishment of convertibility of currencies and of fixed but adjustable exchange rates, and the encouragment of international flows of capital for productive purposes. The IMF and the World Bank were to assist in the attainment of these objectives. The economic accomplishments of the postwar period are in part the result of the effectiveness of these institutions.

*Source:* World Development Report 1985 *(1985: 15).*

dollar was preferred to gold for use by other countries to manage their balance-of-payments and savings accounts. Dollars earned interest, which gold did not; they did not incur storage and insurance costs; and they were needed to buy imports necessary for survival and postwar reconstruction. Thus the postwar economic system was not simply a modified gold standard system; it was a dollar-based system. Dollars became a major component of the international reserves used by national monetary authorities in other countries and of the "working balances" used by private banks, corporations, and individuals for international trade and capital transactions.

In addition to these functions, the dollar became a ***parallel currency:*** It was universally accepted as the "currency against which every other country sold or redeemed its own national currency in the exchange markets" (Triffin, 1978–1979). To maintain the value of their currencies, central banks in other countries either bought or sold their own currencies, using the dollar to raise or depress their value. Such intervention was often necessary because under the Bretton Woods agreement, states had committed themselves to keeping fluctuations in their exchange rates within very narrow limits. In other words, the Bretton Woods monetary regime was based on *fixed exchange rates,* which ultimately required a measure of government intervention for its preservation.

A central problem of the immediate postwar years was how to get U.S. dollars into the hands of those who needed them most. One vehicle was the Marshall Plan, which provided Western European nations with $17 billion in assistance with which to buy the U.S. goods necessary to rebuild their war-torn economies. The United States also encouraged deficits in its own balance of payments as a way of providing international liquidity in the form of dollars.

In addition to providing liquidity, the United States assumed a disproportionate share of the burden of rejuvenating Western Europe and Japan. It supported European and Japanese trade competitiveness, permitted certain forms of protectionism (such as Japan's restrictions against products imported from the United States), and condoned discrimination against the dollar (as in the European Payments Union, a multilateral European group that promoted intra-European trade at the expense of trade with the United States). The United States willingly incurred these short-run costs because the growth that they were expected to stimulate in Europe and Japan was expected eventually to provide widening markets for U.S. exports. The perceived political benefits of strengthening the Western world against the threat of communism helped to rationalize acceptance of these economic costs.

"The system worked well. Europe and Japan recovered and then expanded. The U.S. economy prospered partly because of the dollar outflow, which led to the purchase of U.S. goods and services" (Spero, 1990). Furthermore, the top currency role of the dollar facilitated the U.S. ability to pursue an unrestrained "globalist" foreign policy (Ambrose, 1993). Indeed, U.S. foreign economic and military aid programs were made possible by acceptance of the dollar as the means of paying for them. Business interests could readily expand abroad because U.S. foreign investments were often considered desirable, and American tourists could spend their dollars with few restrictions. In effect, the United States operated as the world's banker. Other countries had to balance their financial inflows and outflows. In contrast, the United States could operate internationally without the constraints of limited finances. The dominant position of the United States also meant that its internal economic circumstances affected other nations in significant ways. Through the ubiquitous dollar, the United States thus came to exert considerable influence on the political and economic affairs of most other countries.

Yet there were costs. The enormous number of dollars held by others made the U.S. domestic economy vulnerable to financial shocks abroad. U.S. policymakers sought, of course, to insulate the U.S. economy from these shocks, but their task was made more difficult because some tools available to others were proscribed by the status of the dollar as a reserve currency.

For most countries, an imbalance in their balance of payments is readily corrected by raising or lowering their currency exchange rate. But this simple mechanism, which lies at the heart of international financial adjustments, was more difficult for the United States because of the dollar's pivotal role. Devaluation of the dollar, for example, would adversely affect political friends and military allies who had chosen to hold large amounts of dollars as reserve currency—and who were especially important in the context of U.S. competition with Soviet communism. Furthermore, a devaluation could easily be offset by others adversely affected by the U.S. action simply by devaluing their own currencies. Understandably, therefore, the United States was reluctant to devalue the dollar.

By the late 1950s, concern began to mount about the long-term viability of an international monetary system based on the dollar (see Triffin, 1978–1979). Analysts worried that such a system would be unable to provide the world with the monetary reserves necessary to ensure growing economic activity. They also feared that the number of foreign-held dollars would eventually overwhelm the ability of the United States to convert them into gold. This undermined the confidence others had in the soundness of the dollar and the U.S. economy and led eventually to a severing of the link between the dollar and gold.

### Hegemony under Stress

As early as 1960 it was clear that the dollar's top currency status was on the wane. Subsequently, the dollar-based international monetary system unilaterally managed by the United States became increasingly a multilaterally managed system under U.S. leadership. There are several reasons for the dollar's declining position.

If too few dollars was the problem in the immediate postwar years, by the 1960s the problem became one of too many dollars. The costs of extensive U.S. military activities, foreign economic and military aid, and massive private investments produced increasing balance-of-payments deficits. Although encouraged earlier, the deficits were by this time out of control. Furthermore, U.S. gold holdings in relation to the growing number of foreign-held dollars fell precipitously. Given these circumstances, the possibility that the United States might devalue the dollar led to a loss of confidence by others and to their unwillingness to continue to hold dollars as reserve currency. Under the leadership of Charles de Gaulle, France went so far as to insist on exchanging dollars for gold, although admittedly in part for reasons related more to French nationalistic pride than to the viability of the U.S. economy.

Along with the glut of dollars, the increasing monetary interdependence of the First World's industrial economies led to massive transnational movements of capital. The internationalization of banking, the internationalization of production via multinational corporations, and the development of a Eurocurrency market outside direct state control all accelerated this interdependence.[4] An increasingly complex relationship between the economic policies engineered in one country and their effects on another was the result. This in turn spawned a variety of comparatively formal groupings of the central bankers and finance ministers from the leading economic powers who devised various ad hoc solutions to their common problems. The decision was also made to create a form of "paper gold" known as Special Drawing Rights (SDRs) in the IMF to facilitate the growth of international liquidity by means other than increasing the outflow of dollars.[5]

Although the United States was the chief proponent and supporter of the various management techniques devised during the 1960s, none proved sufficient to counter the "dollar crises" that surfaced in the late 1960s and early 1970s. An important reason underlying these crises is that the Bretton Woods regime never operated in quite the way it was intended.

The Bretton Woods system obliged each country to maintain the value of its currency in relation to the U.S. dollar (and through it to all others) within the confines of the agreed-upon exchange rate. The purpose was to stabilize and render predictable the value of the currencies needed to carry on international financial transactions. The rules permitted states to devalue their currencies if maintenance of the agreed-upon rates became difficult due to persistent structural weaknesses in a country's economy. Despite this provision, devaluations "proved to be traumatic politically and economically. . . . [They] were taken as indications of weakness and economic failure by states and, thus, were resisted" (Walters and Blake, 1992).

Other changes in the international political economy also contributed to states' unwillingness to continue to hold U.S. dollars. By the 1960s the European and Japanese recovery from World War II was complete, which meant that U.S. monetary dominance and the dollar's privileged position were no longer politically acceptable. The United States nonetheless continued to exercise a disproportionate influence over these other states, even while it was unreceptive to their criticisms.

The Europeans and Japanese especially came to resent the prerogatives that the United States derived from its position as the world's banker and from its ability to determine the level of international liquidity through its balance-of-payments deficits. Not only did these prerogatives affect their economies; they also enabled the United States to spend money for foreign policy purposes with which they disagreed. U.S. involvement in Vietnam was a primary example. Détente between the United States and the Soviet Union, the superpowers' official policy beginning in 1969, also eroded

---

[4] Eurocurrencies are dollars and other currencies held in Europe as bank deposits and lent and borrowed outside the country of origin.

[5] SDRs are reserve assets that countries' central banks agree to accept to settle their official financial transactions. Because their value is set in relation to a "basket" of major currencies, SDRs tend to be more stable than either gold or a single currency.

the willingness of others to follow U.S. leadership because the diminishing perception of a military threat reduced the willingness of the Western democracies to subordinate their economic disagreements to enhance Western security.

The United States, of course, had enjoyed its preponderant status for years. It therefore came to see its own economic health and that of the world political economy as one and the same. In the case of the monetary regime in particular, U.S. leaders treasured the dollar's status as the top currency and interpreted attacks on it as attacks on international economic stability (see Walters and Blake, 1992). That view in turn reflected the interests and prerogatives of a hegemon. Fred L. Block elaborates:

> The exercise of American political and military power on a global basis [had] been designed to gain foreign acceptance of an international monetary order that institutionalizes an open world economy, giving maximum opportunities to American businessmen. It would be absurd for the United States to abandon its global ambitions simply to live within the rules of an international monetary order that was shaped for the purpose of achieving these ambitions. So it [was] hardly surprising that the United States continued to pursue its global ambitions despite the increasing strains on the international monetary order. The fundamental contradiction was that the United States had created an international monetary order that worked only when American political and economic dominance in the capitalist world was absolute. That absolute dominance disappeared as a result of the reconstruction of Western Europe and Japan, on the one hand, and the accumulated domestic costs of the global extension of U.S. power, on the other. With the fading of the absolute dominance, the international monetary order began to crumble. The U.S. [balance-of-payments] deficit was simply the most dramatic symptom of the terminal disease that plagued the postwar international monetary order. (Block, 1977: 163)

### Hegemony in Decline

The United States sought to stave off challenges to its leadership role, but its own deteriorating economic situation made that increasingly difficult. Mounting inflation—caused in part by the unwillingness of the Johnson administration to raise taxes to pay either for the Vietnam War or the Great Society at home—was particularly troublesome, as it reduced the competitiveness of U.S. goods overseas.

Historically, the United States had enjoyed favorable balances of trade. This was important, because the trade surpluses were used to offset its balance-of-payments deficits, which by the end of the 1960s had become chronic. In 1971, for the first time in the twentieth century, the United States actually suffered a modest trade deficit (of $2 billion). This deficit worsened thereafter. As a result, demands by industrial, labor, and agricultural interests for protectionist trade measures designed to insulate them from foreign economic competition began to grow.

Policymakers laid partial blame for the trade deficit at the doorstep of the major U.S. trading partners. Japan and West Germany in particular were criticized for maintaining undervalued currencies (that is, currencies that did not accurately reflect the cost of goods in those countries). This made their goods attractive internationally (and to the American consumer), which in turn enabled these countries to generate balance-of-payments surpluses by selling more overseas than they bought. At the same time, the relative position of the United States in international trade was deteriorating, with the U.S. share declining and Europe's and Japan's increasing.

Faced with these circumstances, the United States took several steps to shore up the sagging U.S. position in the world political economy. In August 1971 President Richard M. Nixon abruptly announced that the United States would no longer exchange dollars for gold. He also imposed a surcharge on imports into the United States as part of a strategy designed to force a realignment of others' currency exchange rates. These startling and unexpected decisions, which came as a shock to the other Western industrial nations, marked the end of the Bretton Woods regime.

A system of free-floating exchange rates replaced the Bretton Woods fixed-exchange-rate system. In this kind of system, market forces rather than government intervention determine currency values. The theory underlying the Bretton Woods replacement is that a country experiencing adverse economic conditions will see the value of its currency in the marketplace decline in response to the choices of traders, bankers, and investors. This will make its exports cheaper and its imports more expensive, which in turn will pull the value of its currency back toward equilibrium—all without the need for central bankers to support their currencies (see Box 7.2).

Based on the theory underlying a free-floating exchange-rate system, policymakers hoped that the politically humiliating devaluations of the past could be avoided. What they did not foresee was that the new system would introduce an unparalleled degree of uncertainty and unpredictability into international monetary affairs.

The strident actions taken by the United States in 1971 were in part a reaction to its growing dependence on the rest of the world and its realization that it could no longer unilaterally regulate international monetary affairs. In this sense its actions were a predictable response to the U.S. decline in the world political economy. For the global economy as a whole, it was now clear that the political basis on which the Bretton Woods system had been built lay in ruins. U.S. leadership was no longer accepted willingly by others or exercised willingly by the United States. Power had come to be more widely dispersed among states, and the shared interests that once bound them together had dissipated.

## From Hegemony toward Multilateral Management

The world political economy would face serious challenges in the wake of Bretton Woods' demise. Where hegemony once reigned, various groups of industrial nations now evolved a series of quasi-official negotiating forums to cope with monetary and other economic stresses.

### *The OPEC Decade*

Formal negotiations on reform of the international monetary system began in 1972. Before new agreements were devised, however, policymakers faced new crises in the form of two oil shocks administered by the Organization of Petroleum Exporting

# Box 7.2
## WHY DO EXCHANGE RATES FLUCTUATE?

• • •

Money works in several ways and serves different purposes: It must be acceptable, so that people earning it can use it to buy goods and services from others. It must serve as a store of value, so that people will be willing to keep some of their wealth in the form of money. And it must be a standard of deferred payment, so that people will be willing to lend money knowing that when the money owed them is repaid in the future, it will still have purchasing power.

Inflation occurs when the government creates too much money in relation to the goods and services produced in an economy. As money becomes more plentiful and hence less acceptable, it cannot serve well as a store of value or a medium of exchange to satisfy debts. Governments work to make certain that their currencies do the jobs intended for them, which means, among other things, that they try to maintain an inflation-free environment.

In the international monetary system, movements in a state's exchange rate occur in part when changes occur in assessments made of the underlying economic strength of a country or the ability of its government to maintain the value of its money change. A deficit in a country's balance of payments, for example, would likely cause a decline in the value of its currency relative to others, because the supply of the currency would be greater than the demand for it. Similarly, when those engaged in international economic transactions change their expectations about the future value of a currency, they might reschedule their lending and borrowing; fluctuations in the exchange rate could follow.

Speculators—those who buy and sell money in an effort to make it—may also affect the stability of a country's currency internationally. Professional speculators make money by making guesses about the future. If, for example, they believe that the Japanese yen will be worth more in, say, three months than it is now, they can buy yen today and sell them for a profit three months hence. Conversely, if they believe that the dollar will be worth less in ninety days, they can sell some number of yen today for a certain number of dollars and then buy back the same yen in ninety days for fewer dollars, thus making a profit.

On what basis do speculators make these kinds of decisions? One is their reading of the health of the currency in which they are speculating. If they believe the U.S. dollar is weak because the U.S. economy itself is weak, they may conclude that the U.S. government will permit a devaluation of the dollar. Another, closely related consideration is whether a government is perceived as having the political will to devise effective policies to ensure the value of its money, particularly against inflation. If speculators think that it does not, they would again be wise to sell dollars today and buy them back tomorrow at the (anticipated) lower price. In the process, of course, speculators may create self-fulfilling prophecies: They may "prove" that the dollar needs to be devalued simply because of the volume of seemingly unwanted dollars offered for sale.

In the same way that governments seek to protect the value of their currencies at home, they try to protect them internationally by intervening in the marketplace. Their willingness to do so is especially important to importers and exporters, who depend on orderliness and predictability in the value of the currencies they deal in to carry on their transnational exchanges. Governments intervene when countries' central banks buy or sell currencies to change the value of their own currencies in relation to others. Unlike speculators, however, they are pledged not to manipulate exchange rates so as to gain unfair advantage.

Countries (OPEC). The first came in 1973–1974, shortly after the 1973 Yom Kippur War in the Middle East, when the price of oil increased fourfold. The second occurred in 1979–1980 in the wake of the revolution in Iran and resulted in an even more dramatic jump in the world price of oil.

Since the United States was then (and remains today) the world's largest oil consumer and importer (U.S. CIA, 1992a: 120–128), the impact of the two oil shocks on the United States was especially pronounced, all the more so as each coincided with a decline in U.S. domestic energy production and a rise in consumption. A dramatic increase in U.S. dependence on foreign sources of energy to fuel its advanced industrial economy and a sharp rise in the overall cost of U.S. imports resulted.

As dollars flowed abroad to purchase energy resources (a record $40 billion in 1977 and $74 billion in 1980), others began to worry about the dollar's value—which augmented its marked decline on foreign exchange markets in the late 1970s and early 1980s. Demand for oil in the United States and elsewhere softened in the early 1980s as a consequence of conservation measures, economic recession, and a shift to alternative sources of energy. Oil prices also began to ease as a result and then plummeted after 1986, due largely to the worldwide oil glut that followed the decision of key members of OPEC to increase their output in an effort to regain market shares lost earlier to others. The decline in oil prices helped to contain inflation and stimulated economic growth in the United States and elsewhere. Simultaneously, the dollar experienced a rapid surge in value (see Figure 7.2 on page 221). Thus the world political economy weathered the immediate effects of the two OPEC oil shocks. However, their long-term effects would persist for years.

## The Aftermath of the OPEC Decade

Global economic recession followed each oil shock. The close relationship between the changing fortunes of the dollar and the price of oil was due in part to the way in which the leading industrial powers chose to cope with the recessions. In response to the first, they relied on fiscal and monetary adjustments to stimulate economic recovery and to avoid unemployment levels deemed politically unacceptable. In response to the second, which proved to be the longest and most severe economic downturn since the Great Depression of the 1930s, they shifted their efforts to controlling inflation through strict monetarist policies (that is, policies designed to reduce the money supply in the economy). Large fiscal deficits and sharply higher interest rates resulted. Both were particularly apparent in the United States. The other industrial countries also experienced higher levels of unemployment than they had been willing to tolerate before.

In an era of complex interdependence, none could escape the impact of these developments, including the Third World. In response to the two oil shocks, many developing countries borrowed extensively from abroad to pay for the increased cost of energy as a way to prevent reductions in domestic economic activity. Borrowing was possible because of the billions of "petrodollars" that flowed to the oil-producing states and that private banks and various multilateral institutions helped to recycle. In the process, however, the debt burden of many states assumed ominous proportions, particularly as interest rates climbed following the second oil shock. The threat of massive defaults by countries unable to service their debts pushed the international monetary regime to the brink of crisis in the early 1980s and again at mid-decade. The crisis atmosphere receded later, but the debt problem persisted (see Chapter 8).

High interest rates in the United States compared with other countries contributed not only to the debt burden of Third World states; they also contributed measurably to the changing fortunes of the U.S. dollar, as increased demand for dollars drove up the exchange rate. Renewed economic growth in the United States, a sharp reduction in inflation, and the perception that the United States was a safe haven for financial investments in a world otherwise marked by political instability and violence also helped to restore faith in the dollar. Foreign investors therefore rushed to acquire the dollars necessary to take advantage of profitable investment opportunities in the United States. This situation contrasted sharply with the 1970s, when the huge foreign indebtedness of the United States, often called the "dollar overhang," was a principal fear.

For the United States, the appreciation of the dollar was a mixed blessing. On the one hand, it reduced the cost of imported oil. On the other hand, it increased the cost of U.S. exports to foreign buyers, thus reducing the competitiveness of U.S. products in overseas markets. This meant the loss of tens of thousands of jobs in U.S. industries that produced for export. It also resulted in a series of record trade deficits—$132 billion in 1985, $155 billion in 1986, and $170 billion in 1987—as imports from abroad became relatively cheaper and hence more attractive to American consumers. "During the 1980s, the red ink in U.S. merchandise trade exceeded one trillion dollars, and it is still not clear when U.S. exports will once again equal or surpass U.S. imports" (Fry, Taylor, and Wood, 1994: 254–255). (The U.S. trade deficit in 1993 ballooned to $115 billion from $84 billion in 1992.)

The budget deficit of the U.S. government has also climbed to record levels since the late 1980s. To deal with the deficit, the United States began to borrow at a record rate from abroad. The result of these combined trends was a rapid erosion in the international investment position of the United States. As the debt climbed and interest payments on it compounded, the United States became for the first time in more than half a century a debtor nation as it moved from being the world's biggest creditor in 1980 to being its largest debtor in 1990 (see Figure 7.1). "At the beginning of 1992, the United States owed foreigners $362 billion more than they owed Americans," and at the end of 1993 the federal government's cumulative debt had risen 400 percent since 1980 to over $4.5 trillion, an uncomfortable 4 percent of gross domestic product (Fry, Taylor, and Wood, 1994: 254, 256–257). By 1994, U.S. federal borrowing was consuming over two-thirds of net private savings (Peterson, 1994: 4) and the national debt equalled about $17,000 for each U.S. citizen. The debt legacy constrains the policy choices the government can draw on to deal with economic

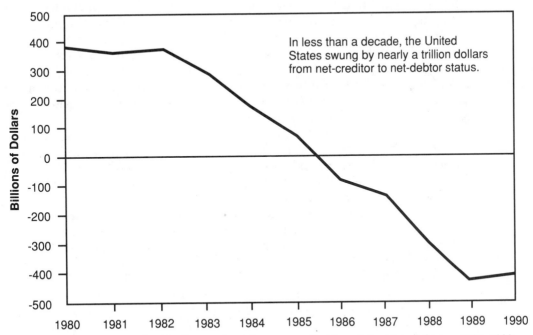

**Figure 7.1**    The Net International Investment Position of the United States, 1980–1990
*Source:* U.S. Department of Commerce, as presented in the Foundation for Teaching Economics and the United Nations Association of the USA (1992: 56).
*Note:* Foreign direct investment is valued at current cost.

downturns. The U.S. debt burden also became a symbol of America's relative economic decline and growing vulnerability to foreign competition.

For a time during the 1980s the high levels of U.S. government spending alongside its staggering budget deficits sustained high interest rates, which in turn triggered a rise in the value of the dollar. Eventually, however, the chronic trade and budget deficits became overwhelming, precipitating a long decline in the value of the dollar from the lofty heights it had achieved by mid-decade (see Figure 7.2). A renewed sense of global economic uncertainty plagued decision makers in the advanced industrial societies, whose economic fates had become increasingly intertwined. Their interdependence was dramatized in October 1987, when stock prices in markets throughout the world plummeted overnight, resulting in billions of dollars in lost equity. The shocking events demonstrated the extent of an interdependent global market, as well as the extent to which its health critically depended on the value of the U.S. dollar and the underlying strength of the U.S. economy.

## Macroeconomic Policy Coordination

Historically, the United States had been loath to intervene in the international marketplace to affect the value of the dollar. By 1985, however, the erosion of U.S. trade competitiveness in overseas markets due to the overvalued dollar had become unpalatable domestically (Destler and Henning, 1989). In response, the Group of Five (or *G-5* composed of the United States, Britain, France, Japan, and West Germany) met secretly in the Plaza Hotel in New York and decided on a coordinated effort to bring down the overvalued dollar. The landmark agreement proved important not only because it signaled an end to the benign neglect toward the vulnerabilities of interdependence that the United States had previously exhibited, but it also committed the major economic powers to greater collective coordination of their economic policies through management of exchange rates internationally and interest rates domestically. This meeting marked the emergence of Japan as a full partner in international monetary management (Spero, 1990) and led to formalization of the *G-7* or Group of Seven (the G-5 plus Canada and Italy) meetings at the Tokyo Economic Summit in 1986. The most powerful capitalist countries had previously convened only informally and intermittently since 1975.

The Plaza agreement failed to realize all the goals that had been intended, however. The Group of Five financial ministers therefore reconvened in Paris at the Louvre in February 1987 to again discuss international monetary management. The agreement they reached pledged to sustain exchange rates within a target range and to coordinate domestic monetary and fiscal policies for this purpose. Only Japan kept its promise, and partly as a result of this failure of policy coordination, in October 1987 international equity markets around the world collapsed. It was only after the Group of Seven restored liquidity that a repeat of the Wall Street crash of 1929, which presaged the worldwide depression, was avoided.

Since 1987, G-7 cooperation has appeared to lose momentum, leading some to suggest that domestic obstacles can only be overcome in times of severe crisis or systemic threat. Critics

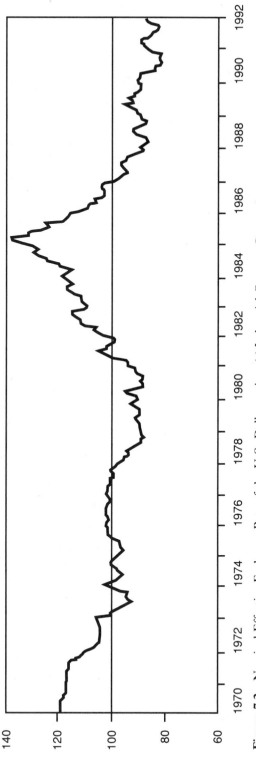

**Figure 7.2** Nominal Effective Exchange Rate of the U.S. Dollar against 16 Industrial-Country Currencies, 1970–1992
*Source*: Various issues of the International Monetary Fund's *Directory of Trade Statistics*, as summarized by the Foundation for Teaching Economics and the United Nations Association of the USA (1992: 44).

*Note*: This trend line reports monthly averages, with 1980–1982 = 100 (base).

argue that the Louvre/crash period showed the dangers of G-7 coordination; advocates argue that it reflected a new collective capacity to sustain the system under new global conditions, in a new policy process. As the case of the 1987 crash illustrates, however, the knowledge level and resources needed to steer the brave new world of global capitalism are still far from sufficient. (Gill, 1993a: 370)

The inability of the United States to devise a politically acceptable budget-deficit reduction strategy played a critical role in the disintegration of macroeconomic policy coordination in the late 1980s. Some modest reductions in U.S. deficits later were achieved. But the forecasts were not promising.

The obstacles to macroeconomic coordination through multilateral diplomacy among the richest countries are also shown by the problems encountered in the pressing need to stabilize the U.S. dollar, the currency of the globe's key monetary actor. When Iraq invaded Kuwait in August 1990, a new financial crisis confronted the rich countries, most of whom were, like the United States, dependent on oil exports while also still in need of a stable dollar for their own economies' stability. A marked downward trend in the value of the dollar was evident even before the Persian Gulf War, but unlike the situation following the 1987 stock market crash, this time there was little disposition among the other industrial countries to cooperate with the United States to rescue the dollar. The value of the U.S. dollar in the international marketplace declined precipitously in the weeks following the onset of the Persian Gulf crisis, as G-7 cooperation failed to materialize to avert the dollar's drop. Instead, those capitalist rivals to the United States acted in accordance with different calculations of where their interests lay. The normal pattern is that a country viewed as a "safe haven" for investments during times of crisis will see the value of its currency appreciate. Typically this had been the United States. In the Persian Gulf case, however, investors concluded Europe and Japan were better bets. The setting for international investment had changed, and these changes portended greater competition and less coordination.

## Toward a Regionalized Monetary Arrangement

The dollar remains preeminent in the world political economy, as does the U.S. economy, but the continuing challenges to U.S. supremacy reflect long-term processes that are impossible to ignore. Reinforcing those processes are movements that portend the possible emergence of a monetary order in which the dollar will play a less pervasive role. Potentially the most important change involves Europe, where the European Union (EU) has launched a European Monetary System (EMS) designed to stabilize the currency values of the European Union's member countries against one another and against the dollar. Although the promise and performance of the EMS have sometimes diverged, the goal of securing a "zone of monetary stability in Europe" has been reached (Spero, 1990), and "it appears highly probable that groups of states [within the EU] will move toward greater economic coordination, such as monetary union" (Hughes, 1995).

To move beyond currency stability toward monetary union, a three-stage process was put in motion, whose ultimate goals were the creation of a European System of

Central Banks (ESCB) and a single European currency unit (ECU). In the eyes of its advocates, monetary union through the EU's Exchange Rate Mechanism (ERM) would foster the eventual political union of the EU.

Whether these lofty goals will someday be achieved is by no means certain. The history of the European Community (now the European Union) is replete with postponed and unrealized plans. In part this is because emergent problems have often deflected the European Union from pursuit of its most visionary unification goals. The financial strains caused by the merger of East and West Germany and the subsidies pledged to draw the former Soviet bloc countries' fledgling market economies into the EU network are two recent examples. Still, the EMS and overloaded ERM may contain the seeds of a regional international monetary arrangement based on a single European currency. The prospects for the proposed "economic and monetary (and political) union (EMU), adopted at Maastricht . . . in December 1991 . . . brightened . . . in May 1993 following a second Danish referendum in which the EMU proposal passed by a comfortable margin after modifications had been made in it" (Mitchell, 1993). Should the initial insemination come to fruition, the European Union will emerge to dominate Europe and those areas of Africa and the Caribbean linked by treaty to it. That development in turn could stimulate similar arrangements in Asia and the Western Hemisphere, where Japan and the United States dominate.

As the preponderant economic power in the 1990s and as in previous decades, the United States is likely to resist regionalization, at least rhetorically. But trade patterns have evolved very far in this direction, and the United States can no longer realize its preferences unilaterally. The United States is necessary for the effective management of the monetary regime, but it is not sufficiently dominant to fulfill its earlier hegemonic role. Negotiations with the other developed market economies are necessary to manage successfully the competing and sometimes contradictory demands that economic interdependence and the desire for sovereign autonomy impose. In short, as "the still-embryonic process of the internationalization of economic policymaking" (Gill, 1993a) continues to develop, "the U.S. economy and American economic decision-making must now be adapted to an emerging global economy that no longer revolves around the United States" (Aho and Stokes, 1991).

## TRADE STRATEGIES IN AN INTERDEPENDENT WORLD . . . . . . . . . . . . . . . .

The volume and value of international trade have grown exponentially, "and the growth has recently accelerated. 1992 was the ninth consecutive year in which world trade grew more rapidly than world output" (Mitchell, 1993: 164). "Although growth in volume of world trade slowed in 1993 to 2.5 percent, the slowest in a decade" (*The Economist* 330, April 19, 1994: 7), the pace still once again continued to exceed the growth rate of world output generally.

This trade expansion has been one of the primary engines driving economic growth and raising living standards throughout the world to levels never before achieved. Continuation of these trends is problematic, however. Increased trade protectionism and the corresponding prospect of regionalization, already apparent in capital markets, the monetary system, and even the trade regime itself, now threaten to dampen further trade growth.

Trade protectionism threatens closure of the open (liberal) multilateral trade regime created after World War II. *Nondiscrimination* is the central norm of the regime, and the World Trade Organization (WTO) created in 1994 in the wake of the General Agreement on Tariffs and Trade (GATT) is the principal international organization that seeks to promote and protect it. Nondiscrimination is embodied in the ***most-favored-nation*** (MFN) principle. According to that principle, the tariff preferences granted to one country must be granted to all others exporting the same product. That is, every trading state is to be treated the same as the most favored one (provided, of course, that the trading partners have previously agreed to grant one another MFN status). Thus the principle stands for nondiscrimination in the way that countries treat one another; its purpose is to eliminate preferential treatment in trade concessions.

Despite widespread enthusiasm for free, nondiscriminatory trade, the political case for trade protectionism is often compelling. When, for example, during the recession of the early 1980s an estimated 30 million people in the industrial world were unemployed, many people felt that low-wage imports were responsible for the loss of domestic jobs. However, cutting off imports denies the benefits that free trade promises. Laura Tyson, chairperson of the U.S. Council of Economic Advisers estimated in May 1994 that trade barriers were costing American consumers between $100 and $200 billion a year.

## Free Trade and Protectionism

As noted, there is a strong correlation between the growth of world trade and global welfare. Moreover, because the costs of protectionism are high and the benefits of free trade clear, the rise of protectionist sentiment in the world political economy is puzzling.

Classical (liberal) economic theory shows conclusively that when all states special-ize in the production of those goods in which they enjoy a ***comparative advantage*** and trade them for goods in which others enjoy an advantage, a net gain in welfare will result. Still, states sometimes practice ***neomercantilism*** in an effort to enhance domestic welfare, even if it undermines their relations with their trade partners. Furthermore, classical theory does not acknowledge the possibility that states may create comparative advantages. That is the purpose of the *strategic trade* policies now widely practiced by Japan and others. These reflect states' sensitivities to their *relative gains* from trade, not just their *absolute gains*.

### Comparative Advantage

In principle, economic relations between states are voluntary exchanges that, either through private entities or public enterprises, they enter into freely for mutual benefit. Indeed, the *raison d'être* of foreign trade is that it offers advantages to both parties in the exchange.

According to the principle of ***comparative advantage,*** any two nations will benefit if each specializes in those goods that it produces comparatively cheaply and acquires, through trade, goods that it can only produce at a higher cost. Trade is encouraged because those countries most efficiently producing cars, textiles, wines, or other products will, because of their lower cost, make them attractive to foreign consumers. Those countries that produce for export will also have incentives to import other goods that may be acquired at lower cost from foreign sources. Specialization and trade therefore permit each to enjoy a higher standard of living than would be possible without them. Thus, when trade is unfettered by nonmarket forces or politically imposed barriers, all countries stand to share in the gains in welfare that trade produces, as illustrated in Box 7.3. This simple conclusion—that the net gain in welfare to most countries is greater as a consequence of their exchange of goods with one another—is the basis of liberal international trade theory. Benjamin Franklin summarized the liberal premise aphoristically more than two centuries ago when he concluded "no nation was ever ruined by trade."

The actual recouping of the benefits from trade is, of course, far more complicated than this simple illustration suggests. Under a free-trade system, states should specialize in the production of goods in which they enjoy competitive advantages, but in practice they routinely interfere with free trade for a variety of political reasons. Moreover, because they are not equal economically (some are endowed with greater resources and productive capacities than others), political competition among the unequals undermines international support for free trade. Indeed, the search for self-advantage at the expense of others—captured in the terms "beggar-thy-neighbor policies" and "neomercantilism"—is commonplace, not the exception.

## *Neomercantilism*

***Beggar-thy-neighbor policies*** are designed to enhance domestic welfare by promoting trade surpluses that can be realized only at other countries' expense. They reflect the efforts by one country to reduce its unemployment through currency devaluations, tariffs, quotas, export subsidies, and other strategies that adversely affect its trade partners.

The practice of beggar-thy-neighbor policies has a long history. During the 1890s, for example, the United States imposed the McKinley tariff in response to high European agricultural tariffs. France retaliated with the Meline tariff that levied still higher duties.

National economic strategies such as these were especially prevalent during the 1930s. Currency devaluations, foreign exchange controls, and restrictive tariffs (such as the U.S. Smoot-Hawley Act of 1930) were implemented at that time to improve states' domestic economic conditions at the expense of other states. In the end, their efforts to generate trade surpluses by cutting imports led to a breakdown of the entire international trade system.[6]

---

[6] See Susan Strange (1985) for a rival interpretation that argues it was not protectionism but financial uncertainty and the shrinking of credit that slowed trade and growth in the 1930s (and again in the recession of the 1980s).

# Box 7.3
## COMPARATIVE ADVANTAGE AND THE GAINS FROM TRADE

• • •

Start with two countries, for example, the United States and the United Kingdom. Each produces steel and cloth. The hypothetical figures below show output per hour for workers in each country. It's clear that the U.S. has an absolute advantage; American workers are more productive in turning out both products than the British workers.

### WORKER PRODUCTIVITY

|  | U.S. | U.K. |
|---|---|---|
| Steel, units of output/hour | 9 | 4 |
| Cloth, units of output/hour | 3 | 2 |

Does this means that there is no possibility for trade between the two countries? If the U.K. wants to trade with [the U.S.], should it try to produce something else in which it has an advantage? And if trade occurs, should the U.S. continue to allocate its scarce resources in the same way it has done? The answer to all these questions is no.

Each country should specialize in those items in which it has the best comparative cost advantage or least comparative cost disadvantage, and trade with others. Here's why.

Since the U.S. is three times more productive in steel than cloth, it should direct more of its resources into steel. One cost of producing more steel is lost cloth output. But the U.S. can turn out three additional units of steel for every unit of cloth production given up, while the U.K. can obtain only two units of cloth.

In the U.K. workers are also more productive in steel than in cloth making. But greater emphasis should be placed on cloth production because Britain is at a smaller disadvantage, compared with America, in this area. If the U.K. specializes in cloth and the U.S. in steel, and they trade, each will benefit.

The chart shows that by moving resources in the U.S. to steel production and in the U.K. to cloth production, the same total inputs will cause steel and cloth output to rise 10 units each. This gain indicates a more efficient allocation of resources. Benefits to both countries can be realized when the U.S. trades its extra steel for British cloth. Indeed, the U.S. ends up with more steel than before specialization and trade and with the same quantity of cloth. The U.K. finds itself with more cloth and the same amount of steel. More output in both countries means higher living standards.

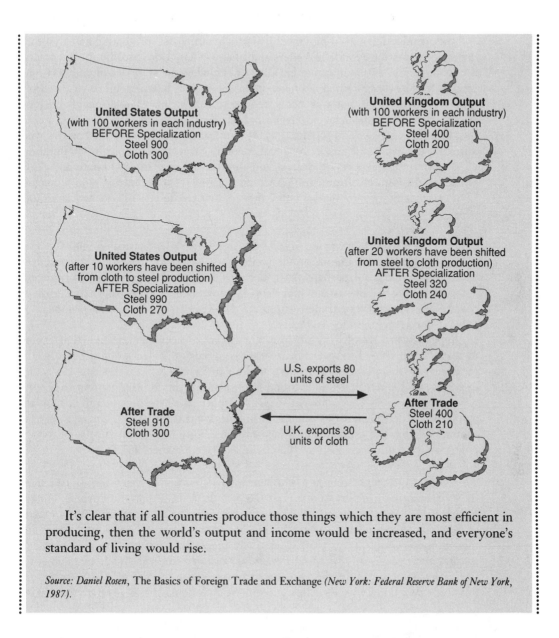

United States Output
(with 100 workers in each industry)
BEFORE Specialization
Steel 900
Cloth 300

United Kingdom Output
(with 100 workers in each industry)
BEFORE Specialization
Steel 400
Cloth 200

United States Output
(after 10 workers have been shifted
from cloth to steel production)
AFTER Specialization
Steel 990
Cloth 270

United Kingdom Output
(after 20 workers have been shifted
from steel to cloth production)
AFTER Specialization
Steel 320
Cloth 240

After Trade
Steel 910
Cloth 300

U.S. exports 80
units of steel

U.K. exports 30
units of cloth

After Trade
Steel 400
Cloth 210

It's clear that if all countries produce those things which they are most efficient in producing, then the world's output and income would be increased, and everyone's standard of living would rise.

*Source: Daniel Rosen*, The Basics of Foreign Trade and Exchange *(New York: Federal Reserve Bank of New York, 1987).*

*Neomercantilism* describes today's beggar-thy-neighbor strategies. The term itself derives from the mercantilist policies that imperial states pursued early in the history of the modern state system, when they sought supremacy over others by the accumulation of precious metals and by exporting as much and importing as little as possible (see Chapter 5). In the contemporary context, neomercantilism refers to "a trade policy whereby a state seeks to maintain a balance-of-trade surplus and to promote

domestic production and employment by reducing imports, stimulating home production, and promoting exports" (Walters and Blake, 1992). More broadly, neomercantilism is state intervention in economic affairs to enhance the state's economic fortunes.
Japan is frequently described as a neomercantilist power, having achieved tremendous
export growth in the postwar years because of an intimate government–business
alliance that both subsidizes promising industries so they can achieve dominance in
the global marketplace and restricts imports from abroad. If these trade barriers were
dismantled, estimates a report by the Economic Strategy Institute in Washington,
U.S. merchandise exports to Japan would climb by more than $50 billion, and, U.S.
adviser to the Clinton administration Clyde Prestowitz predicts, this would increase
U.S. gross domestic product by 1 to 2 percent and create 1.5 million American jobs
(Kaslow, 1994: 4).

**IMPORT QUOTAS** Among industrial states, neomercantilism—and the case
against free trade—is commonly rationalized by the perceived need for protection from
cheap foreign labor, or perhaps from more technologically sophisticated producers.
Already established industries may, for example, seek safeguards in the form of
government assistance or trade restrictions targeted at specific foreign producers as
a way to protect domestic producers.

*Import quotas* usually specify the quantity of a particular product that can be
imported from abroad.[7] Governments impose quotas to protect domestic producers,
regardless of their efficiency relative to foreign producers. In the late 1950s, for
example, the United States established import quotas on oil, arguing that they were
necessary to protect U.S. national security. Hence the government, rather than the
marketplace, determined the amount of imports, and from whom. Sugar is another
commodity that the United States has subjected to quotas in pursuit of its foreign
policy objectives, particularly in the Caribbean (see Krasner, 1978).

**EXPORT QUOTAS** *Export quotas* also impose barriers to free trade. In this sense
they are similar to import quotas, but the two differ in important respects. Import
quotas are unilateral instruments of policy while export quotas are imposed as a result
of negotiated agreements between producers and consumers. The United States and
the European Union, in particular, routinely press other countries to accept *orderly
market arrangements* (OMAs) and *voluntary export restrictions* (VERs) in an effort
to protect domestic industries threatened by foreign imports.[8] Of the roughly one
hundred major known VERs in operation in the mid-1980s, fifty-five restricted exports

---

[7] Import quotas differ from voluntary export restrictions (VERs), discussed later, in that the former are
normally applied on a global, nondiscriminatory basis, whereas the latter are negotiated bilaterally.

[8] Voluntary export restriction (or restraint) is a generic term for all bilaterally agreed-upon restraints on
trade. It usually arises from pressure on an exporting country by an importing country and can be thought
of as "voluntary" in the sense that the exporting country may prefer it to other trade barriers that the
importing country might impose. An OMA is a voluntary export restriction that involves a government-
to-government agreement and often specific rules of management and consultation rights and calls for
monitoring trade flows (see Boonekamp [1987] for a discussion of the nature of VERs, why they were
introduced, and their economic effects).

to the then-European Community, and thirty-two restricted exports to the United States (Boonekamp, 1987: 3). Sectors subject to OMAs and VERs include automobiles, footwear, steel, ships, electronic products, and machine tools.

In some cases there are even networks of agreed-upon export restrictions. The classic example is in textiles and clothes, which has a long history.

> In the 1950s, when domestic interests began putting pressure on the U.S. Government for protection against cheap cotton-textile imports from the Far East, Washington negotiated several informal VERs with Japan and, later, Hong Kong. Ostensibly "temporary," they soon were imitated by major European importers; and in 1961 all were formally consolidated into the first of a series of multilateral cotton-textile agreements later expanded to include woolens and synthetic fibers as well. Now called the Multifiber Arrangement, and involving some forty countries in all, the scheme has evolved into an elaborate international market-sharing agreement that allows virtually no room at all for significant structural adjustment. Importing countries troubled by excess domestic capacity and deteriorating demand are determined not to allow lower-cost Third World exporters to threaten employment at home. Consequently, a disproportionate fraction of their workers remain tied to a stagnant industry. (Cohen, 1983: 10)[9]

Estimates suggest that some 10 percent of total world trade is subject to the distorting effects of OMAs and VERs (Boonekamp, 1987: 3). Moreover, their prevalence grew substantially in the 1980s, particularly as applied to the exports of Japan and the Newly Industrialized Countries (NICs) of East Asia. Although these restrictions on exports are arguably not illegal under GATT's rules, which are concerned primarily with governmental actions affecting imports, they doubtless contravene its broad goal of trade liberalization.

**NONTARIFF BARRIERS**   Import and export quotas are two examples of a class of trade restrictions known as ***nontariff barriers*** (NTBs). NTBs are now a more important form of protection than tariffs, which, in the area of industrial products at least, are comparatively inconsequential. "Formal trade barriers are tiny. Tariffs average 3.5 percent, and quotas apply only to a handful of farm products. But," explains Robert J. Samuelson (1993: 52), trade protection through "informal obstacles abound."

NTBs have become particularly ubiquitous with the rise of the welfare state. Their effects, sometimes inadvertent and sometimes intentional, often restrain trade. As complex societies strive to protect the welfare of their citizens through numerous and often complex government regulations regarding health and safety, foreign-produced goods frequently cannot compete. Examples are the emission-control and safety standards imposed on the auto industry by the U.S. government in order to reduce air pollution and the risk of serious injury. When initiated, these standards, although meeting domestic needs, put burdens on certain foreign auto producers.

Health and safety standards are now regarded as necessary and legitimate forms

---

[9] The Multifiber Arrangement was renegotiated in 1986 and was scheduled for renewal again in 1991. Negotiators had hoped to bring textile trade into the GATT framework during the Uruguay Round of multilateral negotiations, but their efforts were put on hold when the Uruguay Round stalled in late 1991.

of government regulation. They have no necessary bearing on international trade, but if their purpose is to limit external competition—and only secondarily, if at all, to safeguard domestic welfare—then they become legitimate objects of attack by free-trade advocates. The problem lies in the difficulty of distinguishing legitimate NTBs from regulations designed primarily to limit foreign competition. The French and British, for example, suspect that U.S. noise regulations imposed some years ago to restrict the supersonic Concorde passenger plane were really an attempt to limit competition in the aircraft industry after the decision of the United States not to produce the Boeing supersonic transport.

Nontariff barriers range widely in their extensiveness and variety. Over 40 percent of First World imports are subject to the nontariff measures, and the proportion has grown sharply since the mid-1960s (*World Development Report 1991*, 1991: 104–105). Just as health and safety regulations may be legitimately designed to protect a country's citizens, measures taken to limit foreign imports in contravention of what liberal trade theory would otherwise see as mutually beneficial to all—a free-trade regime—are often deemed justified (see Box 7.4 for an amusing illustration). Even though the goods produced by one country may be superior in quality and cheaper in price than those produced in another, the latter may still use import quotas, export quotas, and other nontariff barriers to keep out the superior, less expensive, foreign-produced goods. It will do so if it perceives that the foreign goods' superior performance results not from purely market forces but from government subsidies granted to the export industries in the producing country.

**INFANT INDUSTRIES** The neomercantilist practices described above are widespread among industrialized countries. Among developing countries, for whom the absence of protection from the First World's more efficient firms may prohibit the realization of their domestic industrialization goals, the *infant industry* argument is more often used to justify policies restricting free trade. According to this argument, tariffs or other forms of protection are necessary to nurture young industries until they can mature and until their eventually lower-cost production enables them to compete effectively in the global marketplace. Protectionism is the product of such policies.

**THE COSTS OF PROTECTIONISM** One of the costs of trade protectionism is that it may postpone needed structural changes in national economies, as technological changes alter the relative efficiencies of different industries. A well-known international economist makes the case against protectionism this way:

> Import protection is like the toadstool—superficially attractive but potentially deadly. What protectionists prefer to ignore is that while individual industries might well profit from protectionism, at least for a time, the economy as a whole will suffer as increasingly more resources are locked into inefficient, low-growth activities. A healthy economy must be capable of adapting continuously to changes in the competitive environment. Capital and labor must be able to shift readily into growing, high-productivity sectors. Otherwise overall economic growth—the ultimate guarantor of jobs—gradually will be stifled. History is replete with tragic examples of economies that have choked on a diet of protectionism. (Cohen, 1983: 10)

## Box 7.4
## THE NEW PROTECTIONISM: THE "POITIERS EFFECT"

• • •

The "new protectionism" usually refers to the use of nontariff barriers such as VERs and orderly marketing arrangements. But it only takes a little ingenuity to introduce an administrative regulation which can be an effective barrier to trade.

In October 1982, citing a "Japanese invasion" in consumer electronics, the French government decreed that all imports of videocassette recorders (VCRs) would have to pass through Poitiers. Although not the most obvious point of entry, Poitiers could hardly be better suited to the purpose. It is a town hundreds of miles inland from France's northern ports where the VCRs are landed. It has a tiny customs crew that is obviously inadequate to the task of clearing hundreds of thousands of VCR imports. As the town where the French repelled an earlier invader, the Moors, Poitiers seemed an apt choice.

Moreover, a particularly long and tedious set of customs regulations were strictly enforced at Poitiers. All the accompanying documents were thoroughly examined and each container opened. A large number of VCRs were taken out of their boxes by the customs inspectors, who carefully checked their serial numbers and made sure that the instructions were written in French. Finally, a number of VCRs were dismantled to make sure that they were actually built in their reported country of origin. The regional customs director responsible for Poitiers said of the new regulations: "Before the new policy, it took a morning to clear a lorry-load of video recorders. Now it takes two to three months. We are still clearing consignments that arrived here [three months ago] when the policy went into effect. . . ."

As planned, the "Poitiers effect" severely limited VCR imports into France. Before the use of Poitiers, more than 64,000 VCRs, mostly from Japan, entered France each month for the first ten months of 1981. Afterward, less than 10,000 VCRs cleared the customs point at Poitiers each month, while the rest of the supply waited in bonded warehouses throughout the town. Exporters did not passively concede to the French barriers. Denmark, the Federal Republic of Germany, and the Netherlands, which also export VCRs to France, filed a complaint with the EC Executive Committee in Brussels, which in turn brought charges against France at the European Court of Justice for breach of EC free trade rules. Japan brought its complaint to the GATT and then suspended or curbed VCR shipments to France.

It is not clear what the French hoped to gain from the use of the Poitiers weapon. The French electronics firm Thomas-Brandt did not make its own VCRs, but sold Japanese VCRs under its own label. It experienced a shortage of these when the government required all the imports to go through Poitiers. Shortly after the establishment of Poitiers, the EC Commission negotiated a VER limiting Japan's exports to the entire European Community. This was followed by an agreement between Thomas-Brandt and Japan's JVC to manufacture component parts in France and later the lifting of the Poitiers restrictions. It is likely that several complex issues concerning intragovernment and government-industry relations played a role in the Poitiers scheme. Yet, although the motives remain somewhat obscure, the protective effect of it is clear.

*Source:* World Development Report 1987 *(1987: 141).*

Although they are commonplace, beggar-thy-neighbor trade strategies cannot work for everyone; not everyone can run a balance-of-trade surplus. As in the similar case of balances of payments, when one country is in a surplus position, another *must* have a deficit. Moreover, a contrary view to that described above maintains that the consequences of protectionism may be less devastating than the advocates of free trade sometimes allege (see Box 7.5). In either event, the practice of neomercantilism with varied tactics is widespread. Often this means that consumers either pay higher prices or must settle for commodities inferior to those otherwise available from abroad.

## *Strategic Trade*

In contrast with policies designed to protect inefficient industries, realist advocates of neomercantilist strategic trade policy see it as a means of ensuring that a country's industries will remain competitive in the rapidly changing, high-tech environment of the future.

Classical liberal trade theory shows how international trade contributes to the welfare of trading partners. By implication, it also demonstrates why states may choose to cooperate with one another to reduce trade barriers. What classical theory does not deal with is the fact that comparative advantages may change.

Classical theory attributes the basis for trade to underlying differences among states: Some are better suited to the production of agricultural products, such as coffee, because they have vast tracts of fertile land, for example, while others are better suited to the production of labor-intensive goods, such as consumer electronics, because they have an abundance of cheap labor. Increasingly, however, economists now recognize that comparative advantages take on a life of their own.

Much international trade . . . reflects national advantages that are created by historical circumstance, and that then persist or grow because of other advantages to large scale either in development or production. For example, the development effort required to launch a new passenger jet aircraft is so large that the world market will support only one or two profitable firms. Once the United States had a head start in producing aircraft, its

# Box 7.5
## THE COSTS OF TRADE CONFLICT

• • •

A hypothetical scenario may be useful for understanding what the costs of protection are, and why they are more modest than many people seem to think.

Let's imagine that most of the world's market economies were to group themselves into three trading blocs—one centered on the United States, one centered on the European [Union], and one centered on Japan. And let's suppose that each of these trading blocs becomes highly protectionist, imposing a tariff against goods from outside the bloc of 100 percent, which we suppose leads to a fall in imports of 50 percent.

So we are imagining a trade war that cuts the volume of world trade in half. What would be the costs of this trade war?

One immediate response would be that each bloc would lose jobs in the industries that formerly exported to the others. This is true; but each bloc would correspondingly gain a roughly equal number of jobs producing goods it formerly imported. There is no reason to expect that even such a major fragmentation of the world market would cause extra unemployment.

The cost would come instead from reduced efficiency. Each bloc would produce goods for itself that it could have imported more cheaply. With a 100 percent tariff, some goods would be produced domestically even though they could have been imported at half the price. For these goods there is thus a waste of resources equal to the value of the original imports.

But this would be true only of goods that would have been imported in the absence of tariffs, and even then 100 percent represents a maximum estimate. Our three hypothetical trading blocs would, however, import only about 10 percent of the goods and services they use from abroad even under free trade.

A trade war that cut international trade in half, and which caused an *average* cost of wasted resources for the displaced production of, say, 50 percent, would therefore cost the world economy only 2.5 percent of its income (50 percent × 5 percent = 2.5 percent).

This is not a trivial sum—but it is a long way from a Depression. (It is roughly the cost of a 1 percent increase in the unemployment rate.) And it is the result of an extreme scenario, in which protectionism has a devastating effect on world trade.

If the trade conflict were milder, the costs would be much less. Suppose that the tariff rates were only 50 percent, leading to a 30 percent fall in world trade. Then 3 percent of the goods originally used would be replaced with domestic substitutes, costing at most 50 percent more. If the typical domestic substitute costs 25 percent more, then the cost of the trade conflict is 0.75 percent of world income (25 percent × 3 percent = 0.75 percent).

*Source: Paul Krugman (1990: 105).*

position as the world's leading exporter became self-reinforcing. So if you want to explain why the U.S. exports aircraft, you should not look for underlying aspects of the U.S. economy; you should study the historical circumstances that gave the United States a head start in the industry. (Krugman, 1990: 109)

If the contemporary pattern of international trade reflects historical circumstances, then states may conclude that it is in their interests to try to create advantages that will redound to the long-run benefit of their economies. Curiously, then, the logic of comparative advantage can itself be used to justify government interference in the free market. This rationale underlies *strategic trade*—a form of "managed trade" and industrial policy that seeks to create comparative advantages by targeting government subsidies toward particular industries (for example, computers, semiconductors, high-definition television) so as to gain a competitive edge vis-à-vis foreign producers. Although studies indicate that the returns on strategic trade policies are often marginal (Krugman, 1990; Samuelson, 1993), the fact that some states (such as Japan) engage in such practices encourages others to do likewise. To illustrate, consider the 1993 statement by Laura Tyson, chairperson of President Clinton's Council of Economic Advisors, "Our approach is to say to our trading partners, 'If you continue to subsidize your high-tech industries, we will do the same.'"

## Free Trade and Hegemonic Decline

Economic considerations encourage states to pursue strategic trade policies, but important political considerations also motivate them. As noted above, the absence of world government encourages states to be more concerned with how they fare in relation to others—their relative gains—than with how they fare individually—their absolute gains. Strategic trade, because of "its emphasis on how economies of scale in industries present states with incentives to interfere in trade to gain market shares" (Snidal, 1991b), illustrates how the pursuit of relative gains may impede the logic of comparative advantage and free trade. Thus strategic or managed trade is pursued because states are prone to "forgo some of the benefits of cooperation or economic exchange in the short run, in order to assure security, broadly defined, over the long run" (Mastanduno, 1991).

The concept of relative gains and states' concern for position in their relations with others also shed light on the reasons why the United States, the principle advocate of free trade in the post–World War II era, has itself increasingly engaged in restrictive trade practices. The U.S. "assertive trade policies" make it look in this regard less like a hegemon and more like an "ordinary country" in an intensely competitive trade system. An understanding of the changing role of the United States in the international trade regime, as in the international monetary regime, is essential to understanding the developments that now threaten maintenance of the free-trade alliance.

## THE TRANSFORMATION OF THE INTERNATIONAL TRADE REGIME . . . . . . . . .

Many of the same forces that nudged the crisis-prone international monetary system away from the precepts of the postwar Liberal International Economic Order have also tempted states to reduce their support for free trade. Increasingly, maintenance of the LIEO is often perceived as being less important than meeting countries' domestic economic goals. In a sense, ironically, the very success of the open, multilateral trade regime threatens to undermine its continuation, as growing interdependence increases policymakers' incentives to protect their established market share from foreign competition. Thus, many of the conditions that formerly encouraged support for free trade may erode. The demise of U.S. hegemony is central here, as the United States is today less willing and able to bear the costs of leadership as it had previously. The end of the Cold War is another important ingredient, as anxiety about the Soviet threat has been transferred to anxiety about trade competition among capitalists.

The forces that now challenge the liberal trade regime can be better understood by examining its postwar history and the role played by the United States in shaping it.

## Creating the Liberal Trade Regime: America's Leadership Role

The importance of the United States to the international trade system derives from the size of its economy and the value of its production sold abroad. In 1991, for example, U.S. exports equaled 7.4 percent of its gross domestic product. This contrasts sharply with many other countries that are comparatively more "involved" in the world economy. Japan's exports-to-GNP ratio in the same year, for example, was 13.3 percent, Britain's 20.2 percent, Germany's 32.6 percent, the Netherlands' 53.5 percent, and Taiwan's 42.3 percent (U.S. CIA, 1992a: 16, 18). Despite these higher ratios, however, only Germany's exports rivaled in value the more than $422 billion of U.S. production sold abroad (Japan's exports were $315 billion). In fact, the ranking among these six countries according to their exports-to-GNP ratio is nearly the opposite of their ranking according to the size of their economies.

In 1991 the gross domestic product of the United States was more than four times Germany's and more than thirty times greater than Taiwan's (by 1993 Taiwan, with only twenty million people, held the largest reserves in the world). In general, therefore, and despite the relative decline in American economic dominance, the U.S. economy and its foreign economic policies are much more important to other countries than their economies and policies are to the United States. What U.S. Trade Representative Reuben Askew said in 1980 is still accurate today: "True, we are no longer the single, pre-eminent economic power in the world. But we are still the strongest."

### The U.S. Role in the Bretton Woods Period

The importance of the United States to the world political economy was especially pronounced in the period immediately following World War II. Today the United States accounts for about 23 percent of the world's aggregate GNP; in 1947 it accounted for nearly half. Not surprisingly, therefore, after World War II the United States became the dominant voice in trade as well as monetary affairs.

As with the monetary system, the liberal trading system the United States promoted drew on the lessons policymakers perceived in the 1930s. The zero-sum, beggar-thy-neighbor policies associated with the intensely competitive economic nationalism of the interwar period were widely regarded by those concerned with postwar reconstruction to have been a major cause of the economic catastrophe of the 1930s that precipitated global warfare. To avert a repetition of such a scenario, priority was assigned to removing barriers to trade, particularly tariffs. The decline in the average U.S. tariff rate since the late 1940s reflects this acceptance of liberal free trade (see Figure 7.3).

The United States envisioned that an International Trade Organization (ITO) would be created to seek lower restrictions on trade and set rules of commerce. Thus the new organization would perform the role in trade policy that the IMF and World Bank were designed to perform in international monetary management. However, the ITO was stillborn. It failed to win approval when the liberal trading system envisioned in its proposed charter, popularly known as the Havana Charter, generated congressional opposition: "Protectionists opposed the arrangement for being too liberal, and liberals were against it for being too protectionist. . . . Without U.S. support the ITO was dead" (Isaak, 1991). In its place, the United States sponsored a new multilateral treaty that created the General Agreement on Tariffs and Trade (GATT). GATT became the cornerstone of the liberalized trade regime originally embodied in the ITO.

Under GATT in 1947 and the most-favored-nation principle, a series of multilat-

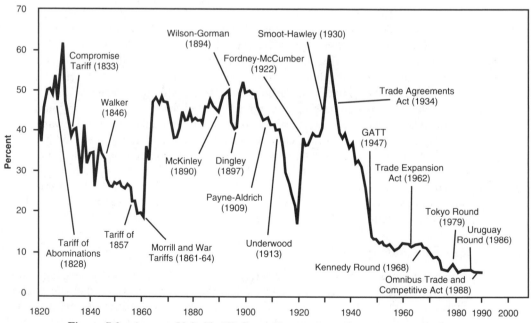

**Figure 7.3**  Average U.S. Tariffs Rates Since 1820
*Source:* Adapted and modified U.S. Department of Commerce statistics as presented in the Foundation for Teaching Economics and the United Nations Association of the USA (1992: 35).

eral trade negotiations aimed at tariff reductions were initiated with broad participation in the capitalist community. The eighth of these sessions, the Uruguay Round, began in 1986 in Punta del Este, Uruguay. It was originally scheduled to have been completed in 1990 to reaffirm and extend the free-trade regime. But the negotiating partners failed to reach agreement on important issues and experienced a logjam on the comprehensive trade reform package. In the process, GATT developed the cynical reputation as the General Agreement to Talk and Talk. In the end, on December 15, 1993, the talks did finally culminate in a new pact. To understand why and how, the evolution of this process needs to be understood.

An important catalyst in the postwar momentum toward a liberalized trading system, notably on industrial products, was the Kennedy Round of negotiations, which actually took place during the Johnson administration (1964–1967). In this, as well as in all previous multilateral trading conferences, the United States was the principal mover.

As hegemony demands, the United States was willing to accept fewer immediate benefits than were its trading partners, due to anticipation of the longer-term benefits of freer international trade. In effect, the United States was the locomotive of expanding world production and trade. By stimulating its own growth, the United States became an attractive market for the exports of others, and the outflow of U.S. dollars stimulated the economic growth of other countries in the "American train." Evidence that supports the wisdom of this strategy, particularly the association between tariff reductions and export growth, is that as the average duty levied on imports to the United States declined by more than half between the late 1940s and the early 1960s, world exports nearly tripled.

The Kennedy Round did not deal successfully with tariff barriers on agricultural products, however. Lack of progress on this issue, and later disagreements over it, began to raise doubts among U.S. policymakers about the wisdom of the U.S. expansionary policies. The immediate challenge was posed in 1966 in the Common Agricultural Policy (CAP) instituted by the European Economic Community (EEC). To outsiders, the CAP was seen as a protectionist tariff wall designed to maintain politically acceptable but artificially high prices for farm products produced within the EEC. Its "egregiously mercantilist" program of internal supports and import levies curtailed foreign competition and stimulated large surpluses that were then dumped on the world market through export subsidies (Babai, 1993: 344). CAP effectively restricted U.S. agricultural exports to the EEC (which by the 1960s had become a principal trading partner of the United States).

The Trade Expansion Act of 1962, passed by the U.S. Congress in an effort to improve the U.S. competitive trade position in relation to that of the European Economic Community, provided the U.S. domestic base for the Kennedy Round. The president's authority to negotiate trade matters under the earlier Trade Expansion Act expired with the end of the Kennedy Round. Thereafter, Presidents Johnson and Nixon fought a rearguard action against the rising protectionist forces that bombarded Congress with trade-restriction demands.

The challenge of an economically revitalized and politically uniting Europe was among the factors that led to the waning of U.S. support for a multilateral free-trade regime. Other contributing factors included the EC's extension of preferential trade treatment to countries in Africa, the Mediterranean, and the Caribbean; the expansion of the Common Market from six members to nine in 1973; the extension of associate status to others; and the growing perception that Japan's highly protectionist trade policies violated the liberalized trading scheme in which others remained in voluntary compliance (Spero, 1990).

At a broader level, the postwar trade regime was threatened by many of the same forces that were undermining the international monetary system. The latter's collapse inhibited progress on trade matters, as did the shifting constellation of political forces within the Western world and between it and the communist world. The loss of U.S. leadership was a consequence.

## The Regime under Stress

In much the same way that the monetary disorder of the 1970s reflected the inability of the Bretton Woods system to master the international economic forces then unleashed, the erosion of the liberal trade regime of the 1950s and 1960s reflected the inability of GATT to keep pace with the new developments. As described by a former counsel to the U.S. special trade representative:

> GATT was formed to promote free-market competition among a maximum number of countries under a relatively few simple rules: nondiscrimination (the United States must treat Japanese and European products equally, for example); no barriers to imports other than declining tariffs; and no protection of faltering industries from import competition except through temporary measures taken publicly in emergency cases. These were rules for a simpler era, when trade was a fraction of its present volume, tariffs were the main trade barrier, a few Western countries dominated international trade and postwar optimism for international free enterprise was high—at least in the United States, which was the preeminent economic superpower. Although by the 1970s all of these circumstances had changed drastically, the GATT rules remained substantially the same and, as a result, were widely ignored. Without viable international rules, trade relations quickly revert to the law of the jungle. (Graham, 1979: 52)

## Challenges to American Leadership and the Liberal Trade Regime

Europe's maintenance of agricultural product prices above market values reveals an important underpinning of protectionist logic: It appeals to influential domestic political interests that perceive the costs of free trade as greater than its benefits.

### The Tokyo Round of Multilateral Trade Negotiations

In part to cope with growing protectionist sentiments in the United States, the Nixon administration sought a new grant of authority from Congress to negotiate lower tariff barriers with other nations. The result was the Tokyo Round of multilateral trade negotiations, which was concluded in 1979 after nearly six years of bargaining.

The Tokyo Round began in a radically different environment from that of the previous GATT sessions. The world political economy had experienced an exponential growth in trade value, the level of economic interdependence among the world's leading industrial countries stood at unprecedented levels, tariffs no longer posed the principal barriers to trade, and the United States no longer enjoyed the prerogatives of an economic giant without rivals. In this new setting, addressing nontariff barriers to trade and reducing barriers to the free flow of agricultural products took on greater urgency.

The Tokyo Round produced new international rules to deal with such issues as subsidies, duties, dumping, government purchasing, product standards, custom valuation and licensing, and trade with developing countries. Still, it did not clearly reaffirm the precepts underlying GATT and the liberal trade regime (Krasner, 1979). Nor did it deal effectively with agricultural trade issues and with the growing incidence of neomercantilist and strategic trade practices that were of special concern to the United States.

It was clear by the time the Tokyo Round concluded that the promise and practice of free trade diverged widely. Part of the reason is that states differ in their assessment of the role that government should play in regulating economic behavior. Where they fall along the continuum between an open and a closed economic system and what they therefore view as appropriate government intervention in market-oriented economies predict their position on international trade issues.

The United States became increasingly reluctant to assume the costs of leadership in an environment in which others were perceived to be playing by a different set of rules. Lee Iacocca, the president of the Chrysler Corporation, reflected popular sentiment by charging in 1983 that "because the U.S. government still clings to free trade rules, America lacks a trade policy responsive to new realities of international competition. For American businessmen and workers—sent out into the global marketplace to compete without government help—the playing field is not level; it's tilted against them." The playing field analogy stresses not the issue of free trade but *fair trade*.

### The Uruguay Round of Multilateral Trade Negotiations

It was against the background of a trade system increasingly rife with restrictive barriers, subsidies, the intentional use of product standards that others cannot meet, and other unfair trade practices and "gray-area" measures (such as VERs) that go beyond the principles of GATT that the United States urged a new round of trade negotiations to "level the playing field."

FREE TRADE VERSUS FAIR TRADE   The trade policies of the continental European states, Japan, and less developed countries were of special concern to the United States. Governments there routinely intervened actively in economic life and played entrepreneurial and developmental roles. Such action violated what the United States, in principle, rhetorically regarded as government's proper role.

Soon after 1986, when the Uruguay Round was in full swing, others began to view the United States, which by then had become the world's largest debtor, as part of the problem. The U.S. trade deficit ranged well beyond $100 billion annually and its trade imbalance with particular countries, notably Japan, had burgeoned to seemingly intractable levels (reaching in 1993 $59 billion with Japan and in 1992 $18 billion with China) (Harper, 1994). Still, America's trade partners were not quick to accept the U.S. analogy of an uneven playing field skewed in their favor (see Kuttner, 1991). One observer caustically described the U.S. position by noting that "the more inefficient and backward an American industry is, the more likely the U.S. government will blame foreign countries for its problems" (Bovard, 1991).

Despite their understandable pique, the world's trading states were sensitive nonetheless to the need to keep protectionist sentiments in the United States at bay. Because U.S. imports stimulated the economic growth of its trade partners, they conceded that new trade talks were necessary in order to cope with issues of special concern to the United States. The Reagan administration simultaneously used the proposed trade talks to thwart growing protectionist sentiments at home, where, at one time during 1985 (when Congress began to debate what eventually became the Omnibus Trade and Competitiveness Act of 1988), some 300 trade protection bills were pending before Congress. These bills offered protection to almost every industrial sector, ranging from steel, copper, lumber, and automobiles to shoes, textiles, neckties, and waterbeds.

**New Issues, Old Problems** Coping with traditional tariff issues and bringing voluntary export restrictions and other forms of the new protectionism under multilateral management preoccupied the United States during the protracted Uruguay Round between 1986 and December 1993. In addition, the United States pushed hard to reduce barriers to trade in services (for example, insurance), trade-related intellectual property rights (known as TRIPs), computer software, and trade-related investment matters (TRIMs). These areas traditionally were outside the GATT framework, but they were of special interest to the United States and other advanced industrial societies who enjoyed comparative advantages in them.

As the comparative advantage in the production of manufactured goods, such as consumer electronics and automobiles, was moving toward advanced developing countries like the Newly Industrialized Countries (NICs), the importance of trade in services and intellectual property grew. The task confronted by the Uruguay Round negotiations was to develop rules that protected their countries' present or potential advantages while easing the passage of manufactures production to developing countries. From the viewpoint of the developing countries, however, severe impediments to the enhancement of their advantages in manufactured products already existed in the form of nontariff and other barriers to First World markets. This perception doubtless hardened the Third World countries' bargaining position on issues salient to the industrial societies.

Agriculture was another issue of special importance to the United States. World trade in agriculture evolved outside the main GATT framework and thus did not benefit from the same liberalizing influences as industrial products (Spero, 1990). It remains especially controversial because agricultural industries are deeply enmeshed in the domestic politics of producing states.

At the core of differences on agricultural trade were the enormous subsidies that governments of the leading producers in the First World paid farmers to keep them competitive in world markets, where prices were often much lower than in Europe or North America. In 1986, for example, the European Community spent over $20 billion, or more than two-thirds of its budget, on agricultural subsidies. The United States, for its part, spent about $30 billion in farm support programs, an amount that exceeded the net income of U.S. farms (Wallis, 1986: 2).

The perceived need for such subsidies reflected fundamental structural changes in the global system of food production. As with textiles, these subsidies were difficult to manage because of the potentially adverse domestic political consequences in those countries for which the global market was an outlet for surplus production, such as the United States and members of what is now formally called the European Union. The difficulty was exacerbated by the emergence of new competitors among Third World producers and by the shrinkage of traditional First World markets as a consequence of technological innovations. The latter have enabled expanded agricultural production in countries that previously experienced food deficits (see also Chapter 9).

During the Uruguay Round, the U.S. push to phase out all agricultural subsidies and farm trade protection programs within a decade was fiercely resisted by the European Community, which sought to maintain its own Common Agricultural Policy. The dispute over agriculture eventually led to an impasse in the Uruguay Round negotiations, which postponed its conclusion despite the success achieved in reaching agreements in services, textiles, property rights, and rules for dispute resolution.

In late 1993, however, the stalemate was finally broken. In a crisis atmosphere, the 117 members of GATT, after seven long years of talk, had to either put up or shut up. Extending the talks beyond the December 15, 1993 announced deadline was widely viewed as impossible. "The current system," warned GATT Director-General Peter Sutherland, was "collapsing," and "failure would be one of the biggest collective follies of this century."

In order to kick-start the troubled global economy and forestall trade wars, the GATT negotiators finally overcame their differences and signed the comprehensive liberal trade reform pact in Marrakesh, Morocco, in April 1994. The war of words ended, and the pattern of missed deadlines was finally broken. Designed to smash export barriers (slashing tariffs on manufactured goods by an average of 37 percent) and to create jobs around the world, the 400-page agreement, which covers everything from paper clips to jet aircraft, from potato chips to computer chips, is the most comprehensive trade deal in history (see Schott, 1994). For example, for the first time agricultural products are covered, and the accord orders an initial cut in members' farm subsides by an average of 21 percent. The result of the eighth GATT round of negotiations is a projection of the continuing reduction of the average tariffs of the industrial countries since 1940, which portends their potential elimination in the twenty-first century (see Figure 7.4).

Fear of failure was undoubtedly an important incentive to the accord, for collapse

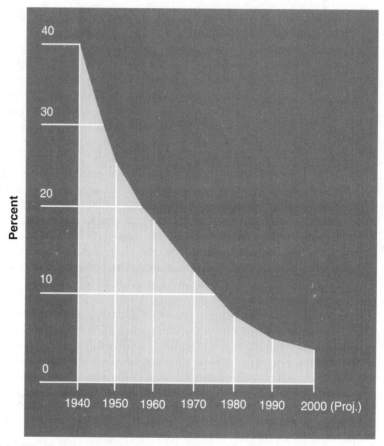

**Figure 7.4**   The Termination of Tariffs? The Decline of the Average Tariffs of Industrialized Countries, 1940–2000
*Source:* Office of the U.S. Trade Representative and the Centre for International Economics, as aggregated by *Time* (December 27, 1993: 16).

of the world trade talks, it was widely perceived, could also have easily led to the collapse of world trade and with it worldwide recession and political instability.[10] The desire for growth was an equally powerful incentive. Most analysts estimated that the terms of the world trade agreement negotiated under the auspices of the Uruguay Round of the GATT would increase global wealth by more than $200 billion *per year* by 2005. Indeed, many economists predict that the trade liberalization holds the promise of expanding global output by $6 trillion over the 1993–2003

---

[10] Fear of the potential erosion of the agreements reached was reflected in the pact's creation of a new ***World Trade Organization*** (WTO) with tougher enforcement powers to succeed the General Agreement on Tariffs and Trade. Instead of relying on the good faith of its members, the WTO's judicial powers require it to rule on member complaints within the year (as opposed to a half decade under GATT procedures). The reform was made possible when the United States became convinced that the new multilateral agency would not be able to overturn U.S. trade laws.

decade. For the United States—in 1993 the world's largest exporter and "once again the world leader in productivity-output per worker-hour" (Lacayo, 1993)—the returns promised to be substantial, as high as $1 trillion over the next decade. U.S. Trade Representative Mickey Kantor predicted that the pact would generate two million jobs over the next decade, and President Clinton claimed that the agreement would "cement our position of leadership in the new global economy." Perhaps these reasons provided incentive for the U.S. Congress to approve the deal by the June 1994 deadline, despite domestic lobbying from producers whose businesses would be hurt by the overall cut of more than 33 percent of the U.S. border taxes on thousands of products that the agreement enacts. Perhaps, too, another rationale for the agreement's approval was operative—growing recognition that recent transformations in the patterns of global production and commerce have removed them largely from the sphere of meaningful government regulation. As multinational "firms are becoming increasingly mobile . . . and are fast forming alliances with competing [foreign] firms" (Richardson, 1995), they have severed their affiliation with any state, and, in an increasingly interdependent global marketplace, have placed their activities beyond the reach of any government's control. Hence, to "open" borders to free trade is to accept the fact that it may no longer be possible for governments to impose barriers to foreign imports (see Box 7.6)

**U.S. BILATERAL AND UNILATERAL INITIATIVES** While the United States was pursuing resolution of outstanding trade issues through the multilateral GATT mechanism in the late 1980s and early 1990s, it also pursued important bilateral negotiations and undertook unilateral measures. Among these was conclusion of free-trade agreements with Israel and Canada. Although these initiatives were rationalized as consistent with GATT, analysts worried that they violated GATT's rule of nondiscrimination (otherwise known as general reciprocity) underlying the liberal trade system.[11]

The United States also unilaterally pursued remedies in response to what it regarded as the unfair trade practices of other governments. The 1988 Omnibus Trade Act required that the president identify countries believed to engage in unfair trade practices. Those countries either had to negotiate remedies or face U.S. retaliation. Although the Super 301 provisions of the law authorizing the U.S. government to investigate and retaliate against specific foreign trade barriers believed to be unfair were "almost unanimously viewed abroad as a clear violation of the GATT" (Walters and Blake, 1992), the provisions reflected particular U.S. resentment of the trade policies of Japan and the four Asian NICs (Hong Kong, Singapore, South Korea, and Taiwan). The intent of Super 301 was to level the playing field with those perceived most in violation of the rules of free trade "by imposing 100 percent tariffs on exports from those nations unless they satisfy U.S. demands," so as to right the overall U.S. imbalance of trade (Bovard, 1994).

The persistent U.S. trade deficit underlies the determination of the United States to take unilateral action against those deemed to play unfairly, such as China, which

---

[11] Raymond Vernon (1982) points out that the United States continued to preach free trade even though it knowingly violated the rule of nondiscrimination because "it has had trouble envisaging a coherent world trading system without such a rule."

## Box 7.6
### Beyond Trade Regulation? The Mobility of the Modern Multinational Mode of Production and Commerce

• • •

By the 1980s a new pattern of corporate behavior was developing. . . . Many . . . firms . . . began moving their manufacturing and other advanced operations abroad in order to meet the cost structures of their new, foreign competition. . . .

The second change underway . . . is the rapid trend toward strategic alliances with foreign companies in the same industry. Some of these are long-term partnerships, anchored in equity ownership—thus, Ford now owns 25 percent of rival Mazda while Honda owns 20 percent of rival Rover. Other alliances are more transient and project-specific, giving rise to the term "virtual corporations." Generally speaking, there are two purposes these various alliances can serve. First, an alliance with a rival may serve to achieve economies of scale. The Chrysler–Mitsubishi assembly plant in Illinois produces virtually identical cars under different nameplates for the two companies. (Originally the Diamond-Star assembly plant in Normal, Illinois, was equally owned by each firm. In 1991, Chrysler sold its half of the plant to Mitsubishi on the condition that certain Chrysler components continue to be used there and that Chrysler-badged vehicles continue to be produced there.) Second, an alliance can allow each firm to complement the other's most distinctive talents and simultaneously learn from its partner's expertise. In addition, these alliances are often complex: Mitsubishi works with Chrysler in North America and meanwhile cooperates in far-flung electronic and automotive ventures with Germany's Daimler–Benz and in automobile coproduction with the Volvo–Renault alliance in the Netherlands.

These cases show that states are being drawn into disputes that are given new form by the growth of those global alliances. Policymakers can easily misunderstand the consequences of their [efforts to arrest foreign imports when] they are seemingly oblivious to the mobility of relevant firms even as they futilely expend diplomatic good will in sometimes rancorous negotiations with other governments. . . .

What is a member of the U.S. Congress to think when lobbied by the "Big Three" U.S. automakers for much higher tariff protection against Japanese minivans? Would the official know that Ford and Nissan jointly produce a minivan in the United States already? That the Dodge Colt minivan is imported from Japan? Would she or he appreciate that, because Japanese minivans have only a very small market share in the United States, Detroit would gain little from such a diplomatically costly decision? Few government leaders in the major trading states are likely to have such trade expertise.

*Source: Neil R. Richardson (1995: 286–287, 289)*

in 1993 had benefited from an enormous and rapidly growing trade surplus with the United States. The causes of the chronic overall U.S. trade deficit estimated in 1993 at $116 billion (the worst since 1988) (Harper, 1994), however, include factors besides trade.

As noted earlier, the dollar exchange rate also is important to an understanding of the trade deficit. As the dollar soared in the first half of the 1980s, the ability of U.S. exporters to compete in the global marketplace plummeted, resulting in thousands of lost jobs among those who depend on exports. Even as the dollar declined in the latter half of the decade, however, the trade deficit, while reduced, persisted. U.S. imports from abroad continued their upward trend in response to the aggressive strategies of major exporters to the U.S. market, who sought to protect their coveted market shares. Moreover, by this time capital flows were playing a more dominant role than trade in the global economy, with the result that exchange-rate fluctuations no longer varied in tandem with changes in the direction of international trade (Bhagwati, 1991).

In addition, the U.S. trade deficit was influenced by the long-term decline in productivity resulting from a loss to Japan and others of the technological edge that the United States enjoyed in the 1950s and 1960s. Insufficient domestic savings and insufficient investment in civilian research and development as well as in basic education contributed to the erosion of the country's trade competitiveness (see Fallows, 1994; Thurow, 1992).

Analysts and policymakers alike often attribute Japan's spectacular export growth since the 1960s to its intimate government–business alliance. Because *keiretsu*—loose groups of companies—channel sales among members, cartels smother price competition, and government support impedes foreigners from entering Japan's market, many conclude that Japan is the world's preeminent neomercantilist power. The enormous trade imbalance between Japan and the United States—surpluses that collectively exceeded $500 billion between 1980 and 1993—reinforced the widespread belief that Japan's trade policies are inherently detrimental to U.S. business. "Japan is unique among developed nations in maintaining closed markets" was the way U.S. Trade Representative Mickey Kantor expressed the view in March 1994.

The United States and Japan have engaged in protracted negotiations designed to right their trade imbalance. The Structural Impediments Initiative (SII) was a recent example. Yet the goal proved elusive. A number of factors explained this, including the preference of millions of Americans for products made in Japan, Japanese tariff and nontariff barriers that limit the ability of U.S. producers to penetrate the Japanese market, and a cultural tradition in Japan that views foreign products as ill-suited to the Japanese consumer. Furthermore, the domestic savings rate in Japan is considerably higher than the average savings rate among the other Western industrialized countries, and its domestic consumption is also low. This means Japanese industry must look overseas for growth; in other words, its surplus of savings over investment, and of production over consumption, gravitates abroad (Feldstein, 1985).

Since the mid-1980s Japan's economic strategy has emphasized domestic demand rather than export promotion. Yet, as noted, this has not rectified Japan's chronic trade imbalance with the United States and others.[12] That imbalance is now a part of the larger trade deficit that has developed between the United States and Asia generally, which has skyrocketed with the remarkable surpluses China's new market economy has generated. Retarded from 1991 to 1993 by the slowest economic growth since the mid-1970s, Japan's proportion of Asian trade has declined while China's exports have risen, climbing 9.4 percent in 1992 (Mitchell, 1993: 164).

When the expansion of the Asian Tigers is included in the trends, it is self-evident that the Pacific Rim will play an increasingly influential role in the global marketplace. Because of Asia's size and its rising prominence in world trade, establishing a reasonable balance between Asia and its trading partners outside the region, as well as integrating these economic powers into the management of the international trading system, will be a central challenge for the remainder of the century.

## From Multilateralism to Regionalism

For some time the possibility that the multilateral trading system would splinter into several regional trading blocs has concerned analysts. They worry that escalating regionalism will lead to the closure of the open trading regime central to the Liberal International Economic Order and precipitate the collapse of the free-trade alliance recently reinforced by the approval of the GATT pact in December 1993.

The European Union in particular is often perceived as the greatest threat to preservation of the open, liberal regime. Its determination under the slogan "Europe 1992" to create a market completely free of internal barriers reinforced that fear. As George Bush put it early in his presidency, "We must all work hard to ensure that the Europe of 1992 will adopt the lower barriers of the modern international economy, not the high walls and the moats of medieval commerce."

At the same time that the United States expressed concern about trends in Europe, the 1988 U.S.–Canada Free Trade Agreement raised fear that the United States was moving toward the same kind of regionalized monetary and trade system that it opposed in Europe. That concern was further heightened on October 7, 1992, when the leaders of Canada, Mexico, and the United States announced their desire to pursue the *North American Free Trade Agreement* (NAFTA). Its purpose was to bring Mexico into the free-trade zone that already linked the United States and Canada in order to create the world's largest market—a $6.5 trillion market with nearly 370

---

[12] It was partly in frustration that President Clinton in March 1994 signed an executive order that reinstated the "Super 301" provision of the 1988 Trade Act (which was phased out in 1990). By renewing it, Clinton hoped to signal that he was serious about unfair trade practices, for the order gave him the authority to impose punitive tariffs of up to 100 percent against exports from countries deemed to have the most restrictive barriers to U.S. goods and services. Instructively, the European Union, which in 1993 registered a trade deficit with Japan about half that of the United States ($30 billion), undertook planning for a combined effort with the United States to force Japan to open its markets, despite criticism that the threat could provoke a wider trade war. "Maybe we're already in a trade war," warned Clyde Prestowitz, an adviser to the Clinton administration, as "we're responding in a different way to a war we've been involved in for a long time."

million people. This goal built on the trade increases that were already occurring. In 1986, Mexico began to liberalize and open its economy. Despite a tariff wall against U.S. products prior to NAFTA that averaged 10 percent, the liberalization in 1986 produced immediate dividends for the trade partners. Between then and 1992, U.S. exports rose 228 percent—from $12.4 billion to $40.6 billion. NAFTA was written to accelerate this growth.

The creation of the world's largest free-trade zone, stretching from the Yukon to the Yucatan, was motivated by more than an appetite for profit and new jobs:

> NAFTA is not really about global free trade. It does remove trade and investment barriers among the United States, Canada and Mexico, but it retains and erects (in the form of "rules of origin") barriers between the three countries and the rest of the world.
>
> Appearances aside, NAFTA is a prudent step toward creating a regional trading bloc that would withstand the devolution of Western Europe and Asia into rival blocs. The treaty's free trade proponents would never admit this, but NAFTA's underlying thrust is toward managed trade and investment. (Judis, 1993a: 32)

Hence, the drive to institute the North American Free Trade Agreement can be interpreted as a defensive response by the United States, Canada, and Mexico to the growing threat of the barriers and competition arising from Asia and the European trade bloc. As U.S. Senator Bill Bradley, an advocate of the agreement, explained, "If we don't do this, Japan and Europe will move in." And similarly the Clinton White House was "ready with a catchy 1990 theme against NAFTA critics if the treaty [was not approved by the Congress]—'Who Lost Latin America?'" (Borger, 1993).

The failure to approve NAFTA would have sent a message that the United States was not really sincere in its claims that it truly believed in liberalizing trade in GATT and bilaterally with other trade partners. And that signal would have stemmed the spectacular economic growth and job creation made possible by the removal of barriers to free trade after World War II. (The widely used formula projects that every $1 billion in exports supports 19,100 jobs.) Canada, which ratified the treaty, was free to walk away from it, and had the treaty been defeated, Mexico was expected to abandon its recent market-oriented reforms and return to its old nationalist, anti-Yankee ways. As U.S. Secretary of State Warren Christopher described it, NAFTA was "good economic policy and good foreign policy. It is a once-in-a-generation opportunity . . . that must not be lost." The fact that the agreement was approved serves as a signpost for the future of the world trade regime. Indeed, NAFTA's passage undoubtedly contributed greatly to the GATT reforms that were approved a month later and to the enthusiasm for creation of a hemispheric free trade area reaching from the northern tip of Canada to the southernmost point in Chile. Still, barriers to trade remain, and uncertainty about the future prospects for further reductions persists, especially in light of the continuing political instability in Mexico symbolized by the assassination in 1994 of ruling-party presidential candidate Luis Donaldo Colosio.

What *is* certain about the future is that the growing regionalization of trade, and with it the formation of competitive trade blocs, will continue. So-called "regional neomercantilism" (Sandholtz et al., 1992) is on the horizon. The efforts of the November 1993 Asia–Pacific Economic Co-operation (APEC) forum in Seattle represented an attempt to arrest the threats to free global trade that regional blocs pose. The meeting brought together the leaders of APEC's seventeen members, which embraces countries as diverse as Australia, Canada, Indonesia, Japan, and the United States. Yet the meeting symbolized the existence of the danger of regionalized trade blocs as much as hope that it can be alleviated.

At present there is no official initiative under way to create a formal Asian trading system centered on Japan and China, whose exchanges escalate. In 1992, Japan sold $12 billion and bought $17 billion worth of Chinese goods, and Japan, Hong Kong, and Taiwan were responsible for 85 percent of the $11 billion foreign investment in China, which rose 160 percent over the prior year (Weiner, 1993: 6). The continuing economic integration of North America and Europe may eventually nudge Asian economic integration forward.[13] More than a third of total world trade already takes place *within* the three major trading blocs, whose per-capita GNPs are becoming increasing equal. Examine the regionalization of trade as illustrated in Figure 7.5, which shows that "a big trend in the world economy is towards 'regionalism' and the reassertion of economic geography" (*The Economist* 329, November 20, 1993). Thus, as a United Nations (1991a) report concluded, "Today the question is not whether these [trade] blocs will be formed, but rather how encompassing they will be and how to ensure that they will not harm the [global] trading system."

Regional trade schemes like those in Europe and North America do not necessarily contravene the WTO's rules regarding nondiscrimination in trade. Nor do analysts agree on the question of whether regionalization is good or bad from the point of view of the effective functioning of the world political economy. Some see economic competition spilling into political conflict (Thurow, 1992; Hart, 1992), while others disagree with this projection. But nearly all worry about the adverse effects that rival trading blocs may have on individual countries, including in particular the United States (see Tyson, 1993).

According to this viewpoint, the regionalization of the world trade (and monetary) regimes into three primary blocs—in Europe, Asia, and the Western Hemisphere—would find the United States the leader of the weakest bloc of the three (Mead, 1990) and increasingly squeezed out of the others, where its trade imbalances are already enormous. The conclusion is that "the United States and Canada are too much like twins to grow rich trading largely with each other"; that prolonged economic weakness characterizes many of the other economies in the Western Hemisphere, whose cultures in any event direct them more toward Europe rather than the United States; that the U.S. dollar, while remaining "the key international currency" is "but a ghost of its former self"; and that the United States is, and will remain, dependent on oil imports from the volatile Middle East (Mead, 1990).

---

[13] The hypothesis underlying this prediction is the tendency for efforts to regionalize growth in one trade zone to stimulate similar efforts in other trade zones. Consider Southeast Asia. Fearing that it would be left out by the formation of trade blocs in North America, Europe, and Northeast Asia, the Association of South East Asian Nations (ASEAN) in 1993 responded. It formed an *ASEAN Free Trade Area* (AFTA) to foster intra-ASEAN economic cooperation by creating a less restrictive market to expand intraregional trade. This follows ASEAN's participation in the 1989 meeting of the first Asia–Pacific Economic Cooperation (APEC) forum—a move then taken to give ASEAN a greater voice in the consultative grouping and thereby prevent its isolation.

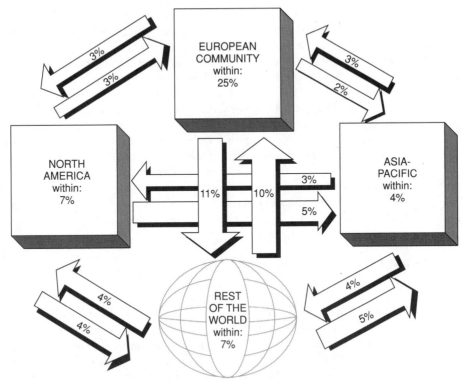

**Figure 7.5** Share of World Exports within and between Trading Areas, 1990
*Source:* United Nations (1991a: 6).
*Note:* North America: Canada, Mexico, United States; European Union; Belgium, Denmark, France, Germany, Ireland, Italy, Luxembourg, the Netherlands, Portugal, Spain, United Kingdom; Asia-Pacific: Hong Kong, Japan, Malaysia, Republic of Korea, Singapore, Thailand.

Beyond these concerns about trade rivalries among the richest countries and blocs, there looms the larger question of what effect the end of the Cold War will have on the regionalization of the multilateral trade system and, more generally, on the world political economy. Many analysts see the eventual integration of the countries of Eastern Europe into the European Union or perhaps some other, even larger European economic entity as both possible and probable. Less certain is the fate of Russia and the fledgling market economies of the other republics that formerly made up the Soviet Union. They would like to integrate their new free market economies into the world capitalist system to foster their prosperity. But the political instabilities and ethnic conflicts that plague their active entry into international trade demand a preoccupation on domestic problems and reforms for the time being. The sizable foreign assistance of $95.5 billion the international community extended between 1990 and 1992 (U.S. CIA, 1992a: 205) is designed to help. But the obstacles are tremendous. Until Russia and these other republics recover, their participation in the global marketplace is likely to remain limited. The proportion of former Soviet bloc countries' trade with the three major trade blocs is even more difficult to project over the long run.

To prevent Russia from becoming a "permanently developing country" (Winiecki, 1989) and to halt the erosion of living standards apparent for some years, leaders in Moscow (and elsewhere in Eastern Europe) have intensified their efforts to transform their moribund economies into market systems. The transition promises to be difficult, and success is by no means assured. The sobering fact is that for most of the new market economies, reforms are likely to be slow, with the "shock therapy" of Poland's quick jump to a market economy in a "single leap" an exception to the "gradualism" likely elsewhere (Bhagwati, 1994).

A major conclusion suggested by recent decades is that growth accelerates and trade expands only when domestic tranquility prevails and interstate tensions ease. The prospects for fully integrating the former socialist economies into the global capitalist market seem to be contingent on their prior ability to institutionalize internally free market, democratic reforms. Until that precondition is met, the full participation of these states in the world economy is problematic.

## THE TURBULENT 1990s: TRIUMPH OR TROUBLE? . . . . . . . . . . . . . . . . . .

The world will need to come to grips with the changing position of the United States in the global economic hierarchy. Some voices in the United States see in the demise of Soviet communism an opportunity for U.S. disengagement from world politics so as to rebuild U.S. power and leadership capabilities without the burdens of past commitments (Tonelson, 1991). Others see this as a unique period in world history, a "unipolar moment" that leaves the United States unchallenged in the world and "the only country with the military, diplomatic, political and economic assets to be a decisive player in any conflict in whatever part of the world it chooses to involve itself" (Krauthammer, 1991b).

Still others worry that the very exercise of U.S. power throughout the world is a misapplication of its resources that could spell its ultimate demise. "Although the United States is at present still in a class of its own economically and perhaps even militarily," historian Paul Kennedy (1987; also 1992) predicts, "it cannot avoid confronting the two great tests which challenge the *longevity* of every major power that occupies the 'number one' position in world affairs: whether, in the military/strategical realm, it can preserve a reasonable balance between the nation's perceived defense requirements and the means it possesses to maintain those commitments; and whether . . . it can preserve the technological and economic bases of its power from relative erosion in the face of ever-shifting patterns of global production."

The many issues and problems discussed in this chapter touch directly on the shifting patterns of economic power that shape the contours of contemporary world politics. If "welfare, not warfare, will [increasingly] shape the rules . . . and dictate the agenda" (Joffe, 1990), as many analysts believe, political leaders will have incentives to substitute "an ethics of 'shared sovereignty' and mutual assistance for the conventional realpolitik ethics of self-help and national competition" (Kegley, 1992). Because the "world's economies, now interdependent, all suffer together," only cooperation can alleviate the suffering and increase general prosperity (Wessel, 1992).

The prospect of further competition among rich "rival capitalists" (Hart, 1992) is to be taken seriously, however. In an interdependent world, leaders' preoccupations are drawn to expanding the material well-being of their own citizenry and their states' relative power position abroad; in this sense, interdependence is, paradoxically, a force promoting economic nationalism. It undermines the willingness of traders to put their countries' fate in the hands of free market dynamics.

Economic nationalism and a retreat from multilateral cooperation threaten to undermine the overall prospects for the world economy's growth. They encourage states to focus on local short-term needs rather than to confront shared long-term problems. "The assertion that 'all foreign policy is ultimately local' is closer to the mark than many . . . admit" (U.S. Department of State, 1993b). Thus the principles on which the Liberal International Economic Order have rested could again come under attack precisely when, as in the period following World War II, they may be most needed, especially by the very rich countries whose interests they have most clearly served. "The industrial countries," former U.S. Secretary of State Henry A. Kissinger (1982) has noted, "are still groping to reconcile the imperatives of their domestic policies with the realities of interdependence." How they finally manage that will have profound effects throughout the world.

## SUGGESTED READINGS

Bovard, James. *The Fair Trade Fraud*. New York: St. Martin's Press, 1991.

Caporaso, James A., and David P. Levine. *Theories of Political Economy*. New York: Cambridge University Press, 1992.

Cerny, Philip G. ed. *Finance and World Politics: Markets, Regimes and States in the Post-hegemonic Era*. Aldershot, UK: Edward Elgar, 1993.

Encarnation, Dennis J. *Rivals Beyond Trade: America versus Japan in Global Competition*. Ithaca, N.Y.: Cornell University Press, 1992.

Gilpin, Robert. *The Political Economy of International Relations*. Princeton, N.J.: Princeton University Press, 1987.

Lairson, Thomas D., and David Skidmore. *International Political Economy: The Struggle for Power and Wealth*. Orlando, Fla.: Harcourt Brace Jovanovich, 1993.

Rueter, Theodore. *The United States in the World Political Economy*. New York: McGraw-Hill, 1994.

Schott, Jeffrey J. *The Uruguay Round: An Assessment*. Washington, D.C.: Institute for International Economics, 1994.

Spero, Joan Edelman. *The Politics of International Economic Relations*, 4th ed. New York: St. Martin's Press, 1990.

Thurow, Lester C. *Head to Head: Coming Economic Battles among Japan, Europe, and America*. New York: Morrow, 1992.

Tyson, Laura D'Andrea. *Who's Bashing Whom: Trade Conflicts in High-Technology Industries*. Washington, D.C.: Institute for International Economics, 1993.

Walters, Robert S., and David H. Blake. *The Politics of Global Economic Relations*, 4th ed. Englewood Cliffs, N.J.: Prentice-Hall, 1992.

# CHAPTER 8

· · ·

# THE THIRD WORLD IN THE NEW GLOBAL MARKETPLACE: TRADE, AID, DEBT, AND DEVELOPMENT

· · ·

*There is no such thing as a coherent worldview of the South. But the failure to understand the [Third World] and to translate such understanding into effective diplomatic, economic, political, and military strategies will have profound consequences. Partnership between North and South remains a possibility, although arguably an improbable one. Antipathy and confrontation are also possible, and made more likely by Northern complacency.*

Shahram Chubin,
Specialist in Middle East Politics, 1993

*The challenge . . . is twofold: to compete successfully in commercial terms and to organize that competition to serve the interests of an expanding world economy. . . . We must be clear that international economic policy is foreign policy.*

U.S. Department of State
Management Task Force, 1993

The international monetary and multilateral trading regimes that evolved after World War II served the interests of the First World capitalist powers that built them. Developing countries on the rich countries' periphery had little influence over those regimes' design or operation. Yet the remaining vestiges of colonial economic linkages entangled the Third World in industrial countries' systems, over which, however, they had little control. From their perspective, the end of colonialism merely ushered in a more subtle and devious exploitation that the new international economic structures helped to perpetuate.

The most strident effort by developing countries to gain status and equality in the world political economy occurred in the 1970s, when they called for a **New International Economic Order** (NIEO). The debate that followed engaged primarily the First and the Third Worlds. The then-communist countries formed political alliances with one side or the other from time to time, as their political advantage dictated. However, because of the so-called socialist states' own lack of economic ties with the South and their belief that they bore no responsibility for colonialism, Second World countries were not active participants in the most intense debates between the North and the South about the structure and management of the world political economy.

Today the New International Economic Order rhetoric is little more than a footnote to the North–South debate of the past. Now the central issue is what impact the end of the Cold War will exert on the developing world. Will it lead to a period of benign neglect, as the advanced industrial countries turn their attention to their own domestic problems and to those of the fledgling democracies in Eurasia? Or will the policy and financial resources once devoted to military defense be redirected toward the urgent needs of the South and toward resolution of long-standing problems that divide North and South despite their bonds in a common fate?

In this chapter we will examine the trade, aid, debt, and development issues that animate the South's drive for equality with the North. Explored through the eyes of the Third World, the inquiry includes an examination of the NIEO debate, how those issues have evolved since, and how continuing economic disparities now shape Third World countries' goals in a rapidly transforming global marketplace.

## THE NEW CLIMATE FOR ECONOMIC DEVELOPMENT . . . . . . . . . . . . . . .

The 1980s were a period of economic expansion. Still, by the time the decade ended, the Third World remained far from being a full partner in prosperity. With nearly 84 percent of the world's population, the Third World in 1991 accounted for only 21 percent of its economic output and 22 percent of world trade (*World Development Report 1993*, 1993: 260, 264). As a group, therefore, the developing countries are far from being equal participants in the global economy.

The twilight of the twentieth century will be pivotal for the Third World. A critical question is how the industrial countries will treat it after the Cold War: "The South itself is seized by the profound anxiety that the termination of the East–West struggle will cause the industrial democracies to forget about it. Accustomed to an age where conflict proved a magnet for . . . foreign policy attention, the developing world now fears falling off the North's agenda" (Feinberg and Boylan, 1991; see also Chapter 5).

For many reasons, it is likely that the South will continue to be important to the North, even in an environment where strategic incentives have receded (see Schraeder, 1993; Sewell, 1992). Nonetheless, because policymakers' views are colored by subjective as well as objective reality, the perception that the North will lose interest in the South for all except perhaps humanitarian reasons is a cause for Third World leaders' anxiety.

In this changing context, world trade, finance, capital flows, and energy supplies will powerfully affect the prospects for Third World development. No clear direction is yet apparent. As summarized in Box 8.1, the climate for Third World development is amenable to both pessimistic and optimistic predictions.

We can begin to understand the prospects and obstacles developing countries face as they seek to become full partners in the global political economy by taking a retrospective look at the issues and events that surrounded their drive for a New International Economic Order.

## THE NORTH–SOUTH DIALOGUE: A HISTORICAL OVERVIEW . . . . . . . . . . . .

The end of colonialism freed Third World countries from their political bondage, but it did not end their economic dependence on the former imperial powers. Nor did it guarantee self-sustained economic development. Thus, as noted in Chapter 5, Third World leaders came to believe that the structure of the international economic system was responsible for their plight and sought structural reforms of the world marketplace to make it more hospitable for their countries' development.

Many Third World leaders believed that international economic institutions, such as the International Monetary Fund (IMF) and General Agreement on Tariffs and Trade (GATT), and the political processes they governed, were "deeply biased against developing countries in their global distribution of income and influence" (Hansen, 1980). The perception was buttressed by the legacy of colonial exploitation and the continued existence in many parts of the Third World of levels of poverty and deprivation unknown in the North. The South's response was thus a call for not only a redistribution of income and wealth from rich countries to poor but also a similar transfer of political influence. Simply put, the goal sought was *regime change*—a revision of the rules and procedures of the industrial North's Liberal International Economic Order to the benefit of the Third World (Krasner, 1985). The hope was that a New International Economic Order (NIEO) governing the transnational flow of goods, capital, and technology would replace the inherently exploitative Liberal International Economic Order (LIEO).[1]

## The New International Economic Order

The historical roots of the developing countries' demands for a new order can be traced to the 1964 United Nations Conference on Trade and Development (UNCTAD), when the developing countries banded together to form the *Group of*

---

[1] The developing countries did not challenge the state system itself, only how it functions. Thus, the choice of the word *international* rather than *global* or *world* is significant. "The growing assertiveness of the developing countries cannot be found to herald the beginning of a new world," declares Robert W. Tucker (1980). "It is not the state system per se that is condemned, but the manner in which the system operated in the past and presumably continues to operate even today. It is primarily through the state that the historically oppressed and disadvantaged nations seek to mount a successful challenge to what governing elites of developing countries view as persisting unjust inequalities."

# Box 8.1
## The Climate for Development in the 1990s

• • •

| Pessimistic | Optimistic |
|---|---|

**World trade**

[World Trade Organization fails to implement GATT trade agreement]; unilateral policies by large industrial countries lead to trade wars; trade declines overall, though by less within regional blocs.

[World Trade Organization] makes real progress; regional GATT-compatible agreements produce dramatically greater integration in Europe, Asia, and the Western Hemisphere; world trade expands rapidly.

**Capital flows**

International capital markets are overcautious, and transfers to developing countries fail to pick up.

Capital flows to the developing countries resume; greater confidence spurs direct foreign investment.

**World finance**

Major institutions fail in Japan and the United States, leading to high risk premiums, low investment, a prolonged economic slowdown, and possibly higher inflation; the debt crisis continues to impede growth in the developing regions.

Major institutions muddle through; financial reforms and regulatory changes reduce systemic risks; economic recovery is rapid; Brady Initiative and its successors gradually reduce developing-country debt burdens.

**Industrial–country policy**

Large industrial countries fail to cooperate; they follow poor macroeconomic policies, and financial instability and low growth result.

Macroeconomic policies of the large industrial countries stabilize financial markets and lead to sustained growth.

**Security**

The decline of the superpowers leads to regional crises and ethnic strife within and among countries; arms races divert economic resources; terrorism, drugs, and poverty undermine internal security.

End of Cold War reduces tensions among superpowers; new international security arrangements are developed through a strengthened United Nations.

*(continued on page 256)*

|  | Pessimistic | Optimistic |
|---|---|---|

**Technology**

| Pessimistic | Optimistic |
|---|---|
| Technologies required for competitive products become more and more sophisticated and labor-saving; technology flows are restricted by protectionist policies and firm strategies; developing-country advantages resulting from cheap labor and raw materials diminish. | New technologies improve health and productivity (especially in agriculture); multinationals develop wider global production networks; computers reduce advantages of large markets; better communications make it easier for countries with adequate human capital to catch up in productivity. |

**Energy**

| Pessimistic | Optimistic |
|---|---|
| Oil prices remain volatile because of ongoing political and social instability in the Middle East, which continues to be the main supplier of oil. | New political arrangements in the Middle East, combined with constructive dialogue between producers and consumers of petroleum, lead to a period of unusual stability in real oil prices. |

**Environment**

| Pessimistic | Optimistic |
|---|---|
| Damage to the environment mounts, with economic repercussions; global resources dwindle; the frequency of local environmental disasters increases. | Environmental ill effects prove less costly and less immediate than predicted; new national and international policies take adequate steps to protect scarce resources. |

*Source:* World Development Report 1991 *(1991: 22).*

77 as a coalition of the world's poor to press for concessions from the rich. Known in diplomatic circles as the *G-77,* the coalition combined forces with the ***Nonaligned Movement*** (NAM) during the 1973 Algiers summit, when issues relating to economic as well as political "liberation" came to the fore. Algeria, then the spokesperson for the nonaligned countries, led the call for what became in 1974 the Sixth Special Session of the UN General Assembly. Using their superior numbers, the G-77 succeeded in passing the Declaration on the Establishment of a New International Economic Order.

Significantly, both the special UN session and the declaration on the NIEO occurred during the food and energy crises of the 1970s. Until then, the advanced industrial countries of the North did not give serious attention to the demands of the developing countries of the South. But the former could not ignore OPEC's (Organization of Petroleum Exporting Countries) success in cartelizing the world market for oil. In this climate, the voice of the Third World began to be heard.

OPEC's success surged the stridency of the poor countries' demands for equality in a new order. Inspired by the belief that "commodity power" endowed the Third World with the political strength necessary to challenge the North, the developing countries felt that their superior numbers would enable them to wield influence in the UN, UNCTAD, the IMF, the World Bank, the Third United Nations Law of the Sea Conference, and various other global and regional forums. They sought a North–South dialogue on their general development demands. These included proposals and pleas on a wide spectrum of topics, ranging from increased transfers of resources from industrial to developing countries and a more equitable system for trade competition to debate about aid, foreign investment, foreign ownership of property, multinational corporations, debt relief, commodity price stabilization, compensatory financing mechanisms, price indexation, and the like.

Although the South forced the industrial countries to listen, the North rejected—and still does reject—the view that the Third World's economic woes are a product of structural deficiencies in the global marketplace. Instead, the North locates the causes (and potential cures) of the poor countries' problems in the domestic systems of Third World countries themselves. Accordingly, proposals to radically alter existing international economic structures as well as the more modest elements of the Third World program met with resentment and resistance. Intransigence was especially apparent during the 1980s in the United States, as the Reagan administration approached the Third World primarily from the vantage point of its role in the East–West conflict. The United States showed little interest in the South's efforts to revise the Liberal International Economic Order. Thus the North–South dialogue gradually degenerated into a dialogue of the deaf.

## The Demise of the NIEO

Because UNCTAD has long served as a spokesperson of the world's poor, it has been a central forum for the North–South dialogue. Ever since the G-77 was first formed, the periodic meetings of UNCTAD focused attention on Third World problems and priorities. Box 8.2 summarizes the principal issues addressed during the eight UNCTAD meetings held between 1964 and 1992.

This brief summary illustrates the extent to which the demands and concerns of the Third World have changed over time. For instance, UNCTAD VI (1983) and VII (1987) exhibited greater concern with immediate issues than with the long-term goals of structural reform and regime change that had dominated the agenda in earlier meetings. The new mood was summarized by Farouk Sobhan of Bangladesh, chairman of the Group of 77, in 1983: "We cannot change institutions overnight. We have to do this gradually with a sense of purpose and pragmatism." This posture extended into the eighth UNCTAD conference, held in Cartagena de Indias, Colombia, in 1992, where structural reform of UNCTAD itself was a primary issue. The debate took place against the background of a broad consensus on the value of market-

## Box 8.2
## The Evolving Stages of UNCTAD

• • •

### UNCTAD I, Geneva 1964

- The creation of a forum to attract attention to issues supporting the developing countries not covered by existing institutions.
- The formulization of the Group of 77 and beginning of discussion on a few issues such as terms of trade, resource gap, and Generalized System of Preferences (GSP).

### UNCTAD II, New Delhi 1968

- Between 1964 and 1968 the UNCTAD secretariat focused more seriously but still sporadically on GSP, the needs of the developing countries for assistance, terms of trade, technology transfer, and selected development policies.
- The Conference led the OECD to initiate work on a scheme of preferences.
- Dr. Raúl Prebisch retired in 1969 as the Secretary-General of the UNCTAD.

### UNCTAD III, Santiago 1972

- Unlike the Geneva and New Delhi meetings, where these issues were considered separately, UNCTAD III saw discussion on interrelationships between trade, money, finance, and development at a technical level.
- Initiation of an effort by Mr. Robert McNamara, President of the World Bank, to mobilize global support for the poor, suggesting ways to integrate the bottom 40 percent of the population in the development process.

### UNCTAD IV, Nairobi 1976

- Stocktaking of progress in various forums (CIEC, GATT) on decisions taken at the Sixth and Seventh Special Sessions of the UN General Assembly in 1974 and 1975, respectively, particularly in the light of the oil price increase, monetary instability, recession, inflation, increased balance of payments gap of the non-oil developing countries, decline in commodity prices, and the uncertainty that the minimum development needs in many developing countries would be met.
- Main emphasis on commodities (Integrated Programme for Commodities–Common Fund) and to a lesser degree on external debt.
- Resolution on a Common Fund symbolized G-77 unity.

## UNCTAD V, MANILA 1979

- Emphasis on trade and financial flows aspects of the relationships between developed and developing countries.
- Emphasis on growing interdependence between different parts of the world economy.
- Efforts to bring socialist countries into the dialogue on economic issues.
- Emphasis on trade liberalization and concern about expanding protectionism.

## UNCTAD VI, BELGRADE 1983

- Movement by G-77 toward immediate issues relating to the global economy and Third World development and away from demands for structural reform.
- Emphasis on a common analysis of the world economic situation and an agreed strategy for economic recovery and development.
- Continued concern for the issue of trade protectionism.
- Recognition of the important role of the World Bank and International Monetary Fund as multilateral development institutions.

## UNCTAD VII, GENEVA 1987

- Broad agreement on the need for macroeconomic policy coordination among major industrial countries.
- Acceptance of the need for growth-oriented adjustment among developing countries, including the need for adequate external support.
- Focus on four substantive issues: resources for development, including the Third World debt problem; commodity prices; the role of trade in economic development; and the problem of the Least Developed of the Less Developed Countries (LLDCs).

## UNCTAD VIII, CARTEGENA DE INDIAS 1992

- Emergence of a broad consensus on importance of market-oriented economic policies and political pluralism as basis for development.
- Reform and revitalization of UNCTAD to ensure its continuing relevance on trade and development issues.
- Agreement to place future emphasis on consensus building and appropriate domestic policies rather than negotiations aimed at binding international agreements.

*Sources: Mahmud A. Burney (1979: 18); Shahid Javed Burki (1983: 18–19); Carlston B. Boucher and Wolfgang E. Siebeck (1987: 14–16); Grant B. Taplin (1992: 37–38).*

oriented economic policies and political pluralism in fostering development (Taplin, 1992).

What accounts for the Third World's apparent retreat from its earlier, militant posture toward regime change? The following five developments are especially potent:

- North and South alike experienced a general and prolonged economic slump in the early 1980s, but for many Third World countries the effects were especially damaging. As their economic growth rates deteriorated, some developing regions, particularly Africa, actually experienced "negative growth." The prices of the commodities exported by Third World countries fell sharply compared with the prices they had to pay for their imports. Faced with reduced export earnings and higher interest rates, many Third World countries incurred debt burdens of ominous proportions. Thus acute economic problems at home caused many Third World leaders to focus pragmatically on immediate policy problems rather than ideologically on the longer-term drive for structural reform launched a decade or more earlier.

- The erosion of the Third World's bargaining leverage added to the softening of its militancy. OPEC's clout faded during the worldwide oil glut of the 1980s, which removed incentives for the North to make major concessions to Southern demands. Thus the NIEO fell victim to "the lack of will on the part [of the] powerful, and the lack of power on the part of the willing" (Laszlo et al., 1980).

- As the unifying force of commodity power receded, latent fissures within the Group of 77 widened. The South no longer spoke as a united group. The differences between the more advanced of the developing countries, on the one hand, of which the Newly Industrialized Countries (NICs) stand out, and the less well-off, especially the least developed of the less developed countries (LLDCs), on the other, became especially pronounced.[2] Others among the more advanced developing countries, particularly in Latin America, were hardest hit by the debt crisis (discussed below). This, too, had the effect of dividing the Third World into competing groups rather than uniting them behind a common cause.

- An increased preference for free markets and a corresponding loss of enthusiasm for "statism" as a development strategy undermined support for the core tenets of the NIEO ideology, including in particular the belief that the capitalistic system was the source of Third World poverty.

- As support for trade protectionism in the industrialized countries rose, many developing countries recognized that GATT's rules for liberal trade offered them the best defense. Many Third World countries accordingly in the 1990s reversed their former opposition by joining GATT.

---

[2] The percentage share of the poorest 20 percent of the globe's economies is far worse than the Third World generally: In 1991 they accounted for 1.4 percent of global GNP, 0.9 percent of global trade, and 1.1 percent of global domestic investment (UNDP, 1994: 63). The ratio of the richest fifth's share of global income to the poorest grew from 30 to 1 in 1960 to 61 to 1 in 1991 (Postel, 1994: 5; UNDP, 1994: 35).

Against the background of these changes, the Third World drive for a New International Economic Order might properly be conceived not as the "beginning of the end" of the Liberal International Economic Order but "as the 'end of the beginning,'" a period of transition to a more complex order with a different international division of labor and different economic and political prospects for different Third World states" (Rothstein, 1988).

## The Political Economy of North–South Relations

Historically, many Third World leaders found four elements particularly irksome in their economic relationships with the North. W. Arthur Lewis, the Nobel Prize-winning economist, summarizes them as follows:

> First, the division of the world into exporters of primary products and exporters of manufactures.
>
> Second, the adverse factoral terms of trade for the products of the developing countries.
>
> Third, the dependence of the developing countries on the developed for finance.
>
> Fourth, the dependence of the developing countries on the developed for their engine of growth. (Lewis, 1978: 3).

Third World countries no longer actively seek to address these issues through structural reforms of the world political economy, but all remain central to an understanding of the evolving international division of labor and the economic and political prospects of different Third World countries within it. Each warrants examination in greater detail.

### The Shifting Composition of North–South Trade

Trade-related issues are uppermost in the Third World's complaints about the structure of the global marketplace. The trade relationships between many developed and developing countries formed during the age of imperialism, when colonies were controlled for the financial benefit of their colonizers. Frequently this meant that the colonies were sources of primary products, such as agricultural produce and minerals, and markets for the finished goods manufactured in the metropole. This pattern continued long after the practice and policy of economic imperialism disappeared.

As shown in Table 8.1, the developing countries rely on primary products for their export earnings (the money necessary to buy goods from abroad) to a much greater extent than do developed countries. In 1980, for example, nearly 80 percent of Third World exports were primary products, and only about 20 percent were manufactured goods. The developed countries in the First World, in contrast, relied on primary products for less than a quarter of their earnings, with manufactured products accounting for nearly 75 percent.

TABLE 8.1 FIRST AND THIRD WORLD TRADE COMPOSITION, 1970–1990 (PERCENTAGES)

| | Third World | | | | | First World | | | | |
|---|---|---|---|---|---|---|---|---|---|---|
| | 1970 | 1975 | 1980 | 1985 | 1990 | 1970 | 1975 | 1980 | 1985 | 1990 |
| **Exports** | | | | | | | | | | |
| Primary Products | 74.2 | 82.6 | 77.6 | 62.1 | 41.6 | 22.5 | 23.3 | 24.0 | 22.2 | 17.4 |
| Mineral fuels and related materials | 32.4 | 59.4 | 59.7 | 43.2 | 24.6 | 3.4 | 5.1 | 7.0 | 7.9 | 4.3 |
| Other primary products[a] | 41.8 | 23.2 | 17.9 | 18.9 | 17.0 | 19.1 | 18.2 | 17.0 | 14.3 | 13.1 |
| Manufactured Products | 23.7 | 17.0 | 21.5 | 36.9 | 57.5 | 75.4 | 75.2 | 73.8 | 75.4 | 80.2 |
| Other | 2.1 | 0.3 | 0.9 | 1.1 | 0.8 | 2.1 | 1.5 | 2.2 | 2.3 | 2.4 |
| **Imports** | | | | | | | | | | |
| Primary Products | 26.6 | 31.0 | 34.7 | 33.5 | 22.6 | 34.8 | 42.5 | 43.5 | 34.1 | 23.4 |
| Mineral fuels and related materials | 7.5 | 14.6 | 18.0 | 17.8 | 8.8 | 9.8 | 22.2 | 27.1 | 19.2 | 9.6 |
| Other primary products[a] | 19.1 | 16.4 | 16.7 | 15.7 | 13.8 | 25.0 | 20.3 | 16.4 | 14.9 | 13.8 |
| Manufactured Products | 68.8 | 65.8 | 62.8 | 62.9 | 74.1 | 63.5 | 56.3 | 54.4 | 64.1 | 74.5 |
| Other | 4.6 | 3.2 | 2.5 | 3.6 | 3.3 | 1.6 | 1.2 | 2.1 | 1.9 | 2.1 |

*Source:* Adapted from United Nations, *International Trade Statistics Yearbook*, various issues.

[a] Food, beverages, tobacco, crude materials (excluding fuels), oil and fats.

## A New International Division of Labor?

Although many developing countries continue to depend heavily on primary-product exports, during the past two decades the Third World's exports have shifted sharply toward manufactured goods. In 1990, for example, manufactured products accounted for two-thirds of the exports of non-OPEC developing countries (UN *Monthly Bulletin of Statistics* 48, May 1994: Special Table C). Thus, it is no longer accurate to picture developing countries as simply exporters of primary products and importers of manufactures.

The shift in the composition of Third World exports challenges empirically the rhetoric many Third World leaders used during the height of the NIEO debate. As a World Bank official observed, "The developing countries . . . persistently argued their case for changing the structure of a global economic order on the grounds that . . . they are unequal partners with the industrial nations. While this concept may be politically attractive, it is increasingly inaccurate as a framework for analysis of the dynamics of current world economic development" (Burki, 1983).

Thus a "new international division of labor" may be replacing the one characterized by the terms *core* (the industrial world) and *periphery* (the developing world) central to both world-system theory and dependency theory (see Chapter 5). In this new global marketplace, the developing countries, traditionally the suppliers of primary and semiprocessed goods, now provide First World countries with an increasing supply of manufactured and processed goods and diminishing proportions of raw materials and agricultural products.

## Growth Strategies

Third World countries have pursued two strategies in an effort to build their own industrial bases: ***import-substitution industrialization*** (ISI) and ***export-led industrialization*** (ELI).

Import-substitution industrialization was once the preferred tactic. Particularly popular in Latin America, the strategy encouraged domestic entrepreneurs to manufacture products otherwise imported from abroad, but it eventually fell into disfavor, in part because Third World manufacturers often found that they still relied on technology and even component parts imported from the North to produce goods for their domestic markets (Sklair, 1991; also Black, 1991).

More recently, a preference has grown for the development of export industries capable of competing in overseas markets. "The idea behind this was the mirror image of ISI. What had enriched the rich was not their insulation from imports (rich countries do, in fact, import massively all sorts of goods) but their success in manufactured exports, where higher prices could be commanded than for Third World raw materials" (Sklair, 1991).

The remarkable strides achieved since the late 1960s by the Newly Industrialized Countries, notably the four Asian Tigers (Hong Kong, Singapore, South Korea, and Taiwan), is testimony to the success of export-led industrialization. Others, impressed by this achievement, have tried to emulate the NICs' experience. But how many will succeed is questionable. The conditions in the world economy are no longer as favorable as when the NICs embarked on their development strategies (Broad and Cavanagh, 1988). Massive debt now burdens many would-be NICs, for example. In addition, competition for external markets has intensified at the same time that protectionist measures threaten to slow the growth of trade. Against these barriers, "few of the countries undertaking structural adjustment have turned into tigers. Most have turned into turkeys" (Massing, 1990–1991).

Some analysts question how "new" the new international division of labor really is. As noted in Chapter 5, world-system and dependency theorists use *semiperiphery* and *dependent development* to describe the perpetuation of long-standing patterns in exchanges between rich and poor countries. "Even when manufactures are exported to the core," one analyst notes, "they remain of the sort that has always defined the semi-periphery's role in the world division of labor. The new industries of the semiperiphery are the old, declining industries of the core. By relying on the now easily transferred technology of traditional mass production using semi-skilled labor, the semi-periphery can use the advantage of low wages to capture a segment of the market. . . . Hence, world-system theorists view recent developments in the semi-periphery not as some sort of unprecedented economic breakthrough, but as extensions of the normal role of that zone in the world-economy" (Shannon, 1989).

## *Preferential Trade*

Because of the importance of trade to the realization of Third World aspirations, gaining access to the industrial world's markets is crucial. "Trade, not aid" is a persistent Third World plea, as many developing countries believe the industrial countries have intentionally denied them access to First World markets through both tariff and nontariff barriers to trade.

Beginning as early as 1964, during the first UNCTAD conference, the Third World sought preferential (as opposed to most-favored-nation) trade treatment as a means to overcome the obstacles to its access to First World markets. Preferential treatment, the Third World argues, will enable it to build diversified export industries capable of competing on equal terms with those of the North.

In partial response to that view, the industrial countries agreed in the 1970s to establish within GATT a system of trade preferences for developing states. Known as the Generalized System of Preferences (GSP), the scheme permits First World countries to grant preferences to developing countries without violating GATT's nondiscrimination principle, long a centerpiece of the LIEO.

Despite this apparent Northern concession, its effects are in dispute. For example, some of the countries that have benefited most from the trade preferences, such as Hong Kong and South Korea, have needed them least (Spero, 1990). In addition, following the insistence of the United States, the GSP provisions approved during the Tokyo Round of GATT negotiations included a "graduation clause." It stipulated that, as developing countries reached higher levels of development, they would receive less special treatment and have to compete on a more equal footing with Northern states. No precise guidelines were formulated to determine when graduation would occur, a matter of concern to the South, but it was on the basis of this provision (written into U.S. law in 1984) that the United States in 1989 revoked the preferential treatment earlier granted the Asian NICs.

The Tokyo Round that legitimized the GSP also failed to grapple with the North's protectionist practices that were often directed at products in which some developing countries already enjoyed comparative advantages, such as clothing, footwear, textiles, and steel. In 1986, for example, 21 percent of the industrial countries' imports from the Third World were subject to "hard-core" nontariff barriers,[3] compared with only 16 percent of the imports from the North (*World Development Report 1991*, 1991: 105). If other restraints are added, such as health and safety standards, the proportion would be even larger—and the trends point toward more restraints, not fewer.

Because of their belief that the Tokyo negotiations did not address protectionist sentiments in the North, the developing countries, many of which did not then belong to GATT, generally shunned the accords. However, the greater attention to nontariff barriers in the Uruguay Round drew many developing countries into the regime. In part this acceptance stemmed from the fact that GATT's rules prohibiting selective tariffs for particular countries provided the Third World protection against trade restrictions that otherwise might be imposed. "Every country in [the World Trade Organization], rich and poor, stands to benefit from the unquantifiable results of the [1993 GATT agreement, although] it is entirely possible that the GATT round will make particular developing countries worse off in the short term" (*The Economist* 329, December 18, 1993: 66).

The emerging regionalized trade blocs (see Chapter 7) pose another kind of challenge. "For the developing countries, the prospect of a world divided into separate regional centers is disconcerting. It leaves too many countries out of the system altogether, and even those it encompasses are left relatively weaker as their bargaining power is divided. So, even though developing countries in the past have regarded the GATT as a 'rich man's club,' today they see it as a guardian for the clear and fair rules they need if they are to enter the international arena successfully" (Philips and Tucker, 1991). Still, it remains problematic whether the developing countries will benefit from participation in a more open but highly competitive global marketplace and whether they can participate freely and fully in the regionalized trade blocs that are crystallizing.

## Commodity Exports and the South's Adverse Terms of Trade

As noted, a large and growing proportion of manufactured product exports now originate in the Third World. For many countries, however, primary products continue to dominate their exports. Indeed, many Third World countries can be classified as "vulnerable single-commodity-dependent countries" (see Map 8.1). The poorest of

---

[3] "Hard-core" NTBs (nontariff barriers) comprise that subset of all NTBs most likely to have significant restrictive effects, including "import prohibitions, quantitative restrictions, voluntary export restraints, variable levies, MFA restrictions, and nonautomatic licensing" (*World Development Report 1987*, 1987).

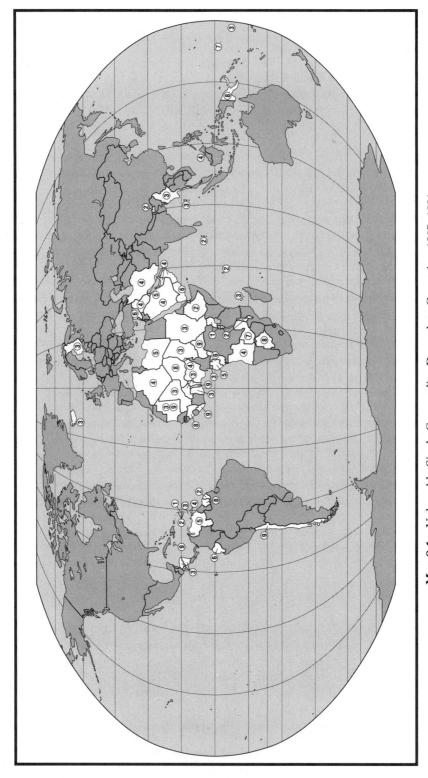

**Map 8.1** Vulnerable Single-Commodity-Dependent Countries, 1987–1991
*Source:* U.S. CIA (1992a: 170–171).

266

① Agriculture and Fishing accounting for more than 80% of total export earnings:

| | | |
|---|---|---|
| Dominica (bananas) | Rwanda (coffee) | Uganda (coffee) |

② Agriculture and Fishing accounting for 60–80% of total export earnings:

| | | |
|---|---|---|
| Bhutan (spices) | Guadeloupe (bananas) | Martinique (bananas) |
| Barundi (coffee) | Malawi (seafood) | St. Lucia (bananas) |
| Ethiopia (coffee) | Maldives (seafood) | Seychelles (seafood) |
| French Guiana (seafood) | | |

③ Agriculture and Fishing accounting for 40–59% of total export earnings:

| | | |
|---|---|---|
| Benin (cotton) | El Salvador (coffee) | Iceland (seafood) |
| Burkina (cotton) | Equatorial Guiana (cocoa, lumber) | Kiribati (copra, seafood) |
| Burma (lumber, opium) | Finland (wood products) | Mali (cotton) |
| Chad (cotton) | Ghana (cocoa) | Mauritania (seafood) |
| Cocos (Keeling) Islands (copra) | Grenada (spices) | Nicaragua (coffee) |
| Comoros (spices) | Honduras (bananas) | Sudan (cotton) |

④ Crude Oil and Petroleum products accounting for more than 80% of total export earnings:

| | | |
|---|---|---|
| Algeria | Iraq | Qatar |
| Angola | Kuwait | Saudi Arabia |
| Brunei | Nigeria | Trinidad & Tobago |
| Iran | Oman | United Arab Emirates |

⑤ Crude Oil and Petroleum products accounting for 60–80% of total export earnings:

| | |
|---|---|
| Bahrain | Libya |
| Gabon | Venezuela |

⑥ Crude Oil and Petroleum products accounting for 40–59% of total export earnings:

| | |
|---|---|
| Congo | Syria |
| Ecuador | Yemen |

⑦ Metals and Minerals accounting for more than 80% of total export earnings:

| | |
|---|---|
| Nauru (phosphates) | Zambia (copper) |

⑧ Metals and Minerals accounting for 60–80% of total export earnings:

| | | |
|---|---|---|
| Botswana (diamonds) | Niger (uranium) | Suriname (aluminum) |
| Guinea (aluminum) | Papua New Guinea (copper) | |

⑨ Metals and Minerals accounting for 40–59% of total export earnings:

| | | |
|---|---|---|
| Central African Republic (diamonds) | Jamaica (aluminum) | Togo (phosphates) |
| Chile (copper) | Liberia (iron ore) | |
| | Mauritania (iron ore) | |

poor countries, particularly in Africa, are typically among them. Thus each of these exporting countries is particularly susceptible to external forces that affect both short- and long-term commodity prices.

## The Terms of Trade

The dependence of many developing countries on a narrow range of primary-product exports underlies the *terms of trade* between North and South. The phrase refers to the ratio of export prices to import prices. For the developing countries, the terms of trade have been unfavorable: The prices they receive for their exports have varied erratically in the short run and fallen in the long run, while the prices of the manufactured goods that they import have increased steadily.

According to world-system and dependency theory, the Third World's deteriorating terms of trade are produced by the structural characteristics of the global marketplace. The South remains critically dependent on the North not only for manufactured goods but also for technology (see Head, 1989; also Chapter 5). The North's greater technological sophistication enables it to convert natural resources into finished goods more efficiently. Powerful labor unions and giant corporations institutionalize (through wage and fringe benefit programs) the comparatively high cost of the technologically sophisticated products manufactured in the North. Meanwhile, worldwide advertising campaigns sustain demand for these products.

Developing countries are unable to compete equally against the North's advanced technologies, the argument continues. Unlike the North, the South cannot bid up the prices for the materials it produces. In a global market where those with the most money determine prices, Third World countries are disadvantaged by their inability to meaningfully affect the prices for the products they trade.

There is no question that prices for the developing countries' primary-product exports fluctuate sharply in the short run; but they have experienced a general downward trend over the long run. As shown in Figure 8.1, nonfuel commodity prices dropped sharply in the early 1980s during the recession induced by the second oil shock, for example, when they fell to a lower level in real terms than at any time since World War II. Prices have remained stagnant since, thus making the general downward trend of the developing countries' terms of trade since the early 1980s appear entrenched (UN *Monthly Bulletin of Statistics* 48, January 1994: Special Table B).

Other evidence is consistent with the arguments about the structural roots of the Third World's unfavorable terms-of-trade circumstances. Between 1900 and 1986, for example, nonfuel commodity terms of trade declined an average of 0.6 percent a year (*World Development Report 1991*, 1991: 106).

Yet ambiguities surround the interpretation of this evidence.[4] For example, it is unclear whether trends over shorter periods are due to a structural deterioration in

---

[4] There are reasons to be cautious with such data, however. For one thing, the choice of the base year for comparison matters. If one chooses 1920 rather than 1900, for example, the terms of trade declined only 0.3 percent per year, rather than 0.6 percent.

Index (1979–1981 = 100)

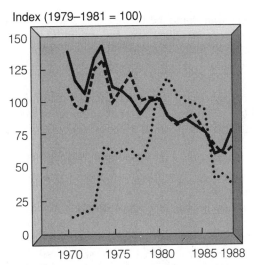

**Figure 8.1** Commodity Prices, 1970–1988
*Source: World Development Report 1989* (1989: 11).
*Note:* Real prices are annual average prices in dollars, deflated by the annual change in the manufacturing unit value (MUV) index, a measure of the price of industrial country exports to developing countries. Prices for nonfuel primary commodities are based on a basket of thirty-three commodities.

the terms of trade or to short-term perturbations related to changes in the business cycle. Moreover, the quality of manufactured products has increased over time, and the increase in the volume of trade offsets some of the decline in the terms of trade (see GATT, 1993). But regardless, because beliefs and perceptions influence Third World leaders, these, rather than reality, will continue to shape the South's posture and rhetoric in the North–South dialogue. As political scientist Robert L. Rothstein notes (1979), "Many economists doubt that there has been a secular decline in the terms of trade for commodities, but what is believed or assumed—taken on faith—is more important here than analytical argument."

## Price Stabilization

Reversing the unfavorable terms-of-trade pattern is a long-term goal of the Third World. A more immediate goal is reducing the fluctuations in the prices developing countries receive for their commodities.

Creation of a new commodities regime was a principal objective of the Group of 77 and UNCTAD during much of the 1970s. It was the central issue during the 1976 UNCTAD IV meeting in Nairobi, Kenya, when the G-77 won adoption of a proposed Integrated Programme for Commodities. As originally formulated, the Integrated Programme called for a revolutionary approach to international decision making and management of trade in commodities (see Rothstein, 1979).

Eventually, attention focused on proposals for a Common Fund designed to stabilize prices of several commodities. The Common Fund would finance creation of buffer stocks that could be bought and sold as supply and demand dictated.[5] The G-77 pushed for a $6 billion fund and a significant voice in its management (Rothstein, 1979; Schechter, 1979). The industrial countries opposed both the amount, most of which they would have to finance, and the management proposals, which favored the South.

What finally emerged was far different from the ambitious goals that the Group of 77 and the UNCTAD secretariat had originally sought. A 1979 agreement created a $750 million pool of funds to help individual commodity organizations purchase buffer stocks of raw materials, which would be used to keep commodity prices within predetermined ranges. The agreement also anticipated creation of an international aid organization to help poorer developing countries expand, diversify, and market their commodity exports.

It would be another decade before the Common Fund secured the number of signatories and ratifications necessary to make it operational. Even then, some key actors, notably the United States, were not among them. Furthermore, the fund's ability to stabilize commodity prices is still questioned. Success has been compromised because only commodity agreements involving producers and consumers may be parties to the arrangement, and agreements do not exist in all of the commodities envisaged by the fund. Moreover, concluding new agreements has proved difficult, and even those that were forged have not been very effective.

Other avenues are available for dealing with commodity problems. Associations of producing countries, for example, avoid the difficulties inherent in international commodity agreements, which require balancing consumer and producer interests. Compensatory financing arrangements, which seek to stabilize export earnings through financial aid rather than buffer-stock manipulation of prices, are another alternative. The International Monetary Fund, for example, maintains a Compensatory and Contingency Financing Facility designed to assist Third World countries facing balance-of-payments difficulties caused by shortfalls in their export earnings or unforseen price increases (as in the case of oil following Iraq's invasion of Kuwait in 1990).

The European Union operates a compensatory financing scheme known as STABEX, the intellectual forerunner of UNCTAD's original proposal for an integrated commodity program. It is part of the Lomé Convention, concluded in 1975 (and since extended to 1999) between the then-European Community and sixty-six so-called ACP (African, Caribbean, and Pacific) countries that are mostly former European colonies. Through the convention the EU grants the ACP countries preferential trade access to the European market without the requirement of reciprocity for the EU nations. The EU also makes foreign aid available to the ACP countries while giving them a voice in the management of aid projects. But the centerpiece of Lomé is STABEX, a compensatory financing arrangement designed to stabilize ACP export earnings in forty-eight agricultural products (mineral exports are covered in a

---

[5] As originally envisaged, eighteen products were to be covered by the Common Fund: bananas, bauxite, cocoa, coffee, copper, cotton, hard fibers, iron ore, jute, manganese, meat, phosphates, rubber, sugar, tea, tropical timber, tin, and vegetable oils.

separate agreement).[6] "Ground-breaking" and "politically genuinely significant" were terms describing STABEX at its inception (Gruhn, 1976).

Despite this initial optimism, the contribution of STABEX to commodity price stabilization is unclear. As the World Bank (*World Development Report 1986*, 1986) put it in commenting on both STABEX and the IMF compensatory financing facility: "To be successful, compensatory schemes must have clear objectives, permit quick identification of shortfalls, and provide prompt payments without complicated conditions. Neither the [IMF scheme] nor STABEX has been ideal in these respects." Furthermore, it became apparent at the time Lomé was first renegotiated that the very economic problems that make compensatory financing mechanisms attractive to producing countries often breed conflict between producing and consuming countries over the coverage and operation of the system (Islam, 1982).

Thus, just as the Common Fund seems unlikely to have the measurable impact on commodity trade once sought by advocates of the New International Economic Order, the STABEX experience suggests that alternative approaches to commodity price stabilization are also unlikely to produce easy solutions to Third World commodity problems. The reason is simple: "Supporting and stabilizing the prices of commodities and providing compensatory financing for Third World exporters both require that resources be transferred from consuming to producing countries, which invariably means from developed to developing countries. Here the major obstacle has been, and remains, Northern unwillingness to make the required transfers" (Puchala, 1983).

Finally, it should be noted that changes in the world political economy raise the possibility that stabilizing commodities' prices may not offer realistic solutions to the problems of Third World commodity exporters. Commodities have increasingly become "uncoupled" from industrial economies as the material intensity of manufacturing has steadily diminished (Drucker, 1986). Hence, commodities are simply less important than previously.

## Development Finance and Foreign Aid

The developing countries may prefer trade to aid, but aid has a long heritage in the relations between rich and poor countries. Moreover, in many ways aid remains a preferred weapon in the developed countries' arsenal for coping with the South, in part, perhaps, because it is more easily tailored to the pursuit of specific foreign policy objectives.

The developing countries, for their part, often view aid as a moral obligation of the rich to the poor necessary to redress the injustices of the imperial past. Not surprisingly, therefore, they are sensitive to the "strings" sometimes attached to the aid they receive. They have also been critical of what they regard as the comparatively meager resources channeled from the rich countries to the poor.

---

[6] The minerals scheme is known as MINEX. It was negotiated in 1979 and designed to give mineral producers the same benefits that STABEX earlier granted to producers of agricultural commodities, principally tropical produce (see Shonfield, 1980).

## The Form and Function of Foreign Aid

"Foreign aid" comes in a variety of forms and is used for a variety of purposes. Some aid consists of outright grants of money, some consists of loans at concessional rates, and some consists of shared technical expertise. Most foreign aid is bilateral, meaning it flows directly from one country to another, but some is channeled through international institutions like the World Bank, and hence is known as multilateral aid.

The purposes of aid are as varied as its forms. Security objectives are typically pursued through military assistance of one kind or another, but economic aid is also used for these purposes. The United States, for example, "paid" for military base rights in many Third World countries during the Cold War with varying amounts of economic as well as military aid. It also continues to target Israel and Egypt as major recipients of U.S. economic assistance because of their critical role in furthering U.S. political and security goals in the Middle East.

Disaster relief and other humanitarian purposes are also met with grants and loans, but the economic development of the Third World has been a primary aim of most foreign aid donors since World War II. The assumption that development will support other goals, such as commercial advantage and the growth of free markets and democratic political systems (see Table 8.2), rationalizes most donors' assistance programs.

## The Volume and Value of Foreign Aid

During the height of their drive for a New International Economic Order, developing countries charged that the foreign aid flowing from North to South was "unjustifiably low" (Hansen, 1979). How do those charges stack up against the evidence?

Certainly by some standards the economic assistance funneled to developing countries has been considerable. The United States alone provided more than $172 billion in nonmilitary assistance between 1945 and 1992. On an annual basis its allocation of "official development assistance"—a term used to capture the concessional element in donors' aid allocations—has averaged about $9 billion annually since the early 1980s.

Today the United States is only one of many major foreign aid donors. Various multilateral institutions are among the others, including the World Bank, the United Nations Development Programme, the Inter-American, Asian, and African Development banks, the European Union, and various OPEC and Arab institutions.

The other major industrial powers also make significant foreign aid contributions. Collectively, they constitute the Development Assistance Committee (DAC) of the Organization for Economic Cooperation and Development (OECD).[7] The official

---

[7] DAC members are Australia, Austria, Belgium, Canada, Denmark, Finland, France, Germany, Ireland, Italy, Japan, the Netherlands, New Zealand, Norway, Sweden, Switzerland, the United Kingdom, the United States, and the Commission of the European Union. Members of the OECD include the above countries plus Greece, Iceland, Luxembourg, Portugal, Spain, Turkey, and Mexico (which became the first new member in 21 years when it joined in April 1994).

TABLE 8.2  THE FOREIGN POLICY AND ECONOMIC GOALS OF FOREIGN AID DONORS

| Time Frame | Primary Objectives | Expected Byproducts | Types of Donors |
|---|---|---|---|
| Long-range | 1. Economic development; reduce poverty<br>2. Eventual self-sufficiency of recipient | 1. Political stability<br>2. Democratization<br>3. Arab/Muslim solidarity | 1. Western<br>2. Western<br>3. Arab (OPEC) |
| Medium-range | 1. Maintain diplomatic presence in recipient<br>2. Symbolize friendships and commitments to, and support for, recipient<br>3. Maintain access to, and influence over, recipient's domestic and foreign policies | 1. Commercial, trade opportunities<br>2. Enrich bilateral relations | 1. All donors<br>2. All donors<br>3. Great powers |
| Immediate | 1. Change recipient's current domestic or foreign policies<br>2. Sustain a recipient's regime in power<br>3. Humanitarian emergency relief | 1. Obtain support for donor's foreign policies<br>2. Protect donor's core objectives<br>3. Possible future goodwill | 1. Great powers<br>2. Great powers<br>3. All donors |

Source: Abridged from K. J. Holsti (1992: 199).

273

development assistance of DAC members grew from less than $30 billion annually in 1970 to nearly $50 billion two decades later, when, interestingly, Japan replaced the United States as the world's foremost aid donor.

Alongside the members of DAC, which are the largest aid donors, other states have also assisted in the aid effort. The communist countries, for example, made grants of between $2 billion and $3 billion annually from the early 1970s until well into the 1980s, when, on the eve of their collapse, their own domestic ills forced them to concentrate on their chronic internal economic problems. That in turn led to the end of their aid effort (with sometimes dramatic effects on recipient countries, notably Cuba) and, in fact, initiated a new period in which the former communist countries became *recipients* of development assistance (see Figure 8.2). The OPEC countries have also been significant players in the aid game, particularly when global oil prices were high. OPEC's role diminished following the decline of oil prices in the mid-1980s, however. In fact, many OPEC countries found themselves seeking

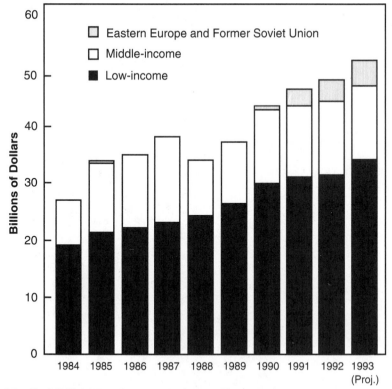

**Figure 8.2** Real Official Development Assistance Flows, 1984–1993
*Source:* The World Bank (1993: 15).
*Note:* Flows are expressed in 1992 U.S. dollars, deflated by the World Bank's import unit value index. Middle-income countries exclude Eastern Europe and the former Soviet Union.

external sources of funds to cope with the balance-of-payments deficits they suddenly faced.

Against this background, what is the basis for the charge that the volume and value of foreign aid has been unjustifiably low? In one sense, of course, the charge is simply wrong: The flow of aid has been substantial, and, since 1984, it has steadily grown (see Figure 8.2). In other ways, however, the charge has merit.

Consider, for example, the "aid burden." The generally agreed-upon standard for measuring the burden of aid is the ratio between aid and a donor's income as measured by gross national product. The principle widely accepted in diplomatic circles is that the rich should transfer to the poor countries resources equivalent to 0.7 percent of their GNP. The OPEC states generally exceeded this target until the mid-1980s, whereas the DAC donors (and particularly the communist countries) have fallen far short of it. Furthermore, the trend has been flat rather than upward, largely a consequence of the downward turn in the relative aid effort of the United States, long the largest aid donor. Since 1960, U.S. development assistance as a proportion of its GNP has declined by more than 70 percent—plummeting from 1.03 percent in 1960 to 0.18 percent in 1992 (Bandow, 1992: 78; UNDP, 1994: 74). By this criterion, the United States now ranks at the bottom of the list of 15 DAC donors.

The rapid *relative* decline in U.S. foreign economic aid reflects its refusal to increase aid commensurately with either real increases in GNP or with rising prices. This policy change is explained by a combination of three factors: "donor fatigue" with the seeming intractability of the development process, the growing conviction that domestic needs should take priority over foreign ones, and, from time to time, U.S. disenchantment with the performance of the multilateral lending agencies. Most recently, the end of the Cold War has prompted a sharp shift from U.S. aid to friendly governments toward—with less assistance—promoting "sustainable development," democracy, and peace (see Goshko and Lippmann, 1993; Krueger, 1993).

Furthermore, the United States, like most aid donors, "ties" its aid to purchases in the United States, even though it may not be the lowest-cost producer of the goods that the developing countries need.[8] The reason: For donors, foreign aid is allocated primarily to subsidize businesses at home. The "foreign" aid must be spent on goods and services supplied by the donors' domestic companies and public and private organizations. At the same time, because developing countries have experienced dramatic population increases in recent decades, the per-capita impact of aid has declined equally dramatically. Adding these two facts to the picture, it becomes clear that the volume of foreign aid received by Third World countries is comparatively small and that its value is shrinking.

Finally, a consideration of other expenditures magnifies the comparative insignifi-

---

[8] Tying means that the aid recipients are required to spend their aid dollars to purchase goods produced in the donor country. C. Fred Bergsten (1973: 104) estimated that "tying alone reduces the real value of aid by 10 to 30 percent below its nominal value." For more recent data on the proportion of aid tied by individual DAC donors, see *Development Cooperation: 1991 Report* (1991: 206).

cance of development assistance. Global military spending, for example, outpaced official government-to-government economic aid in 1992 by a margin of roughly fourteen to one. The disparity is more conspicuous in particular cases. Take the United States. Even after reductions in U.S. military spending began in 1990, Americans still spent more than three times as much on tobacco products and nearly five times as much on alcoholic beverages as their government spent on official development assistance (Philips and Tucker, 1991: 34).

## Conditionality

Beyond criticism of the meager volume and value of aid, complaints about its political strings are legion. The complaints grow out of a long (and understandable) history of donors' efforts to use foreign aid to serve the multiple foreign policy goals summarized in Table 8.2.

We noted above, for example, that the United States has used aid to foster U.S. security interests in the Middle East. During the 1980s it pursued similar strategies in the Caribbean and Central America, where security considerations, not development objectives, were overriding concerns. Similarly, the United States officially (but unsuccessfully) made states' UN voting support for the U.S. position on resolutions the prime criterion for receiving U.S. foreign assistance (see Kegley and Hook, 1991).

The self-interested behavior of the United States is not unusual. OPEC allocates the largest percentage of its aid to Arab countries, with much of the rest spread among Asian and African nations with sizable Muslim populations. Similarly, Britain and France give much of their aid to their former colonies. Noting the failure of many recipients of foreign aid to improve their economies, some observers (Hayter, 1971, for example) have even suggested that foreign aid is often a neo-imperialistic tool used by the North to perpetuate neocolonial and neo-imperial ties by further subordinating the weak and poor while promoting the welfare of those already strong and rich.

Although developing countries are sensitive to the strings attached to foreign aid flows, conditionality is widespread and often involves not only changes in recipients' economic systems but also political reforms. Japan, for example, has guidelines for development assistance that "include reductions in recipient countries' military expenditures (including arms production and trade), introduction of market-oriented economies, promotion of democracy, and respect for human rights" (Philips and Tucker, 1991).

The trend toward Third World democratization, which the Japanese guidelines seek to encourage, is heralded in the liberal First World as a positive consequence of foreign assistance. As shown in Figure 8.3, the number of elected Third World heads of state has increased dramatically since the mid-1980s. If these practices take root, presumably they will produce economic benefits that will help alleviate the suffering of the poor in the Third World. But will the democracies survive? (According to Freedom House, the number of "free" and "partly free" Third World countries declined in 1992 and 1993 [see Figure 3.1].)

Ensuring a successful transition to democracy "has triggered an intense debate

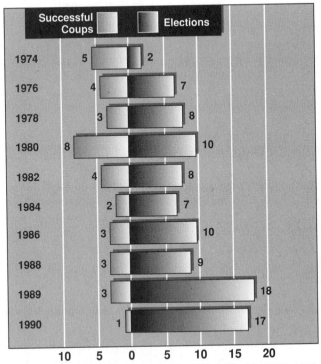

**Figure 8.3** The Trend toward Democracy in the Third World, 1974–1990
*Source:* Rosemarie Philips and Stuart K. Tucker (1991: 16).

about what role [the industrial democracies] and the international financial institutions [IMF and the World Bank] should play in supporting this process." In this context, the view now increasingly shared in the North, embedded in liberal and neoliberal theory (see Chapter 2), is that "political democracy is not only compatible with, but even a precondition for, economic development" (Philips and Tucker, 1991). Yet some question this emerging conventional wisdom:

> Neither empirical evidence nor historical experience substantiate the view that democracy is a necessary precondition for development. Where powerful special interests or a small self-serving elite control the electoral process; where patronage is a significant force in the political parties; where ethnic or regional tensions could provoke conflict or disintegration; or where terrorists, guerrillas, or drug barons control much of public life, rapid political liberalization could result in disproportionate influence on the part of some, rather than increased influence on the part of all. Moreover, political pluralism may conflict with other important policy goals such as economic reform, poverty-oriented development measures, environmental protection, control of the drug trade, or control of terrorism. (Philips and Tucker, 1991: 17)

From this perspective, the connection between democracy and development is unclear, and the contribution that foreign aid might make in encouraging democracy may prove as elusive as its role in promoting economic development. Nonetheless, donor countries (like the United States in the Clinton administration) now officially endorse the use of their economic leverage to encourage Third World reforms designed to promote democratic capitalism, while some recipients regard the promotion of democratization a naked "neocolonial" effort to "westernize" the Third World (Shaw, 1991; UNDP, 1994).

## Third World Dependence on First World Investment: Are Multinational Corporations Engines of Growth?

The preceding discussion demonstrates how profoundly the developed North affects the South's developing economies. Whether those effects are purposeful or not, beneficial or adverse, remain controversial. They comprise a final category of debate in the North–South dialogue.

Until very recently, the South's position was largely informed by dependency theory, which purports to have the answer. Recall from Chapter 5 dependency theory's core arguments:

- The relationship between the advanced countries and those at the periphery is exploitative.
- Underdevelopment in a hierarchical world division of labor is a consequence of the relationship between core and peripheral states.
- Capitalism's need for external sources of demand and profitable investment outlets leads to the penetration of peripheral countries.
- Penetration leads to technological dependence and "cultural imperialism."
- Multinational corporations (MNCs), driven by the profit motive, are a primary agent of this penetration process.
- MNCs transfer profits from the penetrated countries to their home states, thus retarding the peripheral states' growth.
- Local elites within penetrated countries, whose own fortunes become tied to the dominant powers, sustain the inherently exploitative linkages that bind core and periphery together.

Multinational corporations figure prominently in dependency theorists' arguments, as the preceding summary shows. Thus it is appropriate to return to the question of the costs and benefits of multinational corporations that we raised in Chapter 6, but this time from the perspective of the Third World.

### The Benefits of Multinational Corporations

Multinational corporations doubtlessly dominate developing countries' economies, but are they necessarily detrimental to the latter's economic growth? Some analysts think not.

For all the talk (and the reality) of imperialist domination, most of the underdeveloped nations want domestic foreign investment, European and/or American, for a variety of reasons. The multinationals pay higher wages, keep more honest books, pay more taxes, and provide more managerial know-how and training than do local industries. Moreover, they usually provide better social services for their workers, and certainly provide fancy career opportunities for a favored few of the elite. They are, in addition, a main channel through which technology, developed in the West, can filter into the backward nations. To be sure, the corporations typically send home more profits than the capital that they originally introduce into the "host" country; but meanwhile that capital grows, providing jobs, improving productivity, and often contributing to export earnings. (Heilbroner, 1977: 345–346)

These perceived consequences may explain the widespread Third World quest now evident for multinational corporations' investments. Increasingly, multinationals have invested in Third World countries, with foreign direct investment rising from $15 billion in 1987 to more than $48 billion in 1992 (World Bank, 1993: 8). Part of the reason for this resurgence in investment activity since 1987 (see Figure 8.4) is because developing countries (especially states committed to export-led industrialization) now aggressively compete to attract these investments. One observer explains the attractiveness of and "nearly universal demand for substantial MNC activity" thusly:

In many fields the most attractive technology and expertise does not come in "unbundled" form; the advantages in foreign market access that are inherent in most manufacturing MNCs often cannot be duplicated except at a very high price. A rapid and premature jettisoning of the MNC—even in natural resource industries—has led some countries to economic disaster. (Kudrle, 1987: 241)

Partly as a result of this reality, the UN's Transnational Corporations and Management Division in 1992 "departed sharply from much of the international rhetoric of the 1970s by maintaining that transnational corporations serve as an engine of growth in developing countries" (Mitchell, 1993).

### The Costs of Multinational Corporations

From another Third World perspective, however, the costs associated with MNCs are excessive. "The capital, jobs and other benefits they bring to developing economies are recognized, but the terms on which these benefits come are seen as unfair and exploitive and as robbing the new nations of their resources" (Cutler, 1978).

One of the alleged costs is technological dependence. According to one argument, technology imported from the North impedes local development. The technology transferred is often inappropriate to the Third World setting, where the diffusion effects of industrial activity are limited.

Another argument points to multinationals' repatriation of profits. Because MNCs seek to maximize profits for their shareholders, who more often than not live in the parent state rather than in the host state, there is little reinvestment in the country of production. Instead, capital finds its way into someone else's hands. Moreover,

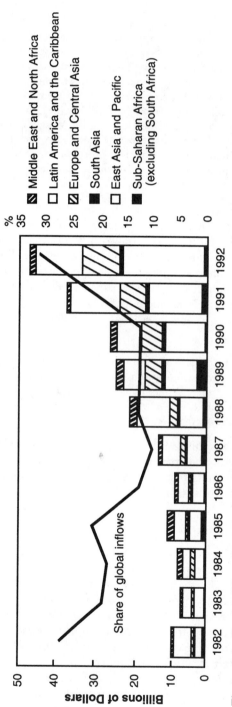

**Figure 8.4** Foreign Direct Investment in Developing Countries, by Region and as Share of Global Inflows, 1982–1992
*Source:* World Bank (1993: 8), with estimates based on balance-of-payments data reported by the International Monetary Fund and data on net foreign investment reported by the Organization for Economic Co-operation and Development.

the returns are sometimes excessive. Between 1975 and 1978, for example, the profit on U.S. direct foreign investment in the First World averaged 12.1 percent, but in the Third World it averaged nearly 26 percent (Spero, 1990: 241).

Critics also charge that profits represent only a small part of the effective return to parent companies. "A large part of the real return comes from the licensing fees and royalties paid by the subsidiary to the parent for the use of technology controlled by the parent" (Spero, 1990). Admittedly, parent companies must absorb the research and development costs of new technologies used abroad. Nonetheless, critics argue that

> subsidiaries in less-developed countries pay an unjustifiably high price for technology and bear an unjustifiably high share of the research and development costs. The monopoly control of technology by the multinational corporation enables the parent to exact a monopoly rent from its subsidiaries. And the parent chooses to use that power and to charge inordinately high fees and royalties to disguise high profits and avoid local taxes on those profits, according to the critics. (Spero, 1990: 242)

Critics also point to the **transfer-pricing mechanism** as another device used by MNCs to increase their profits and minimize their tax burdens. The raw, semi-processed, or finished materials produced by a parent's subsidiaries located in different countries are in effect traded among the subsidiaries. Because the same company sits on both sides of the transaction, it can manipulate the sales or "transfer" prices of these import–export transactions so as to benefit the parent firm. "Some firms do this as objectively as they can, without regard to tax considerations. But there are also some who exercise this discretion so as to minimize their global taxes and maximize their after-tax earnings. Since tax rates vary around the world, they accomplish this by recording profits in jurisdictions where taxes are relatively low" (Cutler, 1978). Increased capital flow from South to North is the net effect. Poverty in the host country is allegedly the primary product (Müller, 1973–1974). So, too, is "the possibility of adverse environmental impacts and dualistic economic structures" (Mitchell, 1993).

Much of the critical literature considers "the remission of 'excessive' profits the key mechanism by which the host country's balance of payments is adversely affected by multinational corporations." Political economist Raymond Vernon (cited in Bierstecker, 1978) argues instead "that the annual income remissions are insignificant compared to the local value added annually by such corporations." Vernon (1975) also challenges the capital-outflow and technology-dependence arguments, alleging that the former "is fallacious because of its failure to measure the implications of changes in domestic output" while the latter is subject to "an overwhelming propensity on the part of well-trained and well-informed critics to oversimplify the issue and to disregard the nonconforming evidence." In a similar vein, international economist Charles Kindleberger (1969) contends that, despite MNCs' monopolistic and exploitative tendencies, multinationals as a whole have, paradoxically, expanded competition and enhanced world economic efficiency.

In sum, then, the economic consequences of MNCs' activities are not always discernible or easily agreed on, which is perhaps why evaluations differ so widely. As Joan Spero (1990) observes, "It is impossible to reach any general or definitive conclusion about the overall effect of multinationals on development. The influence of foreign investment varies from country to country, from firm to firm, and from project to project. Some case studies demonstrate the beneficial impact of direct foreign investment; others, the detrimental effects." She continues by noting that "the principal effect of the criticism of multinationals that began in the 1970s has been to alter the political reality of foreign investment in the developing countries. No longer do governments assume that foreign investment will automatically promote development. Instead, . . . developing country governments have tried to regulate that investment to maximize the rewards and minimize the costs to the host economy" (see also Sklair, 1991).

To grasp the future that awaits Third World countries in the new global market-place, it is necessary to introduce still another dimension that today also influences their potential for development: their monetary circumstances.

## Money Matters: Third World Debt and the Management of Interdependence

As noted above, OPEC's success in cartelizing the global oil regime during the 1970s galvanized the non-oil-producing developing countries into the belief that commodity power would enable them to "force" the North into replacing the Liberal International Economic Order with one more conducive to their development goals. Ironically, however, the two oil shocks of the 1970s created an environment in which many Third World countries thought it was wise to borrow heavily from abroad, while they simultaneously eroded the economic bases on which repayment of those loans depended. The result was a "debt crisis" that "dominated—some would say 'consumed'—international economic discussions in the 1980s" in what effectively became the "debt decade" (Nowzad, 1990). Its causes and consequences weave together many of the strands of the tapestry of North–South relations in the world political economy.

### Dealing with Third World Debt

As it first emerged in the early 1980s, the debt crisis spread to a broad group of countries, ranging from Poland in Eastern Europe to Brazil in Latin America, from the Philippines in Asia to Nigeria in Africa. It grew out of a combination of heavy private and public borrowing from private and public sources during the 1970s that led to an accumulated Third World debt above $600 billion by 1980 and nearly three times that amount by 1993 (see Figure 8.5). Many debtor countries found that they needed to borrow more money not to finance new projects but to meet their debt service obligations (interest and principal payments) on previous loans.

The specific event that triggered the debt crisis was the threat in August 1982 that Mexico would default on its loans. In addition to Mexico, others with the largest debts, including Poland, Argentina, and Brazil, required special treatment to keep them from going into default when they announced they did not have the cash necessary to pay their creditors. Eventually Third World debtors, especially those in Latin America, received the most attention.

### Averting Disaster

The foreign debt accumulation of the 1970s was part of a process that saw private loans and investments and official nonconcessional loans become more important than public foreign aid for all but the poorest of the poor countries (Burki, 1983).[9] The first oil shock gave impetus to the "privatization" of Third World capital flows. As dollars flowed from oil consumers in the West to oil producers in the Middle East ?nd elsewhere, the latter, unable to invest all of their newfound wealth at home, "recycled" their "petrodollars" by making investments in the First World. In the process the funds available to private banks for lending to others increased substantially.

Many of the non-oil-exporting developing countries became eager consumers of the funds private banks offered for investment. The fourfold rise in oil prices induced by the OPEC cartel hit these countries particularly hard. To pay for the sharply increased cost of imported oil along with their other imports, they could either tighten their belts at home to curb their economic growth or borrow from abroad to sustain that growth and pay for needed imports. Many chose the latter, and they often preferred private banks to other governments or multilateral agencies because the banks usually placed fewer restrictions on the use of the borrowed money than did the public sources. Private banks for their part were willing lenders, as they believed "sovereign risk" — the risk that governments might default—was virtually nonexistent.

Just as many of the now-industrial states were net borrowers from the world when they were building their own economies in the past, countries that seek to industrialize today often must rely on external capital. As long as the exports needed to earn the money to pay back the loans grow at the same rate, the accumulation of more debt is no problem. Moreover, there can be long-run payoffs in that investments made today in development projects, such as roads, hydroelectric dams, and steel plants, may eventually more than make up the cost of the original loans by generating new income, employment, and exports.

Whether developing countries always spent their borrowed money wisely is questionable. Argentina, for example, spent billions of dollars on sophisticated military

---

[9] Since the 1970s private financial institutions began to rival not only official bilateral aid but also multilateral institutions as the principal source of financial capital available to Third World countries. "Between 1970 and 1992 [private] flows increased from $5 billion to $102 billion" (UNDP, 1994: 61). The result in many cases was a condition of "indebted industrialization" (Frieden, 1981) as governmental agencies in state-capitalist regimes became actively involved in promoting industrial growth. A decade later many state-capitalist regimes (such as Mexico) came to the conclusion that disengagement of the state from direct involvement in industrialization activities, often through a process of *privatization*, was a necessary internal reform needed to cope effectively with the debt crisis. That process has now spread widely in the Third World and underpins the growth strategies of the Russian Federation, China, and the former socialist countries of Eastern Europe.

equipment later used against Britain during the Falkland Islands (Malvinas) War. And Brazil, the largest debtor, used foreign loans to finance several extraordinarily expensive "white elephants," including three nuclear power plants, the world's largest hydroelectric dam, and a railroad, all either unworkable or never completed (Henry, 1987).

Massive "capital flight" from debtor countries was another problem. Unscrupulous political leaders or well-heeled elites funneled much of the money into private accounts in the very banks extending the loans to the governments in the first place. The outflow of money reduced what was available for the investments that create new jobs and new wealth.

At the same time that developing countries' debt mounted, however, so did the resources needed to service it. As a result, the burden of the growing debt was essentially the same in 1980 as it was in 1970. But that situation changed sharply after 1980 as the drop in commodity prices associated with the worldwide recession caused the ratio of Third World debts to exports to rise markedly after 1981. Economic growth slowed as the prices of the commodities needed to pay for the debt dropped and the money needed to pay off the loans failed to materialize.

Thereafter, the appreciation of the U.S. dollar in foreign exchange markets added to the debt burden, as many developing countries' loans are denominated in dollars. Similarly, the strict monetarist policies adopted by the Western industrial countries as a way of coping with their persistent inflation caused interest rates to rise, with the result that developing countries' debt obligations, tied to those rates, also climbed. For developing countries as a whole, the ratio of debt service payments to export earnings rose sharply, ranging between 16 and 24 percent between 1982 and 1993 (Krueger, 1993: 88; World Bank, 1993: 33). The magnitude of the debts from all sources also grew to staggering proportions and have continued to increase through 1993 (see Figure 8.5) (*The Economist* 329, December 18, 1993: 7). In fact, the total external debt of the developing countries now exceeds their revenues from exports (Krueger, 1993).

The International Monetary Fund's programs to provide debt relief for Third World countries imposed strict conditions for the debtors' reforms. Included were insistence on policies to curb inflation, limit imports, restrict public spending, and expose protected industries. Because the IMF also urged those it helped to increase their exports, the label "export-led adjustment" described the IMF's approach to the debt problem.

The conditions attached to the IMF's help added to the strains on the political and social fabric of debtor countries. Because of this, some commentators asked whether its policies might not have been self-defeating. The IMF austerity program pushed vigorously until 1985 could claim considerable success from a strictly financial viewpoint (see Amuzegar, 1987), but the domestic burdens and the political costs it imposed were too overwhelming (Sachs, 1989). Analysts blamed austerity for the overthrow of the Sudanese government of President Jaafar Nimeri in 1985, for example. Debt and related financial issues also inflamed domestic political conflict in many others among the most heavily indebted countries, including Argentina, Brazil, Chile, Mexico, and Nigeria. Meanwhile, proposals surfaced for creating a "debtors' cartel"

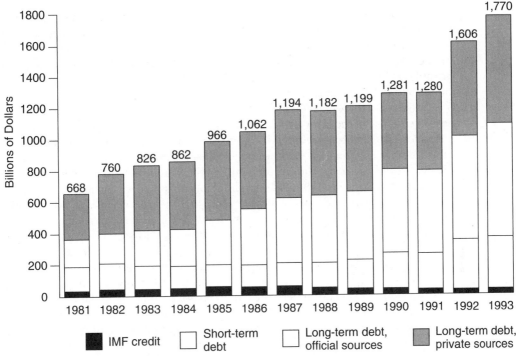

**Figure 8.5** The Developing Countries' Growing External Debt, 1981–1993.
*Source:* The Foundation for Teaching Economics and the United Nations Association of the USA (1992: 26); World Bank (1993: 33).

that would confront the creditor countries with a unified approach for easing their problems, as political leaders in the debtor countries adopted a defiant posture toward the predicament they faced.

### The Search for Long-term Solutions

In this emotionally charged atmosphere the United States abandoned its earlier arm's-length policy and proposed a new plan, known as the Baker initiative, to deal with the debt crisis.[10] The plan sought new loans from private banks and coupled these with renewed efforts to stimulate Third World economic growth via domestic economic reforms in debtor countries. Thus it emphasized a "market approach" to the debt problem rather than the austerity imposed through IMF conditionality. This approach failed, however, when it proved incapable of delivering the promised new resources. In fact, new loans of all sorts became increasingly scarce after 1982 (Philips

---

[10] The adverse impact of the debt crisis on the industrialized countries' commercial interests was underscored by the fact that their exports to the Third World fell from 30 percent of all exports in 1981 to only 20 percent in 1987 (Spero, 1990: 198). Thus the developed countries shared an interest in reducing the debt burden in order to stimulate economic growth and expand the markets the Third World provided for many First World exports.

and Tucker, 1991: 31), with the result that developing countries were paying more to their creditors than they were receiving in new loans. Moreover, because most foreign direct investment occurs in the industrial countries, not the Third World (see Figure 8.4 and Chapter 6), most developing countries could not seek loans from private creditors and increasingly had to rely on their own resources for investment capital and debt servicing (UNDP, 1994).

Two events in 1987 added renewed urgency to the imperative of finding long-term solutions to the debt problem. In February Brazilian President José Sarney announced that his country would suspend interest payments on the bulk of its $108 billion debt, declaring, "We cannot pay the debt with our people's hunger"; and in May Citicorp Chairman John Reed astonished the financial world when he announced that the giant U.S. bank would take a billion-dollar loss to cover its shaky international loans. Other major U.S. banks quickly followed suit. Meanwhile, the debt burden of the most hard-pressed debtors continued to mount, as did bitterness among the debtors toward their creditors, who resented being told that the poor should not borrow more than they could repay. Peruvian President Alan Garcia reflected the sentiments when he asserted in 1987 that "Each of us has the right . . . to not pay more than what its economy can pay. . . . That is the moral law of the debtors."

Events in 1989 again underscored the explosive domestic situation exacerbated by foreign indebtness, as widespread rioting broke out in Venezuela in protest of the government's austerity measures. "In the course of a few days an estimated 300 people died. This was particularly shocking since Venezuela had long been regarded as one of the most stable Latin American democracies" (Sachs, 1989). Yet the occurrence could easily have been repeated elsewhere.

Again the United States stepped forward to offer a new plan. The Brady initiative, announced in early 1989, sought to reduce the debt of all debtors by as much as 20 percent over three years. It focused on debt relief rather than debt restructuring. The plan signaled that "the foreign policy concerns over the deteriorating situation in the debtor countries finally came to the fore" (Sachs, 1989). Previously, concern for the banks had taken precedence. Still, the initiative depended on voluntary actions by creditors to bring about the debt reductions, which are difficult to achieve. In this respect the Brady initiative was an extension of the Baker strategy for containing the debt crisis, not an alternative to it (Cohen, 1989). Like its predecessor, the Brady plan failed to rectify the problem.

## The Debt Burden: Retrospect and Prospect

Among debt-burdened developing countries, the 1980s "debt decade" exacted a devastating toll. Figure 8.6 provides some sense of its cost by charting trends in the per-capita gross domestic product of the industrial countries and two groups of developing countries, those burdened by debt service difficulties and those relatively free of them. The differences are striking: The per-capita income of those without debt-servicing difficulties soared by more than 60 percent between 1978 and 1991, while

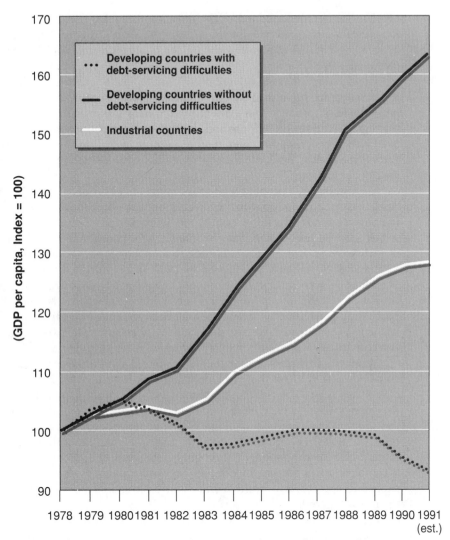

**Figure 8.6**  Per-capita Economic Performance by Country Groups, 1978–1991
*Source:* Rosemarie Philips and Stuart K. Tucker (1991: 32).

the incomes of those burdened by debt were actually less than they had been in 1978. The reality was especially acute in Latin America, where the 1980s are known as "the lost decade."

The trauma and hostility caused by the debt crisis that first exploded in August 1982 are difficult to exaggerate. "It called into question the soundness of the international financial and banking system. It was accused of stunting economic growth in the developing countries. It was blamed for social and political instability, specifically for endangering nascent democratic tendencies in certain countries. It mobilized religious, environmental, and other interest groups that usually remain outside the financial fray. It led to calls for repudiation, solidarity, the formation of debt cartels, and the exploitation of financial obligations to obtain concessions in unrelated areas" (Nowzad, 1990).

The debt crisis has not been resolved. In 1993 the South was collectively indebted to foreigners by more than $1.7 trillion dollars—more than a third of its combined gross domestic product. For Africa, foreign debt was equal to the annual GDP of the region. And for the African and South American debtors, payments on accumulated past debts consumes more than 25 percent of the income earned from exports. Lifting themselves from the debt burden thus will doubtlessly continue to pose an enormous challenge.

Against this grim prophesy, reasons for hope have surfaced in the 1990s. Forecasts suggest that economic growth, stimulated by trade liberalization, will help alleviate the poverty levels afflicting much of the Third World. Some developing countries, which lead in the rate of their economies' growth through the rapid expansion of their exports, are certain to benefit from a world estimated to become between $212 and $274 billion a year richer by 2002 as a result of the 1993 GATT trade-liberalization accord (UNDP, 1994: 63). These newly industrialized countries are, simply put, "catching up" to their First World counterparts. Already, by 1992, at purchasing-power parity, "five of the world's largest economies are those of developing countries. China, India, Russia, Brazil, and Mexico have GDPs bigger than Canada's, currently the G-7's seventh man" (*The Economist* 330, January 8, 1994: 102).

Moreover, this recovery for the Third World's middle-income countries has occurred despite the fact that their debt burdens have increased. Perhaps the major reason has been "the remarkable turnaround in private capital flows . . . to the developing world [which] have risen more than two and a half times since 1990. For the first time in a decade, the volume of private flows has been larger than the volume of official flows" (World Bank, 1993: 3). The 1990s increases in net financial inflows to the Third World (especially through private sources) have raised expectations that a combination of foreign investment and other income transfers will permit the expanding economies of Third World countries to escape the poverty that has afflicted them (see Figure 8.7).

Hence, on the optimistic side, as the World Bank sees it,

> For the commercial banks and some of their middle-income developing-country borrowers, the debt crisis . . . is largely over. Developing-country debt no longer poses a systematic threat to the international banking system, and for some of the previously debt-distressed middle-income countries, renewed portfolio flows are part of a wider (albeit still fragile) return to market access. The crisis is certainly far from over, however, for many other developing countries. External viability remains elusive for many low- and lower-middle-income countries (especially in Sub-Saharan Africa), who are indebted largely to official bilateral creditors and whose debt burdens are, in some cases, unsustainably high. Furthermore, for some smaller middle-income countries, resolution of commercial debt problems has still to be achieved through Brady-type [debt-reduction] agreements. (cited in Mitchell, 1993: 158)

Thus, the debt problem is likely to cast its shadow over the future of many

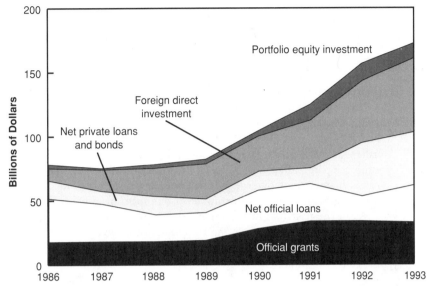

**Figure 8.7** The 1990s Financial Landscape: Aggregate Net Resource Flows to All Developing Countries, 1986–1993

*Source:* World Bank (1993: 4).

*Note:* All flows are deflated by an import price index for developing countries at constant 1993 dollars; 1993 data are estimated.

Third World countries for years, unless resources (particularly through foreign direct investments) continue to flow, and (like a rising tide lifts all ships) these lift the Third World out of its previous impoverished and indebted condition.

Regardless of how sound and responsible their policies may be, the developing countries' future will be profoundly shaped by circumstances in the industrial world and how those rich states respond to them. In this sense the debt curse resembles the conflicts raised in the debates over the proposed New International Economic Order. Developing countries blamed the structure of the world political economy for their ills, and the First World responded with the charge that forces indigenous to the Third World were at fault. The lessons of the debt crisis suggest that both may be right. The global economy is today truly interdependent and increasingly indivisible.

## NORTH–SOUTH RELATIONS AT CENTURY'S END . . . . . . . . . . . . . . . . . . .

How might Third World aspirations for development in all of its manifestations be satisfied and properly managed? Despite the contentious rhetoric surrounding the North–South debate in the past and the persistent global inequalities on which it was based, it is clear that the South cannot force the North to submit to its demands, nor will the North do so voluntarily. A more reasonable scenario depicts piecemeal adjustments in North–South relations born of the realization that the well-being of each is dependent on the health of the other and that "because trade moves in all directions, it needs a worldwide (not regional) set of rules" (*The Economist* 329, November 20, 1993: 15).

The end of the Cold War creates new opportunities for a realistic assessment of where the interests of North and South intersect. The diversity inherent among Third World countries ensures less uniformity of outlook than in the past. Similarly, the emergence of three major economic clusters, centered on Europe, Asia, and North America, portends diverging interests as the three coalescing trade blocs assess the challenges and opportunities posed by the developing countries. The superpowers' competition for allies and influence in the Third World characteristic of the Cold War is history, but divergent interests and perspectives in North and South alike ensure that competition and conflict of one form or another will continue.

As in the past, political economy issues will likely spark conflict between North and South. Other issues relating to population growth, resource consumption, environmental stress, and sustainable development will also define the future parameters of North–South conflict and cooperation. It is to these issues that we now turn.

## SUGGESTED READINGS

Chubin, Shahram. "Southern Perspectives on World Order," pp. 166–179 in Charles W. Kegley, Jr. and Eugene R. Wittkopf, eds., *The Global Agenda*, 4th ed. New York: McGraw-Hill, 1995.

Feinberg, Richard E., and Delia M. Boylan. *Modular Multilateralism: North–South Economic Relations in the 1990s*. Washington, D.C.: Overseas Development Council, 1991.

Ferraro, Vincent, and Melissa Rosser. "Global Debt and Third World Development," pp. 332–355 in Michael T. Klare and Daniel C. Thomas, eds., *World Security: Challenges for a New Century*. New York: St. Martin's Press, 1994.

Head, Ivan L. *On a Hinge of History: The Mutual Vulnerability of South and North*. Toronto: University of Toronto Press, 1991.

Hook, Steven W. *National Interest and Foreign Aid*. Boulder, Colo.: Lynne Rienner, 1994.

Helleiner, G. K. *The New Global Economy and the Developing Countries*. Brookfield, Vt.: Edward Elgar, 1990.

Krasner, Stephen D. *Structural Conflict: The Third World Against Global Liberalism*. Berkeley, Calif.: University of California Press, 1985.

Krueger, Anne O. *Economic Policies at Cross-Purposes: The United States and Developing Countries*. Washington, D.C.: Brookings Institution, 1993.

Sewell, John W. "The Metamorphosis of the Third World: U.S. Interests in the 1990s," pp. 222–238 in Charles W. Kegley Jr. and Eugene R. Wittkopf, eds., *The Future of American Foreign Policy*. New York: St. Martin's Press, 1992.

Schwartz, Herman M. *States versus Markets: History, Geography, and the Development of the International Political Economy*. New York: St. Martin's Press, 1994.

The South Centre. *Facing the Challenge: Responses to the Report of the South Commission*. London: Zed Books, 1993.

Tisch, Sarah J., and Michael B. Wallace. *Dilemmas of Development Assistance: The What, Why, and Who of Foreign Aid*. Boulder, Colo: Westview Press, 1994.

# CHAPTER 9

• • •

# THE GLOBAL COMMONS: POPULATION PRESSURES AND THREATS TO THE ENVIRONMENT

• • •

*If you contemplate the potential growth of population in the future, you can terrify yourself.*

William Colby, Former Director of
the U.S. Central Intelligence Agency, 1993

*Sometimes the developing countries are right. We [industrial countries] have a disproportionate impact on the global environment. We have less than a quarter of the world's population, but we use three-quarters of the world's raw materials and create three-quarters of solid waste.*

Al Gore,
U.S. Vice President, 1993

The forces that will determine the globe's future condition are not confined to economic, political, and military factors. They also include the interdependent relationships between humankind and the biological and geophysical environments within which human interactions occur.

The *ecological perspective*, which makes this dimension of world politics its impact central, views the global environment as a system of delicately and tightly integrated components. Its major concern is the interrelatedness of biological, economic, political, social, technological, and geographic subsystems. This obvious but often ignored linkage underscores the limits nature imposes, namely, that the planet's *carrying capacity*—its ability to support human and other life forms—is not infinite.

How many people can the earth support? What is its ultimate carrying capacity? These questions have been asked for millennia, but the answers remain elusive, in part because rapidly advancing technology has continuously stretched the boundaries. Thus the earth will doubtless accommodate the growth projected for today's 5.6 billion inhabitants into the next century, but at what cost—to human freedom, human welfare, and ultimately to the environment necessary to sustain humankind?

The *tragedy of the commons* is a metaphor widely used to explain the impact of human behavior on ecological systems. It was first articulated in 1833 by the English political economist William Foster Lloyd and later popularized and extended to contemporary world problems by the human ecologist Garrett Hardin (1968). If we assume that the search for self-advantage drives humankind, the metaphor provokes inquiry about the probable human approach to resources held in common in the absence of regulation. If advancing their personal welfare is the primary interest that motivates individuals, what consequences should be anticipated for the finite resources held in common, and hence for all?

Consider, as Hardin did, what occurred in nineteenth-century English villages. The village green was typically common property on which all herders were permitted to graze their cattle. Sharing the common grazing area worked well as long as the number of cattle did not exceed the land's carrying capacity, for if that occurred, the pasture would be ruined and the number of cattle it could support would decline drastically. Still, individual herders had powerful incentives to increase the size of their herds as much as possible because this was the only way they could maximize their individual gain. If pushed, individual herders might concede that reductions in the size of their herds would serve the collective interest of all, which was to preserve the commons. Without guarantees that other herders would follow suit, however, self-restraint was costly. There were few incentives to voluntarily reduce the number of one's own cattle to relieve the pressure on the common village green. Indeed, no one could guarantee that others would follow suit.

On the other hand, the addition of one more animal to the village green would produce a personal gain whose costs would be borne by everyone. Hence, a regard for self-interest encouraged all herders to increase indiscriminately the size of their herds, and it discouraged self-sacrifice for the general welfare. In the end, the collective impact of the effort by each herder to maximize individual gain was to place more cattle on the village green than it could sustain. Destruction of the common village green was the inevitable result. "Ruin is the destination toward which all men rush," Hardin concluded, "each pursuing his own best interest in a society that believes in the freedom of the commons."

The tragedy of the commons is widely used to understand environmental politics because it illuminates so well the sources of many human predicaments.[1] Its relevance to global ecopolitical problems is obvious when we draw an analogy between the village commons in England before the enactment of closure laws and contemporary planetary "common property," such as the oceans, fisheries,

---

[1] Thomas Schelling (1978) observes that the commons image is widely used as a kind of shorthand "for situations in which people so impinge on each other in pursuing their own interests that collectively they might be better off if they could be restrained, but no one gains individually by self-restraint." He goes on to point out that "the commons are a special but widespread case out of a broader class of situations in which some of the costs or damages of what people do occur beyond their purview, and they either don't know or don't care about them."

and the atmosphere, from which individual profit is maximized on the basis of a first-come, first-serve principle but which largely remain beyond regulation. Overuse, even abuse, of common property is apparent when some countries take more fish from ocean fisheries than their yields are able to sustain or when the oceans and atmosphere become sinks for environmental pollution perpetrated by a few but whose costs are borne by many. The task in both instances becomes one of devising regulations for an ecopolitical environment that thrives on freedom of choice (see Soroos, 1995).

A major unregulated freedom of choice on which Hardin (1968) focused is the human freedom to propagate. "The most important aspect of necessity that we must now recognize," he wrote, "is the necessity of abandoning the commons in breeding. Freedom to breed will bring ruin to all. . . . The only way we can preserve and nurture other and more precious freedoms is by relinquishing the freedom to breed, and that very soon. . . . Only so, can we put an end to this aspect of the tragedy of the commons."

Not everyone will agree with the ethical implications of Hardin's arguments. Few decisions, in fact, are more intensely personal or more intimately tied to the social and cultural fabric of a society than those of individual couples about marriage and the family. Furthermore, just as the ultimate carrying capacity of the global ecosystem has proved elastic, the impact of unregulated population growth on environmental quality remains unclear (see Repetto, 1987). Nonetheless, the balance of both theory and evidence points to a world in which unrestrained population growth will result in lost economic opportunities, environmental degradation, domestic strife, and incentives—perhaps imperatives—for governmental restraints on individual choice. As the 1992 statement "Warning to Humanity" signed by 102 Nobel laureates put it, "No more than one of a few decades remain before the chance to avert the threats we now confront will be lost and the prospects for humanity immeasurably diminished. . . . A new ethic is required" (in Postel, 1994).

A world interdependent ecopolitically as well as economically is certain to share the consequences (Homer-Dixon, 1991). Even those countries not experiencing excessive population growth contribute to the problems by placing a disproportionate strain on global resources and the ability of the ecosystem to withstand environmental abuse. That is nowhere more clear than with *global warming,* a quintessential transnational problem whose causes and potential solutions are presently lodged not in the world's most populous countries but in its most prosperous.

Our purpose in this chapter and the next is to explore how changes in demography, the environment, and resources interactively influence world politics. Here we focus on demographic variables and their correlates. We direct particular attention to how projected global trends in births, deaths, and migration will shape the character of our world in the new millennium. This sets the stage for Chapter 10, where we examine how population and environmental changes will affect the world political economy and trends in energy production and consumption as well as the uses made of such policy responses as economic sanctions to deal with the problems these pressures create.

## GLOBAL DEMOGRAPHIC PATTERNS AND TRENDS . . . . . . . . . . . . . . . . . . . . .

The dramatic growth in world population in the decades following World War II is without historical precedent. It took two million years for world population to reach one billion people. As Figure 9.1 illustrates, world population reached two billion around 1930. Since then, additional billions have been added even more rapidly: Three billion was reached by 1960, four billion in 1975, and five billion in 1987. At this rate, it will take only eleven years to reach the next billion (*WorldWatch* 7, January–February 1994: 39). If these trends unfold at the present 1.6 percent growth rate, or about 100 million additional people each year, the world will reach the 6.0-billion figure on the eve of the twenty-first century and finally stabilize at more than 11 billion sometime in the twenty-second century. That projection depends, however, on the assumption that the norm worldwide will have become an average family size of no more than two children, as is presently the case in most of the more developed countries but rarely elsewhere.

The rapid growth of world population since World War II is described by a simple mathematical principle articulated in 1798 by the Reverend Thomas Malthus, namely, that population when unchecked increases in a geometric or exponential ratio (1 to 2, 2 to 4, 4 to 8, and so forth), whereas subsistence increases in only an arithmetic ratio (1 to 2, 2 to 3, 3 to 4). When population increases at such an accelerating rate, the compound effect can be staggering.

Consider, for example, the results that flow from the simple decision of whether to have two children or three. If parents decide to have three children and if each of their children and their children's children also decide to have three, by the third generation thirty-nine people will have been born—three in the first, nine in the second, and twenty-seven in the third. If, however, the initial decision is to have two children instead of three, and if each child makes the same choice, in three generations only sixteen people will have been born (two in the first, four in the second, and

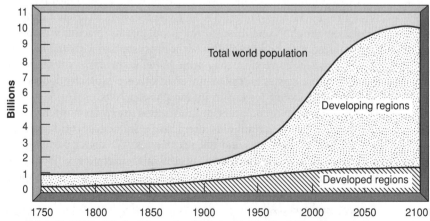

**Figure 9.1**  World Population Growth, Global and Regional Trends, 1750–2100
*Source:* Thomas W. Merrick (1988: 4).

eight in the third). Extrapolating these patterns to whole societies, the cumulative results can be enormous. For example, the population of the United States in 1968 was 200 million. Assuming two-child families (and no immigration), U.S. population will grow to 300 million by the year 2015. However, if we assume three-child families, 300 million will be reached before the turn of the century, and the population will have doubled to over 400 million by 2015. Extending these projections over a century, the population of the United States in 2068 will exceed 800 million if three-child families are the rule but will remain well under 400 million with two-child families.

Another way to contemplate how sensitive world population is to even small, incremental changes in its rate of growth (the difference between births and deaths) is to consider how long it will take the population to double given a particular growth rate. Just as money deposited in a savings account will grow more rapidly if it earns interest not only on the original investment but also on the interest payments, population growth is a function of increases in the original number of people plus those accruing from past population growth. Thus a population growing at a 1 percent rate will double in sixty-nine years, while a population growing at a 2 percent rate will double in only thirty-five years[2] (see Box 9.1).

Worldwide, the rate of population growth peaked at slightly over 2 percent in the late 1960s and then declined to 1.6 percent by the 1990s. The dip, though modest, is an important step toward stabilizing the world's ultimate population size. It means, for example, that by the year 2000 the world's population will be 20 percent less than the 7.5 billion people that the birth and death rates of the 1950s would have produced had they continued uninterrupted. Still, the pressures associated with population growth continue. In the 1990s world population was expected to grow by 100 million people annually, an amount equivalent to adding more than the entire population of Bolivia every month or populating the Bahamas again each day (U.S. CIA, 1993). "Each day, the equivalent of a city the size of Newark or Akron is added to the world; each month, a city the size of New York" (Rowan, 1993). Even more will be added each year in the future. In fact, as Figure 9.2 illustrates, more people will be added to the world's population in the last fifth of the twentieth century than at any other time in history. Put differently, it took the earth's human population two million years to grow to its first billion; it will take only eleven years for the world's population to grow to its next billion (WorldWatch 7, January–February 1994: 39).

Not all countries will share equally in the phenomenon, however. In fact, rapid population growth in the Third World is the most striking demographic development in the post–World War II era, and it will persist into the future at the same time that the more developed countries move toward zero population growth (see Figure 9.2). Ours has become a demographically divided world, with the low-growth countries in the North and the high-growth countries in the South. As with other cleavages between North and South, the globe's demographic divisions promise to widen even

---

[2] This is merely another way of saying that the population grows exponentially rather than arithmetically. The impact of different growth rates on doubling times can be calculated by dividing sixty-nine by the percentage of growth. Thus a population growing at 1 percent will double in sixty-nine years, but a population growing at 3 percent will double in twenty-three years.

## Box 9.1
### Understanding Growth Rates:
### The Secret of the Persian Chessboard

• • •

The way I first heard the story, it happened in ancient Persia. But it may have been India, or even China. Anyway, it happened a long time ago. The Grand Vizier, the principal adviser to the King, had invented a new game. It was played with moving pieces on a board of 64 squares. The most important piece was the King. The next most important piece was the Grand Vizier—just what we might expect of a game invented by a Grand Vizier. The object of the game was to capture the enemy King, and so the game was called, in Persian, *shahmat—shah* for king, *mat* for dead. Death to the King. In Russia it is still called *shakhmaty*, which perhaps conveys a lingering revolutionary ardor. Even in English there is an echo of the name—the final move is called "checkmate." The game, of course, is chess.

As time passed, the pieces, their moves and the rules evolved. There is, for example, no longer a piece called the Grand Vizier—it has become transmogrified into a Queen, with much more formidable powers.

Why a king should delight in the creation of a game called "Death to the King" is a mystery. But, the story goes, he was so pleased that he asked the Grand Vizier to name his own reward for such a splendid invention. The Grand Vizier had his answer ready: He was a humble man, he told the King. He wished only for a humble reward. Gesturing to the eight columns and eight rows of squares on the board he devised, he asked that he be given a single grain of wheat on the first square, twice that on the second square, twice *that* on the third, and so on, until each square had its complement of wheat.

No, the King remonstrated. This is too modest a prize for so important an invention. He offered jewels, dancing girls, palaces. But the Grand Vizier, his eyes becomingly lowered, refused them all. It was little piles of wheat he wanted. So, secretly marveling at the unselfishness of his counselor, the King graciously consented.

When the Master of the Royal Granary began to count out the grains, however, the King was in for a rude surprise. The number of grains starts small enough: 1, 2, 4, 8, 16, 32, 64, 128, 256, 512, 1024. . . . But by the time the 64th square is approached, the number becomes colossal, staggering. In fact the number is nearly 18.5 quintillion grains of wheat. Maybe the Grand Vizier was on a high-fiber diet.

How much does 18.5 quintillion grains of wheat weigh? If each grain were 2 millimeters in size, then all the grains together would weigh around 75 billion metric tons, which far exceeds what could have been stored in the King's granaries. In fact, this is the equivalent of about 150 years of the world's present wheat production. . . .

A sequence of numbers like this—where each is a fixed multiple of the previous one—is called an exponential increase. Exponentials show up in all sorts of places. Compound interest, for example: If an ancester of yours put $10 in the bank for you 200 years ago, and it accrued a steady 5% annual interest, then by now it would be worth $10 × (1.05)$^{200}$, or $172,925.81—where (1.05)$^{200}$ simply means 1.05 times itself 200 times. If that ancestor could have gotten a 6% rate, you'd now have over $1 million; for 7%, over $7.5 million; and for an extortionate 10%, a tidy $1.9 billion.

*Source: Carl Sagan (1989: 14).*

further in the decades ahead. We can better understand the inevitability of this result—and how demographic trends will affect world politics—if we go beyond the simple arithmetic of population growth and explore its dynamics.

## Factors Affecting Population Growth: National and Regional Variations

The population growth rate in the United States in 1993 was 0.8 percent. This is an annual rate similar to that of other industrial countries of the North, where births and deaths have nearly stabilized. Hence, the difference between a typical industrial country and the world growth rate of 1.6 percent is largely attributable to a population

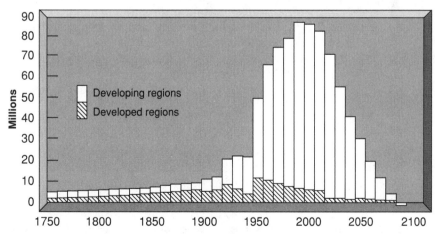

**Figure 9.2** Average Annual Increase in World Population in Numbers per Decade, Global and Regional Trends, 1750–2100
*Source:* Thomas W. Merrick (1988: 4, 19).

surge in the South's less developed countries, where sharply lower death rates since World War II have resulted from advances in medical science, agricultural productivity, and public sanitation. The paradox posed by reduced death rates is that this favorable development has contributed to accelerating population growth rates in precisely those countries least able to support a burgeoning number of people.

Variations in national and regional population growth virtually ensure that today's demographic division of the world will grow wider in the future. As illustrated in Figure 9.1, the 3.7 billion people who inhabited the Third World in 1985 will have grown to 4.8 billion by the year 2000, while the comparable increase among the developed countries will be only from 1.2 billion to 1.3 billion (Merrick, 1988: 13). High fertility rates in much of the Third World today combined with increases in the sheer number of children that will be born underlie these projections.

## Fertility Rates

In 1993, on average, 3.3 children were born by each woman in the world. In the developed world the total fertility rate (the average number of children a woman would have in a lifetime) stood at 1.8, which is actually below "replacement fertility" (one couple replacing themselves with two children), but in the developing world it stood at 4.4 (Population Reference Bureau, *1993 World Population Data Sheet*). In many Third World countries, notably in Africa, the preferred family size is actually much larger than this.[3] But world population will not stabilize until replacement fertility is reached everywhere, for only then will the number of births equal the number of deaths.

The developing countries' high fertility rates derive from a variety of sources. Besides the pleasures that children provide, religious norms often encourage the bearing of children (particularly male offspring in some cultures) as both a duty and a path to a rewarding afterlife. In addition, cultural traditions sometimes ascribe prestige and social status to women according to the number of children they bear. And most important perhaps, high fertility rates are explained by economic factors. Large families add more hands to a family's labor force today and may be a future source of social security for parents who live in societies that have no public programs to provide for the elderly. When the infant mortality rate is high, the incentives for many progeny are even greater—the larger the number of children born, the greater the chance that some will survive.

Even in the face of increasing life expectancy throughout the world, over fourteen million children die each year before they reach the age of five (World Resources Institute, 1990: 253). Child death rates remain particularly high in much of Asia and Africa. In Afghanistan, for example, more than 30 percent of the children will die before the age of five, and in many places in Africa more than 20 percent will die

---

[3] Excluding China from this figure, the total fertility rate among developing countries stood at 4.4. China's rate was only 1.9 as a result of its extremely regulative population control measures to slow the growth of China's huge population, estimated in 1993 to be 1.18 billion. It should also be noted, however, that the desired family size has declined measurably during the past two decades in every world region, even in high-fertility, low-contraceptive areas in Asia and Africa (Starke, 1994).

by that age. Sadly, most communicable diseases, which kill mainly children, are simple to prevent, and medication for them is relatively inexpensive. Noncommunicable disease could be largely eliminated simply by changing adults' behavior. Yet for health conditions to improve even more, what is needed is not more money, but better management of existing health spending.[4] Fertility rates are often highest where poverty in all its manifestations is most widespread; the tragedy is that such high rates often reinforce the persistence of poverty.

## Population Momentum

Even more important to understanding today's population surge in the Third World (which is a result of high, but declining, birthrates and rapidly falling death rates) for tomorrow's world is the "momentum" factor. It helps explain why in the last quintile of the twentieth century more people will be added to the world's population than at any other time in history. Like the momentum of a descending airliner when it first touches down on the runway, population growth simply cannot be halted even with an immediate, full application of the brakes. Instead, many years of high fertility mean that more women will be entering their reproductive years than in the past. Even if all of them gave birth to only two offspring, the absolute number of children born would continue to grow well into the future. The process will continue until the size of the generation giving birth to children is no larger than the generation among which deaths are occurring.

Consider, for example, the three age and sex population profiles shown in Figure 9.3. Kenya's profile shows a "rapid growth" population, because each new age group or cohort contains more people than did the one before it. In contrast, the United States has a "slow growth" profile, because recent cohorts have been smaller than preceding ones and U.S. society as a whole has been aging. Finally, Austria's profile is that of a "declining" population, because it has both low birthrates and a large number of people who survive middle age. Thus Austria's "mature" or "old" age structure is a product of its prior extended period of low birthrates and low death rates.

Although some developing countries have moved toward zero population growth (and many toward Austria's negative growth profile), many others mirror the Kenyan pattern. Because each cohort is typically larger than the one before it, the number of young men and women entering their reproductive years will also grow. Thus the developing countries' age profiles explain the sheer momentum of population growth in the Third World. Figure 9.4 projects the developing world's expected larger propor-

---

[4] The World Bank (*The Economist* 329, July 10, 1993: 58) identifies four major problems:

- Public money is misallocated in that it is spent on treatments that are not cost effective while many diseases that can be treated effectively (such as tuberculosis) do not receive funding.

- Government health spending goes disproportionately to the wealthy through subsidized hospital care and health insurance.

- Inefficient spending takes place with regard to pharmaceuticals and medical equipment.

- In middle-income developing countries, spending on health care is rising faster than income.

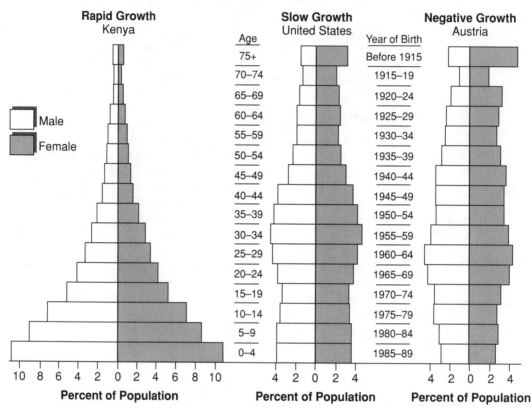

THREE PATTERNS OF POPULATION CHANGE

**Figure 9.3** Three Patterns of Population Change
*Source:* Population Reference Bureau (1990: 9).

tion of fertile age groups and shows why the demographic momentum already in place will produce quite different population growth in the developed and the developing worlds.

In general, population growth will continue after replacement-level fertility is achieved for as many as fifty to seventy years. If the goal of replacement-level fertility is reached worldwide around the year 2020, some seventy years later this would lead to a steady-state population of around eleven billion people (see Figure 9.5). If replacement-level fertility is not reached by this time, of course, the world's ultimate population size will be much greater. Conversely, if replacement-level fertility could be achieved earlier, the impact would be equally substantial. As Robert S. McNamara (1984), former president of the World Bank, has pointed out, "if the date at which replacement-level fertility is reached could be advanced from 2020 to 2000 . . . the ultimate population would be approximately 3 billion less, a number equivalent to 75 percent of today's world total. This reveals in startling terms the hidden penalties of failing to act, and act immediately, to reduce fertility."

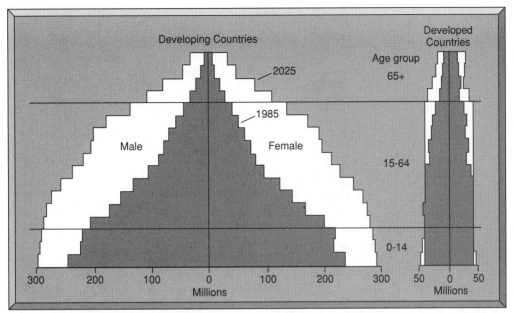

**Figure 9.4**  Population Age Pyramids for Developed and Developing Countries, 1985 and 2025
*Source:* Thomas W. Merrick (1988: 4, 19).

The obvious question, then, is how to achieve replacement-level fertility. The demographic transition theory, which is the most widely accepted explanation of population changes over time, suggests some answers.

### The Demographic Transition Theory

The ***demographic transition theory*** explains the change that Europe and later North America experienced between 1750 and 1930, when a condition of high birthrates combined with high death rates was replaced by a condition of low birthrates and low death rates. The transition started when death rates began to fall, presumably because of economic growth, rising standards of living, and improved control of disease. In such circumstances, the potential for substantial population growth was, of course, great. But then birthrates also began to decline, and during this phase population growth slowed (see Figure 9.6).

According to the theory, birthrate declines occur because economic growth alters people's preferred family size. In preindustrial societies, children are economic bonuses. As industrialization proceeds, they become economic burdens, as they inhibit social mobility and capital accumulation. The move from large to small families, with the associated decline in fertility, is therefore usually exhibited when industrialization takes place.

The fourth stage in the demographic transition was achieved in Europe and North America when both the birth and death rates reached very low levels. With fertility

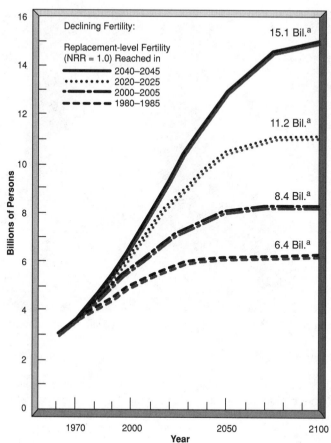

**Figure 9.5** Momentum of World Population Growth
*Source:* U.S. Department of State (1978: 50).
[a] Stabilization level.

rates near the replacement level, the result was a very low rate of population growth, if any at all. The panel on the left in Figure 9.6 depicts the demographic transition experienced by most developed countries.

By contrast, the panel on the right in Figure 9.6 makes clear that the developing countries have not yet experienced rapidly falling birthrates, despite the extraordinarily rapid increase in life expectancy that has occurred in the Third World since World War II. In fact, the precipitous decline in death rates was largely the result of more effective "death-control" measures introduced by the outside world.[5] The

---

[5] Sri Lanka illustrates the effect of public-health measures on the developing countries' death rates. Malaria and malaria-related diseases were a major cause of the historically high death rates in Sri Lanka, which in 1945 stood at twenty-two per one thousand. In 1946 the insecticide DDT was introduced to eradicate the mosquitoes that carry malaria. In a single year the death rate dropped 34 percent, and by 1955 it had declined to about half the 1945 level (Ehrlich et al., 1977: 197).

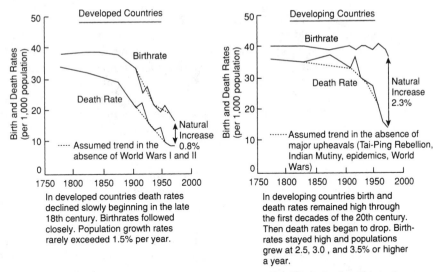

**Figure 9.6**  The Demographic Transition in Developed and Developing Countries
*Source:* U.S. Department of State (1978: 52; based on United Nations data).

decline in the developing countries' death rates thus differs sharply from the long-term, slow declines that Europe and North America experienced. They have been the result of externally introduced and rapid environmental changes rather than the fundamental and evolutionary changes that affect a country's policies, institutions, or cultural traditions. In particular, the developing countries have not experienced the decline in fertility rates that normally follows the decline in mortality rates when sustained economic growth occurs. A population "explosion" is the inevitable result.

## Population Projections

Although developing countries have yet to move toward replacement-level fertility, demographers expect this will happen. Consider the projections in Figures 9.1 and 9.2 (pages 294 and 297). They predict that the transition to low fertility and mortality will occur and that fertility will decline to replacement level by 2040. Based on those assumptions, even if replacement-level fertility had been achieved by 1990, population would continue to grow "until it reached 8.5 [billion] in 2150 because of all the young people already alive" (Starke, 1994: 38).

### Uncertain Death Rates

Projections far into the future are inevitably subject to error. Uncertainty about death rates is one reason. A "limited" nuclear war, for example, could occur, inducing a climatic catastrophe through "nuclear winter" (see Sagan and Turco, 1993) that would abruptly destroy billions of people and make contemporary population projections meaningless. The destructiveness of modern weapons guarantees that even conventional wars could cause mass destruction (see Chapter 11).

A more populous world is also a more vulnerable one. Consider, for example, the difference in population density in Bangladesh and the state of Louisiana in the United States, two delta lands of similar size. Four and a half million people lived in Louisiana in 1993; 114 million lived in Bangladesh, giving it a population density of over two thousand people per square mile. A natural disaster in Bangladesh—where typhoons are commonplace—carries a proportionately greater threat to life and property. In fact, a 1988 typhoon in Bangladesh killed over a thousand people and made twenty-five million homeless.

Death due to malnutrition and starvation and from inadequate health care also may affect the long-term growth of the world's population. Twice in recent years, in the 1970s and again in the 1980s, broad stretches of the Sahel area in Africa experienced life-threatening drought and famine. Sub-Saharan Africa is also more threatened than other regions. Large proportions of people are infected with the human immunodeficiency virus (HIV), which gives them a high risk of contracting AIDS (acquired immune deficiency syndrome). "It is quite likely that 1 of every 100 people will have HIV by the end of this decade" (Sachs, 1994: 102). The World Health Organization (WHO) estimated in 1994 that over 25 million cumulative HIV cases have occurred, about 80 percent in the developing world.

More than 17 million new HIV infections throughout the world are projected in the 1990s, more than half of them in the developing world (*World Development Report 1993*, 1993: 33). "Almost all HIV infections eventually result in cases of full-blown AIDS and . . . AIDS is almost 100 percent fatal" (Sachs, 1994). On conservative estimates, AIDS could cause at least 2 million additional deaths a year within a decade (*The Economist* 329, July 10, 1993: 58). Projections that AIDS could triple the current death rate in Africa are not unrealistic (*World Development Report 1993*, 1993: 33).[6] In addition to Africa, the potentially fatal virus is spreading rapidly in South and Southeast Asia, Latin America, and the Caribbean. (The United States has the largest number of reported AIDS cases at the present time.)

Whether AIDS will become the plague of the twenty-first century comparable to the Black Death of the Middle Ages, as some predict, remains problematic. But the claim AIDS will make on the world's health resources and its contribution to rising mortality in many areas of the world will doubtless grow, especially in developing countries.

## Uncertain Birthrates

Unanticipated changes in birthrates will also affect the accuracy of today's world population projections. Here incompleteness in the demographic transition theory,

---

[6] AIDS is a particular threat to Africa because "it appears to have spread among its limited pool of professional and technical elite. . . . AIDS could, in a sense, decapitate some African countries. The growing epidemic . . . aggravates an already severe shortage of skilled people and raises the prospect of economic, political and social disorder" (Harden, 1987).

which is based primarily on the European experience prior to World War II, may reduce their accuracy.

The demographic transition theory envisages four phases: (1) high birthrate, high death rate; (2) high birthrate, falling death rate; (3) declining birthrate, relatively low death rate; (4) low birthrate, low death rate. The experience in Europe since the 1970s suggests a possible fifth phase: low death rate, declining birthrate. Some have called this Europe's "second" demographic transition (van de Kaa, 1987).

The fertility rate in Europe during the past two decades did not stabilize at the replacement level, as the demographic transition theory predicts. Instead, for Europe as a whole it fell to 1.7, with the highest rate in Romania (2.3) and the lowest in Italy and Spain (1.3) (in most of Africa, by comparison, it is over 6) (Population Reference Bureau, *1993 World Population Data Sheet*). As a result, a secular decline of Europe's population is now in motion: It will take over three thousand years for Italy's population to double, and a German population less than three-fourths its current size is now foreseeable (Starke, 1994: 37). What these data suggest is that fertility rates vary widely across countries (and within some of them). "In a number of countries, such as Brazil, Egypt, Indonesia, Mexico, and Thailand, fertility rates have been dropping as they did in the 1970s in China and India. At the same time, many developing countries have not entered the demographic transition" (Starke, 1994: 37).

A second puzzle that the theory of demographic transition does not solve applies to developing countries; some are seemingly stuck somewhere between the second and third stages of the transition. In such widely separated places as Costa Rica, Korea, Sri Lanka, and Tunisia, for example, death rates have fallen to very low levels, but fertility rates seem to have stabilized well above the replacement level (Merrick, 1988). Perhaps the reason lies in the absence of change in social attitudes toward family size of the sort Europe and North America experienced.

The status of women in society, and especially their education, have an important influence on preferences toward family size.

> Women who have completed primary school have fewer children than those with no education. Having an education usually means that women delay marriage, seek wage-paying jobs, learn about and have more favorable attitudes toward family planning, and have better communication with their husbands when they marry. Educated women have fewer infant deaths; high infant mortality is associated with high fertility. Similarly, when women have wage-paying jobs, they tend to have fewer children (and conversely, women with fewer children find it easier to work). (Population Reference Bureau, 1981: 5)

Education also has an impact on the health of families, for not only do better-educated women tend to have their children later in life, they are also more likely to get prenatal care and to keep their homes and children cleaner (*The Economist* 329, July 10, 1993).

Despite the positive impact of education, women throughout the world continue to be disadvantaged relative to men across a broad spectrum of educational statistics, such as literacy rates, school and college enrollments, and targeted educational resources. Women also enjoy less access to advanced study and training in professional fields, such as science, engineering, law, and business; within occupational groups they are almost always in less prestigious jobs; and everywhere women receive less pay than men (MacFarquhar, 1994). As the UN's study *The World's Women 1970–1990* concludes, in many parts of the developed world these and other differences between men and women have narrowed in recent decades, but in most countries the complex social, cultural, economic, and political forces that underlie inequalities remain firmly rooted. Enhancing the educational opportunities of women and elevating their status in society as a route toward lower fertility rates will not be easily achieved, as feminist theories of international relations explain (see Chapter 2).

## Global Patterns of Emigration and Immigration

Fertility, mortality, and migration are the three basic demographic variables that determine all population changes. Migration often receives less attention than the others, but its political importance was nowhere more dramatically evident than in the massive migration of Germans from East to West in 1989 in what became a precursor to the fall of the Berlin Wall, a symbol for nearly three decades of the Cold War division of Europe. Whether migration from one side of the "Iron Curtain" to the other precipitated its final collapse may never be known for sure, but the dissatisfaction with their political and economic fate that so many thousands demonstrated could not be ignored by the political leaders in the former socialist states. Nor should we overlook the consequence of the political unification of the German people. Because of unification, Germany with 81 million people today ranks with the United States, Japan, and Russia as one of the world's most powerful countries, as measured by such traditional indicators of capabilities as population size, territorial breadth, and economic vitality.

Germany is an exceptional case, but transnational migration has also affected many other countries in Europe and elsewhere. Israel has absorbed a flood of migrants during recent years, particularly from the Russian Federation, whose presence promises to shape Israeli politics and society for years to come. The Middle Eastern oil producers have also received large numbers of migrants in recent years, and, of course, the United States has traditionally provided refuge and opportunity for millions from throughout the world (see Map 9.1).

### Causes of Migration

Migrants are of two types: political refugees who move because of threats to their convictions or fear for their lives and those who move for economic reasons. The United Nations High Commission for Refugees keeps tabs on refugees throughout the world. Their number has grown from 1.5 million in 1951, to about 3 million in the mid-1970s, and to 19.7 million in 1992 (Lewis, 1993b: A7). More than half are in the Middle East, and about a third are in Africa. Refugees are often byproducts of war (see also Chapter 12). The 1980s Afghanistan war drove more than 6.6 million people seeking asylum from their homeland into Pakistan and Iran. Similarly, many of the Asian immigrants to the United States in the early 1980s were victims of the

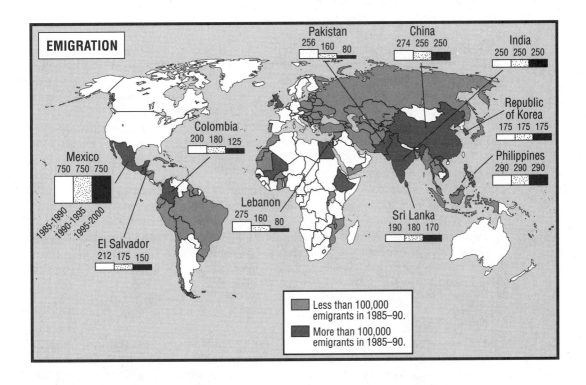

EMIGRATION

Pakistan
256  160   80

China
274  256  250

India
250  250  250

Republic
of Korea
175  175  175

Philippines
290  290  290

Colombia
200  180  125

Mexico
750  750  750

1985-1990
1990-1995
1995-2000

El Salvador
212  175  150

Lebanon
275  160   80

Sri Lanka
190  180  170

Less than 100,000
emigrants in 1985–90.

More than 100,000
emigrants in 1985–90.

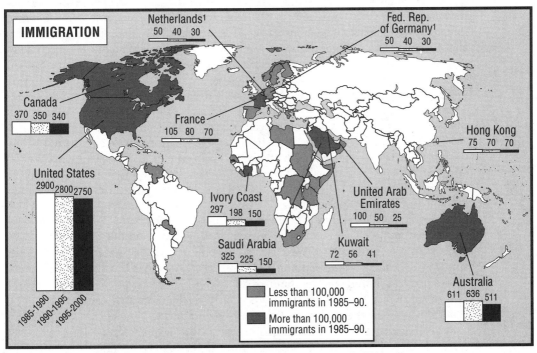

IMMIGRATION

Netherlands[1]
50  40  30

Fed. Rep.
of Germany[1]
50  40  30

Canada
370  350  340

France
105  80  70

Hong Kong
75  70  70

United States
2900 2800 2750

Ivory Coast
297  198  150

United Arab
Emirates
100  50  25

Saudi Arabia
325  225  150

Kuwait
72  56  41

1985-1990
1990-1995
1995-2000

Australia
611  636  511

Less than 100,000
immigrants in 1985–90.

More than 100,000
immigrants in 1985–90.

**Map 9.1**   Patterns of Emigration and Immigration, 1985–2000
*Source:* Fred Arnold (1990: 46–47).

Vietnam War. Political turmoil and civil strife in Cuba, El Salvador, Guatemala, Haiti, Nicaragua, and elsewhere in Central America and the Caribbean also hastened the influx of migrants from these areas. In addition, more than a million refugees have left the former Yugoslavia since 1992 to escape the ethnic warfare that escalated from persecution to "ethnic cleansing," atrocities, and genocide.

Other than refugees, migrants typically leave their homelands in search of a better standard of living. "At least 35 million from the South have taken up residence in the North in the past three decades. . . . The number of illegal international migrants is estimated to be around 15 to 30 million" (UNDP, 1994: 35). Moreover, increasingly many migrants are also "environmental refugees"—people forced to abandon lands no longer fit for human habitation due to environmental degradation. Their number is estimated to be at least ten million, which rivals the number of political refugees (Jacobson, 1989: 60). Some become environmental refugees due to catastrophic events, such as the 1986 explosion of the nuclear power plant at Chernobyl in Ukraine; others leave to escape the consequences of long-term environmental stress, such as excessive land use that results in desertification.

## Consequences of Migration

Migrants are often willing to travel to faraway lands to take jobs shunned by local inhabitants. Typically this means they earn less than do the native people but more than they would earn in their homelands, even performing the same tasks. Host (receiving) countries often welcome migrants, not only because they accept low wages for jobs that natives do not want, but also because the host pays little if anything for migrants' health, education, and welfare needs. On the other hand, the home (sending) countries sometimes encourage people to emigrate as a way of reducing unemployment and because migrants usually repatriate considerable portions of their income to their families at home.

Although receiving countries often benefit from migration, its extent and consequences have been matters of growing controversy in Europe, the Middle East, and the United States, as the demographic composition of their societies undergoes change. Among the industrial societies in particular, where fertility levels are already below the replacement level, greater cultural diversity can be expected, as a larger proportion of their future populations will be made up of recent immigrants from nations culturally different from their descendants. In fact, for Northern countries, migration, not growth, is *the* population problem.

Consider the United States. With fertility in the United States below the replacement level, immigration is now the primary demographic variable stimulating U.S. population growth. Nearly one-fourth of the some 20 million foreign-born residents entered the United States between 1985 and 1990, the 1990 U.S. census reported. The late-1980s immigrants accounted for a third of U.S. population growth, a proportion higher than at any time since early in the twentieth century. In 1990, about 8 percent of the U.S. population was born abroad.

Even more important is the dramatic shift in the origins of the immigrants over recent decades. Most U.S. citizens came from Europe during its first 150 years. This was true even into the mid-twentieth century. Between 1931 and 1960, for example, nearly three-fifths of all immigrants to the United States were of European origin. During the 1980s, by contrast, Europeans counted for little more than 10 percent of new Americans, with immigrants from Asia (40 percent) and Latin America (38 percent) accounting for the bulk of them (De Vita, 1989: 9). Most were legal immigrants in conformity with U.S. law, which in 1992 placed a ceiling of 830,000 new immigrants each year. But the United States has also absorbed large numbers of illegal aliens—estimates vary from as few as 200,000 to as many as two million annually—most of whom enter through Mexico. The costs are high, as "more than $1.1 billion a year goes for educating illegal aliens" (Barnes, 1993: 14).

In Europe, immigrants were especially important after World War II when they provided much of the unskilled labor needed to aid in reconstruction. Others migrated from former colonies, notably the British Commonwealth, to settle in the "mother" country. The mid-1970s was the peak of the "guest worker" era, when one of every seven manual workers in Germany and Britain was a migrant, as were a quarter of those in France, Belgium, and Switzerland (Barnet, 1979: 56). However, as unemployment became the primary economic problem in Europe, migrants were no longer as welcome. In Germany, for example, where the West German government once offered incentives to entice people of other nationalities to emigrate to the Federal Republic, and which in the early 1980s was the home of some four million guest workers, new incentives to encourage emigration were devised to arrest ethnic and racial tensions. However, many foreigners in Germany and elsewhere prefer to stay despite the harassment and hostility they experience. Clashes have been recurrent between Germans and Turks, between Britons and Indians and Pakistanis, between French people and migrants from North Africa, and between Russian and non-Russian ethnic groups.

The Middle East is also the scene of migrant-related tensions. In the 1980s oil money attracted immigrants, who comprised two-thirds of the labor force in many of the host countries (*Population in Perspective*, 1986: 27). Many came from other Arab countries, but large numbers also came from outside the region, mainly from India, Pakistan, Thailand, and South Korea. Tensions stemming from the differences in culture and religion of the non-natives remain high.

The United States is a nation born of immigrants. Despite a heritage that includes the entry of more than 59 million people from abroad between 1820 and 1992, U.S. public attitudes in recent years have turned in favor of limiting the number of legal immigrants and preventing the entry of illegal aliens. "As charted by Gallup, only 33 percent of Americans in 1965 favored fewer immigrants. That grew to 42 percent in 1977, 49 percent in 1986 and 65 percent [in 1993]" (Barnes, 1993: 12). As elsewhere, such nationalistic attitudes favoring a moratorium on immigration reflect a growing concern about the impact of immigrants on traditional values. Others worry that U.S. immigration laws, which use family reunification as the primary basis for determining who will be permitted to enter the United States and who will be denied asylum, are insensitive to the skills workers will need if the United States is to remain competitive in the global marketplace. Current regulations, they argue, do not give enough weight to the potential contributions specialized immigrant labor offers to the U.S. economy (see Chiswick, 1990). The issue is becoming hot, perhaps defining, in American politics. In response, Vice President Al Gore averred in 1993 that "We will make it tougher for illegal aliens to get into our country," and President Bill Clinton pledged, "We must say 'no' to illegal immigration so we can say 'yes' to legal immigration."

The situation faced by the United States offers but a glimpse of the larger demographic forces that will shape national politics and economics for decades to come (see Masson, 1990). Third World population growth will create pressures toward outward movement, and the aging of the industrial societies will encourage those rich states to accept foreign labor. These forces promise to place migration at the center of national political agendas.

## OPTIMISTS, PESSIMISTS, AND PUBLIC POLICY

In 1974, the United Nations sponsored a World Population Conference to address the population "problem," which essentially meant Third World population growth. The lessons of the demographic transition theory informed the view of many of the delegates from the Third World. They argued that if declining fertility rates follow more or less automatically from improvements in the standard of living, the appropriate approach to overpopulation is to improve the quality of life. The population problem will then take care of itself. The slogan "development is the best contraceptive" reflects this view. It summarizes the early European experience, when industrialization and new wealth promoted rapid declines in fertility rates. Other views were apparent among Third World representatives, including, for example, various proponents of marxism who ascribed the lack of economic progress not to population growth but to the absence of equitable income distributions between as well as within countries.

Many First World countries, on the other hand, advocated a more direct attack on the population problem than the protracted solution implied by the "development is the best contraceptive" approach. Led by the United States, they argued that the control of birthrates could by itself substantially address the immediate problem and thereby more rapidly promote subsequent economic development. This policy position echoed the emphasis placed on family planning programs until that time in the foreign aid and development assistance programs of the United States and many other governments and international organizations.

A decade later, in 1984, a second World Population Conference was held in Mexico City. By that time a new consensus had converged around the proposition that family planning was critically important. Curiously, the United States, previously a major advocate of this viewpoint, then departed from this emerging global sentiment. Reflecting the conservative political sentiments prevalent in Washington at the time, the U.S. delegation asserted that free market principles ought to take precedence over government intervention in economic and population matters. The Reagan administration also vigorously opposed abortion as an approach to family planning. As a result, the United States withheld support for multilateral as well as bilateral efforts to assist family planning programs in developing countries.

Although the views of the United States in 1984 were clearly in the minority, they reflected a growing sense of dissatisfaction with the conclusions and policy prescriptions of earlier analyses of the global ecopolitical implications of population growth, especially *The Limits to Growth*, published by the Club of Rome (Meadows et al., 1974), and *The Global 2000 Report to the President*, published by the U.S. government in 1980 (see also Ehrlich and Ehrlich, 1990). Both came to be characterized as products of "neo-Malthusians" or "growth pessimists" (many of whom are human ecologists), whose arguments were informed by the metaphor of the tragedy of the commons described earlier. The position reflected by the U.S. delegation to Mexico City, on the other hand, was that of the "growth optimists" (see, for example, Simon and Khan, 1984; also Wattenberg, 1989), who criticized the earlier limits-to-growth analyses. Sometimes called "cornucopians," optimists (many of whom are economists) argue that unregulated markets produce balances among population, resources, and the environment. They point out that human ingenuity has developed resource-saving (or -substituting) innovations in response to shortages created by population growth, so that population growth is a stimulus, not a deterrent, to economic advancement.

The debate between optimists and pessimists has continued, and became the primary issue at the U.N. International Conference on Population and Development held in September 1994 in Cairo, Egypt. Legalized abortions, the spreading use of contraceptives, the sanctioning of alternative lifestyles, and family values—these are complex issues for which determining who is right is difficult. We can better appreciate this by considering some probable consequences of demographic changes.

## CONSEQUENCES OF DEMOGRAPHIC CHANGES

As trends in births, deaths, and migration unfold worldwide into the twenty-first century, demographic changes will promote changes in world politics. At issue is how these trends will affect traditional national security considerations, economic development opportunities, and the prospects for achieving global food security.

## Demographic Changes and Diminished National Security?

As noted earlier, population growth is far more rapid in the Third World than in the developed countries. In the future, a declining fraction of world population will live in developed countries. The demographic division between the world's have and have-not countries is widening:

> Current UN projections for the year 2025 depict an American population slightly smaller than Nigeria's, an Iranian population almost as large as Japan's and an Ethiopian population nearly twice that of France. Today's industrial democracies would almost all be "little countries." Canada, one of the Big Seven industrial democracies today (alongside the United States, Germany, Japan, Britain, France and Italy), would have a smaller population than such countries as Madagascar, Nepal and Syria. (Eberstadt, 1991: 128)

Political realists argue that a country's population size is an important source of political power. Given this, reduction of the world's most populous states to lesser ranks may itself be a concern. The relative power of the world's states will affect their national security. For example, the low fertility rates in developed states combined with their aging populations will make it more difficult to maintain large armies. In contrast, the abundant youth in developing societies will provide ample supplies of soldiers.

Differential fertility rates among various ethnic populations will also have internal and international consequences. In Israel, for example, the Jewish population may one day become the minority, as fertility rates among Arabs and Palestinians within Israel's borders outstrip those of Israel's Jews. Analogous trends are already evident in South Africa, where the white population is expected by the year 2020 to comprise only one-ninth to one-eleventh of the total population compared with the one-fifth it accounted for in the early 1950s (Eberstadt, 1991: 121). Similarly, the shifting ethnic composition of the Russian Federation is likely to undermine that area's future stability, as fertility rates among non-Russians, particularly Muslims, are measurably higher. Already Russians are less than a majority of the military-age population and will make up less than a majority of the working-age population by the turn of the century.

It is difficult to determine but equally difficult to ignore the stimulus to domestic political strife and external political conflict that changes in the ethnic composition of societies provoke. In virtually every world region and within every major power, different demographic growth rates among ethnonational groups have fanned the flames of political and social unrest. In an interdependent world, the national security of all states is undermined (Homer-Dixon, 1991; see also Chapters 6 and 12).

## Demographic Changes and Economic Underdevelopment?

Growth pessimists stress the adverse effects of population growth on economic development. What they often ignore, however, is that the world has enjoyed unprecedented levels of economic growth and unparalleled population increases simultaneously. Even those countries with the highest rates of population increase are arguably better off economically today than they were at the dawn of the twentieth century. Declining infant mortality and rising life expectancy coincide with improved living standards throughout the world, even if, ironically, these are the very forces that drive population growth.

Still, the pessimism of growth pessimists stems from valid concerns. Population growth contributes to the widening income gap between the world's rich and poor. It also contributes to lower standards of living for many, as poor people tend to have more children to support than do those who are relatively better off. Furthermore, by depressing wage rates relative to rents and returns to capital, "rapid population growth devalues what poor households have to sell—their labor. Property owners gain relative to wage earners when the labor force grows quickly" (Repetto, 1987).

It is also true, however, that "politics and economic policies influence the distribution of income within countries far more than population growth rates do" (Repetto, 1987). This fact lies close to what is emerging as the conventional view among demographers and development economists about the effects of population growth on economic development. Contrary to the view of growth pessimists, the emerging consensus casts population "not as the sole cause of underdevelopment, but an accomplice aggravating other existing problems" (*The New Population Debate*, 1985). The larger proportion of young people in developing countries places strains on certain social institutions, for example, whereas the larger proportion of older people in the developed countries creates other problems. Recommended are new rules and institutions that address environmental concerns while promoting economic growth and development (see Esty, 1994).

## The Third World

In developing countries, dependent children (those younger than fifteen years old) typically make up about 40 percent of the total population (compared with 22 percent in the developed world) (Merrick, 1989: 9). This means there is only about one working-age adult for each child under fifteen in the Third World, compared with nearly three working-age adults in the developed countries. Such a large proportion of dependent children burdens public services, particularly the educational system. It also encourages the immediate consumption of economic resources rather than their reinvestment in social infrastructure to promote future economic growth.

As the children mature, the demands for new jobs, housing, and other human needs multiply, but the resources to meet them are typically scarce and inadequate. In Mexico, for example, a million new jobs are required every year to absorb the wave of young people entering the labor market. On a global scale, the International Labor Organization estimates that the total labor force in developing countries will be 600 million to 700 million larger in the year 2000 than it was in 1980. "To employ all those additional workers, the developing countries would have to create more jobs than now exist in Western Europe, Japan, the United States, the [former Soviet Union], and the other industrialized nations combined" (Fallows, 1983).

The search for jobs augments the growth of urban areas, which has recently proceeded at an unprecedented rate. In 1950 less than a third of the world's population lived in cities; by 1990 the proportion had grown to over 40 percent; and by the year 2020 as many as 60 percent will live in urban areas. Urbanization is a global phenomenon, but increasingly the world's largest cities will be in the Third World. London, New York, and Shanghai were the only cities with populations of ten million or more in 1950. By the turn of the century some two dozen cities will be this large—all but six of them in the less developed countries of Africa, Asia, and Latin America, where a combination of natural population growth and a desire to escape poverty in the countryside will fuel the expansion of the megalopolises.

Wherever urbanization occurs it taxes severely the capacity for effective governance. Urbanization places added pressures on the demand for expanded social services, as urban development requires more investment in infrastructure than does rural development. Urbanization also increases the pressures on local agricultural systems because there are fewer hands in the countryside to feed the growing number of mouths in the city. Urbanization thus adds to the need to import food from abroad. And the often deplorable living conditions within urban areas themselves contain the seeds of violence and political turmoil. Already thousands upon thousands of urban dwellers live in crowded, cramped, shantytown hovels without adequate water, sanitation, health, education, and other social services and in the constant shadow of pervasive crime and violence. Being outside the urban elite and middle class, they are "acutely aware of the great disparity in wealth and poverty about them," which "contributes to alienation and frustration on a massive scale" (U.S. Department of State, 1978). Such were the conditions in Israel's West Bank and Gaza Strip where, in 1993, 2,503 Palestinians were cramped per square mile (*Harper's* 209, November 1993: 15). It is not surprising that crime and violence were ubiquitous.

A number of developing countries, particularly in Asia and Latin America, are now poised for a reduction in the number of people under fifteen and over sixty-five. If the experience of Europe, North America, and especially Japan is a guide, this should facilitate economic gains (Woods, 1989). Ironically, however, the demographic life cycle also portends that the countries that now have the greatest burden of a burgeoning population of young people also will be those with a growing number of older dependents, as today's youth grow to maturity and old age fifty years hence. Although the Third World today contains more than three-quarters of the world's people, it contains only half of those over sixty. By 2025, the population pyramid for developing regions shown in Figure 9.4 on page 301 will begin to turn upside down because of declining birthrates and increased longevity, and the Third World will increase its share of the "gray generation" to three-quarters ("The Age of Aging," 1982: 82). As the experience of the more developed economies demonstrates, there is a long-term downside to this, as demands for social services, particularly expensive health care, will multiply, thus burdening the Third World in a different way.

### The First World

As noted earlier, the United States has recently moved toward zero-population growth, but in many other parts of the industrial world below-replacement fertility is now the norm. Population *decline* is the inevitable result (see Austria's population profile in Figure 9.3 on page 300). As longevity increases, an aging population is also inevitable.

The aging of people in the First World is especially striking in Japan, where the demographic transition began later than elsewhere but was completed more rapidly. Today Japan is the most rapidly aging society in the world. The number of elderly (over 65) Japanese is expected to increase from 12.5 million in 1985 to 31.5 million in 2025, by which time they will comprise nearly a quarter of the population (Martin, 1989: 7). Already the median age of Japanese workers is over forty (Merrick, 1989: 11). As it continues to rise, Japan will have to confront troublesome questions about its ability to continue the vigorous economic productivity and high domestic saving rates that have been key factors in the projection of Japan's economic power abroad.

Beyond the particular case of Japan's export-oriented economy, some gerontologists (those who study aging and its consequences) argue that because the move toward zero or negative population growth in advanced industrial societies will reduce demand for products on which their economies depend, economic growth will decline. Others speculate that a gradually aging society will be a more conservative one politically. Evidence refutes both of these views (see Weller and Bouvier, 1981). Still, what is beyond dispute is that an increasing number of older people will escalate the need for costly age-related social services such as health care.

Providing for the increasing number of dependent elderly people relative to the number of productive workers is already a political concern throughout the First World. The Japanese term "child shock" dramatizes the growing crisis forecast by the decline in workers and growth in pensioners. The Japanese government and private-sector groups have joined forces to promote pronatalist attitudes among the Japanese people to raise fertility rates. However, unlike similar efforts undertaken during the 1930s (when war between Japan and the United States loomed on the horizon), the response to these contemporary efforts to stimulate birthrates has been unenthusiastic.

In Western Europe the wisdom of pursuing pronatalist policies is intensely debated. Much of the dialogue turns on questions of individual versus collective welfare. Proponents of pronatalist measures are concerned with the "continued vitality of national populations that do not replace themselves: no children, no future, is the key phrase" (van de Kaa, 1987; see also Wattenberg, 1989). National pride, concern for the country's place among the world powers, and the prominence of European culture in a world where non-European countries grow much faster also propel pronatalists.

Opponents of pronatalist measures, on the other hand, "dismiss as exaggerated the specter of Europe as a decrepit society of ruminating octogenarians." They "attach no special value to their own cultures" and oppose stimulating population growth in a world where overpopulation is already a serious problem. They believe that "economic resources rather than military resources or population size determine a country's international standing" and that "economic integration is a much more effective way to maintain Europe's international position than stimulating the birth rate." Finally, they question whether it makes sense to stimulate births when Europe already suffers from chronic high unemployment. "With modern technology eliminating jobs, workers are encouraged to work shorter hours, part-time, or retire early and immigration is halted," the argument continues, "so why should we have more people?" (van de Kaa, 1987).

## Demographic Trends and Global Food Security

The gloomiest of Thomas Malthus's predictions made two centuries ago was that the world's population would eventually outstrip its capacity to produce enough food to sustain its growing numbers. As noted above, Malthus based his prognosis on what he regarded as the simple mathematical fact that population grows exponentially, while agricultural output grows only arithmetically. What he did not foresee is that agricultural output would also grow at an increasing rate due to technological innovations.

## Trends in Agricultural Production

Increases in the world's food output were particularly impressive after World War II. In the thirty-five years from 1950 to 1985, world grain harvests increased from less than 750 million tons to 1.7 billion tons. Even though the world experienced unprecedented population growth during this period, the growth in food production was so spectacular that it permitted a 25 percent increase in per-capita food supplies and a corresponding increase in meeting minimum nutritional standards (O'Brien, 1988: 395).

The greatest increases in food production occurred as a result of the increased productivity of First World farmers, but impressive gains were also recorded in many Third World countries as a result of expanding acreage devoted to agriculture and, later, the Green Revolution (the introduction of new high-yield strains of wheat and rice). By the 1980s Indonesia, once a massive importer of food, had largely been removed from the import market, and India, once regarded as a permanent candidate for the international dole, had actually become a modest grain exporter.

Whether world food production will continue to grow as it has in the past is uncertain, yet that will have to happen if output is to keep pace with an expanding world population and improvements in living standards. "In the next two to four generations, world agriculture will be called on to produce as much food as has been produced in the entire 12,000-year history of agriculture" (Freeman, 1990: 16). Growth optimists confidently predict the challenge will be met, believing that technology, particularly genetic engineering, will greatly improve agricultural productivity. Growth pessimists, on the other hand, worry that the recent impressive gains cannot continue. Noting that few further gains in the global food harvest have occurred since the mid-1980s (Postel, 1994) and that "many countries have reached the point where using additional fertilizer does little to boost food output," they conclude that "the diminishing crop response to the additional use of fertilizer, the negative effect of environmental degradation on harvests, and the lack of any new technology to replace fertilizer as the engine of agricultural growth are each contributing to a potentially hungry future for much of humanity" (Brown, 1991).

The pessimists' views are reinforced by what has happened to the world stock of surplus grains (large amounts of which are produced in the North America) since the mid-1980s. As global food production flattened out, these carryover stocks, which in effect provide the world with a food-security buffer during lean years, dwindled. In 1988, excessive heat and drought in the United States and elsewhere sharply reduced global food production. Little rebuilding has occurred since, despite record harvests; "between 1993 and 1994, world carryover stocks of grain . . . are projected to drop from 351 million to 294 million tons, and these grain stocks, as measured in the days needed to consume all reserves, "has fallen since 1988 to an estimated 62 days in

1994, nearing the 55-day low in 1973" (Brown, 1994: 36; Dillin, 1994: 8). "From 1984 until 1993, grain output per person fell 11 percent. Historians may well see 1984 as a watershed year, one marking the transition from an era of rapid growth in food production to one of much slower growth" (Brown, 1994). This recent experience suggests that "agriculture is likely to be the sector that first illustrates how profoundly environmental degradation will eventually shape global economic trends" (Brown, 1991).

## Food Security

*Food security* is defined as the "access by all people at all times to enough food for an active, healthy life."

> Its essential elements are the availability of food and the ability to acquire it. Conversely, food insecurity is the lack of access to sufficient food and can be either chronic or transitory. Chronic food insecurity is a continuously inadequate diet resulting from the lack of resources to produce or acquire food. Transitory food insecurity, on the other hand, is a temporary decline in a household's access to enough food. It results from instability in food production and prices, or in household incomes. The worst form of transitory food insecurity is famine. (Reutlinger, 1985: 7)

Achieving food security became an item on the North–South agenda during the 1970s when, at about the same time as the first OPEC-induced oil crisis, sufficient food for the world's growing billions was not available. However, despite a widespread commitment to the goal of food security since then, the distribution of food remains uneven and its accessibility beyond the reach of many.

UNEVEN DISTRIBUTION  Among the developed countries, increases in per-capita food production since the 1950s have generally moved upward in tandem with increases in total food production. But among the developing countries, per-capita food production has generally lagged behind. Moreover, even in countries of the South where the Green Revolution has produced spectacular production gains, the distribution of its rewards has often been quite uneven; today, there exists "famine amid the world feast" as some regions "can't buy into the agricultural revolution" (Rensberger, 1994).

As a generalization, population growth accounts for the difference between total and per-capita production of food in developed and developing countries. Yet, as Figure 9.7 illustrates, there exist widely differing experiences among developing countries themselves. Using 1970 as the baseline for comparison, the figure demonstrates that China and other Asian centrally planned economies (notably Vietnam) have greatly increased per-capita food availability; that the Asian countries have been able to keep slightly ahead of the population curve; that Near Eastern and Latin American countries have seen their total food production move roughly in tandem with their population growth; and that Africa has experienced a serious and prolonged deterioration in its food–population equation.

Most analysts believe that the introduction of market incentives was critical in stimulating increased food production in China and Vietnam. In 1978 the Chinese

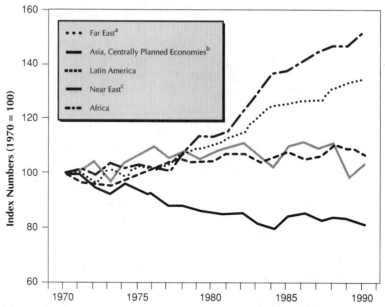

**Figure 9.7** Index of Per-capita Food Production in Developing Regions, 1970–1990

*Source:* Food and Agriculture Organization of the United Nations (FAO), unpublished data, March 1991.

*Notes:* [a] Far East = Bangladesh, Bhutan, Brunei Darussalam, East Timor, Hong Kong, India, Indonesia, Republic of Korea, Lao People's Democratic Republic, Macao, Malaysia, Maldives, Myanmar, Nepal, Pakistan, Philippines, Singapore, Sri Lanka, Thailand; [b] Asia, Centrally Planned Economies = Cambodia, China, Democratic People's Republic of Korea, Mongolia, Vietnam; [c] Near East = *Africa:* Egypt, Libyan Arab Jamahiriya, Sudan. *Asia:* Afghanistan, Bahrain, Cyprus, Gaza Strip (Palestine), Islamic Republic of Iran, Iraq, Jordan, Kuwait, Lebanon, Oman, Qatar, Kingdom of Saudi Arabia, Syrian Arab Republic, Turkey, United Arab Emirates, Yemen Arab Republic, Democratic Yemen.

government shifted from a commune-organized to a market-based agricultural system that offered farmers more financial incentives to produce. The reforms worked, as agricultural productivity and farm income increased dramatically. A decade later Vietnam experienced similar famine-to-feast increases in rice production in response to changes in government policies regarding land tenancy and related economic reforms (Richburg, 1990).

Africa stands in stark contrast. Nowhere does Malthus's grim prediction that population growth would outstrip food production appear more apt than here. During the 1970s, Africa's food production increased by only 1.8 percent annually, but its population grew at a rate of 2.8 percent. Starvation and death became daily occurrences in broad stretches of the Sahel, ranging from Ethiopia in the east to Mauritania in the west. The situation was repeated a decade later when, in Ethiopia in particular, world consciousness was awakened by the tragic specter of tens of thousands suffering from malnutrition and dying of famine at a time of unprecedented food surpluses worldwide. As population growth has moved hand in hand with desecration of the environment, sub-Saharan Africa has experienced the tragedy of the commons in all of its most remorseless manifestations. Civil strife and war have been a consequence.

At various times during the past two decades, civil unrest and major armed conflict affecting tens of millions of people have ravaged a third or more of the countries in sub-Saharan Africa. In some cases, as in Ethiopia, Somalia, and the Sudan, food was actively used as a political weapon. In the words of Shun Chetty of the U.N. High Commission for Refugees, "He who controls roads controls food. He who controls food controls the people."

**UNEQUAL ACCESS** According to the microeconomic principle known as Engel's law, poorer families typically spend a much greater percentage of their budget on food than do higher-income groups. Yet the ability to acquire more food depends on having the income necessary to buy more food. Many people in the developing countries are simply incapable of registering an *effective demand* for food. As Richard Barnet (1980) has observed, "Most people who stop eating do so not because there is insufficient food grown in the world but because they no longer grow it themselves and do not have the money to buy it."

Many people live in *absolute poverty:* "a condition of life so limited by malnutrition, illiteracy, disease, squalid surroundings, high infant mortality, and low life expectancy as to be beneath any reasonable definition of human decency." In the mid-1990s their numbers were estimated to be "at least 800 million" (Rensberger, 1994: 38) and projected to increase.

At the other end of the spectrum are the world's affluent. Many of the agricultural products produced in developing countries (such as sugar, tea, coffee, and cocoa) are exported abroad, where they are dietary supplements (with little nutritional value) for the world's rich.

Wealth also affects dietary habits. As personal income rises, people climb the *food ladder:*

> In the poorer countries the average person can get only about 180 kilograms of grain per year—about a pound per day. With so little to go around, nearly all grain must be consumed directly if minimal energy needs are to be met. But as incomes rise, so do grain comsumption levels. In the wealthier industrial societies such as the United States . . . the average person consumes four-fifths of a ton of grain per year. Of this, only 90 to 140 kilograms is eaten directly as bread, pastries, and breakfast cereals; most is consumed indirectly as meat, milk, and eggs.
>
> In effect, wealth enables individuals to move up the biological food chain. Thus, the average . . . American uses roughly four times the land, water, and fertilizer used by an Indian, a Colombian, or a Nigerian. (Brown, 1978: 134)

The food ladder describes the changing consumption patterns evident since World War II. "While fewer than 200 million people had made the transition to diets with a quarter or more of their calories from livestock products by the mid-1950s, more than 600 million people had made the transition by the early 1980s. An added 650 million consumers in the middle-income countries had also begun the transition" (O'Brien, 1988: 398).

Whether the world will be able to sustain a similar transition up the food ladder for billions more in the future is, however, unlikely:

> As the nineties unfold, the world is facing a day of reckoning. Many knew that this time would eventually come, that at some point the cumulative effects of environmental degradation and the limits of the earth's natural systems would start to restrict economic expansion. But no one knew exactly when or how these effects would show up. Now we see that they are slowing growth in food production—the most basic of economic activities and the one on which all others depend. After nearly four decades of unprecedented expansion in both land-based and oceanic food supplies, the world is experiencing a massive loss of momentum. (Brown, 1994: 177)

Affluence and rising consumption alongside population growth will greatly strain the ability of food producers to ensure global food security. This proposition applies to other resources as well.

## DEMOGRAPHIC GROWTH AND THE PRECARIOUS GLOBAL COMMONS

The environmental toll of population growth and rising affluence seemingly binds humanity in a common fate, but, as the tragedy of the commons suggests, countries do not share the costs and benefits associated with the exploitation equally. Herein lies what many describe as the "planetary predicament." The symptoms and sources of environmental deterioration are discussed from different perspectives.

### Third World Ecological Dangers

Soil erosion, desertification, and deforestation are worldwide phenomena, but they are often most acute where population growth and poverty are most evident (see Postel, 1994). The search for fuelwood is a major source of deforestation and a primary occupation in developing countries. Deforestation and soil erosion also occur when growing populations without access to farmland push cultivation into hillsides and tropical forests ill-suited to farming. "Tropical deforestation," the World Resources Institute reports, "averaged 0.8 percent a year in the 1980s, which means an area three times the size of France was converted to other uses" (Knickerbocker, 1994: 7). In the Sahel area of Africa, growing populations of livestock as well as humans hastened the destruction of productive land, producing a desert that led to famine—a graphic illustration of the tragedy of the commons.

Where population growth rates remain high, a kind of "ecological transition" occurs that is "almost the reverse of the demographic transition in that its end result is disastrous."

> In the first stage, expanding human demands are well within the sustainable yield of the biological support system. In the second, they are in excess of the sustainable yield but still expanding as the biological resource itself is being consumed. And in the final stage, human consumption is forcibly reduced as the biological system collapses. (Brown et al., 1987: 26-27)

Tragically, an ecological transition applies to much of the developing world. In sub-Saharan Africa, more than a quarter of the land area is "moderately to very severely desertified" and vast areas have "permanently" lost their agricultural potential (World Resources Institute, 1990: 91). But human-induced land degradation through overgrazing, deforestation, and agricultural mismanagement is not confined to the Third World, as the degraded area as a share of total vegetated land in Europe (23 percent) exceeds that of Africa and Asia (Postel, 1994: 10).

## First World Threats to Ecological Preservation

Excessive population growth doubtless strains the environment and contributes to destruction of the global commons, but excessive consumption is even more damaging. In this respect it is not the South's disadvantaged four-fifths of humanity who place the greatest strains on the global habitat but the affluent one-fifth in the consumption-oriented North. Consider some evidence:

- A typical resident of the industrialized . . . world uses 15 times as much paper, 10 times as much steel, and 12 times as much fuel as a Third World resident. The extreme case is . . . the United States, where the average person consumes most of his or her own weight in basic materials each day—18 kilograms of petroleum and coal, 13 kilograms of other minerals, 12 kilograms of agricultural products, and 9 kilograms of forest products. (Durning, 1991: 161)

- The average Japanese consumes nine times as much steel as the average Chinese, and Americans use more than four times as much steel and 23 times as much aluminum as their neighbors in Mexico. U.S. paper consumption per person is over a dozen times the average for Latin America, and Americans use about 25 times as much nickel apiece as someone who lives in India. (Young, 1991:40)

- The United States and the former Soviet Union together contribute 32.8 percent of the emission of "greenhouse" gases, and the European Union accounts for another 12.4 percent. (Knickerbocker, 1994: 7)

A consuming society is also a throwaway society. "The Japanese use 30 million 'disposable' single-roll cameras each year, and the British dump 2.5 billion diapers. Americans toss away 180 million razors annually, enough paper and plastic plates and cups to feed the world a picnic six times a year, and enough aluminum cans to make 6,000 DC-10 airplanes" (Durning, 1991: 161). Each American threw away an average of 1,460 pounds of garbage in 1988, and the amount is expected to grow to nearly 1,800 pounds per person by 2010 (Young, 1991: 44). As the mountains of garbage grow, disposing of it has become increasingly difficult.

The growing volume of solid waste in the North mirrors the exponential increase in consumption that has occurred in industrial societies since World War II. Again consider some evidence:

- In the United States . . . people today own twice as many cars, drive two-and-a-half times as far, use 21 times as much plastic, and travel 25 times as far by air as did their parents in 1950. Air conditioning spread from 15 percent of households in 1960 to 64 percent in 1987, and color televisions from 1 to 93 percent.

- The Japanese of today consume more than four times as much aluminum, almost five times as much energy, and 25 times as much steel as people in Japan did in 1950. They also own four times as many cars and eat nearly twice as much meat.

- Taken together, France, West Germany, and the United Kingdom almost doubled their per capita use of steel, more than doubled their intake of cement and aluminum, and tripled their paper consumption since mid-century. (Durning, 1991: 154-155)

## Military Might and Environmental Degradation

Disposing of industrial societies' solid wastes is now more difficult not only because of their magnitude but also because the proportion of plastics and toxic substances has increased markedly (Young, 1991). Peacetime military preparations magnify the problem even further. "The military is quite likely the largest operator of hazardous wastes in the United States and, rivaled by only the [former] Soviet armed forces, the world. In recent years, the Pentagon generated between 400,000 and 500,000 tons of toxics annually, more than the top five U.S. chemical companies. Its contractors produced tens if not hundreds of thousands of tons more. And these figures do not even include the large amounts of toxics spewing from the Department of Energy's nuclear weapons complex" (Renner, 1991: 143; see also Shulman, 1992).

War itself often directly desecrates the global environment. Rome sowed salt on a defeated Carthage to prevent its resurgence; the Dutch breached their own dikes to allow ocean saltwater to flood fertile farmlands in an attempt to stop the advancing Germans during World War II; and the United States used defoliants on the dense jungles in Vietnam in an effort to expose enemy guerrillas. More recently, Iraq practiced "environmental terrorism" when it released millions of gallons of oil into the Persian Gulf during the 1991 Gulf War. Retreating Iraqis also set nearly 600 oil wells on fire and blew up hundreds of other wells, storage tanks, refineries, and other facilities. Extinguishing the fires took months. Meanwhile, tons of smoke with toxic pollutants belched thousands of meters skyward, from where environmental experts expected they would affect near-term the regional climate, food production, and water quality. Experts also expected the disruption of the delicate desert ecosystem caused by military activities in the Persian Gulf to last for decades (Barnaby, 1991).

## Global Warming

What are the long-term consequences of the disproportionate impact of the world's rich countries on global resource consumption, particularly fossil fuels (examined in

Chapter 10)? During the 1970s, growth pessimists warned that the exhaustion of global resources was inevitable. Today the concern lies "less in running out of resources . . . than in the continuing damage that their extraction and processing impose on the environment" (Young, 1991). The consequence of continued heavy dependence on oil in transportation and industry is illustrative: "Rising levels of carbon dioxide in the atmosphere make it unlikely the world will run out of oil before the environmental cost of its use—in the form of global warming—becomes prohibitive" (Young, 1991).

*Global warming* is shorthand for the prospective climate changes that the insulating effect of the earth's atmosphere may cause. The atmosphere permits radiation from the sun to penetrate to the earth, but gas molecules form the equivalent of a greenhouse roof by trapping heat remitted from earth that would otherwise escape into outer space. Carbon dioxide ($CO_2$) accounts for about half of the greenhouse gases. Methane (natural gas), nitrous oxide, ozone, and chlorofluorocarbons (CFCs) make up the rest. (CFCs are artificial chemicals widely used in refrigerators and air conditioners as refrigerants, in Styrofoam cups, in cleansers for computer components, and as aerosol propellants for such things as deodorants.)

In all cases consumption patterns are the chief cause of the volume of greenhouse gases released into the atmosphere.[7] Thus the developed countries of the North are the chief perpetrators of the growing amount of greenhouse gases in the atmosphere. As Figure 9.8 shows, the developed countries, which make up less than a quarter of the world's population, are responsible for 54 percent of the heating effect caused by greenhouse gas emissions. In contrast, developing countries, which make up nearly 80 percent of the world's population, account for less than half. Among the developed countries the United States again stands out, accounting for nearly 18 percent of the heating effect of the greenhouse gases emitted but less than 5 percent of world population. Brazil is the main culprit among developing countries because of the adverse consequences of deforestation of the Amazon basin.[8]

---

[7] Carbon dioxide, CFCs, and methane are the three most important greenhouse gases. The carbon dioxide in the atmosphere is now growing at a rate of 0.05 percent per year, CFCs by 5 percent, and methane by 1 percent (Mathews, 1992: 367). As noted below, fossil-fuel combustion and deforestation account for the bulk of the increased concentration of $CO_2$, and the source of CFCs (which can remain active in the atmosphere for more than a century) is well known, as they are man-made chemicals. The causes of the buildup of methane concentration are unclear, however. "It may be that there are so many links between methane and human activity—from cattle ranching to rice paddies to leaky gas pipelines—that methane emissions are simply tracking population growth" (Mathews, 1992). At present rates of increase, the concentration of greenhouse gases would double by 2030 (Topping, 1990: 5).

[8] The data on greenhouse gas emissions graphed in Figure 9.8 are an index designed to ascertain the contribution individual countries and regions make to global warming. The index is designed to measure two elements: "first, the proportion of the annual release of each greenhouse gas which remains in the atmosphere at the end of a given year and, second, a factor which measures the instantaneous effect of this amount of gas on the earth's energy balance" (McCully, 1991). The prestigious World Resources Institute, which designed the index, argues that it provides an important policy-making base by permitting intercountry comparisons that demonstrate the global proportions of the problem of global warming in both cause and effect, but critics argue that the index assigns disproportionate responsibility for global warming to developing countries and thus directs the attention of policymakers away from the primary source of the problem, which is the industrial world (see McCully, 1991).

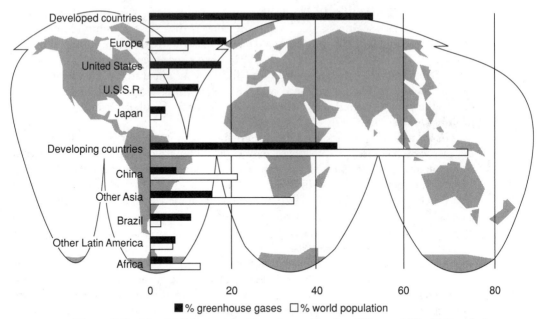

**Figure 9.8** Net Additions to the Greenhouse Heating Effect and World Population (Percentages)

*Source:* Based on data drawn from World Resources Institute (1990: 348–349) and Population Reference Bureau, *1991 World Population Data Sheet.*

*Note:* Population data are for 1991; greenhouse gas data are circa 1985–1987. Greenhouse gas heating effects are based on an index of carbon dioxide and methane emissions and chlorofluorocarbon use; the index includes an estimate of carbon dioxide emissions caused by changes in land use, principally deforestation.

There is widespread agreement on the fact that the gases that cause heat to be trapped in the atmosphere are increasing at unprecedented rates. What remains in dispute is whether continued high rates of greenhouse gas emissions will lead to global warming (and, we might add, with what consequence), in part because too many determinants of climate change are inadequately understood (see World Resources Institute, 1990). Not surprisingly, therefore, global warming is a contentious issue on the global agenda.

### Causes of Global Warming

Deforestation is one of the human activities that accelerate global warming. Green plants routinely remove carbon dioxide from the atmosphere during photosynthesis. The natural processes that remove greenhouse gases are destroyed when forests are cut down, and, as the forests decay or are burned, the amount of $CO_2$ discharged into the atmosphere increases. This makes deforestation doubly destructive. Yet many governments have permitted the destruction of forests, which are being depleted at an alarming rate. For many years it was believed that an area the size of Austria was deforested every year, but recent evidence indicates that the magnitude of the destruction of the world's forests may be even greater (World Resources Institute, 1990: 101–104). Tropical deforestation is notably acute in places like Indonesia, Myanmar (formerly Burma), Cameroon, Costa Rica, and especially Brazil, where vast tracts of rain forests have been cleared and burned to make room for farms and ranches (whose cattle, incidentally, add to the staggering volume of methane released into the atmosphere).

Although deforestation contributes heavily to the greenhouse process, the burning of fossil fuels is an even greater culprit. It accounts for three-quarters of the excess carbon released into the atmosphere, or roughly a ton of atmospheric $CO_2$ for every man, woman, and child on earth. (Deforestation, in contrast, accounts for 25 percent of the excess carbon [Mathews, 1992: 367].)

Along with manufacturing, the utilities industry contributes heavily to atmospheric pollution. In part this is because it produces atmospheric sulfur and nitrogen oxides. These pollutants return to earth, typically after traveling long distances, in the form of "acid rain," which adds to the acidification of lakes, the corrosion of materials and structures, and the impairment of ecosystems. (Acid rain has fallen in measurable amounts in the Scandinavian countries and in the United States and Canada, where it has been a source of transnational controversy.) And the burning of coal, widespread among utilities, releases more $CO_2$ than does the burning of other fossil fuels. Automobiles also emit large quantities of greenhouse gases. The average American car driven an average ten thousand miles a year releases its own weight in carbon into the atmosphere every year (McKibben, 1989: 48).

Energy is the engine of economic growth and improved living standards throughout the world. Today the North's industrial countries consume over seventy percent of the world's energy. Moreover, their access to the world's energy supplies has materially benefited their societies. Interestingly, however, the greatest increases in the *rate* of energy consumption now occur in the developing South's countries. This also means that the Third World will make the largest contribution to increases in atmospheric pollution due to fossil-fuel combustion. If, as now expected, for example, China increases its per-capita gross national product to just fifteen percent of the U.S. per-capita GNP, it will have to burn so much fossil fuel that "the increase in $CO_2$ emissions would equal the total $CO_2$ released from all the coal currently consumed by the United States" (Owen, 1989: 40).

Even without economic growth, the expected doubling of the world's present 5.6 billion people will require an enormous increase in fossil-fuel consumption simply to maintain living standards at their current levels. Thus the population growth now unfolding may seriously disrupt the world's climate and delicate ecosystems in the decades ahead even in the unlikely event that the process of global warming has not already begun.

## Consequences of Global Warming

Is the temperature of the world's atmosphere rising inexorably? The 1980s witnessed the six warmest years on record, and the decade as a whole was the hottest ever.

These facts are consistent with a trend evident over the past century (see Figure 9.9). Since 1880 the average temperature rose by as much as 0.7 degrees Celsius (World Resources Institute, 1990: 20). During the same period the amount of $CO_2$ in the atmosphere increased by twenty-five percent and the amount of methane doubled (Schneider, 1989: 72). Still, scientists do not agree on whether the 1980s heat wave was itself a consequence of the greenhouse effect taking hold. The thesis that the globe is warming remains controversial. As the *New York Times* (May 24, 1992: E10) editorially summarized, "the evidence remains murky. Average world temperatures rose 1 degree Farenheit over the past century, but whether greenhouse gases or other factors were responsible isn't known. Disconcertingly, temperatures flattened or fell from 1940 to 1970 just as greenhouse emissions were soaring, perhaps because other pollutants cooled the earth by blocking sunlight. [In 1992] after a string of hot years, temperatures [were] expected to fall again because of particles from a volcanic eruption. It could take a decade or two for scientists to square the conflicting signals."

Nonetheless, global warming is likely to be a portent of the future, as the earth's average temperature rose slightly in 1993 (Roodman, 1994). If greenhouse gases in the atmosphere mount, global temperatures will rise further. Some researchers predict that by 2050 global temperatures will climb on average four degrees (Celsius) higher than now. The consequences are not easily predicted (see Woodwell, 1990; Wyman, 1991), but some that are widely discussed include a melting of the polar ice caps, which will raise ocean levels significantly and lead to the destruction of coastal areas and wetlands; an increase in the frequency and severity of droughts, dust storms, forest fires, and hurricanes; and a marked alteration of rainfall and other traditional weather patterns critical to agricultural production.

While not all projected changes will be detrimental, collectively they will precipitate profound changes in global patterns of production, trade, capital flows, and migration. The global power pyramid may be transformed in the process. The deserti-

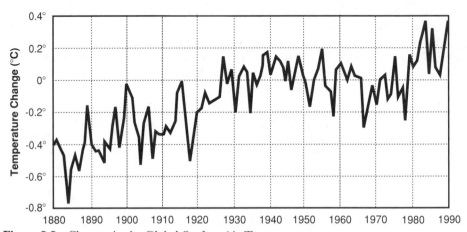

**Figure 9.9** Changes in the Global Surface Air Temperature
*Source:* Foundation for Teaching Economics and the United Nations Association of the USA (1992: 109), as reported originally in S. Fred Singer (1988: 18).

fication of the rich agricultural lands in the heartland of the United States and the emergence of Siberia as a major food-producing region are common prognoses; if they occur, important economic and political changes will follow. Similarly, a warmer Canada could induce large numbers of Americans to migrate there, with the result that Canada may emerge as a great power in the twenty-first century. Thus changes in the world's climate promise to transform world politics profoundly.

## TOWARD A MANAGED GLOBAL COMMONS? PROSPECTS FOR INTERNATIONAL COOPERATION

Other examples of environmental stress associated with affluence include soil erosion caused by the expansion of energy-intensive, mechanized agriculture to marginal lands; the reduction of the world's supply of water per capita by 1994 to only a third of what it was in 1970 (UNDP, 1994: 29); and depletion of ocean fisheries caused by technology-intensive overfishing and pollution of spawning beds. In Eastern Europe and the former Soviet Union, the central planning that placed intense emphasis on rapid industrialization also led to widespread abuse and destruction, which now requires extensive environmental reconstruction (French, 1990). Still, global warming may be the ultimate tragedy of the commons. It was intended by none yet is seemingly beyond the control of all who will bear its costs.

The unequal distribution of power in the international system and the sovereign equality of its members both ensure that national interests will dominate considerations of the common (global) interest. Nonetheless, as the world has become increasingly interdependent ecologically as well as economically, there is a greater awareness that what is in the best interest of all may also be in the best interest of each. The changes taking place are reflected in the "greening" of politics in many countries, particularly in the industrial world, as sensitivity to environmental issues multiplies, as well as in the growing commitment worldwide to the principle of *sustainable development*.

Sustainable development is the central concept in *Our Common Future*, the 1987 report of the World Commission on Environment and Development (1987), popularly known as the Brundtland Commission after the Norwegian prime minister who was its chair. The commission concluded that the world cannot sustain the growth required to meet the needs and aspirations of the world's projected population unless it adopts radically different approaches to basic issues of economic expansion, equity, resource management, energy efficiency, and the like. The commission did not embrace the "limits of growth" maxim popular among growth pessimists during the 1970s; instead, it emphasized "the growth of limits." Thus sustainability means learning to live off the earth's interest, without encroaching on its capital (see MacNeill, 1992; World Resources Institute, 1992).

The Brundtland Commission report is an important landmark in the rapid emergence of environmental concerns as a central issue on the global political agenda. The process began in 1972, when the UN General Assembly convened the first United Nations Conference on the Human Environment in Stockholm. In the ensuing years other conferences were held on a wide range of topics related to the environment, including, for example, population, desertification, food, and the oceans. New international agencies were created to monitor developments in their respective areas and to promote international cooperation in dealing with both national and transnational problems within their jurisdictions. In the process new principles were articulated, which by 1992 were embedded in more than 170 environmental protection treaties that direct the world's countries toward the goal of preserving the global habitat for future generations.

Many of these agreements helped set the stage for the Second United Nations Conference on Environment and Development, held in Rio de Janeiro in 1992, the twentieth anniversary of the first conference. Preparing for the conference, popularly known as the Earth Summit, proved difficult, as many of the differences between the 100 world leaders representing rich and poor countries shaped perceptions of their national interests in environmental issues. Still, the conference, attended by representatives of 7,892 nongovernmental organizations from 167 countries (Linden, 1992: 44), marked another milestone in the growing acceptance of basic principles of national conduct to promote a sustainable future for all of humankind. These are embedded in "Agenda 21," the global action plan drawn up at the Earth Summit.

To monitor global progress on conservation projects such as the Earth Summit's Convention on Biodiversity, 2,000 world environmental leaders representing 62 governments, 99 government agencies, and 575 nongovernmental organizations (NGOs) met in January 1994 in Buenos Aires for the World Conservation Union (IUCN) general assembly. Its purpose was to take a hard look at the effectiveness of the existing international treaties on global warming and biodiversity signed in Rio and to consider reshaping UN institutions to enforce environmental protection agreements. "The IUCN assembly in Buenos Aires will be the first opportunity for the entire IUCN membership, governments as well as NGOs, to discuss the actions we need to take to make a reality out of the rhetoric of Rio," IUCN Director-General Martin Holdgate explained.

Although the machinery for international cooperation on environmental issues is extensive and its prospects for development promising, its past effectiveness in coping with emerging environmental problems such as climate change remains far from satisfactory (Sand, 1991; Soroos, 1995). If there is cause for optimism, it is perhaps best exemplified by the concerted action that depletion of the stratospheric ozone layer has stimulated.

## Coping with Ozone Depletion

Ozone is a pollutant in the lower atmosphere, but in the upper atmosphere it provides the earth with a critical layer of protection against the sun's harmful ultraviolet radiation. Scientists have discovered a marked depletion of the ozone layer—most notably an "ozone hole" over Antarctica that grows at times to be larger than the continental United States—and they have conclusively linked the thinning of the layer to chlorofluorocarbons and a related family of compounds known as halons. Depletion of the ozone layer exposes humans to increased health hazards of various sorts, particularly skin cancer, and threatens other forms of marine and terrestrial life. The release of CFC gases in turn adds measurably to the accumulation of greenhouse gases that threaten dramatic climate change through global warming.

Scientists began to link CFCs to ozone depletion in the early 1970s. Even before their hypotheses were conclusively confirmed, the United Nations Environment Programme (a UN agency created in the aftermath of the 1972 Stockholm conference) began to seek some form of regulatory action. The scientific uncertainty surrounding the issue eased the sense of urgency some felt, and differences between the interests of the chemical industry in the United States (where bans were placed on some CFCs, such as aerosol propellants) and Europe (where they were not) slowed efforts to devise controls. Nevertheless, in 1985 the Vienna Convention on Protection of the Ozone Layer, whose purpose was to control ozone-modifying substances, was concluded. This landmark decision "represented the first international effort to deal formally with an environmental danger before it erupted" (Benedick, 1991).

Two years later a second and even more significant agreement was reached, the Montreal Protocol on Substances That Deplete the Ozone Layer, signed by twenty-three states and the Commission of the European Community. The signatories agreed at that time to reduce their CFC emissions to half of their 1986 levels by the turn of the century. The agreement was widely heralded, as the countries that reached the accord accounted for more than 80 percent of global CFC emissions. Even further cuts were proposed later, and in 1990 a global pact was drafted that called for the phaseout of CFCs by 1996. The new environmental treaty still under negotiation seeks to extend this protection by controlling gases that trap heat in the atmosphere.

The rapid move since 1985 to restrict the use of CFCs and related compounds reflected growing scientific certainty about the connection between CFCs and ozone depletion. Still—and unlike what the tragedy of the commons metaphor would lead us to expect—the success is attributable to states' ability to put their long-term collective interests in environmental protection ahead of short-term individual interests in protecting investments and jobs in the chemical industry.

> Perhaps the most extraordinary aspect of the Montreal Protocol was that it imposed substantial short-term economic costs in order to protect human health and the environment against speculative future dangers—dangers that rested on scientific theories rather than proven facts. Unlike environmental agreements of the past, this was not a response to harmful developments or events, but rather *preventive* action on a global scale. (Benedick, 1991: 129)

Will the success achieved in reducing ozone-depleting gases stimulate efforts to reduce the emissions that threaten to change the world's climate through global warming? There are reasons to be cautious, even skeptical (Grubb, 1990; Sebenius, 1991). They have to do with the magnitude of the problem and the distribution of costs and benefits associated with alternative solutions. The scientific uncertainty surrounding the evidence on global warming even further muddles efforts to deal with it and encourages so-called "eco-revisionists" who, claiming that no threat to health exists, have led a backlash revolt against the environmental protection movement.

## Coping with Global Warming

The magnitude of the problems related to global warming are truly enormous, not simply because of the global character of climate change and its anticipated consequences but also because of who will be affected by policy choices designed to slow it. These facts distinguish global warming from the process that dealt with ozone depletion.

> Negotiating and sustaining serious substantive actions to mitigate greenhouse gas emissions will be far more difficult. . . . The number of significant CFC-producing countries was small. The economic costs, required institutional changes, and affected industries were relatively limited. Those firms that expected to be able to produce CFC substitutes could benefit compared with their competitors and thus could even gain from the treaty. Few of these conditions apply to limits on carbon and other greenhouse emissions. (Sebenius, 1991: 118)

The expected consequences of reducing carbon emissions could be especially severe in the United States, the world's largest consumer of fossil-fuel energy. The Bush administration—characterized as "wed to the gloomiest economic predictions"—estimated that the U.S. GNP would decline by 3 percent (roughly $150 billion) as a result of efforts to halt global warming through increased energy efficiency (Weisskopf, 1991: 33). This perhaps explains why the United States—at least until the surprising discovery in 1992 of significant ozone depletion over North America—talked more of the uncertain extent and consequences of global warming than of positive steps to halt it. Accordingly, the United States "took a hang-tough, U.S.-against-the-world approach toward the Earth Summit," demanding and winning "a weakened version of a treaty on climate change on the grounds that accepting tough new rules to limit carbon dioxide emissions would hurt economic growth" (Greenhouse, 1992). Specifically, stressing its belief that tradeoffs exist between employment and environmental protection, the United States refused to join other industrial nations in a commitment to reduce carbon dioxide emissions to 1990 levels by the year 2000.

At the same time that the United States waxed resistant, countries in western Europe and even Japan (which previously had followed the U.S. lead on greenhouse policy) began to formulate national policies designed to reduce radically carbon dioxide emissions, which are the largest source of greenhouse heating. Thus, "without intending to, or even fully realizing that it has done so, Europe has assumed the mantle of international leadership on this central environmental issue, leaving the United States increasingly isolated" (Mathews, 1990). Furthermore, "if Japan and the West Europeans are correct and the greenhouse phenomenon proves to be a trend that must soon be reversed, their recent decisions to take remedial action could hold bad news for U.S. economic competitiveness. The means by which carbon dioxide emissions will be cut depend on advances in energy supply technologies, in transportation, agriculture, industry, appliances, building construction—in short in every corner of the economy where energy use is important" (Mathews, 1990).

The industrial countries of the North today account for the bulk of greenhouse gas emissions, but, as noted earlier, the most rapid rate of increase in carbon emissions is in the South. Even if the industrial countries are able to reduce their carbon dioxide emissions by 20 percent over the next three decades, the volume would still nearly double as a result of Third World carbon output (Stetson, 1991: 24).

Developing countries are understandably wary about efforts by the rich to solve environmental problems they (the developing countries) did not cause, all the more so if they are denied access to the very technologies that stimulated the economic growth of the now developed world. "Leaders struggling with the hand-to-mouth survival of millions find that 'sacrifice today to save tomorrow' is bitter medicine, especially when those administering it have already reaped the benefits of unlimited greenhouse effusions" (Stetson, 1991) They also regard efforts to blame developing countries as a form of "environmental colonialism."

> The bulk of Third World contributions to climate change . . . comes from agriculture and forests, in the form of methane from cows and rice paddies and carbon released from burning trees. These "survival emissions," as Third World countries call them, are the by-products of life-sustaining activities that generate food and income. They are different from the "luxury emissions" of the North, which come from cars and electricity for appliances in every home. (Stetson, 1991: 23)

During 1991, as preparations continued for the 1992 UN Conference on Environment and Development, substantial efforts were made to hammer out a global climate treaty that would balance the interests of the developed and developing worlds. With the notable exceptions of the United States and the Russian Federation, a consensus among the industrial countries favoring a rapid reduction of carbon emissions began to crystallize.

Third World participation in such efforts is critical if the rate of global temperature increases projected for the next century is to be slowed. Importantly, many Third World countries have agreed to consider voluntary reductions in their carbon dioxide emissions, provided, however, that the industrial countries also reduce their emissions. Developing countries (and Russia) also look for assistance from the rich countries in acquiring the technology to reduce their own pollutants (Sebenius, 1991). The strategy is similar to that devised in 1990 for dealing with ozone depletion, when an agreement was reached on the creation of a special fund (to be administered through the World Bank) that would finance the introduction in developing countries of products and technologies that would substitute for those known to cause depletion of the ozone. Thus halting steps have been taken toward a managed commons arrangement even in the absence of a regulatory (supranational) agency.

## The Freedom of the Commons

Garrett Hardin (1968) warned in his well-known popularization of the tragedy of the commons metaphor that "ruin is the destination toward which all . . . rush . . . in a society that believes in the freedom of the commons." Will the world's countries give up that measure of individual freedom necessary to avert global disaster? The tentative steps toward a managed commons arrangement to cope with climate change are reassuring, but optimism must be tempered by a recognition that issues like global warming involve "the interaction of two vast and complex systems, the planet's ecosystem and the human socioeconomic system" (Skolnikoff, 1990). Substantial inertia works against policy change to delay a collective response, especially in an issue-area where the needs to promote economic growth and trade, on the one hand, appear to conflict with the need to protect the environment, on the other (Esty, 1944; Marlin-Bennett, 1993).

Global warming is an inherently transnational policy problem. Its solution, how-ever, continues to rest in the hands of states, as the generally tentative steps taken at the 1992 Earth Summit amply demonstrated. Maurice Strong, organizer of the twelve-day conference, worried that the summit's outcome reflected "agreement with-out sufficient commitment." "I believe," he lamented, "we are on the road to tragedy." Thus, the logic of state sovereignty (read individual freedom) continues to work against collective global action in a system where the benefits of inaction are shared nationally but the costs are borne transnationally.

## SUGGESTED READINGS

Brown, Lester R., Hal Kane, and David Malin Roodman. *Vital Signs 1994: The Trends That Are Shaping Our Future*. New York: Norton, 1994.

Cassen, Robert. *Population Policy: A New Consensus*. Washington, D.C.: Overseas Development Council, 1994.

Choucri, Nazli, ed. *Global Change: Environmental Challenges and International Responses*. Cambridge, Mass.: MIT Press, 1993.

Gore, Al. *Earth in the Balance: Ecology and the Human Spirit*. Boston: Houghton Mifflin, 1992.

Kritz, Mary M., Lin Lean Lim and Hania Zlotnik, eds. *International Migration Systems: A Global Approach*. New York: Oxford University Press, 1992.

Myers, Norman. *Ultimate Security: The Environmental Basis of Political Security*. New York: Norton, 1993.

Ostrom, Elinor. *Governing the Commons: The Evolution of Institutions for Collective Action*. Oxford: Oxford University Press, 1992.

Pirages, Dennis. "Demographic Change and Ecological Insecurity," pp. 314–331 in Michael T. Klare and Daniel C. Thomas, eds., *World Security: Challenges for a New Century*. New York: St. Martin's Press, 1994.

Postel, Sandra. "Carrying Capacity: Earth's Bottom Line," pp. 3–21 in Lester Brown et al., *State of the World 1994*. New York: Norton, 1994.

Read, Peter. *Responding to Global Warming: The Technology, Economics and Politics of Sustainable Energy*. Atlantic Highlands, New Zealand: Zed Books, 1994.

World Resources Institute. *World Resources 1994–95*. New York: Oxford University Press, 1994.

Young, Oran R., and Gail Osherenko, eds. *Polar Politics: Creating International Environmental Regimes*. Ithaca, N.Y.: Cornell University Press, 1993.

# CHAPTER 10

• • •

# FUELING GROWTH: OIL, ENERGY, AND RESOURCE POWER

• • •

*Whoever controls world resources controls the world in a way that mere occupation of territory cannot match.*

Richard J. Barnet,
Political Scientist, 1980

*Vital economic interests are at risk. . . . An Iraq permitted to swallow Kuwait would have the economic and military power, as well as the arrogance, to intimidate and coerce its neighbors—neighbors who control the lion's share of the world's remaining oil reserves. We cannot permit a resource so vital to be dominated by one so ruthless.*

George Bush,
U.S. President, 1990

In April 1990, the average price for a barrel of internationally traded crude oil was less than $15. Five months later, in September, it was more than $40. For the third time in less than two decades, the world suffered an "oil shock" as the price paid for the most widely used commercial energy source skyrocketed.

The first oil shock occurred in 1973–1974, when, shortly after the 1973 Yom Kippur War, the price of oil increased fourfold as a result of the major Middle Eastern oil producers' collective action. The second jump in world oil prices produced by the oil-exporting countries occurred in 1979–1980 in the wake of the revolution in Iran. Iraq's invasion of Kuwait on August 2, 1990, precipitated the third shock.

Iraq's aggression catapulted the foremost military power in the Arab world into control of a fifth of the oil produced by the Organization of Petroleum Exporting Countries (OPEC) and more than a quarter of its proven reserves of crude oil. In part for this reason, the world community, under the leadership of the United States, launched a dual response. The United Nations first authorized economic sanctions against Iraq in an effort to force its withdrawal from Kuwait. Failing this, on November 29, 1990, the UN Security Council took an unprecedented step when it authorized the use of "all necessary means" to force Iraq from Kuwait. Seven weeks later, on January 16, 1991, the Persian Gulf War began when a coalition of UN forces launched

• • •

the most intensive aerial bombardment ever. Then, in February, coalition forces easily routed Iraqi troops in a 100-hour ground campaign. With Iraq's surrender, the United Nations again used economic sanctions to prod Iraq's compliance with the terms of the truce. Meanwhile, the price of oil reverted to its prewar levels.

Rapid and recurring changes in world oil prices are a major source of global financial and political disruptions. Moreover, access to oil at reasonable prices is a major national security priority, as the Persian Gulf War proved. OPEC formerly used oil successfully to exercise "commodity power" and is now poised to do so again (Stanislaw and Yergin, 1993). The repeated use of economic sanctions as an instrument of states' foreign policies in the past, and potential in the future, underscores the centrality of resource politics in international relations.

The purpose of this chapter is to explore the role of energy resources and economic sanctions in world affairs. The inquiry will focus on several related topics, including policies toward alternative energy sources and the consequences of resource dependence. We begin with an examination of the forces giving rise to the OPEC decade.

## THE POLITICAL ECONOMY OF OIL . . . . . . . . . . . . . . . . . . . . . . . . . . . . . .

The phrase **OPEC decade** captures OPEC's centrality in the world political economy since October 1973, when members of the organization, in response to war in the Middle East, imposed an embargo on the supply of oil and cut overall production levels. OPEC then chose to raise the price of its oil—a decision that precipitated the first of three oil shocks.

The OPEC decade ended in March 1983, when, in response to a worldwide oil glut, OPEC cut its official price of oil and its aggregate production levels. For the remainder of the 1980s and into the 1990s, the production, price, and supply of energy exhibited much variation, adding uncertainty to a global economy already buffeted by other problems and reducing policymakers' ability to make decisions based on reliable forecasts. The Persian Gulf War fueled anxieties anew and underscored the chronic character of oil crises. As we will see, uncertainty and fear continue to characterize today's global energy picture.

### Global Patterns of Energy Consumption

The behavior of individuals in different national settings influences the dynamics that govern global energy supply and demand, price and production. Just as people in the world's rich countries place a disproportionate burden on the global commons, they also consume a disproportionate share of its energy resources. Figure 10.1 illustrates the enormous gap between developed and developing countries in the energy consumed per person. Western Europe uses more than three times as much energy per capita as the developing world, Eastern Europe and the former Soviet Union more than four times as much, and Canada and the United States nearly eight

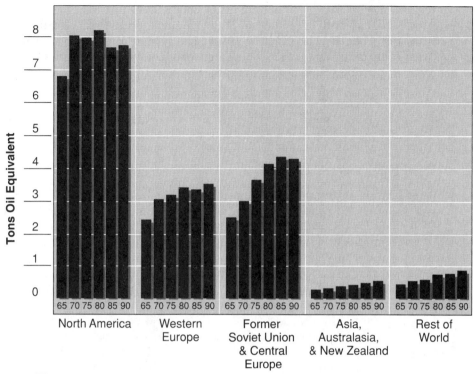

**Figure 10.1** Energy Consumption per Capita, 1965–1990
*Source: BP Statistical Review of World Energy* (1991: 36).

times as much. The differences parallel the gap between the world's rich and poor countries apparent in so many other dimensions of contemporary world politics.

Energy consumption is critical to the production of goods and services. Thus it tends to move in tandem with changes in the gross national product (GNP). During the roughly fifty years from the 1930s to the 1980s, the world's demand for energy increased at almost the same rate as did the aggregate world gross domestic product (GDP) (International Energy Agency, 1982: 69), reflecting in important ways industrial countries' substitution of energy for labor to facilitate production and transportation. Not surprisingly, therefore, the developing countries of the South, which have not yet become as mechanized, see energy as the key to their economic development and higher standards of living. The greatest increases in energy consumption today are occurring in developing countries.

Although the correlation between income and energy use is high, wide differences within given levels of economic output are apparent. Pakistan and Ghana, for example, had identical per-capita incomes in 1991, but Pakistan used over 50 percent more energy per capita than Ghana. Similarly, Belarus and Mexico had almost the same per-capita incomes in 1991 but Belarus used more than twice the energy per person than did Mexico (*World Development Report 1993*, 1993: 238–239, 246–247).

Even more striking are the differences among developed countries. In 1991, for example, the major developed countries (the United States, Japan, and the countries in what is now called the European Union) had approximately equivalent per-capita incomes, but the energy consumption (barrels of oil equivalent per capita) of the United States at 56 per person was more than twice that of its rich-country counterparts (U.S. CIA, 1992a; 16). In comparison, as Figure 10.2 illustrates, Japan and the European Union have historically been more energy-efficient than the United States despite (or perhaps because of) their heavy dependence on imported oil, but the energy efficiency of all three have declined in lockstep with the price of energy in the world market.

## Fossil Fuel Dependence

Rapid increases in energy usage in general and petroleum in particular are primarily post–World War II phenomena. In 1950, when world population stood at roughly 2.5 billion people, world energy consumption was 2.5 billion tons of coal-equivalent energy. Population increased rapidly during the next quarter-century, but energy use increased almost twice as fast. By 1979 the world's 4.4 billion people were consuming 8.7 billion tons of coal-equivalent energy (Sivard, 1981: 6). This increase was closely tied to the unprecedented level of economic growth that the world experienced. From 1950 to 1973, the world economy expanded at a rate of 4 percent annually, spurred by the 7 percent growth in world oil output during this period; on a per-capita basis, this meant that the amount of oil available increased from an average of 1.5 barrels per person in 1950 to over 5.3 barrels in 1973 (Brown, 1979: 17–18). (One barrel of oil equals forty-two U.S. gallons.) Rapidly rising production made oil the world's principal source of commercial energy.

Little more than a century ago, fuelwood was the principal energy source. As the mechanical revolution altered the nature of transportation, work, and leisure, coal began to replace fuelwood. Early in the twentieth century, coal became the dominant source of energy throughout the world. By 1913 it accounted for 75 percent of global energy consumption (Sivard, 1979a: 7).

New technological developments, particularly the internal combustion engine, spurred the shift from coal to oil and, somewhat less so, natural gas. The United States, well endowed with petroleum resources, led the development of oil-based technologies, above all in the automotive and petrochemical industries. Although oil accounted for less than a third of world energy production in 1950, by 1965 it equaled coal production. In the next decade it rapidly outpaced coal as the main energy source.

Everywhere the reasons for the shift to oil were the same. Energy derived from oil (and gas) was cleaner and less expensive than coal. (The cost of once-inexpensive coal also rose in response to labor demands for higher wages, rules to protect the environment, and more costly safety standards.) From the end of the Korean War until the early 1970s, world oil prices actually declined compared with the prices of other commodities. Natural gas prices showed a similar decline in the United States, where it was used more extensively than elsewhere.

The long-term stability of world oil prices is striking. As shown in Figure 10.3, World Wars I and II each produced small increments in the price of oil, but essentially

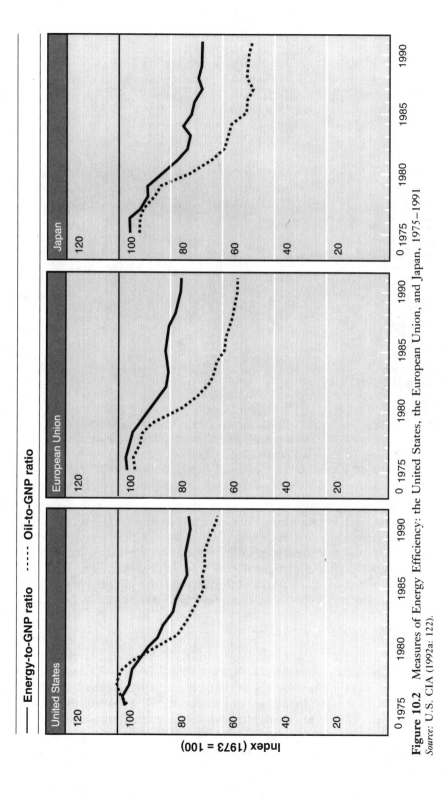

**Figure 10.2** Measures of Energy Efficiency: the United States, the European Union, and Japan, 1975–1991
*Source:* U.S. CIA (1992a: 122).

337

**U.S. dollars per barrel**

| World events | Pennsylvanian oil boom | Russian oil exports begin | Discovery of Spindletop, Texas | Fears of shortage in U.S.A. | Post-war reconstruction | Loss of Iranian supplies | OPEC introduce netback pricing and, later, production quotas |
|---|---|---|---|---|---|---|---|
| | | Sumatra production begins | Growth of Venezuelan production | East Texas field discovered | Suez crisis | Yom Kippur war | Iranian revolution |

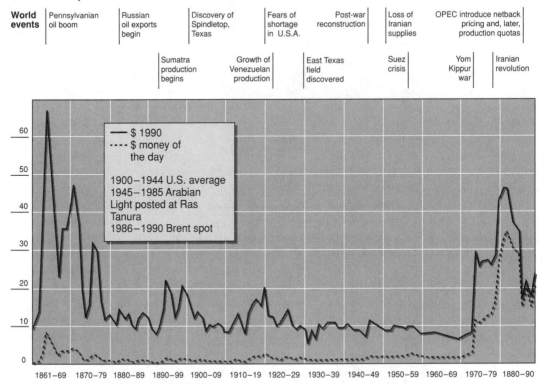

Legend within figure:
— $ 1990
---- $ money of the day

1900–1944 U.S. average
1945–1985 Arabian
Light posted at Ras Tanura
1986–1990 Brent spot

x-axis: 1861–69  1870–79  1880–89  1890–99  1900–09  1910–19  1920–29  1930–39  1940–49  1950–59  1960–69  1970–79  1880–90

**Figure 10.3** Crude Oil Prices since 1861
*Source: BP Statistical Review of World Energy* (1991: 12).

it remained stable. As the price of other commodities as well as manufactured goods rose, oil became relatively cheaper. It therefore made good economic sense to use it in large quantities. As a result, by 1979—the peak year of world oil consumption since the first well was drilled in the middle of the nineteenth century—over 31,000 gallons of petroleum were used every second. The United States alone consumed more than a fourth of this amount. Not until the onset of the first OPEC oil shock was this upward consumption trend interrupted.

## *The Role of the "Majors"*

The chief actors propelling the worldwide shift from coal to oil were eight multinational corporations (MNCs) known as the "majors"—Exxon, Gulf, Mobil, Standard Oil of California, Texaco (all U.S. based), British Petroleum, Royal Dutch Shell, and Compagnie Française des Petroles. In the mid-1970s these eight firms (the first seven of which are often referred to as the *seven sisters*) controlled nearly two-thirds of the world's oil production (Abrahamsson, 1975: 80). Their operations encompassed every aspect of the business from exploration to the retailing of products at their gas stations.

The majors were largely unhindered in their search for, production of, and marketing of low-cost oil. Concessions from countries in the oil-rich Middle East and elsewhere were easy to get. The communist states were virtually the only oil-producing countries that barred the majors.

A buyer's market existed, which meant that the majors had to control production to avoid glut and chronic oversupply. They did this by keeping other competitors, known as *independents,* out of the international oil regime, by engaging in joint ventures and otherwise cooperating among themselves to restrict supply and by avoiding price competition (Spero, 1990). The oil companies were thus able to maintain oil prices at a level profitable for themselves even though its price declined relative to other commodities.

An abundant supply of oil at low prices facilitated the recovery of Western Europe and Japan from World War II and encouraged consumers to use energy-intensive technologies, such as the private automobile. The overall result was an enormous growth in the worldwide demand for and consumption of energy.

To sustain the high growth rates, there was a continual need to find and exploit new oil deposits. The incentives for developing petroleum reserves outside the Middle East waned, however, as the real cost of oil failed to keep pace with increases in the cost of other commodities, goods, and services. And incentives for developing technologies for alternative energy sources, such as coal, were virtually nonexistent.

## The Rise of OPEC

Several factors explain the emergence of OPEC as a successful commodity cartel. One, just noted, was the absence of energy alternatives in the face of growing worldwide demand for oil. A second was the world's growing dependence on Middle Eastern oil. By 1973, the Middle East provided about a third of the world's oil supply, and Iran and Saudi Arabia alone produced nearly a quarter of the entire world's oil. The major industrial states (Japan, the Western European countries, and, less so, the United States) in particular were increasingly dependent on oil imports from the Middle East.

A third factor that contributed to OPEC's success was its ability to wrest control of production and pricing policies from the multinational oil companies. This occurred gradually as the MNCs' bargaining advantages vis-à-vis the host governments of the producing countries deteriorated. OPEC's formation in 1960 was part of the process whereby the oil-producing countries sought to increase their own economic returns as well as their leverage with the majors. Their efforts were bolstered by an increase in the number of independent oil companies after the 1950s, which made for a more competitive market.

Libya provided the catalyst for the first oil shock. A coup d'etat in September 1969 brought to power a radical government headed by Colonel Muammar Qaddafi. Shortly thereafter, Libya targeted Occidental Petroleum, an independent, as Libya asserted control over its resources by cutting oil production and increasing prices. Other oil-producing states quickly learned from Libya's action. They discovered both "the vulnerability of the independent oil companies . . . and the unwillingness of the Western consumers or the majors to take forceful action in their support" (Spero, 1990). The foundation was thus laid for using production controls, not just pricing policies, to generate oil revenues for the governments of the producing countries.

The possibility of using oil as a political weapon to affect the outcome of the unsettled Arab–Israeli dispute was not lost on the Arab members of OPEC. Their common desire to defeat Israel was a principal element uniting them. Thus, when the Yom Kippur War broke out between Israel and the Arabs on October 6, 1973, the stage for using the oil weapon was set.

Less than two weeks after the outbreak of war, the OPEC oil ministers seized the right to determine prices unilaterally, and the Arab producing countries decided to reduce their production levels. Thus, control over production and prices—which quadrupled between October 1973 and January 1974—was transferred from the oil companies to the host governments. Furthermore, the Arab members of OPEC cut production and embargoed exports to consuming countries considered too pro-Israeli, principally the Netherlands and the United States.

This transforming episode suggested several lessons. One was that the oil weapon, brandished successfully for political purposes, could be used again. The inability of the major multinational oil companies to control the international oil regime, as they had done for decades, was a second. Finally, the events showed that as its self-sufficiency in oil production declined, even the world's foremost economic and military power, the United States, was vulnerable to foreign economic pressures.

## The U.S. Role in OPEC's Ascendance

Given the enormity of overall U.S. consumption, its policies and practices exerted a disproportionate influence on the entire global energy picture. Growing U.S. vulnerability to OPEC's production and pricing decisions in a seller's market was instrumental to OPEC's rising power.

The United States has long been a major producer as well as consumer of oil. In 1938 it accounted for nearly two-thirds of the world's crude-oil production. By 1973, however, the proportion had slipped to 16 percent (*BP Statistical Review of World Energy*, 1984: 5).

As U.S. oil production declined, domestic demand increased. Imported oil made up the balance, accounting for 37 percent of consumption by 1973 (compared with about 20 percent in the mid-1960s) (Wald, 1993: A1). Growing U.S. oil import dependence thus helped make OPEC's 1973–1974 price hikes and production controls possible.

Historically, energy was abundant and cheap in the United States, a circumstance that removed incentives to develop efficient energy practices and conservation programs. Preferences for automobiles and trucks for transportation also accelerated U.S. oil consumption. In 1973, Americans drove their cars and trucks 1.3 trillion miles a year; in 1993, they drive 2.2 trillion (Wald, 1993: A1).

Despite the adverse economic consequences of the first oil shock, U.S. oil consumption continued to grow between 1973 and 1978, while domestic production continued to decline. This further increased U.S. reliance on foreign sources of oil. It also set the stage for the second oil shock, which came in 1979–1980 in the wake of the Iranian revolution that led to the creation of the revolutionary Islamic republic headed by the Ayatollah Khomeini. As world oil prices more than doubled, a global economic recession and the Third World debt crisis followed (see Chapters 7 and 8).

## OPEC's Demise

During the OPEC decade the Western industrial countries sought to reduce their dependence on foreign supplies of oil. For example, in February 1974, U.S. President Richard Nixon proposed to "re-establish [U.S.] capability for self-sufficiency" by 1980 and called for "an acceptable pattern of world trade in petroleum." And the new conservation measures and a shift to alternative sources of energy (alongside an economic recession) did, indeed, combine to push down the demand for oil.[1] As Figure 10.4 shows, the industrial countries' oil consumption declined to 58 percent of total world consumption by 1983, compared with its peak proportion of total consumption in 1979.

Oil prices also began to soften following their 1981 peak and went into a near free-fall in 1986 (see Figure 10.3). Many pressures accelerated the drop (see Morse, 1986), but the most important was a worldwide oil glut resulting from the decision of key members of OPEC, notably Saudi Arabia, to increase their output to generate revenues.

By the early 1990s, however, a sense of *déjà vu* began to punctuate the global energy environment. Demand increased steadily from the trough of the early 1980s, surpassing the 1979 peak in 1989 (see Figure 10.4).[2] Although subject to short-term gyrations, prices increased from a low of about $8 per barrel in 1986 to around $20 in 1990. Moreover, nearly all of the increase in world demand for oil was met by

---

[1] A shift to alternative energy sources contributed to the reduced reliance on OPEC oil. Coal, for example, again became a major source of U.S. energy. Similarly, Japan increased its import of coal to meet a growing proportion of its electrical generation and industrial needs, and China relied heavily on coal as its primary source of fossil fuel. Elsewhere, nuclear power was the alternative. The French, for example, increased their electrical generation through nuclear power more than seventeenfold between 1973 and 1986 (U.S. Department of Energy, 1987: 118) to help reduce dependence on imported oil. Brazil invested heavily in the generation of fuel ("gasohol") extracted from agricultural products. And the German government encouraged a shift from oil to natural gas.

[2] U.S. consumption rose an average of 1,850 barrels per day between 1983 and 1990 (*BP Statistical Review of World Energy*, 1991: 8). The result, of course, was that the United States was again exposed to another oil shock, in part because the Reagan administration failed to implement a strategic energy plan (see Renner, 1987). Reduced U.S. production since the early 1980s magnified U.S. vulnerability. The combination of rising consumption and declining production meant that U.S. imports increased "from about one-third of total U.S. consumption in 1983 to over 40 percent in 1990. Moreover, the fraction of total oil imports coming from the Persian Gulf nations . . . increased from about 4 percent of total U.S. oil consumption [10 percent of total U.S. oil imports] to over 11 percent [25 percent of gross U.S. oil imports in 1990]" (U.S. Office of Technology Assessment, 1991: 4).

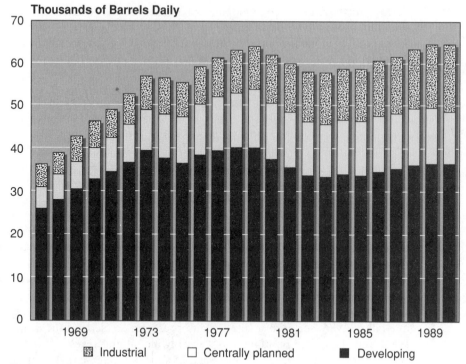

**Figure 10.4** Oil Consumption by Industrial, Centrally Planned, and Developing Economies, 1967–1990
*Source:* 1967–1979 adapted from *BP Statistical Review of World Energy* (1987: 9); 1980–1990 adapted from *BP Statistical Review of World Energy* (1991: 8).
*Note:* Data before 1980 may not be entirely comparable to data beginning with that year.

OPEC producers (Amuzegar, 1990). By 1990, OPEC's share of world oil production had returned to a high level of 38 percent (*BP Statistical Review of World Energy*, 1991: 5). Earlier predictions of "a coming crisis" (for example, Pirages, 1986) suddenly seemed prophetic.

The crisis occurred shortly thereafter, when Iraq invaded Kuwait. Suddenly and unexpectedly, the world experienced a shortage of 4 million barrels of oil per day, or approximately 6 percent of the world oil supply (Sterner, 1990–1991: 43). The shortfall caused the price of oil to double to more than $40 per barrel.

Thus the Persian Gulf crisis again riveted policymakers' attention on the costs and consequences of dependence on fossil-fuel energy, notably oil, in an environment of declining supply and rising demand. The domestic turmoil in and subsequent collapse of the Soviet Union, the world's largest oil producer and its second largest exporter, added to the sense of urgency.

Petroleum will still play a key role in the global energy picture for the remainder of this century and perhaps beyond. This raises questions about OPEC's potential future role as a price setter and production leader.

## OPEC Resurgent?

Though the future cannot be predicted with confidence, further price fluctuations and rapid changes within the oil industry can be expected that will doubtless have global ramifications. Already a return to previous patterns is discernable:

> Oil demand, left stagnant if declining by the 1970s' oil crisis, only began to grow again after the 1986 price collapse. By 1989, world consumption finally regained the previous record level of 1979, and is continuing to grow. Indeed, if Russia is excepted, world oil demand is currently increasing at 1.8 percent per year, even in the midst of a weak global economy. . . . If a disruption occurred in a tight market a few years from now, perhaps at a time of economic growth around the world, the effects could be quite sharp, both as measured in inflation and recession and in terms of raising international tensions. (Stanislaw and Yergin, 1993: 89, 91)

The capacity of OPEC to act together will be decisive. OPEC's members differ widely in their financial needs, oil reserves, governments, foreign policy goals, and political aspirations. They are also geographically distant, with widely disparate sociocultural systems, population sizes, levels of income, internal problems, and external challenges. These factors have often made OPEC a fragile organization. A new partnership between oil-producing countries and the oil multinationals could strengthen OPEC and again permit it to exercise the kind of "commodity power" its members formerly used with such success.

There now appear reasons to believe that OPEC is again positioned to dominate the global marketplace.

> The Arab-dominated Organization of Petroleum Exporting Countries, which after the Arab oil embargo played a declining role in world oil trade, is making a comeback. OPEC now supplies about 40 percent of world oil production, compared with 30 percent in 1985. And if some forecasts are accurate, it will again be providing half of the world's oil output by the end of the next decade—just about the same share as in 1973. What's more, three-fourths of the world's proven oil reserves are in OPEC countries; two-thirds are in the Middle East. Such [trends] suggest the United States and other industrial nations—indeed, the world in general—may become increasingly vulnerable to supply "disruptions." (Lawrence, 1993: A7)

OPEC oil is thus growing in importance. The six Persian Gulf members of the thirteen-member organization, which hold most of the world's proved oil reserves (see Figure 10.5) and also control most of OPEC's production, are now again in a prevailing position, much like the three previous occasions in which they were dominant. Their ability to convert this position into control, however, is likely to be determined by future trends in global demand.

**THIRD WORLD DEMAND**   Growing demand for fossil-fuel energy in the developing world will contribute to the Persian Gulf states' resurgent power. Hastened by rapidly rising population, high economic growth rates, and structural changes resulting from the development process, Third World energy consumption in 2020 could be as much as three times higher than in 1985 (U.S. Office of Technology

**Thousand million barrels**

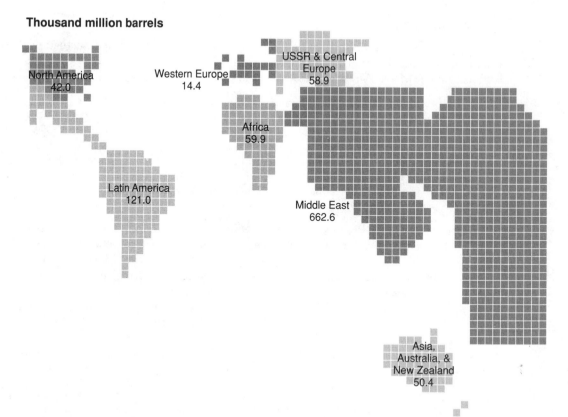

**Figure 10.5**  Proved Reserves of Oil, 1990
*Source: BP Statistical Review of World Energy* (1991: 3).

Assessment, 1991: 34) (see Figure 10.6). As these and related changes take place in the oil-producing countries themselves, some of them—such as Algeria, Ecuador, Gabon, Indonesia, and Nigeria—will need to direct their production to domestic needs rather than the export market (Ebinger, 1985).

Although the long-term trend is toward greater energy use in the Third World, fluctuations in the supply and price of oil will exact a toll. As noted in Chapter 8, seeds of the Third World debt crisis were sown by the first two oil shocks. Many Third World countries borrowed heavily from abroad to cover higher energy costs, only to find that the resources necessary to repay the loans failed to materialize in the recession of the early 1980s. On the other hand, when oil prices in turn fell, import-dependent countries, such as Brazil and Chile, benefited from reduced energy costs. Furthermore, as inflation caused by the rising costs of oil eased, interest rates also eventually declined, reducing the burden of many debt-ridden Third World countries whose obligations were tied directly to the cost of borrowing. To many of these same countries, the threat posed by Iraq's attack on Kuwait was that the process would revert to its earlier pattern.

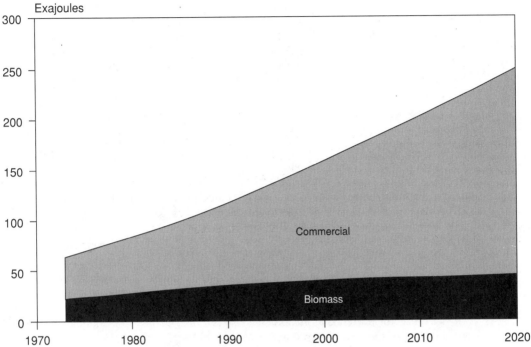

**Figure 10.6** Historical and Projected Energy Consumption in the Developing Countries
*Source:* U.S. Office of Technology Assessment (1991: 34).

As it turned out, the Persian Gulf crisis was relatively short-lived. Even so, its costs (apart from the war itself) both globally and locally were high. World oil prices averaged $30 per barrel between August 1990 and January 1991. The Overseas Development Council (1991: 1) estimated that reduced world economic activity during this period caused a 1 percent cut in developing countries' exports, amounting to a $6 billion cut in earnings. It also estimated that the effects of "higher oil import costs, loss of migrant remittances, and loss of export markets" for a group of thirty-five low- and middle-income countries exceeded $12 billion, or 1 percent of their GNP—"a UN criterion used in assessing the need for disaster relief" (Overseas Development Council, 1991: 2). Future threats to energy security and price stability are difficult to predict, but the Third World's experience with the three prior oil shocks proves they will be costly indeed.

**NON-OPEC PRODUCTION** A second development that will enhance the importance of OPEC's Persian Gulf producers is the expected decline of production among the non-OPEC states. As the North Sea and Alaskan oil finds of the 1970s reach their maximum production levels and then begin to drop in the years ahead, Middle East oil will loom larger in importance.

Certainly, there are signs of new production coming on stream in places like Yemen, Brazil, India, Norway, Angola, Malaysia and Papua New Guinea. These sources may provide a total of 1.5 million to 2 million barrels a day of incremental supply by 1995. But there is nothing on the horizon to match the giant oil fields discovered in the 1960s and 1970s in non-OPEC countries. These discoveries enabled Alaska's North Slope production to go from scratch to nearly 2 million barrels daily, Mexican production to rise by 2 million barrels daily, and North Sea output to add nearly 4 million. (Morse, 1990–1991: 44)

In a related development, the output of "mature" non-OPEC producers, including Mexico and the United States, two of the world's largest oil producers, will drop rapidly during the 1990s (Morse, 1990–1991). This in turn will create upward pressure on prices and production elsewhere.

So, too, will Russia's withdrawal from the global oil-supply equation. Oil production in Russia dropped in 1993 to 7 million barrels per day from 11.5 million in 1988 (Stanislaw and Yergin, 1993: 86). Some predict that Russia will become a net oil importer. To stem current production declines and increase future output, Western companies have entered into joint ventures and otherwise provided capital and technology to exploit Russia's vast resources. The risks to Western firms are great, but the change in attitude is extraordinary. "The Soviet Union . . . nationalized its oil industry nearly three-quarters of a century ago," observed the authoritative *Petroleum Intelligence Weekly* shortly before the breakup of the Soviet Union. "Reopening the Soviet oil sector portends a phenomenal reversal of the sometimes rampant resource nationalism of the past twenty years" (Morse, 1990–1991).

**U.S. Oil Import Vulnerability and Dependence**  As the world's largest energy consumer, the United States must be highly sensitive to the vulnerability caused by its growing import dependence on foreign oil supplies. "The United States uses almost as much oil as it did [in 1973], but imports 46.6 percent of it, up from 37.2 percent in 1973. At the time of the embargo, 5.3 percent of the oil used [in the United States] came from Arab members of OPEC; [in 1993] it [reached] 11.6 percent" (Wald, 1993: A1).

Growing dependence on oil imports from the politically volatile Middle East is cause for special U.S. concern for several reasons.

1. Greater reliance on oil from foreign sources magnifies the potential impacts of import curtailments on U.S. oil supplies and the economy.
2. Oil imports contribute to U.S. balance-of-payments deficits, and as oil imports (and/ or prices) rise, more U.S. export earnings must be allocated to paying for oil rather than devoted to domestic consumption. In 1990 the bill for oil imports amounted to $65 billion, more than half of [the U.S.] $101 billion balance-of-payments deficit.
3. The threat of potential economic and social dislocations that could accompany major oil supply or price disruptions could constrain U.S. policymakers in foreign affairs, national security and military matters where oil supplies might be affected.
4. The ready availability of cheap imported oil in the United States is a powerful financial disincentive for oil-saving investments in efficiency and alternative energy sources or the development of higher-cost domestic oil. Unlike Japan and most Western European countries that are highly dependent on oil imports and where oil is heavily taxed, U.S.

oil prices are comparatively low and do not fully reflect many of the external costs of oil use. Among the most notable of these externalities are, for example, the environmental damage from production, oil spills, and emissions from refining and combustion, and the costs of maintaining and deploying military forces to protect supplies. The defense costs in particular have applied disproportionately to the United States relative to European countries and Japan. (U.S. Office of Technology Assessment, 1991: 12–13)

In light of these considerations, it is not surprising that the United States has seen a strong link between oil and national security. This is, in an economically interdependent global marketplace, a global issue.

## OIL AND NATIONAL SECURITY . . . . . . . . . . . . . . . . . . . . . . . . . . . . .

The Persian Gulf War underscored the importance of oil to national security. U.S. President George Bush never openly admitted that oil was a principal factor propelling the U.S. decision to oppose Iraq's Saddam Hussein. However, in early September 1990 he did acknowledge that short-sighted energy policies had made the United States unduly dependent on Middle Eastern oil to fuel its industrial economy. "We had moved in the wrong direction," he said. "Now we must act to correct that trend."

### Oil and the Persian Gulf War

Oil figured prominently in Iraq's decision to invade Kuwait. Its eight-year war with Iran, which ended in 1988, caused severe economic dislocations, including an $80 billion foreign debt. Lower oil prices, caused in part by increased production by other OPEC members, made it more difficult for Iraq to meet its obligations. "In theory, Iraq might have managed the economic pressures by trimming its costly military program, by tightening its belt, and by intimidating its brethren in the Organization of Petroleum Exporting Countries to curtail their production in order to push prices higher. . . . Saddam [Hussein], however, saw a quicker fix for the economic ills of his country—sharply higher oil prices and the vast wealth of Kuwait, including its $100 billion in foreign assets" (Quandt, 1991).

> By the spring of 1990 he was making his demands known. He wanted Saudi Arabia and Kuwait to write off the billions of dollars of loans extended during the Iran-Iraq War; he wanted Kuwait to come up with an additional $10 billion in aid; he wanted OPEC to push oil prices to $25 per barrel; and he wanted Kuwait to yield two islands that controlled access to Iraq's port at Umm Qasr, as well as to pay some $2.4 billion for oil taken from the Rumailah oil field. At a meeting of the Arab League in May, and later in a letter from his foreign minister, Saddam made these points explicit. According to Arab sources, Saddam acknowledged at the Arab League meeting that his demands might sound like blackmail, but he did not care. Iraq was determined to get its way. (Quandt, 1991: 52)

There were political as well as economic reasons motivating Saddam Hussein, including an aspiration to dominate the Arab world. Thus control over Kuwaiti oil was a means to an end as well as an end in itself. Nonetheless, the Middle East was once more plunged into open warfare, causing alarm throughout the world. In the end, nearly forty countries contributed to the UN-authorized military response to Iraq's aggression.

The Gulf crisis touched the entire world through skyrocketing oil prices, but this was only a symptom of the causes of the world's collective response.

> Three factors distinguished the Iraqi invasion of Kuwait as a situation that demanded an international response. First, Kuwait's importance to the international economy is far beyond its size. It sits atop the fourth largest oil reserve in the world. If Saddam Hussein could have added Kuwait's oil reserves to Iraq's and used his superior military might to bully Saudi Arabia and the smaller Gulf oil states into supporting Iraq's positions in [OPEC], he could have dominated oil production and pricing policies. Oil prices still would have been tied to supply and demand, but Hussein would have been in a position to push prices up, thereby straining the world economy. Second, Iraq's efforts to acquire nuclear weapons and its existing conventional, chemical, and biological weapons capabilities made that country a long-term military threat to the entire Middle East and perhaps beyond. Third, Iraq's government had demonstrated an appetite for military conquest and a capacity for brutality. Since 1980, Iraq had invaded Iran, resorted to the use of chemical weapons against Iranian soldiers and ballistic missiles against Iranian citizens, and used poison gas against its own Kurdish population during a campaign to snuff out the Kurdish resistance movement. (*The Middle East*, 1991: 315–316)

The Persian Gulf War culminated two decades of Middle Eastern turmoil. Yet it was representative of a larger principle: the long-term tightening link between Middle East oil and global stability. That linkage continues to remain tight today. Indeed, it is not a gross exaggeration to suggest that the great powers' prospects for prosperity and peace depend on the preservation of order in the volatile Middle East, whose oil is critical to their economic fortunes. Ensuring access to the region's oil is a national security priority. At issue is not only the ability to protect its vast oil fields from terrorist or other attacks, but also to avert a repetition of the internal political disruptions that have often plagued the region.

The national security importance of this problem is illustrated well by the U.S. perspective. Recall the 1979 example, when the Soviet Union intervened militarily in Afghanistan, poising it perilously close to the Middle Eastern oil lifeline to the West. U.S. security was jeopardized. In response, U.S. President Jimmy Carter enunciated the **Carter Doctrine,** pledging that "an attempt by an outside force to gain control of the Persian Gulf region will be regarded as an assault on the vital interests of America and such an assault will be repelled by any means necessary, including military force." Oil, the Carter Doctrine made clear, mattered—greatly. The ascribed security importance was later underscored in August 1990 when the Bush administration effectively made good on the Carter Doctrine's pledge by dispatching 200,000 troops to Saudi Arabia—although the threat was then from Iraq, not the Soviet Union. Hence, the principle is suggested that great powers will use force to ensure their access to energy. Avoiding that in the future will likely be contingent on the availability of adequate sources of energy.

## Ensuring Energy Security

When vulnerability to oil-supply suspensions first was taken seriously in the 1970s, the United States responded to its growing oil-import dependence by announcing that it intended to develop a strategic petroleum reserve from which it could draw stockpiled oil in the event of a supply interruption. In 1974 it also sponsored creation of the International Energy Agency (IEA) to oversee the sharing of oil among the Western industrial countries in an emergency. In a related move, it embarked on a diplomatic offensive to enhance its ability to ensure the security of supply routes out of the volatile and geopolitically sensitive Middle East to oil-short markets in Japan, Western Europe, and elsewhere.

Ensuring global energy security and an adequate supply of oil requires not only access at the wellhead but also secure routes to refiners and consumers.[3] The two most important routes are from the Persian Gulf area to the Cape of Good Hope at the tip of Africa and from there to Europe and North America, and eastward from the Persian Gulf through the Strait of Malacca to Japan. The importance of the African route had grown prior to the first OPEC oil crisis. In 1965 most of the crude oil going to Europe traveled through the Suez Canal, but after its closure during the 1967 Arab-Israeli War (it was reopened in 1975), the canal receded in importance and, a decade later, became less critical as a sea-lane with the creation of supertankers too large to pass through it. Thus the African route became far more important and remains so today (see Map 10.1).

In 1987, in response to the fear that the continuing war between Iran and Iraq might widen and thereby interrupt the flow of oil from the Middle East, the United States substantially increased its naval presence in the Persian Gulf region and made the controversial decision to escort Kuwaiti oil tankers through the Persian Gulf and the perilous Strait of Hormuz, where oil tankers had become routine targets in the war. Other means to ensure energy security were tried, including, as noted earlier, a shift to alternative energy sources to reduce reliance on OPEC oil. As part of that strategy, Western European countries agreed to help the Soviet Union build a pipeline designed to transport natural gas from Siberia to markets in Germany and elsewhere.

The national security underpinnings of U.S. oil policy is illustrated by another example from the Cold War period. In the early 1980s the United States imposed stiff controls on the export of oil and gas technology to the Soviet Union in an effort to dissuade Western Europe from completing the pipeline. The United States feared that Western European dependence on Soviet energy supplies would make Europe subject to Moscow's dictates and provide it with much-needed hard currency. European leaders did not agree, and argued that the alternative—greater dependency on

---

[3] In 1990 Canada, the United States, and Western Europe accounted for 39 percent of the world's crude-oil refining capacity. The Middle East, in contrast, accounted for only 7 percent (*BP Statistical Review of World Energy*, 1991: 14). The discrepancies were even more striking after the first energy crisis, when in 1976 the West accounted for 53 percent of the world's refining capacity and the Middle East only 4 percent (*BP Statistical Review of World Energy*, 1987: 16).

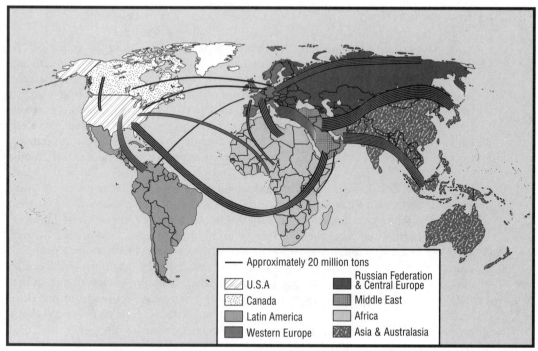

**Map 10.1**  Main Oil Trade Movements
*Source: BP Statistical Review of World Energy.*

politically insecure sources of gas and oil in Africa or the Middle East—was less palatable (Ebinger, 1985). Eventually the United States backed away from its efforts to stop the Siberian pipeline project. Still the fracas with its NATO allies underscores how much security considerations shape U.S. energy policies. The case also illustrates the extent to which other industrial powers are willing to make alliance ties subordinate to their overriding interest in retaining access to energy supplies.

## ALTERNATIVE ENERGY SOURCES

Since the first oil crisis the industrial countries have experimented with comprehensive energy programs that might ease their dependence on foreign oil. More broadly, many of these initiatives have sought to develop alternatives to fossil-fuel energy. Two decades later, following the third oil shock, the issues and prescriptions remain much the same as after the first shock. "Excluding some sort of accommodation with major oil exporters, major oil importing countries . . . still . . . have to adopt a comprehensive domestic energy policy to reduce consumption and increase fuel efficiency, and they must embark on serious efforts to develop alternative, renewable energy sources" (Amuzegar, 1990). The new wrinkle that any program must confront now is the necessity of controlling the environmental hazards that burning fossil fuels produce.

On the basis of current ratios of production to known reserves, oil will last only until about the year 2035 (see Figure 10.7). The mere 1.2 billion barrels the International Energy Agency holds in strategic stockpiles for its members are only adequate to cushion a cutoff of supplies (Lawrence, 1993: A7). It will not postpone the need to find oil substitutes. Declining oil supplies will not lead to declining energy supplies if economically and politically viable energy alternatives are found and utilized. In addition to increased reliance on coal and natural gas, greater use of nuclear and hydropower could ease the transition to a non-oil-based energy system. Oil derived from unconventional sources, such as tar sands and shale, and renewable forms of energy, such as solar, tidal, and wind power, geothermal energy, and bioconversion, might also become viable technologically and economically.

The decline of oil prices (both absolutely and relative to other goods) in the post-OPEC decade has stifled efforts to devise energy alternatives. Most economists agree that higher oil costs will accelerate the search for substitute energy sources. How high prices must rise is, of course, uncertain. But if oil prices skyrocket, unconventional energy technologies will become financially attractive. Coal, natural gas, hy-

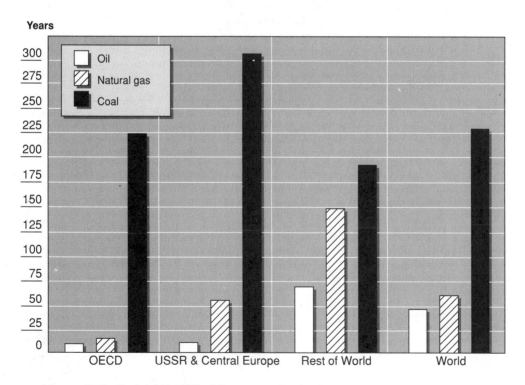

**Figure 10.7**   Ratio of Fossil-Fuel Reserves to Production, 1990
*Source: BP Statistical Review of World Energy* (1991: 36).

dropower, and nuclear power are the major alternatives to oil. Each, however, is beset with economic, environmental, and political uncertainties.

## Coal

Estimates of the world's reserves of fossil fuels are imprecise, but all agree that coal is vastly more abundant than either oil or natural gas. Based on the current ratio of reserves to production, coal will last for more than two centuries.

China, the United States, and the Russian Federation account for more than 60 percent of world coal reserves. Trade in coal increased by 40 percent during the 1980s and, unless constrained by growing environmental concerns, is expected to increase another 40 percent by the year 2000 (World Resources Institute, 1990: 143). Still, most coal is consumed where it is produced, making it less susceptible to supply disruptions than oil. China, in fact, "is trying to do something that is nearly unique today—fueling its rapid economic expansion almost entirely with coal. Indeed, coal now accounts for a remarkable 76 percent of the country's total commercial energy supply" (Flavin, 1992: 30).

As noted earlier, coal use increased sharply as an alternative to oil in the aftermath of the first two oil shocks, growing 30 percent since the mid-1970s (Flavin, 1991–1992: 4). Coal is now the leading alternative to oil, accounting for 27 percent of the world's primary energy use in 1990, compared with 39 percent for oil and 22 percent for natural gas (*BP Statistical Review of World Energy*, 1991: 34). The social costs or "externalities" associated with its widespread use are substantial, however, which has caused a slowdown in the coal boom as environmental concerns and tighter regulations make it less attractive.

As noted in Chapter 9, coal contributes heavily to the acidification of precipitation and to the release of carbon that contributes to global warming. "Because coal has a higher carbon content than other fossil fuels, rising levels of coal combustion accounted for more than half the increase in carbon emissions between 1975 and 1990. By then coal was responsible for 42 percent of the world's carbon emissions from fossil fuels, virtually the same share as oil" (Flavin, 1991–1992: 4).

Because of coal's environmental hazards, its heavy use by China is a growing international concern. "Carbon emissions [in China] have increased 60 percent in the past decade and account for 37 percent of the Third World total. China is already the world's third largest carbon emitter, and is likely to surpass the [Russian Federation] within the decade. Redirecting China's energy economy is fast becoming as important to the global atmosphere as changing those of Europe and the United States" (Flavin, 1992: 30–31).

## Natural Gas

Natural gas is cleaner and more convenient to use than either oil or coal (see Flavin, 1992). Natural gas supplies, based on the current reserve/production ratio, will last for nearly sixty years (Figure 10.7). Unlike coal, however, natural gas is distributed very unevenly on a regional basis, which means that its continued development will depend on export trade.

The two largest natural gas markets are the United States and Russia which in 1990 consumed, respectively, 28 percent and 33 percent of the 72.6 trillion cubic feet of total world production (U.S. CIA, 1992a: 15). Russia is also a major producer of gas and possesses the largest reserves, with 38 percent of the world's proved reserves in 1990. The United States, on the other hand, has only 4 percent of the world's gas reserves (*BP Statistical Review of World Energy*, 1991: 18). Historically the United States has met virtually all of its need for gas from domestic sources, but it seems likely that it will increasingly have to look to imports to sustain its high demand. As with oil, the Middle East is a likely source, as it holds nearly a third of the world's proved reserves but consumes less than 6 percent of world production.

Getting gas from the wellhead to consumers is a primary problem. Pipelines are the preferred method of transport, but they are expensive and massive engineering projects that also pose environmental dangers and thus encounter resistance. Liquefied natural gas is an alternative, perhaps the only one for transshipment from the Middle East to North America or to the growing European and Japanese markets, but experts disagree about its safety. That concern combined with cost considerations and sensitivity to dependence on OPEC sources has limited the development of new liquefied natural gas projects, at least in the United States. Still, because natural gas produces considerably less carbon emissions than either coal or oil, its attractiveness will grow, thus providing incentives to increase its useability throughout the world.

## Hydropower

Hydropower accounts for about 7 percent of world energy use. North America is the primary consumer of electricity generated by hydropower, followed by Latin America, Europe, and Asia (*BP Statistical Review of World Energy*, 1991: 34). Severe drought in the 1980s curtailed water supplies, particularly in the United States, thus reducing the amount of energy available from hydropower. Hydropower has distinct advantages over fossil fuels in that it does not pollute the atmosphere, but water availability, land management issues, and financial considerations, especially in the developing world, will constrain its further development.

## Nuclear Energy

In 1990 nuclear power accounted for 5.7 percent of global energy use. By the end of 1992 some 777 commercial reactors were in operation in 58 countries (Sivard, 1993: 13). In roughly half of these countries, electricity derived from nuclear power accounted for at least a quarter of their electrical use. The United States is the single largest consumer of nuclear energy (followed by France, Japan, and the Russian Federation), but France uses it most intensively, deriving 30 percent of its total energy use (in 1991) from nuclear power (U.S. CIA, 1992a: 123, 137).

Among known technologies, nuclear energy was once seen as the leading alternative to dependence on fossil fuels, but that is no longer the case. Technical and financial problems have forced some countries to reduce or abandon their programs, and in others the political climate has turned markedly against nuclear power, with safety a principal point of contention. Two well-publicized nuclear accidents, one in the United States at the Three Mile Island nuclear power plant in Pennsylvania in 1979 and a second at Chernobyl in Ukraine in 1986, dramatized the risks and seemed to vindicate the skeptics who had warned about the dangers posed by nuclear energy.

Catastrophe was averted at Three Mile Island, but even without the threatened meltdown of the reactor core, the accident released the largest-ever level of radioactive contamination by the U.S. commercial nuclear industry. At Chernobyl, however, catastrophe did strike—and only now is the full magnitude of the world's worst nuclear disaster being revealed. "The fallout from Chernobyl—the equivalent of 10 Hiroshima bombs—. . . left a swath of agricultural land the size of Holland permanently poisoned. About 200,000 people [were] evacuated from their homes. Nearly 4 million people live in contaminated areas. . . . The official death toll remains 31, which was the number of Chernobyl workers and firefighters killed in the immediate aftermath of the explosion. But unofficial estimates run between 5,000 and 10,000" (Dobbs, 1991: 10).

The effects of the Chernobyl explosion ranged well beyond Ukraine. Within days "much of Europe was experiencing the highest levels of radioactive fallout ever recorded there, and within two weeks, minor radioactivity was detected throughout the northern hemisphere. . . . The health of Europe could be affected for decades. Estimates of resulting cancer deaths by researchers in the field range from less than 1,000 to almost 500,000. . . . Rarely have so many countries been so affected by a single event" (Flavin, 1987: 5).

No new reactors were commissioned in the Russian Federation following Chernobyl, construction on thirty-nine others was halted, and the Ukrainian parliament voted to shut down the three remaining reactors at Chernobyl by 1995 and switch to alternative sources of energy. "Chernobyl woke us up," Yavorivskii, the Ukrainian legislator and writer, observed. "It made us understand that we were not masters of our own land" (Dobbs, 1991).

Or *did* Chernobyl wake up Ukraine's leaders? The disaster's lessons may still not be grasped. To the alarm of its European neighbors, Ukraine's economically desperate leaders announced in October 1993 that they planned to leave the Chernobyl power plant in operation, thus reversing their decision to shut down the power station because of safety concerns.

The risks of nuclear power beyond the safety of nuclear energy, narrowly defined, work against its further development as technology is now configured. How and where to dispose of highly radioactive nuclear wastes, for example, is a contentious political issue in Europe and Japan as well as the United States. Spent fuel from nuclear-generating facilities must be removed periodically. It is then "cooled" in water to remove some of the most intense radioactivity before being reprocessed, a procedure that separates still-useful uranium and plutonium from other waste materials. No safe procedure for handling nuclear waste—some of which remains dangerous for hundreds of thousands of years—has yet been devised.[4] In the meantime, large quantities have accumulated, posing a substantial threat to environmental safety.

A related fear is that nuclear know-how might be acquired by countries that do not already possess it, thereby giving them the means to develop nuclear weapons. Proliferation is essentially a national security issue, but it is technologically linked to nuclear power production for peaceful purposes. Nuclear-generating facilities produce weapons-grade material, specifically highly enriched uranium and plutonium. Neither of these materials, which can be used to create a nuclear weapon, is used commercially as fuel in the current generation of nuclear power reactors.[5] Yet at projected rates of production, the amount of such material created will eventually make available enough weapons-grade material to place within reach the construction of tens of thousands of nuclear bombs every year. Preventing the spread of nuclear weapons is therefore tied to the development of safeguards in the commercial nuclear industry, which remain lax (see also Chapter 11).

Even before Chernobyl and Three Mile Island, these and related issues caused the nuclear industry to scale down its previous expansion plans. Virtually all of the industrial world determined in the wake of the first oil shock that a rapid buildup of nuclear power was necessary, but only in France did the nuclear industry develop as planned (Stobaugh, 1982). In the United States, in contrast, many of the earlier orders for nuclear power plants were canceled (since 1978 no new plants have been built), and construction of numerous plants already under way was halted. Elsewhere (for example, Australia, Austria, Denmark, New Zealand, and Norway), the nuclear industry's earlier ambitious plans for new power-generating facilities were postponed indefinitely. Even where nuclear power continued to expand—Japan, the Russian Federation, and the United Kingdom—the pace was slowed. The number of nuclear power plants that developing countries had planned to build was also cut to less than half the number expected in the mid-1970s (Stobaugh, 1982). Three Mile Island and Chernobyl thus merely reinforced existing stiff resistance to the further development of nuclear energy.

This brief exploration of alternatives to energy derived from oil demonstrates that the "energy problematique" is a complex mixture of technical, economic, environmental, political, and security issues. Preparing for a postpetroleum world therefore requires a frontal attack on a multitude of well-entrenched challenges, not the least of which is preservation of the standard of living to which much of the developed

[4] The problem is especially perplexing for financially strapped states who also are dependent on nuclear energy. Consider Russia. Nearly broke, Russia in October 1993 reluctantly agreed to stop dumping liquid radioactive nuclear waste into the Sea of Japan, but had to ask Japan for $100 million to help process the waste for burial on land.
[5] Commercial generating facilities generally use natural uranium, in which the fissile isotope U-235 occurs in low concentrations (less than 1 percent), or slightly enriched uranium (3 to 4 percent). Nuclear weapons, by contrast, require highly enriched uranium, which at present can be produced by only a few states.

Plutonium is an artificial element produced as a by-product of uranium-burning reactors. If separated from spent fuel by chemical reprocessing, it can be used to produce additional electrical generating capacity. However, only about ten kilograms of plutonium are needed to make a nuclear weapon (U.S. Arms Control and Disarmament Agency, 1979: 23).

world has grown accustomed and to which others aspire. Mustering the political will to address the challenges may prove the most formidable task.

## The (Dis)utility of Resource Power ........................

The impact of oil price and production policies on the world political economy derives from the uneven distribution of the demand for and supply of oil. Should there be another oil crisis, it, like the previous ones, will spring from this imbalance. Are there other commodities with similar characteristics? Are other OPECs therefore possible? Might they, too, become vehicles for the use of commodity power to enhance the economic welfare of their members or to realize political purposes?

Table 10.1 displays the Third World's volume and share of world commodity exports in the late 1980s. The data support the proposition that developing countries hold substantial commodity power (for comparisons of individual Third World countries see Map 8.1 on p. 266). Note, for example, that they account for 97 percent of the world's exports of rubber, 90 percent of its cocoa, 89 percent of its coffee, 82 percent of its tea and bananas, and 78 percent of its palm oil and tin. (The proportions have not changed substantially since.)

Such an apparently high degree of global dependence on a few exporters of commodities, some regarded as "critical" or "strategic" resources, has been a serious concern among policymakers in many importing countries, especially after their experiences with the OPEC cartel. In the early years of the Reagan administration U.S. policymakers frequently talked about an impending "resource war," as resource-dependent industrial countries clamored to ensure secure access to resources vital to their advanced economies. Yet no resource war broke out. And even though producers'

### TABLE 10.1 Major Primary Commodity Exports of Developing Countries ($ Billions and Percentage of Total World Exports)

| Commodity | $ | % | Commodity | $ | % |
|---|---|---|---|---|---|
| Rubber | 3.1 | 97.4 | Rice | 1.9 | 58.2 |
| Cocoa | 2.7 | 90.2 | Oilseed cake and meal | 2.8 | 53.1 |
| Coffee | 11.0 | 89.0 | Cotton | 2.9 | 48.8 |
| Bananas | 1.4 | 82.4 | Tobacco | 1.9 | 48.7 |
| Tea | 1.8 | 81.6 | Iron ore | 3.0 | 44.0 |
| Palm oil | 1.6 | 77.9 | Aluminum and bauxite | 3.1 | 24.8 |
| Tin | 1.2 | 77.8 | Soybeans | 1.4 | 24.8 |
| Sugar | 6.9 | 72.9 | Maize | 1.7 | 23.1 |
| Phosphate rock | .9 | 64.3 | Timber | 3.9 | 21.9 |
| Copper | 5.0 | 64.0 | | | |

*Source:* Based on unpublished World Bank data.

associations have at one time or another since existed in many of these commodity markets, none has come under monopoly control in the same way that oil once did. Why not? And what do these apparently failed prognoses regarding impending war and dashed hopes about commodity power portend for the future?

## Resource Dependence and Commodity Power

The ability of Third World producers to wield commodity power—and the incentives that the First World importing countries might have to use armed force to ensure their access to essential resources—depend on a peculiar combination of circumstances. Dependency is the critical factor, but it can take on various manifestations. As political scientist Bruce Russett observes:

> Fears of dependence in industrialized economies arise from several different economic and political possibilities. The first involves changes in market conditions that suppliers impose deliberately, for economic reasons: in effect, the possibility of significant price increases imposed by a single supplier or, more likely, by a cartel in order to reap monopoly (or oligopoly) profits. . . .
>
> A second possibility concerns changes in market conditions imposed deliberately, but for political purposes, by suppliers or hostile third parties. Here we refer chiefly to embargoes, boycotts, or trade sanctions, such as the American economic sanctions against the Soviet Union for its action in Poland and Afghanistan. . . . (Russett, 1984: 483)

As we noted earlier, OPEC was motivated by political and economic aspirations, both of which created fears of resource dependence in the North. The oil embargo against the United States and the Netherlands in the immediate aftermath of the Yom Kippur War sought to alter their support of Israel. Thereafter, most of OPEC's efforts were motivated by a desire to maximize economic returns to its members. To understand why OPEC was able for awhile to succeed and to predict whether its strategy might be repeated in other commodity markets, several factors critical to the successful exercise of commodity power need to be evaluated.

### *Economic Factors*

The two market conditions necessary for effective monopoly power are (1) a lack of responsiveness to prices by consumers and (2) a lack of responsiveness in the supply of the commodity growing out of increases in its price. These conditions are known technically as the *price inelasticity of demand and supply*.

The demand for a commodity is price inelastic if the amount consumed changes little in response to price increases. The price inelasticity of demand is essential to a producers' cartel whose goal is to maximize the amount of foreign exchange it earns from its product. If the demand is price elastic, the total money earned will be less at the new, higher price than at the old, lower price, because of reduced consumption. If, however, the demand is price inelastic, the total revenues will be greater at the higher prices.

The price inelasticity of supply operates in much the same way. If the supply of a commodity is price inelastic, new producers will not (or cannot) enter the market to take advantage of the higher rates of return. If new producers do enter the market, meaning the supply is price elastic, the increased supply will likely drive prices back down, making the foreign exchange earned no greater (and perhaps less) than before. Even if prices do not return to previous levels, producers' monetary receipts will diminish because of the reduced market share each will control. Clearly, then, the price inelasticity of supply is also essential.

OPEC's experience illustrates how important these economic factors are. The crucial role that oil had come to occupy in the world energy picture at the onset of OPEC's assertiveness was apparent by the near absence of any change in global demand following the fourfold increase in the price of oil during the winter of 1973–1974. On the supply side, the long lead time required to develop new petroleum sources (demonstrated by the time required to bring the Alaskan and North Sea finds into production) combined with the absence of energy alternatives to perpetuate dependence on OPEC oil. Eventually both the demand for and supply of oil proved to be more price elastic than most analysts had predicted, as consumers responded to higher prices by reducing consumption and new energy producers entered the marketplace more rapidly than expected. Both forces contributed substantially to the denouement of OPEC's control. But in the immediate aftermath of the first oil shock, supply, like demand, generally proved price inelastic.

How do other commodities compare with oil? In the near term it would appear that many commodity producers could enjoy the benefits of monopoly control, as both demand and supply are sufficiently price inelastic that the producers could enjoy the benefits of increased export earnings if they could cooperate to control prices and output (Krasner, 1974). In the long term, however, the price elasticity of demand for many of the major commodities traded internationally, particularly minerals, is clearly not conducive to effective cartelization (see Varon and Takeuchi, 1974). Three factors capable of altering market conditions are important in explaining this: stockpiles, recycling, and substitutes.

Many commodities are easily stockpiled. The United States, for example, has maintained since 1939 large "strategic stockpiles" of certain minerals. As noted earlier, it now maintains a modest strategic petroleum reserve as well. These inventories give the United States a cushion against foreign producers.

Recycling is another means of affecting commodity supplies. Recovering metal from scrap material is one example; recycling aluminum soft-drink cans is another. Developing recycling capacity may take time, and the resulting product may be comparatively expensive, but the important point is that many minerals are not completely used when they are consumed.

Substitution is a third way to undermine producers' cartels. If aluminum becomes too expensive for making cans, tin can be substituted. If tin becomes too expensive, glass or plastic might be used. Even oil has its substitutes in coal, natural gas, hydropower, and nuclear energy. In the long run, then, there exist few Third World commodities whose potentials for market control are not undermined by simple economic forces.

## Political Factors

What about political factors? Is there some combination of these that might enhance poor countries' bargaining power by increasing the rich countries' fear of them?

Several "political" factors are necessary for translating control over the supply of a commodity (especially nonrenewable resources compared with renewable resources, such as agricultural products) into effective political power (defined as the use of resources to realize political returns, not simply economic or commercial benefits). Three are especially important: (1) *scarcity*—"the global, physical availability of the raw material in question, relative to other natural resources as well as possible substitutes"; (2) *distribution*—"the political and economic character of the market for the specific raw material, its existence in reserve form among the consuming nations, and its pattern of consumption"; and (3) *essentiality*—"the intrinsic importance of the raw material . . . either in security or in economic terms" (Arad and Arad, 1979).

One survey of the applicability of these prerequisites to a range of nonrenewable natural resources concluded that oil was the only resource that met all three criteria (Arad and Arad, 1979; see also Russett, 1984). (Even oil, however, as the experience of the 1980s showed, proved not to meet these three basic requirements.) Several circumstances explain why.

First, many First World countries depend on imports of minerals and other products to sustain their sophisticated economies, but this does not mean they are dependent on Third World exports. Canada is a principal source of many critical U.S. mineral imports, for example. Similarly, other developed countries are suppliers of commodities that enter world trade. Australia is an important producer of bauxite and alumina; South Africa is an important source of manganese, chromium, platinum, and gold; and the republics of the former Soviet Union are important producers of these same four minerals. In fact, most minerals are exported by developed as well as developing countries. This situation is unlikely to change. (The producers of many internationally traded agricultural commodities that enhance the dietary intake of people in the world's rich countries are concentrated in the Third World, but their products fail to meet the criterion of product essentiality.)

Second, because the exporters of many essential products are diverse economically, their prospects for building unified producers' cartels are low. Add to this the fact that many of the principal producers of the minerals traded internationally consist of traditional political rivals. Adversaries seldom cooperate for mutual gain. Hence creating and sustaining effective producers' cartels are very difficult.

Finally, just as many First World countries depend on foreign imports for economic growth, many Third World commodity producers depend on exports to sustain their economies (see Chapter 8). Most, therefore, are risk-averse because they cannot afford to jeopardize losing trade revenues by efforts to cartelize export markets to maximize gains. Indeed, one of the striking lessons from the OPEC experience is that its success depended in large part on the ability of the cartel's key members to bear the brunt of production reductions so as to maintain higher oil prices. This meant that the "swing producers," mainly Saudi Arabia and, less so, Kuwait, had to have enough money (foreign exchange) "in the bank" so as to absorb the costs of production cutbacks.

But the second lesson is more important: OPEC's success as a political force resulted from its most important Arab members' shared political values. It was ideological solidarity that enabled OPEC for a short time to act not simply as another commodity producers' association but as an effective political coalition. Antipathy toward Israel was the unifying value animating the desire of OPEC's most important members to use the oil weapon to its advantage in the long-standing and bitter Middle East conflict. Perhaps more than anything else, this political factor distinguished OPEC from other producers' cartels.

## ECONOMIC SANCTIONS AS INSTRUMENTS OF FOREIGN POLICY . . . . . . . . . . .

When the Arab members of OPEC placed an embargo on the shipment of oil to the United States and the Netherlands in 1973, their purpose, as noted, was to change these countries' policies toward the Arab-Israeli conflict. When the UN Security Council decided in August 1990 that the world organization should cease trade with Iraq, its purpose was to accomplish the immediate and unconditional withdrawal of Iraqi forces from Kuwait. Both are examples of the use of *economic sanctions,* that is, "deliberate government actions to inflict economic deprivation on a target state or society, through the limitation or cessation of customary economic relations" (Leyton-Brown, 1987).

Economic sanctions are part of the broad array of instruments of economic statecraft available to governments (see Baldwin, 1985). An alternative to applying military force, sanctions are enacted to express outrage and to change the target's behavior. Sanctions are increasingly popular. Since World War I, there are observable 120 episodes of foreign policy sanctions, 104 of which were enacted since World War II (Hufbauer, Schott, and Elliott, 1990).

Despite their frequent use, most efforts to apply economic sanctions have failed. This fact has led many policy analysts to question their cost effectiveness (see, for example, Knorr, 1975, 1977). Why is failure so prevalent? And why, then, have economic sanctions "become the weapon of choice in diplomatic confrontation in the wake of the Cold War" (Hoagland, 1993b)? Let us address these questions by looking at some prominent sanctions cases.

## Superpower Sanctions: Three Cases of U.S. Failure

Between 1945 and 1990, when "sanctions [had] become an international fact of life, . . . more than two-thirds were initiated by the United States" (Lopez and Cortright, 1993: 15). Three conspicuous cases of the U.S. application of economic sanctions illustrate their shortcomings: those applied against Castro's Cuba beginning in 1960; against the Soviet Union following its intervention into Afghanistan in 1979; and against Poland and the Soviet Union between 1981 and 1982 following Poland's imposition of martial law in December 1981.

## Cuba

The United States placed sanctions on the Castro regime shortly after it assumed power in 1960. The U.S. began with a cut in the amount of sugar permitted to enter the United States under its quota system. Later the United States extended the sanctions to a full ban on all U.S. trade with Cuba, and it pressured other countries to follow suit. The U.S. goals were twofold. Initially, it sought the overthrow of the Castro government. Failing that, from about 1964 onward the aim was containing the Castro revolution and Cuban interventionism in Central and South America and Africa.

Through mid-1994 the United States remained unsuccessful in securing Castro's overthrow, and prior to then it was only marginally successful in containing Cuba's promotion of revolution abroad. "The major accomplishment of the U.S. economic embargo . . . consisted of increasing the cost to Cuba of surviving and developing as a socialist country and of pursuing an international commitment" (Roca, 1987). Cuba's ability to withstand this pressure from the globe's foremost economic and military power for more than thirty-three years stemmed from several factors. Especially potent was the Soviet Union's prolonged subsidies of "as much as $2–3 billion annually" to Cuba (Elliott, 1993: 35), U.S. inability to persuade its Western allies to curtail trade with and investment in Cuba, and Castro's charismatic leadership and popular support. The U.S. economic sanctions extracted a heavy burden on the target but did not accomplish its political goals. "Our embargo policy has not changed in over 30 years," declared Victor Marreno, the U.S. envoy to the UN General Assembly in November 1993, "because Cuba's repressive regime has not changed." The U.S. did not get its way and was snubbed by its key allies. In a symbolic vote of defiance, in 1993 they voted 88–4 in favor of a UN resolution repudiating the U.S. embargo, asserting that the embargo infringed upon their sovereignty, free trade, and navigation rights. Without support and cooperation from others, the U.S. trade sanctions simply could not succeed.

## The Soviet Union and Afghanistan

Following the Soviet Union's 1979 intervention in Afghanistan, the United States imposed a partial embargo on the sale of grain to the Soviet Union and attempted to organize a boycott of the 1980 Moscow Summer Olympics. Among other aims, the sanctions sought "to punish the Soviet Union while at the same time limiting the damage to the economic interests of important domestic groups" (Falkenheim, 1987).

The grain embargo failed to stop the flow of agricultural produce to the Soviet Union, largely because other countries (principally Argentina) increased their exports to make up the shortfall in U.S. exports. The U.S. sanctions did produce suffering for Soviet citizens, but did not force their leaders to reverse their foreign policy. There were two reasons for this. First, the Soviet economy was then largely self-sufficient, which lessened the impact of trade compression on its economy. Second, because Soviet leaders were determined to resist external pressures, the U.S. sanctions increased their resolve (Falkenheim, 1987).

### The Soviet Union and Poland

Similar lessons apply to Poland. Following the imposition of martial law by the Polish government in 1981 to forestall continued labor unrest, the Reagan administration restricted U.S. government credits for Polish purchase of food and other commodities, banned high-technology exports to Poland, and suspended Poland's most-favored-nation trade status. To stiffen the sanctions' impact, the United States also targeted Poland's patron and primary trade partner, the Soviet Union. The United States restricted the flow of Western goods and technology needed for the trans-Siberian gas pipeline to bring Soviet energy into Western European markets, in the hope also of increasing the economic strains under which both Poland and the Soviet system would have to operate (Marantz, 1987).

The strategy failed to achieve these objectives, however, as the Reagan administration was forced to seek a face-saving compromise with its European allies on the pipeline issue, which permitted its continued construction. The compromise preserved a degree of unity in the Atlantic alliance in the face of the inability of the U.S. sanctions to alter Soviet behavior. The absence of consensus among the NATO allies was itself a factor contributing to the sanctions' failure. Other factors included the Soviet Union's ability and willingness to support its client, namely Poland. Thus in the end the sanctions may have had some liberalizing influence on Poland, but the Soviet Union did not budge.

These examples suggest that a superpower's successful use of economic sanctions faces substantial obstacles. The initiator often pays a high price (lost markets to exporters, increased costs to consumers) and receives a low payoff. In general, the more ambitious the goal, the less successful have been the efforts. "Sanctions are seldom effective in impairing the military potential of an important power, or in bringing about major changes in the policies of the target country" (Hufbauer, Schott, and Elliott, 1990).

Yet, as inventories of the use of economic sanctions indicate, states are increasingly prone to rely on them. The advantages rationalizing their use are suggested by cases that met with relatively greater success.

## Relatively Successful Sanctions: Two Controversial Examples

The utility of economic sanctions as instruments of foreign policy enjoys at best a checkered history. The ability of sanctions to produce policy dividends and the constraints on their use are illustrated by the cases of South Africa and Iraq, respectively.

### South Africa and Apartheid

For many years, the Pretoria regime in South Africa practiced a punitive policy of racial separation known as *apartheid*. To force elimination of this morally unjustifiable practice, the United Nations, at the behest of Third World countries, imposed a voluntary arms embargo against South Africa in 1963, which became "mandatory" in 1977. Later, an oil embargo was imposed on South Africa.

Because U.S. corporations held major investments in South Africa and the United States was a primary importer of the many critical minerals of which South Africa enjoys vast reserves, the U.S. attitude toward South Africa was of special concern to the opponents of apartheid. A frequent argument in the United States during the long years of debate about the appropriate U.S. response to apartheid focused on who would be the targets of internationally applied sanctions: South African blacks, already the victims of a policy of systematic racial discrimination, or the white minority regime who perpetuated apartheid? In 1981, the Reagan administration adopted a policy of "constructive engagement" toward South Africa, whose broad purpose was a soft diplomatic approach to the Pretoria regime. In 1985, however, in an unusual domestic political development, the U.S. Congress legislated, over a presidential veto, harsh mandatory sanctions against South Africa, hoping to change the policies that Congress found objectionable.

Four years later, in 1989, F. W. de Klerk, a reformer, came to power in South Africa. He released Nelson Mandela, leader of the African National Congress (ANC) and a political prisoner for twenty-seven years. De Klerk also lifted the ban on the ANC and other anti-apartheid groups, which opened the door to negotiations on political reforms between the South African government and the ANC. Thus the process of dismantling apartheid finally began and culminated in a historic agreement in 1993 that ended apartheid, restored democracy for all South Africa's citizens, and made possible black majority rule. A new era opened. As trade restrictions were lifted, investors rushed into the vacuum and South Africa rejoined the community of nations. It no longer was an international pariah.

Were the sanctions responsible for setting South Africa on a path toward reform and majority rule? While the sanctions were being applied, analysts' evaluations differed (compare Doxey, 1990, with Claiborne, 1990, and Minter, 1986–1987). But now that apartheid has been officially lifted, most now believe that the sanctions eventually did produce the long-awaited payoff. In this case, the concerted cooperation of many states in combination with the human rights activities of international institutions and nongovernmental organizations throughout the globe produced a return, even if great patience was required before the economic sanctions achieved the political ends sought.

## Iraq and the Crisis over Kuwait

Restraints on the protracted use of economic sanctions for political purposes are illustrated by the 1990 case of Iraq. The first response of the international community to the crisis over Iraq's invasion of Kuwait was the imposition of sanctions. All exports to and imports from Iraq were prohibited except humanitarian shipments of medicine and some food.

> The embargo was designed to cause economic hardship in Iraq that would compel the Iraqi government to withdraw from Kuwait. It also was intended to weaken Iraq militarily

by creating shortages of spare parts, munitions, and fuel and by stalling further progress on its chemical weapons and ballistic missile industries and its pursuit of nuclear weapons. Finally, the United States and its allies hoped that the embargo might foment enough discontent within Iraq to cause the ouster of the Hussein regime. (*The Middle East*, 1991: 321)

In the months that followed, a vigorous debate took place at the United Nations and in various national capitals over the utility of the sanctions. Would they force Saddam Hussein from Kuwait? How long should they be applied before resorting to military power?

Iraq was especially vulnerable to a total embargo because it imported nearly three-quarters of its food and depended almost completely on oil exports for its foreign exchange (*The Middle East*, 1991: 321). Its oil could pass through only two routes, by ship through the Persian Gulf, which was easily blockaded, or overland through pipelines across other countries (see Map 10.1). In December 1990, the director of the U.S. Central Intelligence Agency reported that "more than 90 percent of imports and 97 percent of exports have been shut off." He also reported, however, that "we see no indication that Saddam is concerned at this point that domestic discontent is growing to levels that may threaten his regime or that problems resulting from the sanctions are causing him to rethink his policy on Kuwait. . . . There is no assurance or guarantee that economic hardships will compel Saddam to change his policies or lead to internal unrest that would threaten his regime." Little more than a month later, military power replaced economic sanctions to force Iraq from Kuwait.

During the debate over force and sanctions, two former chairmen of the U.S. Joint Chiefs of Staff urged that sanctions be given a year or more to work. "If in fact the sanctions will work in twelve to eighteen months instead of six months, the trade-off of avoiding war with its attendant sacrifices and uncertainties would, in my view, be worth it," Admiral William J. Crowe testified before the U.S. Congress. Historically, however, sanctions applied over long periods have seldom produced success, the exceptions of the South African and, before it, the Rhodesian racial cases notwithstanding:

> Sanctions imposed slowly or incrementally may simply strengthen the target government at home as it marshals the forces of nationalism. Moreover, such measures are likely to be undercut over time either by the sender's own firms or by foreign competitors. Sanctions are generally regarded as a short-term policy, with the anticipation that normal relations will be reestablished after the resolution of the crisis. Thus, even though popular opinion in the sender country may welcome the introduction of sanctions, the longer an episode drags on, the public support for sanctions dissipates. (Hufbauer, Schott, and Elliott, 1990: 100–101)

Largely for these reasons, and growing concern for how long the coalition against Iraq would hold together, the economic sanctions were abandoned in favor of the use of overwhelming military force. Whether this was wise or foolish remains debatable. But the case illuminates the limits of economic statecraft in crisis circumstances where the need for immediate results is pronounced.

## Why Sanction?

The long and generally unsuccessful history of international economic sanctions lead many critics to conclude that sanctions are a weak tool in statecraft (Elliott, 1993; Førland, 1993). Their arguments reason that

- A typical response to economic coercion in the sanctioned society is a heightened sense of nationalism, a *laager* mentality (circle the wagons to face oncoming enemies), which stimulates resistance in the target state.

- Sanctions sometimes hurt the disempowered people they seek to help. "Sanctions substitute for military action against rulers who have total disregard for the economic hardships faced by their subjects. The logic of the policy [unrealistically] seems to be to make unarmed citizens desperate enough to rise up and throw off brutal regimes that . . . other powers are not willing to use the world's best armies to topple" (Hoagland, 1993b).

- Governments often covertly act to support the sanctioned state even as they profess their support of sanctions publicly.

- "Midsized countries can thwart sanctions, when local dictators are able to quell dissent with a powerful military and divert pain to citizens with no influence" (Hufbauer, 1994).

- The credibility of the state(s) imposing sanctions is often low, given their transparent costs.[6]

- Widespread and sustained cooperation from the international community and international organizations seldom materializes, and unilateral sanctions seldom succeed in an interdependent global marketplace with many competitive suppliers of embargoed goods.

The suitability of sanctions as foreign policy instruments is therefore customarily questioned whenever they are proposed or imposed. (The Clinton administration's 1993 embargo of Haiti to force the ruling junta to step down, of North Korea to dissuade it from building a nuclear bomb, and against the rebel army UNITA in Angola are recent examples.) Critics invariably argue that

> Policymakers often have inflated expectations of what sanctions can and cannot accomplish. . . . At most there is a weak correlation between economic deprivation and political willingness to change. The *economic* impact of sanctions may be pronounced, both on the sender and the target country, but other factors in the situational context almost always overshadow the impact of sanctions in determining the *political* outcome. (Hufbauer, Schott, and Elliott, 1990: 94)

---

[6] It is important to note that sanctions often impose costs on the initiators as well as the targets. Poland, for example, reportedly lost $1 billion in arms sales and construction contracts with Iraq, its main economic partner in the Middle East, as a result of the Iraqi sanctions (Burgess and Auerbach, 1990: 21). Earlier, in the case of the U.S. grain embargo against the Soviet Union, American farmers who depended on exports were especially hard hit by Washington's policies.

If they usually encounter opposition and seldom prove effective, why are "sanctions a New Age growth industry" and increasingly being used (Hoagland, 1993b)?

The most convincing answer resides in the primary purposes underlying policymakers' preferences. Political scientist James M. Lindsay (1986) argues that sanctioning countries' goals fall into five basic categories:

- *compliance* ("to force the target to alter its behavior to conform with the initiator's preferences"), as in the case of the 1982 U.S. embargo of Libya designed to force it to end its support of terrorism;

- *subversion* ("to remove the target's leaders . . . or overthrow the regime"), as in the case of the U.S. trade embargo on Haiti in 1993 and 1994.

- *deterrence* ("to dissuade the target from repeating the disputed action in the future"), as in the case of the Soviet grain embargo by the United States;

- *international symbolism* ("to send messages to other members of the world community"), as in the case of the British sanctions against Rhodesia following its unilateral declaration of independence in 1965; and

- *domestic symbolism* ("to increase its domestic support or thwart international criticism of its foreign policies by acting decisively"), as in the case of U.S. sanctions against Iran following its seizure of U.S. diplomats in 1979.

The cases described earlier suggest that *symbolism* is a primary motivation behind policymakers' decisions to use international economic sanctions. They enable a leader to show leadership without bearing the costs and dangers that other policy options, particularly military force, entail. "When military options are not feasible or desirable and the initiator wants to respond forcefully to the target's behavior, sanctions provide a means of 'doing something'" (Lindsay, 1986).

Whether the "symbolic utility" of economic sanctions in the face of their otherwise "apparent disutility" is a cause for applause or concern may be disputed. "Critics may deride the symbolic uses of trade sanctions as empty gestures, but symbols are important in politics. This is especially so when inaction can signal weakness and silence can mark complicity" (Lindsay, 1986).

Thus, economic sanctions often fail to achieve the most visible aims for which they are implemented:

> Although sanctions were successful . . . in 34 percent of 115 cases [between 1914 and 1989] (the overall U.S. success rate was 32 percent), success has become increasingly elusive in recent years. . . . The success rate among [46] cases begun after 1973 was a little less than 26 percent. Even more striking is the decline in the effectiveness of sanctions imposed in pursuit of modest goals—mostly sought by the United States—which plummetted from 75 percent to 21 percent. (Elliott, 1993: 34)

Nonetheless, sanctions serve important functions. They provide a policy alternative to the use of force to publicize and condemn unacceptable behavior and intolerable situations, and thereby to express outrage and make it appear that something is being done. And under particular conditions "sanctions work—if imposed by a major power against a much weaker, unstable, and economically dependent foe with no friends among the rival powers" (Elliott, 1993). "Sanctions can be used to deter aggression, defend human rights, and discourage nuclear proliferation" (Lopez and Cortright, 1993). For these reasons we can expect sanctions to remain popular.

## TOWARD THE FUTURE

Although economic sanctions often fall short of the objectives their proponents seek, they will continue to be used as instruments of foreign policy when states seek to register protest and force compliance by means short of military force (Martin, 1993). They are increasingly used multilaterally with the cooperation of many countries, especially through the United Nations. The 1993–1994 UN oil embargo against Libya to pressure it to release two suspects in the 1988 terrorist bombing of a jetliner over Lockerbie, Scotland, is exemplary. Resource power is an attractive instrument for countries to influence one another. A world interdependent economically multiplies the opportunities to use economic instruments. Yet interdependence produces vulnerability to disruptions in external economic exchanges on which most states' economic welfare depends. This means that the resort to resource power will result in domestic disruptions—a cost leaders will often be reluctant to bear.

Among Third World countries, the euphoria that once greeted OPEC's efforts to convert resource power into political leverage has dissipated. States that once thought of reliance on commodity exports as a form of dependence viewed OPEC's experience as a demonstration that commodity cartels might enable them to use their very dependence as a form of strength. That idea has proved illusory. Still, commodity associations of one form or another may be pursued by developing countries as they seek to cope with their underdog status in the global pecking order, and they may cause disruptions in various national economies as well as the global marketplace (Spero, 1990). The oil supply and price disruptions that began with the OPEC decade suggest that if a future oil crisis occurs, as some predict it will (Stanislaw and Yergin, 1993), the disruptions could be great.

The world's present crisis-prone energy environment, characterized by dependence on fossil fuels, is being forced in new directions by three major considerations.

The first is the availability of fossil fuels, particularly the most economic and versatile one—petroleum. The constraint is not the global resource base but the geographical and political limits of having nearly two-thirds of the world's current oil reserves in the Persian Gulf region.

The second limit is environmental—the capacity of the world to cope with the overwhelming burden of pollution that is emitted by a $20-trillion world economy run on fossil fuels. The most intractable load is the nearly 6 billion tons of carbon added to the atmosphere each year. As no technical fix appears likely for this problem, slowing global warming will mean placing limits on fossil fuel combustion.

The third constraint is social and political. In recent years, citizens around the globe have rebelled against the energy "solutions" their governments pursued. . . . Political leaders around the world are beginning to realize that people's passionate concerns cannot be swept aside by a tide of technocratic policymaking. (Flavin and Lenssen, 1991: 21–22)

These constraints will become more severe as we move toward the dawn of the twenty-first century and a postpetroleum world. The shape of that future remains clouded nonetheless, as the disjointed energy policies and practices of the world's countries often work at cross-purposes in an increasingly interdependent world, both economically and ecologically. The challenge of preparing for a postpetroleum world alongside sustainable development is not to be underestimated. The welfare of humanity is at stake, and attractive solutions are not available.

## SUGGESTED READINGS

Arad, Ruth W., et al. *Sharing Global Resources*. New York: McGraw-Hill, 1979.

Bromley, Simon. *American Hegemony and World Oil*. University Park, Penn.: Penn State University Press, 1991.

Castles, Stephen, and Mark J. Miller. *The Age of Migration: International Population Movements in the Modern World*. New York: Guilford, 1993.

Ebinger, Charles K. *The Critical Link: Energy and National Security in the 1980s*. Cambridge, Mass.: Ballinger, 1982.

Flavin, Christopher, and Nicholas Lenssen. "Reshaping the Power Industry," pp. 61–80 in Lester R. Brown et al., *State of the World 1994*. New York: Norton, 1994.

Førland, Tor Egil. "The History of Economic Warfare: International Law, Effectiveness, Strategies," *Journal of Peace Research* 30 (May 1993): 151–162.

Fried, Edward, and Philip Trezise. *Oil Security: Retrospect and Prospect*. Washington, D.C.: Brookings Institution, 1994.

Hufbauer, Gary Clyde, Jeffrey J. Schott, and Kimberly Ann Elliott. *Economic Sanctions Reconsidered: History and Current Policy*, 2nd edition. Washington, D.C.: Institute for International Economics, 1990.

Martin, Lisa L. *Coercive Cooperation: Explaining Multilateral Economic Sanctions*. Princeton, N.J.: Princeton University Press, 1992.

Odell, Peter R. *Oil and World Power*. New York: Penguin, 1983.

Stanislaw, Joseph, and Daniel Yergin. "Oil: Reopening the Door," *Foreign Affairs* 72 (September–October 1993): 81–93.

Youngquist, Walter. *Mineral Resources and the Destinies of Nations*. Portland, Ore.: National Book Company, 1990.

# Part IV

# Providing for the Common Defense

. . .

# CHAPTER 11

• • •

# THE MILITARY QUEST FOR NATIONAL SECURITY: ARMS AND THE CHANGING CHARACTER OF POWER

• • •

*The adversaries of the world are not in conflict because they are armed. They are armed because they are in conflict and have not yet learned peaceful ways to resolve their conflicting national interests.*

Richard M. Nixon,
U.S. President, 1969

*The changes of recent years allow us to be hopeful. But common sense reminds us that we must be prepared . . . to ensure that we shall achieve decisive victory should we be called to battle once again. . . . Just as our security cannot rest on a hollow army, neither can it rest upon a hollow economy.*

Bill Clinton,
U.S. President, 1993

The pervasive sense of fear that permeates world politics explains why states are preoccupied with threats to their security and why providing for the common defense is such a priority. Because the anarchical international system requires that states rely on themselves for protection, *national security*—a country's psychological freedom from fear of foreign attack—is a paramount value. Without the ability to ensure survival, all other values are vulnerable. Thus policymakers typically assign national security the most prominent place on their foreign policy agendas.

In this chapter we examine why states feel threatened by others and how they respond to those threats. We begin with the *security dilemma* states face and follow this with an examination of *power* and how it relates to military preparedness and other capabilities. We then consider states' practices designed to diminish threats to their national security. Specifically, we will examine trends in military spending, the arms trade, and weapons technology, and their probable consequences. We will also explore states' military strategies and doctrines for offense (compellence) and defense (deterrence).

• • •

## The Security Dilemma . . . . . . . . . . . . . . . . . . . . . . . . . . . . . . .

What breeds the competition that propels the search for security through preparations for war? In the eighteenth century Jean-Jacques Rousseau argued that "the state . . . always feels itself weak if there is another that is stronger. Its security and preservation demand that it make itself more powerful than its neighbors. It can increase, nourish and exercise its power only at their expense. . . . Because the grandeur of the state is purely relative it is forced to compare itself to that of the others. . . . It becomes small or great, weak or strong, according to whether its neighbor expands or contracts, becomes stronger or declines."

Concern for relative power derives from the fact that states want many of the same things—self-preservation, national identity, freedom from others' control, status, and wealth. They seek these in anarchical conditions that afford scarce protection from the hostile designs of others. Believing their own strength will make them secure, many states attempt to build as much military might as their resources allow. They often compete with one another for position in the rank of states' military capabilities.

Although states ostensibly arm for defensive purposes, others perceive their military might as threatening. Alarmed, their neighbors are provoked to arm in response. Thus, as Rousseau observed, security is a relative phenomenon. Such fear and its reciprocated behaviors create a predicament known as the *security dilemma* (Herz, 1951).

Some scholars also describe this syndrome as the *spiral model* (Jervis, 1976). The imagery is apt, as it captures the tendency of defense-enhancing efforts to result in escalating arms races, which diminish the security of all. Sir Edward Grey described this process well:

> The increase in armaments, that is intended in each nation to produce consciousness of strength, and a sense of security, does not produce these effects. On the contrary, it produces a consciousness of the strength of other nations and a sense of fear. Fear begets suspicion and distrust and evil imaginings of all sorts, till each government feels it would be criminal and a betrayal of its own country not to take every precaution, while every government regards every precaution of every other government as evidence of hostile intent. (Grey, 1925: 92)

As noted, insecurity for all is the unintended result of arms competition. The irony is that no state consciously seeks this unanticipated outcome. Indeed, even without the desire or intention to attack another, fear still prevails.

> None can be sure that others' intentions are peaceful, or will remain so; hence each must maintain power for defense. Since no state can know that the power accumulation of others is defensively motivated only, each must assume that it might be intended for attack. Consequently, each party's power increments are matched by the others, and all wind up with no more security than when the vicious cycle began, along with the costs incurred in having acquired and having to maintain their power. (Snyder, 1984: 461)

Despite the security dilemma that affects all states, leaders still refuse to accept vulnerability and therefore search for strength. They often proceed from the assumptions that (1) security is a function of power, (2) power is a function of military capability, and (3) military might is a measure of national greatness. Each of these assumptions is, of course, consistent with the logic of realpolitik.

Reformers in the neoliberal tradition (recall Chapter 2) question the logic that causes states to engage in the behavior that creates and sustains the security dilemma. To them, "the central theme of international relations is not evil but tragedy. States often share a common interest, but the structure of the situation prevents them from bringing about the mutually desired situation" (Jervis, 1976).

To escape this predicament, liberal reformers call for changes in customary approaches to the problem of national security. Seeing weapons as "indefensible" (Lifton and Falk, 1982), they argue that unarmed or defenseless countries enjoy a flexibility in their foreign policies that their armed neighbors do not. They are freed from the responsibilities that (military) power imposes and do not have to incur the costs of acquiring it. Although they might have to live in the constant shadow of others' missiles, they can take comfort in knowing that they are not the targets of the missiles. Appropriate in this context is U.S. President John F. Kennedy's sober warning that, in the event of another total war, regardless of how it might begin, those most heavily armed would automatically become the primary targets and victims of annihilation.

Not surprisingly, realists are less than sanguine about the idealists' views. Even if leaders and defense planners recognize the threats that arming for security provokes in others, they argue that international anarchy requires that these threats be borne. Since, by definition, there is no escaping a dilemma, the security dilemma explains why states sharing a common interest in security nonetheless engage in individual actions that prevent them from realizing it. Yet, *insecurity* is often the product of their actions.

## POWER IN INTERNATIONAL POLITICS . . . . . . . . . . . . . . . . . . . . . . . . . .

What is this abstraction called *power*, the quest for which political realists depict as states' primary motive? Although definitions abound, power remains an ambiguous concept (see Baldwin, 1989; Claude, 1962; Rothgeb, 1993).

Most leaders assume that power will give them the ability to promote and protect their countries' national interests, to win in bargaining situations, and to shape the rules governing the international system. From this perspective, power is a *political* phenomenon. It manifests itself in the ability of one actor to persuade another to do what it otherwise would not do. Thus, power is the ability to exercise influence. Some also equate power with coercion, and others see influence as manipulation (which is perhaps why politics is often regarded as "dirty"). Indeed, to say that states pursue power is to say that they seek to control and dominate others.

When we view power as the means to control, it is reasonable to ask, Who is stronger and who is weaker? and Who will get their way and who will give in? These invite the more fundamental question: What enables states to achieve their goals?

## The Elements of National Power

To ascertain the comparative power of states, analysts usually rank them according to the kinds of capabilities or resources presumed necessary to attain influence over others. For such purposes, multiple factors measure countries' relative *power potential*. If we could weigh comparatively each state's total capabilities, according to this logic, we could then rank states according to their ability to draw on these resources to exercise influence. Such a ranking would reveal the international system's hierarchy of power, differentiating the strong from the weak, the great from the nongreat.

Of all the components of national power, military capability is usually thought to be the most important. Political realists in particular regard it as the central element in states' power potential. "Throughout history, the decisive factor in the fates of nations has usually been the number, efficiency and dispositions of fighting forces," they argue. "National influence bears a direct relationship to gross national strength; without that, the most exquisite statesmanship is likely to be of limited use" (German, 1960). Because realists assume that the ability to coerce is more important than the ability to reward or to purchase, they believe that military capability is more important than economic capability as a source of power. Against this, other strategic thinkers argue that in the wake of the Cold War, economic competition will be more critical to national strength than military competition and that accordingly the economic foundations of national security should receive primary emphasis (Sandholtz et al., 1992).

Figure 11.1 presents two parallel rankings of the world's twenty most powerful states as seen from the vantage point of their military spending and the size of their armed forces. Both rankings conform to what most people would likely regard as the world's most "powerful" states, but it is instructive to observe the differences in the position of the great powers in these two rankings. Expenditures for defense produce a hierarchy different from that in the great power's armed forces.

In addition to military expenditures and the number of soldiers, power potential also derives from such factors as the size of a state's economy, population and territorial size, geographic position, raw materials, degree of dependence on foreign sources of materials, technological capacity, national character, ideology, efficiency of governmental decision making, industrial productivity, volume of trade, savings and investment, educational level, and national morale and internal solidarity.

There is, however, no consensus on how best to weigh these factors, what their relative importance should be in making country comparisons, or what conditions affect the contribution that each makes in the equation that converts capabilities into influence. Most analysts agree that states are not equal in their ability to influence others, but few agree on how to rank their power potential. Consider, for example, the divergent pictures of the global hierarchy that are produced when the relative capabilities of the great powers are ranked in still other categories that realists define as the most important (see Table 11.1).

Clearly, strength is relative. The leading countries in some dimensions of power potential are not leaders in others. Power comes in many forms. The factors that produce it are varied, and the contributions vary across different circumstances.

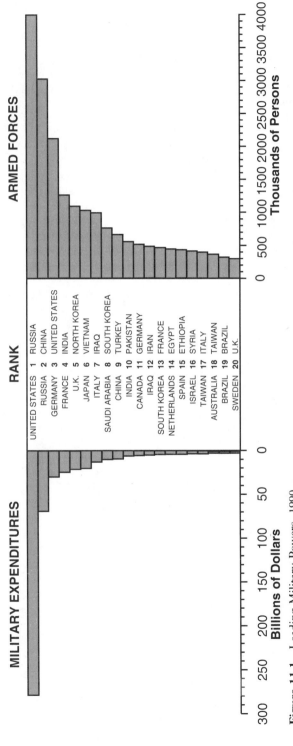

**Figure 11.1** Leading Military Powers, 1990
*Source:* Based on data summarized by Ruth Leger Sivard (1993: 43–45).
*Note:* Military spending is in 1987 constant dollars and exchange rates.

TABLE 11.1 THE POWER POTENTIAL OF THE GREAT POWERS: RANKINGS ACROSS MAJOR DIMENSIONS

| Territorial Size (thousand square km) | | Population (projected for 2010) (millions) | |
| --- | --- | --- | --- |
| 1. Russia | 17,075 | 1. China | 1,135.06 |
| 2. Canada | 9,970 | 2. India | 1,123.48 |
| 3. China | 9,561 | 3. Russia | 327.06 |
| 4. United States | 9,373 | 4. United States | 280.92 |
| 5. Brazil | 8,512 | 5. Indonesia | 246.60 |
| 6. Australia | 7,686 | 6. Brazil | 207.45 |
| 7. India | 3,288 | 7. Pakistan | 205.50 |
| 8. Argentina | 2,767 | 8. Nigeria | 201,27 |
| 9. Kazakhstan | 2,717 | 9. Bangladesh | 188.20 |
| 10. Sudan | 2,506 | 10. Japan | 131.04 |

| Gross National Product, 1992 ($ billions) | | Scientists and Engineers in Research as Percent of World | |
| --- | --- | --- | --- |
| 1. United States | 5,946 | 1. Russia | 19.8 |
| 2. Japan | 3,666 | 2. United States | 18.2 |
| 3. Germany | 1,775 | 3. Japan | 12.2 |
| 4. France | 1,270 | 4. Germany | 5.6 |
| 5. Italy | 1,222 | 5. India | 2.3 |
| 6. United Kingdom | 1,048 | 6. France | 2.2 |
| 7. Spain | 578 | 7. United Kingdom | 2.0 |
| 8. Canada | 569 | 8. Italy | 1.4 |
| 9. China | 434 | 9. Czechoslovakia | 1.3 |
| 10. Russia | 400 | 10. Canada | 1.2 |

*Sources:* Territory, U.S. CIA (1993); population, *The Economist* (1992: 14); GNP, International Institute for Strategic Studies (1993); scientists, Hughes (1994: 82).

## Inferring Power from Capabilities

Part of the difficulty of defining the elements of power is that their potential impact depends on the circumstances in a bargaining situation between actors in conflict and especially on how leaders perceive those circumstances. Such judgments are subjective rather than concrete, as power ratios are not strictly products of measured capabilities. Perceptions matter more.

In addition, power is not a tangible commodity that states can acquire. It has meaning only in terms of others. Power is relational—a state can have power over some other actor only when it can prevail over that actor. Both actual and perceived strength determine who wins in a political contest. To make a difference, an adversary must know its enemy's capabilities and willingness to mobilize them for coercive purposes. It must regard the opponent's threat to use military capabilities as credible, for example. Intentions—and especially perceptions of them—are critically important in this respect. The mere possession of weapons does not increase a state's power if its adversaries do not believe they will be used.

Noteworthy in this context is that, historically, those with the largest arsenals have not necessarily prevailed in political conflicts. Weaker states often successfully resist pressure from their military superiors. A Vietnam that was weak in the conventional military sense succeeded against a vastly stronger France and, later, the United States. An armada of U.S. missiles and bombers capable of inflicting horrendous destruction did not prevent the emergence of a communist government in Cuba only ninety miles from U.S. shores. And superior military power did not prevent seizure of the USS *Pueblo* by North Korea in 1968 or the taking of American diplomats as hostages by Iran a decade later.

Similarly, the Soviet Union's inability, prior to its disintegration, to control political events in Afghanistan, or in its Eastern European satellite empire, or even over its own constituent republics, despite its awesome weapons arsenal, shows that the impotence of military power is not peculiar to the United States. In these and other important instances, so-called second-rate military powers have exerted more influence over the great powers than the great powers have over them. A military power—however strong—is simply not able to dominate weaker states at will.

Despite these caveats, the quest for security through arms and the belief in the utility of military force remain widespread. Most policymakers assume that "while it could be a mistake to assume that political influence is proportional to military strength, it would be an even bigger mistake to deny any connection between the two" (Majeed, 1991). The reason, many believe, is that military capability is a prerequisite to the successful exercise of **coercive diplomacy**, that is, the employment of "threats or limited force to persuade an opponent to call off or undo an encroachment" (Craig and George, 1990). The link between military power and foreign policy has not been severed by the end of Cold War hostility; in fact, it may be "more pervasive and more comprehensive than in earlier periods of history when war was less dangerous" (Majeed, 1991). Perhaps it was this conviction that inspired U.S. President Bill Clinton in May 1993 to assert to the graduating class at West Point that "We have to ensure that the United States is ready, ready to win and superior to all other military forces in the world."

## The Changing Nature of World Power

Military power is central in leaders' conceptualizations of national security. As noted in previous chapters, however, many analysts now argue that "the sources of power are, in general, moving away from the emphasis on military force and conquest that marked earlier eras. In assessing international power today, factors such as technology, education, and economic growth are becoming more important, whereas geography, population, and raw materials are becoming less important" (Nye, 1990). In part this is because military force has often proven ineffectual against certain forces, notably not just belligerent revisionist states but also politically mobilized nationalist and aggressive ethnic movements. Even more so, awareness of the importance of trade competitiveness to national standing has commanded increasing attention to the non-military dimensions of national security.

Economics figure prominently in much of this new thinking. Traditionally, military power was viewed as the basis for the acquisition of wealth, rather than vice versa. That is, military capabilities enabled states to practice imperialism as they colonized foreign territory. Military might also historically allowed states to project power abroad and enhance their leverage over others, thus permitting them to gain economic resources. Now, however, economic capability is viewed increasingly as being as important as military power (Friedberg, 1993). On some issues, at least, the capacity to mobilize capital and resources clearly contributes to the capacity to compete successfully for position in the global hierarchy. Japan's rise to influence as the world's preeminent trading state stands out in this regard.

Political scientist Richard Rosecrance (1986) compares military-political and trade strategies as alternative methods for realizing national security. Increasingly, he argues, the latter has been more effective as a strategy toward political power and material advancement. "Since 1945 a few nations have borne the crushing weight of military expenditure," he observes, "while others have gained a relative advantage by becoming military free-riders who primarily rely on the security provided by others. While the United States spent nearly 50 percent of its research and development budget on arms, Japan devoted 99 percent to civilian production."

In addition to sacrificing other economic opportunities, Rosecrance continues, military spending has direct costs because expensive equipment quickly becomes outdated in the face of rapid technological innovations. Tanks routinely cost $2 million or more per copy, but their capacity is doubtful against modern technology. This creates the need for even more sophisticated and expensive new weapons. Their costs are staggering. The estimated cost to produce the Trident II missile was "a cool $40 billion" (Sivard, 1991: 64), and the new weapons in the 1994 U.S. budget include the F-22 fighter ($2.3 billion), the C-17 transport plane ($3.2 billion) (*The Defense Monitor* 21 [No. 3, 1993]: 2), and the B-2 Stealth bomber ($2.3 billion per plane) (Sivard, 1993: 56). Thus the substantial costs of defense can erode what policymakers hope to defend with military might. Commercial clout and trade competitiveness for national exports may contribute more to national power in a world in which trade bloc competition replaces the military and diplomatic struggles of the past. This thesis is a troublesome idea to which we will return below.

In addition to economic capability, other, less tangible sources of national power now figure more prominently in calculations regarding national defense. "Political leaders and philosophers have long understood that power comes from setting the agenda and determining the framework of a debate. The ability to establish preferences tends to be associated with intangible power resources such as culture, ideology, and institutions." These intangible resources constitute *soft power,* in contrast with the *hard power* "usually associated with tangible resources like military and economic strength" (Nye, 1990). If soft power grows in relative importance, military force ratios will no longer translate into power potential in the way that they once did.

## THE QUEST FOR MILITARY CAPABILITIES . . . . . . . . . . . . . . . . . . . . .

How people spend their money reveals their values. Similarly, how governments allocate their revenues reveals their priorities. Examination of national budgets discloses an unmistakable pattern. Although the sources of world political power may be changing, nearly all states seek security by spending substantial portions of their national treasures on arms.

### Trends in Military Spending

The commitment to purchase military protection is nearly universal, as many countries spend huge amounts of national wealth for arms and armies. Globally, an estimated $767 billion was spent on military preparedness in 1994. This reflects a decline of 3.6 percent annually between 1987, the peak year when global arms spending reached $995 billion, and 1991. The 1991 figure of $855 billion after adjusting for inflation is still 2.6 times that spent in 1960, 1.8 times that of the 1970 outlay, and 1.2 times the 1980 outlay (UNDP, 1994: 48; Sivard, 1993: 42).

Increases in military spending were especially evident during the 1980s, but on closer inspection it is apparent that they merely continued trends in place throughout the twentieth century. Military spending has increased fifteenfold since the mid-1930s, for example, a rate of growth exceeding the growth of world population, the global economy, and even prices since that time (Sivard, 1991).

Historically the rich countries spent the most money on arms acquisitions.[1] The pattern continues today. The industrial countries spent an estimated $630 billion for defense in 1995, in contrast with the developing countries' $114 billion (UNDP, 1994: 48). Thus the developed countries' share of the world total is more than 85 percent. When measured as a proportion of gross domestic product, the developing countries in 1991 spent 3.5 percent on military preparedness, in contrast to the developed countries' 3.4 percent; in 1960 the percentages were 4.2 and 6.3 percent, respectively (UNDP, 1994: 171) (for other estimates, see also Figure 11.2).

---

[1] The United States, for example, spent nearly $3 trillion on defense in the 1980s, or $45,000 for each American household (Sivard, 1991: 3). The end of the Cold War has not reduced this level, even though the national debt of $4.4 trillion—an uncomfortable 4.1 percent of gross domestic product when Clinton became president—exerts pressure for reductions in military spending. As former U.S. Assistant Secretary of Defense Lawrence J. Korb (1993: A13) observed, under the Clinton plan "the Pentagon will spend almost as much as the rest of the world combined on defense and about 85 percent of the level it spent on average during the Cold War." President Clinton has proposed raising the military budget in 1995 "and wants more money than originally planned in the following four years"—a proposal that would permit the military to take "as much as all the rest put together" for discretionary spending (Center for Defense Information Press Release, April 1994).

Although the leading military powers are among the largest and wealthiest countries (see also Figure 11.1 and Table 11.1), the drive to arm militarily is widespread, as the developing countries now mimic the budgetary habits of the rich. Third World military expenditures accounted for 6 percent of the world's total in 1955, but the proportion grew to 15 percent by 1989; "at its height in the late 1970s and early 1980s, Third World military expenditure was some 20 percent of the world total" (Ball, 1994: 217). It is expected by the year 2000 to remain at almost that proportion (UNDP, 1994: 48). Third World military spending has increased sixfold since 1960 (in constant dollars). This exceeds the growth in world military expenditures generally. In 1990, the military expenditures of developing countries was 69 percent larger than their combined education and health expenditures (UNDP, 1993: 205), even though by 1994 in those countries "the chances of dying from social neglect (from malnutrition and preventable disease) are 33 times greater than the chances of dying from external aggression" (UNDP, 1994: 50).

The developing countries' military spending is extremely high given their poverty. The result has been a disproportionately high size of Third World armies. Between 1960 and 1991, the armed forces of the developed world remained relatively constant at a little more than 10 million, but the total in the developing world nearly doubled, growing from 8.4 to 15.9 million—or more than three-fifths of the world total (Sivard, 1993: 42).

## Changes in Military Capabilities

The growing militarization of the Third World manifests itself in other ways. Military capabilities are now more widely spread than ever. "The most striking geostrategic phenomenon of the past few decades," political scientist Michael Klare (1990a) posits, "is the extraordinary diffusion of war-making capabilities from the industrial North to the largely agrarian South. Nations which as recently as 1970 were equipped with a few obsolete tanks and subsonic aircraft, acquired as gifts from the major powers, [now have] large numbers of modern aircraft, tanks, and missiles." Parallel developments in the international arms trade and in the destructiveness of modern weapons underlie this diffusion.

### Changes in the Arms Trade

Kenneth N. Waltz (1975) observes that "states imitate the military innovations contrived by the country of greatest capability and ingenuity. And so the weapons of major contenders, and even their strategies, begin to look much the same all over the world." The international trade in arms, spurred by developing countries' energetic search for armaments commensurate with those of the industrial countries, has fueled the diffusion of military capability throughout the globe. In 1989, 120 countries were recipients of at least $5 million worth of imported weapons (Klare, 1994: 137).

Growth in the value of arms sales attests to the present character of arms trafficking. In 1960 weapons exports were valued at $2.4 billion (Sivard, 1991: 50). By 1991, they had become a $45-billion-a-year business (Pearlstein, 1991: 8). The 1980s witnessed a

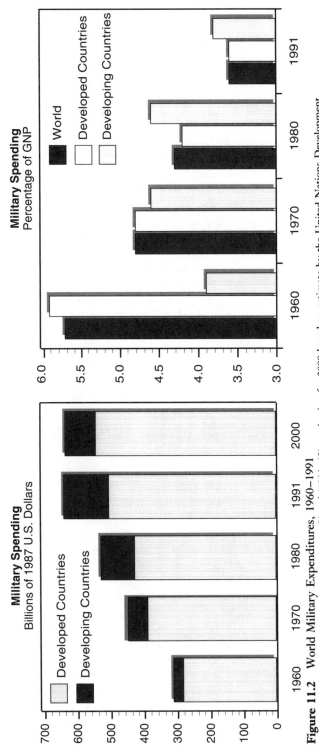

**Military Spending**
Percentage of GNP

World
Developed Countries
Developing Countries

6.0
5.5
5.0
4.5
4.0
3.5
3.0

1960     1970     1980     1991

**Military Spending**
Billions of 1987 U.S. Dollars

Developed Countries
Developing Countries

700
600
500
400
300
200
100
0

1960   1970   1980   1991   2000

**Figure 11.2   World Military Expenditures, 1960–1991**
*Source:* Based on data presented by Ruth Legar Sivard (1993: 42); projection for 2000 based on estimate by the United Nations Development Programme (1994: 48).

slight dip in the upward trend in arms sales, but the surge in new spending following the Persian Gulf War dispelled any notion that a permanent reduction in arms trafficking was in the offing. "As 1992 came to a close, it appeared that global arms sales were headed toward record levels," above the average "of $40–50 billion per year" (Klare, 1994: 136, 134).

As noted, the developing countries have been the leading market for the traffic in arms, accounting since the late 1970s for three-fourths of all trade. They purchased an estimated $430.6 billion in armaments between 1980 and 1992 (U.S. Arms Control and Disarmament Agency [hereafter, ACDA], 1992: 89; *The Defense Monitor* 22 [No. 9, 1993]: 3), including a diverse range of sophisticated equipment. Today, in the face of fierce competition among an expanding number of suppliers, some of the world's most advanced weapons enter the marketplace. Sales during the 1980s included 11,000 tanks and self-propelled cannon, 20,000 artillery pieces, 3,100 supersonic combat aircraft, 37,000 surface-to-air missiles, and 540 warships and submarines (Klare, 1990c: 45).

The sale of advanced technologies is also now commonplace. This permits Third World states themselves to manufacture sophisticated weapons either for their own use or for export to others. The spread of ballistic missiles is one result. In 1992, twenty-three countries had developed the capacity to deliver warheads on foreign targets by rockets reaching fifty miles or more into the atmosphere (*Bulletin of Atomic Scientists* 48 [March 1992]: 31).

**ARMS IMPORTERS** As noted, three-quarters of transnational arms shipments are imported by the less developed South. But the recipients are not spread evenly throughout the Third World. "Just fifteen countries—Afghanistan, Angola, Cuba, Egypt, Ethiopia, India, Iran, Iraq, Israel, Libya, Saudi Arabia, Syria, Taiwan, Turkey, and Vietnam—accounted for 72 percent of all Third World arms imports in the 1985–89 period" (Klare, 1994: 141).

High levels of arms imports have been a continuing characteristic of Middle Eastern countries. In 1967 they accounted for 11 percent of world arms imports; by 1989 the proportion had mushroomed to 33 percent. Alongside the strife-torn Middle East, South Asia and the Far East also account for a disproportionate share of the total arms traffic (Klare, 1994: 141). The concentrations reflect a combination of security concerns and economic developments.

Economically, the surge in world oil prices following OPEC's price shocks in the 1970s enabled the Middle Eastern oil exporters to buy virtually anything they wished. The drop in world oil prices in the 1980s undermined their ability to continue their arms splurge, but the Middle East remains an important recipient region. In 1988 five of the world's top six arms-importing states were in the Middle East: Afghanistan, Iran, Iraq, Israel, and Saudi Arabia (ACDA, 1990: 10).

Strategically, the Middle East was the locus of intense strife and chronic national security problems. It still includes many pairs of competitive states. In the wake of the Persian Gulf War and the 1993 Israeli-Palestine peace accord, rivalries remain between Egypt and Libya, Iran and Iraq, Iran and Saudi Arabia, Iraq and Kuwait, Iraq and Syria, Iraq and Turkey, and Israel and Syria. These states' participation in the global arms market have continued; since the invasion of Kuwait in August 1990 (and July 1993), arms exports to the Middle East from a single supplier, the United States, exceeded $38 billion (Sivard, 1993: 19). In addition, some newly prominent buyers have joined the rush, such as Kuwait and the United Arab Emirates. "Pakistan, which faces a military buildup in both India to its east and Iran to its west, is also likely to increase its arms spending in the years ahead" (Klare, 1994).

It is also possible to predict other areas of activity in the purchases of arms:

> Aside from the Middle East and South Asia, the area that is likely to experience the largest gains in military procurement in the 1990s is East Asia. Here too, the combination of means and motives is critical: the Pacific Rim area harbors some of the world's most vigorous economies (notably those in China, Japan, Malaysia, Singapore, South Korea, Taiwan, and Thailand) as well as some of its most intractable disputes (e.g., those between China and Taiwan, North Korea and South Korea, Thailand and Vietnam). And while the 1990s have brought an increase in trade between these countries, all continue to harbor suspicions about the long-range intentions of their more powerful neighbors and thus have placed great stress on the modernization of their military capabilities. It is likely, therefore, that South Korea, Singapore, and Thailand will join Taiwan on the list of major arms recipients in the later 1990s. (Klare, 1994: 142)

Thus, a shift from the Middle East to Asia in the composition of arms purchasers is under way. In 1992

> Middle East countries bought 22 percent of "major" armaments sold worldwide. . . . However, Asia's share since 1988 has been the largest—approximately 35 percent of all sales of major conventional arms. . . . This shift is particularly significant [because] Asia encompasses more continuing major confrontations than any other region: India-Pakistan, China-Vietnam, China-Taiwan, China-India, North and South Korea, as well as internal strife in Afghanistan, Sri Lanka, Myanmar (Burma), India, and Indonesia-Timor, to name just the major flash points. (*The Defense Monitor* 22 [No. 9, 1993]: 3)

Hence, Asia is likely to be an active arms consumer in the years ahead, if the distribution and identity of purchasers in 1992 continue. At that time six countries—Taiwan, Saudi Arabia, Kuwait, Egypt, Israel, and the United Arab Emirates—ranked in the "top ten both in current arms deliveries and in contracting for new purchases, [and] every nation in the list [was] in either the Middle East or Asia" (*The Defense Monitor* 22 [No. 9, 1993]: 3).

**ARMS EXPORTERS**  In 1963 the United States and the Soviet Union supplied four-fifths of world arms transfers, but by the 1970s they began to face competition from other great powers, notably, Britain, France, Italy, and West Germany. Still, the superpowers continued to dominate the market. Between 1975 and 1990 their share of global arms exports varied between one-half and three-quarters, and in that period the two superpowers together "supplied an estimated $325 billion worth of arms and ammunition to the Third World" (Klare, 1994: 139).

Since the demise of the Soviet Union, the United States has recaptured its position as the "arms merchant of the world" (a phrase used by U.S. President Jimmy Carter to deplore what he sometimes regarded as an unsavory business), as it now "takes the lion's share of arms deals around the world" (Grier, 1994). In fact, the United States has aggressively expanded its sale of military supplies and lined up customers. In 1992 President Bush negotiated a $6 billion sale of 150 F-16 fighter aircraft to Taiwan, a $9 billion sale of F-15 fighters to Saudi Arabia, a $4 billion sale of 256 M-1A2 Abrams tanks to Kuwait, and numerous other high-ticket items to others. Not to be outmatched, the other major arms suppliers announced new sales agreements. "However, the U.S. not only took over the lead in arms sales, it also accounted for approximately 50 percent of all new reported arms agreements for 1991 and 57 percent for 1992." U.S.-approved future arms sale contracts to all recipients totaled $63 billion in 1991, $31.2 billion in 1992, and $35.3 billion in 1993, thus assuring no reduction in the U.S. arms traffic (*The Defense Monitor* 22 [No. 9, 1993]: 3). The total arms actually delivered to just the Third World countries by the major suppliers exceeded $85.5 billion between 1988 and 1992 (SIPRI, 1993: 444); as Table 11.2 illuminates, the future arms sales already under contract assure that the arms trade will remain sizable.

Although the four major suppliers dominate the global arms market, the number of new suppliers has grown steadily, as many developing countries now produce arms for export. The latter's share of world arms exports grew from 4 percent in 1979 to 10 percent in 1989 (ACDA, 1992: 15). By 1990 more than sixty states had entered the business of "peddling arms" (Sivard, 1991: 11). Still, most of these were small producers struggling for a share of the lucrative conventional armaments trade.

A consequence of the increased competition for arms markets is that export controls have been relaxed. The new United Nations Register of Conventional Arms monitors exports and imports of eighty countries but does not curb them. Moreover, the illicit export of Western nuclear, ballistic missile, and chemical weapons technology has not abated. Diversification of suppliers has ended many supplier–consumer ties that earlier had cemented patron–client diplomatic relationships. Every supplier, it seems, is now eager to sell to any purchaser. In 1992 Russia sold $1.2 billion of its military hardware to China, including 24 advanced SU-27 fighters; China sold M-11 ballistic missiles to Pakistan; Taiwan bought 150 American F-16 jet fighters and 60 French

TABLE 11.2 THE CONTINUING SALE OF ARMS TO THE THIRD WORLD AFTER THE COLD WAR, 1990–1992 (CONSTANT 1992 U.S. $ BILLIONS)

| | Global Deliveries | | | | Third World Deliveries | | Third World Sale Contracts | | | |
|------|------|--------|------|--------|------|--------|------|--------|--------|-------|
| Year | U.S. | Russia | U.K. | France | U.S. | Russia | U.S. | Russia | Others | Total |
| 1990 | 10.8 | 9.7 | 1.5 | 2.1 | 4.6 | 6.6 | 19.5 | 11.0 | 11.7 | 42.2 |
| 1991 | 11.7 | 4.5 | .8 | .8 | 4.1 | 4.0 | 14.0 | 5.9 | 8.7 | 28.6 |
| 1992 | 8.5 | 2.0 | .9 | .9 | 3.1 | 1.9 | 13.6 | 1.3 | 9.0 | 23.9 |

*Sources:* Deliveries: SIPRI (1993: 444); Third World: U.S. government agency data, as summarized by *The Defense Monitor* 22 (No. 9, 1993): 2–3.

Mirages; Taiwan also ordered 6 Lafayette frigates from France; Singapore purchased 5 Type-62 corvettes from Germany; Indonesia bought most of the old East German navy; Thailand acquired 6 Jianhhu-class frigates from China; and China illegally acquired U.S. Patriot missiles re-exported by Israel (Gordon, 1993b; Klare, 1993).

**MOTIVES FOR ARMS TRADE** Economic gain is an important rationale for foreign military sales. Israel sells arms abroad to subsidize its arms production at home (Frankel, 1987).[2] The United States uses arms exports to offset its chronic balance-of-payments deficits. And following the disintegration of the Soviet Union, Russia sought to raise desperately needed hard currency by selling at bargain-basement prices its one product mix still in demand—weapons, weapons technology, and weapons expertise. Cash is also the primary motive among other arms suppliers, for whom ideological considerations are virtually nonexistent.

Because the sale of weapons is big business, arms manufacturers comprise a powerful domestic lobby for the continuation of arms sales. In the United States a "gunbelt" military–industrial complex profits at home and abroad from continued arms sales (Markusen, Hall, Campbell, and Deitrick, 1991; see also Kapstein, 1992), and efforts to "dismantle the Cold War military economy" have encountered broad-based, coordinated resistance (Markusen and Yudken, 1992). Russia's inability to hasten "defense conversion" similarly is explainable in part by the resistance of Russia's military–industrial establishment, despite "strong support for [defense] conversion" (Klare, 1994; see also Ustiugov, 1993).

The end of the Cold War promises to increase the incentives to sell arms merely for profit, not in pursuit of foreign policy goals, as historically was the case for the United States and the Soviet Union. States still sell arms (or make outright grants) to support friendly governments, to honor allies' requests, and to earn political loyalty, as illustrated by the U.S. agreements since the 1990 Persian Gulf War for the transfer of $43.8 billion worth of arms to seven Middle Eastern countries (Arms Control Association *Fact Sheet*, October 22, 1993). But the profit motive, fueled in part by the desire of defense contractors to maintain income in a less hostile strategic environment, also continues to drive the spread of weapons worldwide. "The flourishing underground, or black market, trade supplying the wars in the former Yugoslavia and in Somalia" (Sivard, 1993) reveals the grim greed behind suppliers' activities.

Ironically, the treaty on Conventional Armed Forces in Europe (CFE), which entered into force in July 1992, accelerated the arms trade. The treaty called for the elimination from Europe of thousands of tanks, artillery pieces, armored personnel carriers, infantry fighting vehicles, and heavy armament combat vehicles. Many were sold rather than destroyed. Czechoslovakia alone exported more than three-quarters of the equipment that it was required to dispose of under the CFE treaty (*The Defense Monitor* 20 [No. 4, 1991]: 6–7). Some of the other thirty signers of the treaty also sold their weapons on the global arms market.

---

[2] Arms manufacturing is, by its very nature, an expensive proposition. One way to reduce the per-unit cost of a particular weapons system is to produce for foreign consumption as well as for the immediate security needs of the producing state. Selling weapons abroad is thus an attractive option.

THE STRATEGIC CONSEQUENCES OF ARMS SALES  Whether the arming of other countries has accomplished all of its intended goals is open to dispute. During the Cold War, for example, the United States and the Soviet Union thought they could maintain peace by spreading arms to politically pivotal recipients. Between 1983 and 1987 the United States provided arms to fifty-nine Third World countries while the Soviet Union supplied forty-two (Klare, 1990b: 12). Yet many of the recipients engaged in war with their neighbors or experienced internal rebellion. Of the top twenty arms importers in 1988, more than half "had governments noted for the frequent use of violence" (Sivard, 1991: 17). The toll in lives from the some 250 Third World wars since 1945 exceeds 40 million people (Ball, 1994: 216). Undoubtedly, this level of destruction was facilitated by the import of such huge arsenals of weapons from abroad.

The questionable ability of arms suppliers to control the uses to which their hardware is put is also troublesome. The United States armed both sides in several Third World conflicts since World War II, as did the Soviets on occasion. Moreover, loyalty is often a fragile commodity, and supplying weapons can backfire. In 1982 Great Britain found itself shipping military equipment to Argentina just eight days before Argentina's attack on the British-controlled Falkland Islands (Sivard, 1982). Similarly, the day before Iraq sent its troops into Kuwait, the United States approved the sale to the Iraqi government of nearly $700,000 worth of advanced data transmission devices with military applications. "The sale was just one item in $1.5 billion in advanced U.S. products that the Reagan and Bush administrations allowed Iraq to buy from 1985 to 1990" (Auerbach, 1991: 11).

The problem these examples suggest is that the uses of arms by recipients are often beyond the control of the supplier. Betrayal can result when arms sold to an ally, or by an ally to a third party, are later used for purposes that challenge the national interests of the supplier. To cite another example, during the 1980–1988 Iran–Iraq war the United States supplied arms to both sides—as it turned out, to the detriment of its own security. Iran continued to regard the United States as a hostile world power, and U.S. forces sent to the Persian Gulf in 1990 to turn back Iraqi strongman Saddam Hussein's invasion of Kuwait found themselves facing an aggressive force armed with weapons from the West (Timmerman, 1991). "The fact that Saddam Hussein had been able to accumulate such a massive military arsenal—5,500 tanks, 3,700 heavy artillery pieces, 7,500 armored personnel carriers, 700 combat planes, and so on—led many leaders to regret their earlier failure to control the arms trade" (Klare, 1994: 135).

Arms buyers seek weapons for compelling reasons. Many Third World leaders prize military capabilities to symbolize their country's statehood, power, and prestige in the world's pecking order, to increase their position within it, or to deal with internal opposition. Others willingly pay the price because they feel threatened or because they treasure the ability to exercise "forceful persuasion" (George, 1992). Noteworthy is the tendency of arms shipments to gravitate toward regions where the potential for armed conflict is high and the desire to redress grievances strong. The absence of internal security in these trouble spots where ethnic hatreds and nationalistic conflicts reign, and not merely suppliers' greed or the recipients' modernization plans, whets states' appetites for more efficient weapons systems. Through arms, threatened leaders hope to protect their national security and aggressive actors hope to obtain the means to redress perceived past injustices.

## Trends in Weapons Technology

The quest for armaments has led to a potentially explosive global environment. The description is especially apt when we consider not only trends in defense expenditures and the arms trade but also trends in the destructiveness of modern weapons.

NUCLEAR WEAPONS Technological research and development has radically expanded the destructiveness of national arsenals. The largest "blockbuster" bombs of World War II delivered a power of ten tons of TNT. The atomic bomb that leveled Hiroshima had the power of over 15,000 tons of TNT. Less than twenty years later the Soviet Union built a nuclear bomb with the explosive force of 57 megatons (million tons) of TNT. In June 1994, the world's 19,684 nuclear warheads collectively have the explosive force of 900,000 Hiroshima bombs. The combined nuclear stockpiles of the known nuclear powers contain the explosive firepower "of 11,700 megatons of TNT—2.2 tons for each person on the planet" (*The Defense Monitor* 22 [No. 1, 1993]: 1, 2).

The use of such weapons could destroy not only entire cities and countries but, conceivably, the world's entire population.[3] Albert Einstein, the Nobel Prize-winning physicist whose ideas laid the basis for the development of nuclear weapons, was well aware of the threat they posed. He professed uncertainty about the weapons that would be used in a third world war, but he was confident that in a fourth they would be "sticks and stones." He warned that inasmuch as "the unleashed power of the atom has changed everything save our modes of thinking . . . we thus drift toward unparalleled catastrophe."

More bucks have led to more bombs with more bang, making ours an age of overkill. "A nuclear-headed cruise missile, launched from a submarine 1,500 miles at sea, carries thirteen times as much TNT-equivalent explosive as the nuclear bomb that levelled Hiroshima" (Sivard, 1991: 5). A single U.S. bomber can deliver a force level equal to nearly twice the tonnage delivered by all of the participants in World War II. "Far more powerful, of course, are the intercontinental ballistic missiles, which travel 8,000 miles at an incredible speed of 15,000 miles per hour, loaded with multiple warheads and enough explosive force (up to 5,900,000 tons of TNT, over 300 times the power of the Hiroshima bomb) to destroy not just one but several major cities" (Sivard, 1991: 13).

The five principal nuclear weapon states—the United States, the Soviet Union/ Russia, Britain, France, and China—have continuously refined the deadliness of these weapons through testing. Between July 1945 and January 1993 they detonated a

---

[3] Estimates of the number of people who would perish in the event of a nuclear clash vary widely. Former Secretary of Defense Harold Brown (1983) predicted that the "destruction of more than 100 million people in the United States, the Soviet Union, and the European nations could take place during the first half-hour of a nuclear war." For other estimates and scenarios, see Bunge (1988).

combined total of 1,950 nuclear explosions around the world, "on average one explosion every nine days" (*Bulletin of Atomic Scientists* 49 [April 1993]: 49).

The nuclear arsenals of the United States and the former Soviet Union are particularly extensive and sophisticated. When World War II ended, the United States possessed the one atomic bomb still in existence. In 1967, when the U.S. strategic stockpile peaked, the United States had 32,500 warheads in its arsenal, and in 1986, when the Soviet Union was at its peak, it had 45,000 (*Bulletin of Atomic Scientists* 49 [December 1993]: 57). In addition, during the Cold War the United States and the Soviet Union each deployed somewhere between 10,000 and 20,000 tactical nuclear weapons designed for the direct support of combat operations.

The 1987 Intermediate-range Nuclear Force (INF) treaty began the elimination of short- and medium-range delivery vehicles from Europe. Still, "mini-nukes" — nuclear weapons so small they can be carried in a suitcase—pose a continuing threat. So, too, do the nuclear arsenals of the other major nuclear powers. At the end of 1993, if the warheads retired or in reserve awaiting dismantling are included in the inventory of active operational forces, the nuclear stockpiles of the five major powers totaled 49,910 warheads. The U.S. arsenal had 16,750 nuclear warheads and Russia still had 32,000; in addition, France stockpiled an estimated 525 warheads and planned to build up to 1,000; China had 435; Britain retained 200 and planned to more than double its inventory; and Ukraine still controlled 1,240 nuclear warheads or 13 percent of Russia's warhead deployment (*Bulletin of Atomic Scientists* 49 [December 1993]: 57; *Defense Monitor* 22 [No. 1, 1993]: 2).

### Technological Improvements and Weapon Delivery Capabilities
Advances in weapons technology have been rapid and extraordinary. Since the advent of the atomic age with

> the . . . gravity bombs of 1945 . . . a whole warehouse of varied weapons, each with its own special purpose [has been created]; clean bombs; dirty bombs; bombs that burrowed into the earth, seeking underground command posts; bombs that went off undersea, seeking submarines; bombs that went off high over earth, to fry the brains of electrical devices with a huge shower of electromagnetic pulses; bombs that killed tank crews with radiation but didn't flatten towns or cities; bombs delivered by guidance so precise that they could destroy anything with a known location on or near the surface of the earth. . . . The results of this tireless invention were weapons powerful enough to threaten human life on the planet. (Powers, 1994: 123)

Particularly noteworthy have been the technological refinements that enable states to deliver weapons as far away as nine thousand miles within a few hundred feet of their targets in less than thirty minutes. In 1987, seven Western countries (Britain, Canada, France, Germany, Italy, Japan, and the United States) established the Missile Technology Control Regime (MTCR) to curtail the spread of missile technologies, especially those for the delivery of weapons of mass destruction. In 1993 the MTCR's membership included twenty-five states and expanded its coverage to delivery systems for chemical and biological weapons. But this consensual cartel is not a legally binding treaty, includes only a fraction of the missile-technology suppliers, and lacks an institution to monitor and enforce compliance with the voluntary agreement.

Symptomatic of its weakness was the possession in 1993 of short- or medium-range surface-to-air missiles by twenty Third World countries and the fact that seven of them have used missiles in warfare (Arms Control Association *Fact Sheet*, August 10, 1993; see also Zimmerman, 1994). Thus the highly threatening ballistic missile continues outside meaningful international restraints. As a result, the threat of another Iraq, that is, another new "weapon state"—whose characteristics, among others, include "deep grievances against the West and the world order that it has established and enforces" (Krauthammer, 1991a)—has grown.

Other technological improvements have broadened the spectrum of available weapons, as "weapons are just secretions of technologies [and] a military threat is posed by a set of demonstrated technological advances" (Lewis, 1985). The United States and the Russian Federation, for example, equip their ballistic missiles with MIRVs (multiple independently targetable reentry vehicles). These enable a single missile to launch multiple warheads toward different targets simultaneously and with great accuracy. One MIRVed U.S. MX (Peacekeeper) missile carries ten nuclear warheads—enough to wipe out a city and everything else within a fifty-mile radius. The Minuteman III missile carries three warheads with the equivalent of 300 kilotons explosive force; twenty-four missiles on each Trident submarine carry eight warheads with an explosive force of 100 kilotons. As a result of MIRVing, the number of deliverable nuclear warheads in the nuclear powers' arsenals increased far more rapidly than the number of delivery vehicles.

Further technological improvements will lead to steady increases in weapons' speed, accuracy, range, and effectiveness. As Ruth Leger Sivard notes,

> Now, with the improved yield-to-weight ratio, nuclear warheads can be incorporated in artillery shells with a weight of 95 pounds and a range of 18 miles. These have a yield of 2,000 tons of TNT equivalent. More powerful is the nuclear-headed cruise missile which weighs 2,650 pounds. Launched from a submarine at sea, it can travel 1,500 miles under its own power, and release up to 200,000 tons of explosives on the target. (Sivard, 1991: 13)

Other technologies also alter the character of weapons. Laser weapons, nuclear-armed tactical air-to-surface missiles (TASMs), Stealth air-launched cruise missiles (ACMs), and antisatellite (ASAT) weapons that can project force in and wage war from outer space have become a part of the military landscape.

Technological advances are likely to make obsolete both orthodox ways of classifying weapons systems and prior equations for measuring power ratios. As an influential U.S. strategic report predicted:

> Dramatic developments in military technology appear feasible over the next twenty years. They will be driven primarily by the further exploitation of microelectronics, in particular for sensors and information processing, and the development of directed energy. The much greater precision, range, and destructiveness of weapons could extend war across a much wider geographic area, make war much more rapid and intense, and require entirely new modes of operation. Application of new technologies to both offensive and defensive systems

will pose complicated problems for designing forces and assessing enemy capabilities. (Commission on Integrated Long-Term Strategy, 1988: 8)

The 1990 Persian Gulf War provided a glimpse of the future of high-tech weaponry with a dazzling display of military capabilities not previously tried in war. The war revealed elements of the two dimensions of the technological revolution that have transformed the character of so-called conventional weapons:

> One is range coupled with precision guidance. The emphasis is on computerized radars, remotely-piloted vehicles, laser- and television-guided bombs. Satellites and air-borne radar can see far into enemy territory. Targets can be destroyed from great distances. A plane flying at a height of 40,000 feet can hit a target on earth with remarkable precision. A soldier firing a wire-guided weapon can destroy a tank two miles away. A submarine submerged 120 miles at sea can pinpoint a land target with a missile which is guided by the terrain map in its nose. In the war against Iraq in early 1991, the smart bombs and precision-guided missiles quickly established the coalition's air superiority. . . .
>
> On the other hand, the capability for massive destruction has been markedly improved. In one sortie a bomber can drop 50 or more bombs of 500–1,000 pounds each. Explosive power has been greatly enhanced. A single cluster bomb detonates into several hundred bomblets. Fuel air explosives disperse fuel into the air and then detonate the fuel cloud. Both in lethality and in area covered, so-called conventional weapons today approach small nuclear weapons in destructive power. (Sivard, 1991: 13)

Technological improvements, in short, have revolutionized military capabilities. Today's conventional weapons are increasingly destructive, and the precision and power of their means of delivery have improved exponentially. At the same time, the nuclear powers have emphasized quality over quantity, precision and miniaturization over blast and bigness.

For decades a *firebreak* has separated conventional from nuclear wars. The term comes from the firebreaks that fire fighters build to keep forest fires from racing out of control. In the context of modern weaponry, it is a psychological barrier whose purpose is to "prevent even the most intensive forms of conventional combat from escalating into nuclear war." As both nuclear and conventional weapons technologies advance, there is danger that the firebreak is being crossed from both directions—by a new generation of "near-nuclear" conventional weapons capable of "levels of violence approximating those of a limited nuclear conflict" and by a new generation of "near-conventional" nuclear weapons able "to inflict damage not much greater than that of the most powerful conventional weapons" (Klare, 1985).

UNCONVENTIONAL WEAPONS  Chemical and biological weapons pose a special and growing threat. Each is sometimes regarded as a "poor man's atomic bomb" because each can be built at comparatively small cost and cause widespread injury and death. Partly due to the 1972 Biological Weapons Convention prohibiting the development, production, and stockpiling of biological weapons, "no nation is known to possess biological weapons today. But the United States, the United Kingdom, and Japan are known to have developed several types of biological weapons in the past (such stocks have since been destroyed), and Iraq and Syria are strongly suspected of stockpiling such weapons" (Fetter, 1991), as is North Korea (Zimmerman, 1994). In contrast, chemical weapons proliferation is a worldwide concern. Already twenty Third World states are believed to have produced chemical weapons (Fetter, 1991), and in the Middle East "chemical weapons have been used repeatedly [and] most of the countries . . . have chemical weapon development programs" (Arms Control Association *Factfile*, 1993). Among the industrial states, the United States and Russia maintain the largest stockpiles of chemical weapons, but in 1990 they agreed to stop their production and significantly reduce their numbers.

International law prohibits the use of chemical weapons (for example, the 1925 Geneva Protocol banned the use of chemical weapons in warfare, and the ***Chemical Weapons Convention*** [CWC] signed by 147 countries by September 1993 required the destruction of existing stocks).[4] These legal restraints do not assure that states will not use them, however, as Iran's and Iraq's use of gas in warfare demonstrates. (Iraq even used chemical weapons against its own Kurdish people.) Thus the firebreak, the taboo against the use of unconventional weapons, has already been breached. Still, a number of factors limit the military utility of chemical weapons, including weather conditions and the ability to defend against them. Thus the "poor man's atomic bomb" analogy, while appropriate for biological weapons, does not aptly apply to chemical weapons.

Chemical weapons are nonetheless capable of causing widespread death and suffering. Chemical weapons (gas) were used during World War I, for example, "producing about 100,000 fatalities and over 1,000,000 total casualties" (Fetter, 1991: 15). The proliferation of ballistic missiles, particularly among regional rivals in the Middle East, Northeast Asia, and elsewhere, raises the danger because they enable chemical weapons to be readily delivered at great distances. Already twenty-three Third World countries possess a ballistic missile capability, with others likely.

## The Proliferation Problem

Do arms acquisitions promote war? "Many amply supplied armed forces may incline governments to use force rather than to negotiate to resolve conflicts." Even so, "the possession of weapons does not guarantee their use" (Ball, 1991). In fact, as we will discuss in more detail below, the purpose of arming is to *prevent* the use of force (deterrence), not encourage it. Hence, as Michael Klare (1987) reasons, "it would be foolish to argue that increased arms transfers automatically increase the risk of war—the decision to wage war is determined by numerous factors."

Still, he continues, "there is no doubt that the widespread availability of modern arms has made it *easier* for potential belligerents to choose the military rather than

---

[4] "The dual uses of chemical technologies for fertilizers, pesticides and herbicides as well as weapons is even closer than the overlap between commercial and military nuclear facilities" (Nye, 1989–1990). The dual use of chemical agents hampers verification efforts, a principal stumbling block in most arms control efforts for which the ***Organization for the Prevention of Chemical Weapons*** (OPCW), headquartered in the Hague, is designed.

the diplomatic option when seeking to resolve local disputes." Huge arms purchases by Iraq, for example, may have set the stage for its invasion of Kuwait and the subsequent Persian Gulf War. Iraq purchased $75 billion in military equipment during the 1970s and 1980s, or nearly ten percent of all arms transfers. "The weapons . . . may have encouraged Saddam Hussein to believe that his invasion of Kuwait would not be challenged" (Ball, 1991: 20). Thus, even if the arms trade and arms races do not necessarily make the world more violent, they do make it less secure (Johansen, 1995). Hence the proliferation of arms is a great global concern.

## Nuclear Weapons

The addition of new nuclear states is commonly referred to as the *Nth country* problem. The increase in the number of nuclear states is called *horizontal nuclear proliferation*, in contrast with increases in the capabilities of existing nuclear powers, known as *vertical nuclear proliferation*.

Most countries dread the chain reaction that might lead to widespread horizontal proliferation, for it increases the likelihood that one or more states will choose to use nuclear weapons or that an accident or miscalculation will lead to catastrophe. Estimates vary, but experts agree that perhaps as many as thirty other states now have the economic and technological potential to become nuclear powers. By the year 2000, the number could grow to forty (Albright, 1993).

NUCLEAR POWERS, NUCLEAR ASPIRANTS   As Table 11.3 indicates, presently there are only five "official" members of the nuclear club—the United States, Russia, Britain, France, and China. But three others are de facto nuclear weapon states, and three others are on the verge of becoming nuclear powers and are thus classifiable as "states of immediate concern." Five others warrant long-term concern. On the optimistic side of the ledger, four states once regarded as nuclear aspirants have now reversed their former position and thereby joined the nonproliferation regime. On the pessimistic side, "If we totally ignore the mounting threats from non-governmental groups and focus on nation-states alone, we can conclude that approximately 20 countries are either in or are knocking at the door of the Nuclear Club. . . . We may be looking at a world in which a third to a half of all countries have some hideous weapons of mass murder locked away in their arsenals" (Toffler and Toffler, 1993).

THE NONPROLIFERATION REGIME   The Nuclear Nonproliferation Treaty (NPT), first signed in 1968, seeks to prevent further proliferation by prohibiting the transfer of nuclear weapons technology from the now nuclear states to the non-nuclear states. At the same time, however, the nuclear states are obligated to provide others with nuclear information and technology for peaceful purposes. Since entering into force on March 5, 1970, 160 states have become members of the nonproliferation regime.

> NPT membership is divided into two categories: nuclear weapon states and non-nuclear weapon states. Nuclear states are defined as those which "manufactured and exploded a nuclear weapon . . . prior to January 1, 1967." This definition includes only China, France,

## TABLE 11.3 THE STATE OF NUCLEAR PROLIFERATION

**Acknowledged Nuclear Weapons States**
China
France
Russia
United Kingdom
United States

**De Facto Nuclear Weapon States***
India
Israel
Pakistan

**States of Immediate Concern**
Kazakhstan**
North Korea
Ukraine**

**States of Long-Term Concern**
Algeria
Iran
Iraq***
Libya
Syria

**Recent Converts to Nonproliferation**
Argentina
Belarus
Brazil
South Africa

* Possess nuclear weapons or are capable of producing nuclear weapons on short notice.
** Nuclear weapons under Russian control are currently deployed in these countries but both states are committed under the May 1992 Lisbon Protocol to START I to joining the NPT (Nuclear Nonproliferation Treaty) as non-nuclear weapon states "in the shortest possible time."
*** Subject to United Nations and International Atomic Energy Agency inspections and required by Gulf war cease-fire to eliminate all nuclear-related facilities and materials.
*Source:* Arms Control Association *Fact Sheet*, September 1993.

Russia, the United Kingdom, and the United States—all of which are members of the NPT. All other parties to the agreement are non-nuclear weapon states. The three de facto nuclear weapon states—India, Israel, and Pakistan—are not NPT members.

The NPT strikes a bargain between nuclear and non-nuclear weapon states. Under the treaty, the non-nuclear weapon states agree not to acquire nuclear weapons and to accept comprehensive International Atomic Energy Agency (IAEA) safeguards over all of their nuclear materials to ensure that they are used exclusively for peaceful purposes. In exchange, the nuclear weapon states agree to freely share the benefits of peaceful nuclear energy and technology and not to assist other states to acquire nuclear weapons. In addition, the nuclear weapon states pledged to pursue "good faith" negotiations toward an end to the arms race and toward general and complete disarmament. (Arms Control Association *Fact Sheet*, August 1993)

Despite the apparent success of the NPT regime, the obstacles to increased proliferation are fragile, and the incentives to join the nuclear club are strong. There are several reasons.

First, the materials needed to make a nuclear weapon are widely available. In part this is due to the widespread use of nuclear technology for generating electricity. Long-standing concerns about Pakistan's intentions to increase its nuclear weapons capability, for example, intensified in early 1992, when China announced it would export a 300-megawatt nuclear power plant to Pakistan. Today more than 770 nuclear power and research reactors are in operation in fifty-eight countries. In addition to spreading nuclear know-how, states could choose to reprocess the uranium and plutonium that power plants produce as waste for clandestine nuclear weapons production. By the year 2000, commercial reprocessing reactors could be producing enough plutonium to make 37,000 nuclear weapons (Sivard, 1993: 13).

Second, scientific expertise necessary to weapons development has spread with the internationalization of advanced scientific training. "In the near future it will be possible to duplicate almost all past technology in all but the most forlorn of Third World backwaters, and much of the present state-of-the-art will be both intellectually and practically accessible" (Clancy and Seitz, 1991–1992).

Third, export controls designed to stop technology transfer for military purposes are weak. "A large and growing number of states can now export material, equipment, technology, and services needed to develop nuclear weapons" (Potter, 1992), and the leaks in nuclear export controls make "a mockery of the long-revered nuclear nonproliferation regime" (Leventhal, 1992). Conversion of peacetime nuclear energy programs to military purposes can occur either overtly or, as in the case of India, covertly. The safeguards built into the nonproliferation regime are simply inadequate to detect and prevent secret nuclear weapon development programs (Albright, 1993). The ease with which Pakistan made a successful end run around the technology-export controls of the United States and Western European governments illustrates the problem of control. In 1979 Pakistan quietly bought all the basic parts—allegedly with funds supplied by the radical government of Libya—necessary for a uranium-enrichment plant. Similarly, UN inspectors discovered after the Persian Gulf War that Iraq was much closer to building an atomic weapon than previously suspected. Yet Iraq "remained a member [of the nonproliferation regime] in good standing for more than a decade. This was possible because the [NPT] treaty allows members legally to get much too close to weapons capability. . . . The Iraqi experience suggests that it is impossible to effectively safeguard weapons-grade materials" (Mathews, 1991). The fact that no less than eight countries have constructed secret nuclear production plants underscores the difficulties of managing effective inspections and monitoring (Albright, 1993).

Fourth, other states have strong incentives to develop nuclear weapons similar to those once cited by the members of the nuclear club. French President Charles de Gaulle averred that, without an independent nuclear capability, France could not "command its own destiny." Similarly, Britain's Labour Party leader Aneurin Bevan asserted that without the bomb Britain would go "naked into the conference chamber." And in 1993 North Korean President Kim Il Sung defiantly withdrew from the nonproliferation pact and refused to allow even routine monitoring of his country's five declared nuclear sites at Yongbyon. The desire to act independently and to assert North Korea's power and independence were the primary motives. Indeed, North Korea dug in its heels in response to President Clinton's June 1994 pledge that the United States "would not allow North Korea to develop a nuclear bomb."

Many non-nuclear states want the same command of their own fate and the same diplomatic influence that the nuclear powers seem to enjoy. Why, non-nuclear states ask, should they adhere to a nonproliferation agreement that dooms them to others' domination and security guarantees? Consider Iran's sentiments. In January 1992 its spiritual leader, the Ayatollah Ali Khamenenei, declared that the United States had no business questioning his country's nuclear weapons program designed to make it the most powerful military force in the Persian Gulf. "Iran's revolutionary Muslim people recognize no false hegemony for America or any other power," he exclaimed. Similarly, in November 1993 Pakistan's prime minister, Benazir Bhutto, asserted that "it is degrading and humiliating to expect Pakistan to roll back its nuclear program." Pakistan developed a nuclear capability, she explained, to deter India, its archenemy, and "should be rewarded" for stopping short of building a weapon.

Fifth, the breakup of the Soviet Union has spread the number of nuclear weapon states, since 30 percent of Russia's strategic nuclear warheads in early 1994 remained on the soil of now-independent Ukraine, Belarus, and Kazakhstan. Each had incentives to assert continued control over the weapons (although all of them made genuflections in the direction of a joint command over them). Noteworthy was the position that Ukrainian nationalist lawmaker Oles Shevchenko staked out in late November 1993: "We've got to keep nuclear weapons to defend our territory against the eastern aggressor. [Russia's new military doctrine justifying intervention in the 'near abroad' makes it] a thousand times more dangerous for us to disarm." As of June 1994, 3,054 warheads remained in Belarus, Kazakhstan, and Ukraine, and uncertainty remains about the pace with which they will all be dismantled and whether this goal will indeed be accomplished.

### Nuclear Disarmament?

Some see the end of the Cold War as an opportunity to move toward the elimination of nuclear weapons. In 1992 Russia, for example, advocated complete nuclear disarmament. Moreover, the United States and Russia undertook a number of important steps toward meaningful disarmament (see Chapter 13), something unheard of prior to the Cold War's end. Perhaps this will set the stage for expanding the nonproliferation regime, when, in accordance with the provisions of the NPT treaty, the 163 parties to it will gather in 1995 to decide, by majority vote, "whether the treaty shall continue in force indefinitely, or shall be extended for an additional fixed period or periods."

The NPT treaty was last reviewed in 1990 at Geneva. At that time the contracting parties were unable to reach a consensus on the critical nuclear weapons test ban (CTB). That does not augur well for extending, or even maintaining, the nonproliferation regime, much less eliminating nuclear weapons. They, like gods of old, have become symbols of limitless power to which weak states attribute qualities of awe and omnipotence to compensate for their sense of powerlessness (Chernus, 1987). Thus few reasons exist to expect that the nuclear threat will cease. "There's not a snowball's chance in hell we'll eliminate all nuclear weapons from the face of the earth," explains Matthew Bunn, editor of *Arms Control Today*. "That genie is long since out of the bottle and there's no chance of ever getting him back in." Moreover, the security problem posed by a disarmed world is compelling. "The problem is, if you eliminate them all, then any country that built just a few nuclear weapons would have enormous blackmail potential" (Davidson, 1991).

## The Social and Economic Consequences of Military Spending . . . . .

Global patterns of military spending and arms acquisitions testify to the prevalent belief that power can be purchased. What are the effects of this conviction on national well-being?

## The Burden of Defense

The *relative burden* of military spending, defined as the ratio of defense spending to gross national product, is one way to measure the sacrifices military spending requires. In 1991 the relative defense burden for the world as a whole was 4.2 percent; as noted already, the average among developed countries fell to 4.1 percent (a historic low since 1960), but among developing countries it rose to 4.5 percent (ACDA, 1994: 24).

It is customary to show the range in states' willingness to pay a heavy burden for defense by grouping the world's countries according to their share of GNP devoted to the military and to juxtapose this relative burden with their GNP per capita. Such studies reveal wide variations. As shown in Table 11.4, some comparatively wealthy states—for example, Israel and Singapore—bear a heavy burden. In contrast, other states providing a high average income for their citizens pay a low defense burden—for example, Japan and Switzerland. Likewise, the citizens of some very poor countries are heavily burdened, such as Ethiopia and Rwanda, whereas others (Nepal and Nigeria) are not. Thus it is difficult to generalize about the precise relationship between a country's defense burden and its citizens' standard of living or stage of development. Still, the available data do suggest two general patterns.

First, those most burdened by the costs of defense include a disproportionate share of poor countries experiencing civil or international war or threats to their security. Second, the burden of defense in relation to income is more than three times greater in developing than in developed countries. "The countries least able to afford it bore the major share—close to four-fifths—of the world's military burden" (Sivard, 1991: 11). It seems, then, that those least able to afford weapons have made the greatest sacrifices to get them. Hence the costs of arming for security pose "a formidable barrier" to economic development, concludes Ruth Leger Sivard (1991: 11), because the developing countries "lost to the arms race in a single year the equivalent of 187 million human-years of income."

## Military Spending and Social Priorities

The comparatively greater resources military preparedness commands in relation to other problems manifests itself in other ways. Consider some representative indicators, as summarized in Box 11.1 (see page 400).

The data in Box 11.1 show that most countries are more concerned with defending their citizens from foreign attack than they are with protecting them from social, educational, and health insecurities. They also suggest that military spending reduces social welfare. The connection is not direct, but military spending and global deprivation are linked.

Consider, for example, how the United States, first in military spending, ranks (in 1990) among 140 countries across various social indicators (Sivard, 1993: 37, 39, 41):

|  | U.S. Rank Compared with 140 Other Countries |
|---|---|
| • Literacy rate | 4 |
| • Per-capita GNP | 6 |
| • Per-capita public expenditure for education | 9 |
| • Maternal mortality rate | 13 |
| • Per-capita public expenditure for health | 11 |
| • Life expectancy | 10 |
| • School-age population per teacher | 12 |
| • Average scores of students on science and math tests | 13 |

*(continues on page 401)*

## TABLE 11.4 RELATIVE BURDEN OF MILITARY EXPENDITURES, 1991

| Military Expenditures as Percentage of GNP | Gross National Product per Capita | | | | | |
|---|---|---|---|---|---|---|
| | Under $200 | $200–499 | $500–999 | $1,000–2,999 | $3,000–9,999 | $10,000 and Over |
| 10% and over | Ethiopia<br>Afghanistan<br>Mozambique<br>Cambodia | | Iraq<br>Yemen<br>Cape Verde | North Korea<br>Syria<br>Jordan | Saudi Arabia<br>Oman<br>Russian Federation | Kuwait<br>Qatar<br>United Arab Emir. |
| 5–9.99% | Rwanda | Pakistan<br>Chad<br>Liberia | Angola<br>Burma<br>Zimbabwe<br>Albania | Sudan<br>Iran<br>Turkey | Libya<br>Bahrain<br>Cyprus<br>Yugloslavia<br>Greece<br>Taiwan | Israel<br>Singapore |
| 2–4.99% | Tanzania<br>Uganda<br>Burundi<br>Sierra Leonc | Vietnam<br>Nicaragua<br>Laos<br>Burkina Faso<br>Equatorial Guinea<br>Togo<br>Kenya<br>India | Sri Lanka<br>Lesotho<br>Mauritania<br>Egypt<br>Papua New Guin.<br>Bolivia<br>Philippines | Mongolia<br>Botswana<br>Morocco<br>Cuba<br>South Africa<br>Malaysia<br>Venezuela<br>Lebanon | Poland<br>Romania<br>Bulgaria<br>Suriname<br>South Korea<br>Gabon<br>Portugal<br>Czechoslovakia | United States<br>United Kingdom<br>France<br>Norway<br>Sweden<br>Australia<br>Netherlands<br>Germany |

| Mil. exp. (% of GNP) | | | | | | | | |
|---|---|---|---|---|---|---|---|---|
| | | | Guinea-Bissau<br>Zambia<br>Haiti | | | | | Belgium<br>Italy<br>Denmark<br>Canada<br>Finland |
| 1–1.99% | Somali<br>Bangladesh<br>Nepal | Benin<br>Mali<br>Zaire<br>Cen. African Rep.<br>Guinea<br>Niger<br>Madagascar<br>Malawi<br>Guyana<br>Nigeria<br>Ghana<br>Gambia<br>São Tomé & Princ. | Senegal<br>Honduras<br>Cameroon<br>Indonesia<br>Ivory Coast | Algeria<br>Paraguay<br>Swaziland<br>Brazil<br>Peru | Tunisia<br>Chile<br>China<br>Congo<br>El Salvador<br>Thailand<br>Colombia<br>Fiji<br>Uruguay<br>Ecuador | Argentina | Hungary | Switzerland<br>Spain<br>New Zealand<br>Ireland<br>Austria |
| Under 1% | | | Guatemala<br>Dominican Rep. | | Jamaica<br>Mauritius<br>Costa Rica<br>Panama | | Malta<br>Trinidad &<br>Tobago<br>Barbados<br>Mexico | Japan<br>Luxembourg<br>Iceland |

*Source:* U.S. Arms Control and Disarmament Agency (1994: 24).

# Box 11.1
## MILITARY AND OTHER SOCIAL PRIORITIES

• • •

- World military expenditures from 1960 to 1990 add up to $21 trillion ($21,000,000,000,000) in 1987 dollars, equivalent [in 1990] in size to the value of all goods and services produced by and for the 5.3 billion people on the earth. (Sivard, 1991: 11)

- World military spending in 1992 equaled the combined income of 49 percent of the world's people (UNDP, 1994: 48).

- The developed countries spend as much on military power in a year as the poorest 2 billion on earth earn in total income. (Sivard, 1993: 5)

- The price of one ballistic submarine ($1,453,000,000) would double the education budget of 18 poor countries with 129,110,000 children to educate. (Sivard, 1991: 5)

- Between $15 and $20 of every $100 spent by central governments now goes to military purposes, triple their budgets for education, eight times their budgets for housing. (Sivard, 1991: 26)

- For military objectives, governments now invest an average of $36,000 per year per member of the armed forces, thirty times more than they invest in the education of a child enrolled in school. The formidable gap between the two underscores the serious neglect of human capital, and with it, of economic development, in favor of unlimited military power. (Sivard, 1991: 27)

- The developed countries in 1990 provided $56 billion in economic aid to the poorer countries and exported $36 billion in arms to them. (Sivard, 1993: 5)

- The world's armed forces are the single largest polluter on earth; in the U.S. they produce more toxins annually than the top five chemical companies combined. (Sivard, 1991: 5)

- Despite some retrenchment in military spending recently, [Third World] annual outlays still take the equivalent of 180 million man-years of income vs. 56 million man-years for the developed countries. (Sivard, 1991: 11)

- Developing countries have eight times as many soldiers as physicians. (Sivard, 1991: 5)

- At a cost of less than half their military expenditures, the developing countries could have a package of basic health services and clinical care that would save 10 million lives a year. (Sivard, 1993: 5)

|  | U.S. Rank Compared with 140 Other Countries |
| --- | --- |
| • Primary school-age population in school | 15 |
| • Proportion of population protected by public health insurance | 18 |
| • Infant mortality rate | 21 |
| • Population per physician | 22 |
| • Percent population with access to sanitation | 25 |

These rankings and the data in Box 11.1 suggest that high military spending reduces the quality of citizens' lives. Security in the broadest sense means security in the expectation that one will live a full life. Yet arms do not contribute to increased life expectancy or freedom from want. Instead, when expenditures for arms go up, so do disease, illiteracy, and suffering. Thus, high rates of military spending reduce social welfare (see Nincic, 1982; Russett, 1982; UNDP, 1994). As U.S. President Dwight D. Eisenhower observed, "the world in arms is not spending money alone. It is spending the sweat of its laborers, the genius of its scientists, the hopes of its children."

## Military Spending and Economic Growth Rates

How are military expenditures and social welfare linked? Many politicians and experts argue that a tradeoff exists between "guns and butter," that is, between military spending and economic growth. Evidence on the relationship between military spending and economic growth points to "retarding effects through inflation, diversion of investment, use of scarce materials, misuse of human capital" (Sivard, 1979b). One econometric study found that every additional dollar spent on arms in the Third World reduced domestic investment by 25 cents and agricultural output by 20 cents (Klare, 1987: 1279–1280). For most developing countries, when military spending rises the rate of growth declines (Deger and Smith, 1983; also Lipow, 1990; Payne and Sahu, 1993; Väyrynen, 1992) and debt increases (Snider, 1991).

Despite this evidence, the guns-versus-growth issue remains controversial. "Previous research on the impact of military spending on the economy has produced disparate, inconsistent, and unstable results" (Chan, 1987). It has not established a strong correlation that holds for all countries. "The effects of military expenditure on the economy," conclude Ron P. Smith and George Georgiou (1983), "depend on the nature of the expenditure, the prevailing circumstances, and the concurrent government policies." For many advanced industrial economies, for example, military spending often stimulates economic growth, at least in the short run, even though it hinders prosperity in less developed countries (see Payne and Sahu, 1993).

Even if a linkage cannot be shown to hold across all countries, there are strong reasons to believe that the strain of military spending on economic growth is especially

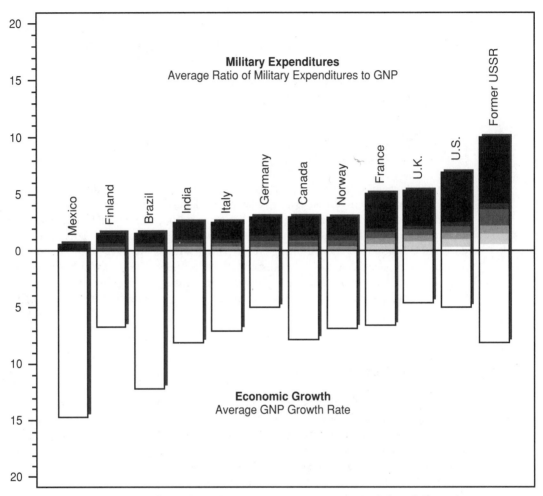

**Figure 11.3** Military Expenditures and Economic Growth, Selected Countries, 1960–1990
*Source:* Based on data presented by Ruth Leger Sivard (1993: 43–45).

severe in many societies. Consider, for example, the data in Figure 11.3, which charts the level of military spending and economic growth rates among a handful of representative countries between 1960 and 1990. The data suggest that the two are negatively correlated. That is, as military spending goes up, economic growth declines.[5] So, too, does a comparison between Japan and Mexico, on the one hand, and the United States and the former Soviet Union, on the other. The former pair of

---

[5] "One of the main reasons for the transformation of the positive contribution of military industrialization into a negative one is the isolation of the military [research and development] and production from the competitive pressures of the market. The bureaucratic interests of the military, its penchant for custom-made technical solutions and the atmosphere of technological mercantilism all favor the disengagement of military industry from the civilian market. There are considerable differences in the technological styles

countries, relatively freed of the burden of funding militarization, expanded their economies greatly. The latter, paying high costs for military power, fell behind economically. Indeed, it appears that excessive military spending was a primary cause of the Soviet Union's demise. "No other industrialized state in the world [had] for so long spent so much of its national wealth on armaments and military forces. Soviet militarism, in harness with communism, destroyed the Soviet economy and thus hastened the self-destruction of the Soviet Empire" (Iklé, 1991–1992: 28).

"The problem in defense spending," President Eisenhower observed in 1956, "is to figure how far you should go without destroying from within what you are trying to defend from without."[6] Paradoxically, the demise of the Soviet Union has added a new wrinkle to the question of the impact of defense spending on the economy. Now the concern is how "downsizing" military establishments geared toward Cold War competition will affect employment levels and research, development, and production opportunities in industries that provide for defense (see Renner, 1990). The goal is "bedeviled by two conflicting objectives: how to shift firms out of defense and into civilian pursuits, and how to preserve a mobilization base to meet conceivable future defense needs" (Adelman and Augustine, 1992). Even the absorption of large numbers of military personnel into the domestic economy has been a matter of concern on both sides of the one-time East–West divide. Just as there may be costs associated with excessive military spending, conversion to a much smaller, "peace-maintaining" military posture may also exact a domestic economic toll. Perhaps this influence explains why the Clinton administration's fiscal 1994 defense budget did "not abolish a single new weapons system." "There is a tendency," observes Robert Reno (1993), "to build an inventory of possible wars to match present levels of defense spending and present levels of manpower, [which is why] defense conversion in Russia will [also] be a very difficult undertaking."

The end of the Cold War poses special problems for the United States, which now stands alone at the pinnacle of world power. What commitments and responsibilities should engage the United States now that the challenges of communist ideology and Soviet expansionism have disappeared? What resources, military and other, should the country devote to those ends? Should the ends sought determine what resources are devoted to the task? Or should the level of available resources dictate the choice of commitments and responsibilities?

There are no easy answers to these questions, but even before the end of the Cold War many analysts worried that U.S. commitments exceeded the country's ability to fulfill them. As noted in previous chapters, historian Paul Kennedy (1987) used the term "imperial overstretch" in his influential book *The Rise and Fall of the Great*

---

of military and civilian industry. Also their approaches to innovation differ; the military–industrial approach is accustomed to the limited nature of its risks, ready availability of funds, the lack of competition and the effort to protect the technology from falling into the adversary's hands. The commercial approach is predicated on the need constantly to increase productivity, to adapt the products for the demands of the market and to live with the reality of national and international competition." (Väyrynen, 1992: 105)

[6] The lingering costs of previous wars also exact a toll. For example, the ratio of U.S. funds spent fighting a war to the funds spent on that war's veterans' benefits are 1 : 3 (*Harper's* [May 1991]: 17).

*Powers* to symbolize concern about a growing imbalance between the ends and means of U.S. foreign policy and the possibility that this imbalance parallels that which led to the fall of hegemonic powers in previous historical periods, notably the Spanish at the turn of the seventeenth century and the British at the turn of the twentieth. Kennedy reiterated that concern in a response to his critics during the 1991 Persian Gulf War, the first crisis of the post–Cold War era:

> So much of the "decline" debate seems to be obsessed with where America is now. . . . My own concern is much more with the future, a decade or more down the road, if the trends in national indebtedness, low productivity increases, mediocre educational performance and decaying social fabric are allowed to continue at the same time that massive American commitments of men, money and material are made in different parts of the globe. Like the late Victorians, we seem to be discovering ever-newer "frontiers of insecurity" in the world that we, the number one power, feel impelled to guard.
>
> . . . It is no use claiming that America is completely different from those earlier great powers when we are imitating so many of their habits—possessing garrisons and bases and fleets in all parts of the globe and acting as the world's policeman on the one hand, running up debts and neglecting the country's internal needs on the other. (Kennedy, 1992: 345–346)

Even those who reject the thesis of ***imperial overstretch*** worry about the solvency of the United States. Political commentator Charles Krauthammer (1991b), for example, responds to the question "Can America long sustain its unipolar preeminence?" with the observation that "an American collapse to second-rank status will be not for foreign but for domestic reasons." Among them are "America's low savings rate, poor educational system, stagnant productivity, declining work habits, rising demand for welfare-state entitlements and new taste for ecological luxuries."

Others worry about the ability of the United States to compete on the economic battlefield. Given the "rising importance of economic power in world affairs," Alan Tonelson (1991) writes, "indifferences to domestic decay" and "disregard for the home front [have] entailed enormous risks and costs" that arguably erode the ability of the United States to guarantee "its safety and well-being."

Maintaining a balance between military preparedness and economic revitalization is a challenge, however. Former U.S. Undersecretary for Defense Fred Charles Iklé (1991–1992) warns that thinking about future security problems and requirements remains "heavily burdened by the Cold War legacy," which includes "old habits of the mind, reinforced by old bureaucratic practices."[7]

Future defense planning *is* clearly influenced by the strategies that were conceived

---

[7] The *New York Times* (February 17, 1992: A1, A5) reported that "the Pentagon envisions seven scenarios for potential foreign conflicts that could draw United States forces into combat over the next 10 years." The seven scenarios are: (1) Iraq invades Kuwait and Saudi Arabia; (2) North Korea invades South Korea; (3) the Iraqi and North Korean invasions occur simultaneously; (4) Russia attacks Lithuania through Poland with help from Belarus; (5) a coup in the Philippines threatens U.S. citizens there; (6) a coup in Panama threatens access to the canal; and (7) a new expansionist superpower emerges. Many members of the U.S. Congress objected that some of the scenarios bordered on the preposterous, but there seemed to be widespread agreement that the Pentagon's exercise was part of its effort to maintain a large military establishment.

during the Cold War. A comparison of the great powers' new defense policies, in light of their previous ones, informs us about the ways states think about arms as they prepare for the common defense.

## STRATEGIC DOCTRINE: PLANNING FOR WAR, DETERRENCE, AND DEFENSE . . . . . . . . . . . . . . . . . . . . . . . . . . . . . . . . . . . . .

The dropping of the atomic bomb on Japan in August 1945 is the most important event distinguishing pre– from post–World War II international politics. In the blinding flash of a single weapon and the shadow of its mushroom cloud, the international arena was transformed from a "balance-of-power" to a "balance-of-terror" system. In the decades that followed, policymakers in the nuclear states had to grapple with two central policy questions: Should they use nuclear weapons? and How can their use by others be prevented?

The questions were especially pertinent to the United States and the Soviet Union, Cold War adversaries who were also the two most heavily armed nuclear powers. Their decisions shaped strategic thinking and doctrines elsewhere. This formative period casts its shadow on defense planning still. We need to look backward in order to grasp the influence of past strategies on present ones.

## Comparing Superpower Military Policies: A Case Study of Continuities and Changes

Although the existence of weapons of mass destruction has been a constant since World War II, the superpowers' postures toward them have changed as technologies, defense needs, capabilities, and global conditions have changed. For analytical convenience, we can treat those postures in terms of two periods. The first began at the end of World War II and lasted until the Cuban missile crisis. U.S. nuclear superiority was the dominant characteristic of this period. The second began in 1962 and lasted until the breakup of the Soviet Union in 1991. Growing Soviet military capability was the dominant characteristic of this period, which meant that the United States no longer stood alone in its ability to annihilate another country without fear of its own destruction.

A third phase in the posture of the nuclear powers toward nuclear weapons began in 1992, as the former Cold War antagonists and the other rising great powers began to restructure their forces and revise their national security doctrines. To better understand this new thinking, we will first examine the superpowers' strategic policies during the precedent-setting Cold War period itself.

### *Coercive Diplomacy, 1945–1962*

Countries that enjoy military superiority vis-à-vis their principal adversaries often think of weapons as instruments in diplomatic bargaining, that is, as tools for the political purpose of changing others' behavior. The United States, the world's first and, for many years, unchallenged nuclear power, was no exception. *Compellence* (Schelling, 1966) described U.S. strategic doctrine when it enjoyed a clear-cut superiority in the nuclear balance of power. Compellence makes nuclear weapons instruments of influence, used not for fighting but to get others to do what they might not otherwise do. Thus it refers to the use of nuclear weapons as instruments of *coercive diplomacy* or "forceful persuasion" (George, 1992).

The United States sought to gain bargaining leverage by conveying the impression that it would actually use nuclear weapons. The posture was especially evident during the Eisenhower administration in the 1950s. To win political victories, Secretary of State John Foster Dulles practiced *brinkmanship*, portraying a willingness to threaten U.S. adversaries with nuclear destruction.

Brinkmanship made sense only as long as the United States enjoyed a position of preponderant strength. It was part of the overall U.S. strategic posture known as *massive retaliation*, employed by the Eisenhower administration as the nuclear arm of the U.S. foreign policy goal of containing communism and Soviet expansionism. Massive retaliation was a *countervalue* posture because it targeted U.S. weapons on objects that the Soviets presumably valued most, their industrial and population centers. The alternative is a *counterforce* strategy, one that targets the enemy's military forces and weapons, thus sparing the general civilian population from immediate destruction.

Massive retaliation and brinkmanship heightened Soviet fears. The Soviet Union had earlier broken the U.S. atomic monopoly, but now, faced with U.S. belligerence, it pursued a twofold response. Following Nikita Khrushchev's ascension to power in the mid-1950s, the Soviets ceased speaking of the utility of military power. Instead, they promoted peaceful coexistence as an alternative means of doing battle with democratic capitalism. Yet, fearing that a nuclear exchange would destroy the Soviet Union but permit U.S. survival, Soviet leaders also expanded their nuclear arsenals. In 1957 the Soviet Union successfully launched the world's first space satellite *(Sputnik)*, demonstrating its potential ability to deliver nuclear weapons far beyond the Eurasian landmass. Thus the superpowers' strategic competition took a new turn, as the United States for the first time began to face a credible military threat to its own geophysical security.

### Mutual Deterrence, 1962–1983

As U.S. strategic superiority eroded, U.S. policymakers began to question whether weapons of mass destruction were useful for political bargaining. They recoiled in horror at the thought of the destruction that could result should compellence provoke a nuclear exchange. The nearly suicidal Cuban missile crisis of 1962 dealt coercive diplomacy a serious blow. Thereafter, the object of nuclear weapons shifted to preventing an attack. That is, strategic policy shifted from compellence to deterrence. In contrast to forceful persuasion, *deterrence* is a strategy designed to prevent an adversary from doing what it would otherwise do.

Both superpowers also pursued *extended deterrence* to prevent an attack on one's allies. Thus, the superpowers sought to protect not only their homelands but also targets outside their adversary's own defense perimeter and alliance network.

Extended deterrence was especially critical to the United States, as its allies were far from its own shores and geographically proximate to the Soviet Union itself. Despite repeated U.S. assurances that it would defend its allies, however, the credibility of its guarantee to the NATO countries in particular was often questioned. Former U.S. Secretary of State Henry Kissinger punctuated the doubt when he noted in 1979 that the promise to defend Europe with nuclear weapons involved "strategic assurances that we cannot possibly mean or if we do mean, we should not execute because if we should execute, we risk the destruction of civilization." The dubious credibility of the U.S. deterrent led some critics to advocate "decoupling" Europe from the U.S. strategic security umbrella and encouraging individual NATO countries to develop their own nuclear capability.

Ironically, the shift from compellence to deterrence stimulated rather than inhibited the U.S.–Soviet arms race. A deterrent strategy depends on the ability to deliver without question unacceptable damage on an opponent. It requires a **second-strike capability** that enables a country to withstand an initial strike by an adversary and still retain the ability to retaliate with a devastating second blow. Such a capability assures a potential aggressor of destruction, thus deterring the contemplated preemptive attack. To ensure a second-strike capability and an adversary's awareness of it, deterrence rationalized an unrestrained search for sophisticated retaliatory capabilities. Any system that could be built was built, because, as President Kennedy explained in 1961, "only when arms are sufficient beyond doubt can we be certain without doubt that they will never be employed."

**MUTUAL ASSURED DESTRUCTION** Policymakers coined the phrase *mutual assured destruction* (MAD) to characterize the strategic balance that emerged during the 1960s and early 1970s. The term accurately described the superpowers' essential military stalemate, for mutual deterrence, based on the principle of assured destruction, rested on the military potential for and psychological expectation of widespread death and destruction for both combatants in the event of a nuclear exchange. Peace—or at least stability—was the product of mutual vulnerability; if one attacked the other, it would do so at the price of its own destruction. Thus nuclear deterrence was "like a gun with two barrels, of which one points ahead and the other points back at the gun's holder. If a burglar should enter your house, it might make sense to threaten him with this gun, but it could never make sense to fire it" (Schell, 1984).

As the United States and the Soviet Union competed with each other, the differences in their strategic capabilities narrowed. By the early 1970s a parity developed in the two superpowers' capabilities. This equality solidified the strategic assumptions of MAD. Thereafter both armed, not to gain superiority but to preserve a rough equivalence in their strategic arsenals. Soviet Premier Leonid Brezhnev in 1978 declared that "approximate equilibrium and parity are enough for defense needs. We do not set ourselves the goal of gaining military superiority. We also know that this very concept loses its meaning with the present enormous stockpiles of nuclear weapons and systems for their delivery." Thus the superpowers tacitly "agreed to stop comparing their overall national power in terms of the size of their respective nuclear arsenals" (Hunter, 1988).

The balance in the superpowers' strategic arsenals laid the basis for negotiations on limiting strategic arms during the 1970s détente phase of the U.S.–Soviet rivalry. Two SALT (Strategic Arms Limitations Talks) agreements were concluded during the 1970s. Both attempted to guarantee each superpower's second-strike capacity, on which stable deterrence rested. Although the pursuit of this shared goal posed difficulties, a precarious peace resulted. Despite the superpowers' sometimes tacit, sometimes formal acceptance of the principles on which assured destruction rested, differences in their interpretation and practical application inevitably led to disagreements. Thus the strategic arms race continued into the 1980s. As it did, the concepts governing the competition began to revert from the principle of deterrence to the previous principle of compellence—which implied the actual utilization of nuclear weapons.

**NUCLEAR UTILIZATION THEORY**   In the early 1980s, superpower confrontation replaced cooperation. A new debate about the role and purpose of nuclear weapons accompanied the change. Should nuclear weapons still be used exclusively for purposes of defense and deterrence? Or, assuming that a first-strike capability could be achieved, might they be used for offensive purposes?

Neither adversary had reason to trust the other. Each assumed that, unless deterred, its opponent would be tempted to use its arsenal for attack. Bad faith and "worst case" analyses governed the reformulation of doctrine.

U.S. statements about the practicability of preemptive strikes and the "winnability" of a nuclear exchange alarmed the world. When U.S. leaders spoke boldly of *damage limitation*, predicated on the belief that one way to avoid the destructive effects of nuclear weapons was to be the first to use them to destroy a portion of the adversary's weapons so that they could not be used in a retaliatory strike, the atmosphere chilled.

As U.S.–Soviet relations worsened, debate in the United States about the best way to protect national security with strategic weapons divided into polar positions. MAD continued to dominate the thinking of some, but others advocated ***nuclear utilization theory,*** or a NUTs approach to the role of nuclear weapons. For the proponents of NUTs, nuclear weapons would not play simply a deterrent role; the United States could also use them in war. Such a posture was necessary, it was argued, because the Soviet Union was preparing to fight—and win—a nuclear war (Pipes, 1977; in contrast, see Holloway, 1983, and Kennan, 1984b). Furthermore, the advocates of NUTs argued that any use of nuclear weapons would not necessarily escalate to an unmanageable, all-out nuclear exchange. Instead, they reasoned that it was possible to fight a protracted "limited" nuclear war. By making nuclear weapons more usable, they argued, the United States could make nuclear threats more credible.

The proponents of MAD, on the other hand, held that deterrence remained the only sane purpose for nuclear weapons. Any use of nuclear weapons, they argued, however limited initially, would surely escalate to an unrestrained exchange. "It is inconceivable to me," former U.S. Secretary of Defense Robert McNamara reflected, "that limited nuclear wars would remain limited—any decision to use nuclear weapons would imply a high probability of the same cataclysmic consequences as a total nuclear exchange." According to this view, the technical requirements necessary to wage a protracted limited nuclear war would surely exceed the human capacity to control it.

Furthermore, the advocates of MAD felt that because the threatened use of even tactical nuclear weapons would lower the nuclear threshold, a nuclear strategy premised on the usability of nuclear weapons in war in fact made war more likely, not less, and thereby diminished the weapons' deterrent capability. From this viewpoint, both superpowers were destined to live in a MAD world, even if, ironically, this meant they would remain bound in the "mutual hostage relationship" in which their earlier weapons decisions had imprisoned them (Keeny and Panofsky, 1981).

As the 1980s nuclear debate raged, U.S. and Soviet leaders both professed their commitment to avoiding nuclear war because it was "unthinkable." This meant expanding the capabilities of both defensive and offensive systems. Accordingly, each superpower continued developing and deploying the kinds of weapons that NUTs required—so-called discriminating low-yield nuclear weapons made possible by new technologies in guidance and precision. These prepared the contestants for warfare short of a massive all-out nuclear attack and sought to provide them with effective deterrents against a conventional war.

Yet this search for new weapons and new ideas to govern their use did little to calm fears. Instead, a vigorous peace movement swept Europe and North America, as mass publics on both sides of the Atlantic voiced their desire for an alternative to the threat posed by nuclear weapons. Accordingly, the purposes that NUTs strategists assigned nuclear arsenals fell into disfavor. As the U.S. Commission on Integrated Long-Term Strategy (1988) concluded, keeping a limited war within bounds involved "a reckless gamble with fate."

### From Offense to Defense, 1983–1993

A new challenge to strategic thinking was launched in 1983, when U.S. President Reagan proposed building a space-based defensive shield against ballistic missiles.

The *Strategic Defense Initiative* (SDI), as it was known officially, called for the development of a "Star Wars" *ballistic missile defense* (BMD) system using advanced space-based technologies to destroy from outer space offensive weapons launched in fear, anger, or by accident. The goal, as President Reagan defined it, was to make nuclear weapons "impotent and obsolete." Thus SDI sought to shift U.S. nuclear strategy away from reliance on offensive missiles to deter attack—that is, away from dependence on mutual assured destruction, which President Reagan deemed "morally unacceptable."

From the start, scientists questioned the feasibility of SDI's technological fix to the security dilemma posed by strategic weapons. There was simply no assurance that a reliable system was possible (Slater and Goldfischer, 1988). Critics also warned that SDI was prohibitively expensive ($24 billion was spent by 1991, and at least another $100 billion in additional costs was projected [*The Defense Monitor* 20 (No. 5, 1991): 2]. Critics thought SDI dangerous, for it could induce an unwarranted sense of safety when in fact it might not work. Worse still, they warned that SDI would stimulate development of a new generation of offensive weapons designed to overwhelm the defensive ones, and, in addition, it "constituted a frontal [legal] assault on the Anti-ballistic Missile (ABM) treaty of 1972" (Graybeal and Krepon, 1994).

Despite this uncertainty and illegality, the United States continued to support SDI even after the end of the Cold War and the demise of the Soviet Union. In the view of the Bush administration, SDI still had a mission: Rather than deter a massive Soviet missile attack on the United States, SDI was now needed to protect the United States against "attacks from the many countries that, regrettably, are acquiring ballistic missile capabilities. In the 1990s strategic defense makes much more sense than ever before."

This rationale reaffirmed the conviction that mutual assured destruction could not provide an adequate defense against missile attacks. SDI was better, Bush claimed, because it could provide "protection from limited ballistic missile assaults, whatever their source," rather than relying on "some abstract theory of deterrence." Yet questions remained. The Pentagon, for example, still generally looked askance at SDI because of the enormous costs, uncertain technological reliability, and the inability of a space-based system to protect against the many other ways that an enemy can deliver tactical weapons (Barnes, 1991), including "short-range missiles or intermediate-range ballistic missiles that fly slightly depressed trajectories" (Fetter, 1991) or even in a hand-carried suitcase.

Announcing "the end of the Star Wars era," U.S. Secretary of Defense Les Aspin in May 1993 called for the creation of what will be called the Ballistic Missile Defense Organization (BMDO). The acronym changed, and the goal was modified. The Pentagon targeted $3.8 billion in 1994 to develop and test "theater missile defenses"—"systems designed to protect a city or battlefield from medium-range missiles"—through the same SDI technologies. Thus, the elusive pursuit of national security continues, although now "without harming the objectives of the ABM treaty" (Graybeal and Krepon, 1994).

## The Mid-1990s Shifting Strategic Situation

The Cold War, the third global conflict of the twentieth century, concluded without bloodshed. To some, this remarkable achievement was attributable to the efficacy of the superpowers' deterrence strategies—the intimidating power of their weapons that made aggression suicidal and the rationality of leaders inspired by their awareness that survival was preferable to victory. To others, the superpowers averted apocalypse despite their awesome arsenals and deterrence doctrines, not because of them (Johansen, 1991; Vasquez, 1991). Thus, like the causes of the onset and end of the Cold War, explaining the most powerful states' avoidance of war will doubtless puzzle historians for decades.

Regardless of its causes, the end of the Cold War rivalry has ended the former adversaries' need to prepare for war against each other. In a radical change, they now perceive their interests served by *reducing* their armaments, not increasing them.

This signals a new age. Disarmament started on the strategic front for the first time. Not long after Mikhail Gorbachev assumed power in the Soviet Union in 1985, and shortly after Reagan's Star Wars speech, the superpowers negotiated a series of dramatic new arms control agreements (see Chapter 13). Reduced fears of an attack in Europe stripped away the rationale for tactical nuclear weapons. The precedent-setting Intermediate-range Nuclear Forces (INF) treaty, followed by the Conventional Armed Forces in Europe (CFE) and then the Strategic Arms Reduction Treaty (START) hastened the emergence of a strategic setting less darkened by the spectre of global conflagration.

The consequences of the reductions in strategic arsenals of the United States and Russia in 1994 are depicted in Figure 11.4. As shown, their post-START disarmament initiatives will cut their diminished arsenals even further by the year 2003. If this "deep cut" occurs, the strategic situation at the turn of the twenty-first century will look radically different. In turn, this would require rethinking traditional assumptions underlying strategic doctrines.

Few expect a war between the great powers in the foreseeable future. Most expect wars to continue in the Third World, however. To deal with the threat presented by this raging disorder, the great powers have sought to restructure their armed forces to deal with the kinds of threats and weapons with which adversaries will fight such wars. This calls for additional reductions of nuclear (strategic) arsenals, U.S. help to the former Soviet republics to destroy their nuclear weapons, and collective great-power efforts to keep nuclear weapons out of the hands of aggressors.

It also calls for increasing the capacity to wage conventional wars in emergent trouble spots. Military preparations have not ceased. Instead, a redirection toward the conduct of short-term wars fought with increasingly sophisticated conventional weapons is evident. The emerging strategies of the great powers now reflect their search for a new security architecture to contain regional conflicts and guard against the rising power of their rivals.

## THE GREAT POWERS' STRATEGIC OPTIONS: COMPETITION OR COOPERATION? . . . . . . . . . . . . . . . . . . . . . . . . . . . . . . .

The clarifying divisions of the Cold War have disappeared. The superpowers have retired their strategic nuclear arsenals more rapidly than they have replaced them, and the size of their strategic arsenals is scheduled to decline to their lowest levels in forty years. The threat to the existence—the survival—of the great powers has therefore greatly receded. The geostrategic landscape of the mid-1990s accordingly bears a scant resemblance to the familiar terrain that existed only a short time ago.

The transformed security environment has raised hopes for great-power coopera-tion. At the same time, it has deprived the strongest states of a clear idea of their role in this new world. When they peer through their blinds at the world outside, leaders see a chaotic and confusing environment. Also troubling is how to prepare

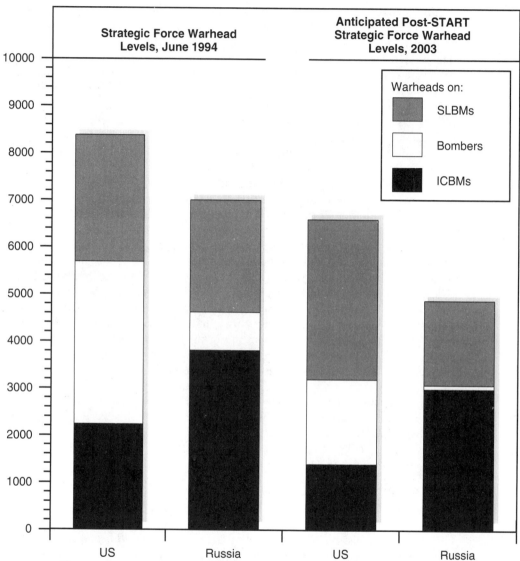

**Figure 11.4** The Changing Strategic Balance, 1994–2003
*Source:* Arms Control Association *Factfile*, 1994.

for their country's defense while protecting national interests and prosperity. Searching for a viable national security policy in an unfamiliar setting without the simplifying rigors of the Cold War presents a formidable challenge. In Washington, Moscow, Beijing, Tokyo, and Berlin, defense planners are struggling to devise workable strategies for peace and defense. The difficulty each great power has had charting its path for an uncertain future is understandable, as the character of the evolving security system has not assumed definition. Knowing with confidence where national interests lie is not possible. As a result, their plans have yet to result in well-defined doctrines.

But in each capital a modicum of consensus has begun to materialize about the principles that will guide the great powers' subsequent national security policies. To capture how the great powers have begun to adapt their national security policies to the new strategic environment, we need to compare their initial efforts to set priorities and delineate aims.

As we noted in Chapter 4, the choices range between the extremes of isolationist withdrawal from participation in world affairs to active international engagement. The options also require choices to be made between *unilateral* self-help actions on one end of the continuum to *multilateral* joint action with others on the other, with *specialized bilateral alliances* and ad hoc partnerships in between.

In examining the strongest powers' preferences and propensities, we can assume, based on their actions and statements since the Cold War ended, that they agree on certain fundamental properties about the emerging twenty-first-century world:

- Forestalling a new major war is a priority, because all other national security interests, such as prosperity, will be jeopardized should peace not endure.
- What is happening economically is of vital importance to military security and to the position of each power in the globe's future hierarchy of power.
- The world pyramid of power is moving to a *multipolar* distribution, in which no hegemon will be dominant and three, four, or more great powers will share approximately equal power.[8]

Given these probabilities, what sort of national security response is visible? We will examine comparatively the emerging security policies of the five major great powers.

## The New Security Policies of the United States

A key to understanding U.S. national security policy is America's economic decline relative to an ascending China, Japan, and Germany. To many observers, America is now more imperiled than imperial: It faces stiff trade competition, and its rivals'

---

[8] Simply put, the contemporary distribution of power in world politics may be said to resemble a layer cake. "The top military layer is largely unipolar, for there is no other military power comparable to the United States. The economic middle layer is tripolar [Europe, Japan, and the United States account for two-thirds of the world's product] and has been for two decades. The bottom layer of transnational interdependence shows a diffusion of power" (Nye, 1994). As former Secretary of State Lawrence Eagleburger has pointed out, we are "returning to a more traditional and complicated time of multipolarity, with a growing number of countries increasingly able to affect the course of events." The primary issue "is how well the United States accomplishes the transition from overwhelming predominance to a position more akin to a 'first among equals' status, and how well America's partners—Japan and Western Europe—adapt to their newfound importance. The change will not be easy for any of the players, as such shifts in power relationships have never been easy." For a fuller description of such a multipolar future and the policy dilemmas it poses, see Kegley and Raymond (1994a) and Kissinger (1994).

economies are growing at a faster pace. In the long run these trends will reduce U.S. influence and the ability to lead in world affairs, and will make a commitment to economic renewal and recovery at home a priority.

Yet this does not mean that military competition and threats will necessarily recede in importance. As U.N. Ambassador Madeleine Albright depicted it in 1993, "wherever we turn, someone is fighting or threatening to fight someone else." "The dangers of the period into which we are going," former Secretary of State Lawrence Eagleburger explained at the same time, "can be as unpleasant, if not as bloody, as most of the first fifty years of this century." We are returning to the raucous multipolarity more reminiscent of the nineteenth century of Bismarck than the past fifty years of the Cold War, he warned. Given this threat, military security will command as important a place in U.S. strategy as will trade, prosperity, and the promotion of free governments and markets throughout the world. "Our interests in democracy and markets do not stand alone," U.S. National Security Adviser Anthony Lake emphasized in 1993.

The tradeoffs between these economic and military objectives have divided Americans about the appropriate U.S. response. With the end of the Cold War, three schools of thought have begun vying to define America's role in world affairs:

> Neo-isolationists want the U.S. to deal only with threats to America's physical security, political independence, and domestic liberty. They find no such threats at present, and therefore argue that the U.S. should let other powers, and regional balances of power, take care of all the world's woes. Realists such as Henry Kissinger want the U.S. to continue to be the holder of the world balance of power, the arbiter of the main regional power groups, and the watchdog against all potential imperialistic trouble-makers. Internationalists want a greater role for multilateral institutions and more emphasis on human needs and rights, the environment and democracy. (Hoffmann, 1992: 59)

It has been the burden of the Clinton administration to attempt to reconcile these divergent needs and outlooks. Clinton has tried to strike a balance, arguing in 1993 that "putting our economic house in order cannot mean that we shut our windows to the world."

The difficulties of forging a viable security policy for this circumstance are great. The stark simplicities and self-evident symmetries of the Cold War have vanished, and "the coming era," summarizes Robert Jervis (1992), "seems odd because it is hard to locate a main axis of conflict." Added to this is the pressing fear that, like Great Britain at the end of the last century, the position of the United States, "though still unrivalled, has already begun eroding" (Zakaria, 1992–1993).

In the nascent multipolar system, the Clinton administration recognized from the start that it would be exceedingly difficult to define the cleavages and coalitions that might arise, and to separate friends from foes. Inasmuch as alignments are likely to depend on the specific issue under consideration, with combinations of like-minded countries in one issue-area (for example, trade policies) being quite different from those in other issue-areas (such as military security), the very nature of multipolarity is likely to require the United States to shift its support as interests and power ratios change and "to concentrate on the capabilities of [its] armed forces to meet a host of threats and not on a single threat" (Powell, 1992–1993).

THE MILITARY QUEST FOR NATIONAL SECURITY • **415**

Former U.S. President Richard Nixon, in his final public words before his death, urged Americans to reject isolationist calls to turn inward and warned that U.S. interests would suffer if the United States failed to lead the world community: "At times it will be necessary to use American power and influence to defend and extend freedom in places thousands of miles away if we are to defend freedom at home. . . . America must lead. . . . It is a role that will require global vision and big plays from President [Clinton] and every successive one in the era beyond peace" (Nixon, 1994).

This conviction was shared by Bill Clinton, who, in his inaugural address, declared that "Clearly America must continue to lead the world we did so much to make. . . . When our vital interests are challenged, or the will and conscience of the international community is defied, we will act—with peaceful diplomacy whenever possible, with force when necessary."

But how to prepare militarily to act? To help define a post–Cold War strategy against unknown threats, the Clinton administration initiated a *Bottom-Up Review*. Released in September 1993, it outlined priorities that pertain to military preparedness:

- Deter the use of nuclear, biological, or chemical weapons against the United States, its forces, and its allies.

- Halt or at least slow the proliferation of such weapons.

- Deter and, if necessary, defeat major aggression in regions important to the United States.

- Be capable of fighting and winning two major regional conflicts nearly simultaneously with a high probability of success, while minimizing American casualties.

- Prepare U.S. forces to participate effectively in multilateral peace enforcement and unilateral intervention operations that could include peacekeeping, humanitarian assistance, counterdrug, and counterterrorism activities.

- Use military-to-military contacts to help foster democratic values in other countries.

- Maintain technological superiority. (Collins, 1994: 5–6)

Viewed in light of this definition of its evolving defense doctrines and military budgets, the United States is thus likely to continue to rely on military might. The emerging U.S. strategy includes the following:

- It moves U.S. strategy from preparing for a war with the Soviet Union and the use of nuclear weapons to preparing for wars that do not threaten the use of these weapons. But it retains high spending for the latter: "The United States will spend $31 billion in 1994, and more than $300 billion over the next ten years to prepare for nuclear war" (*Defense Monitor* 22 [No. 10, 1993]: 2).

- "While strategic nuclear weapons have been cut on paper, little else has changed.

Many U.S. officials have failed to reexamine the basic foundations of U.S. nuclear policy: the strategic nuclear triad of land-based missiles, submarine-based missiles, and bombers [to assure] that if one of these legs is destroyed by a first-strike, the U.S. could still use the remaining two legs to demolish the enemy" (*Defense Monitor* 22 [No. 1, 1993]: 4).

- U.S. doctrine commits the United States to continue to prepare to fight and win two major wars at once. In early 1993, Pentagon planners contemplated adopting a so-called "win-hold-win" strategy under which, if war broke out at the same time in two regions, military force would be used decisively to win one war while air power and a limited number of ground forces would be used to hold the line in another. This sequential strategy was discarded, however. Instead, U.S. defense policy prepares to wage two wars simultaneously.

- U.S. doctrine will mobilize a balanced force structure "to meet any challenge that might emerge" (Cohen, 1991). "The U.S. continues to prepare to be able to intervene militarily around the world" (*Defense Monitor* 22 [No. 7, 1993]: 3). Labeling his policy "democratic realism," President Clinton in February 1993 explained that U.S. security is linked to helping prevent or to resolving conflicts throughout the world. Colin Powell, chairman of the Joint Chiefs of Staff, elaborated: "The central idea in the strategy is the change from a focus on global war-fighting to a focus on regional contingencies" through what Pentagon officials call "mid-intensity conflict" (MIC).

- The military's new doctrine equips the army for "mix-and-match" operations ranging from antidrug actions in Latin America to wars like those in the Persian Gulf and Panama. The doctrine focuses also on preparations for such operations as peacekeeping missions, humanitarian assistance and disaster relief, riot control, and assistance to countries seeking to maintain or convert to democracy. The goal is to enlarge the zone of peace and market democracies "by defending the developed democracies, encouraging the new democracies, getting tough with . . . 'backlash states' and dealing with humanitarian atrocities" (*The New Republic* 209 [October 18, 1993]: 7).

These strategic priorities preserve deterrence as the cornerstone of a revised post–Cold War U.S. strategy. The enemy changes. New threats are identified. Powerful conventional weapons will meet and deter them. And the definition of national security is broadened (see Box 11.2). But the purpose of U.S. military might remains the same: deterring the aggression of any other great power and militarized Third World powers.

Inherent in this strategy is a U.S. preference to share the burden of protecting international security with others where possible. Instead of striving to police the world unilaterally, U.S. strategy seeks to safeguard peace through "assertive multilateralism" (Nixon, 1994). Active use of UN peacekeeping (see Chapter 14) is consistent with this strategy. So, too, was U.S. advocacy of "partnerships for peace" in an expanded NATO that allowed twenty-one formerly neutral or formerly communist bloc countries to participate in some NATO operations (but without guarantees to

## Box 11.2
### REDEFINING THE POST–COLD WAR SECURITY ENVIRONMENT OF THE UNITED STATES

• • •

| OLD WORLD | NEW WORLD |
|---|---|
| **U.S. Perceptions** | |
| Soviet military power | Spread of nuclear weapons |
|  | Terrorism |
|  | Regional thugs |
|  | Drug traffickers |
| Deliberate Soviet attack | Instability in the former Soviet republics |
| Economic power assumed | Japanese economic power |
| High defense budgets | Declining defense budgets |
| Global security concerns paramount | Domestic security concerns paramount |
| **Geopolitical Context** | |
| Bipolar rigidity | Multipolar complexity |
| Predictable | Uncertain |
| Communism | Nationalism/religious extremists |
| U.S. dominant Western power | U.S. militarily No. 1, not economically |
| Fixed alliances | Ad hoc coalitions |
| "Good guys and bad guys" | "Gray guys" |
| UN paralyzed | UN viable |
| **The Threat** | |
| Single (Soviet) | Diverse |
| Survival at stake | Interests/Americans at stake |
| Known | Unknown |
| Deterrable | Nondeterrable |
| Strategic use of nukes | Terroristic use of nukes |
| Overt | Covert |
| Europe-centered | Regional, ill-defined |
| High risk of escalation | Little risk of escalation |

*(continued on page 418)*

| Old World | New World |
|---|---|
| **Military Forces** | |
| Attrition warfare | Decisive attacks on key nodes |
| War by proxy | Direct involvement |
| High-tech dominant | High-medium-low-tech mix |
| Forward deployed | Power projection |
| Forward-based | U.S.-based |
| Host-nation support | Self-reliant |

*Source:* Rep. Les Aspin (1992: 21).

their own security). Likewise, the *Peace, Prosperity and Democracy Act* reorients the foreign assistance program to *enlargement*—to enlarging free-market democracy throughout the globe, as well as encouraging other countries to implement reasonable population policies and to support "sustainable development."

Left unclear is how America's former Cold War adversary, Russia, might fit into this scheme and how it will react to America's new defense doctrines. Also notable is U.S. reluctance to play the role of "balancer" in the newly developing multipolar system by forming temporary alliances with other great powers as circumstances dictate.[9]

## Russian Strategy in the New World Order

For Russia, the primary threat is not an external attack. It is the threat of civil violence from within Russia and the former Soviet Republics on Russia's periphery. At the same time, fears of encirclement and/or isolation from abroad have intensified as Russia's power has plummeted.

Russian strategic planning must confront several tasks. First, it must ensure control over the panoply of nuclear weapons. This requires managing the military establishment, preventing internal differences within the officer corps and between it and enlisted soldiers, institutionalizing civilian authority over the armed forces, and pre-

[9] This runs counter to the advice that some strategists recommend. For example, in regard to Asia, where power ratios are undergoing rapid change, *The Economist* (October 30, 1993) counsels that

> For as far as the eye can see, the only credible way of maintaining a stable balance of power in Asia is for America to hold the scales. The United States is the only country with the power, the interests, the military means and the trust of enough of the concerned parties to be capable of doing this. It would require a line of thinking that Americans are uncomfortable with—that their country should act rather coldly, as Britain did in 19th century Europe, to back first one Asian country and then another to make sure none got too much stronger than the others. Why should America put itself out?

serving command of the nuclear warheads based outside the Russian republic (pending their possible removal altogether). Second, Russia must assure that no foreign power will attack it or intervene militarily to restore order. Third, Russia must seek to contain the escalation of ethnonational civil war in the neighbors on its borders. In this regard China, India, and the Muslim countries to the south present potential, if unknown, threats.

Russian leaders face unusual uncertainties preparing for the kind of threats now probable. As *The Economist* (October 30, 1993) observes, "Russia does not have a foreign policy—it has a couple. One is run by civilians; one by the armed forces. The reason for the involvement of the military men is obvious: the . . . main foreign-policy issues confronting Russia: . . . persuading Ukraine to give up its nuclear weapons, and working out relations with other former Soviet republics—all have strong military overtones. In addition to that, the Ministry of Defence thinks its role in crushing the armed rebellion [against Russian ruler Boris Yeltsin] on October 4th [1993] gives it a right to determine Russia's policy on these issues. What is not so obvious is who takes what policy line."

What, then, are the probable revisions in Russian strategy and force structures? Several components in Russia's existing security policy now define its direction.

- Like the United States, Russian leaders have pledged to keep the Russian arsenal "formidable" (Raphael, 1991). As former Soviet Foreign Minister Alexander Bessmertnykh underscored in January 1992, "Russia will remain a great power. It may not be a superpower, but it will be a great military power and part of the global strategic balance." "Russia will be the continuation of the Soviet Union in the field of nuclear weapons" was the way Russian Foreign Minister Andrei Kozyrev phrased this goal.

- Russian force reconstruction seeks to produce "a more efficient military, but one that is less threatening to the world." Russia most fears wars among its neighbors. "Having emerged from the Cold War," lamented Russian strategist Sergei Karaganov in February 1992, "we now face the prospect of hot war and even several hot wars. All our efforts in diplomacy and defense should be concentrated on avoiding those wars. What were nasty little domestic disputes are now international with the independence of all the former Soviet republics."

- "Instead of preparing to fight the West or keep control of Eastern Europe, the new military is focusing on protecting Russian interests in the former Soviet Union. Instead of huge tank armies, the military's new plans feature rapidly deployable airborne troops and peacekeeping units" (Gordon, 1993a).

- Russian strategy places special emphasis on preserving Russian command of existing nuclear weapons and preventing the loss of their control to the three other former Soviet republics where they in early 1995 were still deployed. Their use against Russia must be deterred. For this a focus on helping to prevent the proliferation of weapons of mass destruction is paramount.

- Russian military planners paid close attention "to the lessons of the Gulf War, particularly because of their persistent past shortcomings in both the strategic and tactical fields. They are applying these lessons even now to a basic revision of their strategic ideas and to their air doctrine. . . . They emphasize the use of advanced non-nuclear weapons throughout the depth of the opponent's military deployment and against all critical means of sustaining the war effort. In fact, they assert that such weapons are capable of accomplishing all of the missions previously reserved for strategic nuclear forces" (Nitze, 1991).

• Russian leaders now look to the West for support and friendship. To this end, Russia in June 1994 joined NATO as a special member of the alliance's *Partnerships for Peace* plan.

These principles were clarified in November 1993 when Russia announced its new defense doctrine. The doctrine rests on two principles. The first is the desire to avoid military conflict with other powers. "There are no potential enemies," President Boris Yeltsin explained, adding that "Russia will engage in warfare only in self- or collective defense." But the need for protection persists, and for this Russia's new defense doctrine explicitly states Russia's continuing reliance on military might in this "transitional period." As Yeltsin put it, "Russia will develop its armed forces in such manner that could allow it to defend itself and its people." General Pavel S. Grachev described this principle's implications by noting that "the danger of a global confrontation or nuclear war had been 'greatly reduced, though not eliminated,' and so the armed forces should become more mobile and prepare to fight regional conflicts" (Schmemann, 1993). The new doctrine justifies using interventionary troops in what the Russians call "the near abroad" (that is, the former Soviet republics and Eastern Europe, as distinct from in the "far abroad" consisting of countries outside the old Soviet empire). The professed aim is to enforce stability and protect the rights of the 25 million Russians living in the "near abroad," but critics fear that this peacekeeping role could be an excuse for the restoration of Russian imperial rule.

Especially instructive is the revision of nuclear strategy that Russia's new doctrine embraces. It drops the pledge of no first use of nuclear weapons in the event of an attack. While it rules out the use of nuclear weapons against nonnuclear states, "as for those states that have nuclear weapons, the doctrine says nothing," General Grachev declared. Presumably, "with Russia's conventional forces in disarray . . . the country evidently [thinks it needs] to remind potential aggressors, especially China, that it is prepared to use nuclear weapons in its defense" (Schmemann, 1993).

Exhibited in all these departures from Cold War strategic doctrines is an acute awareness that Russia's geostrategic position has declined. This sense of vulnerability explains Russia's professed desire to work cooperatively with others to preserve international security while it contends with the threats to Russian security arising from ethnonational uprisings in Russia and along its borders. Symptomatically, Russian Foreign Minister Andrei Kosyrev wrote UN Secretary General Boutros Boutros-Ghali in November 1993 asking for help. He requested UN supervision of Russian troops, arguing that "we consider it high time to seriously consider the possibility of sharing this peacekeeping burden with Russia." This and other pronouncements indicate the likelihood that Russia will seek a multilateral approach to its many security problems (Sestanovich, 1994).

## China's Global Presence and Security Posture

In U.S. and Russian conceptions of security, China figures prominently.

> The rise of China, if it continues, may be the most important trend in the world for the next century. When historians one hundred years hence write about our time, they may well conclude that the most significant development was the emergence of a vigorous market economy—and army—in the most populous country of the world. This is particularly likely if many of the globe's leading historians and pundits a century from now do not have names like Smith but rather ones like Wu.
>
> China is the fastest growing economy in the world, with what may be the fastest growing military budget. It has nuclear weapons, border disputes with most of its neighbors, and a rapidly improving army that may—within a decade or so—be able to resolve old quarrels in its own favor. The United States has possessed the world's largest economy for more than a century, but at present trajectories China may displace it in the first half of the next century and become the number one economy in the world. (Kristof, 1993: 59)

Because China is an economic giant and potential military colossus, its rising ascendance and growing assertiveness have understandably heightened concerns of the other great powers, especially Russia and Japan. China has sought to alleviate their fears, claiming it seeks peaceful relations with all; in 1994, for example, China signed an agreement with Russia aimed at preventing inadvertent or dangerous military confrontations between their forces. Moreover, China asserts that it does not crave military prowess. Yet "the officially disclosed military budget is a bit of a joke, for it does not even include sums spent on weapons procurement or on research and development. Yet, however misleading the official figure is, it is worth noting that between 1988 and 1993 it leaped 98 percent, to $7.5 billion. . . . As a very crude benchmark, . . . total military spending in international prices is much higher, perhaps as much as $90 billion" (Kristof, 1993: 65).

The direction of China's policies seem geared to ensuring its rise to prominence in the Pacific Rim. For that, continuing peace is essential. Hence China can be expected to concentrate on its internal development and trade relations, while seeking to contain domestic instability and divergent Chinese aspirations that threaten to tear national unity apart (especially if ethnic tensions and economic disparities among different regions within China increase). Preserving domestic tranquility and growth is a priority. To this end, China has continued to arm, to test its nuclear weapons, and to equip the globe's second largest (after Russia's) standing army. At the same time, China seems committed to developing the strategic and military might that its status as an economic giant seems to the Chinese to justify. And China has steadfastly refused to take instructions from its great-power rivals, insisting on its right to independently chart a foreign policy guided by China's own perceptions of its national interests.

As yet, this does not mean that China is preparing for foreign military engagement (arguing that defense is the purpose of its military buildup). Still, should that vigorous rearmament inspired by reawakened nationalist pride continue, China's arsenal will position it to play a dominant military role in world affairs. Napoleon Bonaparte counseled in the early nineteenth century that the world should "let China sleep"; now, as he predicted, when China awakens, "the world will tremble."

## Japan's Search for a Strategy

Japan is now an economic superpower, but its "dramatic postwar ascent . . . has not been accompanied by a comparable rise in its international political and strategic weight" (Brown, 1993). Since Japan's defeat in World War II, its policies have adhered to the guidelines of the **Yoshida Doctrine**. As its proponent Prime Minister Shigeru Yoshida argued, Japanese security policy should be to avoid international disputes, keep a low profile on divisive global issues, and concentrate on economic pursuits.

That preference continues to underlie Japan's strategy today. But the new international setting has brought into question the wisdom of this traditional posture, especially in light of the transformed distribution of power in the wake of the decline of U.S. power, the fall of Russia's, and the rise of China's. A larger role and presence are imminent.

Prime Minister Kiichi Miyazawa's policy departures in 1992 signaled the new direction Japan's security policies are likely to take. He won passage of the Peacekeeping Operations Bill, which enabled Japan to deploy a Self-Defense Force to participate in UN peacekeeping operations in Cambodia—the first use of Japanese armed forces abroad since the Second World War. Japan's push for inclusion as a permanent member of the UN Security Council, and its rise to the top of the world's foreign aid donors, also suggest a rise in Japanese international activism.

Japan seeks to discard its isolation and become an involved player in world affairs. Its rising expenditures for defense and efforts to cement cordial relations with its Asian neighbors also speak to this redirection. Japan in 1994 still adhered to its policy of spending no more than one percent of its gross national product on defense and remained committed to its postwar constitution that forbid remilitarization. But Japan's force is impressive, with 250,000 soldiers in uniform and the Pacific's largest navy. This power is a worry to Japan's neighbors, who remember well Japan's violent past. Postwar Japanese pacifism could, with this military clout, give way to resurgent militarism to deal with its simmering territorial disputes with both Russia and China. Regardless of the future use of this military power, Japan faces a wide range of security concerns, which would intensify if the troubled situation in Northeast Asia (especially North Korea) worsens or the United States lowers its presence in Asia. These fears are likely to prompt continuing Japanese participation in the rapid Asian arms race (Klare, 1993).

Even more problematically, with its neighbors arming to the teeth, Japan has begun to have second thoughts about nuclear weapons. It balked at the Clinton administration's attempt to press for a Japanese commitment to support the "indefinite and unconditional extension of the nuclear nonproliferation treaty when it expires in 1995" (Harrison, 1993). This reversal of Japanese doctrine would, indeed, inaugurate a radical departure in Japan's posture toward its military role in the world.

## Germany's Strategic Vision

Now united, Germany is also likely to show signs of a new assertiveness once the immense costs of reunification and rebuilding the former German Democratic Republic are digested. Given its size, economic strength, and geographic location, the challenge for Europeans will be to find a way to absorb Germany within a broad European power-sharing arrangement (Chace, 1992). But according to some analysts, "Germany is too powerful to disappear into a wider European framework." It already accounts for 28 percent of the European Union's gross national product, and its share of the EU budget is "three times the contribution of Great Britain and twice the amount of Great Britain and France combined." Moreover, Belgium, Britain, France, Italy, Luxembourg, the Netherlands, and Spain have linked the value of their currencies to the mark, therein giving Germany enormous leverage over interest rates and economic growth (Garten, 1992). In fact, this extraordinary economic clout assures that Germany will reign dominant within any emergent amalgamated European political entity, whether it is built around the federalist idea of a supranational government or some other, more modest pan-European institutional structure. In either case, "there is nothing in the European [Union], on its own, to balance the power of a united Germany" (O'Brien, 1993a). "Too big for Europe, too small for the world" is the slogan that is used to describe Germany's place in continental affairs.

One consequence of Germany's growing economic strength and diplomatic independence will be greater competition with the United States and other trade rivals. Yet this is not likely to result in a renewed push to flex German military muscle. Despite the January 1993 parliamentary proposal to amend its constitution to permit German troops to take part in international peacekeeping operations, an independent German military presence on the world stage is not likely, and renewed militarism is even less so. Germany's armed forces are still deeply entrenched in and constrained by the joint command in NATO, the Western European Union, and its mutual Franco-German force structure. Germany remains a fervent advocate of the nuclear nonproliferation regime and shows no inclination to build a nuclear weapons capability of its own. Also, German democratization poses a barrier to any return to militarism. Hence, economic rivalry is unlikely to culminate in military activity in the forseeable future.

To be anticipated will be Germany's continuing effort to push for collective security, both within Europe and globally. The drive to become a permanent member of the UN Security Council speaks to Germany's emphasis on multilateral approaches to international security; Germany's 408,200 armed force addresses its abiding desire to be prepared for defense. Similarly, Germany's continuing preference to rely on the United States and NATO for a nuclear guarantee admits Germany's predilection for cooperative partnership in international security. German leaders "have preferred to treat the cynical pleasures of realpolitik with suspicion and to believe that foreign policy could and should be grounded in defense of virtuous principles such as democracy, self-determination, free trade and human rights. [This is reflective of a] strong aversion to militarism" (*Economist* 330, November 20, 1993).

## Other States, Other Security Concerns and Policies

Comparing the policies of the five largest powers in isolation can be misleading. Of perhaps equal importance to future international security is what strategies are forged by the other regional military powers below this great-power tier of the global military hierarchy. As we have seen, a number of states presently outside the circle of dominant military powers are striving to join it. Their armament programs are ambitiously aggressive. The quest for nuclear weapons, and the potential collapse of the nonproliferation regime, would radically transform the globe's security climate.

> Nuclear proliferation in other parts of the world must be reckoned as a high probability. The [U.S.] Central Intelligence Agency estimated that in the early 1990s over fifty countries were working on nuclear, chemical, or ballistic missile capabilities. By the end of the century, some number of these states will certainly develop operational weapons of mass destruction and the means to deliver them. Because nuclear forces could serve as an effective deterrent against retaliation by an outside state, more and more states may be inclined to see nuclear weapons as a serious military option. A nuclear-capable Azerbaijan, for example, could invade Armenia and present the world with a *fait accompli* backed by the threat of using its own nuclear weapons against any third party that would presume to meddle.
>
> Given these political and technological trends, it appears likely that before the end of the twentieth century, a nuclear weapon will be detonated in anger somewhere on the planet. That event, the first use of nuclear weapons since August 1945, could lead to a rapid expansion of the nuclear club as countries with the technical know-how hasten to cross the threshold. Several states are also likely to develop or acquire intermediate-range delivery capabilities. Even if there is no actual use of nuclear weapons, the proliferation of fingers on nuclear triggers will almost inevitably change . . . attitudes toward defense against such weapons. (Kruzel, 1993: 4)

By most assessments, alongside the continuing danger of nuclear warfare, regional and ethnic violence is likely to be a critical locus for military action in the rest of the century. The Third World at the periphery is populated by hypernationalist countries of growing military strength with an interest in controlling events in the areas where their primary security interests lie. This danger has increased the regional focus of the great powers in their immediate spheres of influences. Hence Germany, France, and Great Britain are committed to managing security in Western Europe; Russia is committed to the preservation of order in Eastern Europe and its southern rim; and China and Japan are intent on preserving peace in the rapidly expanding Asian trade zone on which their future prosperity depends, where the globe's "next great arms race" is escalating (Klare, 1993). Nigeria and South Africa are positioned to dominate Africa, and Brazil is similarly positioned in South America. In the Middle East, a large number of military powers are racing for the arms they perceive necessary to protect their interests and security and to exercise influence. The problems that Third World countries face in this situation are numerous and largely intractable (see Chubin, 1995; Singh and Bernauer, 1993).

In combination, global trends in armament and the fragility of stability raise great concerns about the prospects for peace in the twilight of the twenty-first century.

## ESCAPING THE SECURITY DILEMMA? . . . . . . . . . . . . . . . . . . . . . . . . .

The search for national security through preparation for war continues. The quest is understandable in a world where states alone remain responsible for their own self-defense. As President Eisenhower once noted, "until war is eliminated from international relations, unpreparedness for it is well nigh as criminal as war itself." Hence the security dilemma persists.

The fears engendered by visions of national vulnerability also explain why defense planners base their plans on "worst-case" analyses of others' capabilities and intentions. The urge to arm is further stimulated by the ubiquitous influence of defense planners in the policy-making process of most countries and the tendency of political leaders to adopt the vocabulary and concepts of their military advisers.

Asking whether military preparedness risks, rather than increases, national security raises an uncomfortable question. It challenges the orthodox approach to national security prevalent throughout much of the world's history. Yet questioning is required. Many defense experts today recommend redefining national security (for example, Sorensen, 1990; Allison and Treverton, 1992) (see Box 11.3). To their way of thinking, reconceptualization is needed to answer the ultimate questions—Can the world escape the security dilemma and can it remove its vulnerability to annihilation? Less apocalyptically, how can new conceptions of national security gain acceptance?

Because a wide spectrum of problems has risen on political agendas, the concerns of today's foreign policymakers appear different and more diverse from what they were just a short time ago. Though the danger of nuclear weapons and interstate warfare continues, it would be foolish to neglect the dangers posed by such emergent threats as trade-bloc competition, neomercantilism, trade protectionism, the continuing impoverishment of the least developed countries, acid rain, deforestation, global warming, soaring population growth, the AIDS epidemic, international drug trafficking, the depletion of the earth's finite resources, and destruction of its protective ozone layer. These problems command attention, because human survival may depend on mastering these nonmilitary threats. Now that fears of great-power war have receded with the end of the Cold War, the economic and ecological dimensions of national security have assumed relatively greater prominence. Some now believe that in the twenty-first century, "security" should be defined more broadly so as to include all threats to human survival, both military and nonmilitary.

If the pursuit of military might does, indeed, lead to a decrease in national and

## Box 11.3
### REDEFINING "SECURITY" IN THE "NEW WORLD ORDER"
• • •

The concept of "security" must include protection against all major threats to human survival and well-being, not just military threats. Until now, "security"—usually addressed as "national security"—has meant the maintenance of strong military defenses against enemy invasion and attack. This approach may have served us well in the past, when such attack was seen as the only real threat to national survival; today, however, when airborne poisons released by nuclear and chemical accidents can produce widespread death and sickness (as occurred with the Bhopal and Chernobyl disasters), and when global epidemiological and environmental hazards such as AIDS and the "greenhouse effect" can jeopardize the well-being of the entire planet, this perspective appears increasingly obsolete. As individual economies become ever more enmeshed in the world economy, moreover, every society becomes more vulnerable to a global economic crisis. And, as modern telecommunications bring us all closer together, we are made acutely aware of the pain and suffering of those living under oppression, tyranny, and injustice.

Given the fact that our individual security and well-being will depend to an ever-increasing extent on the world's success in mastering complex political, economic, environmental, and epidemiological problems, we must redefine "security" to embrace all of those efforts taken to enhance the long-term health and welfare of the human family. Defense against military aggression will obviously remain a vital component of security, but it must be joined by defenses against severe environmental degradation, worldwide economic crisis, and massive human suffering. Only by approaching the security dilemma from this multifaceted perspective can we develop the strategies and instruments that will be needed to promote global health and stability.

Given the multiplicity of pressing world hazards, the concept of "national security" must be integrated with that of "world security." Until now, most people have tended to rely on the nation-state to provide protection against external threats, and have viewed their own nation's security as being conversely affected by the acquisition of power and wealth of other nations. Thus, in the interests of "national security," nation-states have often engaged in a competitive struggle to enhance their own economic and military strength at the expense of other nations' capabilities. This us-versus-them, zero-sum competition for security is naturally biased toward unilateral solutions to critical problems, frequently entailing military and/or economic coercion. In today's interdependent world, however, the quest for security is rapidly becoming a *positive-sum* process, whereby national well-being is achieved jointly by all countries—or not at all.

*Source: Michael T. Klare and Daniel C. Thomas (1991: 3).*

global security, how then can states escape this dilemma and free themselves from the prospect of destruction? How can they meet these emergent nonmilitary threats, when the threat of warfare in a nationalistic age remains as pervasive as ever?

The security dilemma grants little room for maneuvering. The world has yet to accept "common security" and "nonoffensive defense," strategies that would eliminate offensive capabilities (Møller, 1992). States still build weapons of attack for deterrence, even though conventional deterrence has failed frequently in the past (Huth, 1988; Mearsheimer, 1983). Moreover, deterrence remains an uncertain theory based on a peculiar, almost illogical premise that requires the continuing vulnerability of all states. Despite this, most believe that the threat system must be preserved to counter the threat. Thus security may depend as much on the control of force as on its pursuit. As the British author H. G. Wells long ago prophesied, human destiny may be becoming more and more a race between self-restraint and survival. The alternatives to reliance on preparing for the common defense through armaments will be considered in the next two chapters.

## SUGGESTED READINGS

Baldwin, David A. *Paradoxes of Power*. New York: Basil Blackwell, 1989.

Blackwill, Robert D., and Albert Carnesale, eds. *New Nuclear Nations*. New York: Council on Foreign Relations Press, 1993.

Bundy, McGeorge, William J. Crowe Jr., and Sidney D. Drell. *Reducing Nuclear Danger: The Road Away from the Brink*. New York: Council on Foreign Relations Press, 1993.

Burrows, William E., and Robert Windrem. *Critical Mass: The Dangerous Race for Superweapons in a Fragmenting World*. New York: Simon & Schuster, 1994.

Cassidy, Kevin J., and Gregory A. Bischak, eds. *Real Security: Converting the Defense Economy and Building Peace*. Albany: State University of New York Press, 1993.

Hammond, Grant T. *Plowshares into Swords: Arms Races in International Politics, 1840–1991*. Columbia: University of South Carolina Press, 1993.

Kapstein, Ethan Barnaby. *The Political Economy of National Security: A Global Perspective*. New York: McGraw-Hill, 1992.

Klare, Michael T., and Daniel C. Thomas, eds. *World Security: Challenges for a New Century*, 2nd ed. New York: St. Martin's Press, 1994.

Laurance, Edward J. *The International Arms Trade*. New York: Lexington Books, 1992.

Rothgeb, John M., Jr. *Defining Power: Influence and Force in the Contemporary International System*. New York: St. Martin's Press, 1993.

Shultz, Richard, Roy Godson, and Ted Greenwood, eds. *Security Studies for the 1990s*. Washington, D.C.: Brassey's, 1993.

Taylor, Trevor, and Ryukichi Imai, eds. *The Defence Trade: Demand, Supply and Control*. Washington, D.C.: Brookings Institution, 1994.

# CHAPTER 12

• • •

# RESORT TO FORCE: ARMED CONFLICT BETWEEN STATES AND WITHIN THEM

• • •

*Only the dead have seen the end of conflict.*

George Bush,
U.S. President, 1992

*Mankind must put an end to war or war will put an end to mankind.*

John F. Kennedy,
U.S. President, 1961

Every day, newspapers and television report that human activity revolves around the use of force to settle disputes. Since 1945 not a single day has gone by without war. It is little wonder so many people equate world politics with violence.

In *On War*, the Prussian strategist Karl von Clausewitz advanced his famous dictum that war is merely an extension of diplomacy by other means. This insight underscores the fact that war is an instrument states use to resolve their conflicts. It is also the deadliest instrument. War's onset means that persuasion and negotiations have been unsuccessful. War is, in this sense, as Clausewitz stated, "a form of communication between countries," albeit an extreme form.

This definition pictures war as the use of military force against an adversary to achieve political goals, as distinct from conflict.[1] With this distinction in mind, this chapter examines five ways that armed force is most often used: in *wars* between states, through *coercive diplomacy* that provokes crises and the practice of *low-intensity conflict*, as well as the violence within states that produces *civil wars* and often involves *terrorism*.

---

[1] *War* and *conflict* are different. Conflict occurs when two parties perceive differences between them and seek to resolve those differences to their own satisfaction. Conflict is an intrinsic product of communication and contact. Because some conflict is inevitable when people interact, we should not regard conflict as abnormal. Paradoxically, close contact leads to both friendship and enmity: Cooperation may produce conflict, and conflict may promote cooperation (Coser, 1956). Nor should we regard conflict as altogether undesirable. Conflict promotes social solidarity, clarifies values, stimulates creative thinking, and encourages learning. If managed properly, these functions are constructive to human progress.

• • •

## WARS BETWEEN STATES: CONTINUITIES AND CHANGE . . . . . . . . . . . . . . . .

To trace changes in the frequency and character of war between states, we will break the state system since 1815 into six historical periods, with 1848, 1881, 1914, 1945, and 1989 demarcating the significant "turning points" scholars conventionally regard as major transition points in contemporary history. Table 12.1 summarizes the data that speak to comparisons across these six successive periods.

This evidence measures only sustained wars *between* sovereign states resulting in at least one thousand battle deaths (see Small and Singer, 1982). Measured in this restricted way, the data show that 216 interstate wars erupted between 1816 and 1992, but that the frequency has been fairly stable over time.[2] Furthermore, if we take the expanding number of countries in the system into account, the frequency of the outbreak of wars since 1816 "actually declines from 4 per state per decade prior to World War II to 2 per state per decade since [and even less since the Berlin Wall was dismantled in 1989]. And if we control not for the number of states but the number of *pairs*, the decline appears even more dramatic" (Singer, 1991: 57). Thus, when we adjust for the increasing number of independent countries, the post–World War II era appears comparatively more peaceful than do the periods that preceded it.

Or does it? A different picture emerges when attention focuses on the number of wars *under way*, rather than on the number of wars that start. Interstate war has been under way almost continuously since the Congress of Vienna in 1815. Although there were eighty-two years between 1816 and 1992 in which no wars began, there were

TABLE 12.1 FREQUENCY WITH WHICH 216 WARS HAVE BEGUN OVER SIX HISTORICAL PERIODS, 1816–1992

| Period | Key System Characteristic | No. of Wars | System Size (Average No. of States) |
|---|---|---|---|
| 1816–1848 | Concert of Europe | 33 | 28 |
| 1849–1881 | Wars of European unification | 43 | 39 |
| 1882–1914 | Resurgent imperialism | 38 | 40 |
| 1915–1944 | The Great Depression | 24 | 59 |
| 1945–1988 | The Cold War | 43 | 117 |
| 1989–1992 | Post–Cold War multipolarity | 35 | 172 |

*Source:* Data for 1816–1988 provided courtesy of the Correlates of War Project at the University of Michigan under the direction of J. David Singer and Melvin Small, as retrieved and aggregated by Ricardo Rodriguez. Data for 1989–1992 are based on Peter Wallensteen and Karin Axell (1993) and U.S. CIA (1993).

[2] Estimates of the number of wars depend on the criteria used to define war. Quincy Wright (1942) identified 278 wars from 1480 to 1940; Lewis Fry Richardson (1960b) over 300 from 1820 to 1949; Pitirim Sorokin (1937) 862 from 1100 to 1925; William Eckhardt (1990, 1991) 589 from 1500 to 1990; and R. Paul Shaw and Yuwa Wong (1989: 3) 14,500 over the last 5,600 years, with peace comprising "only 8 percent of the entire recorded history of mankind."

only twenty in which none was under way (Small and Singer, 1982: 149; Singer, 1991: 60–75; Wallensteen and Axell, 1993: 333). The so-called "outbreak of peace" in the post–Cold War is a myth about the facts, as no less than nineteen large-scale wars were under way in each year of the 1989–1992 period (Wallensteen and Axell, 1993: 333).

Let us examine the period since 1945 more closely. Defining war more broadly to include all occasions of armed conflict involving one or more governments and causing the death of 1,000 or more people each year, we observe 149 such incidents from 1945 through 1992 (Sivard, 1993: 20). By this measure, twenty-nine major wars were under way in 1992, and during 1993, forty-two countries were participants in fifty-two major conflicts (UNDP, 1994: 47). Thus, the number of wars, commencing and under way worldwide has remained high since the Cold War ended, providing scant evidence that the world has become more secure. Trends suggest "that the international community has at least some capacity to contain conflicts. The number of protracted conflicts testifies, however, to the inability to find lasting solutions to well-known conflicts" (Wallensteen and Axell, 1993). Figure 12.1 portrays the pattern since 1945 and also estimates the lives destroyed by wars. We will take a closer look at the latter statistic.

## THE CHANGING CHARACTER OF INTERSTATE WAR . . . . . . . . . . . . . . . . .

War has been recurrent in history, but its character has changed markedly in the twentieth century. The reason is found in the nature of modern weapons.

## The Destructiveness of War

One of the most disquieting long-term global trends is the exponential increase in the destructiveness of war, as measured by the loss of human life. According to one estimate, the average time it took for one million people to die in war during the two millennia between the rise of Rome and the beginning of the twentieth century was fifty years, whereas the average time it has taken for that many people to die in war throughout the twentieth century was one year (WorldWatch 7 [March/April 1994]: 39).

> [Since 1500, the world] has lived through 589 wars and lost 141,901,000 lives to them. . . . Beginning with the 17th, every century has registered an increase in the number of wars and in the number of deaths associated with them. The rise in war deaths has far outstripped the rise in population. The 20th century in particular has been a stand-out in the history of warfare. Wars now are shockingly more destructive and deadly. So far, in the 90 years of this century, there have been over four times as many war deaths as in the 400 years preceding. (Sivard, 1991: 20)

Since 1945 all wars either have been between relatively less developed countries or entailed military intervention of the great powers in them; none has occurred *between* the great powers. This is why scholars term the post–1945 period the "long

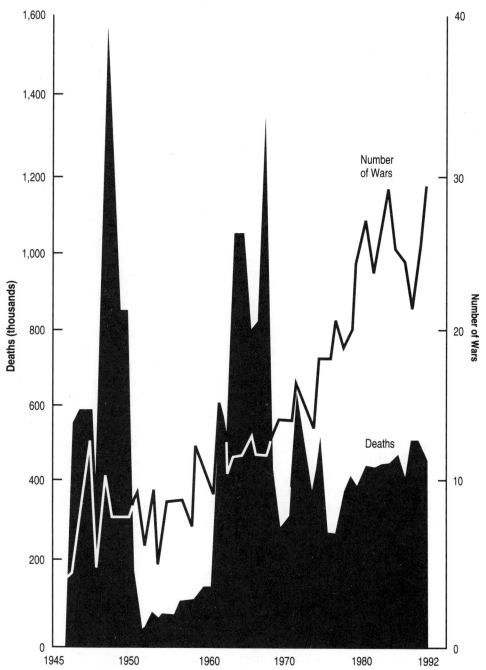

**Figure 12.1** The Fighting Never Stopped: Wars and War-related Deaths, 1945–1992
*Source:* Based on Ruth Leger Sivard (1993: 20).

peace" (Gaddis, 1991a). Still, the fact that since 1945 nearly all wars have occurred outside the great-power "core" in the Third World does not mean that war has ceased to be destructive and bloody. The outcome has been truly tragic (see Figure 12.1). One estimate attributes 40 million deaths to some 250 wars in the Third World since 1945 (Ball, 1994: 216–217).

New, more destructive but nondiscriminating weapons and aerial bombardment have increasingly made noncombatants and civilians wars' main victims. In the twentieth century many more unarmed civilians than professional soldiers have died in wars. Since 1945 more than three-fifths of the human toll from wars were civilians; 14,505,003 noncombatants lost their lives between 1945 and 1992 (Sivard, 1991: 20; 1993: 23).

Nuclear weapons create new dangers that threaten to worsen this trend beyond imagination. Described in Chapter 11, the arsenals of 19,684 nuclear warheads in mid-1994 are far more destructive than those used against Japan during World War II. The U.S. National Security Council estimated in the late 1970s that a superpower exchange at that time would have killed nine times as many Americans and Soviets, not counting the ravaging effects of radiation, as the number who died in all their previous wars (*Defense Monitor* [No. 2, 1979]: 8). The effects of a "limited" war with today's nuclear arms would not be limited. Studies of the immediate and delayed effects of nuclear war (see Sagan and Turco, 1990) picture a postnuclear environment repugnant to contemplate (see Box 12.1). Life as we know it could cease. The danger, moreover, persists: "If all planned cuts in nuclear weapons are implemented, in the year 2003 the world will still have as many as 20,000 nuclear weapons containing the explosive power of more than 200,000 Hiroshima bombs" (*Defense Monitor* 22 [No. 1, 1993]: 1) or "more than 900 times the six million tons of TNT expended in World War II" (Sivard, 1993: 11).

The increasing destructiveness of modern weapons has transformed the character of contemporary warfare in other ways. The length of interstate wars steadily increased between 1816 and World War II, for example, but then began a drastic decline. Wars since 1945 have simply been shorter. Similarly, the average number of countries participating in major wars (which had been rising steadily since 1815) has fallen sharply since World War II (Singer, 1991).

Wars are also more confined geographically and usually involve small countries: Since 1945 92 percent of wars have been between minor states in the developing countries (Sivard, 1993: 20). Hence, major wars have ceased to occur, but the number of smaller ones has increased. This reverses the historic pattern that characterized the previous century, when war between the great powers was comparatively frequent and each took a large toll in human lives.

## Weapons and the Obsolescence of Great-Power War?

Paradoxically, perhaps, the world's most powerful countries have been the most constrained in their use of military strength against one another. The destructiveness

# Box 12.1
## TWO VIEWS OF THE AFTERMATH OF A NUCLEAR ATTACK

• • •

### A PHYSICIAN'S VIEW

A 20-megaton nuclear bomb . . . would create a fireball 1½ miles in diameter, with temperatures of 20 million to 30 million degrees Fahrenheit. . . . All living things would be vaporized within a radius of "ground zero." Six miles from this point, all persons would be instantly killed by a huge silent heat flash traveling at the speed of light. . . . Within a 10-mile radius, the blast wave would slow to 180 mph. In that area, winds and fires would probably kill 50 percent of the population, and injure another 40 percent. . . . Within 20 miles of the center, 50 percent of the inhabitants would be killed or injured by the thermal radiation and blast pressures, and tens of thousands would suffer severe burn injuries. . . . Medical "disaster planning" for a nuclear war is meaningless.

*Source: International Physicians for the Prevention of Nuclear War (Associated Press, March 8, 1980)*

### THE VIEW OF ATMOSPHERIC SCIENTISTS

As bad as the prompt and local effects of nuclear war would be—the delayed and global consequences might be much worse. . . . Forest fires ignited in such a war could generate enough smoke to obscure the sun and perturb the atmosphere over large areas. . . . The smoke from the burning of modern cities would provide a still more serious threat. . . . Provided cities were targeted, even a "small" nuclear war could have disastrous climatic consequences; a global war, . . . might lower average planetary temperatures by 15 to 20°C, darken the skies sufficiently to compromise green plant photosynthesis, produce a witches' brew of chemical and radioactive poisons, and significantly deplete the protective ozone layer. These effects, which had been almost wholly overlooked by the world's military establishments, [are] described as "nuclear winter."

*Source: Carl Sagan and Richard P. Turco (1993: 369)*

of modern weapons may have reduced their practical utility and restrained their use. Winston Churchill articulated this thesis in 1953 when he confessed that on occasion he had "the odd thought that the annihilating character of [nuclear weapons] may bring an utterly unforeseeable security to mankind. . . . It may be that when the advance of destructive weapons enables everyone to kill anybody else no one will want to kill anyone at all." As Churchill mused, "After a certain point has passed, it may be said, the worse things get the better. . . . Then it may be that we shall, by a process of sublime irony, have reached a stage in this story where safety will be the sturdy child of terror, and survival the twin brother of annihilation."

This predicament provides a plausible explanation for the virtual absence since 1945 of wars among the great powers.[3] It was perhaps the incredible costs and risks of fighting that led U.S. President Richard Nixon to say, in the context of the Vietnam War and implicitly in reference to wars between major powers, "I seriously doubt that we will ever have another war. This is probably the very last one." Others also voice this sentiment. Writing "On the Obsolescence of War," John Weltman (1974) asserted, for instance, that "violence as an instrument of foreign policy has increasingly become highly inefficient, if not counterproductive." Even more confidently, Werner Levi (1981) predicted in *The Coming End of War* that the day was nearing when "weapons [will] wipe out war." War, which "antedates the state, diplomacy and strategy by many millennia," may be "ceasing to commend itself to human beings as a desirable or productive . . . means of reconciling discontents" (Keegan, 1994).

Since the Cold War, the great powers appear to have engaged in a "retreat from doomsday" (Mueller, 1989). A "zone of peace" among them has emerged, alongside a "zone of turmoil" in the rest of the world (Singer and Wildavsky, 1993). In early 1992, U.S. President George Bush observed at the United Nations that "today the threat of global nuclear war is more distant than ever before."

This does not mean, however, that the threat has disappeared. Increasing numbers of countries in the globe's large "zone of turmoil" stockpile weapons of mass destruction, both overtly and covertly (see Chapter 11). Warfare is not necessarily the intended purpose, because military strategies today often emphasize not winning in war but deterring an adversary from starting it. Yet there is no guarantee that deterrence will succeed forever. Still, the self-defeating nature of nuclear might has reduced its utility as a tool of coercive diplomacy. As Melvin Laird, U.S. secretary of defense in the Nixon administration, observed, "Nuclear weapons . . . are useless for military purposes." Today nuclear states want not so much to win as to avoid loss.

A rival, more pessimistic explanation is also worth contemplating. The world may have escaped nuclear devastation by sheer luck—"less a consequence of intelligent policy than a fortunate concatenation of conditions" (Singer, 1991). By the laws of probability, so this reasoning goes, the longer nuclear arsenals exist, the more likely it is that a nuclear exchange will occur, as any event that can possibly happen eventually will. The question is not if, but when, for deterrence is inherently unstable and cannot persist forever. The odds for nuclear holocaust through a fatal error, whether of judgment, performance, miscalculation, or accident, are not low simply because the world has avoided that tragedy until now. Moreover, the limits to rationality under conditions of crisis heighten the potential dangers (Holsti, 1989a). So,

---

[3] And it fulfills a prediction made by Alfred Nobel (the Swedish armaments manufacturer whose endowments fund the Nobel Peace Prize and other awards), who speculated in 1892 that "perhaps my dynamite plants will put an end to war sooner than your congresses. On the day two army corps can annihilate each other in one second, all civilized nations will recoil from war in horror."

too, is safety limited by the unreliable decision-making procedures of large-scale organizations and by the probability of additional "close call" accidents (Sagan, 1993).

These apocalyptic thoughts suggest that the widespread belief that nuclear weapons have preserved peace—a *pax atomica*—may be a fanciful "myth" (see Vasquez, 1991). We may also question the corollary proposition that as "the fear of escalating nuclear power reaches further down, [it will inhibit] also the use of lesser force for lesser ends and goals" (Majeed, 1991).

These speculations lead to a related set of questions about the causes of war. Accordingly, it is useful to review contending ideas about the sources from which wars originate.

## THE CAUSES OF WAR: CONTENDING PERSPECTIVES · · · · · · · · · · · · · · · · ·

The resort to force has prompted efforts throughout history to understand its causes. Inventories of the causes of war invariably conclude that they are incomplete (see Blainey, 1988; Howard, 1983; Vasquez, 1993; Waltz, 1954), in part because most agree that war is rooted in multiple sources at various "levels of analysis" (recall Chapter 2).

## War and Human Nature

In one sense, of course, all wars originate from the decisions of national leaders. The choices they make ultimately determine whether war will occur. It is therefore common in discussions of the roots of war to consider the relationship of war to individuals and human choice. For this, questions about human nature are central.

The repeated outbreak of war has led some, such as the famous psychologist Sigmund Freud (1968), to conclude that aggression stems from humans' genetic programming and psychological makeup. Noting that Homo sapiens is the most deadly species, ethologists (those who study animal behavior in order to understand human behavior) such as Konrad Lorenz (1963) similarly argue that humankind is one of the few species practicing "intraspecific" aggression (routine killing of its own kind). Most other species practice "interspecific" aggression (they kill only other species, except in the most unusual circumstances—cannibalism in certain tropical fishes is one exception).

Many question these theories on both empirical and logical grounds. If aggression is an inevitable impulse deriving from human nature, they ask, then should not all humans exhibit this genetically determined behavior? Some people are consistently nonaggressive, however. Genetics also do not explain why individuals are belligerent and nonbelligerent at different times.

Many social scientists thus conclude that war is a learned trait, that it is a part of humankind's cultural heritage, not its biological nature.[4] For example, the 1986 *Seville Statement* endorsed by more than a dozen professional scholarly associations maintains that "it is scientifically incorrect" to say that "we have inherited a tendency to make war from our animal ancestors," "that war or any other violent behavior is genetically programmed into our human nature," "that humans have a 'violent brain,'" or "that war is caused by 'instinct' or any single motivation" (see Somit, 1990). As Ted Robert Gurr (1970) puts it, "The capacity, but not the need, for violence appears to be biologically entrenched in men." Aggression is a propensity acquired early in life as a result of socialization and, therefore, is a learned rather than biologically determined behavior.

The willingness of people to participate eagerly in war because of a sense of duty to their leaders and country is one of history's puzzles, however. It is not to be confused with the genetic roots of war, because individual citizens do not initiate war even if they participate in wars their country's leadership initiate. "The fog of war" is what the Russian author Leo Tolstoy and others have called the fact that people will give their lives in struggles, large and small, whose importance is elusive and purpose sometimes completely obscure. Clearly, this self-sacrifice stems from learned beliefs that some convictions—such as loyalty to the state—are preferable to life and worth dying for. "It has been widely observed that soldiers fight—and noncombatants assent to war—not out of unaggressiveness but obedience" (Caspary, 1993). This does not make human nature a cause of war, even if such learned habits of obedience are a cause of participation in the warfare authorized by others, and even if jaunty public jingoism often encourages leaders to start wars.

Scholars also question the belief that entire nations are predisposed to war—that "national character" predetermines national aggression. National character can express itself in different ways. And it can change; for example, Sweden since 1809 and Switzerland since 1815 have managed conflict without recourse to war, whereas formerly they were aggressive. This suggests that violence is not an inborn national trait that predestines periodic outbreaks of national aggression. Many countries have escaped the tragedy of war. In fact, since 1500 more than one in five states have never experienced war (Sivard, 1991: 20). This variation across different countries nearly 500 years suggests that war is not endemic and unavoidable. "A vision of a ubiquitous struggle for power or of a determining systemic structure explains recurrence without accounting for non-recurrence or the great deviations from an average pattern of recurrence" (Holsti, 1991).

---

[4] Many realists assume that the drive for power is innate and cannot be eradicated and therefore accept the Darwinian conclusion: Life entails a struggle of the fittest for survival, and natural selection eliminates the traits that interfere with successful competition. In opposition, another interpretation of the biological influences on human behavior can be advanced as to why people cooperate and act morally. As James Q. Wilson (1993) argues, Darwinian theory leads to the conclusion that "the moral sense must have adaptive value; if it did not, natural selection would have worked against people who had such useless traits as sympathy, self-control or a desire for fairness in favor of those with the opposite tendencies." The controversy over the nature–nurture question regarding the biological basis of aggression has not been resolved. For reviews of discourse about the issue, see also Caspary (1993), Nelson (1974), and Somit (1990).

Nobel Prize-winner Ralph Bunche argued in an address to the United Nations that "there are no warlike people—just warlike leaders." Similarly, St. Thomas More averred in the sixteenth century that "the common folk do not go to war of their own accord, but are driven to it by the madness of kings." But explaining the role of leaders in making war is not quite that simple. Leaders usually make foreign policies within groups. Both the social–psychological and bureaucratic setting for decision making and the global environment may exert "an influence independent of the actions and beliefs of individual policymakers. . . . War seems less like something decision makers choose than something that somehow happens to them," even as it happens "through them," through the choices they make (Beer, 1981).

The decision for war is better explained, then, not by individual leaders' aggressiveness or by aggressive national characters, but by the many political pressures that influence the government leaders who "ultimately decide the great questions of war and peace" (Holsti, 1991). Therefore, it is relevant to ask, what domestic factors encourage policymakers to choose war?

## Internal Characteristics and War Involvement

Conventional wisdom holds that variations in states' size, ideology, geographical location, population dynamics, ethnic homogeneity, wealth, economic performance, political institutions, military capabilities, and level of educational attainment influence whether they will engage in war.[5] Drawing on the possibility suggested by the Russian political theorist Peter Kropotkin in 1884 that "the word *state* is identical with the word *war*," let us next examine some theories addressing the internal characteristics of states that influence leaders' choices about the use of force.

### Duration of Independence

New nations are more likely to initiate wars than are mature states (Wright, 1942). Newly independent countries usually go through a period of internal political upheaval. This has often served as a catalyst to external aggression. As the recent national rivalries within and conflicts between the newly independent nations of the former Soviet Union indicate, drives to settle long-standing internal grievances and territorial disputes by force often follow the acquisition of independence. Between 1945 and 1992, all but one of the sixty civil wars were fought in emergent nations, and nearly a quarter of them became internationalized as the internal bloodletting expanded

---

[5] Implicit in this approach is the assumption (embraced by "the comparative study of foreign policy" perspective identified in Chapters 2 and 3) that the differences in the types or classes of states will determine whether they will engage in war. A (perhaps dubious) corollary is that the leaders' personalities and perceptual idiosyncrasies are relatively immaterial—that the prospects for war will be conditioned more by the effects of national attributes than by the impact of leaders on the countries they lead. The decision for war, in other words, will be affected more by the circumstances that leaders encounter than by their preferences.

across borders (Singer, 1991: 59, 79). It is thus not coincidental that wars since World War II have been prevalent among the newly independent states of the Third World.

## Cultural Determinants and the Decay of Moral Constraints

Modern countries' international behavior is influenced strongly by the cultural and ethical traditions of their peoples. In the state system governed by the rules advocated by political realism, moral constraints on the use of force do not command wide acceptance. Instead, most governments have encouraged their populations to accept whatever decisions their leaders deem necessary for national security, including warfare against adversaries.

CULTURAL "NUMBING" AND VIOLENCE Most people in most societies, proponents of the cultural sources of war argue, live an everyday experience of disengagement, or "numbness," that disinclines them to oppose their leaders decisions' to wage war. The modern state organizes its society to accept war and "builds a culture that affirms death." Cultural factors allow people to accept senseless carnage:

The significance of this culture critique for war . . . can be specified. Ethical traditions and ethical reasoning, undermined by instrumental rationality [recall Chapter 3], form a frail source of opposition to the technological juggernaut. Experiencing so much death-in-life we shrug our shoulders at war or even welcome it as another source of sensation to break through our deadness. War may even be embraced by some as an apocalyptic release from pain and negativity. (Caspary, 1993: 435)

THE FEMINIST CRITIQUE OF REALISM AND VIOLENCE To other critics—those operating from the perspective of feminist theories of international relations—a source of war worldwide is also largely cultural, but rooted in the "masculinist" ethos of political realism that prepares people to accept war and to respect the "warrior" as a hero (see especially Enloe, 1993, and Tickner, 1992). Gender roles, supported by realist values, contribute to the prevalence of militarism and warfare.

According to feminist critics, international relations theory as it has evolved incorporates "masculinist" prejudices at each of its three levels of analysis: man, the state and war. Realists are "androcentric" in arguing that the propensity for conflict is universal in human nature ("man"); that the logic and the morality of sovereign states are not identical to those of individuals ("the state"); and that the world is an anarchy in which sovereign states must be prepared to rely on self-help, including organized violence ("war"). Feminist theorists would stress the nurturing and cooperative aspects—the conventionally feminine aspects—of human nature; they would expose the artificiality of notions of sovereignty, and their connection with patriarchy and militarism; and they would replace the narrow realist emphasis on security, especially military security, with a redefinition of security as universal social justice. (Lind, 1993: 37)

From this and the foregoing interpretation, the propensity for warfare does not evolve in a vacuum. It is produced by the ways national societies shape the beliefs and norms of their populations. Governments inculcate values in their political culture that condone the practice of war through the educational programs they fund in schools and other institutions. Ironically, in a world of diverse national cultures, the message of obedience and of duty to make sacrifices to the state is common. The belief disseminated is that the state's right to make war should not be questioned and that the ethical principles of religious and secular philosophies prohibiting violence should be made subservient. Hence, to critics, powerful institutions exist that prepare individuals to subconsciously accept warfare as necessary and legitimate.

## *National Poverty*

A country's level of economic development also affects the probability of its war involvement. Advanced industrial societies with comparatively high standards of living tend to be satisfied states less apt to start a war that might risk that valued status. (There are exceptions, of course, such as Germany in 1939.) On the other hand, historically the most warlike states have been poor, and this pattern persists, as the locale of warfare has shifted since 1945 to the developing countries at the periphery. As U.S. Secretary of Defense Robert S. McNamara explained in 1966, "there is no question but that there is evidence of a relationship between violence and economic backwardness." Aggression is a response to frustration and *relative deprivation.* When peoples' expectations of what they deserve rise more rapidly than their material rewards, the probability of conflict grows. That, of course, applies to most of the Third World today.

Before we conclude that poverty breeds war, however, we must note that the *most* impoverished countries have been the least prone to start wars. The poorest countries cannot vent their frustrations aggressively because they lack the military or economic resources to sustain its costs. Thus the poorest states, like the wealthiest, cannot afford to wage war, but for quite different reasons. The former lack the means; the latter hold weapons too destructive to use.

This pattern does not mean that the poorest countries will always remain peaceful. Indeed, if the past is a guide to the future, then the impoverished countries that develop economically will be those most likely to acquire arms and engage in future wars (Chouchri and North, 1975). In particular, many studies suggest that states experience wars *after* sustained periods of economic growth—that is, during periods of rising prosperity in conjunction with upswings in the business cycle when they can most afford them (Cashman, 1993). This bodes ill should Third World economic development rapidly occur.

## *Power Transitions*

An extension of the preceding theory reasons that war is most likely when competitive states' power ratios—the differentials between their capabilities—narrow. Dubbed the *power transition theory,* this holds that

> an even distribution of political, economic, and military capabilities between contending groups of states is likely to increase the probability of war; peace is preserved best when there is an imbalance of national capabilities between disadvantaged and advantaged nations;

the aggressor will come from a small group of dissatisfied strong countries; and it is the weaker, rather than the stronger, power that is most likely to be the aggressor. (Organski and Kugler, 1980: 19)

During the transition from developing to developed status, emergent challengers can achieve through force the power and recognition their new-formed muscles permit them. Conversely, established powers often are willing to employ force to arrest their relative decline. Thus, when advancing and retreating states seek to cope with the changes in their relative power, war between the rising challenger(s) and the declining dominant hegemon(s) becomes especially likely. The rapid *changes* in the power and status that produced the division of Europe among seven powers largely equal in military strength, for example, are often (alongside the alliances they nurtured) interpreted as the tinderbox from which World War I ignited.

As explained in Chapter 13, rapid disruptions in the global distribution of power have often preceded outbursts of aggression, especially when the new distribution nears approximate equality and thereby tempts the rivals to wage war to defeat their challengers. Moreover, the propensity persists for transitions in states' relative capabilities to culminate in wars started by the weaker party, in order to either overtake its rival or to preemptively deter its own subjugation. Presumably, the uncertainty created by a rough equilibrium prompts the challenger's (usually unsuccessful) temptation to risk war against a stronger opponent. Equally persistent is the prediction of the power transition theory that advantages have shifted from the attacker to the defender. "In earlier centuries the aggressor seemed to have a 50-50 chance of winning the war, but this no longer holds. The chances of the starter being victorious are shrinking. In the 1980s only 18 percent of the starters were winners" (Sivard, 1991: 20).

## Militarization

Many leaders assume that a close association exists between a country's military strength and its likely use of force. For this reason they spend much time estimating their country's military power relative to their rivals'.

The age-old question of whether military power is a correlate of war or peace has assumed renewed emphasis in the post–Cold War era. As we noted in Chapter 11, "the race for the most advanced military technology began in the highly industrialized countries, and for awhile it was confined there. It is now rapidly spreading to the Third World, largely with assistance both in equipment and technological aid to . . . the developed countries" (Sivard, 1991). Hence, at issue is whether this dispersion of weapons to the developing countries also will increase the probability of war.

As Third World countries accumulate the economic resources to equip their military establishments, many experts believe that the incidence of warfare will increase further before it recedes. The prediction stems from the evidence that fundamental changes in military capability are an important determinant of the onset of war (Vasquez, 1993), especially as reflected in the historical pattern in Europe as that region developed.

During its transition from relative poverty to the apex of development, Europe was the location of the world's most frequent and deadly wars. The major European states armed themselves heavily and fought about 65 percent of the time in the sixteenth and seventeenth centuries (Wright, 1942). Between 1816 and 1945, 59 percent of all international wars took place in Europe, with one erupting on average every 1½ years (Singer, 1991: 58). Not coincidentally, this happened when the developing states of Europe were most energetically arming in competition with one another. Perhaps as a consequence, the great powers—those with the largest armed forces—were the most involved in, and most often initiated, war (see Cashman, 1993). Since 1945, however, with the exception of war among the now-independent units of the former Yugoslavia (and clashes among the republics of the former Soviet Union), interstate war has not occurred in Europe. As the European countries moved up the ladder of development in later centuries, they moved away from war with each other (internal turmoil is another matter).

In contrast, the developing countries now resemble Europe prior to 1945. If the Third World follows the European pattern, the future may well witness the specter of a peaceful, developed world surrounded by a violent, less developed world.

### Economic System

Recall the distinction drawn in Chapter 7 between open (market) economies, like those in Western Europe and North America, and closed (command) economies, like those in the former socialist systems of Eastern Europe and the Soviet Union, where governments actively regulated commercial transactions. At issue here is whether, as is often claimed, the difference influences the frequency of warfare.

The question has provoked controversy for centuries. Particularly since marxism took root in Russia following the Bolshevik revolution in 1917, communist theoreticians claimed that capitalism *is* the primary cause of war—that capitalists practice imperialism and colonialism (see Chapter 5). According to this theory, capitalism produces surplus capital. The need to export it stimulates wars to capture and protect foreign markets. Thus laissez-faire capitalism rationalized militarism for economic purposes. Citing the demonstrable frequency with which societies that practiced capitalism engaged in aggression, marxists believed that the only way to end international war was to end capitalism.

Contrary to marxist theory is liberal theory's tenet that free market systems promote peace, not war. Defenders of capitalism have long assumed that free market countries that practice free trade abroad are more pacific. The reasons are multiple, but they center on the premise that commercial enterprises are natural lobbyists for world peace because their profits depend on it. War interferes with trade, blocks profit, destroys property, causes inflation, consumes scarce resources, and encourages big government and counterproductive regulation of business activity. By extension, the reasoning continues, as government regulation of internal markets declines, prosperity will increase and fewer wars will occur.

The evidence for these rival theories (like those surrounding all important controversies) is, not surprisingly, mixed. Conclusions depend in part on perceptions about the influence of economics on international behavior, in part because alternative perspectives focus on different dimensions of the linkage. The controversy was at the heart of the ideological debate between East and West during the Cold War, when the relative virtues and vices of two radically different economic systems (communism and capitalism) were uppermost in people's minds. At the time, communists cited the previous record of wars initiated by capitalistic countries (Germany, Japan, and the United States in Vietnam, for example) to lend credence to the marxist interpretation (while ignoring the pacificity of capitalist Sweden, Switzerland, and others).

Communist theory also did not explain communist states' embarrassingly frequent use of force, however. The Soviet Union invaded Finland in 1939 and Afghanistan in 1979; North Korea attacked South Korea in 1950; Communist China attacked Tibet in 1959; Vietnam invaded Cambodia in 1975; and Cuba intervened militarily in Africa in the 1980s. Moreover, communist states repeatedly clashed with one another during the Cold War, as in the case of China and the Soviet Union in 1969, China and Vietnam in 1979 and again in 1987, the Soviet Union and Hungary in 1956, and the Soviet Union and Czechoslovakia in 1968. "Of sixty-one international conflicts of the 1945–1967 period, socialist systems participated in fifteen—approximately 25 percent. This is compared to the fact that only approximately 15 percent of all economies had socialist economies" (Cashman, 1993: 133). Thus the thesis that socialist or communist states were inherently nonaggressive failed empirically.

More than this, communism's failure to produce economic growth hastened its rejection in Eastern Europe and in the very heartland of the communist experiment, the Soviet Union itself. With capitalism's triumph over communism, a phase of history "ended" (Fukuyama, 1992b). By 1994 only Cuba and North Korea still fully endorsed communist economic principles; all other former advocates repudiated communism, preferring free market economies instead.

The revolutionary termination of the communist experiment does not end the historic debate about the link between economics and war, however. The issue of economic influences on international behavior remains. With the end of the Cold War, this basic theoretical question is even likely to command increasing interest, especially given the "shift in the relevance and usefulness of different power resources, with military power declining and economic power increasing in importance" (Huntington, 1991a).

## Type of Government

The neoliberal perspective on international politics predicts that not just free enterprise but also democracy will inhibit the frequency with which governments settle their disputes by force. Between 1974 and 1991, roughly a third of the countries on the planet converted their political systems to democratic rule (recall Figure 3.1). In a short span, a "global resurgence of democracy" was evident (Diamond and Plattner, 1993). Freedom House, a private organization that monitors the progress toward democracy, estimates that as 1992 began, 41 percent of the world's people lived in free countries, 37 percent lived in partly free countries, and 22 percent lived in not-free countries. As we described in detail in Chapter 3, democracy has grown throughout the world to a proportion never before achieved (see Map 12.1).

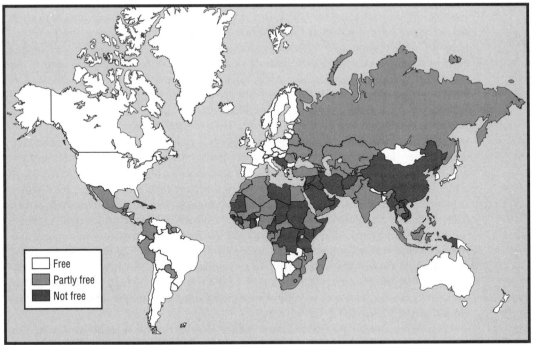

**Map 12.1** The Diffusion of Democracy
*Source:* Based on classifications of freedom in countries by Freedom House, as summarized in *The Wall Street Journal* (December 31, 1991, p. A6).

The recent "third wave of democratization" (Huntington, 1991b) has provoked speculation that Western liberal democracy will become universal, "the final form of government" (Fukuyama, 1992b). If the growth of democracy spreads to the Third World, where in 1992 fifty-one governments were under military control (Sivard, 1993: 23), there is hope that the transition to democratic rule will inaugurate a new era of peaceful world politics. Indeed, this liberal tenet has been embedded in the foreign policy of the United States. Now that the threat of communism has vanished, the United States has defined the promotion of democracy as one of its central purposes. The goal draws on America's idealist diplomatic tradition.

The belief that democratic policy-making institutions will produce peace follows the idealist conviction of eighteenth-century philosopher Immanuel Kant in his 1795 text *Perpetual Peace*, namely that democracies are inherently less warlike than autocracies. He felt that public opinion restrains the freedom of rulers of democratic states to wage war, because in democratic governments the mass public would have to supply the soldiers and bear the human and financial costs of imperial policies, and in democracies and unlike dictatorships the voice of the people protects their right to be heard and to express their opposition to waging war abroad.

History has been kind to Kant's views, which are the bedrock of the liberal and neoliberal challengers to the realist and neorealist theoretical traditions that discount the importance of government type as a determinant of peace (see Baldwin, 1993;

Kegley, 1995). Scholars now take the consequences of democratization seriously, because they have discovered that "Although preventive war has been the preferred response of declining authoritarian leaders, no democracy has ever initiated such a war. Instead, depending on the regime type of the rising challenger, democratic states have chosen accommodation, defensive alliances, or internal balancing" (Schweller, 1992). Simply put, democracies have dealt with conflicts against other democracies by methods other than war (Dixon, 1994; Doyle, 1995; Lake, 1992; Maoz and Abdolali, 1989; Russett, 1993), and this regularity is "as close to anything we have to an empirical law in international relations" (Levy, 1989a). This does not mean that democracies never experience war (see Ray, 1995). "It appears that democracies fight as often as do other types of states" (Morgan and Schwebach, 1992; also Small and Singer, 1976; Wright, 1942) because democracies have been engaged often in "defensive" or preventive wars against dictatorships. But democracies "seldom, if ever, fight one another." Why? The political culture of democratic states embraces norms against aggression as a method of conflict resolution. Institutional procedures reinforce this constraint on leaders' policy choice (Morgan and Schwebach, 1992). Moreover, in democracies constitutions restrict leaders' freedom, political participation and civil liberties such as free speech and a free press encourage opposition and criticism, and leaders' fear of electoral punishment deters them from undertaking wars that the public does not support.

The experience of Western Europe since World War II is consistent with the view that democratic states are unlikely to engage in war with one another. Still, we must be careful not to assume too quickly that democracy is an altogether reliable barrier to war.

> It was, after all, the democratization of conflict in the nineteenth century that restored a ferocity to warfare unknown since the seventeenth century; the bloodiest war in American history remains the one fought between two (by today's standards flawed) democracies—the Civil War. Concentration camps appeared during another conflict between two limited democracies, the Boer War. World War I was launched by two regimes—Wilhelmine Germany and Austria-Hungary—that had greater representation and more equitable legal systems than those of many important states today. And even when modern liberal democracies go to war they do not necessarily moderate the scope of the violence they apply; indeed, sensitivity to their own casualties sometimes leads to profligate uses of firepower or violent efforts to end wars quickly. Shaky democracies fight each other all the time. . . . We must remind ourselves just how peculiar the wealthy and secure democracies of the West are, how painful their evolution to stability and the horror of war with each other has been. Perhaps other countries will find short-cuts to those conditions, but it would be foolish to assume they will. (Cohen, 1995: 39)

Thus, it would be premature and overly optimistic to assume that the growth of democratic governance (if it continues and is not reversed) assures a more peaceful world. The frequency with which democratic states have intervened militarily in authoritarian states in order to force democratic reform is another concern (Stedman, 1993). Waging wars to spread democracy, as Woodrow Wilson did when he sent U.S. Marines into Mexico "to teach them to elect good governments," will not make for a more peaceful world.

## Nationalism

*Nationalism*—love of nation—is widely believed to be the cauldron from which wars often spring (Van Evera, 1994). "The tendency of the vast majority of people to center their supreme loyalties on the nation-state," political scientist Jack S. Levy explains, is a powerful catalyst to war. When people

> acquire an intense commitment to the power and prosperity of the state [and] this commitment is strengthened by national myths emphasizing the moral, physical, and political strength of the state and by individuals' feelings of powerlessness and their consequent tendency to seek their identity and fulfillment through the state, [then] assertive and nationalist policies are perceived as increasing state power and are at the same time psychologically satisfying for the individual and, in this way, nationalism contributes to war. (Levy, 1989a: 271)

The connection between nationalism and war suffers from a long history (see Box 12.2), but it has been especially pronounced in the twentieth century. The English essayist Aldous Huxley once termed nationalism "the religion of the twentieth century."[6] Today, separatist nationalism is particularly virulent and intense: "In our modern age, nationalism is not resurgent; it never died. Neither did racism. They are the most powerful movements in our world today, cutting across many social systems" (Gardels, 1991).

"Predictions for the post–Cold War era have varied from visions of a world in which war had become obsolete to one racked by ethnic and nationalist violence. . . . The bulk of global conflict concerns what is legally described as internal issues" (Wallensteen and Axell, 1993). These are fed by nationalist sentiments that promote "war fever . . . accompanied by overt hostility and contempt toward a caricatured image of the enemy" out of which sadistic violence and genocide have historically emanated (Caspary, 1993).

Today's "binge of nationalism" is international and not just internal in its consequences (see Ryan, 1990). "Nationalism has often generated aggression abroad. Nationalism, including some of the more messianic variations of Zionism, has given us some three dozen costly wars in the Middle East since 1945" (Yoder, 1991). It was the threat of nationalism to world order that led former Soviet President Mikhail Gorbachev to warn in May 1992 that "the demons of nationalism are coming alive again, and they are putting the stability of the international system to the test. Even the United States itself is not immune from the dangerous nationalism." Hence, in an increasingly nationalistic world populated by more than "5,000 different ethnic groups, . . . it is no longer possible to ignore the widespread tenacity of ethnic conflict and the way in which it is deeply influencing current interstate behavior" (Carment, 1993: 137).

This discussion of states' characteristics that influence their war proneness does not exhaust the subject. Many other potential causes internal to the state exist. But

---

[6] Kenneth Boulding has commented on the violence-provoking consequences of this disposition by noting that nationalism is "the only religion that still demands human sacrifice" (cited in Nelson, 1974).

## Box 12.2
### NATIONALISM, ETHNICITY, AND WAR
• • •

*Nationalism* is an attitude of mind, a pattern of attention and desires. It arises in response to a condition of society and to a particular stage in its development. It is a predisposition to pay far more attention to messages about one's own people, or to messages from its members, than to messages from or about any other people. At the same time, it is a desire to have one's own people get any and all values that are available. The extreme nationalist wants his people to have all the power, all the wealth, and all the well-being for which there is any competition. He wants his people to command all the respect and deference from others; he tends to claim all rectitude and virtue for it, as well as all enlightenment and skill; and he gives it a monopoly of his affection. In short, he totally identifies himself with his nation. Though he may be willing to sacrifice himself for it, his nationalism is a form of egotism written large. . . .

Even if most people are not extreme nationalists, nationalism has altered the world in many ways. Nationalism has not only increased the number of countries on the face of the earth, it has helped to diminish the number of its inhabitants. All major wars in the twentieth century have been fought in its name. . . .

Nationalism is in potential conflict with all philosophies or religions—such as Christianity—which teach universal standards of truth and of right and wrong, regardless of nation, race, or tribe. Early in the nineteenth century a gallant American naval officer, Stephen Decatur, proposed the toast, "Our country! In her intercourse with foreign nations, may she be always in the right, but our country, right or wrong." Nearly 150 years later the United States Third Army, marching into Germany following the collapse of the Nazi regime, liberated the huge concentration camp at Buchenwald. Over the main entrance to that place of torture and death, the Nazi elite guard had thoughtfully written, "My Country, Right or Wrong."

*Source: Karl W. Deutsch (1974: 124–125)*

however important domestic influences as a source of war might be, many believe that the nature of the international system is even more important.

## System Dynamics: Cycles of War and Peace

Classical political realism emphasizes that the roots of war inhere in human nature. In contrast, neorealism sees war springing from the decentralized character of the international system, as it requires that sovereign states rely on self-help for their security.

International anarchy may promote war's outbreak, but it fails to provide a complete explanation of its occurrence. To capture war's many structural determinants, we must consider how and why systems change. This requires an exploration of the impact of the distribution of military capabilities, balances (and imbalances) of power, the number of alliances and international organizations, the rules of international law, cultural and moral constraints, economic imperatives, and inequalities in global wealth. At issue is how these systemic factors—the system's attributes and institutions—combine to influence changes in war's frequency. We will examine many of these factors in Chapters 13 and 14. Here we focus attention on cycles of war and peace at the international level.

### Does Violence Breed Violence?

In 1935 U.S. President Franklin D. Roosevelt asserted "war is a contagion." The adage "violence breeds violence" reflects that view and the corresponding notion that the seeds of future wars are found in past wars. From this perspective World War II was an outgrowth of World War I, and the successive wars in the Middle East are seemingly little more than one war with each battle stimulated by its predecessor. Because the frequency of past wars *is* correlated with the incidence of wars in later periods, war appears contagious and its future outbreak inevitable. If so, then something within the dynamics of world politics—its anarchical nature, its weak legal system, its uneven distribution of power, inevitable destabilizing changes in the principal actors' relative power, or some combination of structural attributes—makes the state system a war system.

Those subscribing to the belief in war's inevitability often take their ammunition from the historical fact that war has been so repetitive. We cannot safely infer that past wars have *caused* later wars, however. Hence, we should exercise care in drawing conclusions from chronological sequences, for the fact that a war precedes a later one does not establish that the first caused the ones that followed to occur.

That history has been replete with war does not necessarily mean that we will always have it. War is not a universal institution (see Etzioni, 1968; Kluckhohn, 1944; Mead, 1968; Sumner, 1968). There are societies that have never known war, and, as noted, some countries have been immune to it for prolonged periods. Moreover, the outbreak of war since 1945 has stabilized, despite the large increase in the number of independent countries. This indicates that war is not necessarily inevitable and that historical forces do not control people's freedom of choice or experiences.

### Cyclical Theories

If war is recurrent but not necessarily inevitable, how might we explain changes over time in its outbreak? The absence of a clear trend in the frequency of war, and the periodic outbreak of war after intermittent stretches of peace, suggest that world history oscillates rhythmically between *long cycles* of war and peace.

Arnold J. Toynbee's *A Study of History* (1954) is a classical realist interpretation of history that sees it alternating rhythmically between periods of war and periods of peace. The more recent formal analysis of such cycles is known as ***long-cycle theory***. As noted in Chapter 4, its proponents argue that cycles of world leadership and global war are operative over the past five centuries, with a "general war" erupting approximately once every century, although at irregular intervals (Modelski, 1987b; Modelski and Thompson, 1995; Thompson, 1988).

Long-cycle theory seeks to explain how an all-powerful invisible hand built into the system's dynamics causes such peaks and valleys. Although the theory embraces many contending explanations (see Goldstein, 1988, for a comparison), they converge on the proposition that some combination of systemic properties (economic, military, and political) produce the frequency with which major wars have periodically erupted throughout modern history.

The long-cycle perspective is based on the fact that a great power has risen to a hegemonic (preponderant) position about every one hundred years. Taking the possession of disproportion seapower as a measure of dominance, we observe regularly appearing intervals of hegemony (see Figure 12.2). Portugal and the Netherlands rose at the beginning of the sixteenth and seventeenth centuries, respectively. Britain climbed to dominance at the beginning of both the eighteenth and nineteenth centuries. And the United States became a world leader at the end of World War II. During their reigns, these hegemonic powers monopolized military power and trade and determined the system's rules. Yet no hegemonic power has retained its top-dog position for more than three or four decades. In each cycle, overcommitments, the costs of empire, and ultimately the appearance of rivals led to the delegitimation of the hegemon's authority and to the deconcentration of power globally. As challengers to the hegemon's rule grew in strength, a "global war" has erupted after a long period of peace in each century since 1400 (between 1494–1517, 1580–1609, 1688–1713, 1792–1815, and 1914–1945). At the conclusion of each previous general war, a new world leader emerged dominant (Modelski, 1978, 1987b), and the cyclical process began anew.

Such deterministic theories have intuitive appeal. It seems plausible, for example, that just as long-term downswings and recoveries in business cycles profoundly affect subsequent behaviors and conditions, so a war experience produces aftereffects that may last for generations. A country at war will become exhausted and lose its enthusiasm for another war, but only for a time. This idea is labeled the ***war weariness hypothesis*** (Blainey, 1988). Italian historian Luigi da Porto expresses one version: "Peace brings riches; riches brings pride; pride brings anger; anger brings war; war brings poverty; poverty brings humanity; humanity brings peace; peace, as I have said, brings riches, and so the world's affairs go round." Because it takes time to move through these stages, alternations between periods of enthusiasm for war and weariness of war appear to be influenced by learning, forgetting, and aging.

Empirical tests of cyclical theories lead to conflicting results. Quincy Wright (1942) suggested that if cycles exist, intervals between major outbreaks of war last about fifty years. And Lewis F. Richardson (1960a) and Pitirim Sorokin (1937) estimated that cycles extend over two hundred years from peak to peak (although both were

**Global Wars**

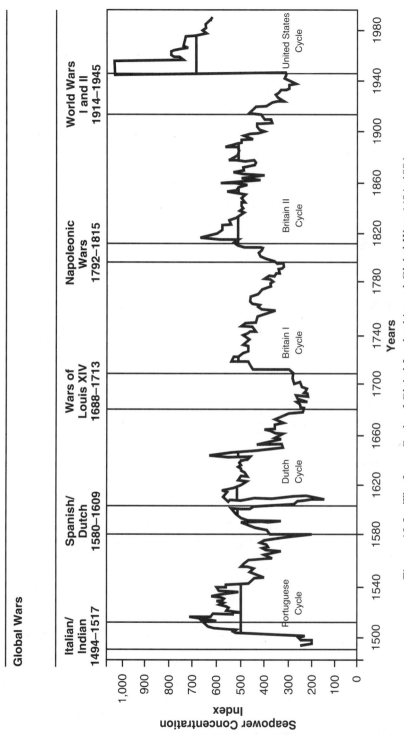

**Figure 12.2**  The Long Cycle of Global Leadership and Global War, 1494–1994
*Source:* Adapted from George Modelski (1987a: 6).

449

somewhat skeptical and cautioned against attaching too much causal importance to their findings).

The validity of cyclical interpretations depends in part on the measures of war's frequency and magnitude that are used (see Goldstein, 1991). The evidence accumulated by the Correlates of War Research Project, for example, fails to establish the existence of a cycle in war's onset since 1815 (Singer, 1981). Moreover, "no cyclical patterns are apparent when we examine the military experiences of the individual nations which participated in several wars" (Small and Singer, 1972). We must therefore question assertions about recurrent cycles in international war.

A different picture emerges when the amount of war *under way* since 1815 rather than the number of wars begun is considered. Here, the evidence "suggests not so much that discrete wars come and go with some regularity, but that, with *some* level of such violence almost always present, there may be certain periodic fluctuations in the amount of that violence" (Small and Singer, 1982).

From several theoretical standpoints, therefore, we must question claims that warfare in the twenty-first century, be it long and destructive or short and less costly, is predetermined. Although the historical record provides little basis for assuming that the war system is obsolete, it does suggest that peace is also possible. Both long periods of peace and long periods of warfare have existed in the past, and either could follow in the approaching new millennium.

If the disappearance of war is problematic over the long run, the character of conflict and violence may nevertheless fundamentally change. We now turn from our exploration of the multiple causes of interstate war to examine other uses of force in world politics.

## Armed Force Short of War . . . . . . . . . . . . . . . . . . . . . . . . . . . . .

Ours is an age of violence. This adage finds expression not only in wars between states but in other ways in which states use the threat of force to exercise influence over others. Three command a central place in thinking about statecraft: the crises that result from the practice of *coercive diplomacy, intervention,* and *low-intensity conflict.*

### Coercive Diplomacy and International Crises

"A crisis is a situation that (1) threatens the high-priority goals of the decision-making unit, (2) restricts the amount of time available for response before the decision is transformed, and (3) surprises the members of the decision-making unit by its occurrence" (Hermann, 1972). Most of the conspicuous crises of our age, such as the Cuban missile crisis, the Berlin blockade, the Sino–Soviet border clash, and the Formosa Straits crisis, exhibited these attributes. Each contained the elements of surprise, threat, and time pressure, as well as the risk of war. In each, a sense of urgency provoked by others' unanticipated military maneuvers was involved. But none crossed the line into overt military hostilities.[7] Instead, all were managed successfully.

Crises result when one actor attempts to force an adversary to alter its behavior. The threat of warfare, or "the strategy of coercive diplomacy (or compellence, as some prefer to call it) employs threats or limited force to persuade an opponent to call off or undo an encroachment—for example, to halt an invasion or give up territory that has been occupied" (Craig and George, 1990). "Military power does not have to be used for it to be useful"; the threat of force may suffice by "coercing a country by demonstrating the quantity of force and highlighting the capability of, and intention to, use force" (Majeed, 1991). "Coercive diplomacy offers the possibility of achieving one's objective economically, with little bloodshed, fewer political and psychological costs, and often with much less risk of escalation than does traditional military strategy" (Craig and George, 1990).

The crises generated by coercive diplomacy thus perform the bargaining function that war often traditionally played, namely, "to resolve without violence, or with only minimal violence, those conflicts that are too severe to be settled by ordinary diplomacy and that in earlier times would have been settled by war" (Snyder and Diesing, 1977).

Figure 12.3 displays the distribution of 390 interstate crises between 1918 and 1988. It reveals a continuous stream of changes "in the intensity of disruptive interactions between two or more states, with a heightened probability of military hostilities that destabilizes their relationships and challenges the structure of an international system" (Brecher, 1993).[8]

The evidence suggests several patterns. First, interstate crises are ubiquitous in the twentieth century; the 390 such situations threatening to escalate to war "occurred in all *regions* and in all of the seven *decades* since the end of World War I." Second, the frequency of crises varies annually, with many peaks and troughs. Third, many—in fact most—states either provoke or experience crises, as the 390 crises involved 826 individual states between 1918 and 1988. "Ninety-nine states triggered one or more crises, and no less than 123 states served as the target of crises." Fourth, some states are "more 'aggressive' in the crisis domain, that is, more prone to initiate crises." Fifth, crises overall tend to be concentrated "in the Third World 'peripheries' of the global system. Africa, Asia, and the Middle East accounted for two-thirds of the 390 international crises after World War I, compared to only 21 percent for Europe, the core of the dominant system" (Brecher, 1993: 68–69, 171).

It goes almost without saying that what makes the use of military threat for

---

[7] For crises to be managed successfully without escalating to war, policymakers, as rational actors, must be able to keep their quarrels within controllable bounds. Ole R. Holsti (1972) questions the validity of this assumption: "There is scant evidence that along with more lethal weapons we have evolved leaders more capable of coping with stress." Crises can easily escalate to war because of the time pressures, inadequate information, fear and anxiety, and impulsive risk-taking that normally accompany decision-making procedures during threatening situations (see Holsti, 1989a; also Rhodes, 1988).

[8] The frequency of international crises is sometimes measured by the incidence of *militarized disputes*, that is, "confrontations short of war characterized by the reciprocated threat, deployment, mobilization, or use of force" (Singer, 1991; also Gochman and Maoz, 1984).

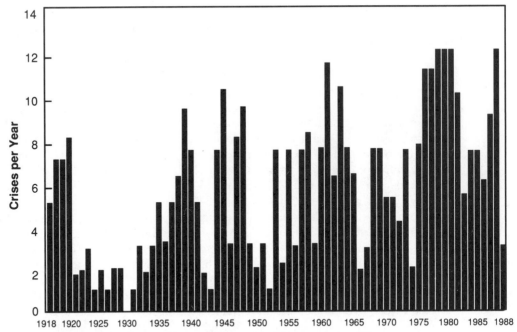

**Figure 12.3** Seventy Years of International Crises, 1918–1988
*Source:* Michael Brecher (1993: 69).

bargaining purposes between states and the crises that result from these activities so important is that crises are the circumstances that trigger war. When crises are not successfully managed, violence results. And this, sadly, has often been the case.[9] Once they erupt, more than 30 percent of all crises escalate to violence, and a large proportion—95 percent—of the most intense crises involve the major powers (Brecher, 1993: 333, 576). Moreover, this record suggests that international tension is not likely to abate in the future. If past experience is a model, we can predict that

> the post–Cold War subsystems retain an abundance of conflicts within which international crises are likely to erupt. . . . The ethnic/nationalist virus has created a context for other crises in the future. . . . The conclusion is disquieting: most anticipated international crises in the coming years are likely to erupt in violence, though its severity will vary from minor clashes to full-scale war. (Brecher, 1993: 546, 548)

## Military Intervention

As noted, coercive diplomacy, which includes threats often associated with crisis, sometimes involves the limited use of force. International military *interventions* provide

---

[9] Examples of violence that were preceded by crisis include World War I (1914), Kashmir (1948), Suez (1956), Tibet (1959), the Bay of Pigs (1961), Goa (1961), and Kuwait (1990). Conversely, some situations popularly termed crises in fact do not meet these criteria. The global energy crisis during the 1970s is an example. Surely the situation involved "threat," but neither "surprise" nor "time pressure" describes it appropriately.

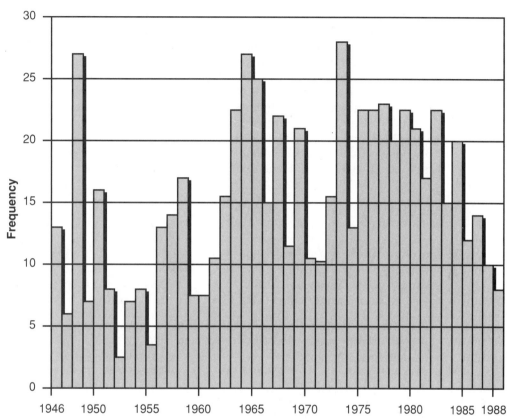

**Figure 12.4** Military Interventions, 1946–1988: Annual Frequencies
*Source:* Adapted from Frederic S. Pearson, Robert A. Baumann, and Jeffrey J. Pickering (1991).

evidence of the application of force in conflict situations, which occurred 667 times throughout the globe between 1946 and 1988 (see Figure 12.4). These frequent great-power interventions into Third World conflicts were intended to expand the great power's control and sphere of influence. Included are seventy-one Cold War interventions by the United States and twenty-five by the Soviet Union (Pearson, Baumann, and Pickering, 1991: Table 1).[10] In addition, "the role played by shadowy, often secret, participants" in these interventions, "who were not central parties to the conflict but gave it support and prolonged it for their own purposes," should be taken into consideration (Sivard, 1993). As a result of overt and covert interventionary activity, a crisis atmosphere prevailed because in most interventions, "any foreign

[10] Another inventory for the same period, using different criteria, counts 269 military interventions by 591 intervening states between 1945 and 1988, of which the great powers initiated one-fourth (Tillema, 1991).

overt military intervention can precipitate or expand war [and] every instance . . . is an incipient war" (Tillema, 1989).

Both crises and military interventions remain ubiquitous, but fortunately the onset of international crises has not precipitated a third world war. All post–World War II crises and instances of military intervention have been managed without recourse to war between the great powers. The most powerful states seem to have learned skills in crisis management and to have developed tacit rules for this purpose (George, 1986; also Tarr, 1991). Fear of the dire consequences should their management efforts fail doubtless contributed to their learning process (Gaddis, 1991a). In contrast, war-threatening disputes between unequals—those between powerful and weak states—continue, with death and destruction a frequent consequence.

## Low-Intensity Conflict

The destructiveness of modern weapons reduces the incentives for great and small powers alike to resort to armed force and increases the propensity to substitute the threat of force for its actual use. Still, violence has not ended, as states increasingly engage in *low-intensity conflict* (LIC).

> [Low-intensity conflict] is warfare that falls below the threshold of full-scale military combat between modern armies (of the sort that occurred in the Korean War and at the onset of the Iran-Iraq War). Under U.S. doctrine, low-intensity conflict encompasses four particular types of operations: (1) *counterinsurgency* . . . combat against revolutionary guerrillas . . . ; (2) *pro-insurgency* . . . support for insurgents . . . ; (3) *peacetime contingency operations* [or] police-type actions . . . ; and (4) military *"shows of force,"* [which threaten] military maneuvers. (Klare, 1988: 12)

These practices are not altogether new. They derive, for example, from the U.S. experiment with counterinsurgency warfare in the Vietnam War and the prior practice of "gunboat diplomacy." The United States used *shows of force* 286 times between 1946 and 1984, or an average of more than seven times a year (Blechman and Kaplan, 1978: 547–553; Zelikow, 1987: 34–36). Similarly, the Soviet Union prior to its fragmentation also engaged in such behavior over 150 times between the mid-1940s and late 1970s (Kaplan, 1981: 689–693).

As the concept is now used, low-intensity conflict is a symbol of warfare between the haves and have-nots. It refers primarily to methods for combating terrorism, insurgency, and guerrilla activities in the Third World to protect the interests of the powerful. Proxy wars, wars fought with mercenaries, psychological operations to terrorize the populace, death squads—these are part and parcel of the modern face of warfare below the level of overt military operations by the soldiers of a state's regular army. "What is crucial to recognize," notes political scientist Michael T. Klare (1988), "is that low-intensity conflict is a form of warfare in which *your* side suffers very little death or destruction, while the other side suffers as much damage as possible without producing undue hardship for your own society. . . . [Low-intensity conflict] doctrine . . . states that the privileged nations of the industrialized 'North' are vitally threatened by the starving, nonwhite masses of the underdeveloped 'South' and that this threat to the industrial West must be met by force short of war."

Low-intensity conflict thus describes the great powers' methods of combating "revolutionary strife, random violence, nuclear terrorism, and drug-running. . . . The strategy for conducting low-intensity war strikes at the heart of the development process, and that is its purpose. Physical attacks on roads, dams, and so forth, with the inevitable collateral damage to houses, schools, and hospitals, is accompanied by a psychological attack on those aspects of a revolutionary government's program that establish its legitimacy" (Barnet, 1990).

Three other characteristics are notable. Low-intensity conflict "is almost certain to be pervasive, is likely to be prolonged, and is often sufficiently unconventional as to defy being labeled as conflict in any traditional sense. It may be indistinguishable from police work; it can always be labeled police action" (Yarmolinsky, 1988). Despite its name, however, low-intensity conflict does not necessarily mean low levels of death or destruction. "The low-intensity conflict in Guatemala, for instance, . . . claimed well over 100,000 lives" (Klare, 1988: 12).

As noted in Chapter 11, great powers like the United States also now prepare for *mid-intensity conflict* (MIC), that is, for the kinds of disruptive localized wars of the sort fought against Saddam Hussein in 1991 (Klare, 1991). New threats are emerging beyond the traditional East–West antagonism of the last forty-five years, President Bill Clinton declared in 1993, and U.S. security is increasingly "linked to helping prevent or resolve conflicts that can grow out of ethnic, regional, or religious tensions throughout the world." Controlling these kinds of problems will loom larger in defense planning, by both the United States and other states.

# WAR WITHIN STATES

Wars within countries—civil wars—have erupted far more frequently than have wars between states since World War II. It is thus internal wars and insurgencies, more than international wars, that tend to capture the headlines. For example, *The New York Times* (February 7, 1993: 12) featured a story that traced the status of no less than forty-eight ethnic insurgencies under way throughout the world.

## Civil Wars

Civil wars resulting in at least one thousand civilian and military deaths per year have erupted 162 times between 1816 and 1992 (Small and Singer, 1982; Singer, 1991: 66–75; Wallensteen and Axell, 1993: 333). The outbreak has been somewhat irregular. At least one civil war began in "only" 84, or less than half, of these years. However, over time civil war has become increasingly frequent (see Table 12.2). Sixty percent of the civil wars since 1816 began after 1945, and the frequency has steadily climbed each decade in this period, with a "sharp increase" in low-intensity

### Table 12.2 The Frequency and Severity of 162 Civil Wars, 1816–1992

| Period | No. of Civil Wars Begun | System Size (Average No. of States) | Battle Deaths | No./Percent of Civil Wars Internationalized through Large-Scale Military Intervention |
|---|---|---|---|---|
| 1816–1848 | 12 | 28 | 93,200 | 3 (25%) |
| 1849–1881 | 20 | 39 | 2,891,600 | 1 (5%) |
| 1882–1914 | 18 | 40 | 388,000 | 3 (17%) |
| 1915–1945 | 14 | 59 | 1,631,460 | 4 (29%) |
| 1946–1988 | 60 | 117 | 6,222,020 | 14 (23%) |
| 1989–1992 | 38 | 172 | Not available | 4 (11%) |
| Totals | 162 | | 11,226,280 + | 29 |

*Source:* Data for 1816–1988 provided courtesy of the Correlates of War Project at the University of Michigan under the direction of J. David Singer and Melvin Small, as retrieved and compiled by Ricardo Rodriguez. Data for 1989–1992 are based on Peter Wallenstein and Karin Axell (1993).

conflicts occurring in 1992 (Wallensteen and Axell, 1993). However, this apparent trend is in part a product of the increase in the number of independent states in the international system, which makes the incidence of civil war more probable statistically.

The amount of civil war *under way* provides a different picture of the worldwide spread of civil war. Civil wars have been under way internationally 83 percent of the time, or 146 years, between 1816 and 1992 (Small and Singer, 1982: 251–267; Singer, 1991: 66–75; Wallensteen and Axell, 1993: 333). "Of the approximately 120 ongoing wars [in the late 1980s], 72 percent (86) were state-nation [states fighting insurgencies] conflicts" (Nietschmann, 1991: 175). In the post–Cold War period since 1989, "the bulk of global conflict concerns what is legally described as internal issues rather than international ones"; 95 percent of all armed conflicts were fought within states, and in 49 percent of these opposition groups battled the government in power (Wallensteen and Axell, 1993: 333). In June 1994, *all* of the thirty-six wars then being fought were civil wars, twenty-one of which had begun more than a decade earlier (*Harper's* 289, July 1994: 11).

The severity of civil wars is another of their troublesome attributes. The number of lives lost in civil violence has remained high since the Napoleonic Wars ended in 1815 (see Table 12.2), and casualty rates show an alarming growth, especially since World War II. One symptom is that ten of the fifteen most destructive civil wars between 1816 and 1980 occurred in the twentieth century; of those ten, seven occurred since World War II (Small and Singer, 1982: 241). Another characteristic is suggested by Ted Robert Gurr (1970: 3), who found that "ten of the world's thirteen most deadly conflicts [between 1815 and 1965] have been civil wars and rebellions." Although data "are insufficient to estimate the total number of deaths due to [internal] armed conflicts" between 1989 and 1992, "it was undoubtedly more than 70,000 in 1992 alone" (Wallensteen and Axell, 1993: 332), as in that year "war deaths were the highest in 17 years, extending a pattern of growing violence and human suffering in local wars" (Sivard, 1993).

## Causes of Civil War

Civil war and revolution have been simultaneously defended as instruments of justice and condemned as the immoral acceptance of violent change. They contain ingredients of both. The revolutionaries who engineered the American, Russian, and Chinese revolutions claimed that violence was necessary to realize social change, political freedom, and independence, while the powers from whom they sought liberation berated the immorality of their methods.

**INTERNAL REBELLION AND SECESSIONIST REVOLTS**  Civil wars stem from a wide range of ideological, demographic, religious, ethnic, economic, social–structural, and political conditions. Internal violence is also a reaction to frustration and deprivation, especially when the distribution of wealth and opportunities is highly unequal (Gurr, 1970). These conditions partially account for the pervasiveness of civil war today in the developing countries. Note in this context that the seeds of civil strife are often sown by national independence movements. "More than one-half (52 percent) of the wars in the post-1945 period were manifestations of the state-creation enterprise" (Holsti, 1991: 311). The growth of new states in Europe and Asia in the aftermath of the Cold War and the breakup of the Soviet Union will likely increase the probability of local wars. Unrest and discontent, long held in check "at the point of a bayonet" (Brogan, 1990), have now been released.

**NATIONALISM AND "NEONATIONALISM"**  Among the sources for civil war, nationalism is today widely regarded to be an especially potent cause. The reasons are tied to the arguments about nationalism as a cause of war noted earlier. But the conditions prevailing today lead many to believe that nationalism will incite civil strife at unprecedented levels. The potential magnitude of nationalistic-inspired war is great:

> More than 95 percent of the world's 168 states are multinational, that is, composed of many nations, some unconsenting. These 168 states assert sovereignty over the world's 3,000 to 5,000 nations and peoples. . . . State governments [are pitted] against guerrilla insurgencies and indigenous nations. Most of these wars are over territory, resources, and identity, not ideology. They are hidden from most people's views because the fighting is against peoples and countries that are not even on the map. (Nietschmann, 1991: 172–173)

If nationalism is a powerful influence on internal wars, what is termed *neonationalism* adds a new ingredient to this traditional cause. Neonationalism and the localized conflicts it spawns differ from the nationalism previously seen in the Third World.

> Earlier stages of Third World nationalism tended to revolve around the national liberation experience, the zeal engendered by the throwing off of colonial ties. . . . Neonationalism is the product of more recent decades, going beyond classical nationalism and [includes] separatist subnationalism; that is, the expression of communal/ethnic aspirations of groups

within the nation-state that are unhappy with their lot: Shiites in Iraq, Sikhs in India, Unighur Turks in Chinese Turkestan. It involves strong new drives toward separatism: the Moros in the Philippines, Georgians in the [former] Soviet Union, Catholics in Northern Ireland, Hungarians in Romania, Biafra in Nigeria, even Quebec in Canada. (Fuller, 1991–1992: 14–15)

Thus, the new nationalism is destabilizing. Rather than seeing nationalism as a benign desire for unification among national groups seeking to create a state by people sharing similar values, the new nationalism breeds conflict. This kind of "hypernationalism" is malign because nationalist doctrines are used "to justify or motivate large-scale violence by one state or group against others. . . . This doctrine justifies on strategic or ethical grounds the conquest or subjugation of other nationalities, or, at a minimum, ruthlessly aggressive means of self-defense" (Snyder, 1993). Similarly, the civil strife that erupted in the Balkans, Somalia, and Rwanda in the mid-1990s was symptomatic of the new wave of ethnic and fractional conflicts that has swept the globe.

ETHNONATIONAL CONFLICT AND CIVIL WAR    Since the Cold War ended, civil wars provoked by ancient ethnic and racial hatreds have been prevalent. "Multi-ethnic states are likely to continue to be a feature of politics both within and between sovereign states" (Ryan, 1990), and from their presence a rash of civil wars throughout the globe has evolved. Between 1945 and 1981, 258 cases of ethnic warfare are observable, 40 percent of which involved high levels of violence (Carment, 1993: 141). More recently, this ancient disease has assumed epidemic proportions. Ted Robert Gurr (1994: Tables 2 and 3), for example, estimated that 26,759,000 refugees were fleeing the fifty major ethnonational conflicts that were occurring in 1993–1994, each of which was responsible for an average 80,000 deaths. As U.S. President Bill Clinton observed in his 7 June 1994 speech before the French National Assembly, "Militant nationalism is on the rise, transforming the healthy pride of nations, tribes, religious and ethnic groups into cancerous prejudice, eating away at states and leaving their people addicted to the political painkillers of violence and demagoguery." Chan Heng Chee, formerly Singapore's ambassador to the United Nations, in 1993 described the opinion shared by most experts when she observed that "with the end of the Cold War . . . the new problems haunting us will be instability arising from ethnic and religious turmoil. . . . The fault line will . . . to a large extent coincide with racial and ethnic divisions."

The origins of this problem are cultural; they derive from people's beliefs. As a 1992 U.N. Commission on Human Rights report put it, a "new racism" based on cultural differences has gained momentum. "In the last analysis, and as in the past," those who fear and refuse to live peacefully with individuals of different ethnic origin or religious beliefs abide by a "racism and xenophobia [that] boil down to intolerance and lead to numerous acts of violence."

Underlying this "new racism" is an ideology based on nationalism. Nationalism, the U.N. report warned, stresses the "insurmountable differences between cultures" and is used to "justify the need to keep human communities apart. . . . Claims about other's inferiority are disguised as respect for other's differences" (cited in Greenway,

1993). The danger, warns Conor Cruise O'Brien (1993b), resides in the fact that nationalism "is something for which people are prepared to kill and die in large numbers, as Serbs, Croats and Bosnian Muslims are now doing [in the former Yugoslavia], and as, at an even more primordial level, warlike Somalian clansmen are doing." Hence, the wave of internal revolts and ethnic warfare sweeping the world is not inspired by political motives and economic aims. These "ethnic cleansing" clashes between cultures that practice genocide stem from deeply rooted racial animosities. Ethnonational clashes differ greatly from the anticolonial secessionist and separatist movements of the past.

**THE ECONOMIC DIMENSIONS OF INTERNAL REBELLION**  The destabilization caused by rapid growth also helps to account for the ubiquity of internal war (see Olson, 1971). In contrast with what intuition might suggest, civil violence often erupts in countries in which conditions are improving, not deteriorating. "Economic modernization," former U.S. Secretary of State Henry Kissinger postulated, "leads to political instability rather than political stability." When modernization generates rising expectations that governments are unable to satisfy, civil war often follows (Gurr, 1970). This is the essence of *relative deprivation* as a cause of internal violence and war.

## Civil Strife and External Aggression

If leaders assume that national cohesion will rise when an external threat exists, then when facing domestic unrest they may seek to manage it by initiating foreign adventures. At least since the ancient Greeks about whom Thucydides wrote, many have noted that leaders can wage war abroad to manage civil disturbance at home. Machiavelli, for instance, in 1513 advised the Prince to undertake foreign wars whenever turmoil within the state became too great. Hermann Goering advocated the same idea in Nazi Germany, contending: "Voice or no voice, the people can always be brought to do the bidding of the leaders. That is easy. All you have to do is tell them they are being attacked and denounce the pacifists for lack of patriotism." John Foster Dulles (1939) expressed this idea also, noting that: "The easiest and quickest cure of internal dissension is to portray danger from abroad. Thus group authorities find it convenient always to keep alive among the group members a feeling that their nation is in danger from one or another of the nation-villains with which it is surrounded."

The ***diversionary theory of war*** is predicated on the expectation that external war will result in increased domestic support for political leaders. "To put it cynically, one could say that nothing helps a leader like a good war. It gives him his only chance of being a tyrant and being loved for it at the same time. He can introduce the most ruthless forms of control and send thousands of his followers to their deaths and still be hailed as a great protector. Nothing ties tighter the in-group bonds than an out-group threat" (Morris, 1969).

Whether political leaders actually start wars to deal with domestic conflict is an empirical question. Many studies have examined the proposition, but few confirm it (see Levy, 1989b; Morgan and Bickers, 1992). It seems reasonable to assume that "war with the outside is sometimes the last chance for a state ridden with inner antagonisms to overcome these antagonisms" (Simmel, 1956), and that "statesmen may be driven to a policy of foreign conflict—if not open war—in order to defend themselves against the onslaught of domestic enemies" (Haas and Whiting, 1956). Yet we cannot demonstrate that leaders frequently undertake these diversionary actions for this purpose. "The linkage depends," Levy (1989b) concludes, "on the kinds of internal conditions that commonly lead to hostile external actions for diversionary purposes." For example, "democratic states are particularly likely to use force externally during an election year, especially when the election occurs at a time of economic stagnation" (Ostrom and Job, 1986; also Russett, 1989). At other times, this linkage does not hold. In most cases "where civil unrest preceded external conflict, war was not usually initiated by the strife-torn state. Instead, most wars were initiated by outside powers, with the internally troubled state in the role of the victim" (Cashman, 1993).

In general, then, the available evidence indicates that we must question the plausible, widely postulated diversionary theory of war. Perhaps the most compelling reason for the absence of a direct linkage is that "when domestic conflict becomes extremely intense it would seem more reasonable to argue that there is a greater likelihood that a state will retreat from its foreign engagements in order to handle the situation at home" (Zinnes and Wilkenfeld, 1971).

## The International Dimensions of War within States

It is tempting to think of civil war as only an internal problem, stemming exclusively from conditions within countries. However, external factors often influence internal rebellions. "Every war has two faces. It is a conflict both between and within political systems; a conflict that is both external and internal. [It is undeniable that] internal wars affect the international system [and that] the international system affects internal wars" (Modelski, 1964).

We can distinguish several waves in the linkage between changes in the international system and the incidence of civil war. First, the effects of imperialism, industrialization, nationalism, mass communication, and ideology spawned the comparatively high levels of civil war between 1848 and 1870. Second, the frequent incidence of civil war between the end of World War II and the 1960s was caused by the breakup of the European colonial empires. And today in the post–Cold War era a third wave is evident. The discipline imposed by Cold War bipolarity has disappeared. As this constraint has been lifted, many states no longer live with the fear that turmoil within their borders will precipitate military intervention on the part of the great powers.

CIVIL WARS AND INTERVENTION  Because the great powers have global interests, historically they have been prone to intervene militarily in civil wars to support friendly governments and to overthrow unfriendly ones. When they did, wars within states become internationalized.

It is often difficult to determine where an internal war ends and an international

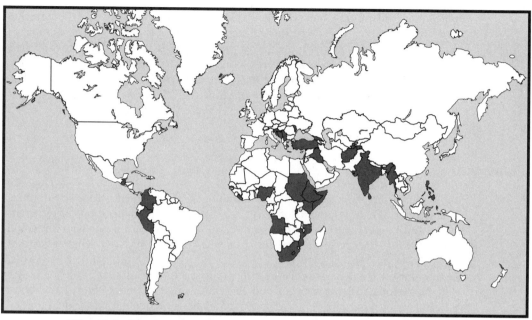

**Map 12.2**  The Locus of War, 1992
*Source:* Adapted from inventory provided by Ruth Leger Sivard (1993: 20).

one begins. As Table 12.2 reveals, since 1816 nearly one in five civil wars has become an interstate war through intervention by an external power. More than three-fifths of these large-scale military interventions have occurred since 1944.[11] Many U.S. and Soviet foreign entanglements during the Cold War were responses to internal instability (as in Lebanon, the Dominican Republic, Korea, Vietnam, Grenada, and Panama in the case of the United States, and Hungary, Ethiopia, and Afghanistan in the case of the Soviet Union). Even today, the Third World remains the site of most violent conflicts in the world (see Map 12.2). Many of them inevitably have been internationalized in one way or another. In an interdependent, increasingly borderless global marketplace, the difference between involvement and intervention is difficult to distinguish.

**MULTILATERAL RESPONSES TO CIVIL WAR?**  Yet since the Cold War began to fade from the scene in 1989, the frequency of unilateral great-power intervention has declined. What intervention has occurred—for humanitarian or other purposes—has been primarily through multilateral responses, such as those organized by the United Nations (see Chapter 14). Many believe that multilateral peacekeeping operations will

---

[11] A military intervention by one state into the civil war in another is said to occur if that participation is direct: One thousand troops or more must be committed to a battle zone, or one hundred casualties sustained. According to this measure, thirty-five cases of third-party intervention were recorded between 1816 and 1988, resulting in the internationalization of twenty-five civil wars (see Small and Singer, 1982; Singer, 1991: 60–75).

replace unilateral military intervention as a collective approach to alleviate the suffering caused by civil war. However, the willingness of the international community to organize and fund these joint humanitarian measures is, at best, problematic, as their costs are substantial and their incentives weak. "Very few people are prepared to die for an altruistic project where no national interests are clearly involved. . . . The United Nations can be useful if it is resorted to with discrimination. At present, it is being overworked, overextended and underfunded" (O'Brien, 1993b).

## Terrorism

Transnational terrorism poses another alarming kind of violence in contemporary world politics. The instruments of terror are varied and the motivations of terrorists diverse, but "experts agree that terrorism is the use or threat of violence, a method of combat or a strategy to achieve certain goals, that its aim is to induce a state of fear in the victim, that it is ruthless and does not conform to humanitarian norms, and that publicity is an essential factor in terrorist strategy" (Laqueur, 1986).

Some terrorist activities begin and end in a single country. However, many transcend national borders. Thus terrorism today has a uniquely transnational character that afflicts many countries. In 1990 terrorists targeted the citizens and property of 73 countries in 533 separate attacks (U.S. Department of State, 1991: 37).

Although terrorism dates to antiquity, it emerged as a significant international problem in the 1960s (Kidder, 1990) and grew to epidemic proportions in the 1970s and 1980s. Figure 12.5 shows the changing prevalence of terrorism in today's world. The general trend suggests an increasing level of transnational terrorist activity since 1968, followed by a decline since 1987. "International terrorist attacks declined during 1992 to 361, the lowest point in 17 years. This [was] roughly 35 percent fewer than the 567 incidents recorded in 1991" (U.S. Department of State, 1993a: 1). In 1993, 427 incidents were reported by the U.S. Department of State (1994: 7).

Terrorism is a tactic of the powerless against the powerful. Thus it is not surprising that political or social minorities and ethnic movements perpetrate many acts of terrorism. Those seeking independence and sovereign statehood, like the Sikh groups who wish to carve out an independent Sikh state called Khalistan ("Land of the Pure") from Indian territory, and the Basques in Spain, typify the kinds of aspirations that animate terrorist activity.

In the industrialized world, terrorism often occurs where discrepancies in income are severe and where minority groups feel deprived of the political freedoms and privileges enjoyed by the majority. Guerrilla warfare normally associated with rural uprisings is not a viable route to self-assertion in the urbanized areas of the industrialized world, but terrorist tactics are.

Consideration of terrorists' motives underscores that terrorism is not perceived by all to be a disease. One person's terrorist may, to another, be a liberator. In fact, both governments and countergovernment movements claim to seek liberty, and both are labeled terrorists by those they oppose. The difference between nationalistic "freedom fighters," whose major complaint is that they lack a country, and the

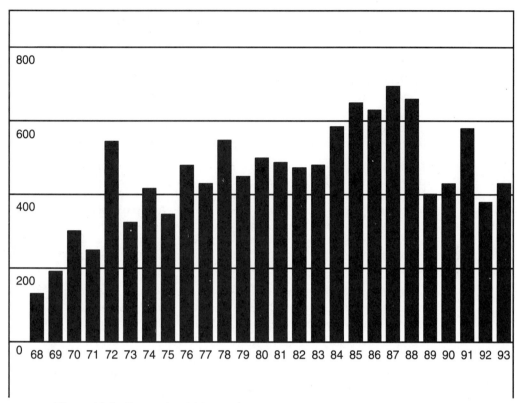

**Figure 12.5**  International Terrorist Incidents, 1968–1993
*Source:* Office of the Coordinator for Counterterrorism, U.S. Department of State (1994).

protectors of freedom often lies in the eye of the beholder. This problem makes the definition of a terrorist group not altogether obvious or noncontroversial.

Seen from this angle, terrorism by ideologically motivated fanatics, extremists, and minorities at the periphery of society may not be very different from the kinds of terrorism conducted by the state governments that they oppose. This is especially true given the way in which modern warfare is often conducted.

> Those who are described as terrorists, and who reject that title for themselves, make the uncomfortable point that national armed forces, fully supported by democratic opinion, have in fact employed violence and terror on a far vaster scale than what liberation movements have as yet been able to attain. The "freedom fighters" see themselves as fighting a just war. Why should they not be entitled to kill, burn and destroy as national armies, navies and air forces do, and why should the label "terrorist" be applied to them and not to the national militaries? (O'Brien, 1977: 56–57)

Although many terrorist groups today are undeniably groups without sovereignty that seek it, a broader definition of terrorism would acknowledge that many terrorist acts are state supported (see Bell, 1990; Crenshaw, 1990). Indeed, some states condone and support the terrorist activities of movements that espouse philosophies they embrace (or challenge the security of states they see as enemies). States have often financed, trained, equipped, and provided sanctuary for terrorists whose activities serve their foreign policy goals. This **state terrorism** is part of the claim that the United States leveled in the 1980s at the behaviors of the Soviet Union, Syria, Iraq, and Libya, among others.[12] In a similar way, others accused the United States of sponsoring terrorist activities in Vietnam, Chile, El Salvador, Nicaragua, and elsewhere (Schlagheck, 1990).

Many terrorist sanctuaries have disappeared with the end of the Cold War. Still,

> it is unlikely that international terrorism is a passing and transitory phenomenon. The trend toward the weakening of central authority in governments, the rise in ethnic and subnational sentiments, and the increasing fractionalization of the global political process point toward its growth as a form of political protest and persuasion. Classic balance of power diplomacy is of little utility in dealing with it, for violent acts of small groups of people, or individuals, are difficult for governments to control. International terrorism is likely to continue and to expand because in the minds of many of its perpetrators it has proven to be "successful." (Pierre, 1984: 85)

Indeed, the dangers posed by terrorism have not receded. Warned Libyan leader Col. Muammar Qaddafi in July 1993, "Whatever takes place in America—and you will see a lot more terrorism there—is a function of perceived injustices in other parts of the world. . . . Acts of terrorism in America will be the answer, and they will be more and more violent and spectacular for television purposes around the world." The terrorist threat thus thrives, as evidenced by the activity percolating in the Cold War's wake in Afghanistan in December 1993 (see Box 12.3).

## THE HUMAN TRAGEDY OF VIOLENT CONFLICT ...................

War exacts a terrible toll on human life. Its indelible mark is commemorated publicly by black flags of mourning that flutter from the homes of the war dead and memorials at grave sites. Monuments honor the courage displayed by the soldiers who gave their lives in their nations' wars, though at the beginning of this century around 90 percent of war casualties were military whereas today about 90 percent of the world's war victims are innocent civilians (UNDP, 1994: 47). Consider the grim statistics reported in UNICEF's *The State of the World's Children, 1992*. More than 1.5 million children were killed in wars during the 1980s, and more than 4 million were "physically disabled—limbs amputated, brains damaged, eyesight and hearing lost—through bombing, land-mines, firearms, torture. Five million children are in refugee camps because of war: a further 12 million have lost their homes" (in Raspberry, 1992: A31).

The tragic human consequences of violence are also revealed every day by the

---

[12] The attack by Libyan embassy personnel on anti-Qaddafi demonstrators in London in April 1984 is an example of terrorist actions conducted by representatives of a state government. Those who retaliate against terrorist attacks become, in the eyes of the target, terrorist attackers. Thus the U.S. air strike against Libya in April 1986 provoked the charge that the United States itself practiced terrorism.

## Box 12.3
### TERRIBLE PAYBACK: THE MODERN ARSENAL OF TRAINED TERRORISTS WHO NOW WAGE WAR AGAINST THEIR ARMS SUPPLIER
• • •

An antisecular war of violence and religious fanaticism throughout the world [is] fueled by the vipers' nest of terrorist-training centers and arms depots left over from the war in Afghanistan. The outposts along the Afghanistan-Pakistan border are home to people [the United States] once called freedom fighters who are now soldiers in a wider war. . . . The CIA concedes that zealots from more than 40 countries now routinely travel to Afghanistan for training in some of the world's nastier weaponry, including the awesome shoulder-mounted Stinger rockets that can easily shoot down passenger planes. . . . But what is the CIA doing about it? The agency has been belatedly authorized to spend $55 million to buy back the rockets it gave to the Afghans. So far the CIA admits that more than 300 of the Stingers are unaccounted for. That means at least 300 have fallen into the hands of movements and governments that have no scruples about knocking a civilian airplane out of the sky.

*Source: Robert Scheer (1993: 45)*

efforts of individuals and families seeking to escape its scourge. They can be observed fleeing from one country in hopes of finding refuge, and perhaps a better life, in another country. Religious preference, the color of one's skin, and the expression of political dissent are some of the factors that motivate refugees. Along with poverty, persecution, and the pain of hunger and starvation, war—whether intranational or international—remains a paramount cause.

The refugee asylum problem has assumed global dimensions. In 1993, the UN High Commissioner for Refugees reported that "the spread of ethnic conflict since the end of the Cold War has pushed the number of refugees to 44 million people, or more than one in every 130 inhabitants of the globe" (Lewis, 1993b: A1) (see Figure 12.6). This tide of humanity seeking sanctuary, about 10,000 on average each day worldwide (*The Economist* [November 13, 1993]: 45), are "victims of protracted wars and civil strife" who cross national borders in the hope of escaping bloodshed and civil violence. They escape by air, they march by foot, and they travel the oceans by boat. Whatever the means and the destination, their goal is the same: to find a place where survival is possible.

The ravages of war are not confined to its human victims. Some of the costs of war are economic, paid by survivors responsible for the debts and damages. This can take generations. Other costs are ecological. Consider here the 1991 Persian Gulf

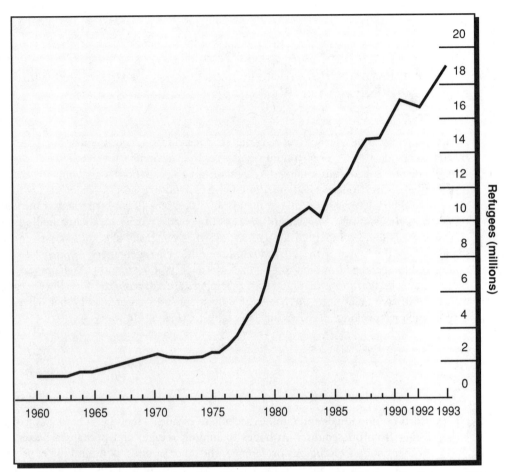

**Figure 12.6** Crossing Borders: The Flight of Refugees Worldwide from the Ravages of War, 1960–1993
*Source:* United Nations High Commissioner for Refugees.

War (see Arkin, Durrant, and Cherni, 1991). The blackened skies have now cleared, but, as we noted in Chapter 9, the environmental damage may take decades to undo.

Could it be that a world so ingenious in perpetrating violence also will learn that war and violence are too costly, too destructive to continue? If so, can it discover viable paths to peace? In the subsequent chapters we will examine some solutions that policymakers and concerned citizens have proposed.

## SUGGESTED READINGS

Betts, Richard K., ed. *Conflict after the Cold War: Arguments on Causes of War and Peace.* New York: Macmillan, 1994.

Brecher, Michael. *Crises in World Politics: Theory and Reality*. Oxford, England: Pergamon Press, 1993.

Cashman, Greg. *What Causes War? An Introduction to Theories of International Conflict*. New York: Lexington Books, 1993.

Coker, Christopher. *War in the Twentieth Century: The Impact of War on Modern Consciousness*. London: Brassey's, 1994.

Freedman, Lawrence, ed. *War*. New York: Oxford University Press, 1994.

Gilpin, Robert. *War and Change in World Politics*. Cambridge, England: Cambridge University Press, 1981.

Holsti, Kalevi J. *Peace and War: Armed Conflicts and International Order 1648–1989*. New York: Cambridge Press, 1991.

Kegley, Charles W., Jr., ed. *International Terrorism: Characteristics, Causes, Controls*. New York: St. Martin's Press, 1990.

Porter, Bruce D. *War and the Rise of the State*. New York: Free Press, 1994.

Sederberg, Peter C. *Fires Within: Political Violence and Revolutionary Change*. New York: Harper-Collins, 1994.

Singer, Max, and Aaron Wildavsky. *The Real World Order: Zones of Peace, Zones of Turmoil*. Chatham, N.J.: Chatham House, 1993.

Vasquez, John A. *The War Puzzle*. Cambridge: Cambridge University Press, 1993.

# CHAPTER 13

· · ·

# MILITARY PATHS TO PEACE: ALLIANCES, THE BALANCE OF POWER, AND ARMS CONTROL

· · ·

*It is an unfortunate fact that we can only secure peace by preparing for war.*

John F. Kennedy,
U. S. Presidential Candidate, 1960

*I went into the British Army believing that if you want peace you must prepare for war. I now believe that if you prepare thoroughly for war you will get it.*

Sir John Frederick Maurice,
British Military Officer, 1883

Many countries can inflict enormous destruction on their enemies. As a consequence, national security remains, as ever, elusive. Because of the escalating dangers of modern weapons, most states' sense of security has diminished, not increased, during this century.

To defend themselves, states have several options. They may (1) arm themselves; (2) form alliances to combine their armaments with those of other countries; (3) shift alliance partners to maintain a balance of power; or (4) negotiate arms control and disarmament agreements so as to reduce the threat of adversaries' weapons. In practice, most leaders usually simultaneously pursue various combinations of these approaches. Nonetheless, each represents a distinct military approach to security.

In Chapter 11 we covered the first defensive option by examining the search for national security through the acquisition of military capabilities and the practice of deterrence strategies. In this chapter we will explore the uses and consequences of the three other approaches to providing for the common defense.

## ALLIANCES · · · · · · · · · · · · · · · · · · · · · · · · · · · · · · · · · · · · ·

Alliances are "formal associations of states for the use (or non-use) of military force, intended for either the security or the aggrandizement of their members, against

· · ·

468

specific other states" (G. Snyder, 1991). Alliances thus are coalitions that adhere to realism's first rule of statecraft: to increase military capabilities. States can do this either by acquiring arms or by acquiring allies, and, as noted, throughout history states have vigorously pursued both methods. But of the two methods, alliances are more economical because they permit the defense burden to be shared.

This advantage might make alliances appear to be the preferred method for increasing military capabilities. Yet this solution has significant disadvantages, and making alliance choices has seldom been easy. It requires weighing the military strength, goals, and reliability of allies and of adversaries.

## Alliances in World Politics: Rival Theories

Three contending schools of thought exist within the boundaries of political realism regarding these calculations.[1] The first image holds that alliances are basically advantageous. The second maintains that the costs of alliances usually outweigh the benefits, and that, because alliances are generally disadvantageous, states should eschew them except when absolutely necessary. The third holds alliances in contempt, arguing that they have proved so dangerous that prudent policymakers must avoid them altogether.

### *The Advantages of Alliance*

Allies provide a means to counterbalance threats posed by potential aggressors in the anarchical international environment. Accordingly, "whenever in recorded history a system of multiple sovereignty has existed, some of the sovereign units when involved in conflicts with others have entered into alliances" (Wolfers, 1968), "even in advance, against [a] probable aggressor" (Morgenthau, 1959); alliances are "typically against, and only derivatively for, someone or something" (Liska, 1962).

Facing common dangers, states have several good reasons to ally. "The primary benefit of alliance is obviously security. . . . Security benefits in a mutual defense alliance include chiefly a reduced probability of being attacked (deterrence), greater strength in case of attack (defense) and prevention of the ally's alliance with one's adversary (preclusion)" (G. Snyder, 1991: 90).

Alliances have seldom been long-lasting, however, and have often dissolved when the common threat receded. For this reason, alliance formation usually is seen not as a goal in itself but as a strategy that includes both the recruitment of allies and the abandonment of them. Recognizing that "alignment and dealignment are the main short-term strategies for increasing security," the basic options consist of seeking "changes in foreign policy commitments, adding or expanding relations with nations that can provide immediate increases in one's security, and eliminating or curtailing relations with nations that are a drain on security" (Scarborough and Bueno de Mesquita, 1988). According to the logic of realpolitik, the only good alliance is one

---

[1] This synthesis of the rival images of alliances in realpolitik follows Kegley and Raymond (1994, 1995).

that can be easily dissolved when the threat to the security of its members declines. As Britain's Lord Palmerston admonished in 1848, states "should have no eternal allies and no perpetual enemies"; their only duty is to follow their interests.

## The Disadvantages of Alliance

The preeminent risk inherent in alliances with others is that they will bind one's state to a commitment that later may become disadvantageous. Throughout history policymakers have been ever mindful of the risk of entanglement. Entrusting their security to the pledges of others reduces their future freedom of action. Consequently, leaders usually adhere to warnings about the costs of commitments to allies, such as George F. Kennan's:

> The relations among nations, in this imperfect world, constitute a fluid substance, always in motion, changing subtly from day to day in ways that are difficult to detect from the myopia of the passing moment, and even difficult to discern from the perspective of the future one. The situation at one particular time is never quite the same as the situation of five years later—indeed it is sometimes very significantly different, even though the stages by which this change came about are seldom visible at the given moment. This is why wise and experienced statesmen usually shy away from commitments likely to constitute limitations on a government's behavior at unknown dates in the future in the face of unpredictable situations. (Kennan, 1984a: 238)

Hence, though alliances provide some measure of protection, binding a state to another reduces states' capacity to make accommodative realignments when conditions change. Indeed, the usefulness of any alliance is destined to diminish when the common external threat that brought the coalition into being declines, as inevitably it will (Wolfers, 1962). Therefore policymakers are often advised not to take a fixed position on temporary convergences of national interests and to forge alliances only to deal with immediate threats. The risks of entrapment and abandonment "tend to vary inversely: reducing one tends to increase the other" (Snyder, 1984). Hence many states' alliance policies are shaped by their acute awareness of the many risks of sharing their fate with allies (see Table 13.1).

## The Dangers of Alliance

Many realists go further and counsel avoiding alliances altogether. They perceive alliance formation as dangerous for five basic reasons. First, alliances enable aggressive states to aggregate resources for offensive wars. Alliances simply do not deter war—they promote it because expansionist states can act more aggressively than they otherwise would when they can count on their allies' assistance. As Adolf Hitler said, "Any alliance whose purpose is not the intention to wage war is senseless and useless."

Second, alliances threaten enemies and provoke them to form counteralliances, with the result that the security of *both* coalitions is reduced.

> Peacetime alliances may occur in order to reduce the insecurity of anarchy or reduce armament costs. If they do they will tend to create relations of enmity as well as alignment.

---

### TABLE 13.1 ALLIANCES: SOME POSTULATED DISADVANTAGES

Alliances . . .
- Foreclose options
- Reduce the capacity of states to adapt to changing circumstances
- Weaken a state's influence capability by decreasing the number of additional partners with which it can align
- Eliminate the advantages in bargaining that can be derived from deliberately fostering ambiguity about one's intentions
- Provoke the fears of adversaries
- Entangle states in disputes with their ally's enemies
- Interfere with the negotiation of disputes involving an ally's enemy by precluding certain issues from being placed on the agenda for debate
- Preserve existing rivalries
- Stimulate envy and resentment on the part of friends who are outside the alliance and therefore are not beneficiaries of its advantages

---

Even if the initial alliance is not directed at a specific opponent, other states will perceive it as a threat and begin to behave as enemies, perhaps by forming a counteralliance. Not only will alliances identify friends and foes, they will create interests consistent with such relations. (G. Snyder, 1991: 88)

In a similar vein, "alliances both reveal any added support that a state may have, and the amount of support that a potential belligerent may need. . . . The reduction of uncertainty brought about by such information may be all that is needed to facilitate an aggressor's desire to attack another state" (Bueno de Mesquita, 1981).

Third, alliance formation may draw otherwise neutral parties into opposed coalitions. As Thomas Jefferson warned, alliances can be dangerously "entangling." They require members to come to one another's aid, so that alliances are likely to involve members in the wars of their partners.

Fourth, once states join forces, they must control the behavior of their own allies. Management of intra-alliance relations is necessary to deter each member from reckless aggression against its enemies that would threaten the security of the alliance's other members. Also, allies must work to deter defection from the alliance.

Fifth, the possibility always exists that today's ally might become tomorrow's enemy. Realists believe that all states are natural enemies, that there are no permanent friends or adversaries. The historical record is noteworthy in this respect. In the period between the Congress of Vienna in 1815 and the 1960s, wars between allies were commonplace. "More than 25 percent of coalition partners eventually [went] to war against each other" (Russett and Starr, 1989: 95). Thus, when alliances form they can increase the prospects for, and the scope of, war.

### Alliances in the Realist and Idealist Images

In an address to the U.S. Senate on January 22, 1917, President Woodrow Wilson proposed that henceforth "all nations avoid entangling alliances which would draw them into . . . a net of intrigue and selfish rivalry." His advice reflected the belief that alliances and secret diplomacy transform limited conflicts into complex, global wars.

Like idealists such as Wilson, realists also stress the dangers and disadvantages of alliances. However, realists qualify their criticism by holding that alliances can be beneficial if policymakers remain flexible and if prevailing international norms support an elastic interpretation of alliance commitments and the rights of neutrals. Most policymakers schooled in the logic of realpolitik contend that entanglements occur only when alliance structures become rigid, when commitments are interpreted as irrevocable pledges, and when states operate from the belief that their commitments oblige them to take sides in their allies' serious disputes.

Let us examine these arguments more closely. Their veracity is best evaluated by observing the possible contribution of alliance formation to the maintenance of the balance of power, a controversial subject to which we now turn.

## THE BALANCE OF POWER

International anarchy places responsibility for national security on each state, and, as the seventeenth-century English political philosopher Thomas Hobbes put it, states are engaged in a perpetual "war of all against all." To political realists and their neorealist colleagues (recall Chapter 2), reforming this self-help competitive system is not realistic because international anarchy is permanent.

Given the continuing popularity of these assumptions, how might policymakers effectively enhance their states' survival in such a disorderly system? To realists, survival and world order rest on the proper functioning of a system of military balances. What is the meaning of this approach, broadly captured in the phrase "balance of power"?

### Assumptions of Balance-of-Power Theory

*Balance of power* is an ambiguous concept used in a variety of ways (see Claude, 1962; Haas, 1953). At the core of its many meanings is the idea that peace will result when military power is distributed so that no one state is strong enough to dominate the others. If one state, or a combination of states, gains enough power to threaten others, compelling incentives exist for those threatened to disregard their superficial differences and unite in a defensive alliance. The aggregation of power resulting from such collusion would, according to this conception, deter the would-be attacker from pursuing expansionism. Hence, from the laissez-faire competition of predatory and defensive rivals would emerge an equilibrium, a balance of contending factions, that would maintain the status quo.

Balance-of-power theory is also predicated on the premises that weakness invites attack and that countervailing power must be used to deter potential aggressors.

Because it is assumed that the drive for expanded power guides every state's actions, then the conclusion follows that all countries are potential adversaries, and each must strengthen its military capability to protect itself. Invariably, this reasoning rationalizes the quest for military superiority because others pursue it as well.

On the surface, these assumptions appear dubious because, self-fulfillingly, the arms races they justify could breed the very outcome most feared—a destructive globalized war. The European policymakers who formulated classical balance-of-power theory in the decades following the Peace of Westphalia in 1648 were not irrational, however (see Gulick, 1955). They reasoned that a system founded on suspicion and competition in which all states were free to act in their perceived national interests would distribute power evenly through realignments, and this would curtail the temptation of any actor to seek to dominate others.

## *The Balance Process*

In classic balance-of-power theory, fear of a third party would encourage alignments because those threatened would need help to offset the power of the mutual adversary. An alliance would add the ally's power to their own and deny the addition of that power to the enemy. As alliances combine power, the offsetting coalitions would give neither a clear advantage. Therefore, war would appear illogical and be averted.

To deter an aggressor, counteralliances were expected to form easily because states sitting on the sidelines could not risk nonalignment. If they refused to ally, their own vulnerability would encourage the expansionist state to attack them at a later time. In theory, the result of these individual calculations would be the formation of coalitions approximately equal in power.[2]

**THE RULES OF THE BALANCE-OF-POWER GAME**  To help maintain an even distribution of power, realists recommended rules of behavior that promoted fluid and rapidly shifting alliances. They recognized that alliance competition would not automatically achieve equilibrium and that a balance would develop only if states practiced certain behaviors. One requirement was that a great power not immediately threatened by the rise of another power or coalition would perform the role of "the balancer" by offsetting the new challenger's power. Great Britain often played this role in the eighteenth and nineteenth centuries, when it gave its support to one or another coalition to ensure that none achieved preponderance. Winston Churchill (1948) described Britain's role in this process, declaring that "for 400 years the foreign policy of England has been to oppose the strongest, most aggressive, most dominating power on the continent, in joining the weaker states."

---

[2] According to the so-called *size principle*, rational actors will tend to form coalitions sufficient in size to ensure victory and no larger; hence political coalitions tend to be roughly equal in size (see Riker, 1962). Hans J. Morgenthau (1985) and Edward Gulick (1955) also discuss the rationality of policies aimed at equalizing the power of competing coalitions, predicated on the willingness to recognize their interest in stopping aggression. As U.S. President Jimmy Carter in 1980 expressed this premise, "History teaches perhaps few clear lessons. But surely one such lesson learned by the world at great cost is that aggression unopposed becomes a contagious disease."

In addition to a balancer, all states had to behave according to the following "essential rules":

> (1) increase capabilities but negotiate rather than fight; (2) fight rather than fail to increase capabilities; (3) stop fighting rather than eliminate an essential actor; (4) oppose any coalition or single actor which tends to assume a position of predominance within the system; (5) constrain actors who subscribe to supranational organizational principles; and (6) permit defeated or constrained essential national actors to reenter the system as acceptable role partners. (Kaplan, 1957: 23)

According to these rules, competition is proper because it leads to the equalization of capabilities among the major competitors. The balance-of-power approach deals with the problem of war in a way that preserves the problem, for war is a way of measuring national power and a means for changing the distribution of power while perpetuating the essential features of the system itself.

**PRECONDITIONS FOR PEACE THROUGH BALANCE** The successful operation of a balance-of-power system also presupposes that the prerequisites for its successful operation be present.[3] For example, to maintain a balance, states must possess accurate information about others' capabilities and motives. Moreover, the theory argues that there must also be (1) a sufficiently large number of independent states to make alliance formation and dissolution readily possible;[4] (2) a limited geographic area; (3) freedom of action for national leaders; (4) relative equality in states' capabilities; (5) a common political culture in which the rules of the system are recognized and respected; (6) a modicum of homogeneity across the system's members; (7) a weapons technology that inhibits quick mobilization for war, prevents preemptive first-strike attacks that defeat the enemy before it can organize a retaliatory response, and reduces the prospects of wars of annihilation; and (8) the absence of international or supranational institutions capable of interfering with states' alignments and realignments.

The preconditions characterize the environment of international politics during much of the period prior to World Wars I and II, but we can question whether they exist today. Are the assumptions underlying classic balance-of-power theory still warranted?

## The Breakdown of Power Balances

Is international order truly a product of alliance formation and power balances, as many (Liska, 1968; Osgood, 1968) believe? Or, instead, when arms races and alliance

---

[3] The conditions believed necessary for the successful operation of the balance-of-power mechanism remain somewhat controversial. Kenneth Waltz (1979) provides a useful review and critique of the conventional reasoning associated with this issue by advancing the neorealist thesis that "balance-of-power politics prevail whenever two, and only two, requirements are met: that the order be anarchic and that it be populated by units wishing to survive."

[4] Morton A. Kaplan (1957) postulates that a stable balance-of-power system requires at least five great powers or blocs of states.

formation combine power into polarized contending blocs, do the states so aligned find that their security actually diminishes and that major wars erupt?

If the assumptions of the balance-of-power theory are correct, then historical periods in which the basic preconditions for the operation of balance-of-power politics were in evidence should also have been periods in which war became less frequent. What does the historical record suggest?

The Eurocentric system that existed from the mid-seventeenth century until World War I is generally regarded as the "golden age" of balance-of-power politics. But even then the balance of power was always precarious at best (Dehio, 1962). Indeed, the regularity with which wars broke out in Europe between the mid-1600s and the early twentieth century, when the fundamental prerequisites for the mechanical "invisible hand" of the balance of power presumably existed, attests to the repeated failure of its mechanisms to preserve peace (see Box 13.1). Although the classical systems may

## Box 13.1
### THE BALANCE OF POWER: A PRECARIOUS AND FAILED SECURITY SYSTEM

• • •

Balance of power theory is concerned mainly with the rivalries and clashes of great powers—above all—what we have come to describe as *world wars*, the massive military conflicts that engulf and threaten to destroy the entire multistate system. It is difficult to consider world wars as anything other than catastrophic failures, total collapses, of the balance of power system. They are hardly to be classed as stabilizing manoeuvres or equilibrating processes, and one cannot take seriously any claim of maintaining international stability that does not entail the prevention of such disasters as the Napoleonic wars or World War I. Mention of those and similar disasters, however, frequently evokes the reminder that the would-be universal emperor—be it Louis XIV or Napoleon or Hitler—was defeated; in accordance with balance of power principles, a coalition arose to put down the challenger and maintain or restore the independence of the various states. In short, the system worked. Or did it? Is the criterion of the effectiveness of the balance of power that Germany lose its bid for conquest, or that it be deterred from precipitating World War I? It is not easy to justify the contention that a system for the management of international relations that failed to prevent the events of 1914–1918 deserves high marks as a guardian of stability or order, or peace. If the balance of power system does not aim at the prevention of world war, then it aims too low; if it offers no hope of maintaining the general peace, then the quest for a better system is fully warranted.

*Source: Claude (1989: 78).*

at times have prolonged the length of peacetime between wars and possibly limited their duration and damage when they occurred, a balancing of power never kept the peace.[5] To be sure, several decades of peace existed during the balance of power in Europe (between the Congress of Vienna in 1815 and the outbreak of war across Europe in 1848, and after the Franco-Prussian War in 1871 until 1914).[6] But more striking is the destructiveness of the general wars that erupted each time a previous balance-of-power system collapsed.

In light of the previous repetitious breakdown of the balance of power, it is noteworthy that the pattern of recurrent general wars ended when the nuclear era began, after World War II. Since then, war among great powers has been virtually nonexistent—a "long peace" (Gaddis, 1986) has taken root. Could it be that nuclear weapons (the "balance of terror") deterred great-power belligerence since 1945 more than did the balance of power? Alliance formation and balance-of-power politics could not have caused this long peace because the rigid alliance blocs during the Cold War precluded the rapid realignments necessary for the equilibrium that balance-of-power theory envisions. Arguably, the destructiveness of sophisticated weapons since the 1950s kept the peace—not the alliances and power balances that the great powers constructed, which, when used in previous systems, failed to deter major wars.

Equally questionable is the balance-of-power assumption that the relative strength of states determines whether peace will result. Contrary evidence suggests that arming countries may actually invite attack upon themselves. In five of the nine wars involving the great powers in the 150 years following the Congress of Vienna, the countries attacked were stronger militarily than those initiating the war (Singer and Small, 1974). This empirical regularity does not speak well for the premise that seeking military advantages over others deters aggression. Instead, the growth of a state's military power may so terrify its adversaries that they are motivated to initiate a preemptive strike in order to prevent their subjugation.

## Collective Security versus Power Balances

The outbreak of World War I, perhaps more than any other event, discredited balance-of-power politics and promoted the search for alternatives to it. The catastrophic proportions of that war led many to view the balance-of-power mechanism as a *cause* of war instead of an instrument for its prevention. Indeed, many critics cited the arms races, secret treaties, and cross-cutting alliances surrounding balance-of-power politics before the outbreak of the war as its causes.

[5] Research shows that during the nineteenth century, alliance formation within the balance-of-power system was associated with the absence of war, but that throughout the first half of the twentieth century this linkage no longer held: As many states became members of alliances, the international system became relatively more war prone (Singer and Small, 1968).
[6] It could be argued that the relative peace of nineteenth-century Europe was *not* the product of an equilibrium resulting from balance-of-power politics but, instead, was a result of the extraordinary preponderance of power possessed and used by Great Britain to keep peace among its European rivals (see Organski, 1968).

## Assumptions Underlying Collective Security

President Woodrow Wilson voiced the most vehement opposition to balance-of-power politics. He and other political idealists hoped to replace the alliances and counteralliances within the balance of power with the principle of *collective security*. As one student of the subject summarizes their thinking:

> Whereas nineteenth century doctrines considered particular alliances as a normal and justifiable feature of international society, collective security must view alliances between particular states with alarm. Such particular alliances are either superfluous or dangerous; superfluous insofar as they provide a security guarantee to particular states which they already enjoy by virtue of their membership in the society of states, and dangerous insofar as they advertise the fact that those states participating in a particular community of states consider their own security of greater importance than the security of states generally. (Hendrickson, 1993: 4–5)

The League of Nations embodied these beliefs, as it was built on the assumption that peace-loving countries could collectively deter—and, if necessary, counter-act—aggression. Instead of accepting war as a legitimate instrument of national policy, collective security sought to inhibit war through the threat of collective action. The theory proposed (1) to retaliate against *any* aggression or attempt to establish hegemony—not just those acts that threatened particular countries; (2) to involve the participation of *all* member states—not just a sufficient number to stop the aggressor; and (3) to create an international organization to identify acts of aggression and to organize a military response to them—not just to let individual states decide for themselves whether to undertake self-help measures. As one authority describes it,

> The rock bottom principle upon which collective security is founded provides that an attack on any one state will be regarded as an attack on all states. It finds its measure in the simple doctrine of one for all and all for one. War anywhere . . . is the concern of every state.
>
> Self-help and neutrality, it should be obvious, are the exact antithesis of such a theory. States under an order of neutrality are impartial when conflict breaks out, give their blessings to combatants to fight it out, and defer judgment regarding the justice or injustice of the cause involved. Self-help in the past was often "help yourself" so far as the great powers were concerned; they enforced their own rights and more besides. In the eighteenth and nineteenth centuries this system was fashionable and wars, although not eliminated, were localized whenever possible. In a more integrated world environment, a conflict anywhere has some effect on conditions of peace everywhere. A disturbance at one point upsets the equilibrium at all other points, and the adjustment of a single conflict restores the foundations of harmony at other points throughout the world. (Thompson, 1953: 755)

To the disappointment of its proponents, collective security was not endorsed by the very powers that after World War I had promoted it. Japan's aggression against Manchuria in 1931 (and China proper in 1937) and Italy's invasion of Ethiopia in 1935 were widely condemned, but collective resistance was not forthcoming. Furthermore, Germany's attack on Czechoslovakia and other European countries in the late 1930s elicited no collective response. When World War II broke out, collective security was discredited.

## The Revival of Balance-of-Power Politics

Following World War II, realists maintained that national self-reliance was the only trustworthy safeguard of security, that peace would come through strength, and that it was necessary to confront a potential aggressor with a preponderance of power to successfully deter its aggression. U.S. President Richard Nixon was one among many leaders who reaffirmed the balance-of-power approach when he opined, "We must remember the only time in the history of the world that we have had any extended period of peace is when there has been a balance of power . . . It will be a safer world . . . if we have a strong, healthy United States, Europe, Soviet Union, China, Japan, each balancing the other."

To evaluate the validity of this proposition and of the balance-of-power theory in general, it is instructive to review the evolution of the international system's polarity structure since World War II during which a long, great-power peace unfolded.

## Post–World War II Models of the Balance of Power

Power can be distributed in different ways. Historically, these have ranged from highly concentrated distributions on one end of the continuum to highly dispersed distributions on the other. The former have included regional empires (such as the Roman Empire), while an example of the latter is the approximate equality of power held by the European powers at the conclusion of the Napoleonic Wars in 1815.

Following the conventional periodizations of analysts, we can identify three major configurations in the distribution of international power since 1945, with a possible fourth one emergent in the post–Cold War period.[7]

### Unipolarity

Most countries were devastated by the global war that ended in 1945, but the United States was left in a clearly superordinate position, with its economy accounting for about half the world's combined gross national product. The United States was also the only country with the awesome new weapon, the atomic bomb. It had already demonstrated its willingness to use that weapon, which underscored to others that the United States was without rival and incapable of being counterbalanced. The United States was not just stronger than anybody—it was stronger than everybody. This immediate postwar power configuration was *unipolar* because power was concentrated in the hands of a single dominant hegemon. This period was short-lived, however.

---

[7] Historians disagree as to the precise dates at which a particular distribution of power collapsed and a new one arose. For discussions of alternative periodizations, see Kaplan (1957), Oren (1984), Rosecrance (1963), and Thompson (1988).

## Bipolarity

The recovery of the Soviet economy, the growth of its military capabilities, the maintenance of a large army, and growing Soviet rivalry with the United States soon gave rise to a new distribution of world power. The Soviets broke the U.S. monopoly of atomic weapons in 1949 and exploded a thermonuclear device in 1953, less than a year after the United States. This achievement symbolized creation of a *bipolar* distribution, as military capabilities became concentrated in the hands of two competitive *superpowers*.

The concentration of power (what scholars term *polarity*) into two dominant actors induced *polarization,* as power combined through alliance formation to form two countervailing *blocs* or opposed coalitions.[8] The concept of polarization, which refers to the propensity of actors to cluster in alliances around the most powerful states, is especially apt in this context because a *pole* is a fit metaphor for a magnet—it both repels and attracts (Nogee, 1975). The formation of the North Atlantic Treaty Organization (NATO), linking the United States to the defense of Western Europe, and the Warsaw Pact, linking the Soviet Union in a formal alliance with its Eastern European clients, were manifestations of the polarization process through which states combined their military resources in countercoalitions to reinforce a bipolar structure. The opposing alliance systems formed partly because the superpowers competed for allies and partly because the less powerful states looked to one or the other of the superpowers for protection. Correspondingly, each superpower's allies gave it forward bases from which to carry on the competition. In addition, the involvement of most other states in the superpowers' struggle globalized the East–West conflict. Few states remained outside the superpowers' rival alliance networks as neutral or nonaligned actors.

By grouping the system's nation-states into two blocs, each led by a superpower, the Cold War's bipolar structure bred insecurity among all (Spanier, 1975). The balance was constantly at stake. Each bloc leader, fearing that its adversary would attain hegemony, viewed every move, however defensive, as the first step toward world conquest. The conflict became "zero-sum" because both sides viewed what one side gained as a loss for the other. Both therefore attached great importance to recruiting new allies, and fear that an old ally might desert the fold was ever present. Bipolarity left little room for compromise or maneuver and worked against the normalization of superpower relations (Waltz, 1993).

## Bipolycentrism

The major Cold War coalitions associated with bipolarity began to disintegrate in the 1960s and early 1970s. As their internal cohesion eroded and new centers of power

---

[8] Note that these concepts are sometimes used interchangeably, but that they refer to distinct dimensions of the two primary ways military power is aggregated (or dispersed) at any point in time in the international system. In the first instance, when states independently build arms at home, their differential production rates change the system's *polarity* or distribution of power. In the second instance, when states combine their arms through alliance formation, the aggregation of power through *polarization* changes the system's balance of power.

emerged, a bipolycentric system (Spanier, 1975) came into being. ***Bipolycentrism*** described the continued military superiority of the United States and the Soviet Union, and their allies' continued reliance on their respective superpower patrons for security. At the same time, increasing room for maneuver by the weaker alliance partners became possible. Hence the term *polycentrism* evolved, indicating the emergence of diverse relationships among the states subordinate to the superpowers at this second tier (such as the friendly relations that were nurtured between the United States and Romania, on the one hand, and those between France and the Soviet Union, on the other). The secondary powers also began to cultivate ties across alliance boundaries (such as between Poland and West Germany) to enhance their bargaining position within their own alliance. The superpowers remained dominant militarily, but this less rigid system allowed other states to perform new foreign policy roles, other than simply aligned or nonaligned.

Rapid technological innovation in the superpowers' major weapons systems was a principal catalyst of change. In particular, intercontinental ballistic missiles (ICBMs) eroded the necessity of forward-base areas for striking at the heart of the adversary and diminished the need to maintain tight, cohesive alliance systems composed of reliable partners.

In addition, the narrowed differences in the superpowers' arsenals loosened the ties that had previously bound allies to one another. The European members of NATO in particular began to question whether the United States would indeed, as it had pledged, protect Paris or Bonn by sacrificing New York. Under what conditions might Washington or Moscow be willing to risk a nuclear holocaust? The uncertainty aroused by such questioning became pronounced as the pledge to extend deterrence to allies by retaliating against their attacker seemed increasingly insincere. As former CIA director Stansfield Turner acknowledged in 1986, "It's not conceivable that any president would risk the very existence of [the United States] in order to defend [our] European allies from a conventional assault."

In partial response to the dilemma this posed, other states, particularly France, decided to protect themselves by developing their own nuclear capabilities, with the result that the diffusion of power already under way gathered momentum.

As these changes unfolded in the 1970s and 1980s, Cold War categories used to classify "free world" (capitalist) and "socialist" (communist) countries' foreign policy alignments lost much of their relevance, as bipolycentrism implies. The revival of democratic capitalism in the late 1980s that led communist states to accept free market principles eroded further the adhesive bonds of ideology that had formerly helped these countries face their security problems from a common posture. Such fissures in both blocs widened, as disputes arose in the Western alliance over strategic doctrine, arms control, U.S. military bases on allies' territory, and especially "out-of-area conflicts" (those beyond the traditional geographical boundaries of NATO). Not only decomposing blocs, but also declining support in general for the sanctity of alliance commitments became evident (see Kegley and Raymond, 1990). As fears of a new world war steadily lessened and the Cold War began to fade, leaders questioned whether defense alliances were still needed.

**THE CRUMBLING OF THE COLD WAR BLOCS** The events that began in 1989 with the tearing down of the Berlin Wall tore apart the post–World War II architecture of competing blocs. With the end of this division, and without a Soviet threat, the consistency of outlook and singularity of purpose that once bound NATO members together dissipated. To many critics, NATO and the Warsaw Pact had institutionalized antagonisms and perpetuated the Cold War—and were no longer needed.

Central to the unfolding debate was "the German question." According to Lord Ismay, the first secretary general of NATO, the original purpose of the Atlantic alliance was "to keep the Russians out, the Americans in, and the Germans down." In 1990, though the Soviet Union feared a "Fourth Reich" — a united, powerful, and potentially expansionist German state—the Soviet Union reversed its long-standing opposition to German unification and agreed to withdraw its military from Europe. It did not make that dramatic concession without conditions, however. It insisted that unification be orchestrated through the active management of *all* the major World War II allies, that Germany reduce its armed forces, and that the United States keep a military presence in NATO on German soil.

Germany met all of these preconditions in 1990. In September the Four Powers (the United States, the Soviet Union, Great Britain, and France) and the two Germanys (the "Two plus Four") negotiated a treaty in Moscow that terminated the Four Powers' rights over Germany. German leaders declared they had no territorial claims to make in Europe, including the territories in Poland that were annexed during and after World War II. Moreover, they pledged to never obtain nuclear weapons, and to reduce their 670,000-person armed forces to 370,000 troops by 1995 (in exchange for the removal of 370,000 Soviet soldiers from Germany). And Germany and the Soviet Union signed a bilateral treaty under which the two powers promised never to attack each other.

The West greeted these agreements (and Soviet concessions) with enthusiasm because they symbolized at once the retreat of the Soviet Union from a region, East Europe, it had long regarded as central to its security and the geostrategic shift of NATO influence into the heartland of the Warsaw Pact, which formally dissolved early in 1991.

**THE TRANSFORMATION OF THE ATLANTIC ALLIANCE**  Although in the early 1990s many perceived the need to replace NATO and the defunct Warsaw Pact with a new security arrangement, most leaders maintained that some configuration of collective defense pacts remained necessary to cement relationships and stabilize the rush of cascading events. President Bush, for example, was a vocal advocate of the continuing need to anchor security in alliances, pledging to keep U.S. troops in Europe and promising that the United States would remain the backbone of NATO, which he (and President Clinton afterward) sought to preserve.

To others, a new Concert of Europe like that which the great powers created in the wake of the Napoleonic Wars in 1815 was needed. Leaders in Moscow and some Western analysts (Mueller, 1990; also Rosecrance, 1992) reasoned that it was useful to preserve NATO if it were restructured not to contain enemies but to control allies. For that, *all* the countries in Europe would be required to coordinate their defense policies. This would incorporate the East European and former Soviet republics pursuing democratization into a European-wide framework and possibly shift peacekeeping responsibilities from NATO to the larger Conference on Security and Cooperation in Europe (CSCE), which in 1994 expanded to fifty-four members when each of the former Soviet republics joined the organization.

An alternative scenario was the conversion of NATO from a military alliance designed for defense against a predetermined enemy to a larger collective security community focused primarily on the political dimensions of security. The 1991 Rome Summit moved in this direction by drafting "The Alliance's New Strategic Concept." The Rome Declaration announced formation of a new North Atlantic Cooperation Council (NACC) "to build genuine partnership among the North Atlantic Alliance and the countries of Central and Eastern Europe." The next meeting of defense ministers months later witnessed the members of NATO sitting at the same table with the former Warsaw Pact states and newly independent Baltic republics, facing a request from Russia to become a member.

> The purpose of NACC is to enhance stability throughout the European Union by providing the nations of the former Warsaw Pact with a forum for dialogue, consultation, and the development of joint projects. In less than two years since its first meeting, the organization has grown in membership (38 countries), in geographic scope ("from Vancouver to Vladivostok . . ."), and in responsibilities. . . . In accordance with this new defense posture, NATO [sought to develop] both immediate reaction forces and more substantial rapid reaction forces. A headquarters [was] established for the ACE Rapid Reaction Corps, and the Corps itself should become operational in 1995. (Stuart, 1993: 17).

These adjustments in role and mission reflected an effort, of course, to keep NATO alive even though the Cold War has died. The old NATO was built on the joint will to resist Soviet aggression. The new NATO sought to survive by preparing to contain ethnonational conflicts and foster disarmament and by remaining a vehicle for preserving U.S. involvement in European security. The latter, NATO's Secretary General Manfred Wörner asserted in November 1993, was "even more important than in the past."

In January 1994 the historic dynamics of balance-of-power realignments again were exhibited. The European balance of power had tilted to the West after the Soviet Union collapsed and the Warsaw Pact dissolved. In response, four countries sought hard to *bandwagon* by shifting to support the strongest alliance, NATO. The most advanced democracies in the former communist bloc—Poland, the Czech Republic, Slovakia, and Hungary—lobbied aggressively for immediate membership. NATO cut a compromise deal with them by offering "Partnerships for Peace." Under these bilateral agreements, the four countries were allowed to participate in some NATO operations. For example, they are able to plan and train together with NATO troops for peacekeeping and crisis management. But they are not extended the same security guarantee of aid in the event that any are attacked and must await the unspecified day when they can become full members of NATO with the collective defense commitment that this membership would provide. Still, in extending NATO to the East, the European security framework was transformed. With this territorial expansion, the balance of power again began to shift (see Map 13.1).

Within a short period of time, this expansion could proved to comprise an im-

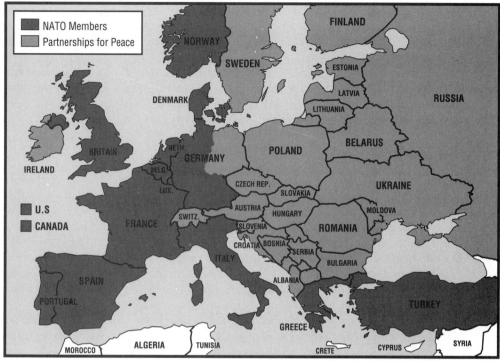

**Map 13.1** NATO's 1994 Expansion and the Shifting European Balance of Power

portant step in the consolidation of all Europe in a common collective security regime—including Russia, which had earlier expressed its hope for closer military cooperation with NATO (Sestanovich, 1994). "We have ushered in a new era of cooperation" through expansion of the alliance, Manfred Wörner, NATO's secretary general explained in February 1994. Elaborating on the purposes envisioned, U.S. Secretary of State Warren Christopher argued that

> the Alliance must embrace innovation or risk irrelevance. . . . The January (1994) summit [opens] the door to an evolutionary process of NATO expansion. This process should be non-discriminatory and inclusive. It should . . . initiate practical military cooperation between NATO forces and those of the East. To that end, we have proposed a Partnership for Peace. The Partnership would be open to all members of the North Atlantic Cooperation Council as well as others. It excludes no nations and forms no blocs.

Shortly thereafter NATO did expand, and began to fashion itself for a single common defense without specifying a single common enemy. In June 1994, as NATO Deputy Secretary-General Sergio Balanzino put it, "a defining moment in shaping the continent" was reached. Russia agreed to join twenty other neutrals and former-Warsaw Pact countries in actively participating in the Partnership for Peace plan, thereby ending months of speculation about whether Moscow would sign the accord. When he put his signature to the agreement, Russian Foreign Minister Andrei Kozyrev stated that "Today Russia took an important step to help shape a safer and more peaceful post-Cold War world. . . . Things that were unthinkable two years ago have now become virtually a routine matter in bilateral cooperation and military exchanges."

This breakthrough creates a far different distribution of power than that which existed in the bipolycentric system of the 1970s and 1980s and the bipolar system that preceded it in the 1950s and 1960s. The waves of change that have unfolded presage the beginning of a new multipolar system.

## Multipolarity

U.S. Secretary of State Lawrence Eagleburger proclaimed in 1989 that "we are now moving into . . . a world in which power and influence is diffused among a multiplicity of states—[a] multipolar world." A *multipolar* system of relatively equal powers similar to the classical European balance-of-power system may indeed best describe the emerging distribution of power. Such a multipolar system might consist of the United States, China, Germany, Japan, and Russia. To these might someday be added a consolidated European Union as a product of the treaty signed in February 1992 that called for the eventual amalgamation of Europe and its pursuit of a common defense policy (see Chapter 14).

What will be the likely character of such a multipolar world? As we have seen, when power has been relatively evenly distributed in the past, each player has been assertive, independent, and competitive; diplomacy has displayed a nonideological, chess-like character; and conflict has been intense as each contender has nervously feared the power of its rivals.

Should a truly multipolar world develop, it is difficult to foresee how each great power's relationship with the others will evolve. Realignments are to be expected. With the probable expansion of the number of great powers to as many as five, new cleavages will inevitably develop, and rivalry will intensify as each pole jockeys for privilege, position, and power. Indeed, a world comprised of five or more independent and approximately equal centers of power will create an enlarged global chessboard of thirty bilateral geostrategic relationships. Such a congested landscape would be fraught with great potential for conflict and much confusion about the identity of friends and foes. To make the setting even more confusing, the interplay is likely to take place simultaneously on two playing fields, the first economic and the second military (recall Chapter 4, Table 4.2 on page 108).

In a new multipolar system, we can expect the major powers to align together against others on particular issues, as interests dictate. Behind the diplomatic smiles and handshakes, one-time friends and allies are likely to grow apart, and formally "specialized" relationships will likely dissolve. Consider the already heated U.S.–Japan–EU rivalry on the economic battlefield (Thurow, 1992; see also Chapter 7).

Multipolarity also presages the potential alignment of former adversaries. The United States and the Russian Federation, allied victors in World War II, are now both apprehensive about the powers they defeated: an ascendant China, Japan, and Germany. As a result, and as balance-of-power theory would predict and Russian strategist Peter Gladkov prescribed in 1992, the United States and Russia may be "natural" allies. Hence, the post–Cold War division of power portends a

> new international order [that] will see many centers of power. . . . History so far has shown us only two roads to international stability: domination or equilibrium. [The United States does] not have the resources for domination, nor is such a course compatible with [U.S.] values. So we are brought back to a concept maligned in much of America's intellectual history—the balance of power. (Kissinger, 1992: 239)

If the fundamental trend toward the dispersion of global power continues, the prospects for peace undoubtably will be affected, as Henry Kissinger postulates. Less certain is the more probable consequence of a changing global balance of power. Which is more likely, war or peace?

## Polarity and Peace?

In the wake of the Cold War and the disintegration of its bipolar structure, the long-standing debate has intensified about which type of power distribution—unipolar, bipolar, or multipolar—is the most stable. Let us compare the conflicting views in this controversy.[9]

### *Unipolarity and Peace*

One position, informed by the concentration of military power during the *pax Romana*, *pax Britannica*, and *pax Americana*, holds that "the periods of known preponderance are periods of peace":

> It is often claimed that a balance of power brings peace. . . . There were periods when an equal distribution of power between contenders actually existed . . . but these . . . were the exception rather than the rule. . . . Closer examination reveals that they were periods of war, not peace. (Organski, 1968: 293)

If this view is accurate, then peace will occur when one hegemonic state acquires enough power to deter others' expansionist ambitions. The proposition springs from the arguments that "an unequal power distribution (or preponderance) promotes peace because the more powerful opponent has no need to go to war, while the weaker side would be foolish to do so," but that "an equal power distribution between opponents increases the likelihood of war because each opponent thinks it can win" (Simowitz, 1982).

If we think of the United States as the hegemonic power in the post–World War II system, these seemingly plausible conclusions about the stability of unipolar systems do not bode well for peace in the future. For if present trends continue, the so-called "unipolar moment" of unchallenged U.S. hegemony (Krauthammer, 1991b) will pass and the late 1990s will likely witness the continuing deconcentration of

---

[9] This discussion follows Kegley and Raymond (1992, 1994).

power. The new world order in this circumstance without a dominant global leader would be increasingly disorderly (see also Chapter 7).

## Bipolarity and Peace

In contrast, a second school of thought maintains that a bipolar world like the one that emerged in the 1950s is the most stable (for example, Waltz, 1964). Here the argument is that the heightened tension accompanying bipolarity compelled the super-powers' caution and restrained their subordinate allies from provoking crises. According to this line of reasoning, stability, ironically, results from "the division of all nations into two camps [because it] raises the costs of war to such a high level that all but the most fundamental conflicts are resolved without resort to violence" (Bueno de Mesquita, 1975). Under such stark simplicities and balanced symmetries, the two leading rivals have incentives to manage crises to prevent them from escalating to war. It is also thought that the clarity surrounding bipolarity keeps leaders alert and promotes their caution.

Those who believe that a bipolar world is inherently more stable than either its unipolar or multipolar counterparts draw support from the fact that in the bipolar environment of the 1950s, when the threat of war was endemic, major war did not occur. True, the superpowers went to the brink of war repeatedly (Brecher, 1993), but they never went over the brink. Extrapolating, these observers (for example, Mearsheimer, 1990) reason that because now a new multipolar distribution of global power makes it impossible to run the world from one or two centers, disorder will result:

> As the world becomes more multipolar—with economic leverage and even political-military power being more widely dispersed among nations—it isn't necessarily becoming a safer, gentler globe. And as nations become more interdependent, they aren't necessarily becoming more cooperative.
>
> [There] is every reason to believe that the world of the 1990s will be less predictable and in many ways more unstable than the world of the last several decades. . . . It is rather basic. So long as there were only two great powers, like two big battleships clumsily and cautiously circling each other, confrontations—or accidents—were easier to avoid. Now, with the global lake more crowded with ships of varying sizes, fueled by different ambitions and piloted with different degrees of navigational skill, the odds of collisions become far greater. (House, 1989: A10)

## Multipolarity and Peace

A third school of thought argues that multipolar systems, not unipolar or bipolar ones, are the least war prone. The reasons advanced differ, but there is a shared belief that polarized systems that either concentrate power, as in a unipolar system, or that divide the globe into two antagonistic blocs, as in a bipolar system, promote struggles for dominance. During the bipolar Cold War, for instance, "the leaders of each bloc [tried] to destroy and revolutionize their rivals [and sought] to wear down the other [by] using force to maintain and expand their blocs" (Pelz, 1991).

Moreover, this school perceives bipolarity as dangerously destabilizing because bipolarity by definition generates the fear that tempts each bloc to destroy the other. As Hans J. Morgenthau (1985) grimly described it, the Cold War's bipolar system reduced the international system "to the primitive spectacle of two giants eyeing each other with watchful suspicion. They [bent] every effort to increase their military potential to the utmost, since this is all they [had] to count on. Both [prepared] to strike the first decisive blow, for if one [did] not strike it the other might. Thus, contain or be contained, conquer or be conquered, destroy or be destroyed, [became] the watchwords of Cold War diplomacy." In contrast to bipolar competition, multipolar systems encompass a larger number of autonomous actors, giving rise to more potential alliance partners, which are essential to the operation of a balance to counterbalance a would-be aggressor, for shifting alliances can occur only when there are multiple power centers (Deutsch and Singer, 1964).

Note that this perspective portrays polarization[10] as hazardous because the structural rigidity it fosters significantly reduces *interaction opportunities*[11] and cross-cutting allegiances that constrain conflict.[12] Under these circumstances, minor disagreements easily become magnified into larger tests of will. Lacking suppleness, polarized configurations of power have historically deteriorated into struggles for preeminence between two armed hostile camps, and this means that "bipolarity can, at times, be just as destabilizing as multipolarity" (Thompson, 1988). Among the examples of unstable bipolar systems are the rivalries in antiquity between ancient Athens and Sparta and between the Greek confederations and the Persians, and, in more modern history, between Hapsburg and Valois in the sixteenth century, England and the Netherlands a century later, and England and France in the eighteenth century.

## Contemplating a Multipolar Future

The emergence of a less polarized international system appears very likely. However, the probable consequences of a new multipolar system are not clear, as the three schools of thought on the relationship between polarity and global stability suggest.[13]

---

[10] A system with multiple power centers can be said to be moving toward a greater degree of polarization if its members form separate blocs whose external interactions are characterized by increasing levels of conflict while their internal interactions become more cooperative (Rapkin and Thompson with Christopherson, 1989). Conversely, polarization decreases when the number of alignments expands.

[11] The concept of *interaction opportunities* refers to the fact that as the number of autonomous actors increases, the probability that more actors will develop relationships with an expanding number of other actors also grows, thereby increasing the number of possible coalitions.

[12] Numerous studies provide evidence that polarized blocs (such as the European system on the eve of World War I) are war prone (for example, Wallace, 1973), whereas a moderate amount of flexibility in the structure of alliances has inhibited the onset of war. Historically, when tight, polarized alliances approximately equal in capability have emerged and alliance networks have tightened, the incidence of war has risen (Kim, 1989).

[13] A large number of investigations suggest that a direct relationship between multipolar systems and the probability of war cannot be safely drawn (see Bueno de Mesquita, 1981; Hopf, 1991; Kegley and Raymond, 1994; Levy, 1985; Ostrom and Aldrich, 1978).

Because "there is no real consensus on whether systems with a certain number of poles are more war prone than others" (Russett and Starr, 1989), it would be imprudent to jump to the conclusion that a new multipolar system will necessarily spell another period of warfare. Different *types* of multipolar systems can emerge involving variant armament ratios and levels of alliances. These combinations can produce very disparate outcomes. Because alternate scenarios are both possible and plausible, and the presence or absence of a particular polarity balance by itself will not dictate whether war will result, we have reasons to both celebrate and mourn the passing of the Cold War's competitive bipolar world as well as the disappearance of the unipolar system in which the United States as the globe's single hegemon dominated.

To conclude, the aggregation of power by states to balance power as a way to preserve peace has a rather checkered history. In the long run, the alliances formed and the distributions of power produced have failed to avert a breakdown of world order. The great powers have been drawn into four "large wars this century by the collapse of the balance of power in either Europe or East Asia or both at the same time" (*Economist*, October 30, 1993). Yet history also suggests that prospects for peace in multipolar systems depend on still other factors. Negotiated arms agreements designed to change the existing balance of power are a critical component, which could alter the past propensity of multipolar systems to culminate in widespread warfare.

## DISARMAMENT AND ARMS CONTROL

Some reformers have attacked the theory that power can be balanced with power to preserve world order, advocating instead the biblical prescription that nations should beat their swords into plowshares. The destructiveness and dispersion of today's weapons have inspired many people once again to take this tenet of liberal theory seriously.

### Controlling Weapons: Rationales and Approaches

Do the weapons of war contribute to its frequency? Several rationales suggest that they do (see Johansen, 1991, 1995). Countries build arms for use in conflict. A country that arms itself signals to others its potentially aggressive designs. If others fear that the weapons are directed toward them, they often feel compelled to arm themselves. Furthermore, the possession of arms may tempt a threatened party to use them in a preemptive strike to defeat the stronger enemy before it can attack.

On the other hand, war cannot occur if the instruments of force are not available. Nor are countries without weapons always the most likely targets of aggression by their armed neighbors (although they are not freed from that fear). Instead, as the Bible argues and as evidence supports, countries that have lived by the sword have died by the sword (see Midlarsky, 1975; Richardson, 1960a). The acquisition of arms may invite attack because weapons elicit fear and aggression in others. If enemies are most dangerous when provoked—and nothing is more provocative than a sophisticated system of delivering destruction—then the creation of intimidating weapons systems with which to threaten enemies may be counterproductive. This principle translates into the observation that each new increment of military power may give states that much *less* security.

The incentives for controlling arms have increased greatly since the horrors of Hiroshima and Nagasaki. The threat that nuclear weapons pose to stability and survival was expressed by President Kennedy in a 1961 address to the United Nations that still retains its relevance:

> Today, every inhabitant of this planet must contemplate the day when this planet may no longer be habitable. Every man, woman and child lives under a nuclear sword of Damocles, hanging by the slenderest of threads, capable of being cut at any moment by accident or miscalculation or by madness. The weapons of war must be abolished before they abolish us.
>
> Men no longer debate whether armaments are a symptom or a cause of tension. The mere existence of modern weapons—ten million times more powerful than any that the world has ever seen, and only minutes away from any target on earth—is a source of horror, and discord and distrust. Men no longer maintain that disarmament must await the settlement of all disputes—for disarmament must be a part of any permanent settlement. And men may no longer pretend that the quest for disarmament is a sign of weakness—for in a spiraling arms race, a nation's security may well be shrinking even as its arms increase.

These words conjure up Soviet Premier Nikita Khrushchev's prediction in 1962 that in the event of a nuclear exchange "the survivors would envy the dead." They call into question the conventional wisdom that arms produce security. Indeed, they question the very right to arm. When the destructiveness of weapons threatens the fate of the earth itself (see Sagan and Turco, 1990), abolishing the source of that threat ceases to appear to be a radical, utopian aspiration.

Before reviewing the historical record of efforts to change through negotiations the global distribution of weapons and the uses to which they can be put, and assessing its implications for peace, we need to recognize two distinctions, one between disarmament and arms control, a second between bilateral and multilateral agreements.

Although many people assume the terms are synonymous, ***disarmament*** is different from ***arms control***. Arms control refers to agreements designed to regulate arms levels either by limiting their growth or by restricting how they might be used. This is a far less ambitious endeavor than disarmament, which seeks to reduce or eliminate weapons.

> In its most general conception, arms control is any type of restraint on the use of arms, any form of military cooperation between adversaries. Arms control can be implicit or explicit, formal or informal, and unilateral, bilateral, or multilateral. It is a process of jointly managing the weapons acquisition processes of the participant states in the hope of reducing the risk of war. . . . Arms control [refers] to formal agreements imposing significant restrictions or limitations on the weapons or security policies of the signatories.

Disarmament rests on a fundamentally different philosophical premise than arms control. It envisions the drastic reduction or elimination of all weapons, looking toward the eradication of war itself. Disarmament is based on the notion that if there were no more weapons there would be no more war. This is a compelling proposition, with enough truth to give it a very long life in the history of thought about war and peace. Arms control, on the other hand, accepts the existence of weapons and the possibility of conflict. Contrary to popular impression, it is not necessarily about reducing arms levels. Arms control attempts to stabilize the status quo and to manage conflict, to encourage peaceful resolution of disputes and limit the resort to military force. Although many visceral opponents would be shocked at the thought, arms control is fundamentally a conservative enterprise. Disarmament, by contrast, is a radical one. Disarmament seeks to overturn the status quo; arms control works to perpetuate it. (Kruzel, 1991: 249)

Furthermore, as suggested, bilateral agreements should be differentiated from multilateral agreements. Because the former refer to agreements between only two countries, they are often easier to negotiate and to enforce than are the latter, which refer to agreements between three or more countries. Negotiating a multilateral agreement simultaneously binding on many states poses many obstacles because states' security interests are very divergent, as are the domestic processes by which governments approve international agreements. As a result, the record of bilateral agreements differs from that of multilateral agreements with respect to both arms control and disarmament.

## Multilateral Diplomacy: The Disarmament and Arms Control Record

It is hardly a novel idea that reducing the world's military arsenals is one way to control war. Yet until very recently one of the few constants in the changing international system has been the repetition with which states have advocated disarmament but failed to implement it. To be sure, in the past, some countries did succeed in reducing their armaments levels.[14] However, these achievements were rare, as many more countries raced to expand their arsenals than tried to cut them. Most disarmament was involuntary, the product of reductions imposed by coercion on the vanquished by the victors in the immediate aftermath of a war, as when the Allied powers after World War I attempted (unsuccessfully) to permanently disarm a defeated Germany. Instances of unilateral disarmament in the absence of coercion historically have been even less frequent. In short, to speak of disarmament is to speak of a phenomenon with few historical examples. With the end of the Cold War, this, as we will see, has begun to change.

---

[14] The Chinese states in 600 B.C.E. formed a disarmament league that produced a peaceful century for the league's members, and in the Rush-Bagot Agreement of 1818 Canada and the United States disarmed the Great Lakes. Disarmament proposals also figured prominently in the League of Nations' abortive World Disarmament Conference of 1932 and rather continuously in the United Nations since 1946 but especially in its "special sessions" on disarmament.

In contrast with disarmament, there are many historical examples of arms control efforts. As early as the eleventh century the Second Lateran Council prohibited the use of crossbows in fighting, and the 1868 St. Petersburg Declaration prohibited the use of explosive bullets. More recent examples include the 1899 and 1907 International Peace Conferences at the Hague, which restricted the use of some weapons and prohibited others, and the agreement among the United States, Britain, Japan, France, and Italy at the Washington Naval Conferences (1921–1922) adjusting the relative tonnage of their fleets (followed and extended by the London Treaties of 1930 and 1936). Other examples include the 1919 St. Germain Convention on the export of arms, the 1925 Geneva Convention on arms trade, and the 1929 Geneva draft convention on arms manufacture. An unsuccessful example is found in the 1921 League of Nations' effort to realize an arms production moratorium.

The post–World War II period saw a variety of new arms control proposals. The Baruch Plan (1946) called for the creation of a United Nations Atomic Development Authority that would have placed atomic energy under an international authority to ensure its use for only peaceful purposes, but the great powers never approved the proposal. (However, beginning in 1957 U.S. and Soviet scientists met informally at the so-called Pugwash Conferences to discuss processes for controlling nuclear weapons.) The Rapacki Plan of 1957, which would have prevented the deployment of nuclear weapons in Central Europe, also failed.

Nonetheless, leaders have made recurrent efforts to resolve differences so formal arms control agreements might be realized. Prominent among them were the arms control summit meetings of the great powers, of which those between the United States and Soviet Union, the world's nuclear superpowers, were the most frequent. Summit talks between the Cold War antagonists began in July 1955, when U.S. President Eisenhower and Soviet leader Nikita Khrushchev met in Geneva and Eisenhower made an "open skies" proposal for aerial reconnaissance to monitor military maneuvers. Among other things, these summits sought, and often resulted in, an improved atmosphere for serious arms control negotiations and paved the way for the ambitious agreements that were reached as the Cold War ended to cement a new world order based on a reduced and stable military power balance (see also Chapter 4).

In addition to summitry, multilateral negotiations on particular issues have sometimes taken on the character of institutionalized efforts to reach arms control agreements. Nine examples illustrate their range and breadth:

- The Mutual and Balanced Force Reductions Talks (MBFR) were conducted from 1973 to 1988 in an effort to realize force reductions between the blocs dividing Europe. These negotiations did not produce a treaty, but during the Cold War they sustained a "consensus that arms control negotiations are a necessary component of alliance defense strategy" and "were helpful in preparing for the Negotiations on Conventional Armed Forces in Europe (CFE)" (Hallenbeck and Shaver, 1991).

- The Comprehensive Test Ban (CTB) negotiations have been held periodically since the late 1950s in an effort to reach agreement on a treaty banning all nuclear explosions. The Reagan administration broke off negotiations in 1982, citing verification obstacles and the need to test nuclear weapons as long as deterrence rested on them, but negotiations on verification protocols resumed in November 1987. New protocols were added to the existing Threshold Test Ban Treaty and the Peaceful Nuclear Explosions Treaty. They provided for three methods of cooperative verification: in-country seismic tests, on-site inspections, and a hydrodynamic system. Since then, negotiations have proceeded on further limits to nuclear testing. In a move strongly advocated by Russia, the Clinton administration announced in June 1993 that the United States would extend its self-imposed moratorium on nuclear tests until September 1994 unless another nuclear weapon state conducts a nuclear test.

- The Conventional Force Reductions in Europe negotiations, which began in March 1989, produced the Conventional Armed Forces in Europe (CFE) treaty signed by the twenty-three participating states in Paris in November 1990. Ratified in December 1991 and extended to newly independent countries in 1992, "CFE is the most significant and ambitious conventional arms control agreement ever negotiated. The treaty established parity at reduced levels in five categories of major conventional arms equipment . . . in the area from the Atlantic to the Urals (ATTU). . . . The treaty left NATO with a clear superiority in conventional armaments and no obvious adversary" (Keeny, 1993).

- The Conference on Security and Cooperation in Europe (CSCE), begun in Helsinki in July 1973, became the leading multilateral institution for managing the transformation of Europe from a system of counterpoised alliances (NATO and the Warsaw Pact) to one based on common principles stretching across the entire continent and North America. The Paris CSCE summit in November 1990 established a permanent CSCE secretariat and Conflict Prevention Center. In early 1992, the former republics of the Soviet Union joined the CSCE. The 1992 Helsinki CSCE meetings discussed the paths by which this enlarged community could apply the provisions of the 1975 Helsinki accords to the new European geopolitical environment. In subsequent meetings, discussion has remained centered on the right of all peoples to self-determination, peaceful border changes, prohibition of the use of force to settle disputes, and the collective control of internal violence.

- The Nonproliferation Treaty (NPT) conferences, following the historic Treaty on Nonproliferation of Nuclear Weapons signed by 138 non-nuclear weapons parties in 1968 (and 163 by June 1994), have held Review Conferences at five-year intervals (1975, 1980, 1985, 1990) to discuss compliance and enforcement programs. The 1995 twenty-five-year review conference in New York will face the difficult task of renewing (extending) the NPT. "Three de facto nuclear weapon states—India, Israel, and Pakistan—are not NPT members [and states] have the right to withdraw from the treaty if their 'supreme national interests' are jeopardized." To keep the NPT in place, the United States, Germany, and Japan have proposed that the NPT be extended without limits after 1995 "while other states have suggested shorter, set periods of extension, ranging from five to 25 years. The length of the Pact's extension will be decided by a majority of the NPT members" (Arms Control Association *Fact Sheet*, August 1993).

• The Conference on Disarmament (CD) emerged from the bilateral negotiations between the United States and the Soviet Union that began in 1976 to ban the production, stockpiling, and use of chemical weapons. In 1981 those closed negotiations moved to the multilateral Conference on Disarmament forum in Geneva, out of which the U.S.–Soviet Chemical Weapons Destruction Agreement was reached on June 1990. At its August 1991 meeting, the thirty-nine-state Conference on Disarmament gave its Ad Hoc Committee on a Nuclear Test Ban a mandate to negotiate a Comprehensive Test Ban Treaty, while pursuing a comprehensive and worldwide multilateral chemical weapons disarmament convention. The Persian Gulf War intensified interest in reaching the accord, which resulted in the 1993 multilateral treaty described below.

• The Review Conferences of the Biological Weapons Convention have convened periodically since the 1972 Bacteriological (Biological) and Toxin Weapons Convention (TWC) was ratified. The 1972 convention was the first multilateral arms control agreement aimed at the complete elimination of an entire category of weapons of mass destruction. It banned the development, production, stockpiling, acquisition, or retention of biological and toxin weapons but did not specifically ban their use. That had already been done by the 1925 Geneva Protocol for the Prohibition of the Use in War of Asphyxiating, Poisonous, or Other Gases and of Bacteriological Methods of Warfare, and the two instruments were seen as complementing each other. From these emanated the new Chemical Weapons Convention (CWC), signed by 147 countries by September 1993, that calls for the destruction of all chemical weapons by the year 2003.

• The Missile Technology Control Regime (MTCR) is an informal arrangement among the globe's most advanced suppliers of missile-related equipment to control the export of ballistic and cruise missiles. Initially designed to deter the spread of nuclear-capable missiles, the MTCR was expanded in January 1993 to prevent the diffusion of delivery systems for chemical and biological weapons. The regime, created by seven founding countries in April 1987, has expanded to include twenty-five additional states, and "several other countries have pledged to abide by the terms of the regime." The agreement relies on voluntary compliance and is "neither an international treaty nor a legally binding agreement." Its weaknesses were illustrated in August 1993 when China, which "pledged in 1992 to abide by the terms of the MTCR . . . was found by the United States to have transferred M-11 missile components to Pakistan in violation of MTCR provisions" (Arms Control Association *Background Paper*, September 1993).

Table 13.2 Major Multilateral Arms Control Treaties and Agreements

| Date | Agreement | No. Signatories, 1994 | Principal Objectives |
|---|---|---|---|
| 1959 | Antarctic Treaty | 40 | Prevents the military use of the Antarctic, including the testing of nuclear weapons |
| 1967 | Outer Space Treaty | 93 | Outlaws the use of outer space for testing or stationing any weapons, as well as for military maneuvers |
| 1967 | Treaty of Tlatelolco | 24 | Creates the Latin America Nuclear Free Zone by prohibiting the testing and possession of nuclear facilities for military purposes |
| 1968 | Limited Test Ban Treaty | 120 | Prohibits nuclear weapons in the atmosphere, outer space, and underwater |
| 1968 | Nuclear Nonproliferation Treaty | 163 | Prevents the transfer of nuclear weapons and nuclear weapons production technologies to non-nuclear weapon states |
| 1971 | Seabed Treaty | 88 | Prohibits the deployment of weapons of mass destruction and nuclear weapons on the seabed beyond a 12-mile coastal limit |
| 1972 | Biological Weapons Convention | 126 | Prohibits the production and storage of biological toxins; calls for the destruction of biological weapons stocks |
| 1977 | Environmental Modifications Convention | 57 | Bans the use of technologies that could alter the earth's weather patterns, ocean currents, ozone layer, or ecology |
| 1981 | Inhumane Weapons Convention | 35 | Prohibits the use of such weapons as fragmentation bombs, incendiary weapons, booby traps, and mines to which civilians could be exposed |
| 1985 | South Pacific Nuclear Free Zone (Roratonga) Treaty | 11 | Prohibits the testing, acquisition, or deployment of nuclear weapons in the South Pacific |
| 1986 | Confidence-Building and Security-Building Measures and Disarmament in Europe (CDE) Agreement (Stockholm Accord) | 29 | Requires prior notification and mandatory on-site inspection of conventional military exercises in Europe |

| Date | Agreement | No. Signatories, 1994 | Principal Objectives |
|------|-----------|-----------------------|----------------------|
| 1987 | Missile Technology Control Regime (MTCR) | 25 | Restricts export of ballistic missiles and production facilities |
| 1990, 1992 | Conventional Armed Forces in Europe (CFE) | 30 | Places limits on five categories of weapons in Europe and lowers balance of forces |
| 1990 | Confidence- and Security-Building Measures (CSBM) Agreement | 53 | Improves measures for exchanging detailed information on weapons, forces, and military exercises |
| 1991 | UN Register of Conventional Arms Transfers | 173 | Calls on states to voluntarily establish universal and non-discriminatory register that introduces greater openness about arms transfers and facilitates monitoring excessive arms build-up in any one country |
| 1992 | Open Skies Treaty | 25 | Permits flights by unarmed surveillance aircraft over the territory of the signatory states |
| 1993 | Chemical Weapons Convention (CWC) | 147 | Requires all stockpiles of chemical weapons to be destroyed within ten years |
| 1993 | UN Register of Conventional Arms | 80 | Requires states to submit information on seven categories of major weapons exported or imported during previous year |

- The United Nations Register of Conventional Arms is "the first international attempt to compile official information on the weapons trade since the League of Nations began assembling a similar list. . . . The Register invites states to submit information voluntarily about their trade in seven categories of major weapons: tanks, armored combat vehicles, heavy artillery, combat aircraft, attack helicopters, warships, and missiles and missile systems. Each of the world's top suppliers—Britain, China, France, Russia, and the United States—have submitted reports . . . and [the UN's October 1993 report contained] 'replies' from 80 countries about imports and exports of conventional arms during 1992" (Arms Control Association *Fact Sheet*, October 22, 1993).

Table 13.2 summarizes the major multilateral arms control agreements that have been reached since 1959. These agreements limit the range of permissible actions and weapons systems available to states, and have helped slow the global arms race and paved the way for still more ambitious proposals. They also contribute important confidence-building measures that reduce the political tensions underlying the urge to arm.


## Bilateral Diplomacy and the Control of Nuclear Arms: Superpower Agreements

Throughout the Cold War, Soviet and U.S. arms control efforts understandably focused on ways to lessen the threat of nuclear war. These efforts intensified with the disintegration of the Soviet Union into separate, independent republics. Table 13.3 summarizes the results of these negotiations, listing the major *bilateral* arms control agreements between the two superpowers since 1960.

To these we might add an indeterminate number of tacit understandings about the level and use of weapons to which the two powers agreed; these are understandings that did not achieve the status of formal agreements but that the two superpowers observed nonetheless. They include occasional pledges to refrain from the offensive use of nuclear arsenals, as indicated by President Carter's and Soviet Foreign Minister Andrei Gromyko's promise that their states would never be the first to use nuclear weapons in any conflict. Such commitments were not legally binding. Indeed, NATO based its *flexible response* strategy on the right to retaliate to an attack with nuclear weapons. And in 1993 Russia's new strategic doctrine reserved the right to use nuclear weapons in the event of an attack. Still, these understandings undeniably help enforce great-power respect for the no-first-use doctrine, as does China's vocal support for the same principle.

Such informal rules have paved the road to creation of greater institutional controls over the use of strategic weapons. Let us examine the major steps to these.


### SALT

Of the superpowers' explicit, formal arms control agreements, the two so-called SALT (Strategic Arms Limitation Talks) agreements were precedent-setting. SALT I, signed in 1972, consisted of (1) a treaty that restricted the deployment of antiballistic missile defense systems to equal and very low levels and (2) a five-year interim accord on strategic offensive arms that restricted ICBM (intercontinental ballistic missile) and SLBM (submarine-launched ballistic missile) launchers. The SALT I agreement was essentially a confidence-building, "stopgap" step toward a longer-term, more comprehensive treaty. The 1979 SALT II agreement, then the most extensive arms control agreement ever negotiated, sought to realize that aim. The agreement called for placing an eventual overall ceiling of 2,250 on the number of ICBM launchers, SLBM launchers, heavy bombers, and ASBMs (air-to-surface ballistic missiles with ranges over six hundred kilometers) permitted each side. These limitations reduced by as many as 8,500 the total number of

## Table 13.3 Major Bilateral Arms Control Agreements between the United States and the Soviet Union/Russia

| Date | Agreement | Principal Objectives |
|------|-----------|----------------------|
| 1963 | Hot Line Agreement | Establishes a direct radio and telegraph communication system between the governments to be used in times of crisis |
| 1971 | Hot Line Modernization Agreement | Puts a hot line satellite communication system into operation |
| 1971 | Nuclear Accidents Agreement | Creates a process for notification of accidental or unauthorized detonation of a nuclear weapon; creates safeguards to prevent accidents |
| 1972 | Anti-ballistic Missile (ABM) Treaty (SALT I) | Restricts the deployment of antiballistic missile defense systems to one area and prohibits the development of a space-based ABM system |
| 1972 | SALT I Interim Agreement on Offensive Strategic Arms | Freezes the superpowers' total number of ballistic missile launches for a 5-year period |
| 1972 | Protocol to the Interim Agreement | Clarifies and strengthens prior limits on strategic arms |
| 1973 | Agreement on the Prevention of Nuclear War | Requires superpowers to consult if a threat of nuclear war emerges |
| 1974 | Threshold Test Ban Treaty with Protocol | Restricts the underground testing of nuclear weapons above a yield of 150 kilotons |
| 1974 | Protocol to the ABM Treaty | Reduces permitted ABMs to one site |
| 1976 | Treaty on the Limitation of Underground Explosions for Peaceful Purposes | Broadens the ban on underground nuclear testing stipulated in the 1974 Threshold Test Ban Treaty; requires on-site observers of tests with yields exceeding 150 kilotons |
| 1977 | Convention on the Prohibition of Military or Any Other Hostile Use of Environmental Modification Techniques | Bans weapons that threaten to modify the planetary ecology |
| 1979 | SALT II Treaty (never ratified) | Places ceilings on the number of strategic delivery vehicles, MIRVed missiles, long-range bombers, cruise missiles, ICBMs, and other weapons; restrains testing |
| 1987 | Nuclear Risk Reduction Centers Agreement | Creates facilities in each national capital to manage a nuclear crisis |
| 1987 | Intermediate-range Nuclear Force (INF) Treaty | Eliminates U.S. and USSR ground-level intermediate- and shorter-range nuclear weapons in Europe and permits on-site inspection to verify compliance |

*(continued on next page)*

Table 13.3 Major Bilateral Arms Control Agreements between the United States and the Soviet Union/Russia *(continued)*

| Date | Agreement | Principal Objectives |
|------|-----------|----------------------|
| 1990 | Chemical Weapons Destruction Agreement | Ends production of chemical weapons; commits cutting inventories of chemical weapons in half by the end of 1999 and to 5,000 metric tons by the end of 2002 |
| 1990 | Nuclear Testing Talks | New protocol improves verification procedures of prior treaties |
| 1991 | START (Strategic Arms Reduction Treaty) | Reduces arsenals of strategic nuclear weapons by about 30 percent |
| 1992 | START I Protocol | Holds Russia, Belarus, Ukraine, and Kazakhstan to strategic weapons reductions agreed to in START by the former USSR |
| 1993 | START II | Cuts the deployed U.S. and Russian strategic nuclear warheads on each side to between 3,000 and 3,500 by the year 2003; bans multiple-warhead land-based missiles |

strategic nuclear weapons that the United States and the Soviet Union would have possessed by 1985 without the agreement.

The obstacles to arms control were illustrated by the problems that SALT II encountered, however. The U.S. Senate deferred ratification of the SALT II treaty indefinitely following the 1979 Soviet invasion of Afghanistan. Although both superpowers continued to abide by the basic terms of SALT II through the early 1980s, the "final result as embodied in SALT II was a clear disappointment to the hopes generated in the early 1970s. In essence, SALT II failed to achieve actual arms reductions. Its basic fault was that it would have permitted substantial growth in the strategic forces of both sides" (U.S. Department of State, 1983).

## START

Against the background of what U.S. leaders labeled "the failed promise of SALT," they set the agenda for new approaches to strategic arms control.[15] In June 1982 the

---

[15] At this time, because of the fear inspired by the relentless arms race and frustration with the lack of progress in the arms control process, the idea of a "nuclear freeze" on the testing, production, and deployment of nuclear weapons gained momentum on both sides of the Atlantic. Freeze advocates were motivated by the view that it was a "delusion" to see "nuclear weapons as just one more weapon, like any other weapon, only more destructive" (Kennan, 1982). To help dispel this delusion, the American Catholic bishops composed a widely read Pastoral Letter that called for an immediate end to the arms race and asserted that the deliberate initiation of nuclear warfare, on however restricted a scale, could not be morally justified. As a policy proposal, a total freeze envisioned a path to disarmament that would first stop production of new weapons systems before starting to reduce the existing ones, built on the premise that

Reagan administration initiated a new round of arms talks aimed at significant reductions in the strategic arsenals of both superpowers. Termed START (Strategic Arms Reduction Talks), the initiative resumed the SALT process but expanded its agenda by seeking to remove asymmetries that had developed in the superpowers' weapons systems.

And, after nine years of bargaining, the negotiators overcame their differences and concluded the START treaty committing each side to *reduce* its strategic forces by one-third. Signed in July 1991, the treaty provided a baseline for future reductions in the two superpowers' capabilities (see Chapter 11, Figure 11.4).

Or did it? The treaty was equally significant for what it did *not* regulate. The 600-page treaty, whose implementation would have taken seven years, only reduced the number of weapons of each side to the level they had when the START negotiations began in 1982. Moreover, the treaty did not achieve as much as many had once expected. As one analysis noted at the time it was concluded:

> The United States will be able to continue its strategic modernization program unencumbered by START and its existing force will be largely unaffected by START. The only modernization effort that may be curtailed is converting the B-1 bomber to carry ALCMs; the START bomber weapon counting rule would deter this conversion. . . .
>
> In other words, the United States will be able to have a modern, more accurate, and lethal force under START than today. In addition, the bomber weapon counting rules would allow the United States to deploy 3,000 to 6,000 weapons that are not counted. . . .
>
> The Soviet Union will for the most part be able to continue its modernization plans. . . . Under START, the Soviets will retain a highly lethal force of modern SS-18 missiles, which is sufficient to destroy with high confidence all U.S. ICBM silos and fixed launch facilities and hardened command posts. The Soviets will also retain a significant survivable mobile ICBM force of SS-24s and SS-25s. (Congressional Research Service, 1991: 53–54)

### The Post–Cold War Disarmament Race

In September 1991, responding to widespread complaints that the START treaty barely started the kinds of arms reductions possible now that the threat of a Soviet attack had vanished, President Bush declared that the United States must seize "the historic opportunity now before us." He called long-range bombers off 24-hour alert, canceled plans to deploy the long-range MX on rail cars, and offered to negotiate with the Soviet Union sharp reductions in the most dangerous kinds of globe-spanning missiles. Bush also proposed to remove short-range nuclear weapons from U.S. bases in Europe and Asia and from U.S. Navy vessels around the world. Asking the Soviet Union, which Bush described as "no longer a realistic threat," to join the United States, the U.S. president warned that the proposed cuts might not be made if the

---

both sides' deterrent capabilities were invulnerable and that a freeze would keep them that way. Once the arms race was curtailed, it was reasoned, arms reductions could then be considered. The "nuclear freeze" movement in the early 1980s helped set the stage for the progress that occurred in the early 1990s when the Cold War no longer constrained negotiations.

Soviet Union did not respond in kind. This set the stage for a showdown on a new race to *dis*arm.

The fragmentation of the Soviet Union and the improved political relationship between Russia and the United States removed the major barriers to disarmament. Instructively, the disarmament process began first through unilateral proposals and gained momentum only later through incremental accords painstakingly negotiated at the bargaining table. But when disarmament agreements finally came, they then came about rapidly.

On January 25, 1992, new Russian President Boris Yeltsin, declaring that his country "no longer consider[ed] the United States our potential adversary," announced the decision to stop targeting U.S. cities with nuclear missiles. This cleared the way for another U.S. response. Four days later, in his State of the Union address, President Bush announced a series of unilateral arms cuts. Among them were the decision to suspend production of the B-2 bomber, halt development of the Midgetman mobile nuclear missile, and cease purchases of advanced cruise missiles. Bush also canceled production of warheads used aboard Trident submarine missiles.

Yeltsin did not wait for his scheduled summit meeting with Bush at Camp David to reply to this initiative. Within hours, Yeltsin recommended that the two powers reduce their nuclear arsenals to only 2,000 to 2,500 warheads each—far below the cuts called for in the START agreement and almost 50 percent greater than the reductions proposed by Bush. In other statements, Yeltsin announced his intention to reduce Russian military spending to less than one-seventh of the previous year's allocation and to trim the Russian army in half. And to emphasize the new climate of Russian–American friendship, Yeltsin proposed creating a joint U.S.–Russian global defense system and a new international agency to oversee the orderly reduction of nuclear weapons. He also proposed eliminating strategic nuclear weapons entirely by the year 2000.

Even in this hopeful climate of reciprocated reductions, during the spring of 1992 obstacles remained to dismantling the weapons with which each superpower had threatened the existence of the other. The differences centered on where the cuts should be made. Bush called for the elimination of all land-based strategic missiles with multiple warheads (MIRVs), the category in which Russia was strongest. But on submarine-launched missiles, where the United States had the advantage, Bush refused to accept reductions beyond a third and fought the Russian quest for across-the-board cuts.

Complicating the situation further, and impeding progress, was the uncertain future of Russia's government. Even more problematic were the other commonwealth republics having nuclear weapons. Ukraine, Kazakhstan, and Belarus signed the May 1992 Lisbon protocol to the START agreement. This pledged their elimination of all nuclear weapons on their territory by 1999 and their willingness to join the NPT as non-nuclear states. But that cooperation and compliance remained much in doubt. It still does. Asked in November 1993 when Ukraine was likely to begin giving up its inherited stockpile of Soviet nuclear warheads, leading parliamentary deputy Serhiy Holvaty said, "Quite frankly, never."

In addition, efforts to modernize arsenals were scheduled to continue at this time.

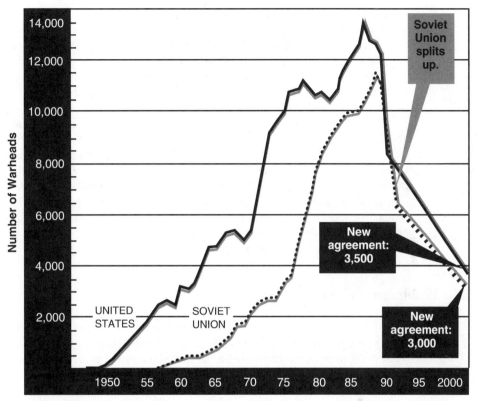

**Figure 13.1**  Countdown to Strategic Parity: The Collaborative Dismantling of the U.S. and Russian Strategic Arsensals since the Breakup of the Soviet Union
*Source: Newsweek* (January 11, 1993): 17

This meant that the former Cold War enemies planned to be heavily armed after their cuts were complete. The lack of realistic targets and the technological breakthrough of miniaturization made most of the discarded weapons obsolete, so those deliberately scrapped did not mean that armament modernization plans had ended. The former adversaries were still militarily preparing to wage war, even with the planned cuts, and even with U.S. assistance to help the Russians destroy their weapons.

Yet, just when it appeared that the disarmament process might lose momentum, a new breakthrough was achieved. At the June 1992 Washington summit, Presidents Yeltsin and Bush made the surprise announcement that Russia and the United States would make additional deep cuts in their strategic arsenals. The formal Joint Understanding accord to the START agreement called for a 60 percent reduction of the two powers' combined total nuclear arsenals from about 15,000 warheads to 6,500 by the year 2003 (see Figure 13.1). But even more dramatically, this so-called "Follow-on" treaty to START reshapes the strategic landscape. Signed January 3, 1993, START II not only cuts by three-fifths the number of actual warheads in each side's strategic arsenal that had been projected under START, but it also alters drastically the kinds of weapons in each country's arsenal. Under the agreement, Russia and the United States would give up all multiple warheads on their land-based ICBM missiles.[16] Specifically, by banning "all MIRVed ICBMs [and reducing] submarine-launched ballistic missile (SLBM) warheads to no more than 1,750," the new agreement "promised a significant enhancement of U.S.–Russian strategic stability since these missiles have long been seen as the most threatening because of their preemptive capabilities" (Keeny, 1993).

If adhered to, the Follow-on START agreement thus could reduce the chances of war by banning the nuclear weapons that both powers would be most likely to use in a preemptive strike, while leaving them with only those weapons they would be likely to use in a retaliatory strike. By reducing the probability of a nuclear war, the agreement thus signaled the potential dawning of a new era. As President Bush put it, "With this agreement the nuclear nightmare recedes more and more for ourselves, for our children, and for our grandchildren." President Yeltsin concurred, noting that with the agreement, "we are departing from the ominous parity where each country was exerting every effort to keep up."

## The Problematic Future of Arms Control

As promising as some of the great powers' recent arms control agreements might appear, the checkered history of their past negotiations testifies to the many obstacles that exist to arms control agreements, as well as the extent to which they are dependent on prior improvement in adversaries' political relations. That history raises questions about whether arms control agreements can restrain the arms race in the long run, as these obstacles could resurface in a new multipolar system characterized by rivalry among five or more great powers and a potentially large number of new nuclear weapon states.

Until perhaps very recently, "the weapons prohibited had little, if any, military importance, and the outlawed activities [had] never been seriously contemplated as methods of war" (Goldblat, 1982). The international agreements reached controlled only those armaments that the parties to them had little incentive for developing in the first place or that had become obsolete. Do states purposely leave the most threatening problems outside negotiations and only seek to control the insignificant ones? Several indicators suggest that states do not take arms control seriously when they perceive their interests and survival to be at stake.

For example, consider first the disregard that some signatories to agreements

---

[16] This comprised a major concession on the part of Russia. As Jack Mendelsohn of the Arms Control Association observed, "On paper, it [looked] like the two forces [would] be reduced equally, but in fact the Russians [gave] up the backbone of their arsenal—land-based multiple warhead missiles—while [the United States] [retained] the area of [its] greatest strength, sea-based ballistic missiles." In effect, the Russians relinquished their most powerful missiles while the United States only had to reduce the number of its most sophisticated missiles on its Trident submarines by 50 percent. The agreement eliminated "the most threatening Russian nuclear weapons while allowing the United States to maintain its most advanced missiles" (Friedman, 1992).

demonstrate toward them. There were twelve alleged instances of the use of chemical and biological warfare between 1975 and 1981 that violated the 1972 Biological Weapons Convention (Goldblat, 1982: 100). Included among the allegations were the Vietnamese forces' use of poison gas against China (1979), the United States' use of chemical weapons in covert action in Cuba (1978–1981), the Iraqis' use of "chemical bombs" in occupied Iranian territory (1980), and the Soviet Union's use of lethal chemical weapons in Laos and Afghanistan over prolonged periods in such quantities as to produce a toxic "yellow rain."

Second, the continued testing of nuclear weapons also speaks to the propensity of states to make improvements in their weaponry a priority over their control. The six known nuclear states conducted 1,950 nuclear explosions between 1945 and 1992, an average of one test every nine days (*Bulletin of the Atomic Scientists* 49 [April 1993]: 49). The pace did not slow as a result of the partial test ban treaty of 1963, which proscribed atmospheric and underwater testing but not underground explosions.[17] In fact, three-quarters of all nuclear tests took place since 1963 after the ban went into effect. Disclosures by the U.S. government in December 1993 revealed 204 previously unannounced secret nuclear weapons tests above the 1,051 officially reported figure between 1945 and 1992, some of which resulted in accidental releases of radioactive gases into the atmosphere. Energy Secretary Hazel R. O'Leary captured the arms race cult by lamenting that "We were shrouded and clouded in an atmosphere of secrecy that compromised safety and environmental considerations. . . . I would call it repression."

Third, recall that the Nuclear Nonproliferation Treaty (NPT) of 1968 obligated the non-nuclear countries not to manufacture or acquire nuclear weapons. Adherence to the agreement has been widespread. Yet the nuclear states' enthusiasm for ever more imposing arsenals showed no signs of abating until 1992. Given their historic appetite for expanded strategic inventories, it is understandable why the non-nuclear members of the NPT question why they should remain restrained while the existing nuclear states continue to develop their nuclear capabilities (Spector and Smith, 1992).

Fourth, consider the sobering lessons suggested by the SALT agreements. SALT I did freeze the number of strategic launchers in operation or under construction but did not cover strategic bombers or prevent the kinds of qualitative improvements that would make quantitative thresholds meaningless. One such improvement was in the number of strategic warheads that a single missile could launch against an enemy. And in fact the number of multiple independently targetable warheads (MIRVs) deployed on missiles by the superpowers in 1977 was four times greater than when the SALT talks began, even though SALT I froze the number of delivery vehicles at the superpowers' disposal. Perhaps this troublesome outcome (experts now conclude that MIRVs were destabilizing and costly and reduced security) led Herbert Scoville,

---

[17] Testing continues even in the wake of the Cold War, as witnessed by the fact that the United States conducted seven nuclear tests in 1991 and six in 1992, and France, the United Kingdom, and China collectively conducted another nine tests between 1991 and 1993 (*Bulletin of the Atomic Scientists* 50 [May/June 1994]: 63), and, in the midst of the threat of war over North Korea's nuclear weapons motives, conducted another test (China's fortieth at its Lop Nor testing site in June 1994.

a former deputy director of the U.S. Central Intelligence Agency, to note at the time of the signing of SALT I that "arms control negotiations [were] rapidly becoming the best excuse for escalating rather than toning down the arms race." The pattern revealed in this and other developments prompted one former U.S. policymaker to conclude that "three decades of U.S.–Soviet negotiations to limit arms competition have done little more than to codify the arms race" (Gelb, 1979).

These Cold War experiences created doubt about the ability of agreements to control the size and dispersion of weapons. Why did states take decisions to arm that apparently imprisoned them in the grip of perpetual insecurity? On the surface, the incentives for meaningful arms control seem numerous. Significant controls would save money, reduce tension and hence the dangers of war, symbolize leaders' desire for peace, lessen health hazards, control the environmental hazards of nuclear waste, reduce the potential destructiveness of war, dampen the incentive for one state to seek a power advantage over others, diminish the possibility of being the target of a preemptive attack, and achieve a propaganda advantage for those advocating peace. To these we can add moral satisfaction and the opportunity to live in a global environment free of fear.

But states did not—and perhaps still do not—control significantly the growth of arms. Multiple reasons exist for reliance on military preparedness as a path to peace. They stem from the fear that is endemic to international anarchy. Most countries are reluctant to engage in arms limitations in a self-help system that requires each state to protect itself. Hence states find themselves caught in a vicious circle of fear. This creates the "security dilemma"—a condition in no actor's interest but one that permits no easy escape. Its influence on behavior is potent and helps explain why throughout the Cold War military establishments subscribed to two basic principles: "(1) 'Don't negotiate when you are behind. Why accept a permanent position of number two?' and (2) 'Don't negotiate when you are ahead. Why accept a freeze in an area of military competition when the other side has not kept up with you?'" (Barnet, 1977). The result of this syndrome is clear: When fearful countries abide by the axiom that they should never negotiate from a position of weakness, then they are left with no option but to refuse to negotiate. Arms bargaining is a game of give and take, but all participants typically want to take much and give little. Given this posture, alongside the powerful restraining impact that domestic politics exerts on the negotiation process (see Caldwell, 1991),[18] it is little wonder that meaningful agreements are so hard to achieve and that states develop weapons systems as bargaining chips for future negotiations.

Even in the post–Cold War world, arms control remains a murky policy area.

---

[18] Many people benefit financially from the perpetuation of arms races and become lobbyists against arms agreements because they can lose their jobs by an abatement of military spending. Military–industrial complexes (see Rosen, 1973; Hooks, 1991; Markusen and Yudken, 1992) exist in all societies whose influence is tied to the continuation of the arms race. The resistance of military planners and defense specialists to reductions in arsenals even in the wake of the Cold War attests to the continuing penchant of defense experts and arms manufacturers to insist that "prudence" dictates preparing for the worst contingency by retaining military preparedness at as high a level as possible. "The business of defense is defending business" is the way one analyst summarized the problem (Mulhollin, 1994).

Seeking to modify the 1972 Anti-ballistic Missile Treaty between the U.S. and the former Soviet Union, the Clinton administration in 1994 sought to further develop Thaad—a heat-seeking interceptor system capable of shooting down medium-range enemy missiles. While arms control groups criticized the proposal and accused it of undermining previous arms control agreements, administration officials argued that "the greater danger is not a superpower arms race but rather Third World governments with shorter-range and medium-range missiles" (Gordon, 1993c). Thus a shifting playing field, accompanied by increasing Third World military capabilities, poses difficulties for the future of arms control. This is especially true under conditions in which "the International Atomic Energy Agency (IAEA), the world's primary means of monitoring clandestine nuclear programs worldwide, remains chronically starved for funding at $60 million and has even been forced to cut inspections (Sommer, 1994: 23).

We should not expect too much of arms control or exaggerate its potential. As one expert concludes,

> The history of the postwar era proves that arms control, if pursued wisely and properly, can reduce the threat; it can never eliminate the risk of war altogether. Arms control is not a substitute for weapons but a complement to them. Arms and arms control, one by creating the means to inflict unacceptable damage on a potential enemy and the other by protecting that capability from enemy attack, are both necessary for national security. A defense policy that fails to pursue the two together, that emphasizes one approach to the exclusion of the other, is dangerous and incomplete. . . .
>
> True international security depends not as much on arms or arms control as on reducing as much as possible the sources of conflict in international relations and on finding effective nonviolent means of resolving the conflicts that remain. (Kruzel, 1991: 268)

## ARMS AND THE SEARCH FOR PEACE

The obstacles to the control of arms are formidable. The idea that a disarmed world would be a more secure one does not have the force of history behind it, whereas the idea that military preparedness produces security does. As long as aggressive states exist, it would be imprudent to disarm. Arms control does not solve the basic problem of rivalry between states because as long as states have and can use weapons, such agreements are little more than cooperative arrangements between adversaries. They define the competition and confine the potential destruction that can result in the event of war but do not remove the *source* of the conflict.

Alternatively, managing political conflicts without violence may be the key to arms control. For arms, after all, are less causes of war than they are symptoms of political tension: "Men do not fight because they have arms. They have arms because [they are afraid and] they deem it necessary to fight" (Morgenthau, 1985). From this perspective, controlling arms is contingent on removing the fears that underlie states' political conflicts, for the quest for national security in an anarchical world springs from states' fear of one another. Yet, because one country's security makes others insecure, nearly all states prepare for war to defend themselves.

States, of course, pursue many paths to the realization of their national goals, of which security is the preeminent one. Thus they seek through deterrence to balance power with power while seeking simultaneously through arms control to remove the incentives for war that arms provide, because the weapons themselves may aggravate political tensions. In this sense the military paths to peace discussed in this chapter are intimately related to the quest for national security discussed in Chapter 11. Whether global security is served by states' military search for their own national security remains at issue, however. Perhaps the seeds of the world's destruction have been sown by the forces that propel the pursuit of peace and security through military might. Nothing makes the search for peace through political means more compelling. Hope may be inspired by the observations of former U.S. Secretary of Defense Robert McNamara: "We have reached the present dangerous and absurd confrontation by a long series of steps, many of which seemed rational in their time. Step-by-step we can undo much of the damage."

## SUGGESTED READINGS

Bremer, Stuart A., and Barry B. Hughes. *Disarmament and Development: A Design for the Future.* Englewood Cliffs, N.J.: Prentice-Hall, 1990.

Bueno de Mesquita, Bruce. *The War Trap.* New Haven, Conn.: Yale University Press, 1981.

Bundy, McGeorge, William J. Crowe Jr., and Sidney D. Drell. *Reducing Nuclear Danger: The Road Away from the Brink.* New York: Council on Foreign Relations Press, 1993.

Carpenter, Ted Galen. "Closing the Nuclear Umbrella," *Foreign Affairs* 73 (March/April 1994): 8–13.

Claude, Inis L., Jr. *Power and International Relations.* New York: Random House, 1962.

Gulick, Edward Vose. *Europe's Classical Balance of Power.* Ithaca, N.Y.: Cornell University Press, 1955.

Johansen, Robert C. "Swords into Plowshares: Can Fewer Arms Yield More Security?," pp. 253–279 in Charles W. Kegley Jr., ed., *Controversies in International Relations Theory: Realism and the Neoliberal Challenge.* New York: St. Martin's Press, 1995.

Kegley, Charles W., Jr., and Gregory A. Raymond. *A Multipolar Peace? Great-Power Politics in the Twenty-first Century.* New York: St. Martin's Press, 1994.

Luard, Evan. *The Balance of Power.* New York: St. Martin's Press, 1992.

Pearson, Frederic S. *The Spread of Arms in the International System.* Boulder, Colo.: Westview Press, 1994.

Powaski, Ronald E. *The Entangling Alliance: The United States and European Security, 1950–1993.* Westport, Conn.: Greenwood Press, 1994.

Sabrosky, Alan Ned, ed. *Polarity and War: The Changing Structure of International Conflict.* Boulder, Colo.: Westview Press, 1985.

# CHAPTER 14

· · ·

# POLITICAL PATHS TO PEACE: INTERNATIONAL LAW, ORGANIZATION, AND INTEGRATION

· · ·

*Everything that is done in international affairs must be done from the viewpoint of whether it will advance or hinder the establishment of world government.*

Albert Einstein,
Physicist, 1946

*For the first time, it is clear that the United Nations is indispensable to us all.*

Carlos Andres Perez,
President of Venezuela, 1992

Since antiquity, the world has pursued two primary paths to peace. One emphasizes the use of *military* power, the other *political* solutions. This chapter examines three political approaches to world order embedded in the liberal theoretical tradition: international law, organization, and integration.

## INTERNATIONAL LAW AND WORLD ORDER · · · · · · · · · · · · · · · · · · · · ·

In international affairs there is much disorder and recurrent warfare. This has led many critics to conclude that international law is "weak and defenseless" (Fried, 1971). Indeed, they ask, Is international law really law?

For many reasons, the answer to this question is yes. Although imperfect, transnational actors regularly rely on international law to redress grievances (see Joyner, 1995; Kim, 1991). They direct most of this activity to regulating routinized transnational intercourse in such areas as commerce, communications, and travel. Sometimes called *private* international law, this legal domain is largely invisible to the public because its accomplishments only infrequently command public attention. Yet private international law is the locus for all but a small fraction of international legal activities. It is here that the majority of transnational disputes are regularly settled, and in which

· · ·

507

the record of compliance compares favorably with that achieved in domestic legal systems (Brownlie, 1990).

In contrast, *public* international law, which addresses government-to-government relations, captures the headlines. It also captures most of the criticism, for here failures, when they occur, are quite conspicuous. This is especially true with respect to the breakdown of peace and security. When states use force, criticism intensifies. Consider, for example, former U.S. Secretary of State Dean Acheson's accusation that international law is "a crock" and Israeli Ambassador Abba Eban's lament that "international law is that law which the wicked do not obey and the righteous do not enforce."

Because this chapter examines the capacity of public international law to control war, our discussion will address only the laws and institutional machinery created to manage interstate conflict. That is, it explores that segment of public international law popularly regarded as most deficient.

## Law at the International Level: Concepts and Principles

Public international law is usually defined as rules that govern the conduct of states in their relations with one another. The *corpus juris gentium* (the body of the law of nations) has grown considerably over the past three centuries, changing in response to transformations in international politics (Kaplan and Katzenbach, 1961). An inventory of the basic legal principles relevant to the control of war clarifies the international system's character.[1]

### Principles of International Law

No principle of international law is more important than state *sovereignty.* Sovereignty means that no authority is legally above the state, except the authority that the state voluntarily confers on supranational organizations that it joins. Indeed, international law "permits a complete freedom of action" (Parry, 1968) to states to preserve their sovereign independence.

Nearly every legal tenet supports and elaborates the cardinal principle that nation-states are the primary subjects of international law. Although the Universal Declaration of Human Rights in 1948 expanded concern about states' treatment of individual people, states remain supreme. "Laws are made to protect the state from the individual and not the individual from the state" (in Gottlieb, 1982). Accordingly, the vast majority of rules address the rights and duties of states, not people. For instance, the principle of the sovereign *equality* of states entitles each state to full respect by other states and full protection of the system's legal rules. As a corollary, the right of independence guarantees states autonomy in their domestic affairs and external relations, under the logic that the independence of each presumes that of all. Similarly,

---

[1] The rules of international law are multiple and difficult to summarize. For authoritative texts that describe the body of existing international legal principles, see Akehurst (1992), Janis (1993), and von Glahn (1992).

the doctrine of *neutrality* permits states to avoid involvement in others' conflicts and coalitions.

Furthermore, the **noninterference principle** forms the basis for *nonintervention*, that is, states' duty to refrain from uninvited involvement in another's internal affairs. This sometimes abused classic rule gives to governments the right to exercise jurisdiction over practically all things on, under, or above their bounded territory. (There are exceptions codified in international law, such as *diplomatic immunity* for states' ambassadors while they represent their country abroad and *extraterritoriality*, which allows control of embassies on other states' terrain. But the precept of territorial integrity remains sacrosanct.)

In practice, domestic jurisdiction permits a state to enact and enforce whatever laws it wishes for its own citizens, including the rules for individuals to become citizens.[2] A state can create whatever form of government it desires without regard to its acceptability to other states. It also has freedom to regulate economic transactions within its boundaries and is empowered to conscript those living on its soil into its armed forces to fight—and die, if necessary—to defend the state.

The Montevideo Convention of 1933 on the Rights and Duties of States summarizes the major components of *statehood*. A state must possess a permanent population, a well-defined territory, and a government capable of ruling its citizens (claiming legitimacy) and managing formal diplomatic relations with other states. Other rules specify how and when these conditions are satisfied. Essentially, the acquisition of statehood is dependent on a political entity's recognition as such by other states. Whether or not a state exists thus rests in the hands of other states; that is, preexisting states are entitled to extend *diplomatic recognition* to another entity. *De facto* recognition is provisional and capable of being withdrawn in the event that the recognized government is superseded by another; it does not carry with it the exchange of diplomatic representatives or other legal benefits and responsibilities. The government that is recognized *de jure*, on the other hand, obtains full legal and diplomatic privileges from the granting state. The distinction emphasizes that recognition is a political tool of international law, through which approval or disapproval of a government can be expressed.

Today, with the exception of Antarctica, which is administered jointly by several states and is outside the jurisdiction of any one of them, no significant land mass remains *terra nullius* (territory belonging legally to no one). Because nearly all of the earth's land surfaces are now within some state's sovereign control, the birth of a new state must necessarily be at the expense of an existing one. Hence, the recognition of a new state almost always means the recognition of a new government's control over a particular piece of territory. Because recognition is a voluntary political act,

---

[2] Appallingly, prior to 1952 "there was no precedent in international law for a nation-state to assume responsibility for the crimes it committed against a minority within its jurisdiction" (Wise, 1993). The citizen of a state was not protected against the state's abuse of human rights. Note that two basic principles govern the way nationality and citizenship are conferred. Under *jus soli*, citizenship is determined by the state on whose territory the birth took place. Under *jus sanguinis*, nationality is acquired by descent from a parent of a national. Some states recognize a combination of these conventions.

*nonrecognition* is a legally institutionalized form of public insult to a government aspiring to be accepted as legitimate by other governments, a form of sanction against an unwanted political regime.

States are free to enter into treaty arrangements with other states. Rules specify how treaties are to be activated, interpreted, and abrogated. International law holds that treaties voluntarily entered into are binding (*pacta sunt servanda*) but also reserves for states the right unilaterally to terminate treaties previously agreed to by reference to the escape clause known as *rebus sic stantibus*—the principle that a treaty is binding only as long as no fundamental change occurs in the circumstances that existed when the treaty was concluded.

### Procedures for Dispute Settlement

In addition to these general principles, international law provides a wide variety of legal methods for states to resolve their conflicts. The laws of *negotiation* do not obligate states to reach agreement or to settle their disputes peacefully, but they do provide rules for resolving conflicts. For example, international law advances explicit procedures for *mediation* (when a third party proposes a nonbinding solution to a controversy between two other states, as illustrated by President Carter's historic mediation at the 1978 Camp David meeting between Egypt and Israel); *good offices* (when a third party offers a location for discussions among disputants but does not participate in the actual negotiations, as Switzerland often does); and *conciliation* (when a third party assists both sides but does not offer any solution). In addition, rules for settling disputes also include *arbitration* (when a third party gives a binding decision through an ad hoc forum) and *adjudication* (when a third party offers a binding decision through an institutionalized tribunal, such as a court).

## The Structural Limitations of the International Legal System

Sovereignty and the legal principles derived from it shape and reinforce international anarchy. The global condition is legally dependent on what governments choose to do with one another and the kinds of rules they voluntarily support. It is a legal system by and for them.

Many theorists consider the international legal system structurally defective because it depends so much on the attitudes and behaviors of those it governs. Because formal legal institutions (like those within states) are absent at the international level, critics make the following points.

First, in world politics a legislative body capable of making laws does not exist. Rules are made only when states willingly observe them or embrace them in the treaties to which they voluntarily subscribe. There is no systematic method of amending or revoking them. Article 38 of the Statute of the International Court of Justice (or World Court), generally accepted as the authoritative statement on the sources of international law, affirms this. It states that international law derives from (1) custom,

(2) international treaties and agreements, (3) national and international court decisions, (4) the writings of legal authorities and specialists, and (5) the "general principles" of law recognized since the Roman Empire as part of "natural law" and "right reason."

Second, in world politics no authoritative judicial body has power to identify the rules accepted by states, record the substantive precepts reached, intepret when and how the rules apply, and identify instances of violation. Instead, states are responsible for performing these tasks themselves. As we discuss below, the World Court does not have the power to perform these functions without states' consent.

Finally, in world politics there is no executive body capable of enforcing the rules. Rule enforcement usually occurs through the self-help actions of the victims of a transgression or with the assistance of their allies or other interested parties. No centralized enforcement procedures exist, and compliance is voluntary. The whole system rests, therefore, on states' willingness to abide by the rules to which they consent and on the ability of each to enforce through retaliatory measures the norms of behavior they value.

In sum, states are accountable to no one and abide by only those regulations they voluntarily subscribe to and enforce through self-help measures. The states themselves, not a higher authority, determine what the rules are, when they apply, and how they should be enforced. This raises the question, When everyone is above the law, is anyone ruled by it?

Still other weaknesses beyond the barriers to legal institutions posed by sovereignty warrant comment.

- *International law lacks universality.* An effective legal system must represent the norms shared by those it governs. According to the precept of Roman law *ubi societas, ibi jus* (where there is society, there is law), shared community values are a minimal precondition for the formation of a legal system. Yet the contemporary international order is culturally and ideologically pluralistic and lacks a common value consensus (McDougal and Lasswell, 1959). Some claim the Western-based international legal order approximates universality, yet state practice and the simultaneous operation of often incompatible legal traditions throughout the world contradict this claim (Bozeman, 1971).

- *International law justifies the competitive pursuit of national advantage without regard to morality or justice.* As in any legal system, in international politics the legal thing to do is not necessarily the moral thing to do (see Nardin, 1983). Indeed, international law legitimizes the drive for hegemony and contributes to conflict (Lissitzyn, 1963). Self-help does not control power; it is a concession to power. By worshiping the unbridled autonomy of sovereign independence, international law follows the realists' "iron law of politics"—that legal obligations must yield to the national interest (Morgenthau, 1985).

- *International law is an instrument of the powerful to oppress the weak.* In a voluntary consent system, the rules to which the powerful willingly agree are those that serve their interests. These rules therefore preserve the existing hierarchy (Friedheim, 1965). For this reason some claim that international law supports the so-called *structural violence* in world politics believed to benefit the strong at the expense of the weak (Galtung, 1969). Because enforcement is left "to the vicissitudes of the distribution of power between the violator of the law and the victim of the violation," political scientist Hans J. Morgenthau (1985) notes, "it makes it easy for the strong both to violate the law and to enforce it, and consequently puts the rights of the weak in jeopardy. A great power can violate the rights of a small nation without having to fear effective sanctions on the latter's part."

- *International law is little more than a justification of existing practices.* When a particular behavior pattern becomes widespread, it becomes legally obligatory, as rules *of* behavior become rules *for* behavior (Hoffmann, 1971). International law is a codification of custom. Hans Kelsen's contention that states ought to behave as they have customarily behaved (see Onuf, 1982) and E. Adamson Hoebel's (1961) dictum that "what the most do, others should do" reflect the positivist legal theory that when a type of behavior occurs frequently it becomes legal.[3] The dependence of rules on *custom* means that the policies of states shape law, not vice versa.

- *International law's ambiguity reduces law to a policy tool for propaganda purposes.* The vague, elastic wording of international law makes it easy for states to define and interpret almost any action as legitimate. "The problem here," observes Samuel S. Kim (1991), "is the lack of clarity and coherence [that enables] international law [to be] easily stretched, . . . to be a flexible fig leaf or a propaganda instrument." This ambivalence permits states to exploit international law to get what they can and to justify what they have obtained (Wright, 1953).

These deficiencies illustrate but do not exhaust the international legal order's alleged inadequacies. Critics note others. In combination, they suggest that international law is least developed in the state system's most critical realm: where national security is at stake.

## The Relevance of International Law

International law *is* fraught with deficiencies. Still, we can question the proposition that it is irrelevant to contemporary international politics.

States themselves do not deem public international law irrelevant. In fact, they attach much importance to it and expend considerable time and energy fighting over

---

[3] Positivists stress states' customs as the most important source from which laws derive. In the absence of formal machinery for creating international rules, for evidence of what the law is, positivists observe leaders' foreign policy pronouncements, repeated usage in conventions voluntarily accepted by states, general practices (by an overwhelmingly large number of states), the judicial decisions of national and international tribunals, and legal principles stated in the resolutions of multinational assemblies such as the UN General Assembly.

its interpretation and attempting to shape its evolution. All are decidedly interested in revising it in ways that serve their purposes and in maintaining those rules already in operation that advance their own interests. Indeed, if law were meaningless, we would not be able to point to the existence of a systematic code of rules repeatedly affirmed by states in multilateral agreements, resolutions, and declarations (Jones, 1991). These treaties, conventions, and formal declarations reflect state opinion and show there *are* basic principles that states formally recognize and agree to respect.

An important reason states value international law and affirm their commitment to it is that they need a common understanding of the "rules of the game." International law is an "institutional device for communicating to the policy makers of various states a consensus on the nature of the international system" (Coplin, 1965). Law helps shape expectations, and rules reduce uncertainty and enhance predictability in international affairs. These communication functions serve every member of the international system, and the benefits they confer explain why states usually support international law and voluntarily accommodate their actions and policies to it. World politics would undoubtedly be more disorderly without this system, however imperfect and primitive it might be.

However, the system's members usually agree on certain general values at the same time that they often fail to recognize the implications of these values for their own behavior (Coplin, 1966). Thus it is tempting to agree with the critics that the lack of a centralized authority having supranational sanctioning powers makes international law useless for its most important function, the control of violence. This conclusion is questionable, however, as it stems from the misleading comparison critics often draw between the international legal order's primitive institutions and nation-states' highly centralized domestic legal systems. Comparison invites the specious conclusion that a formal legal structure (a centralized, vertical system of law) is automatically superior to a decentralized, self-help, horizontal system. The organizational differences between domestic (municipal) and international systems hide similarities and obscure the really important comparative question: Which type of legal order is more effective?

The absence of a reliable procedure of identifying a violation of international law and of an authority monopolizing enforcement instruments does not mean that states exercise their sovereign freedoms without restraint or routinely disobey existing customs and rules. A voluntary compliance system need not be normless. In fact, disobedience is rare. "The reality as demonstrated through their behavior," Christopher Joyner (1995) observes, "is that states do accept international law as law and, even more significant, in the vast majority of instances they usually obey it."

Why is this so? Self-restraint often works because even the most powerful states appreciate its benefits. International reputations are important. Those who play the game of international politics by recognized rules receive rewards. Conversely, those who ignore international law or who opportunistically break customary norms pay costs for doing as they please; other countries thereafter will be reluctant to cooperate with them. Reprisals and retaliation by those victimized by a transgression are also to be feared, as is the loss of prestige. For this reason only the most ambitious or reckless state is apt flagrantly to disregard accepted standards of conduct.

Evidence shows that unorganized or primitive legal systems succeed in containing violence and ensuring compliance with rules (see Masters, 1969). Even in systems without the kinds of institutionalized procedures for punishing rule violation typically found in municipal legal systems (such as tribal societies without formal governments), sanctions often operate effectively (Barkun, 1968). Hence we should not be surprised to learn that "international law is not violated more often, or to a higher degree, than the law of other systems" (Joyner, 1995). The historical record demonstrates that states regularly have resolved their differences through legal procedures. Of 97 inter-state conflicts between 1919 and 1986, we observe no less than 168 attempts by the contending parties to negotiate, mediate, adjudicate, or otherwise settle their disputes through formal procedures of conflict resolution (note that one conflict may entail several types of settlement attempts). More impressively, 68 of these attempts were successful (Holsti, 1988: 420). In other words, since World War I states have been able to resolve their differences 70 percent of the time through use of one or more pacific settlement procedures.

It is also clear that formal institutions for rule enforcement do not guarantee rule compliance. No legal system can deter all of its members from breaking existing laws. Thus it is a mistake to expect a legal system to prevent all criminal behavior or to assert that any violation of the law proves the inadequacy of the legal structure. That asks too much of law. A single murder or burglary in a domestic system does not mean that all people disregard laws. Law is designed to deter crime, but it is unreasonable to expect it to prevent it.

Similarly, we should not view every breakdown of international law as confirming general lawlessness. Conditions of crisis strain all legal systems, and few, when tested severely, can contain all violence. Since 1500 more people have died from civil wars than have perished from wars between sovereign states (Sivard, 1991: 25). Today, with street crime in cities worldwide at epidemic proportions (Taylor, 1993) and ethnonational warfare also exacting a deadly toll within many countries (Gurr, 1993), states' domestic legal systems are patently failing to prevent killing. By this bloody criterion, the allegedly "deficient" international legal system performs its primary job—inhibiting violence—more effectively than the supposedly more sophisticated domestic systems. Perhaps, therefore, the usual criteria by which critics assess legal systems are dubious. Should they be less concerned with structures and institutions, and more with performance?

Even the most skeptical of theorists who claim that leaders act without consideration of the rules must acknowledge that legal norms help order the process of bargaining and the formation of "security regimes" (see Jervis, 1982; Stein, 1993). At the onset of militarized disputes, law "serves as a sort of signal to tell states which of these clashes are acceptable and which are deserving of retaliation" (D'Amato, 1982). Once a crisis erupts, rules eliminate the need to decide on a procedure for deciding—and this is no small service. It would be difficult to imagine a more peaceful world without these rules.

At another level, public international law makes possible the routinized transactions otherwise governed by private international law in such activities as international trade, foreign travel, mail flows, currency exchange, and debt obligations. Parties to the regimes in these areas regard them as binding and abide by their provisions (Kim, 1991; Soroos, 1986). Arguably, by removing disputes from possible resolution by armed force, international law reduces the sources of aggression. This helps make an anarchical world an orderly world nonetheless.

# The Legal Control of Warfare

In the realm of behavior most resistant to legal control, the management of conflict, skeptics often claim that law clearly fails. If under international law states are "legally bound to respect each other's independence and other rights, and yet free to attack each other at will" (Brierly, 1944), international law may actually encourage war. To address this complaint, it is useful to examine the ethical and jurisprudential *just war* tradition from which the laws of war stem.

## *The Just War Doctrine*

Many people are confused by international law because it both prohibits and justifies the use of force. This confusion derives from the *just war* tradition in Christian "realism" in which the rules of war are philosophically based. In the fourth century, St. Augustine questioned the strict view that those who take the life of another on behalf of the state's defense necessarily violate the commandment "Thou shalt not kill." He counseled that "it is the wrong-doing of the opposing party which compels the wise man to wage just wars." The Christian was obligated, he felt, to fight against evil and wickedness. To St. Augustine, the City of Man was sinful, in contrast to the City of God; in the secular world it was sometimes permissible to kill.

From this perspective evolved the modern just war doctrine as developed by such medieval secularists as Hugo Grotius, the widely alleged "parent" of international law. The just war doctrine consists of two categories of argumentation, *jus ad bellum* (the justice *of* a war) and *jus in bello* (justice *in* a war). The former sets the criteria by which a political leader may determine whether a war should be waged. The latter specifies restraints on the range of permissible tactics when a just war is fought.

These distinctions have been hotly debated since their inception. Drawing the line between murder and just war is a controversial task. Yet the just war theory encoded in international law for most of the twentieth century seeks to define these boundaries. According to this legal tradition, all "killing" is not "murder." International law recognizes limited circumstances in which lethal force may be justifiably used and provides guidelines for sanctioned methods.

At the core of the just war tradition is the conviction that the taking of human life may be sanctioned as the "lesser evil" when necessary to prevent life-threatening aggression. It was St. Thomas More's contention that the assassination of an evil leader responsible for starting a war could be justified if the destruction of innocent lives would be prevented.[4] From this premise, a number of other precepts follow: (1) *last resort*—war is permissible only if all other means of resolution have been tried; (2) *legitimate authority*—the decision to go to war can be made only by a duly constituted authority; (3) *right intention*—war is justified only for the purpose of defense and not for revenge; (4) *probability of success*—there must be a reasonable chance that the war will succeed at a reasonable cost of life; (5) *appropriate goal*—a war can be initiated only to restore a peace that would be preferable to the conditions that were likely to materialize if the war had not been fought; and (6) *military purpose*—war is permitted to resist aggression but not to change an aggressor's type of government (Henkin, 1991).

## The Evolving Laws of Warfare

Throughout history, international law has changed in response to changing global conditions. We will illustrate this by reviewing changes in the rules for war's initiation and the means by which it may be waged.

THE USE OF FORCE We can document a gradual but steady decline in the international community's tolerance of war (see Figure 14.1). Over time, the world community has voiced increasing disaffection with the absolute right of states to employ force to achieve their foreign policy objectives.[5]

The Hague conferences of 1899 and 1907 were early developments in shaping new attitudes toward war. It was World War I, however, that revealed more than any other event the dangers springing from the fact that "under general international law, as it stood up to 1914, any state could at any time and for any reason go to war without committing an international delinquency" (Kunz, 1960).

In the aftermath of World War I, states began to revise their support of the legal

---

[4] Today, however, most states subscribe to the ban on killing leaders, no matter how evil, out of expedience—for to assassinate a war-mongering head of state would likely remove the person authorized to surrender and would justify plots of assassination against enemies worldwide—a freedom no leader wants. Perhaps this is why the Bush administration, in conformity with Executive Order 12333 that prohibits assassination of foreign leaders (thereby confirming the 1949 Geneva Conventions prohibiting the international targeting of noncombatants), did not authorize targeting Saddam Hussein during Operation Desert Storm in 1991, despite the fact that he was responsible for the naked aggression against Kuwait. Against this, however, is the counterargument more consistent with More's original view that "the 'proportionality' doctrine of international law supports a conclusion that it is wrong to allow the slaughter of [thousands of] relatively innocent soldiers and civilians if the underlying aggression can be brought to an end by the elimination of one guilty individual" (Turner, 1990).

[5] This is not to suggest that the right to use force to punish wrongdoers in just war theory has been repudiated. The "neo-just war doctrine . . . no longer seriously purports to accept the view that peace is unconditionally a higher view than justice. We have returned to the medieval view that it is permissible . . . to fight to promote justice, broadly conceived. Evil ought to be overturned, and good ought to be achieved, by force if necessary" (Claude, 1988). Indeed, some interpret just war theory to condone savage behavior to end a war quickly and coerce surrender. As the Prussian military theorist Karl von Clausewitz (1832) argued in *On War*, it is necessary to use "force unsparingly, without deference against the bloodshed involved. . . . To introduce into a philosophy of war a principle of moderation would be an absurdity. War is an act of violence pushed to its utmost bounds."

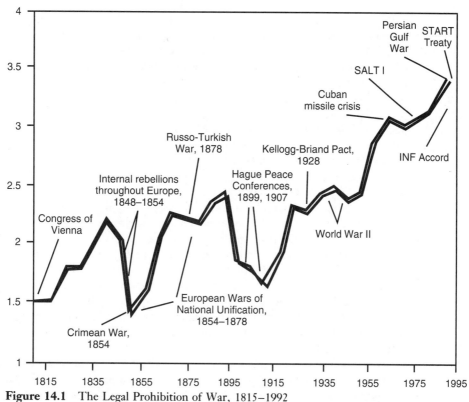

**Figure 14.1** The Legal Prohibition of War, 1815–1992
*Source:* Transnational Rules Indicators Project (TRIP), as described by Charles W. Kegley Jr. and Gregory A. Raymond (1990).

right to use force. The Covenant of the League of Nations, which was incorporated as Part I of the Treaty of Versailles in 1919, implemented a new regime. Articles 11 to 17 stipulated that in no case could a state resort to war until three months after a judicial determination by the League had elapsed and contained provisions subjecting any member "who committed an act of war against another member to sanctions." Another important step was taken in 1928 in the Treaty Providing for the Renunciation of War as an Instrument of National Policy, known as the Kellogg-Briand Pact. The prohibition was reaffirmed in the 1933 Anti-War Treaty of Rio de Janeiro and in the Nuremberg war crimes trials at the end of World War II. Both spoke of war as "the supreme international crime." The United Nations Charter (Article 2) expanded the prohibition by unequivocally outlawing both the threat and initiation of war. At the same time, Article 39 gave the international community the right to determine "the existence of any threat to the peace, breach of the peace or act of aggression," and Article 42 authorized the Security Council "to take such action . . . as may be necessary to maintain or restore international peace and security."

Hence, over time legal injunctions have increasingly restricted states' right to resort to war. The doctrine of *military necessity* clarifies international law's position by justifying "protective" military measures taken to guard national interests but restricting the justification to threats in which the use of retaliatory force is absolutely necessary as a last recourse for defense (Claude, 1988). The modern conception of just war thus still embraces the traditional *jus ad bellum*, but now confines the right to wage a war to the purposes of punishing aggression, deterring attack, protecting innocents' human rights, and generally defending "the system's rules" (Kelsen, 1945). This change modifies the political culture in which states compete: "The willingness of nations to subscribe, even in principle, to the renunciation of their rights to use force (except in self-defense) is a significant step, an expression of willingness to move in one direction rather than the other, and a disclosure of consensus on the most important aspect of political order in world affairs" (Falk, 1965).

Even though attitudes toward the use of force have changed, this has not necessarily caused a reduction in warfare or, even more optimistically, as some believe, its obsolescence. Although the major powers have avoided direct combat with one another since World War II, they have frequently used force against other states. Many of these actions were conducted in ways arguably prohibited by international law despite these states' professed respect for the nonintervention principle (Tillema and Van Wingen, 1982).

Still, because war is no longer licensed, *animus belligerandi* (the intention to make war) is a crime, and those who start a war are now criminals. That normative consensus may be an important psychological restraint on future policymakers' choices. (Political realists, however, would undoubtedly disagree, arguing that aggressive leaders will not be restrained by the mere delegitimization of violence.)

In addition to this prohibition, contemporary international law has sought to grapple with newer forms of conflict, although this has proven difficult. Consider two examples.

First, in response to the scourge of terrorism, international law advances guidelines for states' permissible military response. It restricts that response to cases where another state's responsibility for the act of terrorism is beyond all doubt. Moreover, "this right does not allow retaliation for past attacks. The response in self-defense to an armed [terrorist] attack must be necessary and proportional . . . and the victim of an act of terrorism will have to pursue other remedies against states it believes responsible and against the states that encourage, promote, condone, or tolerate terrorism or provide a haven to terrorists" (Henkin, 1991).

Second, consider the rise of military intervention and arms sales as policy instruments in world affairs, in the context of the concomitant decay since 1945 of the distinction between internal and international situations:

> International law does not forbid one state to sell arms to another state, and upon authentic invitation, a state may introduce military forces into the territory of another to assist the government for various purposes, including maintaining internal order. On the other hand,

a state may not introduce arms or armed forces into a country without the consent of its government, surely not to support any groups hostile to the government. (Henkin, 1991: 63)

**THE RULES FOR WAR'S CONDUCT** Laws regulating the methods that states may use in war—*jus in bello*—have also grown.[6] *In bello* restraints include the principles of *discrimination* and *noncombatant immunity* that restrict military targets to soldiers and supplies in an effort to protect innocent civilians. *Lex talionis* (the laws of retaliation) specify conditions under which certain practices are legitimate. One category, ***reprisals*** (hostile and illegal acts permitted if taken in proportionate response to a prior hostile and illegal act), stipulates procedures for military occupations, blockades, shows of force, and bombardments. Another category, ***retorsion*** (hostile but legal retaliatory acts when taken in response to similar legal acts initiated by other states), provides rules for embargoes, boycotts, import quotas, tariffs, and travel restrictions to redress grievances.

The cynic may conclude that the laws of retaliation (particularly reprisals) are really instructions for killing. That conclusion is unwarranted, however. The restrictions on the weapons that can be used and the permissible methods of fighting, alongside the widening scope of acts regarded as war crimes, reduce killing in warfare. Consider the following examples (from von Glahn, 1992):

- No attacking of unarmed enemies
- No use of forbidden arms or munitions
- No firing on undefended localities without military significance
- No improper use or destruction of privileged (exempt, immune) buildings for military purposes
- No poisoning streams or wells
- No pillaging
- No killing or wounding military personnel who have surrendered or are disabled by wounds or sickness
- No assassinating and hiring of assassins
- No ill-treating prisoners of war
- No compelling the inhabitants of occupied enemy territory to furnish information about the armed forces of the enemy or his means of defense
- No bombarding from the air to terrorize or attack civilian populations

---

[6] The most dramatic evidence of this development was the 1977 Geneva Conference on Humanitarian Law. Two protocols were adopted; one added twenty-eight rules to the one principle governing internal wars since the 1949 Geneva Conventions; the other provided new instruments for "Red Cross law" stipulating regulations for the treatment of noncombatants and prisoners of war. Subsequently, the 1980 United Nations Conference on Prohibition or Restrictions of the Use of Certain Conventional Weapons Which May Be Deemed to Be Excessively Injurious or to Have Indiscriminate Effects adopted a convention and three protocol statements.

- No attacking enemy vessels that have indicated their surrender by lowering their flag
- No destroying civilian cultural objects and places of worship

These illustrative objections to practices once condoned move warfare away from barbarism.

## Law's Contribution to Peace

Cynics who contend that international law is irrelevant to the control of war overlook several dimensions of law's character. First, international law is not intended to prevent all warfare. Aggressive war is illegal, but defensive war is not. It is a mistake, therefore, to claim that international law has broken down whenever war has broken out.

Second, instead of doing away with war, international law preserves it as a sanction against the breaking of rules. Thus war is a device of last resort to punish aggressors and thereby maintain the system's legal framework.

Third, international law is an institutional substitute for war. Legal procedures exist to resolve conflicts before they erupt into open hostilities. Although they cannot deter war, they may make recourse to violence unnecessary by resolving disputes that otherwise might escalate to war.

To illustrate this latter proposition and evaluate the utility of judicial procedures, let us examine the impact of the World Court on states' behavior.

**THE WORLD COURT** The demonstrable capacity of pacific methods to reduce the frequency of war (see Holsti, 1988) does not mean that international adjudicative machinery is well developed or functionally effective. Nowhere is this more evident than with the International Court of Justice. Presumably created as the highest court on earth, in practice the World Court is a very inactive judicial institution. Between 1946 and July 1991 it heard only sixty-four contentious cases between one state and another, rendered judgments on less than half of these, and handed down only nineteen advisory opinions (Riggs and Plano, 1994: 138–139).

Part of the reason behind the World Court's marginal impact is that most judicial conflict settlements take place in the domestic courts of one of the contestants or in other international tribunals. Here there is strong evidence of compliance with decisions that are reached (Falk, 1964; Lillich, 1972). Still other controversies are settled through ad hoc arbitration and adjudication proceedings before they are referred to a court for resolution.

The most important reason, however, is that the court's jurisdiction is not compulsory. Although all 184 UN members are members of the court, at the beginning of 1992 only fifty-four had affirmed their willingness to accept automatically the court's limited compulsory jurisdiction in conflicts involving them, and all but a handful of these have stipulated reservations to their acceptance. The United States, for example, has weakened the Optional Clause in the so-called

Connally amendment that reserves the U.S. right to determine the cases in which it will allow the court jurisdiction.

The World Court's weakness against powerful states was dramatized in 1984, when the United States announced that it would unilaterally withdraw from the World Court's jurisdiction its disputes with several Central American countries following Nicaragua's charge that the U.S. Central Intelligence Agency had illegally tried to "overthrow and destabilize" the elected Sandinista government. In particular, Nicaragua charged that the United States had illegally mined its ports and supplied money, military assistance, and training to the rebel *contra* forces. In denying the tribunal's authority, the United States was certainly not acting without precedent; others had done so previously. But some felt that by thumbing its nose at the court and the rule of law it represents, the United States had become an "international outlaw."[7] Others, however, felt that the United States was acting within its rights. The World Court supported the former view. In 1984, the court (by a vote of fifteen to one), without addressing the jurisdictional issue, ruled as follows:

> The right to sovereignty and to political independence possessed by the Republic of Nicaragua, like any other state of the region or of the world, should be fully respected and should not in any way be jeopardized by any military and paramilitary activities which are prohibited by the principles of international law, in particular the principle that states should refrain in their international relations from the threat or the use of force against the territorial integrity or the political independence of any state, and the principle concerning the duty not to intervene in matters within the domestic jurisdiction of a state. (*New York Times* [May 11, 1984]: 8)

**INTERNATIONAL LAW AND PEACE IN THE TWENTY-FIRST CENTURY**  World order in the new post–Cold War system will depend to a considerable extent on the uses to which states put international law. Its alleged shortcomings lie not with the laws but with their creators—states. The intentions of states acting individually or in concert, and not the slow processes by which legal development grows, will be decisive. Whereas it seems likely that the capacity of international law to curtail aggression has improved now that Cold War competition has ceased to dominate world affairs, many barriers remain to creating, as John F. Kennedy expressed liberal theory's hope, "a new world of law, where the strong are just and the weak secure and the peace preserved." That conclusion leads naturally to a consideration of the role that international organizations play in maintaining world peace.

---

[7] The American Society of International Law voted overwhelmingly on April 12, 1984, to urge the United States to reverse its decision. Harvard Law professor Abram Chayes, who earlier in his career laid the legal foundations for the Kennedy administration's naval quarantine of Cuba during the 1962 missile crisis with the Soviet Union, elected to represent Nicaragua in its suit against the United States. Believing that the Nicaraguan leaders were acting "to uphold the rule of law in international affairs," Chayes stated that he thought it appropriate for the United States, which "purports to be bound by the rule of law," to be judged under "appropriate international procedures." He stated that "there is nothing wrong with holding the United States to its own best standards and best principles" (*New York Times*, April 11, 1983).

## INTERNATIONAL ORGANIZATION AND WORLD ORDER · · · · · · · · · · · · · · · · · · · · · · · · · · · · · ·

Liberals and neoliberals recommend, as a second political path to peace, the creation of international organizations.

> Prevention of war is clearly not the only, or in every case the primary, goal toward which international organizations are directed. There is, nevertheless, substantial justification for the popular expectation that international organizations will pursue that goal. The best known international institutions have been widely advertised as war-preventing agencies. (Claude, 1988: 70)

The growth of international organizations to deal with the problem of war has been persistent, particularly in the twentieth century. To understand this political approach, we must also understand its theoretical underpinnings. The expectations about and performance of the United Nations (UN) exemplify those theoretical premises.

### The United Nations and the Preservation of Peace

Like its predecessor the League of Nations, the UN's primary mission, as its charter states, is the "maintenance of international peace and security." The stipulation that membership is open to all "peace-loving" countries reaffirms this purpose. So does the charter's requirements that members "settle their international disputes by peaceful means."

#### Collective Security

*Collective security* is often viewed as an alternative to competitive alliances and the balance of power as a method for preserving peace. In a balance-of-power system, it is assumed that each state acting in its own self-interest for its individual protection will form coalitions offsetting others and that the resulting equilibrium will prevent war. In contrast, collective security asks each state to share responsibility for every other states' security. Collective security "assumes that every nation perceives every challenge to the international order in the same way, and is prepared to run the same risks to preserve it" (Kissinger, 1992). All states are to take joint action against *any* transgressor, and *all* are to act in concert. This presumes that the superior power of the entire community will deter those contemplating aggression or, failing this, that collective action will defeat any violator of the peace.

In the aftermath of the League's failure to put collective security into practice, critics sadly noted the perhaps illusory expectations on which proponents had built the design. Many of the preconditions necessary for an effective system of collective security were lacking. The League's failures stemmed from the U.S. refusal to join the organization; the other great powers' fear that the League's collective strength might be used against them; disagreement over objectively defining an instance of aggression in which all concurred; states' pervasive dread of inequities in sharing the risks and costs of mounting an organized response to aggression; and states' general penchant for only voicing approval of the value of general peace but willingness to organize resistance only to threats to their own security. In the final analysis, the theory's central fallacy was that it expected a state's desire to see others protected to be as strong as its desire to protect itself. That assumption was not upheld in the interwar period. As a result, the League of Nations never implemented a true collective security system.

The architects of the United Nations were painfully aware of the League's disappointing experience. Thus while they voiced support for collective security, their design restored the balance of power to maintain peace. The United Nations Charter, signed June 26, 1945, permitted any of the Security Council's five permanent members (the United States, the Soviet Union, Great Britain, France, and China) to veto and thereby block any proposed enforcement action which any disapproved. Because the Security Council could act in concert only when the permanent members fully agreed, the UN Charter was a concession to states' sovereign freedom:

> In the final analysis, the San Francisco Conference must be described as having repudiated the doctrine of collective security as the foundation for a general, universally applicable system for the management of power in international relations. The doctrine was given ideological lip service, and a scheme was contrived for making it effective in cases of relatively minor importance. But the new organization reflected the conviction that the concept of collective security had no realistic relevance to the problems posed by conflict among the major powers. (Claude, 1962: 164–165)

To further enhance the authority of the great powers relative to the United Nations, the charter severely restricted the capacity of the General Assembly to mount collective action. The charter authorized it only to initiate studies of conflict situations, bring perceived hostilities to the attention of the Security Council, and make recommendations for peacekeeping initiatives. Moreover, it restricted the role of the secretary general to that of chief administrative officer. Article 99 confined the secretary general, and the working staff of the Secretariat created to aid him, to alerting the Security Council to peace-threatening situations and to providing administrative support for the peacekeeping operations that the Security Council authorized.

The UN's structure compromised the organization's security mission. Still, the United Nations is much more than a mere debating society. It is also more than an arena for the conduct of power politics. During the Cold War the United Nations fell short of many of the ideals its more ambitious founders originally envisioned, principally because its two most powerful members in the Security Council did not cooperate (see Chapter 6). Nevertheless, like any adaptive institution, the United Nations found ways to overcome the compromising legal restrictions that inhibited its capacity to preserve world order.

## From Collective Security to Peacekeeping

The Korean police action in 1950 provided a glimmer of hope that the United Nations might overcome its institutional barriers to preserving world order. However, that episode was an intervention sponsored and fought by the United States under UN auspices and did not set a precedent for equally ambitious initiatives in later conflicts. The disillusioning Korean experience was the UN's last "enforcement" mission to defeat an aggressor until 1990, when, freed from the paralyzing grip of Cold War rivalry, the United Nations mounted a collective response to Iraq's invasion of Kuwait.

During the long interregnum between Korea and Kuwait, the UN adaptively sought to overcome the political obstacles posed by superpower discord. UN experiments with monitoring explosive situations began in its formative period. For example, in 1948 it created the United Nations Truce Supervision Organization (UNTSO) to monitor the ceasefire between Israel and neighboring countries and the United Nations Military Observer Group in India and Pakistan (UNMOGIP) for protecting a ceasefire zone in Kashmir. And, after the Korean War, these initiatives became precedents for a new approach. Acting in response to the Suez crisis under the Uniting for Peace resolution, in 1956 the General Assembly created the United Nations Emergency Force (UNEF) and charged the secretary general with primary responsibility for managing the UN's first *peacekeeping* operation in the Sinai.

The assembly designed UNEF to forestall the superpowers' competitive intrusion into a potentially explosive situation and to overcome the Security Council's inaction. This innovative approach went beyond prior UN fact-finding commissions and observer forces. It was largely improvisational, since the charter had not made provisions for peacekeeping activities authorized by the General Assembly and managed by the secretary general. The principles underlying UNEF were different from collective security. The latter emphasized checking aggression through collective enforcement. UNEF, by contrast, emphasized noncoercive activities aimed at placing the UN's neutral "thin blue line" between the clashing armies to permit time for negotiations to resolve the conflict.

Success can be infectious. Following UNEF, the UN sprang into action to authorize other operations designed to forestall conflicts, which have since become closely identified with the process of peacekeeping. For example, in 1958 the UN Observer Group helped to defuse the crisis in Lebanon. And in 1960 the largest UN peacekeeping force ever entered the Congo to stabilize that newly independent country. Shortly thereafter, in 1964, the UN sent the UNFICYP peacekeeping force to Cyprus. Other increasingly diverse and ambitious UN peacekeeping operations followed from these precedents (see Durch, 1993a). Table 14.1 summarizes the most well-known operations, and Map 14.1 on page 533 displays their location throughout the globe.

Of these operations, it is reasonable to regard only UNYOM, in Yemen, as an outright failure and UNIFIL, in Lebanon, as "limited" in success (Haas, 1986). But "in no case can the setback[s] be attributed to inadequacies of the operation[s]" (Skjelsbaek, 1989). UN missions thus have regularly succeeded in creating buffers between the warring disputants, providing time for negotiating cease-fires, and ensuring compliance with agreements. More impressively, on many occasions they have helped contain conflicts that threatened to escalate to large-scale wars with additional participants. "By keeping the situation quiet on the ground, they [have given] diplomats enough time to do their part of the job" (Skjelsbaek, 1989).

Over time, the roles associated with UN peacekeeping have moved from managing

## TABLE 14.1 UN PEACEKEEPING OPERATIONS, OBSERVER MISSIONS, AND RELATED DISPUTE SETTLEMENT ACTIVITIES, 1945–1994

### LATIN AND CENTRAL AMERICA

**IAPF.** Inter-American Peace Force, 1965–1966: Dispatched by the Organization of American States, and authorized to act with it, UN representatives and military observers moderated civil unrest in the Dominican Republic.

**ONUCA.** UN Observer Group in Central America, 1989–1991: Established to monitor the Guatemala (Esquipulas II) agreement that prohibited cross-border support for the *contra* rebels and, after March 1990, to help manage the voluntary demobilization of the Nicaraguan resistance.

**ONUVEN.** UN Mission for Verification of the Electoral Process in Nicaragua, 1988–present. Established to oversee elections following the truce and ensure continuing respect for democratic procedures.

**ONUSAL.** UN Observer Mission in El Salvador, May 1991–present: Created to implement the human rights agreement between the government of El Salvador and the Farabundo Marti National Liberation Front (FMNL).

**UNOMIH.** UN Observer Mission in Haiti, September 1993–present: Embargo and show-of-force of 1,200 soldiers to restore democracy to Haiti, reestablish domestic order, return President Jean-Bertrand Aristide to power, and train Haitian military to respect human rights.

### AFRICA

**ONUC.** French initials for the UN Operation in the Congo, 1960–1964: Authorized to maintain peace and order while preserving unity in the newly independent former Belgian colony.

**UNTAG.** UN Transition Assistance Group conceived in 1978 and implemented between April 1989 and April 1990: Empowered administrators to supervise free elections in a democratic exercise of self-determination to convert the South African colony of South West Africa to the independent country of Namibia.

**UNAVEM I.** UN Angola Verification Mission, 1988–1991: Verified the redeployment southward and the phased and total withdrawal of Cuban troops from Angola.

**UNAVEM II.** UN Angola Verification Mission, June 1991–present: Established to monitor the implementation of the Angola Peace accords, agreed to by Angola and the political opposition movement UNITA, and to monitor the Angolan police as set out in the Protocol of Estoni.

**MINURSO.** UN Mission for the Referendum in Western Sahara, 1991–present: To oversee elections to determine whether Western Sahara should become independent or integrated into Morocco.

**UNOSOM I.** UN Operation Mission in Somalia, 1992: Observer and escort operation to deliver humanitarian assistance and provide buffer force.

## Table 14.1 UN Peacekeeping Operations, Observer Missions, and Related Dispute Settlement Activities, 1945–1994 *(continued)*

**UNOSOM II.** UN Operation in Somalia, 1993–1994: Provide security by United States for humanitarian aid shipments.

**UNOMOZ.** UN Operation in Mozambique, December 1992–present: Observer force to supervise cease-fire and to prepare for elections.

**UNOMUR.** UN Observer Mission in Uganda/Rwanda, 1993–present: Sent to supervise truce.

**NMOG.** Rwanda Neutral Military Observer Group, 1992–1993: Charged with monitoring cease-fire and creating a demilitarized zone between three warring factions in Rwanda.

**UNAMIR.** UN Assistance Mission in Rwanda, 1993–present: Forces sent in October 1993 to restore order in civil war.

**ECOMOG.** Economic Community of West African States Cease-Fire Monitoring Group, 1990–present: Buffer force and combatant against the Charles Taylor faction in the Liberian civil war.

**UNOMIL.** UN Observer Mission in Liberia, 1993–present: Charged with supervising cease-fire and preparing for local governance.

### EUROPE

**UNMOG.** UN Military Observers in Greece, 1952–1954: Created to restore order along borders separating Albania, Yugoslavia, and Bulgaria.

**UNFICYP.** UN Force in Cyprus, 1964–present: Established to prevent recurrence of fighting between contending Greek and Turkish communities and, since 1974, to supervise the cease-fire and maintain a buffer zone between the disputants.

**UNPROFOR.** UN Observer Mission in Yugoslavia, December 1991–present: Deployed a peacekeeping force of 14,000 to demilitarize fighting between Serbian federal army and Croatian forces in the former Yugoslavia and create a buffer zone while troops are withdrawn and demobilized, coordinate humanitarian escort relief units in Bosnia, and, since 1994, establish control of all heavy weapons within a twelve-mile exclusion zone in Sarajevo.

**UNSCOB.** UN Special Committee on the Balkans, 1947–present: To supervise cessation of hostilities and provide assistance to restore normal relations among Greece, Albania, Bulgaria, and Yugoslavia.

**UNOMIG.** Joint Russian–South Ossetian–Georgian Command Force under UN Supervision, 1993–present: Monitor disengagement corridor and cease-fire buffer zone in Georgia.

**Moldova Force.** Joint Russian-Moldovan-Transdestrian UN Command, 1992–present: Buffer force assigned to monitor a cease-fire between Moldovan and Transdestrian forces, at the two disputants' request.

## TABLE 14.1 UN PEACEKEEPING OPERATIONS, OBSERVER MISSIONS, AND RELATED DISPUTE SETTLEMENT ACTIVITIES, 1945–1994 (*continued*)

### MIDDLE EAST

**UNTSO.** UN Truce Supervision Organization in Palestine, 1948–present: Created to supervise armistice among Israel, Jordan, Lebanon, and Syria, and cease-fire of 1967, it today operates with UNDOF and UNIFIL.

**UNEF I and II.** UN Emergency Force, 1956–1967, 1973–1979: Established to prevent Israel and Egypt from fighting in Sinai and Gaza Strip.

**UNOGIL.** UN Observer Group in Lebanon, June–December 1958: Established to police border dividing Lebanon and Syria.

**UNDOF.** UN Disengagement Observer Force, 1974–1994: Created to monitor the buffer zone on the Golan Heights between Syrian and Israeli forces.

**UNIFIL.** UN Interim Force in Lebanon, 1978–present: Sent to police border dividing Lebanon and Israel, confirm withdrawal of Israeli troops, and establish effective authority in southern Lebanon.

**UNYOM.** UN Yemen Observation Mission, 1963–1964: Created to observe and monitor withdrawal of Saudi Arabian and Egyptian forces.

**UNIIMOG.** U.N. Iran–Iraq Military Observer Group, 1988–1991: Created to supervise cease-fire and police border between Iran and Iraq.

**MFO.** Multinational Force and Observers, 1981–present: To verify the level of forces in the zones created by the peace treaty between Israel and Egypt and ensure freedom of navigation through the Strait of Tiran.

**UNIKOM.** UN Iraq–Kuwait Observation Mission, April 1991–present: Established to create a demilitarized zone between Iraq and Kuwait, deter violations of the boundary, restore Kuwait's independence, ensure Iraqi compliance with the UN's sanctions for Iraq's aggression, and observe hostile or potentially hostile actions.

### ASIA AND THE PACIFIC

**UNMOGIP.** UN Military Observer Group in India and Pakistan, 1948–present: Created to supervise cease-fire in Kashmir.

**UNCFI.** UN Commission for Indonesia, 1949–1951: Sent to settle disputes following Indonesian independence from the Netherlands.

**NNSC.** Neutral Nations' Supervisory Commission for Korea, 1953– present: Established by the Armistice Agreement at the end of the Korean War, the commission is to supervise, observe, inspect, and investigate the armistice and to report on these activities to the Military Armistice Commission. Today its main role is to maintain and improve relations between both sides and thus keep open a channel of communications.

---

TABLE 14.1 UN PEACEKEEPING OPERATIONS, OBSERVER MISSIONS, AND RELATED DISPUTE SETTLEMENT ACTIVITIES, 1945–1994 (*continued*)

**UNGOMAP.** UN Good Offices Mission in Afghanistan and Pakistan, 1988–1991: Deployed military observers to monitor implementation of Geneva accords to assure withdrawal of Soviet troops, noninterference, and nonintervention.

**OSGAP.** Office of the Secretary General in Afghanistan and Pakistan, 1989–present: To assist the Personal Representative of the Secretary General to oversee enforcement of General Assembly Resolution 44/15 in order to help preserve peace.

**UNTEA/UNSF.** UN Temporary Executive Authority and UN Security Force in West New Guinea, 1962–1963: Engineered and monitored a cease-fire between Indonesian and Netherlands forces so that peace negotiations could proceed without further incident.

**UNIPOM.** UN India–Pakistan Observation Mission, 1965–1966: Established to oversee and supervise cease-fire in Rann of Kutch.

**UNAMIC.** UN Advance Mission in Cambodia, 1991–1992: Demobilized armed factions waging war in Cambodia.

**UNTAC.** UN Transitional Authority in Cambodia, March 1992–September 1993: Force of 22,000 disarmed and dispersed rebel factions and Vietnamese troops, organized and oversaw free elections that seated Cambodian national leader Norodom Sihanook at head of democratic government.

---

crises "during incipiency" to bolder security- and confidence-building measures, verification, legal assistance in civil wars, combating terrorism, humanitarian aid, drug interdiction, naval peacekeeping, and other operations beyond the activities originally envisioned for them (Rikhye, 1989).

### The Changing Role of the Secretary General

Drawing on the UN's experience with UNEF, Secretary General Dag Hammarskjöld of Sweden articulated in his 1960 annual report to the world organization what he saw as the new United Nations role in managing peace and security. *Preventive diplomacy* describes Hammarskjöld's vision, a term that since has become virtually synonymous with United Nations peacekeeping:

> Preventive diplomacy . . . is of special significance in cases where the original conflict may be said either to be the result of, or to imply risks for, the creation of a power vacuum between the main blocs. Preventive action in such cases must in the first place aim at filling the vacuum so that it will not provoke action from any of the major parties, the initiative for which might be taken for preventive purposes but might in turn lead to counter-action from the other side. The ways in which a vacuum can be filled by the United Nations so as to forestall such initiatives differ from case to case, but they all have this in common: temporarily . . . the United Nations enters the picture on the basis of its noncommitment to any power bloc . . . so as to provide to the extent possible a guarantee in relation to all parties against initiatives from others.

Hammarskjöld saw preventive diplomacy partly as a response to the need to take bolder conflict-avoidance measures by resolving conflicts before they reached the crisis stage (in contrast to ending wars once they erupt), but it also reflected his frustration with Security Council inaction.

More than his unobtrusive predecessor, Trygve Lie of Norway, who resigned in November 1952, Hammarskjöld saw the secretary general's role as that of an active crisis manager. He independently enlarged the defined responsibilities of the executive organ of the United Nations by using his "good offices" to mediate international disputes and by strengthening the UN's administrative support for peacekeeping operations.

Hammarskjöld met an untimely tragic death in the line of duty in September 1961. Afterward, his successor, U Thant of Burma, pursued a much less activist program through the two terms he held office until 1971. Constrained by increasing pressure from both the United States and the Soviet Union, U Thant concentrated on "quiet diplomacy" to manage crises that not he but the Security Council or the General Assembly identified. This approach was more akin to that which had prevailed in the early 1950s, stressing crisis response rather than crisis prevention.

Kurt Waldheim of Austria, who assumed the post of secretary general in 1972, shared U Thant's preference to avoid offending the great powers. Waldheim did seek to resolve some interstate disputes, as his efforts to obtain release of the U.S. hostages seized in Iran in 1979 illustrate. His initiatives were restrained, however. In his first public statement as secretary general, Waldheim stressed that "in this position one has to know the limits." This passivity endeared Waldheim to the superpowers, who rewarded his submissiveness by supporting his reappointment in 1976 to a second five-year term and by promoting his reelection to a third in 1981. But by this time China, insisting on the election of a candidate from the Third World and vowing to use its veto to prevent Waldheim's reelection, paved the way for the election of a more experienced diplomat with greater ambitions (Jakobson, 1991).

Waldheim's successor, Javier Pérez de Cuéllar of Peru, also held "quiet diplomacy" in respect. Yet Pérez de Cuéllar was outspokenly critical of the "alarming succession of international crises" in which "the United Nations is unable to play as effective and decisive a role as the Charter certainly envisaged for it." To rectify its impotence, he called for renewed use of the Security Council that "too often [finds] itself on the sidelines" because of alleged "partisanship, indecisiveness or incapacity arising from divisions among Member States." He felt the Security Council should "keep an active watch on dangerous situations and, if necessary, initiate discussions with the parties" to defuse them "at an early stage before they degenerate into violence." Lamenting the fact that "the power of exposure" was the secretary general's only authorized power under the charter, in May 1989 Pérez de Cuéllar declared that "I cannot accept that, in each and every case, we need agreement by the two great powers before we can advance." Acting on this principle, he aggressively pursued both *peacemaking* and *peacekeeping* initiatives. He explained his approach in these terms:

> I have tried to simplify the procedures for finding peaceful solutions to international conflicts. The sequence of events is always the same. First you have to get a truce—end the hostilities. That is what we call "peacemaking" in diplomatic parlance. Once that is

achieved and approved by the UN Security Council, we set up operations to keep the peace. That is what we call "peacekeeping."

## Cold War Obstacles to Conflict Prevention

This ambitious departure strengthened the UN's capacity to preserve world peace through efforts organized by the secretary general (see Skjelsbaek, 1991). Still, until the closing days of the Cold War, the UN's record of preventing and settling conflicts attested to the barriers that then existed, for "only about two out of five" of the UN's attempts to mediate conflicts succeeded (Holsti, 1988: 423). Another accounting recorded a total of 319 international disputes in which some fighting occurred between 1945 and 1984, of which only 137, or 43 percent, were referred to the UN for management; moreover, the United Nations failed to abate 47 percent of these disputes and failed to settle fully 75 percent of them (Haas, 1986: 17). Hence, the UN's *peacekeeping* record was more distinguished than its *peacemaking* achievements, for the world organization was more successful in preserving peace than in preventing wars.

Yet the successes that were recorded also demonstrate that the UN was to some extent able to transcend the substantial barriers symbolized by 264 vetoes in the Security Council, or on a third of its resolutions between 1945 and 1992 (Riggs and Plano, 1994: 58). This record of both success and impotence suggests that the UN's efficacy as an instrument of conflict management in the Cold War's inauspicious climate was greatest when a conflict (1) did not involve the superpowers, (2) was outside the context of the East–West rivalry, (3) was opposed by both superpowers and other members of the Security Council, (4) was intense and in danger of spreading geographically, (5) entailed fighting (albeit at a limited level), (6) centered on a decolonization dispute, (7) involved "middle" and "small" states comparatively unprepared militarily, or (8) was identified as a threat to peace by the secretary general, who led efforts to organize UN resistance to its continuation. The record underscores the extent to which, as Trygve Lie noted in 1946, "the United Nations is no stronger than the collective will of the nations that support it. Of itself it can do nothing. It is a machinery through which nations can cooperate. It can be used and developed . . . or it can be discarded and broken."

Given this reality, it is understandable why, while the United Nations was a captive of Cold War competition, the UN directed its activities primarily toward addressing the deep-seated structural causes of war, where it could make a difference. This is seen in its "rear door" efforts to alleviate the conditions of poverty, inequality, frustration, and despair that provoke violence. In other words, for most of its existence the United Nations concentrated its efforts on *peacelessness* in the sphere of low politics, in response to an awareness that poverty causes more death, suffering, and human incapacity than does war (Alger, 1990) and because it is here rather than in the sphere of high politics that the UN's power is greatest.[8]

---

[8] These programs include work on human rights, technical assistance, refugees, decolonization, world trade, drug trafficking, the law of the sea, protection of children, world food, social discrimination, the equality of women, agricultural development, religious discrimination, disaster relief, environmental protection, and a host of other world problems that influence the quality of life and prospects for conditions from which aggression springs.

Despite its weaknesses, the United Nations in many respects is, as John F. Kennedy put it, "our last hope in an age where the instruments of war have far outpaced the instruments of peace." This promise gained new momentum on becoming fulfilled when the Cold War's end opened a new chapter on the UN's quest for world order.

### The UN's Blue Helmets and Multilateral Peacemaking

The United Nations was a victim of superpower rivalry for more than four decades. Now, however, the Cold War no longer stands in the way of the organization's ability to fulfill its security-preserving mission.

U.S. President George Bush characterized Iraq's 1990 invasion of Kuwait as the first major test of the UN's ability to maintain peace in the new world order. Many people agreed. Their hopes were inspired by the UN's prior successes in the late 1980s. In 1988, Security Council Resolution 598 provided a framework for settling the eight-year Iraq–Iran war. A series of equally impressive achievements soon followed. The UN brokered the withdrawal of Soviet troops from Afghanistan, monitored elections in Nicaragua, helped orchestrate the peaceful independence of Namibia, negotiated cease-fires in Central America and the western Sahara, and negotiated a settlement of the long-drawn-out conflict in Cambodia. Bolstered by these accomplishments, the Security Council passed Resolution 678 authorizing "member states cooperating with the Government of Kuwait to use all necessary means" to coerce Iraq's withdrawal from Kuwait. Under the authority of this resolution, on January 16, 1991, President Bush ordered an air war against Iraq's military machine, the fourth largest in the world. Forty-three days later, Iraq agreed to a cease-fire and to a withdrawal from Kuwait.

The successful expulsion of Iraq from Kuwait was the first collective response to aggression under the auspices of the UN Security Council since the Korean War in 1950.[9] Many felt it could become the springboard from which the United Nations might begin to perform a true collective security role. As President Bush described it in his October 1990 address before the United Nations, "This is a new and different world. Not since 1945 have we seen the real possibility of using the United Nations as it was designed, as a center for international collective security." Similarly, President Clinton argued in 1992 that the time was auspicious "to reinvent the institutions of collective security." In September 1993, speaking before the United Nations, Clinton challenged the organization to reform its practices so that the world body could have "the technical means to run a modern, world-class peacekeeping operation."

---

[9] The action was (like the Korean operation) a U.S.-dominated endeavor. The United States took the lead in drafting the UN resolutions and gaining acquiescence from the Security Council's permanent members for a military intervention, in place of the strategy of giving the UN-imposed economic blockade time to work. And the more than 500,000 troops deployed were almost exclusively American. To be sure, some coalition partners (especially France, Great Britain, and Saudi Arabia) also contributed forces, and the Soviet Union agreed to participate as well on condition that the military force operated under the United Nations flag, but that never happened. Hence the United States technically ran the war.

To enable the United Nations "to function in the way it was originally supposed to: as a center for organizing international actions to maintain or restore peace" (Jakobson, 1991), in 1990 Secretary General Pérez de Cuéllar established a planning and monitoring group within the United Nations and recommended that, as originally called for by Article 52 of the charter, the Security Council hereafter actively cooperate with regional defense organizations to police emergent disputes. This began the process by which the UN's capacity to take the lead in peacemaking started to strengthen. This objective was facilitated by the shift of power from the General Assembly back to the Security Council where the five permanent members represent the major poles in an emerging multipolar system. Acting in concert, they authorized the United Nations to launch between 1988 and 1994 nearly twice the peacekeeping missions than it had in the previous forty-three years of its existence (see Map 14.1). In 1994, the UN's 100,000 Blue Helmets were deployed in twenty-two trouble spots on four continents around the globe. Just six years earlier, the UN's blue-helmeted army consisted of only 10,000 peacekeepers active in only seven operations.

Under Secretary General Boutros Boutros-Ghali, the UN's ambitions to maintain world order expanded greatly. Among his bold proposals for this goal was creation of a UN volunteer force. Each member could make available up to one thousand troops to a "peace enforcement unit" that would "enable the United Nations to deploy troops quickly to enforce a ceasefire by taking coercive action against either party, or both, if they violate it" (Boutros-Ghali, 1992–1993). As with UN peacekeeping forces employed during the Cold War, the recommended rapid deployment units would be established by the voluntary contribution of member states, go into action when authorized by the Security Council, and serve under the command of the secretary general. In contrast to traditional peacekeeping operations, however, their use could be ordered without the express consent of the disputants, and they would be trained and equipped to use force if necessary. The UN's strategic role thus would prepare it for a new mission:

> Strategically, the United Nations' new domain resembles a suasion game: because there is no clear-cut aggressor, U.N. forces, by presenting a credible military threat, seek to convince all conflictual parties that violence will not succeed. International force is brought to bear not to defeat but to neutralize the local forces. The political objective is to prevent local force from becoming the successful arbiter of disputes and to persuade combatants that they have no viable alternative but to reach a negotiated settlement. The military objective of the strategy, then, is to deter, dissuade and deny ($D^3$). (Ruggie, 1993: 29)

**BLUE HELMET BLUES** A number of barriers exist to the realization of these collective security goals. One is political; the enlarged size of the United Nations complicates decision making. Between March 1992 and December 1993, nineteen countries joined the United Nations, swelling it to 184 members ranging in size from Russia and China to microstates such as tiny new members Andorra and impoverished Eritrea. The potential expansion of the permanent Security Council to eight or ten members also would make agreements about peacekeeping goals unwieldy because

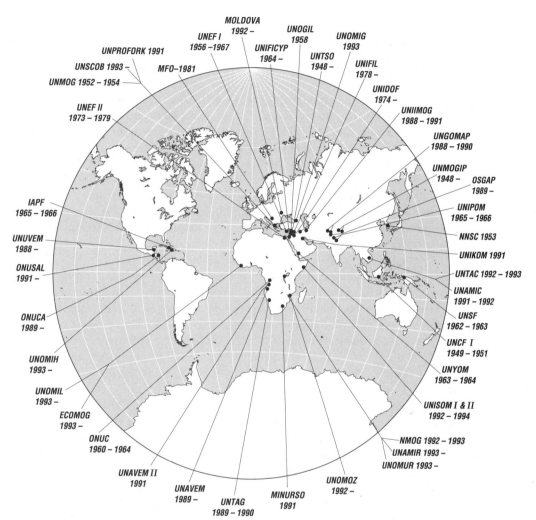

**Map 14.1** UN Peacekeeping Forces and Observer Missions, 1948–1993
*Source:* Inventory based on an update of United Nations, *The Blue Helmets: A Review of United Nations Peacekeeping* (New York: United Nations, June, 1990), and modified to identify new UN operations since 1990.

of the difficulty for large groups to reach a consensus. The UN's members have many divergent interests, and these differences reduce the prospects for consensus and concerted action. Even if the post–Cold War environment is more hospitable to collective security organizations than in the past, implementing collective security through the UN will not be easy. As Inis Claude has put it:

> An automobile does not climb the hill just because its brake has been released, but requires a battery, fuel, and a driver intent on driving up the hill. So it is with collective security, which requires a motive force supplied by states convinced of the wisdom of, and willing

to pay the price of participation in, the universal enforcement of the antiaggression rule. (Claude, 1992: 11)

As in the past, so now the UN's members still have incentives to maximize their individual relative gains rather than share collectively in peacekeeping. There remains a great temptation to support only those peacekeeping operations that affect each member's immediate security interests. Illustrative is the U.S. Presidential Decision Directive 25 (PDD 25) signed by President Clinton in May 1994. It prohibits placing U.S. military forces under a foreign command such as the permanent standby force authorized by Article 43 of the UN Charter, except for highly restricted operations in which U.S. troops are temporarily assigned to a UN commander for control of a particular operation. Furthermore, the new policy specifies that before the United States will agree to participate in a UN military operation there must be an identifiable U.S. interest at stake and an identifiable "exit strategy" for ending the U.S. involvement.

To complicate the politics of collective decision making even further, pervading the UN's membership is a fear that the organization has become a captive of its strongest member at the moment, the United States. American influence is resented by many states, who nonetheless recognize the need for U.S. leadership if the United Nations is to play a peacemaking and peacekeeping role. The Persian Gulf War and subsequent crises have demonstrated that collective security without the United States is not feasible. This creates a dilemma: "Without U.S. leadership and power, the United Nations lacks muscle. With it, the United Nations loses its independent identity" (Gelb, 1993).

A second constraint is institutional. The United Nations remains poorly designed to carry out a full-fledged peacekeeping program. The goals have exceeded the institutional apparatus. UN troops no longer just patrol truce lines. Now they are asked to "monitor elections, protect human rights, train local police, guard humanitarian relief deliveries and take up arms against those who get in their way. The burgeoning operations have not been accompanied by any serious reassessment of the UN's capacity to manage them effectively. [As a UN internal report concluded,] 'the UN lacks the technical, administrative and logistical tools required to implement effectively the peacekeeping agenda'" (Michaels, 1993).

The extraordinary tasks the UN has been asked to perform are illustrated by its UNPROFUR mission in Croatia; after two years, 27,860 troops were not adequate to stop the Serb–Croate carnage that threatens to take the lives of four million. The same "impossible" situations were extant in the UN's Haitian (UNOMIH) and Somalian (UNOSOM II) peacekeeping operations (Ottaway, 1993), and the Security Council's resolution on 21 April 1994 to cut the UN force in Rwanda from 2,500 to 250 was prompted by the same realization that the UN was managing too many crises.

Many observers concur with former Undersecretary General Brian Urquhart's 1993 portrayal of the United Nations as "an enormous ramshackle structure," poorly equipped to police the troubled global village. Attempting to reform the United

Nations while simultaneously coping with the exploding demand for UN peacekeepers has been described by Secretary General Boutros Boutros-Ghali as "like trying to repair a car while you are driving at a speed of 120 miles per hour." The consequence is debilitating. "Now that the UN is free to work as the Founders intended," British Foreign Minister Douglas Hurd lamented in January 1993, "it is in danger of being overwhelmed by the scale of the problems." Agreeing, President Clinton recommended in September of that year that the UN reduce its peacekeeping plans. "The United Nations simply cannot become engaged in every one of the world's conflicts," Clinton said. "The United Nations must know when to say no."

A third barrier is financial. Lack of money works against the UN's managerial security role. Indeed, the United Nations cannot pay for its expanded list of new, expensive peacekeeping missions, let alone take on responsibility for the many new initiatives also under consideration. In 1987 peacekeeping cost UN members $240 million in assessments; by 1993 the bill had risen to $3,043 million, "of which member nations . . . contributed only $2 billion," leaving a shortfall of more than $1 billion for 1993 alone (Stedman, 1993: 10). A larger future UN peacekeeping agenda will require even more resources—a dim prospect since in 1994 the cost of UN peacekeeping missions was "$3.2 billion a year, of which one third [was] unpaid" (*The Economist* [April 30, 1994]: 52). Under severe criticism for financial mismanagement, the UN remains budgetarily crippled, as "the chances that a UN member paid its dues on time" in 1993 was 1 in 12 (*Harper's* 288 [April 1994]: 17). If the UN is to play a leading security role in the waning days of the century, then huge sums of new money will have to be raised. The prospects are remote, however, unless the staggering arrearages owed the UN are paid (see Chapter 6). "Money, money, money—that is the prerequisite for the United Nations playing the role it could play after the Cold War," Secretary General Boutros-Ghali summarized in September 1993.

**COLLECTIVE DANGERS** Together, these problems raise concerns about the UN's future ability to police the many ethnic conflicts and potential civil and interstate wars on the horizon. The UN is not yet a true collective security organization. Its blueprint for global involvement is just that: a blueprint. It is a design without a realistic structure. Gains toward a global civil society have been made nonetheless. But the UN is not yet empowered for the high purposes it has been asked to perform. As a joint statement issued by the five permanent Security Council members in October 1993 concluded, "the demands being made on the United Nations exceed its capabilities and . . . proposed new peacekeeping operations must be reviewed very carefully" (Lewis, 1993a).

Pulling against its success are the impediments that have eroded past collective security mechanisms. Thinking that they could rely on joint action to resist aggression, some states reduced their own military preparedness so as to free-ride on the defense efforts of their peers. Conversely, other states historically have taken the opposite tack in the security organizations they joined: Rather than reneging on their security pledges, they mobilized at the first hint of trouble and thus expanded what might have remained small local conflicts into larger wars. In sum, the history of collective security reveals twin deficiencies—that it may "not work when needed, or that it would work when it should not" (Betts, 1992). Still,

> in the great uncertainties and disorders that lie ahead, the UN, for all its shortcomings, will be called on again and again, because there is no other global institution, because there is a severe limit to what even the strongest powers wish to take on themselves. . . . Either the UN is vital to a more stable and equitable world and should be given the means to do its job, or peoples and governments should be encouraged to look elsewhere. But is there really an alternative? (Urquhart, 1994: 33)

## Regional Security Organizations and Conflict Management

If the United Nations reflects the lack of shared values and a common purpose characteristic of a global community, perhaps geographically restricted regional organizations of states that already share some interests and cultural traditions offer better prospects. That idea is endorsed by UN Secretary General Boutros Boutros-Ghali, who has called on regional bodies to play a larger role in the security affairs of their regions (Durch, 1993b).

During the Cold War, the North Atlantic Treaty Organization (NATO) and the Warsaw Pact (WTO) were the best-known examples of regional security organizations. Others included the ANZUS pact and the Southeast Asia Treaty Organization (SEATO). Regional organizations with somewhat broader political mandates beyond defense include the Organization of American States (OAS), the League of Arab States, the Organization of African Unity (OAU), the Nordic Council, the Association of Southeast Asian Nations (ASEAN), and the Gulf Cooperation Council.

Despite the fact that Article 51 of the United Nations Charter encouraged creation of regional organizations for collective self-defense, it would be misleading to describe NATO and the other Cold War regional organizations as a substitute collective security instrument for the United Nations. They were not. More accurately, they remain regional alliance systems designed to deter a common external enemy. "Collective security properly refers to a global or regional system in which *all* member countries ensure each other against *every* member; no state is singled out in advance as the enemy, and each might be an aggressor in the future. Alliances, however, usually come into existence when the members are agreed on the identity of the enemy and wish to insure each other against him" (Haas, 1969).

Today's regional security organizations are influenced by reductions in their members' perception of a common threat. A sign of the times was NATO's response to the virtual disappearance of the threat of a Soviet invasion that it was created to prevent. At the January 1994 NATO summit in Brussels, the ministers formally opened the door to NATO's expansion so that it might incorporate the former Soviet satellites and Russia itself as participants. The sixteen member states offered "Partnerships in Peace" to all the countries in Europe outside NATO, and by May 1994 eighteen non-NATO countries had joined at the same time that Russian Foreign Minister Andrei Kozyrev sought to negotiate a "special role" for Russia in the plan;

failing that, on June 22, 1994, Russia agreed to work with the alliance under the terms of the "partnership" accord. Yet, as monumental as was this historic step, the expansion did not strengthen NATO's capacity to act as a regional peacekeeping organization. The new "peace partners" were not offered the security guarantee that NATO's full members enjoy—that an attack on one would be considered an attack on all. Hence NATO's security-protecting capacity remains in doubt, and skeptics ask what the military alliances' purposes are without an enemy.

The European setting after the Cold War is one marked by many ethnic conflicts—in Bosnia, parts of the former Soviet Union, and other areas of Eastern Europe, such as Romania. NATO is not postured to deal with this vague kind of threat; nor is it willing. NATO's charter envisioned only one purpose—mutual self-protection from external attack; it never defined policing internal rebellions as a goal. Hence, it is not surprising that neither the sixteen sovereign full members nor the now twenty-one "partners for peace" have sought to call upon NATO to intervene to contain ethnic warfare. (The closest they came occurred in 1993, when NATO put forward financial and administrative requirements for its participation under UN mandate and flag in the Bosnia–Herzegovina peacekeeping operations.) Likewise, in other U.S.-sponsored mutual security systems (particularly the OAS and SEATO), controversies among the coalition partners about the identity of "the enemy" are endemic.

During the Cold War, the Soviet Union was the common threat that stimulated the creation of NATO, and the United States was the perceived enemy of the Warsaw Pact. Thus the two principal Cold War alliance systems were created to enhance mutual security because each faced an external threat. They were not created to prevent interstate or internal aggression generally. The opposing alliances may have contributed to the absence of war in Europe since 1945, but it is difficult to assign NATO and the Warsaw Pact exclusive credit for keeping the "long great-power peace" in Europe. Their existence concurrent with the absence of interstate war during this period does not prove that the former caused the latter.

Similarly unresolved questions exist about whether other regional organizations have operated as effective peacekeeping mechanisms. Between 1945 and 1984, of 319 disputes, 86 (or only 27 percent) were referred to the Organization of American States (OAS), the Arab League, the Organization for African Unity (OAU), and the Council of Europe for management (Haas, 1986: 20), and the regional organizations failed to abate 44 percent and failed to settle 74 percent of these referrals (Haas, 1986: 17). These facts indicate that although regional organizations in some ways perhaps "seek to compensate for the deficiencies of global arrangements" (Haas, 1983) such as those that paralyzed the United Nations during the Cold War, more realistically they complemented the UN more than they acted as a substitute for it.

That role continues today. The crisis in Bosnia is a recent paragon of the obstacles that regional organizations face. When the civil war broke out in June 1991 and Croatia declared its independence, neither NATO nor the European Union was able to agree on action to preserve peace. After the EU, led by Germany, recognized the breakaway republics of Slovenia and Croatia as independent states, both the European Union and NATO relied on the UN to enforce a cease-fire and orchestrate the peace plan. This case and others suggest that regional organizations have the capacity to bring conflict within their territory or in close proximity under control when their members are in agreement, but that they often lack the consensus and political will to control controversial conflicts.

In the long run, regional organizations may help build security communities in which the expectation of peace exceeds the expectation of war. The processes through which such metamorphoses might occur are addressed by the functional and neofunctional approaches to peace.

## POLITICAL INTEGRATION: THE FUNCTIONAL AND NEOFUNCTIONAL PATHS TO PEACE . . . . . . . . . . . . . . . . . . . . . . . . . . .

*Political integration* refers either to the process or the product of efforts to build new political communities and supranational institutions that transcend the nation-state. Their purposes are to remove states' incentives for war and to outline a reform program to transform international institutions from instruments *of* states to structures *over* them.

## World Federalism

Functionalism in its various manifestations does not represent a frontal attack on the nation-state by proposing to replace it with some central authority. That radical remedy is represented by *world federalism.* Federalists follow Albert Einstein's conviction that "there is no salvation for civilization, or even the human race, other than the creation of a world government." They recommend building a political union at the regional and global level like the U.S. federal structure that integrates the fifty states.

If people value survival more highly than relative national advantage, so federalists reason, they will willingly transfer their loyalty to a supranational authority to dismantle the multistate system that produces war and threatens to annihilate the human species. "World government," world federalists believe, "is not only possible, it is inevitable [because it appeals to] the patriotism of men who love their national heritages so deeply that they wish to preserve them in safety for the common good" (Ferencz and Keyes, 1991).

It is not surprising that ardent nationalists have vociferously attacked the revolutionary federalist "top-down" peace plan since it was first advocated. Because the plan seeks to subvert the nation-state system, it threatens many entrenched interests. More abstractly, other critics reject the world federalists' proposition that governments are bad but people are good, wise, and enlightened (see Claude, 1971). Likewise, they challenge the assumption that "necessity" will lead to global institutional innovation, for the need for something will not automatically bring it into existence.

Although still actively promoted by the United World Federalists (an international nongovernmental pressure group), aversion to war and raised consciousness of its dangers have not mobilized widespread grass-roots enthusiasm for a world government. Other approaches to reforming the world political system have attracted more adherents.

## Functionalism

Classical functionalism is a rival but complementary reform movement also in the spirit of neoliberal institutionalism. In contrast to federalism, however, *functionalism* is directed not to the creation of a world federal structure with all its constitutional paraphernalia but, rather, to building "peace by pieces" through transnational organizations that emphasize the "sharing of sovereignty" instead of its surrender. Functionalism advocates a "bottom-up," evolutionary strategy for building cooperative ties among states.

Functionalists see technical experts, not professional diplomats, as the best agents for building collaborative ties bridging national borders, because the latter are overly protective of national interests at the expense of collective human interests. Rather than addressing the immediate sources of national insecurity, the functionalists' peace plan calls for transnational cooperation in technical (primarily social and economic) areas as a first step. Habits of cooperation learned in one technical area (such as physics or medicine), they assume, will *spill over* into others, especially if the experience is mutually beneficial and demonstrates the potential advantages of cooperative ventures in other related functional areas (such as transportation and communication).

To enhance the probability that cooperative endeavors will prove rewarding rather than frustrating, the functionalist plan recommends that less difficult tasks be tackled first. It assumes that successful mastering of one problem will then encourage attacking other problems collaboratively. If the process continues unabated, the bonds among countries will multiply, for no government would oppose the web of functional organizations that provide such clear-cut benefits to its citizens. Hence, "the mission of functionalism is to make peace possible by organizing particular layers of human social life in accordance with their particular requirements, breaking down the artificialities of the zoning arrangements associated with the principle of sovereignty" (Claude, 1971).

Many people found the functionalist approach to peace persuasive because, as its intellectual father David Mitrany (1966) argued in *A Working Peace System*, first published in 1943, it was based on self-interest.

> Functionalism proposes not to squelch but to utilize national selfishness; it asks governments not to give up sovereignty which belongs to their peoples but to acquire benefits for their peoples which were hitherto unavailable, not to reduce their power to defend their citizens but to expand their competence to serve them. It intimates that the basic requirement for peace is that states have the wit to cooperate in pursuit of national interests that coincide with those of other states rather than the will to compromise national interests that conflict with those of others. (Claude, 1971: 386)

The permanent problem-solving organizations created in the 1800s, such as the Rhine River Commission (1804), the Danube River Commission (1857), the International Telegraphic Union (1865), and the Universal Post Union (1874), suggested a process by which states might cooperate to enjoy mutual benefits and hence to launch the more ambitious experiments that functionalists anticipated. Their lessons informed the early organizational ideology that inspired the missions assigned to the UN's specialized agencies and the growth of international intergovernmental (IGO) and nongovernmental (NGO) organizations generally.

Functionalism as originally formulated did not pertain to multinational corporations (MNCs), but it is tempting to speculate that MNCs may facilitate the transformation of world politics in a manner consistent with functionalist logic. Individuals who manage global corporations often think and talk of themselves as a "revolutionary class" possessing a holistic, cosmopolitan vision of the earth that challenges traditional nationalism (Barnet and Müller, 1974). This ideology and the corresponding slogan "down with borders" are based on the assumptions that the world can be managed as an integrated unit, that global corporations can serve as agents of social change, that governments interfere unnecessarily with the free flow of capital and technology, and that the MNCs can promote compromise between contending states.

As a theory of peace and world order, however, functionalism does not take into account some important political realities. First, its assumption about the causes of war is questionable. Do poverty and despair cause war, or does war cause poverty and despair? Indeed, may not material deprivation sometimes breed—instead of aggression—apathy, anomie, and hostility without recourse to violence (see Gurr, 1970)? Why should we assume that the functionalist theory of war is more accurate than the many other explanations of global violence?

Second, functionalism assumes that political differences among countries will be dissolved by the habits of cooperation learned by experts organized transnationally to cope with technical problems. The reality is that technical cooperation is often more strongly influenced by politics than the other way around. The U.S. withdrawal from the International Labor Organization (ILO) and the United Nations Educational, Scientific, and Cultural Organization (UNESCO) because of their politicized nature dramatizes the primacy of politics.

Functionalists sometimes naively argue that technical (functional) undertakings and political affairs can be separated, but they cannot. If technical cooperation becomes as important to state welfare as the functionalists argue it will, states will not step aside. Welfare and power cannot be separated, because the solution of economic and social problems cannot be divorced from political considerations. Whether the authority and competency of transnational institutions can readily be expanded at the expense of national governments is, therefore, unlikely. Functionalism, in short, is an idea whose time has passed.

## Neofunctionalism

A new, albeit derivative, theory arose in the 1950s to question the assumption that ever-expanding functional needs for joint action to address property rights, health, agriculture, and other shared problems would force the resolution of political disputes. Termed *neofunctionalism,* the reconstructed theory sought to address directly the political factors that obtrusively dominate the process of merging formerly independent states.

> *Neofunctionalism* holds that political institutions and policies should be crafted so that they lead to further integration through the process of . . . "the expansive logic of sector integration." For example, [the first] president of the ECSC [European Coal and Steel Community], [Jean] Monnet, sought to use the integration of the coal and steel markets of the six member countries as a lever to promote the integration of their social security and transport policies, arguing that such action was essential to eliminate distortions in coal and steel prices. [The] neofunctionalism of Monnet and others [had] as its ultimate goal . . . the creation of a federal state. (Jacobson, 1984: 66)

Neofunctionalism thus proposes to accelerate the processes leading to new supranational communities by purposely pushing for cooperation in areas that are politically controversial, rather than by avoiding them. Neofunctionalism advocates that the proponents of integration bring political pressure to bear at crucial decision points to persuade their opponents of the greater benefits of forming a larger community among its formerly independent national members.

### *The European Experience*

Western Europe is the preeminent example of the application of neofunctionalist principles to the development of an integrated political community. As described in Chapter 6, within a single generation cooperation across European borders advanced progress toward a single European economic market and, in the 1992 Treaty on European Union, to the promise of a politically integrated European Union (known as the European Community prior to 1993). The treaty set the stage for the European Union's expansion. In 1994 Austria, Finland, Norway, and Sweden agreed to the terms that upon passage by referendums will allow them to join the EU in January 1995. Other applicants for membership include Cyprus, Malta, Switzerland, and Turkey, most of whom are members of the European Free Trade Association. Waiting in the wings as potential new EU members are still others, such as the Czech Republic, Hungary, Poland, and Slovakia, which already have association agreements with the EU (see Map 14.2). Expected to apply in the future are Albania, Bulgaria, Estonia, Latvia, Lithuania, and Romania (*The Economist* 330 [March 26, 1994]: 58), and the former members of the Soviet Union. In June 1994, Russia signed a broad trade and cooperation accord with the European Union that opened the door to negotiations for its application for EU membership. A conference has been scheduled for 1996 to reform the EU's institutions so that it can deal with the enlargement.

Yet despite EU expansion and the opportunities for launching a new chapter of European history that this movement symbolizes, obstacles remain. These were made evident at the Maastricht summit leading to the Union treaty. Alongside its agreement to complete the 1992 single-market program that is the most potent symbol of Europe's new dynamism, the treaty obliges the EU states to cooperate not just in finance and

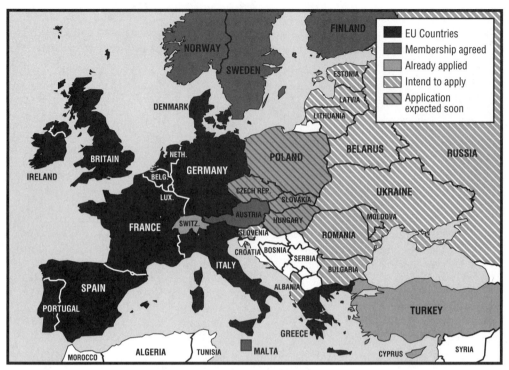

**Map 14.2**   The Expanding European Union, 1994

economics but in defense and foreign policy as well. However, even though, as British Foreign Secretary Douglas Hurd observed, the EU "is no longer fragile," obstacles to consolidation and unity remain, as some problems, including security policy, "at the heart of the functions of the nation-state are better conducted directly between governments answerable to their national Parliaments." That sentiment punctuated the many points at which politics has often impeded the integrative process through which a "United States of Europe" might emerge. Given the chronic suspicion, selfishness, and tenacious national memories of the dark side of Europe's twentieth-century history—alongside the potential for interdependence to provoke competition and struggles for advantage amidst capsizing currencies—it is unclear whether the dream of true European unity in a wider confederation will someday become a reality. The resistance of voters in Denmark, Great Britain, and elsewhere to ratification of the treaty brought the problems into the open in 1993. Disagreement about the desirability of true political unification remains (see Box 14.1).

Yet, although many obstacles to political unification remain, the dream has gained believers and momentum. "We have reached the point of no return," Dutch Prime Minister Rudd Lubbers proclaimed on the eve of the signing ceremonies for the Treaty on European Union.

Even if Europeans do not soon realize their aspiration of political union, Europe has already constructed a "security community" in which the expectation of war has

## Box 14.1
### EUROPEAN UNITY: PROPONENTS AND DOUBTERS

• • •

#### EURO-ENTHUSIASM

"[For Germany, there is] no alternative to closer unity. In the long term, I am firmly convinced that this is also a question of war and peace. It's a grave mistake if people think the horrific pictures from the former Yugoslavia are limited to that area of Europe, or that racism, nationalism, chauvinism and xenophobia in other parts of Europe and in Germany have been banished once and for all. . . . What we have accomplished economically together in the European Community will last only if we bolster it politically. A kind of super free-trade zone is not enough. We need political union."

—Helmut Kohl, German Chancellor,
November 1993

"[It is in Britain's interest] to be in there shaping a new Europe, a new Europe that is larger, more open and less intrusive."

—John Major, British Prime Minister,
April 1993

#### EURO-PESSIMISM

"[A European federal state] is unrealistic dreaming. . . . We don't want to copy the United States of America, but we don't want to return to the 19th century either. . . . The Maastricht treaty does not provide for a federal Europe at all. . . . I want a simple confederation. That means the nation-states maintain their dominant role, at least as far as internal matters are concerned."

—Edmund Stoiber, Premier of Bavaria,
November 1993

"A centralized Europe is no Europe—it's a communist model. It's absolutely utopian."
—Manfred Brunner, former EU Bureaucrat,
Brussels, June 1994

vanished from one of the historically most violence-prone regions of the world (Deutsch and colleagues, 1957). The onset of armed hostility between the EU's democracies is *very* unlikely.[10] Still, the issue of how broad and geographically wide this integrative process will go is highly uncertain (see Chapter 6). And the number of members that ultimately join this "common European home" is likely to prove consequential for European security:

> It has been argued that a more unified western Europe will be better able to withstand the stresses of political upheaval in eastern Europe, and has thus become an imperative. Yet, it also can be argued that as the [European Union] "deepens" it will become more of a closed club, unwilling to accommodate the legitimate demands of . . . other European states for trade and security. Thus, there is a danger that the "one Europe" of the visionaries will in fact be two Europes, one rich and stable and the other poor and unstable. That could be a formula for future conflicts not unlike those of the past. (Melloan, 1991: A15)

## *The Preconditions for Regional Integration*

The record of integrative experiments demonstrates that the factors promoting (or inhibiting) successful integration efforts are many and their mixture complex. It is not enough that two countries choose to interact cooperatively. Research indicates that the probability that such cooperative behavior will culminate in integration is remote in the absence of geographical proximity, steady economic growth, similar political systems, supportive public opinion led by enthusiastic leaders, cultural homogeneity, internal political stability, similar experiences in historical and internal social development, compatible forms of governmental and economic systems, similar levels of military preparedness and economic resources, a shared perception of a common external threat, bureaucratic compatibilities, and previous collaborative endeavors (Cobb and Elder, 1970; Deutsch, 1953). Although not all of these conditions must be present for integration to occur, the absence of more than a few considerably reduces the chances of success. The integration of two or more societies, let alone the entire world, is, in short, not easily accomplished.

European integration has served as a model for the application of the neofunctionalist approach to institution building and the pooling of sovereignty in other regions, including Africa, Asia, Latin America, and, until the demise of the Cold War, Eastern Europe. However, the evidence to date suggests that the integration of nation-states into larger political communities may be peculiarly relevant to the West's advanced industrial democracies but of doubtful applicability to the Third World. The record, moreover, indicates that even where conditions are conducive, there is no guarantee

---

[10] Recall the extreme infrequency with which democracies have waged war against one another, as liberal and neoliberal theories emphasize (see Chapters 2, 3, and 12). Also adding to the improbability of war between the EU's democratic members is the fact that, through NATO and the ten-country Western European Union, an overlapping and integrated military command structure exists through which the member states work together to perform what each country otherwise would have to duplicate individually. Because each state's military is embedded in a joint command, the ability to initiate unilateral military action (such as Germany did in World Wars I and II) is highly remote. These collective institutions constrain the renationalization of defense in Europe and thereby help to deter warfare.

that the sector integration will proceed automatically. Even in Europe, high hopes have alternated with periods of disillusionment. When momentum has occurred, *spillover,* involving either the deepening of ties in one sector or their expansion to another to ensure the members' satisfaction with the integrative process, has led to further integration. But there is no inherent expansive momentum in integration schemes. *Spillback* (when a regional integration scheme fails, as in the case of the East African Community) and *spillaround* (when a regional integration scheme stagnates or its activities become encapsulated) are also possibilities.

## Political Disintegration

The substantial difficulty that most regions have experienced in achieving the same level of institution building as has the European Union suggests the magnitude of existing barriers to the creation of new political communities out of previously divided ones. Furthermore, the paradox that "the planet is falling precipitantly apart *and* coming reluctantly together at the very same moment" (Barber, 1992) confounds predictions. We are witnessing "a convulsive ingathering of nations" (Gardels, 1991), as nations and ethnic nationalities seek to separate themselves from the states that presently rule them. Consider Europe, where important steps toward economic and political integration in the EU were taken in 1992 and 1993 at the precise moment when

- the Soviet Union disintegrated into a loosely tied Commonwealth of Independent States whose members threaten to splinter through ethnonational conflict into still more, smaller independent states;
- Czechoslovakia was formally reconstituted the Czech and Slovak Federal Republic;
- civil war in Yugoslavia ripped the former United Slavic Federation into six independent states, and four proceeded to wage war against each other for control of territory; and
- ethnic conflict in Romania, Bulgaria, Macedonia, and elsewhere threatened to fragment these warring nationalities into new European states.

These disintegrative developments transform the European political terrain. Indeed, in contrast to Western Europe, much of postcommunist Eastern Europe and the Balkans experienced the resumption of the ancient ethnic quarrels and nationalistic passions that have bedeviled the region for centuries and helped cause two world wars. In 1991, fifteen new national flags were adopted to symbolize newly independent countries. Since then, four new states became independent.

This surge of ethnic and religious tensions that are tearing countries apart is not confined to the larger European continent. Equally sobering is the fact that many other aspirant states are in line throughout the globe. Fifty regions worldwide declared themselves autonomous between 1989 and 1991 (*Harper's* [December 1991]: 17). This wave of hypernationalism and quest for independence by minorities and subnational grievance groups under the banner of self-determination threatens to *dismember* formerly integrated sovereign states, including such widely disparate states as Canada, South Africa, and the United Kingdom. Such developments are not new, of course, as the U.S. Civil War in 1861 and the thirty-year civil war in Ethiopia enabling Eritrea to gain independence in 1991 exemplify. But these counterintegrative tendencies remind us that states may either amalgamate or fragment. There is little reason to expect integrative processes, once under way, to progress through the pull of their own momentum. And in a world in which "few modern states—probably fewer than 20—are ethnically homogenous" (Gurr, 1990: 85), the prospects are high that the *disintegrative* process will continue. "The world may fracture into 500 states from the current 200" (Davis, 1994). As Henry A. Kissinger (1994) predicts, "The international system of the twenty-first century will be marked by a seeming contradiction: on the one hand, fragmentation; on the other, growing globalization."

## MULTILATERAL INSTITUTIONS AND WORLD ORDER · · · · · · · · · · · · · · ·

Liberal and neoliberal theories that focus on international law, organization, and political integration see war as deriving from the deficiencies built into the state system. Neoliberal reformers believe the system is the problem, not the solution, because existing arrangements make security dear and global welfare subservient to national welfare. To change this, they advocate legal and institutional methods to pool sovereignty. Seeing the international system as underdeveloped and unstructured, advocates of these reforms believe that a rebuilt state system can best extirpate the roots from which war has so often grown. As one scholar argues, global change requires innovation because "in the world of the 1990s we will face an increasing number of conflicts. During the coming decades global challenges will continue and may increase. . . . There is more and more of an overlap between national interests and global responsibilities. The task of multilateral diplomacy is to cope with new issues, new demands and new situations [through] 'shared responsibilities' and 'strengthened partnership'" (Kinnas, 1992).

To proponents, the problems on the global agenda are transnational in nature (see Box 14.2). They cannot be meaningfully managed unilaterally—they are international and cannot be met with a national response. Be it in trade, the environment, the control of AIDS, or even conflict, arguably a multilateral cooperative approach is required under conditions of interdependence. In this context, U.S. President Bill Clinton has opined that "multilateral action holds promise as never before" and that his administration would therefore seek "collective stands against aggression," providing that multilateral institutions such as the United Nations "reinvent" the way they operate.

The contributions of international law and institutions to this grand purpose have, to date, been rather modest. The use of military power in concert by many countries, in what Madeleine Albright, the U.S. ambassador to the United Nations, dubbed in 1993 "assertive multilateralism," has historically been infrequent. However, the impact of multilateral management of strife-torn areas should not be minimized. As Inis L. Claude avers,

> Particular *organizations* may be nothing more than playthings of power politics and hand-maidens of national ambitions. But international *organization*, considered as an historical process, represents a secular trend toward the systematic development of an enterprising quest for political means of making the world safe for human habitation. It may fail, and peter out ignominiously. But if it maintains the momentum that it has built up in the twentieth century, it may yet effect a transformation of human relationships on this planet which will at some indeterminate point justify the assertion that the world has come to be governed—that mankind has become a community capable of sustaining order, promoting justice, and establishing the conditions of that good life which Aristotle took to be the supreme aim of politics. (Claude, 1971: 447–448, emphasis added)

---

## Box 14.2
### A MULTILATERAL MOMENT? PROPHECIES AND PRESCRIPTIONS
• • •

#### "HELLO, MULTI, FAREWELL, UNI":

"I disagree with those who say that the United States participation in multinational force arrangement is always and by definition a derogation of [U.S.] national interests. I think sometimes it furthers our national interests and saves money."
—U.S. President Bill Clinton, 1993

#### "THE TIME HAS COME FOR AN INTERNATIONAL POLICE FORCE":

"In the post–Cold War world . . . a global political system to manage a global economy (and there's no backing up on the latter) is inevitable. As all nations become more interdependent economically, the development of an international political process that parallels national processes with all their functions becomes a requirement. These include lawmaking, police forces, and tax collection. Over the short term, joint, but voluntary, efforts at policing, such as that in Somalia, and irregular dues collections will be the norm as the community of nations stumbles forward. . . ."
—Llewellyn D. Howell (1993: 49)

## SUGGESTED READINGS

Arend, Anthony Clark, and Robert J. Beck. *International Law and the Use of Force: Beyond the U.N. Charter Paradigm*. New York: Routledge, 1993.

Claude, Inis L., Jr. *States and the Global System: Politics, Law and Organization*. New York: St. Martin's Press, 1988.

D'Amato, Anthony, ed. *International Law Anthology*. Cincinnati, Ohio: Anderson.

Durch, William J., ed. *The Evolution of UN Peacekeeping*. New York: St. Martin's Press, 1993.

Jones, Dorothy V. *Code of Peace: Ethics and Security in the World of the Warlord States*. Chicago: University of Chicago Press, 1991.

Nardin, Terry, and David R. Mapel, eds. *Traditions of International Ethics*. New York: Cambridge University Press, 1992.

Nolan, Janne E., ed. *Global Engagement: Cooperation and Security in the 21st Century*. Washington, D.C.: Brookings Institution, 1994.

Riggs, Robert E., and Jack C. Plano. *The United Nations: International Organization and World Politics*, 2nd ed. Belmont, Calif.: Wadsworth, 1994.

Rochester, J. Martin. *Waiting for the Millennium: The United Nations and the Future of World Order*. Columbia: University of South Carolina Press, 1993.

Simai, Mihaly. *The Future of Global Governance: Managing Risk and Change in the International System*. Washington, D.C.: U.S. Institute of Peace, 1994.

Taylor, Paul. *International Organization in the Modern World: The Regional and Global Process*. London: Pinter, 1993.

Weiss, Thomas G., David P. Forsythe, and Roger A. Coate. *The United Nations and Changing World Politics*. Boulder, Colo.: Westview, 1994.

# Part V

# Toward the
# Twenty-First Century

. . .

**15**
The Global Predicament:
Fifteen Questions for the Dawn of the Millennium

# CHAPTER 15

• • •

# THE GLOBAL PREDICAMENT: FIFTEEN QUESTIONS FOR THE DAWN OF THE MILLENNIUM

• • •

*Trend is not destiny.*

René Dubos,
French author, 1975

*We stand on the brink of shaping a new world of extraordinary hope and opportunity. . . . The new world we seek will not emerge on its own. We must shape the transformation that is underway in a time of great fluidity.*

Warren Christopher,
U.S. Secretary of State, 1993

The convergence of multiple world political trends in the twilight of the twentieth century points toward a new, transformed world order but one whose character has not yet developed sharp definition and vivid coloration. Thus U.S. President George Bush, commenting in late 1991 on the post–Cold War world, justifiably cautioned that "the enemy is uncertainty. The enemy is unpredictability."

What *is* certain is that the pace of change will challenge the wisdom of old beliefs and orthodox visions of the world. Because turmoil and turbulence govern contemporary international affairs, they require our asking unconventional questions about conventional ideas.

In this final chapter we pose fifteen questions about the future based on our preceding analyses of contemporary world politics. How these questions are answered will significantly shape world politics during the remainder of this century and the next.

## 1. Are Nation-States Obsolete?

The changing environment of world politics undermines the traditional preeminence of the territorial nation-state, the primary actor in world politics for more than three centuries.

• • •

One of the hallmarks of human history in the late twentieth century is the increasing internationalization of the world: in production, trade, finance, technology, threats to security, communications, research, education, and culture. One major consequence of this is that the mutual penetration of economic, political, and social forces among the nations of the world is increasingly salient; and it may be the case that the governments of nation-states are progressively losing degrees of direct control over the global forces that affect them. (Smelser, 1986: 1)

Can the nation-state cope with the challenges it now faces? "A myth" is what John F. Kennedy called "the untouchability of national sovereignty." Henry Kissinger, a former U.S. secretary of state, labeled the nation-state "inadequate" and the emergence of a global community an "imperative." Zbigniew Brzezinski, a former U.S. presidential adviser, similarly asserted that "we are witnessing the end of the supremacy of the nation-state on the international scene" and noted that although "this process is far from consummated . . . the trend seems irreversible." These views question the nation-state's capacity to handle global challenges.

The nineteenth-century French sociologist Auguste Comte argued that societies create institutions to address problems and meet human needs, and that institutions disappear when they can no longer perform these functions. Today, the nation-state's managerial capabilities everywhere, irrespective of form of government, fail to inspire confidence. As a recent report concluded,

> The sovereignty of states is eroding. A wide variety of forces has made it increasingly more difficult for any state to wield power over its people and address issues it once considered its sole prerogative. Among these forces are the communications revolution, the rise of transnational corporations, increasing migration, economic integration, and the global nature of economic and environmental problems.
>
> The increasing lack of control, an inability to solve pressing problems, and the fact that few states' boundaries or interests coincide with the nationalities within have exacerbated mistrust of political leaders and institutions in many states. Governments are perceived as not representing the interests of, not delivering security to, and not providing for the well-being of their constituents. As a result, peoples are looking elsewhere for representation of their views and provision of their needs, further eroding the authority of states. (The Stanley Foundation, 1993: 16)

Other forces infuse the nation-state with vigor and encourage its persistence, however. "Obviously in some respects the nation-state is flourishing and in others it is dying," observes French political scientist Pierre Hassner (1968), adding, "it can no longer fulfill some of the most important traditional functions, yet it constantly assumes new ones which it alone seems able to fulfill." Thus, at the core of contemporary international politics lies a paradox: "At a time when the nation-state has appeared to be functionally obsolete, it has been reaffirmed by the same process which would call for its transcendence" (Morse, 1976).

## 2. Is Interdependence a Cure or a Curse?

Global interdependence lies at the heart of the internationalization of domestic politics. It poses a singular threat to the nation-state. Interdependence expands the range of global issues while making their management more difficult, as mutual vulnerabilities reduce states' autonomy and curtail their control of their own destinies.

From one perspective, global interdependence may draw the world's diverse components together in pursuit of mutual survival and welfare. Awareness of the common destiny of all, alongside the inability of sovereign states to address many shared problems through unilateral national action, may energize efforts to put aside national competition. Conflict will recede, according to this reasoning, as few states can afford to disentangle themselves from the interdependent ties that bind them together in the common fate on which their welfare depends. From this perspective, then, we should welcome the continued tightening of interstate linkages, for they strengthen the seams that bind together the fragile tapestry of international relations.

From another, more pessimistic perspective, interdependence will not lead to transnational collaboration, regardless of how compelling the need or how rewarding the benefits may be. Instead, contact and mutual dependence will breed conflict. The absence of a community of nations remains, and nostalgia for the more autonomous nation-state abounds. Intertwined economies will not necessarily prevent relations to sour or the hammer of trade sanctions to fall. Under conditions of fierce competition and resurgent nationalism, the temptation to seek isolation from foreign economic dependence by creating barriers to trade and other transactions may be irresistible. So, too, may be the temptation to use force.

Thus, the tightening web of global interdependence foretells both opportunity and danger. If, on balance, the advantages of interdependence outweigh the disadvantages, then leaders must harness the means for accelerating its development. Conversely, if global interdependence undermines national and international welfare and security, they must try to contain and perhaps reverse its effects.

## 3. What Is the "National Interest"?

What goals should nation-states pursue? In earlier times, the answer was easy: The state should promote the internal welfare of its citizens, provide for the common defense, and preserve the nation's values and way of life.

Leaders pursue the same goals today, but increasingly their domestic and foreign policy options are limited. We live in an age of tradeoffs, as many problems can be resolved only at the risk of exacerbating others. Under such conditions, the quest for narrow self-advantage often carries prohibitively high costs. The historic tendency to define the national interest chauvinistically—my country, right or wrong—can be counterproductive domestically as well as internationally, as no country can long afford to pursue the quest for power in ways that reduce the security and welfare of its competitors.

Those who questioned orthodox definitions of the national interest in the past seldom found support, but this is changing. As the eminent anthropologist Margaret Mead mused, "Substantially we all share the same atmosphere today, and we can only save ourselves by saving other people also. There is no longer a contradiction between patriotism and concern for the world." Former U.S. Secretary of State Cyrus Vance voiced a similar idea, observing that "more than ever cooperative endeavors among nations are a matter not only of idealism but of direct self-interest."

E. H. Carr (1939), a pioneering political realist, was convinced of the realism of idealism, maintaining that opposition to the general interests of humankind does not serve one's self-interest. Nor is it served by a failure to recognize that the plight of others can ultimately threaten oneself—a view underscored by Martin Luther King Jr., who urged that "injustice anywhere is a threat to justice everywhere."

## 4. Is Technological Innovation a Blessing or a Burden?

Technological innovations, like interdependence, offer solutions to some problems but cause others. As noted economist Wassily Leontief warned in 1987, "Technology is now, for better or worse, the principal driving force behind the ongoing rapid economic, social, and political change. Like any irrepressible force, the new technology can bestow on us undreamed of benefits but also inflict irreparable damage." It can create new ways of preventing disease but also new ways of destroying others in war. Discoveries in microelectronics, information processing, transportation, energy, agriculture, communications, medicine, and biotechnology profoundly affect our lives and shape our future.

New technologies propel growth and alter behavior patterns. Still, "there appears to be a fundamental lag between the current rate of technological change and the rate of adjustment to these changes among decision-makers" (Blumenthal, 1988). The technological catalyst of change will promote progress only if it is properly and constructively managed and if the interconnectedness of technological innovation and economic, political, and military imperatives is recognized.

## 5. Of What Value Is Military Power?

Military might in the past enabled states to project power, exercise influence, and dominate others. Today the destructiveness of nuclear weapons and sophisticated conventional and unconventional weapons makes their use risky. Moreover, their threatened use is less convincing than ever. Yet continuing proliferation raises new questions alongside old ones. Security is a psychological phenomenon, but does the acquisition of more weapons augment it? Or are preparations for war and defense responsible for the security dilemma that all countries face?

To be sure, most leaders agree with the ancient Greek philosopher Aristotle, who argued that "a people without walls is a people without choice." Hence most assume that preparing for war is necessary for peace. Yet, as Henry Kissinger explained, "the paradox of contemporary military strength is that the capacity to destroy is difficult to translate into a plausible threat even against countries with no capacity for retaliation." Today, the threat of force often lacks credibility. Military power has become impotent by its very strength.

Weapons may deter resort to force, but if military might no longer exacts compliance from others, then weapons have lost their role as a basis, or substitute, for diplomacy. And if military power is impotent, why pay the price of vigilance? Since no amount of military might can guarantee a state invulnerability, preparations for war can be assessed only in terms of other consequences. Thresholds may exist beyond which the addition of greater destructive power is meaningless, and excessive preparations for war may leave a country heavily fortified with little left to defend, as U.S. President Eisenhower warned in 1961. U Thant, former secretary general of the United Nations, echoed this point when he noted that "the massive sums devoted to armaments . . . serve to feed the escalating arms race, to increase insecurity, and to multiply the risks to human survival."

The end of the Cold War has further eroded justifications for the pursuit of military power. Once implacable enemies now proclaim hope for a new friendship (Kozyrev, 1994). The urge for military preparedness will nonetheless continue in a multipolar world. Hence the relative costs and benefits of preparations for war must be weighed against the kinds of threats to national security that still arise.

## 6. Will Geo-economics Supercede Geopolitics?

Throughout most of recorded history, countries have competed with each other militarily for position and prominence in the global hierarchy of power. World politics, accordingly, has largely been a record of countries preparing, waging, and recovering from wars with each other (Morgenthau, 1985). Military might was equated with prestige, and military conquest was regarded as a means to hegemonic rule. Perhaps now, however, the relationship of economics to national security and national structure has changed rather profoundly (Friedberg, 1993). Successful trading states in the competitive global marketplace are the world's leaders. They lead in the prosperity they provide for their citizens and in their capacity to give them the living standards that make for a full and complete life. Economically dynamic states lead in their ability to defend themselves and to exert military and diplomatic pressure along with their economic might. Successful trading states command international respect and envy; they enjoy that position and prominence that traditionally was associated with large standing armies. With commercial clout also comes political influence.

To some, the next battlefield in world politics will center on economic issues. National destinies will be determined by commercial competition, not military conquest (Rosecrance, 1986). To the extent that so-called geo-economics (Luttwak, 1993) continues to grow in importance and impact relative to conventional geopolitics, the foreign policies of countries—and how they organize their foreign affairs bureaucracies for the management of economic relations—will be required to change.

Whether these transformations will produce a more secure and prosperous world remains to be seen. Trade partners may understand that their best interests lie in trading—not squabbles—with each other. As wealth is converted into political muscle, nationalistic pride can give rise to competition and self-assertiveness. Economic interdependence and tight commercial relationships can collapse in trade disputes and political rivalry, especially in periods of recession. Yet, regardless of the direction that geo-economics eventually takes, the shift of priorities to the economic dimensions of international relations is certain to influence and reorder where individual states will rank in the pyramid of twenty-first-century power.

## 7. Is War Obsolete?

As noted, ideas and institutions wither away when they cease to serve their intended purpose, as the examples of slavery, dueling, and colonialism illustrate. Is war subject to this same phenomenon? Since World War II, legal prohibitions against the use of military force have expanded, and war and interventions have been largely confined to battles among and in developing countries. The period since 1945 has been the longest span of great-power peace since the seventeenth century, thus raising expectations that the major powers have "retreated from doomsday" (Mueller, 1989). Hence the obsolescence of major war may be on the horizon, even if the emergence of trade wars is a distinct possibility.

Whether the seemingly unthinkable use of today's most destructive weapons has truly made war unthinkable is, of course, debatable. Instead, war may eventually disappear in another, far more frightening way—because resort to weapons of mass destruction will obliterate humankind. Thus the puzzle is when and by what means war will become obsolete. As Martin Luther King Jr. put it, "The choice is either nonviolence or nonexistence."

## 8. Can Cultural Conflict Be Controlled?

Throughout the world's history, when distinct cultures have come into contact, the collisions have sparked communication. At times, this has produced a healthy respect for diversity, as the members of each cultural tradition have learned from each other, to their mutual benefit. But on many other occasions, familiarity has bred contempt. Especially when followers embraced the ethnocentric view that their own group's values are inherently superior, animosity and disrespect for differences have been characteristic. Often clash and warfare followed.

Today the ideological contest between communism and capitalism has disappeared, and ancient cultural cleavages and hatreds have reappeared (Huntington, 1993). Tribalism, religious fanaticism, and hypernational ethnicity are again on the move. Ethnic conflict and secessionist revolts are prevalent, and they are now the world's greatest killers. Hypernationalist beliefs rationalize large-scale violence and the subjugation of other nationalities (Snyder, 1993). With ethnocultural contact and clashes have come "ethnic cleansing" efforts to destroy unprotected subgroups and even genocide. Hypernationalistic movements respect neither liberty nor life.

Minorities are at risk throughout the globe (Gurr, 1993, 1994). They have been denied basic human rights, and prejudice has made them the victims of aggression, repression, and persecution. Minorities have had to flee as refugees across borders in order to survive. In 1993 one of every 125 humans on the planet, the U.N. High Commissioner on Refugees estimated, had to escape his or her homeland in search of asylum and sanctuary (*Harper's* 288 [April 1994]: 17).

Armies are not prepared or trained to defend those victims. (Often, they are trained to victimize the defenseless minorities.) Likewise, international organizations are not empowered, in the absence of widespread multilateral cooperation, to stop the carnage. The fact that the weak, the poor, the exploited have no power contributes to their victimization.

Because most states are multiethnic societies, the predictable consequence of ethnonationalism is the disintegration of existing states into smaller and smaller units. The process of national self-determination is not likely to occur often through the ballot, as liberals such as Woodrow Wilson advocated.

> Today liberals are beginning to recoil, because at the same time that economic interdependence is emptying sovereignty of substance, demands for sovereignty are multiplying—leading to a proliferation of conflicts and the risk of endless challenges to existing borders in a futile quest for the perfect "pure" nation state. Meanwhile, migrations old and new have made it almost impossible to avoid the presence of minorities on the soil of any conceivable unit (unless it succeeds in closing off its borders completely and in expelling all such minorities—another recipe for disorder and tragedy). (Hoffmann, 1993: 101)

Of great concern therefore is whether the international community has the modicum of moral outrage necessary to put an end, through concerted action, to the ethnic and cultural conflict that now rages out of control. Will a humanitarian concern for the plight of ethnic minorities crystallize in collaborative responses? Or will the victims of cultural clash perish in a sea of indifference?

## 9. The End of Empire?

Much of world history is written in terms of dreams of world conquest, the quest of rulers for world domination, and the efforts of others to prevent it. Some leaders continue to think and act as though they believe others still actively plan territorial conquest. But the past five decades have witnessed the great powers' race to relinquish their overseas empires, not expand them. Even the Soviet Union, the last world empire of any size, has now disintegrated—by choice, not by coercion from abroad.

Why has the quest for empire seemingly ended? A plausible explanation is that empire did not benefit the imperial powers materially (Boulding, 1978). Political scientist William Langer, writing in the early 1960s, when the decolonization process was at its peak, argued similarly:

> It is highly unlikely that the modern world will revert to the imperialism of the past. History has shown that the nameless fears which in the late nineteenth century led to the most violent outburst of expansionism were largely unwarranted. The Scandinavian states and Germany since Versailles have demonstrated that economic prosperity and social well-being are not dependent on the exploitation of other peoples, while better distribution of wealth in the advanced countries has reduced if not obviated whatever need there may have been to seek abroad a safety-valve for the pressures building up at home. Even in the field of defense, the old need for overseas bases or for the control of adjacent territories is rapidly being outrun. (Langer, 1962: 129)

If imperialism, empire building, and territorial acquisition are no longer in a state's self-interest, why should it continue to prepare for military defense against the imagined expansionist aims of others?

## 10. What Price Preeminence?

The quest for world conquest has waned, but national competition for status in the global pecking order continues. Prestige, respect, and wealth remain the core values of many states and the central goals for which they strive. To become or remain first in the international arena means competing for the political and economic means to bend others to one's will.

The potential long-term results of this competition are disquieting. The problems of primacy are numerous, the disadvantages of advantage many. With global leadership comes the burden of responsibility and the necessity of setting the pace and maintaining world order. Moreover, dominant countries are often the targets of other states' resentment, envy, hostility, fear, and blame.

The quest for military superiority may lose much of its rationale in the aftermath of the Cold War. Today, the increasingly high costs of military preeminence have quieted its appeal in many national capitals. Military spending reduces industrial growth, weakens economic competitiveness, and, ultimately, undermines states' ability to pursue and preserve dominance:

> It has been a common dilemma facing previous "number-one" countries that even as their relative economic strength is ebbing, the growing foreign challenges to their position have compelled them to allocate more and more of their resources into the military sector, which in turn squeezes out productive investment and, over time, leads to the downward spiral of slower growth, heavier taxes, deepening domestic splits over spending priorities and a weakening capacity to bear the burdens of defense. (Kennedy, 1987: 533)

Many will not take this message seriously, however, as the one predicament that nearly every country finds worse than being preeminent is being subject to another's dictates. Thus the pursuit of preeminence continues.

## 11. Is "Realism" Still Realistic and Relevant?

Since the eve of the Second World War, by far the most prevalent theoretical perspective for viewing world affairs has been through the lens of political realism. Leaders and scholars alike have organized their thoughts and images almost exclusively in terms of this dominant paradigm. This reliance on realism to explain and predict international developments was understandable. Realism found a fertile ground in which to flourish during the conflict-ridden fifty-year period between 1939 and 1989. The lust for power, appetite for imperial expansion and struggle for hegemony, a pervasive arms race, and obsession with military security were in strong evidence. Realism accounted for these phenomena better than did any other theoretical perspective.

But now, in the wake of the Cold War conflict, a window has opened to expose quite different dimensions of world politics heretofore largely neglected. The global agenda has shifted as new issues and problems have risen to prominence. Joseph S. Nye Jr. (1992), a U.S. political scientist working in the Clinton administration, writes, "The problem . . . today is not new challengers for hegemony; it is the new challenge of trans-national interdependence." "Welfare, not warfare, will shape the rules [and] global threats like ozone holes and pollution will dictate the agenda" (Joffe, 1990).

To a number of theorists, the broadened and transformed post–Cold War global agenda goes beyond what realism can realistically be expected to address. To their mind, "realist preoccupations operate as a gigantic distraction from the deeper challenges associated with [the] political, economic, and social restructuring" that has occurred in international affairs (Falk, 1992), and "international relations have parts which realist theory cannot reach" (Scholte, 1993). "The approach of classical realism," political scientist Robert Jervis (1992) predicts, "will not be an adequate guide for the future of international politics."

Other critics are disturbed by the inability of realism and neorealism to anticipate the democratic revolutions that accompanied the Cold War's end, the voluntary retreat of the Soviet Union, and global change and cooperation generally. "The wisdom [that] calls itself 'realism'," scolds political scientist Stanley Hoffmann (in Friedman, 1993), "is utter nonsense today." Realism *was* predictively weak. Moreover, critics charge that realism is scientifically inaccurate and fails

> to provide an adequate understanding of the dynamics of peace and war [which are] at the heart of the paradigm (on the topics that realism claims to provide the best answers). . . .
> An entirely new theoretical approach may be needed, that will put both existing findings and unresolved questions into a perspective that makes sense of both. (Vasquez, 1993: 10, 3–4).

If these critics of realism's receding accuracy and relevance are correct, then the question "Is realism finished?" (Zakaria, 1992–1993) will be asked increasingly in the future. Pressure will mount for a new theoretical paradigm to replace orthodox realism and neorealism.

What a new theory will or should look like is not presently obvious, as challengers to realism theories are divergent in their prescriptions (see Kegley, 1995). Yet many agree with the general view that "It is time for a new, more rigorous idealist alternative to realism" (Kober, 1990) and that "there are good reasons for examining aspects of the liberal international legacy once again" (Fukuyama, 1992a) by giving Woodrow Wilson's liberal vision "the fair test it has never received" (Gaddis, 1990). Perhaps a reconstructed theory that fuses the best properties of realism and the new (neo)liberal theories that are emerging (Baldwin, 1993) will provide the intellectual framework needed to understand world politics in the twenty-first century.

## 12. Is the World Preparing for the Wrong War?

To preserve peace, one must prepare for war. That remains the classical formula for national security. But would states not be wiser to prepare to conquer the conditions that undermine prosperity, freedom, and welfare? "War for survival is the destiny of all species," observes philosopher Martin J. Siegel (1983). "In our case, we are courting suicide [by waging war against one another]. The world powers should declare war against their common enemy—the catastrophic and survival-of-the-fittest forces that destroyed most of the species of life that came before us."

Not all world leaders succumb to the single-mindedness of preparing to wage the wrong war. Voices that challenge the prevailing penchant are increasingly heard. President Miguel de la Madrid of Mexico in 1983 noted that "scarce resources are being used to sustain the arms race, thereby hindering the economic development of nations and international cooperation." Similarly, President François Mitterrand of France warned in the same year that "together we must urgently find the solutions to the real problems at hand—especially unemployment and underdevelopment. This is the battlefield where the outlines of the year 2000 will be drawn." And India's Prime Minister Indira Gandhi predicted that "either nuclear war will annihilate the human race and destroy the earth, thus disposing of any future, or men and women all over must raise their voices for peace and for an urgent attempt to combine the insights of different civilizations with contemporary knowledge. We can survive in peace and goodwill only by viewing the human race as one, and by looking at global problems in their totality."

Each of these rhetorical positions doubtless reflected the problems and self-interests the leaders faced at home and abroad, but they nonetheless reveal a minority viewpoint. The war of people against people goes on. Humankind may consequently plummet, not because it lacks opportunities, but because of its collective inability to see and to seize them. "Perhaps we will destroy ourselves. Perhaps the common enemy within us will be too strong for us to recognize and overcome," the eminent astronomer Carl Sagan (1988) lamented. "But," he continued, "I have hope. . . . Is it possible that we humans are at last coming to our senses and beginning to work together on behalf of the species and the planet?"

## 13. What Is Human Well-Being in an Ecologically Fragile Planet?

The once popular "limits to growth" proposition has been replaced by the maxim of sustainability, which emphasizes "the growth of limits." Thus "sustainable development" means learning to live off the earth's interest, without encroaching on its capital.

Gross national product is the common measure of economic well-being throughout the world and "is closely bound up with human welfare. . . . Human welfare has dimensions other than the economic one. But it is rightly held that the economic element is *very* important, and that the stronger the economy the greater the contribution to human welfare" (Daly and Cobb, 1989).

A rise in a state's economic output has different consequences for people currently living in poor societies compared with those in rich societies. For the inhabitants of most Third World countries, growth in GNP may mean more food, better housing, better education, and an increased standard of living. Because the affluent people living in the First World already have these basic amenities, additional increments to their income usually lead to the satisfaction of comparatively trivial needs.

The impact on the global commons of population growth and the continued striving for economic growth is critical nonetheless. "The incremental person in poor countries contributes negligibly to production, but makes few demands on world resources," explains economist Herman Daly (1973). By contrast, "the incremental person in the rich country contributes to his country's GNP, and to feed his high standard of living contributes greatly to depletion of the world's resources and pollution of its spaces." In both cases, then, continued population growth is detrimental—for poor societies, because it inhibits increases in per-capita income and welfare, and for rich societies, because it further burdens the earth's delicate ecological system. Unbridled exploitation and consumption, unhinged from responsibility to others, are ultimately self-destructive. As Mikhail Gorbachev in 1988 warned, we must halt "humanity's aggression against nature."

An alternative to perpetual growth for the world's rich countries is a steady-state economy that seeks a constant stock of capital and population combined with as modest a rate of production and consumption of goods as possible. Because most advanced industrial countries have already approached zero population growth, or a steady state, realizing zero economic growth would require profoundly altered attitudes toward production and consumption. It would also require an alteration in attitudes toward cultural norms regarding leisure and satisfaction. Citizens would have to maximize the durability of goods and recycle more products. And they would have to restrain the profit motive that justifies the need for growth and the craving for unnecessary material goods. Similarly, policymakers would have to devise means of managing conflict other than by doling out increments of an ever-expanding pie—for in a steady-state economy the pie would no longer grow.

These ideas challenge the very foundations of Western civilization. Sustainable development is a more realistic prospect, but even it will be hard to realize. Minimally, it requires rethinking the meaning of human welfare. Economic welfare remains critical to human welfare, but "the first question to ask is whether growth in the economy as measured by GNP actually contributes to the total well-being of people" (Daly and Cobb, 1989). Sustainable economic welfare, like sustainable development, requires sensitivity not only to economic growth but also to natural resource depletion, environmental damage, and the value of leisure and liberty (UNDP, 1993). But is there an alternative? Can growth in a finite world proceed infinitely? How long can finite energy sources sustain uncontrollable consumption before automobiles sputter to a stop, industries grind to a halt, and lights go out? How many pollutants can the atmosphere absorb before irreparable environmental damage is done? And how many people can a delicately balanced ecosystem support?

## 14. The End of History?

To many observers, the history of world affairs is the struggle between tyranny and liberty. The contest has taken various forms since antiquity: between kings and sovereign peoples; authoritarianism and republicanism; despotism and democracy; ideological principle and pragmatic governance. Labels are misleading and sometimes dangerous, but they form the vocabulary of diplomacy and inform theoretical discourse about governance and statecraft. History, in this image, is a battle for the hearts and minds of civilizations, an ideological contest for the allegiance of humankind to a particular form of political, social, and economic organization.

Since the Bolshevik revolution in 1917 brought socialism to power in Russia and made marxism a force in international affairs, the fight for allegiance in the twentieth century has been dominated by the contests between communism, fascism, and democratic capitalism. With the defeat of fascism in World War II and the collapse of the international communist movement a generation later, it has become fashionable to argue that we have witnessed the end of a historic contest of epic proportions—and hence "the end of history":

> The twentieth century saw the developed world descend into a paroxysm of ideological violence, as liberalism contended first with the remnants of absolutism, then bolshevism and fascism, and finally an updated Marxism that threatened to lead to the ultimate apocalypse of nuclear war. But the century that began full of self-confidence in the ultimate triumph of Western liberal democracy seems at its close to be returning full circle to where it started: not to an "end of ideology" of a convergence between capitalism and socialism, as earlier predicted, but to the unabashed victory of economic and political liberalism. (Fukuyama, 1989: 3)

The abrupt repudiation of communism in Moscow and Eastern Europe, China's embrace of a free market economy, and communism's probable demise in Cuba and Vietnam raise expectations that history has indeed "ended" in the sense that democratic governments practicing free market capitalism at home and free trade abroad will become the rule throughout the world. To believers of the liberal faith, this is heartwarming. World order, they believe, can be created best by free governments practicing free trade. As Woodrow Wilson argued, making the world "safe for democracy" would make the world itself safe. From this neoliberal perspective, the diffusion of democratic capitalism bodes well for the future of world politics in the next millennium.

Contrariwise, a less reassuring possibility is that history has not "ended" and that neither the battle between totalitarian and democratic governance nor the inclination of states to struggle among themselves for power is over. Instead, with the end of the ideological dimension to the Cold War, we may be witnessing not history's end but a watershed that, like previous turning points in history, signals history's resumption: the return to the ageless search for barriers against the resurgence of tyranny, nationalism, and war. Especially to followers of realpolitik, the most salient feature of world politics—the relentless competitive struggle for power—is permanent. The end of the Cold War does not assure us that the international community has moved beyond tyranny or interstate competition and war. As former Soviet President Mikhail Gorbachev noted in May 1992, "In the major centers of world politics, the choice, it would seem, has today been made in favor of peace, cooperation, interaction and overall security." However, he warned, "A major international effort will be needed to render irreversible the shift in favor of a democratic world—and democratic for the whole of humanity, not just half of it."

## 15. A Reordered Global Agenda?

The paradox of contemporary world politics is that a world liberated from the paralyzing grip of the Cold War must now face a series of challenges every bit as threatening and as potentially intractable. Global interdependence without the rigidity of Cold War bipolarity has simultaneously enlarged the responsibilities and expanded the issues to be confronted. As U.S. President Bill Clinton in 1993 summarized the globe's circumstances, "Profound and powerful forces are shaking and remaking our world. And the urgent question of our time is whether we can make change our friend and not our enemy."

Alongside the resurgence of nationalism, ethnic conflict, and separatist revolt, the sea changes in recent years have spawned a diffusion of new kinds of threats to world order: acid rain, AIDS, drug trafficking, ozone depletion, global warming, energy and food insecurity, desertification and deforestation, chronic debt, and neomercantilism and trade protectionism, among others.

The potential impact of these new threats is potent because emerging trends suggest that, alongside the continuing threat of arms and ethnic and regional conflict, nonmilitary dangers will multiply. Accordingly, the distinction between high politics and low politics may disappear. "In the post–Cold War world low politics is becoming high politics" (Moran, 1991).

## A NEW WORLD ORDER? . . . . . . . . . . . . . . . . . . . . . . . . . . .

From our vantage point at the twilight of the twentieth century, the world has undergone a fundamental transformation. Previously established patterns and relationships have been obliterated. Something revolutionary, not simply new, has unfolded.

Juxtaposed against the revolutionary is the persistent—the durability of accepted rituals, existing rules, established institutions, and entrenched customs. These resist the pull of the momentous recent changes in world politics. Change and persistence coexist uneasily, and it is this intertwined mixture that makes the future so uncertain.

Two races govern the path between the world that is and the world that will be. The first is the race between knowledge and oblivion. Ignorance stands in the way of global progress and justice. Advances in science and technology far outpace resolution of the social and political problems they generate. Building the knowledge to confront these problems may therefore present the ultimate challenge. "The splitting of the atom," Albert Einstein warned, "has changed everything save our modes of thinking, and thus we drift toward unparalleled catastrophe. Unless there is a fundamental change in [our] attitudes toward one another as well as [our] concept of the future, the world will face unprecedented disaster."

"Knowledge is our destiny," the philosopher Jacob Bronowski declared. If the world is to forge a promising future, it must develop more sophisticated knowledge. Sophistication demands that we see the world as a whole as well as in terms of its individual parts. The temptation to picture others according to our images of ourselves and to project onto them our own aims and values must be overcome. We must discard the belief that there is a simple formula for a better tomorrow and resist single-issue approaches to reform. Toleration of ambiguity, even the pursuit of it, is essential.

The future of world politics also rests on a race between states' ability to act in concert and the forces militating against transnational collaboration. As U.S. Secretary of State James A. Baker urged in 1990, the international community must "use the end of the Cold War to get beyond the whole pattern of settling conflicts by force." Only concerted international cooperation can avert slipping "back into ever more savage regional conflicts in which might alone makes right." The world's capacity to summon the political will to implement the reforms necessary to meet global challenges is being tested.

The world's future is uncertain, but it is our future. The moving words of President Kennedy thus describe a posture we might well assume: "However close we sometimes seem to that dark and final abyss, let no man of peace and freedom despair. For he does not stand alone. . . . Together we shall save our planet or together we shall perish in its flames. Save it we can, and save it we must, and then shall we earn the eternal thanks of mankind."

## SUGGESTED READINGS

Baylis, John, and N. J. Rengger, eds. *Dilemmas of World Politics: International Issues in a Changing World*. New York: Oxford University Press, 1992.

Brown, Lester R., Hal Kane, and David Malin Roodman. *Vital Signs 1994: The Trends That Are Shaping Our Future*. New York: Norton, 1994.

Camilleri, Joseph A., and Jim Falk. *The End of Sovereignty? The Politics of a Shrinking and Fragmenting World*. Aldershot, U.K.: Edward Elgar, 1993.

Fukuyama, Francis. *The End of History and the Last Man*. New York: Free Press, 1992.

Kennedy, Paul. *Preparing for the Twenty-First Century*. New York: Random House, 1993.

Heilbroner, Robert L. *An Inquiry into the Human Prospect: Looked at Again for the 1990s*. New York: Norton, 1992.

Kaplan, Robert D. "The Coming Anarchy," *The Atlantic Monthly* 273 (February 1994): 44–76.

Lundestad, Geir, and Odd Arne Westad, eds. *Beyond the Cold War: New Dimensions in International Relations*. New York: Oxford University Press, 1993.

Puchala, Donald J. "The History of the Future of International Relations," *Ethics & International Affairs* 8 (1994): 177–202.

Rosenau, James N., and Ernst-Otto Czempiel, eds. *Governance without Government: Order and Change in World Politics*. New York: Cambridge University Press, 1992.

Sato, Seizaburo, and Trevor Taylor, eds. *Prospects for Global Order*. Washington, D.C.: Brookings Institution, 1993.

Toffler, Alvin, and Heidi Toffler. *War and Anti-War: Survival at the Dawn of the Twenty-First Century*. New York: Little, Brown, 1993.

# REFERENCES

• • •

ABRAHAMSSON, BERNHARD J. (1975) "The International Oil Industry," pp. 73–88 in Joseph S. Szyliowicz and Bard E. O'Neill (eds.), *The Energy Crisis and U.S. Foreign Policy*. New York: Praeger.

ADELMAN, KENNETH L., AND NORMAN R. AUGUSTINE. (1992) "Defense Conversion," *Foreign Affairs* 71 (Spring): 26–47.

"THE AGE OF AGING." (1982) *UN Chronicle* 19 (July): 82–84.

AHO, C. MICHAEL, AND BRUCE STOKES. (1991) "The Year the World Economy Turned," *Foreign Affairs* 70 (No. 1): 160–178.

AKEHURST, MICHAEL. (1992) *A Modern Introduction to International Law*, 6th ed. London: Unwin Hyman.

ALBRIGHT, DAVID. (1993) "A Proliferation Primer," *Bulletin of the Atomic Scientists* 49 (June): 14–23.

ALGER, CHADWICK. (1990) "The U.N. in Historical Perspective." Paper presented to the International Research Conference on the Future of the United Nations, Ottawa, January 5–7.

ALLISON, GRAHAM T. (1971) *Essence of Decision: Explaining the Cuban Missile Crisis*. Boston: Little, Brown.

ALLISON, GRAHAM, AND GREGORY F. TREVERTON. (eds.) (1992) *Rethinking America's Security: Beyond Cold War to New World Order*. New York: Norton.

AMBROSE, STEPHEN E. (1993) *Rise to Globalism*, 7th ed. New York: Penguin.

AMIN, SAMIR. (1987) "Democracy and National Strategy in the Periphery," *Third World Quarterly* 9 (October): 1129–1156.

———. (1974) *Accumulation on a World Scale: A Critique of the Theory of Underdevelopment*. New York: Monthly Review Press.

AMUZEGAR, JAHANGIR. (1990) "Oil and a Changing OPEC," *Finance and Development* 27 (September): 43–45.

———. (1987) "Dealing with Debt," *Foreign Policy* 68 (Fall): 140–158.

ANGELL, NORMAN. (1910) *The Great Illusion: A Study of the Relationship of Military Power in Nations to Their Economic and Social Advantage*. London: Weidenfeld and Nicholson.

APTER, DAVID E., AND LOUIS W. GOODMAN. (eds.) (1976) *The Multinational Corporation and Social Change*. New York: Praeger.

ARAD, RUTH W., AND UZI B. ARAD. (1979) "Scarce Natural Resources and Potential Conflict," pp. 23–85 in Ruth W. Arad et al., *Sharing Global Resources*. New York: McGraw-Hill.

ARKIN, WILLIAM D., DAMIAN DURRANT, AND MARIANNE CHERNI. (1991) *On Impact: Modern Warfare and the Environment: A Case Study of the Gulf War*. Washington, D.C.: Greenpeace.

ARNOLD, FRED. (1990) "International Migration: Who Goes Where?" *Finance & Development* 27 (June): 46–47.

ART, ROBERT J. (1973) "Bureaucratic Politics and American Foreign Policy: A Critique," *Policy Sciences* 4 (December): 467–490.

ASHLEY, RICHARD K. (1984) "The Poverty of Neorealism," *International Organization* 38 (Spring): 255–286.

ASHLEY, RICHARD K., AND R. B. J. WALKER. (eds.) (1990) "Speaking the Language of Exile: Dissident Thought in International Studies," Special issue, *International Studies Quarterly* 34 (September): 259–417.

ASPIN, LES. (1992) "National Security in the 1990s: Defining a New Basis for U.S. Military Forces." Statement presented to the Atlantic Council of the United States, January 6.

ATKINSON, RICK. (1994) "Germany's Economic Reach into Eastern Europe Raises Fears of Empire Building," *Washington Post National Weekly Edition* 11 (May 2–8): 15.

AUERBACH, STUART. (1991) "Made in America, Used by Iraq," *Washington Post National Weekly Edition* 9 (March 18–24): 11.

AXELROD, ROBERT, AND ROBERT O. KEOHANE. (1985) "Achieving Cooperation under Anarchy: Strategies and Institutions," *World Politics* 38 (October): 226–254.

• • •

AZAR, EDWARD E., AND THOMAS J. SLOAN. (1973) *Dimensions of Interaction*. Pittsburgh: Center for International Studies, University of Pittsburgh.

BABAI, DON. (1993) "General Agreement on Tariffs and Trade," pp. 342–348 in Joel Krieger (ed.), *The Oxford Companion to Politics of the World*. New York: Oxford University Press.

BALDWIN, DAVID A. (ed.) (1993) *Neorealism and Neoliberalism: The Contemporary Debate*. New York: Columbia University Press.

———. (1989) *Paradoxes of Power*. New York: Basil Blackwell.

———. (1985) *Economic Statecraft*. Princeton, N.J.: Princeton University Press.

BALL, GEORGE W. (1971) "Cosmocorp: The Importance of Being Stateless," *Columbia Journal of World Business* 6 (November–December): 25–30.

BALL, NICOLE. (1994) "Demilitarizing the Third World," pp. 216–235 in Michael T. Klare and Daniel C. Thomas (eds.), *World Security*. New York: St. Martin's Press.

———. (1991) *Briefing Book on Conventional Arms Transfers*. Boston: Council for a Livable World Education Fund.

BANDOW, DOUG. (1992) "Economic and Military Aid," pp. 75-96 in Peter J. Schraeder (ed.), *Intervention into the 1990s*. Boulder, Colo.: Lynne Rienner.

BARAN, PAUL. (1968) *The Political Economy of Growth*. New York: Monthly Review Press.

BARBER, BENJAMIN R. (1992) "Jihad vs. McWorld," *Atlantic* 269 (March): 53–63.

BARKUN, MICHAEL. (1968) *Law without Sanctions: Order in Primitive Societies and the World Community*. New Haven, Conn.: Yale University Press.

BARNABY, FRANK. (1991) "The Environmental Impact of the Gulf War," *Ecologist* 21 (July/August): 166–172.

BARNES, FRED. (1993) "No Entry," *The New Republic* 209 (November 8): 10–14.

———. (1991) "Brilliant Pebble," *The New Republic* 207 (April 1): 10–11.

BARNET, RICHARD J. (1992) "The Disorders of Peace," *The New Yorker* (January 20): 62–74.

———. (1990) "U.S. Intervention: Low-Intensity Thinking," *Bulletin of the Atomic Scientists* 46 (May): 34–37.

———. (1980) *The Lean Years*. New York: Simon & Schuster.

———. (1979) "Challenging the Myths of National Security," *New York Times Magazine* (April 1): 25, 56 passim.

———. (1977) *The Giants: Russia and America*. New York: Simon & Schuster.

BARNET, RICHARD J., AND RONALD E. MÜLLER. (1974) *Global Reach: The Power of the Multinational Corporations*. New York: Simon & Schuster.

BARON, SAMUEL H., AND CARL PLETSCH. (eds.) (1985) *Introspection in Biography: The Biographer's Quest for Self Awareness*. Hillsdale, N.J.: Analytic Press.

BEER, FRANCIS A. (1981) *Peace Against War: The Ecology of International Violence*. San Francisco: Freeman.

BELL, CORAL. (1990–1991) "Why Russia Should Join NATO," *The National Interest* 22 (Winter): 37–47.

BELL, DANIEL. (1987) "The World in 2013," *New Society* 116 (Summer): 1–31.

BELL, J. BOWYER. (1990) "Explaining International Terrorism: The Elusive Quest," pp. 178–184 in Charles W. Kegley Jr. (ed.), *International Terrorism: Characteristics, Causes, Controls*. New York: St. Martin's Press.

BENDOR, JONATHAN, AND THOMAS H. HAMMOND. (1992) "Rethinking Allison's Models," *American Political Science Review* 86 (June): 301–322.

BENEDICK, RICHARD ELLIOT. (1991) "Protecting the Ozone Layer: New Directions in Diplomacy," pp. 112–153 in Jessica Tuchman Mathews (ed.), *Preserving the Global Environment*. New York: Norton.

BENNETT, A. LEROY. (1988) *International Organizations*, 4th ed. Englewood Cliffs, N.J.: Prentice-Hall.

BERGESEN, ALBERT. (1980) "From Utilitarianism to Globology: The Shift from the Individual to the World as a Whole as the Primordial Unit of Analysis," pp. 1–12 in Albert Bergesen (ed.), *Studies of the Modern World-System*. New York: Academic Press.

BERGESEN, ALBERT, AND RONALD SCHOENBERG. (1980) "Long Waves of Colonial Expansion and Contraction, 1415–1969," pp. 231–277 in Albert Bergesen (ed.), *Studies of the Modern World-System*. New York: Academic Press.

BERGSTEN, C. FRED. (1973) "The Threat from the Third World," *Foreign Policy* 11 (Summer): 102–124.

BERTELSEN, JUDY S. (ed.) (1977) *Nonstate Nations in International Politics*. New York: Praeger.

BETTS, RICHARD K. (1992) "Systems for Peace or Causes of War? Collective Security, Arms Control, and the New Europe," pp. 199–237 in Sean M. Lynn-Jones and Steven E. Miller (eds.), *America's Strategy in a Changing World*. Cambridge, Mass.: MIT Press.

BHAGWATI, JAGDISH. (1994) "Shock Treatments," *The New Republic* 210 (March 28): 39–43.

———. (1991) *The World Trading System at Risk.* Princeton, N.J.: Princeton University Press.

BIERSTECKER, T. J. (1978) *Distortion or Development: Contending Perspectives on the Multinational Corporation.* Cambridge, Mass.: MIT Press.

BISSELL, RICHARD E. (1991) "After Foreign Aid—What?" *Washington Quarterly* 14 (Summer): 23–33.

———. (1990) "Who Killed the Third World?" *Washington Quarterly* 13 (Autumn): 23–32.

BLACK, JAN KNIPPERS. (1991) *Development in Theory and Practice.* Boulder, Colo.: Westview.

BLAINEY, GEOFFREY. (1988) *The Causes of War*, 3rd ed. New York: Free Press.

BLECHMAN, BARRY M., AND STEPHEN S. KAPLAN, WITH DAVID K. HALL, WILLIAM B. QUANDT, JEROME N. SLATER, ROBERT M. SLUSSER, AND PHILIP WINDSOR. (1978) *Force without War.* Washington, D.C.: Brookings Institution.

BLIGHT, JAMES G., AND DAVID A. WELCH. (1989) *On the Brink: Americans and Soviets Re-examine the Cuban Missile Crisis.* New York: Hill and Wang.

BLOCK, FRED L. (1977) *The Origins of International Economic Disorder.* Berkeley: University of California Press.

BLUMENTHAL, W. MICHAEL. (1988) "The World Economy and Technological Change," *Foreign Affairs* 66 (No. 3): 529–550.

BOONEKAMP, CLEMENS F. J. (1987) "Voluntary Export Restraints," *Finance and Development* 24 (December): 2–5.

BORGER, GLORIA. (1993) "Clinton vs. the Populists on NAFTA," *U.S. News & World Report* (October 11): 55.

BOSWELL, TERRY. (1989) "Colonial Empires and the Capitalist World-Economy: A Time Series Analysis of Colonization, 1640–1960," *American Sociological Review* 54 (April): 180–196.

BOUCHER, CARLSTON B., AND WOLFGANG E. SIEBECK. (1987) "UNCTAD VII: New Spirit in North–South Relations?" *Finance and Development* 24 (December): 14–16.

BOULDING, KENNETH E. (1978) *Stable Peace.* Austin: University of Texas Press.

———. (1959) "National Images and International Systems," *Journal of Conflict Resolution* 3 (June): 120–131.

BOUTROS-GHALI, BOUTROS. (1992–1993) "Empowering the United Nations," *Foreign Affairs* 72 (Winter): 89–102.

BOVARD, JAMES. (1994) "A U.S. History of Trade Hypocrisy," *Wall Street Journal* (March 8): A16.

———. (1991) "Fair Trade Is Unfair," *Newsweek* (December 9): 13.

BOZEMAN, ADDA B. (1971) *The Future of Law in a Multicultural World.* Princeton, N.J.: Princeton University Press.

*BP Statistical Review of World Energy.* (1991) London: British Petroleum Company.

*BP Statistical Review of World Energy.* (1987) London: British Petroleum Company.

*BP Statistical Review of World Energy.* (1984) London: British Petroleum Company.

BRAUCHLI, MARCUS W. (1994). "Asia, on the Ascent, Is Learning to Say No to 'Arrogant' West," *Wall Street Journal* (April 13): 1, 6.

BRAUDEL, FERNAND. (1984) *Civilization and Capitalism: 15th–18th Century*, Vol 3. New York: Harper and Row.

———. (1982) *Civilization and Capitalism: 15th–18th Century*, Vol 2. New York: Harper and Row.

———. (1981) *Civilization and Capitalism: 15th–18th Century*, Vol 1. New York: Harper and Row.

BRECHER, MICHAEL. (1993) *Crises in World Politics: Theory and Reality.* Oxford, England: Pergamon.

BRIERLY, JAMES L. (1944) *The Outlook for International Law.* Oxford, England: Clarendon Press.

BROAD, ROBIN, AND JOHN CAVANAGH. (1988) "No More NICs," *Foreign Policy* 72 (Fall): 81–103.

BROGAN, PATRICK. (1990) *The Fighting Never Stopped: A Comprehensive Guide to Conflict since 1945.* New York: Vintage.

BRONFENBRENNER, URIE. (1971) "The Mirror Image in Soviet–American Relations," *Journal of Social Issues* 27 (No. 1): 46–51.

BROWN, EUGENE. (1993) *Japan's Search for Strategic Vision.* Carlisle Barracks, Penn.: Strategic Studies Institute, U.S. Army War College.

BROWN, HAROLD. (1983) *Thinking About National Security: Defense and Foreign Policy in a Dangerous World.* Boulder, Colo.: Westview.

BROWN, LESTER R. (1994) "Facing Food Insecurity," pp. 177–197 in Lester R. Brown et al. *State of the World 1994.* New York: Norton.

———. (1991) "The New World Order," pp. 3–20 in Lester R. Brown et al., *State of the World 1991.* New York: Norton.

———. (1979) *Resource Trends and Population Policy: A Time for Reassessment.* WorldWatch Paper No. 29. Washington, D.C.: WorldWatch Institute.

———. (1978) *The Twenty-Ninth Day.* New York: Norton.

———. (1972) *World without Borders.* New York: Vintage Books.

BROWN, LESTER R., ET AL. (1987) *State of the World 1987.* New York: Norton.

BROWN, SEYOM. (1994) "World Interests and the Changing Dimensions of Security," pp. 10–26 in Michael T. Klare and Daniel C. Thomas (eds.), *World Security: Challenges for a New Century.* New York: St. Martin's Press.

BROWNLIE, IAN. (1990) *Principles of Public International Law*, 4th ed. New York: Oxford University Press.

BRZEZINSKI, ZBIGNIEW. (1994) "The Premature Partnership," *Foreign Affairs* 73 (March/April): 67–82.

BUENO DE MESQUITA, BRUCE. (1981) *The War Trap*. New Haven, Conn.: Yale University Press.

———. (1975) "Measuring Systemic Polarity," *Journal of Conflict Resolution* 22 (June): 187–216.

BUENO DE MESQUITA, BRUCE, AND DAVID LALMAN. (1992) *War and Reason: Domestic and International Imperatives*. New Haven, Conn.: Yale University Press.

BULL, HEDLEY. (1977) *The Anarchical Society: A Study of Order in World Politics*. New York: Columbia University Press.

BUNDY, MCGEORGE. (1990) "From Cold War to Trusting Peace," *Foreign Affairs* 69 (No. 1): 197–212.

BUNGE, WILLIAM. (1988) *Nuclear War Atlas*. New York: Basil Blackwell.

BURGESS, JOHN, AND STUART AUERBACH. (1990) "Many Losers but Some Winners in the Gulf Crisis," *Washington Post National Weekly Edition* 7 (August 20–26): 21.

BURKI, SHAHID JAVED. (1983) "UNCTAD VI: For Better or for Worse?" *Finance and Development* 20 (December): 16–19.

BURMAN, STEPHEN. (1991) *America in the Modern World: The Transcendence of United States Hegemony*. New York: St. Martin's Press.

BURNEY, MAHMUD A. (1979) "A Recognition of Interdependence: UNCTAD V," *Finance and Development* 16 (September): 18.

BUZAN, BARRY, CHARLES JONES, AND RICHARD LITTLE. (1993) *The Logic of Anarchy: Rethinking Neorealism*. New York: Columbia University Press.

CALDWELL, DAN. (1991) *The Dynamics of Domestic Politics and Arms Control*. Columbia: University of South Carolina Press.

———. (1978) "A Research Note on the Quarantine of Cuba, October 1962," *International Studies Quarterly* 22 (December): 625–633.

———. (1977) "Bureaucratic Foreign Policy Making," *American Behavioral Scientist* 21 (September–October): 87–110.

CALLEO, DAVID. (1994) "American National Interest and the New Europe," pp. 175–192 in Eugene R. Wittkopf (ed.), *The Future of American Foreign Policy*. New York: St. Martin's Press.

CALVOCORESSI, PETER, GUY WINT, AND JOHN PRITCHARD. (1989) *Total War: The Causes and Courses of the Second World War*, 2nd ed. New York: Pantheon.

CAPORASO, JAMES A. (1992) "International Relations Theory and Multilateralism: The Search for Foundations," *International Organization* 46 (Summer): 599–631.

———. (1980) "Dependency Theory: Continuities and Discontinuities in Development Studies," *International Organization* 34 (Autumn): 605–628.

———. (ed.) (1978) "Dependence and Dependency in the Global System," Special issue, *International Organization* 32 (Winter): 1–300.

CARMENT, DAVID. (1993) "The International Dimensions of Ethnic Conflict," *Journal of Peace Research* 30 (May): 137–150.

CARR, E. H. (1939) *The Twenty-Years' Crisis, 1919–1939*. London: Macmillan.

CARTER, ASHTON B. (1990–1991) "Chairman's Note," *International Security* 15 (Winter): 3–4.

CASHMAN, GREG. (1993) *What Causes War? An Introduction to Theories of International Conflict*. New York: Lexington Books.

CASPARY, WILLIAM R. (1993) "New Psychoanalytic Perspectives on the Causes of War," *Political Psychology* 14 (September): 417–446.

CENTRE ON TRANSNATIONAL CORPORATIONS. (1991) *World Investment Report 1991: The Triad in Foreign Direct Investment*. New York: United Nations.

———. (1987) *Foreign Direct Investment, the Service Sector, and International Banking*. New York: United Nations.

CHACE, JAMES. (1992) *The Consequences of Peace: The New Internationalism and American Foreign Policy*. New York: Oxford University Press.

CHALIAND, GÉRALD, AND JEAN-PIERRE RAGEAU. (1992) *A Strategic Atlas*, revised edition. New York: Harper Perennial.

———. (1990) *A Strategic Atlas*. New York: Harper and Row.

CHAN, STEVE. (1987) "Military Expenditures and Economic Performance," pp. 29–37 in U.S. Arms Control and Disarmament Agency, *World Military Expenditures and Arms Transfers 1986*. Washington, D.C.: U.S. Government Printing Office.

———. (1984) "Mirror, Mirror on the Wall . . .: Are the Free Countries More Pacific?" *Journal of Conflict Resolution* 28 (December): 617–648.

CHATTERJEE, PARTHA. (1993) *The Nation and Its Fragments*. Princeton, N.J.: Princeton University Press.

CHERNUS, IRA. (1987) *Dr. Strangegod: On the Symbolic Meaning of Nuclear Weapons*. Columbia: University of South Carolina Press.

CHILDE, V. GORDON. (1962) *Man Makes Himself*. New York: Mentor Books.

CHISWICK, BARRY R. (1990) "Reopening the Golden Door," *Washington Post National Weekly Edition* 7 (October 15–21): 25.

CHOUCHRI, NAZLI, AND ROBERT C. NORTH. (1975) *Nations in Conflict*. San Francisco: Freeman.

CHUBIN, SHAHRAM. (1995) "Southern Perspectives on World Order," pp. 166–178 in Charles W. Kegley Jr. and Eugene R. Wittkopf (eds.), *The Global Agenda*, 4th ed. New York: McGraw-Hill.

CHURCHILL, WINSTON. (1948–1953) *The Second World War*. Boston: Houghton Mifflin.

———. (1948) *The Second World War: The Gathering Storm*. Boston: Houghton Mifflin.

CLAIBORNE, WILLIAM. (1990) "South Africa's Quiet Revolution," *Washington Post National Weekly Edition* 7 (January 22–28): 24–25.

CLANCY, TOM, AND RUSSELL SEITZ. (1991–1992) "Five Minutes Past Midnight—and Welcome to the New Age of Proliferation," *The National Interest* 26 (Winter): 3–17.

CLAUDE, INIS L., JR. (1992) "Collective Security after the Cold War," pp. 7–28 in Inis Claude, Sheldon Simon, and Douglas Stuart, *Collective Security in Europe and Asia*. Carlisle Barracks, Penn.: Strategic Studies Institute, U.S. Army War College.

———. (1989) "The Balance of Power Revisited," *Review of International Studies* 15 (January): 77–85.

———. (1988) *States and the Global System: Politics, Law, and Organization*. New York: St. Martin's Press.

———. (1971) *Swords into Plowshares*, 4th ed. New York: Random House.

———. (1967) *The Changing United Nations*. New York: Random House.

———. (1962) *Power and International Relations*. New York: Random House.

von CLAUSEWITZ, KARL. (1976 [1832]) *On War*. Princeton, N.J.: Princeton University Press.

COBB, ROGER, AND CHARLES ELDER. (1970) *International Community*. New York: Harcourt, Brace & World.

COHEN, BENJAMIN J. (1989) "A Global Chapter 11," *Foreign Policy* 75 (Summer): 109–127.

———. (1983) "Trade and Unemployment: Global Bread-and-Butter Issues," *Worldview* 26 (January): 9–11.

———. (1973) *The Question of Imperialism*. New York: Basic Books.

COHEN, ELIOT A. (1995) "The Future of Military Power: The Continuing Utility of Force," pp. 35–43 in Charles W. Kegley Jr. and Eugene R. Wittkopf (eds.), *The Global Agenda*, 4th ed. New York: McGraw-Hill.

———. (1991) "After the Battle: A Defense Primer for the Next Century," *The New Republic* 207 (April 1): 19–26.

COLCLOUGH, CHRISTOPHER, AND JAMES MANOR. (eds.) (1991) *States or Markets? Neo-Liberalism and the Development Policy Debate*. New York: Oxford University Press.

COLLINS, JOHN M. (1994) *Military Preparedness: Principles Compared with U.S. Practices*. Washington, D.C.: Congressional Research Service.

COLLINS, SUSAN M., AND DANI RODRIK. (1991) *Eastern Europe and the Soviet Union in the World Economy*. Washington, D.C.: Institute for International Economics.

COMMAGER, HENRY STEELE. (1983) "Misconceptions Governing American Foreign Policy," pp. 510–517 in Charles W. Kegley Jr. and Eugene R. Wittkopf (eds.), *Perspectives on American Foreign Policy*. New York: St. Martin's Press.

COMMISSION ON TRANSNATIONAL CORPORATIONS. (1991) "Recent Developments Related to Transnational Corporations and International Economic Relations," U.N. Doc. E/E.10/1991/2, United Nations Economic and Social Council.

CONGRESSIONAL RESEARCH SERVICE. (1991) *Soviet–U.S. Relations*. Washington, D.C.: U.S. Congressional Research Service.

CONOVER, PAMELA J., AND STANLEY FELDMAN. (1984) "How People Organize the Political World: A Schematic Model," *American Journal of Political Science* 28 (February): 95–126.

COPLIN, WILLIAM D. (1971) *Introduction to International Politics*. Chicago: Markham.

———. (1966) *The Functions of International Law*. Chicago: Rand McNally.

———. (1965) "International Law and Assumptions About the State System," *World Politics* 17 (July): 615–634.

COSER, LEWIS. (1956) *The Functions of Social Conflict*. London: Routledge & Kegan Paul.

COX, MICHAEL. (1991) "From the Truman Doctrine to the Second Superpower Detente: The Rise and Fall of the Cold War," *Journal of Peace Research* 27 (February): 25–41.

CRAIG, GORDON A., AND ALEXANDER L. GEORGE. (1990) *Force and Statecraft*, 2nd ed. New York: Oxford University Press.

CRENSHAW, MARTHA. (1990) "Is International Terrorism Primarily State-Sponsored?" pp. 163–169 in Charles W. Kegley Jr. (ed.), *International Terrorism: Characteristics, Causes, Controls*. New York: St. Martin's Press.

CUSACK, THOMAS R., AND RICHARD J. STOLL. (1990) *Exploring Realpolitik*. Boulder, Colo.: Lynne Rienner.

CUSHMAN, JOHN H., JR. (1993) "Cold War Secret Revealed: 204 Nuclear Blasts by U.S.," *New York Times* (December 8): A12.

CUTLER, LLOYD N. (1978) *Global Interdependence and the Multinational Firm*. Headline Series No. 239 (April). New York: Foreign Policy Association.

D'AMATO, ANTHONY. (1982) "What 'Counts' as Law?" pp. 83–107 in Nicholas Greenwood Onuf (ed.), *Law-Making in the Global Community*. Durham, N.C.: Carolina Academic Press.

DALY, HERMAN E. (1973) "Introduction," pp. 1–29 in Herman E. Daly (ed.), *Toward a Steady-State Economy*. San Francisco: Freeman.

DALY, HERMAN E., AND JOHN B. COBB JR. (1989) *For the Common Good*. Boston: Beacon Press.

DARMSTADTER, JOEL, AND HANS H. LANDSBERG. (1976) "The Economic Background," pp. 15–37 in Raymond Vernon (ed.), *The Oil Crisis*. New York: Norton.

DAVID, STEVEN R. (1994) "Why the Third World Still Matters," pp. 236–246 in Eugene R. Wittkopf (ed.), *The Future of American Foreign Policy*. New York: St. Martin's Press.

DAVIDSON, KEAY. (1991) "Slashing U.S. Nuclear Arsenal Now Thinkable," *Sunday Advocate* (Baton Rouge, La.) (November 10): E1.

DAVIS, BOB. (1994) "Global Paradox: Growth of Trade Binds Nations but It Can Also Spur Separatism," *Wall Street Journal* (June 20): A1, A10.

DEGER, SAADET, AND RON SMITH. (1983) "Military Expansion and Growth in Less Developed Countries," *Journal of Conflict Resolution* 27 (June): 335–353.

DEHIO, LUDWIG. (1962) *The Precarious Balance*. New York: Knopf.

DENTZER, SUSAN. (1993) "Meet the New Economic Bogymen," *U.S. News and World Report* (October 18): 67.

DER DERIAN, JAMES, AND MICHAEL J. SHAPIRO. (eds.) (1989) *International/Intertextual Relations: Postmodern Readings of World Politics*. Lexington, Mass.: D.C. Heath.

DeRIVERA, JOSEPH H. (1968) *The Psychological Dimension of Foreign Policy*. Columbus, Ohio: Merrill.

DE RUYT, JEAN. (1989) *European Political Cooperation: Toward a Unified European Foreign Policy*. Washington, D.C.: Atlantic Council of the United States.

DESTLER, I. M., AND C. RANDALL HENNING. (1989) *Dollar Politics: Exchange Rate Policymaking in the United States*. Washington, D.C.: Institute for International Economics.

DE TOCQUEVILLE, ALEXIS. (1969 [1835]) *Democracy in America*. New York: Doubleday.

DEUDNEY, DANIEL, AND G. JOHN IKENBERRY. (1992) "Who Won the Cold War?" *Foreign Policy* 87 (Summer): 123–138.

———. (1991–1992) "The International Sources of Soviet Change," *International Security* 16 (Winter): 74–118.

DEUTSCH, KARL W. (1974) *Politics and Government*. Boston: Houghton Mifflin.

———. (1953) "The Growth of Nations: Some Recurrent Patterns in Political and Social Integration," *World Politics* 5 (October): 168–195.

DEUTSCH, KARL W., SIDNEY A. BURRELL, ROBERT A. KANN, MAURICE LEE JR., MARTIN LICHTERMAN, RAYMOND E. LINDGREN, FRANCIS L. LOEWENHEIM, AND RICHARD W. VAN WAGENEN. (1957) *Political Community and the North Atlantic Area*. Princeton, N.J.: Princeton University Press.

DEUTSCH, KARL W., AND RICHARD L. MERRITT. (1965) "Effects of Events on National and International Images," pp. 132–187 in Herbert C. Kelman (ed.), *International Behavior*. New York: Holt, Rinehart & Winston.

DEUTSCH, KARL W., AND J. DAVID SINGER. (1964) "Multipolar Power Systems and International Stability," *World Politics* 16 (April): 390–406.

*Development Cooperation: 1991 Report*. (1991) Paris: Organisation for Economic Co-operation and Development.

DE VITA, CAROL J. (1989) *America in the 21st Century: A Demographic Overview*. Washington, D.C.: Population Reference Bureau.

DIAMOND, LARRY, AND MARC F. PLATTNER. (eds.) (1993) *The Global Resurgence of Democracy*. Baltimore: Johns Hopkins University Press.

DIETRICH, WILLIAM S. (1992) *In the Shadow of the Rising Sun: The Political Roots of American Economic Decline*. University Park: Penn State Press.

DILLIN, JOHN. (1994) "Earth's Vital Signs: A Mixed Bag," *Christian Science Monitor* June 15: 8.

DiRENZO, GORDON J. (ed.) (1974) *Personality and Politics*. Garden City, N.Y.: Doubleday-Anchor.

DIXON, WILLIAM J. (1994) "Democracy and the Peaceful Settlement of International Conflict," *American Political Science Review* 88 (March): 14–32.

DOBBS, MICHAEL. (1991) "Disaster, Nuclear and Bureaucratic," *Washington Post National Weekly Edition* 8 (May 6–12): 10–11.

DORAN, CHARLES F. (1991) *Systems in Crisis: New Imperatives of High Politics at Century's End*. Cambridge: Cambridge University Press.

DOXEY, MARGARET. (1990) "International Sanctions," pp. 242–261 in David G. Haglund and Michael K. Hawes (eds.), *World Politics: Power, Interdependence, and Dependence*. Toronto: Harcourt Brace Jovanovich.

DOYLE, MICHAEL W. (1995) "Liberalism and World Politics Revisited," pp. 83–106 in Charles W. Kegley Jr. (ed.), *Controversies in International Relations Theory: Realism and the Neoliberal Challenge*. New York: St. Martin's Press.

DRUCKER, PETER F. (1986) "The Changed World Economy," *Foreign Affairs* 64 (Spring): 768–791.

DULLES, JOHN FOSTER. (1939) *War, Peace, and Change*. New York: Harper.

DURCH, WILLIAM J. (1993a) *The Evolution of UN Peacekeeping*. New York: St. Martin's Press.

———. (1993b) *The United Nations and Collective Security in the 21st Century*. Carlisle Barracks, Penn.: U.S. Army War College.

DURNING, ALAN THEIN. (1993) "Supporting Indigenous Peoples," pp. 80–100 in Lester R. Brown et al., *State of the World 1993*. New York: Norton.

———. (1991) "Asking How Much Is Enough," pp. 153–169 in Lester R. Brown et al., *State of the World 1991*. New York: Norton.

———. (1990) "Ending Poverty," pp. 135–153 in Lester R. Brown et al., *State of the World 1990*. New York: Norton.

———. (1989) *Poverty and the Environment: Reversing the Downward Spiral*. WorldWatch Paper No. 92. Washington, D.C.: Worldwatch Institute.

EASTON, DAVID. (1969) "The New Revolution in Political Science," *American Political Science Review* 63 (December): 1051–1061.

EASTON, STEWART C. (1964) *The Rise and Fall of Western Colonialism*. New York: Praeger.

EBERSTADT, NICHOLAS. (1991) "Population Change and National Security," *Foreign Affairs* 70 (Summer): 115–131.

EBINGER, CHARLES. (1985) "A 'Complacent' U.S. Courts New Oil Crisis," *U.S. News and World Report* (May 27): 37–38.

ECKHARDT, WILLIAM. (1991) "War-Related Deaths since 3000 BC," *Bulletin of Peace Proposals* 22 (December): 437–443.

———. (1990) "Civilization, Empires and Wars," *Journal of Peace Research* 27 (February): 9–24.

*The Economist*. (1992) *World in Figures, 1993 Edition*. London: The Economist Books.

EHRLICH, PAUL R., AND ANNE H. EHRLICH. (1990) *The Population Explosion*. New York: Simon & Schuster.

EHRLICH, PAUL R., ANNE H. EHRLICH, AND JOHN P. HOLDREN. (1977) *Ecoscience*. San Francisco: Freeman.

ELLIOTT, KIMBERLY ANN. (1993) "Sanctions: A Look at the Record," *Bulletin of the Atomic Scientists* 49 (November): 32–35.

EMMANUEL, ARGHIRI. (1972) *Unequal Exchange: An Essay on the Imperialism of Trade*. New York: Monthly Review Press.

ENLOE, CYNTHIA. (1993) *The Morning After: Sexual Politics at the End of the Cold War*. Berkeley: University of California Press.

ESTY, DANIEL C. (1994) *Greening the GATT: Trade, Environment, and the Future*. Washington, D.C.: Institute for International Economics.

ETZIONI, AMITAL. (1968) "Toward a Sociological Theory of Peace," pp. 403–428 in Leon Bramson and George W. Goethals (eds.), *War*. New York: Basic Books.

EUROPEAN COMMUNITY IN THE NINETIES, THE. (1992) Washington, D.C.: Delegation to the United States.

EVANS, PETER B. (1993) "Dependency," pp. 231–233 in Joel Krieger (ed.), *The Oxford Companion to Politics of the World*. New York: Oxford University Press.

FALCOFF, MARK. (1990) "First World, Third World, Which World?" *The American Enterprise* 1 (July/August): 13–14.

FALK, RICHARD A. (1992) *Explorations at the Edge of Time: The Prospects for World Order*. Philadelphia: Temple University Press.

———. (1970) *The Status of Law in International Society*. Princeton, N.J.: Princeton University Press.

———. (1965) "World Law and Human Conflict," pp. 227–249 in Elton B. McNeil (ed.), *The Nature of Human Conflict*. Englewood Cliffs, N.J.: Prentice-Hall.

———. (1964) *The Role of Domestic Courts in the International Legal Order*. Syracuse, N.Y.: Syracuse University Press.

FALKENHEIM, PEGGY L. (1987) "Post-Afghanistan Sanctions," pp. 105–130 in David Leyton-Brown (ed.), *The Utility of International Economic Sanctions*. New York: St. Martin's Press.

FALLOWS, JAMES. (1994) *Looking at the Sun: The Rise of the New East Asian Economic and Political System*. New York: Pantheon.

———. (1983) "Immigration: How It's Affecting Us," *The Atlantic* 252 (November): 45–52.

FEINBERG, RICHARD E., AND DELIA M. BOYLAN. (1992) "Modular Multilateralism: North–South Economic Relations in the 1990s," *Washington Quarterly* 15 (Winter): 187–199.

———. (1991) *Modular Multilateralism: North–South Economic Relations in the 1990s*. Washington, D.C.: Overseas Development Council.

FELD, WERNER J., AND ROBERT S. JORDAN, WITH LEON HURWITZ. (1994) *International Organizations: A Comparative Approach*, 3rd ed. Westport, Conn.: Praeger.

FELDSTEIN, MARTIN. (1985) "American Economic Policy and the World Economy," *Foreign Affairs* 63 (Summer): 995–1008.

FERENCZ, BENJAMIN B., AND KEN KEYES JR. (1991) *PlanetHood*. Coos Bay, Ore.: Love Line Books.

FERGUSON, YALE H., AND RICHARD W. MANSBACH. (1988) *The Elusive Quest: Theory and International Politics*. Columbia: University of South Carolina Press.

FESTINGER, LEON. (1957) *A Theory of Cognitive Dissonance*. Evanston, Ill.: Row, Peterson.

FETTER, STEVE. (1991) "Ballistic Missiles and Weapons of Mass Destruction: What Is the Threat? What Should Be Done?" *International Security* 16 (Summer): 5–42.

FIELDHOUSE, D. K. (1973) *Economics and Empire, 1830–1914*. Ithaca, N.Y.: Cornell University Press.

"Financing the United Nations." (n.d.) UNA-USA Fact Sheet. United Nations Association of the United States of America.

FISCHER, FRITZ. (1967) *Germany's Aims after the First World War*. New York: Norton.

FLAVIN, CHRISTOPHER. (1992) "Building a Bridge to Sustainable Energy," pp. 27–45 in Lester R. Brown et al., *State of the World 1992*. New York: Norton.

———. (1991–1992) "The Global Challenges of the Coming Energy Revolution," *Harvard International Review* 14 (Winter): 4–6, 60–61.

———. (1987) *Reassessing Nuclear Power: The Fallout from Chernobyl*. WorldWatch Paper No. 75. Washington, D.C.: WorldWatch Institute.

FLAVIN, CHRISTOPHER, AND NICHOLAS LENSSEN. (1991) "Designing a Sustainable Energy System," pp. 21–38 in Lester R. Brown et al., *State of the World 1991*. New York: Norton.

FØRLAND, TOR EGIL. (1993) "The History of Economic Warfare: International Law, Effectiveness, Strategies," *Journal of Peace Research* 30 (May): 151–162.

FOSTER, GREGORY D. (1989) "Global Demographic Trends to the Year 2010: Implications for U.S. Security," *Washington Quarterly* 12 (Spring): 5–24.

FOUNDATION FOR TEACHING ECONOMICS AND THE UNITED NATIONS ASSOCIATION OF THE USA. (1992) *International Economic Diplomacy*. Davis, Calif., and New York: Foundation for Teaching Economics and the United Nations Association of the USA.

FRANK, ANDRE GUNDER. (1969) *Latin America: Underdevelopment or Revolution*. New York: Monthly Review Press.

FRANKEL, GLENN. (1987) "Weapons: The Global Commodity," *Washington Post National Weekly Edition* 4 (January 12): 6–7.

FREEMAN, ORVILLE L. (1990) "Meeting the Needs of the Coming Decade: Agriculture vs. the Environment," *Futurist* 24 (November–December): 15–20.

FRENCH, HILARY F. (1991) "The EC: Environmental Proving Ground," *WorldWatch* 4 (December): 26–33.

———. (1990) *Green Revolutions: Environmental Reconstruction in Eastern Europe and the Soviet Union*. WorldWatch Paper No. 99. Washington, D.C.: WorldWatch Institute.

FREUD, SIGMUND. (1968) "Why War," pp. 71–80 in Leon Bramson and George W. Goethals (eds.), *War*. New York: Basic Books.

FRIED, JOHN H. E. (1971) "International Law—Neither Orphan nor Harlot, Neither Jailer nor Never-Never Land," pp. 124–176 in Karl W. Deutsch and Stanley Hoffmann (eds.), *The Relevance of International Law*. Garden City, N.Y.: Doubleday-Anchor.

FRIEDBERG, AARON L. (1993) "The Changing Relationship between Economics and Security," pp. 99–110 in Demetrios Caraley and Cerentha Harris (eds.), *New World Politics: Power, Ethnicity and Democracy*. New York: The Academy of Political Science.

———. (1992) "Is the United States Capable of Acting Strategically?" pp. 95–111 in Charles W. Kegley Jr. and Eugene R. Wittkopf (eds.), *The Future of American Foreign Policy*. New York: St. Martin's Press.

FRIEDEN, JEFF. (1981) "Third World Indebted Industrialization: International Finance and State Capitalism in Mexico, Brazil, Algeria, and South Korea," *International Organization* 35 (Summer): 407–431.

FRIEDHEIM, ROBERT L. (1965) "The 'Satisfied' and 'Dissatisfied' States Negotiate International Law," *World Politics* 18 (October): 20–41.

FRIEDMAN, THOMAS L. (1993) "Friends Like Russia Make Diplomacy a Mess," *New York Times* (March 28): E5.

———. (1992) "Reducing the Russian Arms Threat," *New York Times* (June 17): A7.

FRY, EARL H., STAN A. TAYLOR, AND ROBERT S. WOOD. (1994) *America the Vincible*. Englewood Cliffs, N.J.: Prentice-Hall.

FUKUYAMA, FRANCIS. (1992a) "The Beginning of Foreign Policy," *The New Republic* 207 (August 17 and 24): 24–32.

———. (1992b) *The End of History and the Last Man*. New York: Free Press.

———. (1989) "The End of History?" *The National Interest* 16 (Summer): 3–16.

FULLER, GRAHAM E. (1991–1992) "The Breaking of Nations—and the Threat to Ours," *The National Interest* 26 (Winter): 14–21.

GADDIS, JOHN LEWIS. (1992) *The United States and the End of the Cold War: Implications, Reconsiderations, Provocations*. New York: Oxford University Press.

———. (1991a) "Great Illusions, the Long Peace, and the Future of the International System," pp. 25–55 in Charles W. Kegley Jr. (ed.), *The Long Postwar Peace*. New York: HarperCollins.

———. (1991b) "Toward the Post–Cold War World," *Foreign Affairs* 70 (Spring): 102–122.

———. (1990) "Coping with Victory," *The Atlantic* 265 (May): 49–60.

———. (1986) "The Long Peace: Elements of Stability in the Postwar International System," *International Security* 10 (Spring): 99–142.

———. (1983) "Containment: Its Past and Future," pp. 16–31 in Charles W. Kegley Jr. and Eugene R. Wittkopf (eds.), *Perspectives on American Foreign Policy*. New York: St. Martin's Press.

———. (1972) *The United States and the Origins of the Cold War*. New York: Columbia University Press.

GALTUNG, JOHAN. (1969) "Violence, Peace, and Peace Research," *Journal of Peace Research* 6 (No. 3): 167–191.

GARDELS, NATHAN. (1991) "Two Concepts of Nationalism," *New York Review of Books* 38 (November 21): 19–23.

GARDNER, LLOYD C. (1970) *Architects of Illusion*. Chicago: Quadrangle.

GARTEN, JEFFREY E. (1992) *A Cold Peace: America, Japan, Germany and the Struggle for Supremacy*. New York: Random House.

GELB, LESLIE H. (1993) "Tailoring a U.S. Role at the U.N.," *International Herald Tribune* (January 2–3): 4.

———. (1979) "The Future of Arms Control: A Glass Half Full," *Foreign Policy* 36 (Fall): 21–32.

GELB, LESLIE H., AND MORTON H. HALPERIN. (1973) "The Ten Commandments of the Foreign Affairs Bureaucracy," pp. 250–259 in Steven L. Spiegel (ed.), *At Issue*. New York: St. Martin's Press.

GENERAL AGREEMENT ON TARIFFS AND TRADE (GATT). (1993) *1993 Statistics: International Trade*. Geneva: General Agreement on Tariffs and Trade.

GEORGE, ALEXANDER L. (1993) *Bridging the Gap: Theory and Practice in Foreign Policy*. Washington, D.C.: U.S. Institute of Peace.

———. (1992) *Forceful Persuasion: Coercive Diplomacy as an Alternative to War*. Washington, D.C.: United States Institute of Peace.

———. (1986) "U.S.–Soviet Global Rivalry: Norms of Competition," *Journal of Peace Research* 23 (September): 247–262.

———. (1972) "The Case for Multiple Advocacy in Making Foreign Policy," *American Political Science Review* 66 (September): 751–785.

GERMAN, F. CLIFFORD. (1960) "A Tentative Evaluation of World Power," *Journal of Conflict Resolution* 4 (March): 138–144.

GILL, STEPHEN. (1993a) "Group of 7," pp. 369–370 in Joel Krieger (ed.), *The Oxford Companion to Politics of the World*. New York: Oxford University Press.

———. (1993b) "Hegemony," pp. 385–386 in Joel Krieger (ed.), *The Oxford Companion to Politics of the World*. New York: Oxford University Press.

GILL, STEPHEN, AND DAVID LAW. (1988) *The Global Political Economy*. Baltimore: Johns Hopkins University Press.

GILPIN, ROBERT. (1987) *The Political Economy of International Relations*. Princeton, N.J: Princeton University Press.

———. (1985) "The Politics of Transnational Economic Relations," pp. 171–194 in Ray Maghroori and Bennett Ramberg (eds.), *Globalism versus Realism: International Relations' Third Debate*. Boulder, Colo.: Westview.

———. (1984) "The Richness of the Tradition of Political Realism," *International Organization* 38 (Spring): 287–304.

———. (1981) *War and Change in World Politics*. Cambridge: Cambridge University Press.

———. (1975) *U.S. Power and the Multinational Corporation*. New York: Basic Books.

VON GLAHN, GERHARD. (1992) *Law among Nations*, 6th ed. New York: Macmillan.

GLEDITSCH, NILS PETTER. (1992) "Democracy and Peace," *Journal of Peace Research* 29 (November): 369–376.

GOCHMAN, CHARLES S., AND ZEEV MAOZ. (1984) "Militarized Interstate Disputes, 1816–1976: Procedures, Patterns, and Insights," *Journal of Conflict Resolution* 28 (December): 585–616.

GOLDBLAT, JOZEF. (1982) *Agreements for Arms Control: A Critical Survey*. London: Taylor & Francis.

GOLDSTEIN, JOSHUA S. (1994) *International Relations*. New York: HarperCollins.

———. (1991) "The Possibility of Cycles in International Relations," *International Studies Quarterly* 35 (December): 477–480.

———. (1988) *Long Cycles: Prosperity and War in the Modern Age*. New Haven, Conn.: Yale University Press.

GOODGAME, DAN. (1993) "Trading Punches," *Time* (June 21): 24.

GORDON, MICHAEL R. (1993a) "As Its World View Narrows, Russia Seeks a New Mission," *New York Times* (November 29): A1, A7.

———. (1993b) "Israel Sells China Arms, C.I.A. Says," *New York Times* (October 13): A7.

———. (1993c). "U.S. Seeking to Ease 1972 Treaty Limits on Missile Defenses," *New York Times* (December 3): A7.

GORE, AL. (1992) *Earth in the Balance: Ecology and the Human Spirit*. Boston: Houghton Mifflin.

GOSHKO, JOHN M., AND THOMAS. W. LIPPMANN. (1993) "Foreign Policy Painted with a Broader Brush," *Washington Post National Weekly Edition* 11 (December 6–12): 18.

GOTTLIEB, GIDON. (1982) "Global Bargaining: The Legal and Diplomatic Framework," pp. 109–130 in Nicholas Greenwood Onuf (ed.), *Law-Making in the Global Community*. Durham, N.C.: Carolina Academic Press.

GRAHAM, THOMAS R. (1979) "Revolution in Trade Politics," *Foreign Policy* 26 (Fall): 49–63.

GRANT, REBECCA, AND KATHLEEN NEWLAND. (eds.) (1991) *Gender and International Relations*. Bloomington: Indiana University Press.

GRAYBEAL, SIDNEY N., AND MICHAEL KREPON. (1994) "Its Not Son of Star Wars," *The Bulletin of the Atomic Scientists* 50 (March/April): 16–17.

GREENHOUSE, STEVEN. (1992) "Ecology, the Economy and Bush," *New York Times* (June 14): 1, 6.

GREENSTEIN, FRED I. (1987) *Personality and Politics*. Princeton, N.J.: Princeton University Press.

GREENWAY, H. D. S. (1993) "Racism Can Wear Multicultural Cloak," *The State* (Columbia, S.C.) (June 14): A9.

GREGG, ROBERT W. (1977) "The Apportioning of Political Power," pp. 69–80 in David A. Kay (ed.), *The Changing United Nations*. New York: Academy of Political Science.

GREY, EDWARD. (1925) *Twenty-five Years, 1892–1916*. New York: Frederick Stokes.

GRIECO, JOSEPH M. (1995) "Anarchy and the Limits of Cooperation: A Realist Critique of the Newest Liberal Institutionalism," pp. 151–171 in Charles W. Kegley Jr. (ed.), *Controversies in International Relations Theory: Realism and the Neoliberal Challenge*. New York: St. Martin's Press.

———. (1990) *Cooperation among Nations: Europe, America, and Non-Tariff Barriers to Trade*. Ithaca, N.Y.: Cornell University Press.

———. (1988) "Realist Theory and the Problem of International Cooperation: Analysis with an Amended Prisoner's Dilemma Model," *Journal of Politics* 50 (August): 600–624.

GRIER, PETER. (1994) "United States Takes Lion's Share of Arms Deals around the World," *Christian Science Monitor* (April 5): 3.

GRUBB, MICHAEL. (1990) "The Greenhouse Effect: Negotiating Targets," *International Affairs* 66 (January): 67–89.

GRUHN, ISEBILL V. (1976) "The Lomé Convention: Inching toward Interdependence," *International Organization* 30 (Spring): 241–262.

GULICK, EDWARD VOSE. (1955) *Europe's Classical Balance of Power*. Ithaca, N.Y.: Cornell University Press.

GURR, TED ROBERT. (1994) "Peoples against States: Ethnopolitical Conflict and the Changing World System," *International Studies Quarterly* 38 (September): 347–377.

———. (1993) *Minorities at Risk: A Global View of Ethnopolitical Conflicts*. Washington, D.C.: United States Institute of Peace.

———. (1990) "Ethnic Warfare and the Changing Priorities of Global Security," *Mediterranean Quarterly* 1 (Winter): 82–98.

———. (1970) *Why Men Rebel*. Princeton, N.J.: Princeton University Press.

HAAS, ERNST B. (1986) *Why We Still Need the United Nations: The Collective Management of International Conflict, 1945–1984.* Berkeley: Institute of International Studies, University of California.

———. (1983) "Regime Decay: Conflict Management and International Organizations, 1945–1981," *International Organization* 37 (Spring): 189–256.

———. (1969) *Tangle of Hopes.* Englewood Cliffs, N.J.: Prentice-Hall.

———. (1953) "The Balance of Power: Prescription, Concept, or Propaganda?" *World Politics* 5 (July): 442–477.

HAAS, ERNST B., AND ALLEN S. WHITING. (1956) *Dynamics of International Relations.* New York: McGraw-Hill.

HAGAN, JOE D. (1993) *Political Opposition and Foreign Policy in Comparative Perspective.* Boulder, Colo.: Lynne Rienner.

HAGGARD, STEPHAN, AND BETH A. SIMMONS. (1987) "Theories of International Regimes," *International Organization* 41 (Summer): 491–517.

HALL, JOHN A. (1993) "Liberalism," pp. 538–542 in Joel Krieger (ed.), *The Oxford Companion to Politics of the World.* Oxford: Oxford University Press.

HALLENBECK, RALPH A., AND DAVID E. SHAVER. (eds.) (1991) *On Disarmament.* New York: Praeger.

HAMMOND, GRANT T. (1993) *Plowshares into Swords: Arms Races in International Politics, 1840–1991.* Columbia: University of South Carolina Press.

HANRIEDER, WOLFRAM F. (1978) "Dissolving International Politics: Reflections on the Nation-State," *American Political Science Review* 72 (December): 1276–1287.

HANSEN, ROGER D. (1980) "North–South Policy—What's the Problem?" *Foreign Affairs* 58 (Summer): 1104–1128.

———. (1979) *The North–South Stalemate.* New York: McGraw-Hill.

HANSON, PHILIP. (1991) "Soviet Economic Reform: Perestroika or 'Catastroika'?" *World Policy Journal* 8 (Spring): 289–318.

HARDEN, BLAINE. (1987) "AIDS May Replace Famine as the Continent's Worst Blight," *Washington Post National Weekly Edition* 4 (June 15): 16–17.

HARDIN, GARRETT. (1968) "The Tragedy of the Commons," *Science* 162 (December): 1243–1248.

HARPER, LUCINDA. (1994) "Trade Deficit Narrowed in December, but Gap for '93 was Largest in 5 Years," *Wall Street Journal* (February 18): A2.

HARRIS, NIGEL. (1987) *The End of the Third World*, Vol 1. Harmondsworth, England: Pelican.

HARRISON, SELIG S. (1993) "Japan's Second Thoughts about Nuclear Weapons: With Its Neighbors Armed to the Teeth, Will Tokyo Join the Club?" *Washington Post National Weekly Edition* 11 (November 8–14): 23–24.

HART, JEFFREY A. (1992) *Rival Capitalists: International Competitiveness in the United States, Japan, and Western Europe.* Ithaca, N.Y.: Cornell University Press.

HASSNER, PIERRE. (1968) "The Nation-State in the Nuclear Age," *Survey* 67 (April): 3–27.

HAYTER, TERESA. (1971) *Aid as Imperialism.* Baltimore: Penguin.

HEAD, IVAN L. (1989) "South–North Dangers," *Foreign Affairs* 68 (Summer): 71–86.

HEILBRONER, ROBERT L. (1991) *An Inquiry into the Human Prospect: Looked at Again for the 1990s.* New York: Norton.

———. (1977) "The Multinational Corporation and the Nation-State," pp. 338–352 in Steven L. Spiegel (ed.), *At Issue: Politics in the World Arena.* New York: St. Martin's Press.

HEILIG, GERHARD, THOMAS BÜTTNER, AND WOLFGANG LUTZ. (1990) "Germany's Population: Turbulent Past, Uncertain Future," *Population Bulletin* 45 (No. 4). Washington, D.C: Population Reference Bureau.

HELMAN, UDI. (1990) "Environment and the National Interest: An Analytical Survey of the Literature," *Washington Quarterly* 13 (Autumn): 193–206.

HENDRICKSON, DAVID C. (1993) "The Ethics of Collective Security," *Ethics and International Affairs* 7: 1–15.

HENKIN, LOUIS. (1991) "The Use of Force: Law and U.S. Policy," pp. 37–69 in Stanley Hoffmann et al. (eds.), *Right v. Might: International Law and the Use of Force*, 2nd ed. New York: Council on Foreign Relations.

HENRY, JAMES S. (1987) "Brazil Says: Nuts," *New Republic* 202 (October 12): 25, 28–29.

HERMANN, CHARLES F. (1988) "New Foreign Policy Problems and Old Bureaucratic Organizations," pp. 248–265 in Charles W. Kegley Jr. and Eugene R. Wittkopf (eds.), *The Domestic Sources of American Foreign Policy.* New York: St. Martin's Press.

———. (1972) "Some Issues in the Study of International Crisis," pp. 3–17 in Charles F. Hermann (ed.), *International Crises.* New York: Free Press.

HERMANN, CHARLES F., CHARLES W. KEGLEY JR., AND JAMES N. ROSENAU. (eds.) (1987) *New Directions in the Study of Foreign Policy.* Boston: Allen & Unwin.

HERMANN, MARGARET G. (1988) "The Role of Leaders and Leadership in the Making of American Foreign Policy," pp.

266–284 in Charles W. Kegley Jr. and Eugene R. Wittkopf (eds.), *The Domestic Sources of American Foreign Policy*. New York: St. Martin's Press.

———. (1987) "Role Theory and Foreign Policy Dynamics: The African Arena," pp. 161–198 in Stephen G. Walker (ed.), *Role Theory and Foreign Policy Analysis*. Durham, N.C.: Duke University Press.

———. (1976) "When Leader Personality Will Affect Foreign Policy: Some Propositions," pp. 326–333 in James N. Rosenau (ed.), *In Search of Global Patterns*. New York: Free Press.

HERMANN, MARGARET G., AND CHARLES F. HERMANN. (1989) "Who Makes Foreign Policy Choices and How: An Empirical Inquiry," *International Studies Quarterly* 33 (December): 361–387.

HERZ, JOHN H. (1951) *Political Realism and Political Idealism*. Chicago: University of Chicago Press.

HIGGINS, BENJAMIN, AND JEAN DOWNING HIGGINS. (1979) *Economic Development of a Small Planet*. New York: Norton.

HILSMAN, ROGER. (1967) *To Move a Nation*. New York: Doubleday.

HOAGLAND, JIM. (1993a) "A Breakthrough for Clinton Too," *Washington Post National Weekly Edition* 10 (September 20–26): 29.

———. (1993b) "Economic Sanctions Sometimes Do More Harm Than Good," *The State* (Columbia, S.C.) (November 11): A12.

HOEBEL, E. ADAMSON. (1961) *The Law of Primitive Man*. Cambridge, Mass.: Harvard University Press.

HOFFMANN, STANLEY. (1993) "The Passion of Modernity," *The Atlantic Monthly* 272 (August): 101–109.

———. (1992) "To the Editors," *The New York Review of Books* 40 (June 24): 59.

———. (1971) "International Law and the Control of Force," pp. 34–66 in Karl W. Deutsch and Stanley Hoffmann (eds.), *The Relevance of International Law*. Garden City, N.Y.: Doubleday-Anchor.

———. (1961) "International Systems and International Law," pp. 205–237 in Klaus Knorr and Sidney Verba (eds.), *The International System*. Princeton, N.J.: Princeton University Press.

———. (1960) *Contemporary Theory in International Politics*. Englewood Cliffs, N.J.: Prentice-Hall.

HOLLOWAY, DAVID. (1983) *The Soviet Union and the Arms Race*. New Haven, Conn.: Yale University Press.

HOLSTI, KALEVI J. (1992) *International Politics: A Framework for Analysis*, 6th ed. Englewood Cliffs, N.J.: Prentice-Hall.

———. (1991) *Peace and War: Armed Conflicts and International Order, 1648–1989*. Cambridge: Cambridge University Press.

———. (1988) *International Politics: A Framework for Analysis*, 5th ed. Englewood Cliffs, N.J.: Prentice-Hall.

———. (1982) *Why Nations Realign: Foreign Policy Restructuring since World War II*. London: Allen & Unwin.

———. (1970) "National Role Conceptions in the Study of Foreign Policy," *International Studies Quarterly* 14 (September): 233–309.

HOLSTI, OLE R. (1989a) "Crisis Decision Making," pp. 8–84 in Philip E. Tetlock, Jo L. Husbands, Robert Jervis, Paul C. Stern, and Charles Tilly (eds.), *Behavior, Society, and Nuclear War*. New York: Oxford University Press.

———. (1989b) "Models of International Relations and Foreign Policy," *Diplomatic History* 13 (Winter): 15–43.

———. (1972) *Crisis Escalation War*. Montreal: McGill-Queen's University Press.

———. (1962) "The Belief System and National Images: A Case Study," *Journal of Conflict Resolution* 6 (September): 244–252.

HOMER-DIXON, THOMAS F. (1991) "On the Threshold: Environmental Changes as Causes of Acute Conflict," *International Security* 16 (Fall): 76–116.

HOOKS, GREGORY. (1991) *Forging the Military-Industrial Complex*. Urbana, Ill.: University of Illinois Press.

HOPF, TED. (1991) "Polarity, the Offense-Defense Balance, and War," *American Political Science Review* 85 (June): 475–493.

HOUSE, KAREN ELLIOT. (1989) "As Power Is Dispersed among Nations, Need for Leadership Grows," *Wall Street Journal* (February 21): A1, A10.

HOWARD, MICHAEL E. (1983) *The Causes of War*. Cambridge, Mass.: Harvard University Press.

———. (1978) *War and the Liberal Conscience*. New York: Oxford University Press.

HOWELL, LLEWELLYN D. (1993) "The Time Has Come for an International Police Force," *USA Today* 122 (September): 49.

HUFBAUER, GARY CLYDE. (1994) "The Futility of Sanctions," *Wall Street Journal* (June 1): A14.

———. (1989–1990) "Beyond GATT," *Foreign Policy* 77 (Winter): 64–76.

HUFBAUER, GARY CLYDE, JEFFREY J. SCHOTT, AND KIMBERLY ANN ELLIOTT. (1990) *Economic Sanctions Reconsidered: History and Current Policy*, 2nd ed. Washington, D.C.: Institute for International Economics.

HUGHES, BARRY B. (1995) "Evolving Patterns of European Integration and Governance," pp. 223–243 in Charles W.

Kegley Jr. (ed.), *Controversies in International Relations Theory: Realism and the Neoliberal Challenge*. New York: St. Martin's Press.

———. (1994) *Continuity and Change in World Politics: The Clash of Perspectives*, 2nd ed. Englewood Cliffs, N.J.: Prentice-Hall.

HUNTER, ROBERT E. (1988) "Changing Roles for Military Power," *Los Angeles Times* (January 5): 7.

HUNTINGTON, SAMUEL P. (1993) "The Clash of Civilizations?" *Foreign Affairs* 72 (Summer): 22–49.

———. (1991a) "America's Changing Strategic Interests," *Survival* 33 (January/February): 3–17.

———. (1991b) *The Third Wave: Democratization in the Late Twentieth Century*. Norman: University of Oklahoma Press.

———. (1989) "No Exit: The Errors of Declinism," *The National Interest* 17 (Fall): 3–10.

———. (1973) "Transnational Organizations in World Politics," *World Politics* 25 (April): 333–368.

HURWITZ, JON, AND MARK PEFFLEY. (1987) "How Are Foreign Policy Attitudes Structured? A Hierarchical Model," *American Political Science Review* 81 (December): 1099–1120.

HUTH, PAUL. (1988) *Extended Deterrence and the Prevention of War*. New Haven, Conn.: Yale University Press.

HYLAND, WILLIAM G. (1990) "America's New Course," *Foreign Affairs* 69 (Spring): 1–12.

IKLÉ, FRED CHARLES. (1991–1992) "Comrades in Arms," *The National Interest* 26 (Winter): 22–32.

IMPOCO, JIM. (1993) "Smashing Trade Barriers," *Time* (October 11): 71.

INTERNATIONAL ENERGY AGENCY. (1982) *World Energy Outlook*. Paris: Organisation for Economic Co-operation and Development.

INTERNATIONAL INSTITUTE FOR STRATEGIC STUDIES. (1993) *The Military Balance 1993–1994*. London: Brassey's.

ISAAK, ROBERT A. (1991) *International Political Economy: Managing World Economic Change*. Englewood Cliffs, N.J.: Prentice-Hall.

———. (1975) *Individuals and World Politics*. North Scituate, Mass.: Duxbury.

ISLAM, SHADA. (1982) "STABEX Sour Note as Brussels Rings Changes," *South* 24 (October): 71–72.

JACKSON, ROBERT. (1990) *Quasi-States: Sovereignty, International Relations, and the Third World*. Cambridge: Cambridge University Press.

JACOBSON, HAROLD K. (1984) *Networks of Interdependence: International Organizations and the Global Political System*. New York: Knopf.

JACOBSON, JODI. (1989) "Abandoning Homelands," pp. 59–76 in Lester R. Brown et al., *State of the World 1989*. New York: Norton.

JAKOBSON, MAX. (1991) "Filling the World's Most Impossible Job," *World Monitor* 4 (August): 25–33.

JAMES, PATRICK. (1993) "Neorealism as a Research Enterprise: Toward Elaborated Structural Realism," *International Political Science Review* 14 (No. 2): 123–148.

JANIS, IRVING. (1982) *Groupthink: Psychological Studies of Policy Decisions and Fiascoes*, 2nd ed. Boston: Houghton Mifflin.

JANIS, MARK W. (1993) *An Introduction to International Law*, 2nd ed. Boston: Little, Brown.

JENSEN, LLOYD. (1982) *Explaining Foreign Policy*. Englewood Cliffs, N.J.: Prentice-Hall.

JERVIS, ROBERT. (1992) "A Usable Past for the Future," pp. 257–268 in Michael J. Hogan (ed.), *The End of the Cold War*. New York: Cambridge University Press.

———. (1991–1992) "The Future of World Politics: Will It Resemble the Past?" *International Security* 16 (Winter): 39–73.

———. (1991) "Will the New World Be Better?" pp. 7–19 in Robert Jervis and Seweryn Bialer (eds.), *Soviet–American Relations after the Cold War*. Durham, N.C.: Duke University Press.

———. (1982) "Security Regimes," *International Organization* 16 (Spring): 357–378.

———. (1976) *Perception and Misperception in World Politics*. Princeton, N.J.: Princeton University Press.

JOFFE, JOSEF. (1990) "Entangled Forever," *The National Interest* 21 (Fall): 35–40.

———. (1985) "The Foreign Policy of the Federal Republic of Germany," pp. 72–113 in Roy C. Macridis (ed.), *Foreign Policy in World Politics*, 6th ed. Englewood Cliffs, N.J.: Prentice-Hall.

JOHANSEN, ROBERT C. (1995) "Swords into Plowshares: Can Fewer Arms Yield More Security?" pp. 253–279 in Charles W. Kegley Jr. (ed.), *Controversies in International Relations Theory: Realism and the Neoliberal Challenge*. New York: St. Martin's Press.

———. (1991) "Do Preparations for War Increase or Decrease International Security?" pp. 224–244 in Charles W. Kegley Jr. (ed.), *The Long Postwar Peace*. New York: HarperCollins.

JONAH, JAMES O. C. (1991) "Critical Commentary: A Third World View of the Implications of Superpower Collaboration," in Thomas G. Weiss and Meryl A. Kessler (eds.), *Third World Security in the Post–Cold War Era*. Boulder, Colo.: Lynne Rienner.

JONES, DOROTHY V. (1991) *Code of Peace: Ethics and Security in the World of the Warlord States.* Chicago: University of Chicago Press.

JOYNER, CHRISTOPHER. (1995) "The Reality and Relevance of International Law in the Post–Cold War Era," pp. 211–224 in Charles W. Kegley Jr. and Eugene R. Wittkopf (eds.), *The Global Agenda,* 4th ed. New York: McGraw-Hill.

JUDIS, JOHN B. (1993a) "The Divide: History of NAFTA," *The New Republic* 209 (October 11): 26–32.

———. (1993b) "The Foreign Unpolicy," *The New Republic* 209 (July 12): 16–20.

KAISER, DAVID. (1990) *Politics and War: European Conflict from Philip II to Hitler.* Cambridge, Mass.: Harvard University Press.

KAPLAN, MORTON A. (ed.) (1968) *New Approaches to International Relations.* New York: St. Martin's Press.

———. (1957) *System and Process in International Politics.* New York: Wiley.

KAPLAN, MORTON A., AND NICHOLAS DeB. KATZENBACH. (1961) *The Political Foundations of International Law.* New York: Wiley.

KAPLAN, ROBERT. (1994) "The Coming Anarchy," *The Atlantic* 273 (February): 44–76.

KAPLAN, STEPHEN S. (1981) *Diplomacy of Power.* Washington, D.C.: Brookings Institution.

KAPSTEIN, ETHAN BARNABY. (1992) *The Political Economy of National Security: A Global Perspective.* New York: McGraw-Hill.

———. (1991–1992) "*We Are Us:* The Myth of the Multinational," *National Interest* 26 (Winter): 55–62.

KASLOW, AMY. (1994) "Clinton's Trade Tactics Taken to Task, Home and Abroad," *Christian Science Monitor* (March 8): 1, 4.

KEEGAN, JOHN. (1994) *A History of Warfare.* New York: Knopf.

KEENY, SPURGEON M., JR. (1993) "Arms Control during the Transition to the Post–Soviet World," pp. 175–197 in Joseph Kavzel (ed.), *American Defense Annual,* 8th ed. New York: Lexington Books.

KEENY, SPURGEON M., JR., AND WOLFGANG K. H. PANOFSKY. (1981) "MAD vs. NUTS: Can Doctrine or Weaponry Remedy the Mutual Hostage Relationship of the Superpowers?" *Foreign Affairs* 60 (Winter): 287–304.

KEFALAS, A. G. (1992) "The Global Corporation: Its Role in the New World Order," *National Forum* 72 (Fall): 26–30.

KEGLEY, CHARLES W., JR. (ed.) (1995) *Controversies in International Relations Theory: Realism and the Neoliberal Challenge.* New York: St. Martin's Press.

———. (1994) "How Did the Cold War Die? Principles for an Autopsy," *Mershon International Studies Review* 38, Supplement 1 (March): 11–41.

———. (1993) "The Neoidealist Moment in International Studies? Realist Myths and the New International Realities," *International Studies Quarterly* 37 (June): 131–146.

———. (1992) "The New Global Order: The Power of Principle in a Pluralistic World," *Ethics and International Affairs* 6: 21–42.

———. (ed.) (1991) *The Long Postwar Peace: Contending Explanations and Projections.* New York: HarperCollins.

KEGLEY, CHARLES W., JR., AND STEVEN W. HOOK. (1991) "U.S. Foreign Aid and U.N. Voting: Did Reagan's Linkage Strategy Buy Deference or Defiance?" *International Studies Quarterly* 35 (September): 295–312.

KEGLEY, CHARLES W., JR., AND GREGORY A. RAYMOND. (1995) "Networks of Intrigue? Realpolitik, Alliances, and International Security," forthcoming in Frank Wayman and Paul Diehl (eds.), *Reconstructing Realpolitik.* Ann Arbor: University of Michigan Press.

———. (1994) *A Multipolar Peace? Great-Power Politics in the Twenty-first Century.* New York: St. Martin's Press.

———. (1992) "Must We Fear a Post–Cold War Multipolar World?" *Journal of Conflict Resolution* 36 (September): 573–582.

———. (1990) *When Trust Breaks Down: Alliance Norms and World Politics.* Columbia: University of South Carolina Press.

KEGLEY, CHARLES W., JR., AND EUGENE R. WITTKOPF. (1991) *American Foreign Policy: Pattern and Process,* 4th ed. New York: St. Martin's Press.

KELMAN, HERBERT C. (ed.) (1965) *International Behavior: A Social–Psychological Analysis.* New York: Holt, Rinehart & Winston.

——— (1970) "The Role of the Individual in International Relations," *Journal of International Affairs* 24 (No. 1): 1–17.

KELSEN, HANS. (1945) *General Theory of Law and State.* Cambridge, Mass.: Harvard University Press.

KEMP, GEOFFREY. (1990) "Regional Security, Arms Control, and the End of the Cold War," *Washington Quarterly* 13 (Autumn): 33–51.

KENNAN, GEORGE F. (1993) *Around the Cragged Hill: A Personal and Political Philosophy.* New York: Norton.

———. (1984a) *The Fateful Alliance: France, Russia, and the Coming of the First World War.* New York: Pantheon.

———. (1984b) "Soviet–American Relations: The Politics of Discord and Collaboration," pp. 107–120 in Charles W. Kegley Jr. and Eugene R. Wittkopf (eds.), *The Global Agenda*. New York: Random House.

———. (1982) *The Nuclear Delusion*. New York: Pantheon.

———. (1976) "The United States and the Soviet Union, 1917–1976," *Foreign Affairs* 54 (July): 670–690.

———. (1967) *Memoirs*. Boston: Little, Brown.

———. (1954) *Realities of American Foreign Policy*. Princeton, N.J.: Princeton University Press.

———. (1951) *American Diplomacy, 1900–1950*. New York: New American Library.

———. ["X"] (1947) "The Sources of Soviet Conduct," *Foreign Affairs* 25 (July): 566–582.

KENNEDY, PAUL. (1993) *Preparing for the Twenty-First Century*. New York: Random House.

———. (1992) "A Declining Empire Goes to War," pp. 344–346 in Charles W. Kegley Jr. and Eugene R. Wittkopf (eds.), *The Future of American Foreign Policy*. New York: St. Martin's Press.

———. (1987) *The Rise and Fall of the Great Powers*. New York: Random House.

KEOHANE, ROBERT O. (1989) "International Relations Theory: Contributions from a Feminist Standpoint," *Millennium* 18 (Summer): 245–253.

———. (ed.) (1986a) *Neorealism and Its Critics*. New York: Columbia University Press.

———. (1986b) "Realism, Neorealism and the Study of World Politics," pp. 1–26 in Robert O. Keohane (ed.), *Neorealism and Its Critics*. New York: Columbia University Press.

———. (1984) *After Hegemony: Cooperation and Discord in the World Political Economy*. Princeton, N.J.: Princeton University Press.

———. (1983) "Theory of World Politics: Structural Realism and Beyond," pp. 503–540 in Ada Finifter (ed.), *Political Science: The State of the Discipline*. Washington, D.C.: American Political Science Association.

KEOHANE, ROBERT O., AND STANLEY HOFFMANN. (1991) "Institutional Change in Europe in the 1980s," pp. 1–39 in Robert O. Keohane and Stanley Hoffmann (eds.), *The New European Community: Decisionmaking and Institutional Change*. Boulder, Colo.: Westview.

KEOHANE, ROBERT O., AND JOSEPH S. NYE JR. (1989) *Power and Interdependence*, 2nd ed. Glenview, Ill.: Scott, Foresman/Little Brown.

———. (1988) "Complex Interdependence, Transnational Relations, and Realism: Alternative Perspectives on World Politics," pp. 257–271 in Charles W. Kegley Jr. and Eugene R. Wittkopf (eds.), *The Global Agenda*, 2nd ed. New York: Random House.

———. (1977) *Power and Interdependence*. Boston: Little, Brown.

———. (1975) "International Interdependence and Integration," pp. 363–414 in Fred I. Greenstein and Nelson W. Polsby (eds.), *International Politics: Handbook of Political Science*, Vol. 8. Reading, Mass.: Addison-Wesley.

KIDDER, RUSHWORTH, M. (1990) "Why Modern Terrorism?" pp. 135–138 in Charles W. Kegley Jr. (ed.), *International Terrorism: Characteristics, Causes, Controls*. New York: St. Martin's Press.

KIDRON, MICHAEL, AND DAN SMITH. (1991) *The New State of War and Peace: An International Atlas*. New York: Simon & Schuster.

KIM, SAMUEL S. (1991) "The United Nations, Lawmaking and World Order," pp. 109–124 in Richard A. Falk, Samuel S. Kim, and Saul H. Mendlovitz (eds.), *The United Nations and a Just World Order*. Boulder, Colo.: Westview.

KIM, WOOSANG. (1992) "Power Transitions and Great Power War from Westphalia to Waterloo," *World Politics* 45 (October): 153–172.

———. (1989) "Power, Alliance, and Major Wars, 1816–1975," *Journal of Conflict Resolution* 33 (June): 255–273.

KINDLEBERGER, CHARLES P. (1973) *The World in Depression, 1929–1939*. Berkeley: University of California Press.

———. (1969) *American Business Abroad*. New Haven, Conn.: Yale University Press.

KINNAS, J. N. (1992) "Global Challenges and Multilateral Diplomacy," pp. 23–48 in Ludwik Dembinski (ed.), *International Geneva Yearbook*. Berne, Switzerland: Peter Lang.

KISSENGER, HENRY A. (1994) *Diplomacy*. New York: Simon & Schuster.

———. (1992) "Balance of Power Sustained," pp. 238–248 in Graham Allison and Gregory F. Treverton (eds.), *Rethinking America's Security: Beyond Cold War to New World Order*. New York: Norton.

———. (1982) *Years of Upheaval*. Boston: Little, Brown.

———. (1979) *White House Years*. Boston: Little, Brown.

———. (1969) "Domestic Structure and Foreign Policy," pp. 261–275 in James N. Rosenau (ed.), *International Politics and Foreign Policy*. New York: Free Press.

————. (1964) *A World Restored*. New York: Grosset and Dunlap.

KLARE, MICHAEL T. (1994) "Adding Fuel to the Fires: The Conventional Arms Trade in the 1990s," pp. 134–154 in Michael T. Klare and Daniel C. Thomas (eds.), *World Security*. New York: St. Martin's Press.

————. (1993) "The Next Great Arms Race," *Foreign Affairs* 72 (Summer): 136–152.

————. (1991) "Behind Desert Storm: The New Military Paradigm," *Technology Review* 94 (May–June): 28–36.

————. (1990a) "An Arms Control Agenda for the Third World," *Arms Control Today* 20 (April 1990): 8–12.

————. (1990b) "Wars in the 1990s: Growing Firepower in the Third World," *Bulletin of the Atomic Scientists* 46 (May): 9–13.

————. (1990c) "Who's Arming Who? The Arms Trade in the 1990s," *Technology Review* 93 (May/June): 45–50.

————. (1988) "Low-Intensity Conflict," *Christianity and Crisis* 48 (February 1): 11–14.

————. (1987) "The Arms Trade: Changing Patterns in the 1980s," *Third World Quarterly* 9 (October): 1257–1281.

————. (1985) "Leaping the Firebreak," pp. 168–173 in Charles W. Kegley Jr. and Eugene R. Wittkopf (eds.), *The Nuclear Reader: Strategy, Weapons, War*. New York: St. Martin's Press.

KLARE, MICHAEL T., AND DANIEL C. THOMAS. (eds.) (1991) *World Security: Trends and Challenges at Century's End*. New York: St. Martin's Press.

KLUCKHOHN, CLYDE. (1994) "Anthropological Research and World Peace," pp. 143–152 in L. Bryson, Laurence Finkelstein, and Robert MacIver (eds.), *Approaches to World Peace*. New York: Conference on Science, Philosophy, and Religion.

KNICKERBOCKER, BRAD. (1994) "Report on Environment Paints Sober Picture of World's Future," *Christian Science Monitor* (March 23): 7.

KNORR, KLAUS. (1977) "International Economic Leverage and Its Uses," pp. 99–126 in Klaus Knorr and Frank N. Trager (eds.), *Economic Issues and National Security*. Lawrence: Regents Press of Kansas.

————. (1975) *The Power of Nations*. New York: Basic Books.

KNORR, KLAUS, AND JAMES N. ROSENAU. (eds.) (1969) *Contending Approaches to International Politics*. Princeton, N.J.: Princeton University Press.

KNORR, KLAUS, AND SIDNEY VERBA. (eds.) (1961) *The International System*. Princeton, N.J.: Princeton University Press.

KNUDSEN, BAARD BREDRUP. (1984) *Europe versus America: Foreign Policy in the 1980s*. Paris: Atlantic Institute for International Affairs.

KOBER, STANLEY. (1990) "Idealpolitik," *Foreign Policy* 79 (Summer): 3–24.

KOHN, HANS. (1944) *The Meaning of Nationalism*. New York: Macmillan.

KORANY, BAHGAT. (1986) *How Foreign Policy Decisions Are Made in the Third World*. Boulder, Colo.: Westview.

KORB, LAWRENCE J. (1993) "Inman Has Skills to Keep Clinton from Being Rolled by the Pentagon," *The State* (Columbia, S.C.) (December 21): A13.

KOZYREV, ANDREI. (1994) "The Lagging Partnership," *Foreign Affairs* 73 (May–June): 59–71.

KRASNER, STEPHEN D. (1985) *Structural Conflict: The Third World against Global Liberalism*. Berkeley: University of California Press.

————. (1983) *International Regimes*. Ithaca, N.Y.: Cornell University Press.

————. (1982) "Structural Causes and Regime Consequences," *International Organization* 36 (Spring): 185–206.

————. (1981) "Transforming International Regimes: What the Third World Wants and Why," *International Studies Quarterly* 25 (March): 119–148.

————. (1979) "Tokyo Round: Particularistic Interests and Prospects for Stability in the Global Trading System," *International Studies Quarterly* 23 (December): 491–531.

————. (1978) *Defending the National Interest*. Princeton, N.J.: Princeton University Press.

————. (1974) "Oil Is the Exception," *Foreign Policy* 14 (Spring): 68–84.

————. (1972) "Are Bureaucracies Important? (Or Allison Wonderland)," *Foreign Policy* 7 (Summer): 159–179.

KRATOCHWIL, FRIEDRICH, AND JOHN GERARD RUGGIE. (1986) "International Organization: A State of the Art on the Art of the State," *International Organization* 40 (Autumn): 753–775.

KRAUTHAMMER, CHARLES. (1991a) "The Lonely Superpower," *The New Republic* (July 29): 23–27.

————. (1991b) "The Unipolar Moment," *Foreign Affairs* 70 (No. 1): 23–33.

KRISTOF, NICHOLAS D. (1993) "The Rise of China," *Foreign Affairs* 72 (November/December): 59–74.

KRUEGER, ANNE O. (1993) *Economic Policies at Cross-Purposes: The United States and Developing Countries*. Washington, D.C.: Brookings Institution.

KRUGMAN, PAUL. (1990) *The Age of Diminished Expectations: U.S. Economic Policy in the 1990s.* Cambridge, Mass.: MIT Press.

KRUZEL, JOSEPH. (1993) "American Security Policy in a New World Order," pp. 1–23 in Joseph Kruzel (ed.), *American Defense Annual*, 8th ed. New York: Lexington Books.

———. (1991) "Arms Control, Disarmament, and the Stability of the Postwar Era," pp. 247–269 in Charles W. Kegley Jr. (ed.), *The Long Postwar Peace.* New York: HarperCollins.

KUDRLE, ROBERT T. (1987) "The Several Faces of the Multinational Corporation: Political Reaction and Policy Response," pp. 230–241 in Jeffry A. Frieden and David A. Lake (eds.), *International Political Economy.* New York: St. Martin's Press.

KUHN, THOMAS S. (1970) *The Structure of Scientific Revolutions.* Chicago: University of Chicago Press.

KUNZ, JOSEF L. (1960) "Sanctions in International Law," *American Journal of International Law* 54 (April): 324–347.

KUTTNER, ROBERT. (1991) "Another Great Victory of Ideology Over Prosperity," *Atlantic Monthly* 283 (October): 32 et passim.

LACAYO, RICHARD. (1993) "America's New Competitive Muscle," *Time* (November 29): 28–29.

LAKE, DAVID A. (1992) "Powerful Pacifists: Democratic States and War," *American Political Science Review* 86 (March): 24–37.

LANGER, WILLIAM L. (1962) "Farewell to Empire," *Foreign Affairs* 41 (October): 115–130.

LASZLO, ERVIN, JORGE LOZOYA, A. K. BHATTACHARYA, JAIME ESTEVEZ, ROSARIO GREEN, AND VENKATA RAMAN. (1980) *The Obstacles to the New International Economic Order.* Elmsford, N.Y.: Pergamon Press.

LAQUEUR, WALTER. (1986) "Reflections on Terrorism," *Foreign Affairs* 65 (Fall): 86–100.

LAWRENCE, RICHARD. (1993) "New Oil Crisis Approaching," *The State* (Columbia, S.C.) (November 1): A7.

LEBOW, RICHARD NED. (1981) *Between Peace and War: The Nature of International Crisis.* Baltimore: Johns Hopkins University Press.

LEBOW, RICHARD NED, AND JANICE GROSS STEIN. (1994) *We All Lost the Cold War.* Princeton, N.J.: Princeton University Press.

LEVENTHAL, PAUL L. (1992) "Plugging the Leaks in Nuclear Export Controls: Why Bother?" *Orbis* 36 (Spring): 167–180.

LEVI, ISAAC. (1990) *Hard Choices: Decision Making under Unresolved Conflict.* New York: Cambridge University Press.

LEVI, WERNER. (1981). *The Coming End of War.* Beverly Hills, Calif.: Sage.

LEVY, JACK S. (1995) "War in the Post–Cold War Era: Structural Perspectives on the Causes of War," pp. 64–74 in Charles W. Kegley Jr. and Eugene R. Wittkopf (eds.), *The Global Agenda*, 3rd ed. New York: McGraw-Hill.

———. (1992) "An Introduction to Prospect Theory," *Political Psychology* 13 (June): 171–186.

———. (1991) "Long Cycles, Hegemonic Transitions, and the Long Peace," pp. 147–176 in Charles W. Kegley Jr. (ed.), *The Long Postwar Peace.* New York: HarperCollins.

———. (1990–1991) "Preferences, Constraints, and Choices in July 1914," *International Security* 15 (Winter): 151–186.

———. (1989a) "The Causes of War: A Review of Theories and Evidence," pp. 209–333 in Philip E. Tetlock, Jo L. Husbands, Robert Jervis, Paul C. Stern, and Charles Tilly (eds.), *Behavior, Society, and Nuclear War.* New York: Oxford University Press.

———. (1989b) "The Diversionary Theory of War: A Critique," pp. 259–288 in Manus I. Midlarsky (ed.), *Handbook of War Studies.* Boston: Unwin Hyman.

———. (1985) "The Polarity of the System and International Stability: An Empirical Analysis," pp. 41–66 in Alan Ned Sabrosky (ed.), *Polarity and War.* Boulder, Colo.: Westview.

LEWIS, KEVIN N. (1985) "Balance and Counterbalance: Technology and the Arms Race," *Orbis* 29 (Summer): 259–268.

LEWIS, PAUL. (1993a) "Five Key Nations Urge Prudence in Setting Peacekeeping Goal," *New York Times* (October 1): A2.

———. (1993b) "Stoked By Ethnic Fighting, Refugee Numbers Grow," *New York Times* (November 10): A1, A7.

LEWIS, W. ARTHUR. (1978) *The Evolution of the International Economic Order.* Princeton, N.J.: Princeton University Press.

LEWONTIN, R. C., STEVEN ROSE, and LEON J. KAMIN. (1984) *Not in Our Genes: Biology, Ideology, and Human Nature.* New York: Pantheon.

LEYTON-BROWN, DAVID. (1990) "The Roles of the Multinational Enterprise in International Relations," pp. 224–241 in David G. Haglud and Michael K. Hawes (eds.), *World Politics: Power, Interdependence, and Dependence.* Toronto: Harcourt Brace Jovanovich.

———. (1987) "Introduction," pp. 1–4 in David Leyton-Brown (ed.), *The Utility of International Economic Sanctions.* New York: St. Martin's Press.

LIFTON, ROBERT JAY, AND RICHARD FALK. (1982) *Indefensible Weapons: The Political and Psychological Case against Nuclearism.* New York: Basic Books.

LIJPHART, AREND. (1974) "The Structure of the Theoretical Revolution in International Relations," *International Studies Quarterly* 18 (March): 42–49.

LILLICH, RICHARD B. (1972) "Domestic Institutions," pp. 384–424 in Cyril E. Black and Richard A. Falk (eds.), *The Future of the International Legal Order.* Princeton, N.J.: Princeton University Press.

LIND, MICHAEL. (1993) "Of Arms and the Woman," *The New Republic* 209 (November 15): 36–38.

LINDBLOM, CHARLES E. (1977) *Politics and Markets.* New York: Basic Books.

LINDEN, EUGENE. (1992) "Rio's Legacy," *Time* (June 22): 44–45.

LINDSAY, JAMES M. (1986) "Trade Sanctions as Policy Instruments: A Re-examination," *International Studies Quarterly* 30 (June): 153–173.

LIPOW, JONATHAN. (1990) "Defense, Growth, and Disarmament: A Further Look," *Jerusalem Journal of International Relations* 12 (June): 49–59.

LISKA, GEORGE. (1968) *Alliances and the Third World.* Baltimore: Johns Hopkins University Press.

———. (1962) *Nations in Alliance: The Limits of Interdependence.* Baltimore: Johns Hopkins University Press.

LISSITZYN, OLIVER J. (1963) "International Law in a Divided World," *International Conciliation* 542 (March): 3–69.

LISTER, FREDERICK K. (1986) *Fairness and Accountability in U.N. Financial Decision-Making.* New York: United Nations Association of the United States of America.

LITTLE, DAVID. (1993) "The Recovery of Liberalism," *Ethics and International Affairs* 7: 171–201.

LOPEZ, GEORGE A., AND DAVID CORTRIGHT. (1993) "Sanctions: Do They Work?" *Bulletin of the Atomic Scientists* 49 (November): 14–15.

LORENZ, KONRAD. (1963) *On Aggression.* New York: Harcourt, Brace & World.

LUDLOW, PETER. (1991) "The European Commission," pp. 85–132 in Robert O. Keohane and Stanley Hoffmann (eds.), *The New European Community: Decisionmaking and Institutional Change.* Boulder, Colo.: Westview.

LUTTWAK, EDWARD N. (1993) *The Endangered American Dream: How to Stop the United States from Becoming a Third World Country and How to Win the Geo-Economic Struggle for Economic Supremacy.* New York: Simon & Schuster.

———. (1990) "From Geo-Politics to Geoeconomics," *National Interest* 20 (Summer): 17–23.

MACFARQUHAR, EMILY. (1994) "The War against Women," *U.S. News & World Report* (March 28): 42–48.

MACKINDER, SIR HALFORD. (1919) *Democratic Ideals and Reality.* New York: Henry A. Holt.

MACNEILL, JIM. (1992) "Sustainable Development: What Is It?" pp. 379–387 in Charles W. Kegley Jr. and Eugene R. Wittkopf (eds.), *The Global Agenda*, 3rd ed. New York: McGraw-Hill.

MACRIDIS, ROY C. (ed.) (1989) *Foreign Policy in World Politics*, 8th ed. Englewood Cliffs, N.J.: Prentice-Hall.

MAHAN, ALFRED THAYER. (1890) *The Influence of Sea Power in History.* Boston: Little, Brown.

MAJEED, AKHTAR. (1991) "Has the War System Really Become Obsolete?" *Bulletin of Peace Proposals* 22 (December): 419–425.

MAOZ, ZEEV, AND NASRIN ABDOLALI. (1989) "Regime Types and International Conflict," *Journal of Conflict Resolution* 33 (March): 3–36.

MARANTZ, PAUL. (1987) "Economic Sanctions in the Polish Crisis," pp. 131–146 in David Leyton-Brown (ed.), *The Utility of International Economic Sanctions.* New York: St. Martin's Press.

MARKUSEN, ANN, AND JOEL YUDKEN. (1992) *Dismantling the Cold War Economy.* New York: Basic Books.

MARKUSEN, ANN, PETER HALL, SCOTT CAMPBELL, AND SABINA DIETRICK. (1991) *The Rise of the Gunbelt: The Military Remapping of America.* New York: Oxford University Press.

MARLIN-BENNETT, RENÉE. (1993) *Food Fights: International Regimes and the Politics of Agricultural Trade Disputes.* London: Gordon and Breach.

MARTIN, LINDA G. (1989) "The Graying of Japan," *Population Bulletin* 44 (No. 2). Washington, D.C.: Population Reference Bureau.

MARTIN, LISA L. (1993) "Credibility, Costs, and Institutions: Cooperation on Economic Sanctions," *World Politics* 45 (April): 406–432.

MASSING, MICHAEL. (1990–1991) "'Structural Adjustment' in the Third World Has Been a Bust," *Washington Post National Weekly Edition* 9 (December 31–January 6): 24.

MASSON, PAUL R. (1990) "Long-term Macroeconomic Effects of Aging Populations," *Finance and Development* 27 (June): 6–9.

MASTANDUNO, MICHAEL. (1991) "Do Relative Gains Matter? America's Response to Japanese Industrial Policy," *International Security* 16 (Summer): 73–113.

MASTANDUNO, MICHAEL, DAVID A. LAKE, AND G. JOHN IKENBERRY. (1989) "Toward a Realist Theory of State Action," *International Studies Quarterly* 33 (December): 457–474.

MASTERS, ROGER D. (1969) "World Politics as a Primitive Political System," pp. 104–118 in James N. Rosenau (ed.), *International Politics and Foreign Policy*. New York: Free Press.

MATHEWS, JESSICA T. (1992) "Coping with the Uncertainties of the Greenhouse Effect," pp. 366–372 in Charles W. Kegley Jr. and Eugene R. Wittkopf (eds.), *The Global Agenda*, 3rd ed. New York: McGraw-Hill.

———. (1991) "Iraq's Nuclear Warning," *Washington Post National Weekly Edition* 9 (July 22–28): 19.

———. (1990) "The Greenhouse Effect: Apparently It's for Others to Worry About," *Washington Post National Weekly Edition* 8 (July 9–15): 29.

McCULLY, PATRICK. (1991) "Discord in the Greenhouse: How WRI Is Attempting to Shift the Blame for Global Warming," *Ecologist* 21 (July/August): 157–165.

McDOUGAL, MYRES S., AND HAROLD D. LASSWELL. (1959) "The Identification and Appraisal of Diverse Systems of Public Order," *American Journal of International Law* 53 (January): 1–29.

McGOWAN, PATRICK J., WITH THE ASSISTANCE OF BOHDAN KORDAN. (1981) "Imperialism in World-System Perspective," *International Studies Quarterly* 25 (March): 43–68.

McKIBBEN, BILL. (1989) "Reflections: The End of Nature," *New Yorker* (September 11): 47–48 passim.

McNAMARA, ROBERT S. (1984) "Time Bomb or Myth: The Population Problem," *Foreign Affairs* 62 (Summer): 1107–1131.

MEAD, MARGARET. (1968) "Warfare Is Only an Invention—Not a Biological Necessity," pp. 270–274 in Leon Bramson and George W. Goethals (eds.), *War*. New York: Basic Books.

MEAD, WALTER RUSSELL. (1990) "On the Road to Ruin: Winning the Cold War, Losing Economic Peace," *Harper's* 280 (March): 59–64.

MEADOWS, DONELLA H., DENNIS L. MEADOWS, JØRGEN RANDERS, AND WILLIAM W. BEHRENS III. (1974) *The Limits to Growth*. New York: New American Library.

MEARSHEIMER, JOHN J. (1992) "Europe after the Superpowers: Why We Will Soon Miss the Cold War," pp. 158–167 in Charles W. Kegley Jr. and Eugene R. Wittkopf, eds., *The Global Agenda*, 3rd ed. New York: McGraw-Hill.

———. (1990) "Back to the Future: Instability in Europe after the Cold War," *International Security* 15 (Summer): 5–56.

———. (1983) *Conventional Deterrence*. Ithaca, N.Y.: Cornell University Press.

MEISSNER, DORIS. (1992) "Managing Migrations," *Foreign Policy* 86 (Spring): 66–83.

MELANSON, RICHARD A. (1983) *Writing History and Making Policy: The Cold War, Vietnam, and Revisionism*. Lanham, Md.: University Press of America.

MELLOAN, GEORGE. (1991) "Maastricht's Ghost of Europes Past, and Future," *Wall Street Journal* (December 9): A15.

MERRICK, THOMAS W. (1989) *America in the 21st Century: A Global Perspective*. Washington, D.C.: Population Reference Bureau.

———. (1988) "World Population in Transition," in *Population Bulletin* 41 (No. 2). Washington, D.C.: Population Reference Bureau.

MICHAELS, MARGUERITE. (1993) "Blue-Helmet Blues," *Time* (November 15): 66–67.

*The Middle East*. (1991) 7th ed. Washington, D.C.: Congressional Quarterly, Inc.

MIDLARSKY, MANUS I. (1988) *The Onset of World War*. Boston: Unwin Hyman.

———. (1975) *On War*. New York: Free Press.

MILLS, C. WRIGHT. (1956) *The Power Elite*. New York: Oxford University Press.

MINTER, WILLIAM. (1986–1987) "South Africa: Straight Talk on Sanctions," *Foreign Policy* 65 (Winter): 43–63.

MITCHELL, GEORGE H., JR. (1993) "Economics and Development," pp. 145–169 in John Tessitore and Susan Woolfson (eds.), *A Global Agenda: Issues Before the 48th General Assembly of the United Nations*. Lanham, Md.: University Press of America.

MITRANY, DAVID. (1966) *A Working Peace System*. Chicago: Quadrangle.

MITTELMAN, JAMES H. (1993) "Third World," pp. 908–910 in Joel Krieger (ed.), *The Oxford Companion to Politics of the World*. New York: Oxford University Press.

MODELSKI, GEORGE. (ed.) (1987a) *Exploring Long Cycles*. Boulder, Colo.: Lynne Rienner.

———. (1987b) "The Study of Long Cycles," pp. 1–15 in George Modelski (ed.), *Exploring Long Cycles*. Boulder, Colo.: Lynne Rienner.

———. (1978) "The Long Cycle of Global Politics and the Nation-State," *Comparative Studies in Society and History* 20 (April): 214–235.

———. (1964) "The International Relations of Internal War," pp. 14–44 in James N. Rosenau (ed.), *International Aspects of Civil Strife.* Princeton, N.J.: Princeton University Press.

MODELSKI, GEORGE, AND WILLIAM R. THOMPSON. (1995) *Leading Sectors and World Powers.* Columbia: University of South Carolina Press.

———. (1989) "Long Cycles and Global War," pp. 23–54 in Manus I. Midlarsky (ed.), *Handbook of War Studies.* Boston: Unwin Hyman.

MØLLER, BJØRN. (1992) *Common Security and Nonoffensive Defense: A Neorealist Perspective.* Boulder, Colo.: Lynne Rienner.

MONIAC, RÜDIGER. (1992) "NATO Revises Nuclear Strategy for the Post–Cold War Age," *The German Tribune* (October 30): 1–2.

MOON, BRUCE E., AND WILLIAM J. DIXON. (1985) "Politics, the State, and Basic Human Needs: A Cross-National Study," *American Journal of Political Science* 29 (November): 661–694.

MORAN, THEODORE H. (1991) "International Economics and U.S. Security," *Foreign Affairs* 69 (Winter): 74–90.

MORAWETZ, DAVID. (1977) *Twenty-five Years of Economic Development, 1950 to 1975.* Washington, D.C.: World Bank.

MORGAN, T. CLIFTON, AND KENNETH N. BICKERS. (1992) "Domestic Discontent and the External Use of Force," *Journal of Conflict Resolution* 36 (March): 25–52.

MORGAN, T. CLIFTON, AND SALLY HOWARD CAMPBELL. (1991) "Domestic Structure, Decisional Constraints and War," *Journal of Conflict Resolution* 35 (June): 187–211.

MORGAN, T. CLIFTON, AND VALERIE L. SCHWEBACH. (1992) "Take Two Democracies and Call Me in the Morning: A Prescription for Peace?" *International Interactions* 17 (No. 4): 305–320.

MORGENTHAU, HANS J. (1985) *Politics among Nations,* 6th ed. Revised by Kenneth W. Thompson. New York: Knopf.

———. (1983) "Defining the National Interest—Again," pp. 32–39 in Charles W. Kegley Jr. and Eugene R. Wittkopf (eds.), *Perspectives on American Foreign Policy.* New York: St. Martin's Press.

———. (1969) "Historical Justice and the Cold War," *New York Review of Books* 16 (July 10): 10–17.

———. (1959) "Alliances in Theory and Practice," pp. 184–212 in Arnold Wolfers (ed.), *Alliance Policy in the Cold War.* Baltimore: Johns Hopkins University Press.

———. (1948) *Politics among Nations.* New York: Knopf.

MORRIS, DESMOND. (1969) *The Human Zoo.* New York: Dell.

MORSE, EDWARD L. (1990–1991) "The Coming Oil Revolution," *Foreign Affairs* 69 (Winter): 36–56.

———. (1986) "After the Fall: The Politics of Oil," *Foreign Affairs* 64 (Spring): 792–811.

———. (1976) *Modernization and the Transformation of International Relations.* New York: Free Press.

MUELLER, JOHN. (1990) "A New Concert of Europe," *Foreign Policy* 77 (Winter): 3–16.

———. (1989) *Retreat from Doomsday: The Obsolescence of Major War.* New York: Basic Books.

MULHOLLIN, GARY. (1994) "The Business of Defense Is Defending Business," *Washington Post National Weekly Edition* 11 (February 14–20): 23.

MÜLLER, RONALD. (1973–1974) "Poverty Is the Product," *Foreign Policy* 13 (Winter): 71–103.

MURPHY, CRAIG N. (1983) "What the Third World Wants: An Interpretation of the Development and Meaning of the New International Economic Order Ideology," *International Studies Quarterly* 27 (March): 55–76.

NARDIN, TERRY. (1983) *Law, Morality, and the Relations of States.* Princeton, N.J.: Princeton University Press.

NARDIN, TERRY, AND DAVID R. MAPEL. (eds.) (1992) *Traditions of International Ethics.* New York: Cambridge University Press.

NATHAN, JAMES A. (ed.) (1992) *The Cuban Missile Crisis Revisited.* New York: St. Martin's Press.

NAU, HENRY R. (1990) *The Myth of America's Decline.* New York: Oxford University Press.

NELSON, STEPHAN D. (1974) "Nature/Nurture Revisited: A Review of the Biological Bases of Conflict," *Journal of Conflict Resolution* 18 (June): 285–335.

*The New Population Debate: Two Views on Population Growth and Economic Development.* (1985) Washington, D.C.: Population Reference Bureau.

NICHOLSON, MICHAEL. (1992) *Rationality and the Analysis of International Conflict.* Cambridge: Cambridge University Press.

NIEBUHR, REINHOLD. (1947) *Moral Man and Immoral Society.* New York: Scribner's.

NIETSCHMANN, BERNARD. (1991) "Third World War: The Global Conflict Over the Rights of Indigenous Nations," pp. 172–176 in Robert M. Jackson (ed.), *Global Issues 91/92.* Guilford, Conn.: Dushkin.

NINCIC, MIROSLAV. (1992) *Democracy and Foreign Policy: The Fallacy of Political Realism*. New York: Columbia University Press.

———. (1982) *The Arms Race: The Political Economy of Military Growth*. New York: Praeger.

NITZE, PAUL. (1991) "After Iraq, Nukes Can Be Junked," *Wall Street Journal* (December 24): A6.

NIXON, RICHARD. (1994) *Beyond Peace*. New York: Random House.

NOGEE, JOSEPH L. (1975) "Polarity: An Ambiguous Concept," *Orbis* 28 (Winter): 1193–1224.

NOWZAD, BAHRAM. (1990) "Lessons of the Debt Decade," *Finance and Development* 27 (March): 9–13.

NYE, JOSEPH S., JR. (1994) "What New World Order?" pp. 50–60 in Eugene R. Wittkopf (ed.), *The Future of American Foreign Policy*. New York: St. Martin's Press.

———. (1992) "The Changing Nature of World Power," pp. 117–129 in Charles W. Kegley Jr. and Eugene R. Wittkopf (eds.), *The Global Agenda*. New York: McGraw-Hill.

———. (1990) *Bound to Lead: The Changing Nature of American Power*. New York: Basic Books.

———. (1989–1990) "Arms Control after the Cold War," *Foreign Affairs* 68 (Winter): 42–64.

———. (1988) "Neorealism and Neoliberalism," *World Politics* 40 (January): 235–251.

———. (1987) "Nuclear Learning and U.S.–Soviet Security Regimes," *International Organization* 41 (Summer): 371–402.

———. (1971) *Peace in Parts*. Boston: Little, Brown.

NYE, JOSEPH S., JR., AND ROBERT O. KEOHANE. (1971) "Transnational Relations and World Politics: An Introduction," *International Organization* 25 (Summer): 329–349.

OBERDORFER, DON. (1991) *The Turn: From the Cold War to a New Era*. New York: Poseidon.

O'BRIEN, CONOR CRUISE. (1993a) "Germany Resurgent," *Harper's* 286 (March): 15–17.

———. (1993b) "The Wrath of Ages," *Foreign Affairs* 72 (November/December): 142–149.

———. (1977) "Liberty and Terrorism, *International Security* 2 (Fall): 56–67.

O'BRIEN, PATRICK M. (1988) "Agricultural Productivity and the Global Food Market," pp. 394–408 in Charles W. Kegley Jr. and Eugene R. Wittkopf (eds.), *The Global Agenda*, 2nd ed. New York: Random House.

OLSON, MANCUR. (1982) *The Rise and Decline of Nations*. New Haven, Conn.: Yale University Press.

———. (1971) "Rapid Growth as a Destabilizing Force," pp. 215–227 in James C. Davies (ed.), *When Men Revolt and Why*. New York: Free Press.

ONUF, NICHOLAS GREENWOOD. (1989) *World of Our Making: Rules and Rule in Social Theory and International Relations*. Columbia: University of South Carolina Press.

———. (1982) "Global Law-Making and Legal Thought," pp. 1–82 in Nicholas Greenwood Onuf (ed.), *Law-Making in the Global Community*. Durham, N.C.: Carolina Academic Press.

ONUF, NICHOLAS, AND THOMAS JOHNSON. (1995) "Republicanism and International Thought," pp. 179–197 in Charles W. Kegley Jr. (ed.), *Controversies in International Relations Theory: Realism and the Neoliberal Challenge*. New York: St. Martin's Press.

OREN, NISSAN. (ed.) (1984) *When Patterns Change: Turning Points in International Politics*. New York: St. Martin's Press.

ORGANSKI, A. F. K. (1968) *World Politics*. New York: Knopf.

ORGANSKI, A. F. K., AND JACEK KUGLER. (1980) *The War Ledger*. Chicago: University of Chicago Press.

OSGOOD, ROBERT E. (1968) *Alliances and American Foreign Policy*. Baltimore: Johns Hopkins University Press.

OSTROM, CHARLES W., JR., AND JOHN H. ALDRICH. (1978) "The Relationship between Size and Stability in the Major Power International System," *American Journal of Political Science* 22 (November): 743–771.

OSTROM, CHARLES W., AND BRIAN L. JOB. (1986) "The President and the Use of Force," *American Political Science Review* 80 (June): 554–566.

OTTAWAY, DAVID B. (1993) "Giving Up on Peace in Croatia," *Washington Post National Weekly Edition* 11 (November 15–21): 16.

OVERSEAS DEVELOPMENT COUNCIL. (1991) "The Gulf Crisis: Impact on Developing Countries," *Policy Focus*, No. 6. Washington, D.C.: Overseas Development Council.

OWEN, OLIVER S. (1989) "The Heat Is On: The Greenhouse Effect and the Earth's Future," *Futurist* 23 (September–October): 34–40.

PACKENHAM, ROBERT. (1992) *The Dependency Movement: Scholarship and Politics in Dependency Studies*. Cambridge, Mass.: Harvard University Press.

Parenti, Michael. (1969) *The Anti-Communist Impulse*. New York: Random House.

PARRY, CLIVE. (1968) "The Function of Law in the International Community," pp. 1–54 in Max Sørensen (ed.), *Manual of Public International Law*. New York: St. Martin's Press.

PAYNE, JAMES E., AND ANANDI P. SAHU. (eds.) (1993) *Defense Spending and Economic Growth.* Boulder, Colo.: Westview.

PEARLSTEIN, STEVEN. (1991) "A Wholesale Change in the Arms Bazaar," *Washington Post National Weekly Edition* 8 (April 15–21): 8–9.

PEARSON, FREDERIC S., ROBERT A. BAUMANN, AND JEFFREY J. PICKERING. (1991) "International Military Intervention: Global and Regional Redefinitions of Realpolitik." Paper presented at the Annual Meeting of the American Political Science Association, Washington, D.C., August 29–September 1.

PELZ, STEPHEN. (1991) "Changing International Systems, the World Balance of Power, and the United States, 1776–1976," *Diplomatic History* 15 (Winter): 47–81.

PERLE, RICHARD. (1991) "Military Power and the Passing Cold War," pp. 33–38 in Charles W. Kegley Jr. and Kenneth L. Schwab (eds.), *After the Cold War: Questioning the Morality of Nuclear Deterrence.* Boulder, Colo.: Westview.

PETERSON, PETER G. (1994) "Entitlement Reform: The Way to Eliminate the Deficit," *New York Review of Books* 41 (April 7): 39–47.

PETERSON, V. SPIKE, AND ANNE SISSON RUNYAN. (1993). *Global Gender Issues.* Boulder, Colo.: Westview.

PHILIPS, ROSEMARIE, AND STUART K. TUCKER. (1991) *U.S. Foreign Policy and Developing Countries: Discourse and Data 1991.* Washington, D.C.: Overseas Development Council.

PIERRE, ANDREW J. (1984) "The Politics of International Terrorism," pp. 84–92 in Charles W. Kegley Jr. and Eugene R. Wittkopf (eds.), *The Global Agenda.* New York: Random House.

PIPES, RICHARD. (1977) "Why the Soviet Union Thinks It Could Fight and Win a Nuclear War," *Commentary* 26 (July): 21–34.

PIRAGES, DENNIS. (1986) "World Energy Crisis 1995," *Futures Research Quarterly* 2 (Fall): 31–47.

*Population in Perspective.* (1986) Washington, D.C.: Population Reference Bureau.

POPULATION REFERENCE BUREAU. (1990) *World Population: Fundamentals of Growth.* Washington, D.C.: Population Reference Bureau.

POPULATION REFERENCE BUREAU. (1981) *World Population: Toward the Next Century.* Washington, D.C.: Population Reference Bureau.

POSTEL, SANDRA. (1994) "Carrying Capacity: Earth's Bottom Line," pp. 3–21 in Lester R. Brown et al., *State of the World 1994.* New York: Norton.

POTTER, WILLIAM C. (1992) "The New Nuclear Suppliers," *Orbis* 46 (Spring): 199–210.

POTTS, MARK. (1991) "Going Hunting for the Biggest Game in Town," *Washington Post National Weekly Edition* 8 (February 18–24): 18–19.

POURGERAMI, ABBAS. (1991) *Development and Democracy in the Third World.* Boulder, Colo.: Westview.

POWELL, COLIN L. (1992–1993) "U.S. Forces: Challenges Ahead," *Foreign Affairs* 71 (Winter): 32–45.

POWERS, THOMAS. (1994) "Downwinders: Some Casualties of the Nuclear Age," *The Atlantic* 273 (March): 119–124.

PUCHALA, DONALD J. (1988) "The Integration Theorists and the Study of International Relations," pp. 198–265 in Charles W. Kegley Jr. and Eugene R. Wittkopf (eds.), *The Global Agenda*, 2nd ed. New York: Random House.

———. (ed.) (1983) *Issues Before the 38th General Assembly of the United Nations, 1983 and 1984.* New York: United Nations Association of the United States of America.

PUTNAM, ROBERT. (1988) "Diplomacy and Domestic Politics: The Logic of Two-Level Games," *International Organization* 42 (Summer): 427–460.

QUANDT, WILLIAM B. (1991) "The Middle East in 1990," *Foreign Affairs* 70 (No. 1): 49–69.

RAPHAEL, THERESE. (1991) "The Yeltsin Military Strategy," *Wall Street Journal* (August 30): A6.

RAPKIN, DAVID P. (ed.) (1990) *World Leadership and Hegemony.* Boulder, Colo.: Lynne Rienner.

RAPKIN, DAVID, AND WILLIAM THOMPSON, WITH JON A. CHRISTOPHERSON. (1989) "Bipolarity and Bipolarization in the Cold War Era," *Journal of Conflict Resolution* 23 (June): 261–295.

RASPBERRY, WILLIAM. (1992) "Seeing Past the Children," *Washington Post* (January 1): A31.

RAY, JAMES LEE. (1995) *Democracy and International Conflict: An Evaluation of the Democratic Peace Proposition.* Columbia: University of South Carolina Press.

RAYMOND, GREGORY A. (1994) "Democracies, Disputes, and Third Party Intermediaries," *Journal of Conflict Resolution* 38 (March): 24–42.

Reardon, Betty. (1985) *Sexism and the War System.* New York: Teachers College Press.

Reich, Robert. (1990) "Who Is Us?" *Harvard Business Review* 68 (January–February): 53–64.

———. (1983) "Why Democracy Makes Economic Sense," *The New Republic* 199 (December 19): 25–32.

RENNER, MICHAEL. (1991) "Assessing the Military's War on the Environment," pp. 132–152 in Lester R. Brown et al., *State of the World 1991.* New York: Norton.

———. (1990) "Ending Poverty," pp. 135–153 in Lester R. Brown et al., *State of the World 1990.* New York: Norton.

———. (1987) "Shaping America's Energy Future," *World Policy Journal* 4 (Summer): 383–414.

RENO, ROBERT. (1993) "Defense Conversion Bombs Out," *The State* (Columbia, S.C.) (April 2): A15.

RENSBERGER, BOYCE. (1994) "Famine Amid the World's Feast," *Washington Post National Weekly Edition* 11 (March 7–13): 38.

REPETTO, ROBERT. (1987) "Population, Resources, Environment: An Uncertain Future," *Population Bulletin* 42 (No. 2). Washington, D.C.: Population Reference Bureau.

REUTLINGER, SHLOMO. (1985) "Food Security and Poverty in LDCs," *Finance and Development* 22 (December): 7–11.

RHODES, EDWARD. (1988) "Nuclear Weapons and Credibility: Deterrence Theory beyond Rationality," *Review of International Studies* 14 (January): 45–62.

RICHARDSON, LEWIS F. (1960a) *Arms and Insecurity.* Pittsburgh: Boxwood Press.

———. (1960b) *Statistics of Deadly Quarrels.* Chicago: Quadrangle.

RICHARDSON, NEIL R. (1995) "International Trade as a Force for Peace," pp. 281–293 in Charles W. Kegley Jr. (ed.), *Controversies in International Relations Theory: Realism and the Neoliberal Challenge.* New York: St. Martin's Press.

RICHBURG, KEITH B. (1990) "Going from Famine to Feast—Literally," *Washington Post National Weekly Edition* 7 (May 21–27): 18.

RIGGS, ROBERT E., AND JACK C. PLANO. (1994) *The United Nations: International Organization and World Politics,* 2nd ed. Belmont, Calif.: Wadsworth.

RIKER, WILLIAM H. (1962) *The Theory of Political Coalitions.* New Haven, Conn.: Yale University Press.

RIKHYE, INDAR JIT. (1989) *The Future of Peacekeeping.* New York: International Peace Academy.

RITTBERGER, VOLKER. (ed.) (1993) *Regime Theory and International Relations.* Cambridge: Clarendon Press.

ROCA, SERGIO. (1987) "Economic Sanctions against Cuba," pp. 87–104 in David Leyton-Brown (ed.), *The Utility of International Economic Sanctions.* New York: St. Martin's Press.

ROODMAN, DAVID MALIN. (1994) "Global Temperature Rises Slightly," pp. 66–67 in Linda Starke (ed.), *Vital Signs 1994.* New York: Norton.

ROSECRANCE, RICHARD. (1992) "A New Concert of Powers," *Foreign Affairs* 71 (Spring): 64–82.

———. (1986) *The Rise of the Trading State: Commerce and Conquest in the Modern World.* New York: Basic Books.

———. (1963) *Action and Reaction in World Politics.* Boston: Little, Brown.

ROSEN, DAVID. (1987) *The Basics of Foreign Trade and Exchange.* New York: Federal Reserve Board of New York.

ROSEN, STEVEN J. (ed.) (1973) *Testing the Theory of the Military-Industrial Complex.* Lexington, Mass.: Heath.

ROSENAU, JAMES N. (1980) *The Scientific Study of Foreign Policy.* New York: Nichols.

ROSENAU, PAULINE MARIE. (1992) *Post-Modernism and the Social Sciences.* Princeton, N.J.: Princeton University Press.

ROSENTHAL, JOEL H. (1991) *Righteous Realists.* Baton Rouge: Louisiana State University Press.

ROSTOW, W. W. (1960) *The Stages of Economic Growth.* Cambridge: Cambridge University Press.

ROTHGEB, JOHN M., JR. (1993) *Defining Power: Influence and Force in the Contemporary International System.* New York: St. Martin's Press.

ROTHSTEIN, ROBERT L. (1993) "New International Economic Order," pp. 628–629 in Joel Krieger (ed.), *The Oxford Companion to Politics of the World.* New York: Oxford University Press.

———. (1988) "Give Them a Break: Third World Debtors and a Cure for Reaganomics," *The New Republic* 204 (February 1): 20–24.

———. (1979) *Global Bargaining: UNCTAD and the Quest for a New International Economic Order.* Princeton, N.J.: Princeton University Press.

ROWAN, CARL. (1993) "U.S. Has Big Stake in Worldwide Family Planning," *The State* (Columbia, S.C.) (December 5): D3.

RUGGIE, JOHN GERARD. (1993) "Wandering in the Void: Charting the U.N.'s New Strategic Role," *Foreign Affairs* 72 (November/December): 27–31.

———. (1983) "Continuity and Transformation in the World Polity: Toward a Neorealist Systhesis," *World Politics* 35 (January): 261–285.

RUMMEL, RUDOLPH. (1983) "Libertarianism and International Violence," *Journal of Conflict Resolution* 27 (March): 27–71.

RUSSETT, BRUCE. (1993) *Grasping the Democratic Peace: Principles for a Post–Cold War World.* Princeton, N.J.: Princeton University Press.

———. (1990) *Controlling the Sword: The Democratic Governance of National Security.* Cambridge, Mass.: Harvard University Press.

———. (1989) "Economic Decline, Electoral Pressure, and the Initiation of Interstate Conflict," pp. 123–140 in Charles Gochman and Allen Ned Sabrosky (eds.), *Prisoners of War? Nation-States in the Modern Era.* Lexington, Mass.: D.C. Heath.

———. (1984) "Dimensions of Resource Dependence: Some Elements of Rigor in Concept and Policy Analysis," *International Organization* 38 (Summer): 481–499.

———. (1982) "Defense Expenditures and National Well-Being," *American Political Science Review* 76 (December): 767–777.

RUSSETT, BRUCE, AND HARVEY STARR. (1989) *World Politics: The Menu for Choice,* 3rd ed. New York: W. H. Freeman.

RUSSETT, BRUCE, AND JAMES S. SUTTERLIN. (1991) "The U.N. in a New World Order," *Foreign Affairs* 70 (Spring): 69–83.

RYAN, STEPHEN. (1990) *Ethnic Conflict and International Relations.* Brookfield, Vt.: Gower.

RYSER, RUDOLPH C. (1985) "Fourth World Wars: Indigenous Nationalism and the Emerging New International Political Order," pp. 304–315 in Menno Boldt and J. Anthony Long in association with Leroy Little Bear (eds.), *The Quest for Justice.* Toronto: University of Toronto Press.

SACHS, AARON. (1994) "HIV/AIDS Cases Rising Steadily," pp. 102–104 in Linda Starke (ed.), *Vital Signs 1994.* New York: Norton.

SACHS, JEFFREY. (1989) "Making the Brady Plan Work," *Foreign Affairs* 68 (Summer): 87–104.

SAGAN, CARL. (1992) "Between Enemies," *Bulletin of the Atomic Scientists* 48 (May): 24–26.

———. (1989) "The Secret of the Persian Chessboard," *Parade* (February 14): 14.

———. (1988) "The Common Enemy," *Parade* (February 7): 4–7.

SAGAN, CARL, AND RICHARD TURCO. (1993) "Nuclear Winter in the Post–Cold War Era," *Journal of Peace Research* 30 (November): 369–373.

———. (1990) *A Path Where No Man Thought: Nuclear Winter and the End of the Arms Race.* New York: Random House.

SAGAN, SCOTT D. (1993) *The Limits of Safety: Organizations, Accidents, and Nuclear Weapons.* Princeton, N.J.: Princeton University Press.

SAMUELSON, ROBERT J. (1993) "Why Are We Fighting?" *Newsweek* (June 21): 52.

SAND, PETER H. (1991) "International Cooperation: The Environmental Experience," pp. 236–279 in Jessica Tuchman Mathews (ed.), *Preserving the Global Environment.* New York: Norton.

SANDHOLTZ, WAYNE, MICHAEL BORRUS, JOHN ZYSMAN, JAY STOWSKY, KEN CONCA, STEVEN VOGEL, AND STEVE WEBER. (1992) *The Highest Stakes: The Economic Foundations of the Next Security System.* New York: Oxford University Press.

SCARBOROUGH, GRACE E. IUSI, AND BRUCE BUENO DE MESQUITA. (1988) "Threat and Alignment," *International Interactions* 14 (No. 1): 85–93.

SCHECHTER, MICHAEL G. (1979) "The Common Fund: A Test Case for the New International Economic Order." Paper presented at the Annual Meeting of the International Studies Association/South, Athens, Ga., October 4–6.

SCHEER, ROBERT. (1993) "Terrible Payback," *Playboy* 40 (December): 45.

SCHELL, JONATHAN. (1984) *The Abolition.* New York: Knopf.

SCHELLING, THOMAS C. (1978) *Micromotives and Macrobehavior.* New York: Norton.

———. (1966) *Arms and Influence.* New Haven, Conn.: Yale University Press.

SCHLAGHECK, DONNA M. (1990) "The Superpowers, Foreign Policy, and Terrorism," pp. 170–177 in Charles W. Kegley Jr. (ed.), *International Terrorism: Characteristics, Causes, Controls.* New York: St. Martin's Press.

SCHLESINGER, ARTHUR, JR. (1986) *The Cycles of American History.* Boston: Houghton Mifflin.

———. (1983) "Pretension in the Presidential Pulpit," *Wall Street Journal* (March 17): 26.

———. (1967) "Origins of the Cold War," *Foreign Affairs* 46 (October): 22–52.

SCHMEMANN, SERGE. (1993) "Russia Drops Pledge of No First Use of Atom Arms," *New York Times* (November 4): A5.

SCHNEIDER, STEPHEN H. (1989) "The Changing Climate," *Scientific American* 261 (September): 70–79.

SCHOETTLE, ENID C. B. (1992) "U.N. Dues: The Price of Peace," *Bulletin of the Atomic Scientists* 48 (June): 14–16.

SCHOLTE, JAN AART. (1993) "From Power Politics to Social Change: An Alternative Focus for International Studies," *Review of International Studies* 19 (January): 3–21.

SCHOTT, JEFFREY J. (1994) *The Uruguay Round: An Assessment.* Washington, D.C.: Institute for International Economics.

SCHRAEDER, PETER J. (1993) "'It's the Third World, Stupid!' Why the Third World Should Be the Priority of the Clinton Administration," *Third World Quarterly* 14 (June): 215–237.

SCHWELLER, RANDALL L. (1992) "Domestic Structure and Preventive War," *World Politics* 44 (January): 235–269.

SEBENIUS, JAMES K. (1991) "Designing Negotiations toward a New Regime: The Case of Global Warming," *International Security* 15 (Spring): 110–148.

SESTANOVICH, STEPHEN. (1994) "Andrei the Giant," *The New Republic* 210 (April 11): 24–27.

SEWELL, JOHN W. (1992) "The Metamorphosis of the Third World," pp. 222–238 in Charles W. Kegley Jr. and Eugene R. Wittkopf (eds.), *The Future of American Foreign Policy*. New York: St. Martin's Press.

———. (1991) "Foreign Aid for a New World Order," *Washington Quarterly* 14 (Summer): 35–45.

SHANNON, THOMAS RICHARD. (1989) *An Introduction to the World-System Perspective*. Boulder, Colo.: Westview.

SHAW, R. PAUL, AND YUWA WONG. (1989) *Genetic Seeds of Warfare: Evolution, Nationalism and Patriotism*. Boston: Unwin Hyman.

SHAW, TIMOTHY M. (1991) "Reformism, Revisionism, and Radicalism in African Political Economy during the 1990s," *Journal of Modern African Studies* 29 (June) 191–212.

SHIVA, VANDANA. (1991) "The Green Revolution in the Punjab," *Ecologist* 21 (March/April): 57–60.

SHONFIELD, ANDREW. (1980) "The World Economy 1979," *Foreign Affairs* 58 (No. 3): 596–621.

SHULMAN, SETH. (1992) *The Threat at Home: Confronting the Toxic Legacy of the U.S. Military*. Boston: Beacon.

SIEGEL, MARTIN J. (1983) "Survival," *USA Today* 112 (August): 1–2.

SIMMEL, GEORG. (1956) *Conflict*. Glencoe, Ill.: Free Press.

SIMON, HERBERT A. (1982) *Models of Bounded Rationality*. Cambridge, Mass.: MIT Press.

———. (1957) *Models of Man*. New York: Wiley.

SIMON, JULIAN L., AND HERMAN KAHN. (eds.) (1984) *The Resourceful Earth: A Response to Global 2000*. Oxford: Blackwell.

SIMOWITZ, ROSLYN. (1982) *The Logical Consistency and Soundness of the Balance of Power Theory*. Denver: Graduate School of International Studies, University of Denver.

SINGER, HANS W., AND JAVED A. ANSARI. (1988) *Rich and Poor Countries*, 4th ed. London: Unwin Hyman.

SINGER, J. DAVID. (1991) "Peace in the Global System: Displacement, Interregnum, or Transformation?" pp. 56–84 in Charles W. Kegley Jr. (ed.), *The Long Postwar Peace*. New York: HarperCollins.

———. (1981) "Accounting for International War: The State of the Discipline," *Journal of Peace Research* 18 (No. 1): 1–18.

———. (ed.) (1968) *Quantitative International Politics*. New York: Free Press.

———. (1961) "The Level-of-Analysis Problem in International Relations," pp. 77–92 in Klaus Knorr and Sidney Verba (eds.), *The International System*. Princeton, N.J.: Princeton University Press.

———. (1960) "Theorizing about Theory in International Politics," *Journal of Conflict Resolution* 4 (December): 431–442.

SINGER, J. DAVID, AND MELVIN SMALL. (1974) "Foreign Policy Indicators: Predictors of War in History and in the State of the World Message," *Policy Sciences* 5 (September): 271–296.

———. (1968) "Alliance Aggregation and the Onset of War, 1815–1945," pp. 247–285 in J. David Singer (ed.), *Quantitative International Politics*. New York: Free Press.

SINGER, MAX, AND AARON WILDAVSKY. (1993) *The Real World Order: Zones of Peace/Zones of Turmoil*. Chatham, N.J.: Chatham House.

SINGER, S. FRED. (1988) "Fact and Fantasy on Greenhouse Earth," *Wall Street Journal* (August 30): 18.

SINGH, JASIT, AND THOMAS BERNAUER. (eds.). (1993) *Security of Third World Countries*. Geneva, Switzerland: United Nations Institute for Disarmament Research.

SIVARD, RUTH LEGER. (1993) *World Military and Social Expenditures 1993*. Washington, D.C.: World Priorities.

———. (1991) *World Military and Social Expenditures 1991*. Washington, D.C.: World Priorities.

———. (1982) *World Military and Social Expenditures 1982*. Leesburg, Va.: World Priorities.

———. (1981) *World Energy Survey*. Leesburg, Va.: World Priorities.

———. (1979a) *World Energy Survey*. Leesburg, Va.: World Priorities.

———. (1979b) *World Military and Social Expenditures 1979*. Leesburg, Va.: World Priorities.

SIVERSON, RANDOLPH M., AND JULIAN EMMONS. (1991) "Democratic Political Systems and Alliance Choices," *Journal of Conflict Resolution* 35 (June): 285–306.

SJOLANDER, CLAIRE TURENNE, AND WAYNE S. COX. (eds.) (1994) *Beyond Positivism: Critical Reflections on International Relations*. Boulder, Colo.: Lynne Rienner.

SKJELSBAEK, KJELL. (1991) "The U.N. Secretary-General and the Mediation of International Disputes," *Journal of Peace Research* 28 (February): 99–115.

——. (1989) "United Nations Peacekeeping and the Facilitation of Withdrawals," *Bulletin of Peace Proposals* 20 (September): 253–264.

SKLAIR, LESLIE. (1991) *Sociology of the Global System.* Baltimore: Johns Hopkins University Press.

SKOLNIKOFF, EUGENE R. (1990) "The Policy Gridlock on Global Warming," *Foreign Policy* 79 (Summer): 77–93.

SLATER, JEROME, AND DAVID GOLDFISCHER. (1988) "Can SDI Provide a Defense?" pp. 74–86 in Charles W. Kegley Jr. and Eugene R. Wittkopf (eds.), *The Global Agenda,* 2nd ed. New York: Random House.

SMALL, MELVIN, AND J. DAVID SINGER. (1982) *Resort to Arms: International and Civil Wars, 1816–1980.* Beverly Hills, Calif.: Sage.

——. (1976) "The War-Proneness of Democratic Regimes, 1816–1965," *Jerusalem Journal of International Relations* 1 (March): 50–69.

——. (1972) "Patterns in International Warfare, 1816–1965," pp. 121–131 in James F. Short Jr. and Marvin E. Wolfgang (eds.), *Collective Violence.* Chicago: Aldine-Atherton.

SMART, IAN. (1976) "Uniqueness and Generality," pp. 259–281 in Raymond Vernon (ed.), *The Oil Crisis.* New York: Norton.

SMELSER, NEIL J. (1986) "External and Internal Factors in Theories of Social Change." Paper presented to the German–American Conference on Social Change and Modernization. Berkeley, Calif., August 26–28.

SMITH, MICHAEL JOSEPH. (1986) *Realist Thought from Weber to Kissinger.* Baton Rouge: Louisiana State University Press.

SMITH, ROGER K. (1987) "Explaining the Non-Proliferation Regime: Anomalies for Contemporary International Relations Theory," *International Organization* 41 (Spring): 251–281.

SMITH, RON P., AND GEORGE GEORGIOU. (1983) "Assessing the Effect of Military Expenditures on OECD Economies: A Survey," *Arms Control* 4 (May): 3–15.

SMITH, STEVE, AND MICHAEL CLARKE. (1985) *Foreign Policy Implementation.* London: Allen & Unwin.

SMITH, TONY. (1981) "The Logic of Dependency Theory Revisited," *International Organization* 35 (Autumn): 755–776.

——. (1979) "The Underdevelopment of Development Literature: The Case of Dependency Theory," *World Politics* 31 (January): 247–288.

SNIDAL, DUNCAN. (1993) "Relative Gains and the Pattern of International Cooperation," pp. 181–207 in David A. Baldwin, ed., *Neorealism and Neoliberalism: The Contemporary Debate.* New York: Columbia University Press.

——. (1991) "International Cooperation among Relative Gains Maximizers," *International Studies Quarterly* 35 (December): 387–402.

——. (1985) "The Limits of Hegemonic Stability Theory," *International Organization* 49 (Autumn): 579–614.

SNIDER, LEWIS W. (1991) "Guns, Debt, and Politics: New Variations on an Old Theme," *Armed Forces and Society* 17 (Winter): 167–190.

SNYDER, GLENN H. (1991) "Alliance Threats: A Neorealist First Cut," pp. 83–103 in Robert L. Rothstein (ed.), *The Evolution of Theory in International Relations.* Columbia: University of South Carolina Press.

——. (1984) "The Security Dilemma in Alliance Politics," *World Politics* 36 (July): 461–495.

SNYDER, GLENN H., AND PAUL DIESING. (1977) *Conflict among Nations: Bargaining, Decision-Making, and System Structure in International Crisis.* Princeton, N.J.: Princeton University Press.

SNYDER, JACK. (1993) "The New Nationalism: Realist Interpretations and Beyond," pp. 179–200 in Richard Rosecrance and Anthony A. Stein (eds.), *The Domestic Bases of Grand Strategy.* Ithaca, N.Y.: Cornell University Press.

——. (1991) *Myths of Empire: Domestic Politics and International Ambition.* Ithaca, N.Y.: Cornell University Press.

SOMIT, ALBERT. (1990) "Humans, Chimps, and Bonobos: The Biological Bases of Aggression, War, and Peacemaking," *Journal of Conflict Resolution* 34 (September): 553–582.

SOMMER, MARK. (1994) "Can Military Strategies Ban the Bomb?" *Christian Science Monitor* (April 29): 23.

SORENSEN, THEODORE C. (1990) "Rethinking National Security," *Foreign Affairs* 69 (Summer): 1–18.

——. (1963) *Decision Making in the White House.* New York: Columbia University Press.

SOROKIN, PITIRIM A. (1937) *Social and Cultural Dynamics.* New York: American Book.

SOROOS, MARVIN S. (1992) "The Tragedy of the Commons in Global Perspective," pp. 388–401 in Charles W. Kegley Jr. and Eugene R. Wittkopf (eds.), *The Global Agenda,* 3rd ed. New York: McGraw-Hill.

——. (1986) *Beyond Sovereignty: The Challenge of Global Policy.* Columbia: University of South Carolina Press.

SPANIER, JOHN. (1975) *Games Nations Play,* 2nd ed. New York: Praeger.

SPECTOR, LEONARD S., AND JACQUELINE R. SMITH. (1992) *Nuclear Threshold: The Spread of Nuclear Weapons 1990–1991.* Boulder, Colo.: Westview.

SPERO, JOAN EDELMAN. (1990) *The Politics of International Economic Relations*, 4th ed. New York: St. Martin's Press.

SPIEGEL, STEVEN L. (1985) *The Other Arab–Israeli Conflict*. Chicago: University of Chicago Press.

SPIEZIO, K. EDWARD. (1990) "British Hegemony and Major Power War, 1815–1939," *International Studies Quarterly* 34 (June): 165–181.

SPROUT, HAROLD, AND MARGARET SPROUT. (1971) *Toward a Politics of the Planet Earth*. New York: Van Nostrand.

———. (1962) *Foundations of International Politics*. Princeton, N.J.: Van Nostrand.

SPYKMAN, NICHOLAS. (1944) *Geography of Peace*. New York: Harcourt Brace.

STANISLAW, JOSEPH, AND DANIEL YERGIN. (1993) "Oil: Reopening the Door," *Foreign Affairs* 72 (October): 81–93.

STANLEY FOUNDATION. (1993) *The UN Role in Intervention*. Muscatine, Iowa: The Stanley Foundation.

STARKE, LINDA. (1994) "Fertility Rates: The Decline Is Stalling," *WorldWatch* 7 (March/April): 37–38.

STEDMAN, STEPHEN JOHN. (1993) "The New Interventionists," *Foreign Affairs* 72 (No. 1): 1–16.

STEIN, JANICE GROSS. (1993) "Reassurance in International Conflict Management," pp. 77–97 in Demetrios Caraly and Cerentha Harris (eds.), *New World Politics*. New York: Academy of Political Science.

STEIN, JANICE GROSS, AND LOUIS W. PAULY. (1993) *Choosing to Cooperate: How States Avoid Loss*. Baltimore: Johns Hopkins University Press.

STERNER, MICHAEL. (1990–1991) "Navigating the Gulf," *Foreign Policy* 81 (Winter): 39–52.

STETSON, MARNIE. (1991) "People Who Live in Green Houses . . .," *WorldWatch* 4 (September–October): 22–29.

STOBAUGH, ROBERT. (1982) "World Energy to the Year 2000," pp. 29–57 in Daniel Yergin and Martin Hillenbrand (eds.), *Global Insecurity*. New York: Penguin.

STOCKHOLM INTERNATIONAL PEACE RESEARCH INSTITUTE (SIPRI). (1993) *World Armaments and Disarmament*. New York: Oxford University Press.

STOESSINGER, JOHN G. (1977) *The United Nations and the Superpowers: China, Russia, and America*. New York: Random House.

STRANG, DAVID. (1991) "Global Patterns of Decolonization, 1500–1987," *International Studies Quarterly* 35 (December): 429–545.

———. (1990) "From Dependence to Sovereignty: An Event History Analysis of Decolonization 1870–1987," *American Sociological Review* 55 (December): 846–860.

STRANGE, SUSAN. (1985) "Protectionism and World Politics," *International Organization* 39 (Spring): 233–259.

———. (1982) "Cave! Hic Dragones: A Critique of Regime Analysis," *International Organization* 36 (Spring): 479–496.

STUART, DOUGLAS. (1993) "NATO's Future as a Pan-European Security Institution," *NATO Review* 41 (August): 15–19.

SUMNER, WILLIAM GRAHAM. (1968) "War," pp. 205–228 in Leon Bramson and George W. Goethals (eds.), *War*. New York: Basic Books.

TALBOTT, STROBE. (1990) "Rethinking the Red Menace," *Time* (January 1): 66–72.

TANTER, RAYMOND, AND RICHARD ULLMAN. (eds.) (1972) *Theory and Policy in International Relations*. Princeton, N.J.: Princeton University Press.

TAPLIN, GRANT B. (1992) "Revitalizing UNCTAD," *Finance and Development* 29 (June): 37–38.

TARR, DAVID W. (1991) *Nuclear Deterrence and International Security: Alternative Security Regimes*. New York: Longman.

TAYLOR, PAUL. (1993) "Cities of Violence," *Washington Post National Weekly Edition* 11 (November 15–21): 6.

TAYLOR, PETER J. (ed.) (1990) *World Government*. New York: Oxford University Press.

THOMPSON, KENNETH W. (1960) *Political Realism and the Crisis of World Politics*. Princeton, N.J.: Princeton University Press.

———. (1953) "Collective Security Reexamined," *American Political Science Review* 47 (September): 753–772.

THOMPSON, WILLIAM R. (1992) "Dehio, Long Cycles and the Geohistorical Context of Structural Transitions," *World Politics* 45 (October): 127–152.

——— .(1988) *On Global War: Historical–Structural Approaches to World Politics*. Columbia: University of South Carolina Press.

THUROW, LESTER C. (1992) *Head to Head: Coming Economic Battles among Japan, Europe, and America*. New York: William Morrow.

TICKNER, J. ANN. (1992) *Gender in International Relations: Feminist Perspectives on Achieving Global Security*. New York: Columbia University Press.

TILLEMA, HERBERT K. (1991) *International Armed Conflict since 1945: A Bibliographic Handbook of Wars and Military Interventions*. Boulder, Colo.: Westview.

————. (1989) "Foreign Overt Military Intervention in the Nuclear Age," *Journal of Peace Research* 26 (May): 179–195.

TILLEMA, HERBERT K., AND JOHN R. VAN WINGEN. (1982) "Law and Power in Military Intervention: Major States after World War II," *International Studies Quarterly* 26 (June): 220–250.

TIMMERMAN, KENNETH. (1991) *The Death Lobby: How the West Armed Iraq.* Boston: Houghton Mifflin.

TODARO, MICHAEL P. (1989) *Economic Development in the Third World,* 4th ed. New York: Longman.

TOFFLER, ALVIN, AND HEIDI TOFFLER. (1993) *War and Anti-War: Survival at the Dawn of the Twenty-First Century.* New York: Little, Brown.

TONELSON, ALAN. (1991) "What Is the National Interest?" *Atlantic Monthly* 268 (July): 35–52.

TOPPING, JOHN C., JR. (1990) "Global Warming: Impact on Developing Countries," *Policy Focus,* No. 6. Washington, D.C.: Overseas Development Council.

TOYNBEE, ARNOLD J. (1954) *A Study of History.* London: Oxford University Press.

TRACHTENBERG, MARC. (1990–1991) "The Meaning of Mobilization in 1914," *International Security* 15 (Winter): 120–150.

TRIFFIN, ROBERT. (1978–1979) "The International Role and Fate of the Dollar," *Foreign Affairs* 57 (Winter): 269–286.

TUCHMAN, BARBARA. (1962) *The Guns of August.* New York: Dell.

TUCKER, ROBERT W. (1990) "1989 and All That," *Foreign Affairs* 69 (Fall): 93–114.

————. (1980) "America in Decline: The Foreign Policy of 'Maturity'," *Foreign Affairs* 58 (No. 3): 449–484.

TURNER, ROBERT F. (1990) "What's Wrong with Killing Saddam Hussein?" *Washington Post National Weekly Edition* 9 (October 15–21): 24.

TYSON, LAURA D'ANDREA. (1993) *Trade Conflicts in High-Technology Industries.* Washington, D.C.: Institute for International Economics.

UNCTAD. (1993) *World Investment Report 1993.* New York: United Nations.

UNITED NATIONS. (1991a) *World Economic Survey 1991.* New York: United Nations.

————. (1991b) *The World's Women 1970–1990: Trends and Statistics.* New York: United Nations.

UNITED NATIONS DEVELOPMENT PROGRAMME (UNDP). (1994) *Human Development Report 1994.* New York: Oxford University Press.

————. (1993) *Human Development Report 1993.* New York: Oxford University Press.

————. (1991) *Human Development Report 1991.* New York: Oxford University Press.

UNITED NATIONS FUND FOR POPULATION ACTIVITIES. (1991) *State of World Population 1991.* New York: United Nations Fund for Population Activities.

UNITED NATIONS PROGRAMME ON TRANSNATIONAL CORPORATIONS. (1993) "World Investment Report 1993," *Transnational Corporations* 2 (August): 99–123.

U.S. ARMS CONTROL AND DISARMAMENT AGENCY (ACDA). (1994) *World Military Expenditures and Arms Transfers 1991–1993.* Washington, D.C.: U.S. Government Printing Office.

————. (1992) *World Military Expenditures and Arms Transfers 1990.* Washington, D.C.: U.S. Government Printing Office.

————. (1990) *World Military Expenditures and Arms Transfers 1989.* Washington, D.C.: U.S. Government Printing Office.

————. (1979) *Arms Control 1978.* Washington, D.C.: U.S. Government Printing Office.

U.S. CENTRAL INTELLIGENCE AGENCY (CIA). (1993) *The World Factbook 1993–94.* New York: Brassey's.

————. (1992a) *Handbook of International Economic Statistics.* Washington, D.C.: U.S. Government Printing Office.

————. (1992b) *World Factbook 1992.* Washington, D.C.: U.S. Government Printing Office.

U.S. COMMISSION ON INTEGRATED LONG-TERM STRATEGY. (1988) *Discriminate Deterrence.* Washington, D.C.: U.S. Government Printing Office.

U.S. CONGRESS, OFFICE OF TECHNOLOGY ASSESSMENT. (1991) *Energy in Developing Countries.* Washington, D.C.: U.S. Government Printing Office.

————. (1981) *Technology and Soviet Energy Availability.* Washington, D.C.: U.S. Government Printing Office.

U.S. DEPARTMENT OF ENERGY. (1987) Energy Information Administration. *Monthly Energy Review* (October).

U.S. DEPARTMENT OF STATE. (1994) *Patterns of International Terrorism 1993.* Washington, D.C.: Office of the Coordinator for Counterterrorism, U.S. Department of State.

————. (1993a) *Patterns of Global Terrorism 1992.* Washington, D.C.: Office of the Coordinator for Counterterrorism, U.S. Department of State.

————. (1993b) *State 2000: A New Model for Managing Foreign Affairs.* Washington, D.C.: Office of Management Task Force, U.S. Department of State.

————. (1991) *Patterns of Global Terrorism: 1990.* Washington, D.C.: U.S. Department of State.

———. (1985) *Atlas of United States Foreign Relations*. Washington, D.C.: U.S. Government Printing Office.

———. (1983) *Security and Arms Control: The Search for a More Stable Peace*. Washington, D.C.: U.S. Government Printing Office.

———. (1978) "World Population: The Silent Explosion—Part 1," *Department of State Bulletin* 78 (October): 45–54.

URQUHART, BRIAN. (1994) "Who Can Police the World?" *New York Review of Books* 41 (May 12): 29–33.

USTIUGOV, MIKHAIL. (1993) "An Embarrassment of Weapons," *Bulletin of the Atomic Scientists* 49 (October): 48–50.

VAN DE KAA, DIRK J. (1987) "Europe's Second Demographic Transition," *Population Bulletin* 42 (No. 1). Washington, D.C.: Population Reference Bureau.

VAN EVERA, STEPHEN. (1994) "Hypotheses on Nationalism and War," *International Security* 18 (Spring): 5–39.

———. (1992) "The United States and the Third World: When to Intervene?" pp. 105–150 in Kenneth A. Oye, Robert J. Lieber, and Donald Rothchild (eds.), *Eagle in a New World*. New York: HarperCollins.

———. (1990–1991) "Primed for Peace: Europe after the Cold War," *International Security* 15 (Winter): 7–57.

VARON, BENSION, AND KENJI TAKEUCHI. (1974) "Developing Countries and Non-Fuel Minerals," *Foreign Affairs* 52 (April): 497–510.

VASQUEZ, JOHN. (1993) *The War Puzzle*. Cambridge: Cambridge University Press.

———. (1991) "The Deterrence Myth: Nuclear Weapons and the Prevention of Nuclear War," pp. 205–223 in Charles W. Kegley Jr. (ed.), *The Long Postwar Peace*. New York: HarperCollins.

VÄYRYNEN, RAIMO. (1992) *Military Industrialization and Economic Development*. Aldershot, England: Dartmouth.

VERBA, SIDNEY. (1969) "Assumptions of Rationality and Non-Rationality in Models of the International System," pp. 217–231 in James N. Rosenau (ed.), *International Politics and Foreign Policy*. New York: Free Press.

VERNON, RAYMOND. (1982) "International Trade Policy in the 1980s: Prospects and Problems," *International Studies Quarterly* 26 (December): 483–510.

———. (1975) "Foreign Operations," pp. 275–298 in James W. McKie (ed.), *Social Responsibility and the Business Predicament*. Washington, D.C.: Brookings Institution.

———. (1971) *Sovereignty at Bay*. New York: Basic Books.

WALD, MATTHEW L. (1993) "20 Years Later, U.S. Foot Still on the Gas," *The State* (Columbia, S.C.) (October 18): A1, A5.

WALDHEIM, KURT. (1984) "The United Nations: The Tarnished Image," *Foreign Affairs* 63 (Fall): 93–107.

WALKER, R. B. J. (1993) *Inside/Outside: International Relations as Political Theory*. Cambridge: Cambridge University Press.

———. (1987) "Realism, Change, and International Political Theory," *International Studies Quarterly* 31 (March): 65–86.

WALKER, WILLIAM O. (1991) "Decision-making Theory and Narcotic Foreign Policy: Implications for Historical Analysis," *Diplomatic History* 15 (Winter): 31–45.

WALLACE, BRIAN. (1978) "True Grit South of the Border," *Osceola* (January 13): 15–16.

WALLACE, MICHAEL D. (1973) "Alliance Polarization, Cross-cutting, and International War, 1815–1964," *Journal of Conflict Resolution* 17 (December): 575–604.

WALLENSTEEN, PETER, AND KARIN AXELL. (1993) "Armed Conflict at the End of the Cold War, 1989–1992," *Journal of Peace Research* 30 (August): 331–346.

WALLERSTEIN, IMMANUEL. (1988) *The Modern World-System III: The Second Era of Great Expansion of the Capitalist World-System, 1730–1840*. San Diego: Academic Press.

———. (1980) *The Modern World-System II*. New York: Academic Press.

———. (1974a) *The Modern World-System: Capitalist Agriculture and the Origins of the European World-Economy in the Sixteenth Century*. New York: Academic Press.

———. (1974b) "The Rise and Future Demise of the World Capitalist System: Concepts for Comparative Analysis," *Comparative Studies in Society and History* 16 (September): 387–415.

WALLIS, ALLEN. (1986) "U.S.–EC Relations and the International Trading System." Address before the Luxembourg Society for International Affairs, October 8. U.S. Department of State, Bureau of Public Affairs, Current Policy No. 889.

WALTERS, ROBERT S., AND DAVID H. BLAKE. (1992) *The Politics of Global Economic Relations*, 4th ed. Englewood Cliffs, N.J.: Prentice-Hall.

WALTZ, KENNETH N. (1995) "Realist Thought and Neorealist Theory," pp. 67–83 in Charles W. Kegley Jr. (ed.), *Controversies in International Relations Theory: Realism and the Neoliberal Challenge*. New York: St. Martin's Press.

———. (1993) "The Emerging Structure of International Politics," *International Security* 18 (Fall): 44–79.

———. (1979) *Theory of International Politics.* Reading, Mass.: Addison-Wesley.

———. (1975) "Theory of International Relations," pp. 1–85 in Fred I. Greenstein and Nelson W. Polsby (eds.), *International Politics: Handbook of Political Science,* Vol. 8. Reading, Mass.: Addison-Wesley.

———. (1970) "The Myth of National Interdependence," pp. 205–223 in Charles P. Kindleberger (ed.), *The International Corporation.* Cambridge, Mass.: MIT Press.

———. (1964) "The Stability of a Bipolar World," *Daedalus* 93 (Summer): 881–909.

———. (1954) *Man, the State, and War.* New York: Columbia University Press.

WATTENBERG, BEN J. (1989) *The Birth Dearth.* New York: Pharos Books.

WAYMAN, FRANK, AND PAUL F. DIEHL. (eds.) (1995) *Reconstructing Realpolitik.* Ann Arbor: University of Michigan Press.

WEINER, TIM. (1993) "C.I.A. Says Chinese Economy Rivals Japan's," *New York Times* (August 1): 6.

WEISSKOPF, MICHAEL. (1991) "Paying the Overheating Bill," *Washington Post National Weekly Edition* 8 (February 11–17): 33.

WELCH, DAVID A. (1992) "The Organizational Process and Bureaucratic Politics Paradigms: Retrospect and Prospect," *International Security* 17 (Spring): 112–146.

WELLER, ROBERT H., AND LEON F. BOUVIER. (1981) *Population: Demography and Policy.* New York: St. Martin's Press.

WELTMAN, JOHN J. (1974) "On the Obsolescence of War," *International Studies Quarterly* 18 (December): 395–416.

WENDT, ALEXANDER. (1992) "Anarchy Is What States Make of It: The Social Construction of Power Politics," *International Organization* 46 (Spring): 391–426.

WENDZEL, ROBERT L. (1980) *International Relations: A Policymaker Focus.* New York: Wiley.

WESSEL, DAVID. (1992) "World's Economies, Now Interdependent, All Suffer Together," *Wall Street Journal* (September 17): A1, A12.

WHITE, RALPH K. (1990) "Why Aggressors Lose," *Political Psychology* 11 (June): 227–242.

WHITING, ALLEN S. (1985) "Foreign Policy of China," pp. 246–290 in Roy C. Macridis (ed.), *Foreign Policy in World Politics,* 6th ed. Englewood Cliffs, N.J.: Prentice-Hall.

WILLIAMS, SHIRLEY. (1991) "Sovereignty and Accountability in the European Community," pp. 155–176 in Robert O. Keohane and Stanley Hoffmann (eds.), *The New European Community: Decisionmaking and Institutional Change.* Boulder, Colo.: Westview.

WILMER, FRANKE. (1993) *The Indigenous Voice in World Politics: Since Time Immemorial.* Newbury Park, Calif.: Sage.

WILSON, JAMES Q. (1993) *The Moral Sense.* New York: Free Press.

WINIECKI, JAN. (1989) "CPEs' Structural Change and World Market Performance: A Permanently Developing Country (PDC) Status," *Soviet Studies* 41 (July): 365–381.

WISE, MICHAEL Z. (1993) "Reparations," *The Atlantic* 272 (October): 32–35.

WITTKOPF, EUGENE R. (1990) *Faces of Internationalism: Public Opinion and American Foreign Policy.* Durham, N.C.: Duke University Press.

WOLFERS, ARNOLD. (1968) "Alliances," pp. 268–271 in David L. Sills (ed.), *International Encyclopedia of the Social Sciences.* New York: Macmillan.

———. (1962) *Discord and Collaboration.* Baltimore: Johns Hopkins University Press.

WOLF-PHILLIPS, LESLIE. (1987) "Why 'Third World'?: Origin, Definitions and Usage," *Third World Quarterly* 9 (October): 1311–1327.

WOLPIN, MILES. (1983) "Comparative Perspectives on Militarization, Repression, and Social Welfare," *Journal of Peace Research* 20 (No. 2): 129–156.

WOODS, ALAN. (1989) *Development and the National Interest: U.S. Economic Assistance into the 21st Century.* Washington, D.C.: Agency for International Development.

WOODWARD, BOB. (1991) *The Commanders.* New York: Simon & Schuster.

WOODWARD, BOB, AND RICK ATKINSON. (1990) "Launching Operation Desert Shield," *Washington Post National Weekly Edition* 7 (September 3–9): 8–9.

WOODWELL, GEORGE M. (1990) "The Effects of Global Warming," pp. 116–132 in Jeremy Leggett (ed.), *Global Warming: The Greenpeace Report.* New York: Oxford University Press.

WORLD BANK. (1993) *World Debt Tables 1993–94.* Vol. 1, *Analysis and Summary Tables.* Washington, D.C.: The World Bank.

WORLD COMMISSION ON ENVIRONMENT AND DEVELOPMENT. (1987) *Our Common Future.* New York: Oxford University Press.

*World Development Report 1993*. (1993) New York: Oxford University Press.

*World Development Report 1991*. (1991) New York: Oxford University Press.

*World Development Report 1989*. (1989) New York: Oxford University Press.

*World Development Report 1987*. (1987) New York: Oxford University Press.

*World Development Report 1986*. (1986) New York: Oxford University Press.

*World Development Report 1985*. (1985) New York: Oxford University Press.

WORLD RESOURCES INSTITUTE. (1992) *World Resources 1992–93*. New York: Oxford University Press.

———. (1990) *World Resources 1990–91*. New York: Oxford University Press.

WRIGGINS, W. HOWARD. (1978) "Third World Strategies for Change: The Political Context of North–South Interdependence," pp. 19–117 in W. Howard Wriggins and Gunnar Adler-Karlsson (eds.), *Reducing Global Inequalities*. New York: McGraw-Hill.

WRIGHT, QUINCY. (1955) *The Study of International Relations*. New York: Appleton-Century-Crofts.

———. (1953) "The Outlawry of War and the Law of War," *American Journal of International Law* 47 (July): 365–376.

———. (1942) *A Study of War*. Chicago: University of Chicago Press.

WYMAN, RICHARD L. (ed.) (1991) *Global Climate Change and Life on Earth*. New York: Routledge, Chapman and Hall.

YARMOLINSKY, ADAM. (1988) "Low-Intensity Conflict: Causes, Consequences, and Questionable Cures," pp. 96–101 in Charles W. Kegley Jr. and Eugene R. Wittkopf (eds.), *The Global Agenda*, 2nd ed. New York: Random House.

YODER, EDWIN M., JR. (1991) "Isolationists Would Put America on a Dangerous Course," *The State* (Columbia, S.C.) (December 14): A10.

YOUNG, JOHN E. (1991) "Reducing Waste, Saving Materials," pp. 39–55 in Lester R. Brown et al., *State of the World 1991*. New York: Norton.

YOUNG, ORAN. (1986) "International Regimes: Toward a New Theory of Institutions," *World Politics* 39 (October): 104–122.

ZACHER, MARK W. (1991) "Toward a Theory of International Regimes," pp. 119–137 in Robert L. Rothstein (ed.), *The Evolution of Theory in International Relations*. Columbia: University of South Carolina Press.

———. (1987) "Trade Gaps, Analytical Gaps: Regime Analysis and International Commodity Regulation," *International Organization* 41 (Spring): 173–202.

ZACHER, MARK W., AND RICHARD A. MATTHEW. (1995) "Liberal International Theory: Common Threads, Divergent Strands," pp. 107–149 in Charles W. Kegley Jr. (ed.), *Controversies in International Relations Theory: Realism and the Neoliberal Challenge*. New York: St. Martin's Press.

ZAGARE, FRANK C. (1990) "Rationality and Deterrence," *World Politics* 42 (January): 238–260.

ZAGORIN, JANET S. (1990) *Europe 1992: Navigating New Waters*. New York: Baker and McKenzie.

ZAKARIA, FAREED. (1992–1993) "Is Realism Finished?" *The National Interest* 30 (Winter): 21–32.

ZELIKOW, PHILIP. (1987) "The United States and the Use of Force: A Historical Summary," pp. 31–81 in George K. Osburn, Asa A. Clark IV, Daniel J. Kaufman, and Douglas E. Lute (eds.), *Democracy, Strategy, and Vietnam*. Lexington, Mass.: Lexington Books.

ZIMMERMAN, TIM. (1994) "Arms Merchant to the World," *U.S. News & World Report* (April 4): 37.

ZINNES, DINA A. (1980) "Prerequisites for the Study of System Transformation," pp. 3–21 in Ole R. Holsti, Randolph M. Siverson, and Alexander L. George (eds.), *Change in the International System*. Boulder, Colo.: Westview.

ZINNES, DINA A., AND JONATHAN WILKENFELD. (1971) "An Analysis of Foreign Conflict Behavior of Nations," pp. 167–213 in Wolfram F. Handieder (ed.), *Comparative Foreign Policy*. New York: McKay.

# GLOSSARY

• • •

**Acid rain:** precipitation that has been made acidic through contact with sulfur dioxide and nitrogen oxides.

**ACP nations:** African, Caribbean, and Pacific developing nations linked to the European Union through treaties of cooperation.

**Adjudication:** a conflict resolution procedure where a third party makes a binding decision through an institutionalized tribunal.

**Aid burden:** the ratio between aid and a donor's income as measured by gross national product.

**Algiers summit conference (1973):** the international meeting that resulted in the Group of 77 joining forces with the nonaligned movement.

**Alliance:** a formal agreement among states for the purpose of coordinating their behavior in the event of certain specified military contingencies.

**Anarchy:** an absence of governmental authority.

**Apartheid:** the South African policy of racial separation.

**Appeasement:** a policy that attempts to buy off a potential aggressor with concessions that may conflict with the country's principles.

**Arbitration:** a conflict resolution procedure where a third party makes a binding decision through an ad hoc forum.

**Arms control:** agreements designed to regulate arms levels.

**ASAT weapon:** antisatellite weapon.

**Asian Tigers:** the four Asian NICs (Hong Kong, South Korea, Singapore, and Taiwan) that experienced rates of economic growth during the 1980s far greater than the more advanced industrial societies of the First World.

**Atlantic Charter:** a declaration issued in 1941 by U.S. President Franklin D. Roosevelt and British Prime Minister Winston Churchill outlining the principles that would guide the construction of a postwar general security system.

**Baker initiative:** a proposal to resolve the Third World debt problem by encouraging domestic economic reforms and seeking new loans from private banks.

**Balance of payments:** a summary statement of a state's financial transactions with the rest of the world, including such items as foreign aid transfers and the income of citizens employed abroad who send their paychecks home.

**Balance of power theory:** a body of thought that contends peace will result when military power is distributed in such a way that no one state can dominate the others.

**Balance of trade:** a state's net trade surplus or deficit, based on the difference in the value of its imports and exports.

**Balancer:** a role played by a state that gives its support to one or another side of a dispute to ensure that no one achieves preponderance.

**Ballistic missile defense (BMD):**   a system to defend against an attack by incoming ballistic missiles.

**Bandung Conference (1955):**   a meeting of twenty-nine Asian and African nations that was held in Bandung, Indonesia to devise a strategy to combat colonialism.

**Bandwagon:**   the process of aligning with the most powerful state.

**Baruch Plan (1946):**   a call for the creation of a UN Atomic Development Authority that would place atomic energy under international authority.

**Beggar-thy-neighbor policy:**   efforts to promote domestic welfare by promoting trade surpluses that can be realized only at other countries' expense.

**Behavioralism:**   an approach to the study of international relations that emphasizes the application of scientific methods.

**Bilateral aid:**   aid that flows directly from one country to another.

**Billiard ball model:**   a metaphor that compares world politics to a game in which billiard balls (states) continuously clash and collide with one another. The actions of each are determined by their interactions with the others, not by what occurs within them.

**Biological Weapons Convention (1972):**   an agreement prohibiting the development, production, and stockpiling of biological weapons.

**Bipolar:**   an international system containing two dominant power centers.

**Bipolarization:**   the clustering of smaller states in alliances around the two dominant power centers.

**Bipolycentrism:**   the existence of military bipolarity between the United States and Soviet Union coupled with multiple political centers of independent foreign policy decisions.

**Bloc:**   a rigid, highly cohesive alliance among a group of states.

**Brady initiative:**   an approach to resolving the Third World debt crisis by reducing the debt of all debtor nations.

**Bretton Woods system:**   the rules, institutions, and decision-making procedures devised during World War II to govern international economic relations in the postwar era.

**Brezhnev Doctrine:**   the assertion by Leonid Brezhnev following the 1968 Soviet invasion of Czechoslovakia that the USSR had the right to intervene to preserve communist party rule in any state within the Soviet bloc.

**Brinkmanship:**   the threat of nuclear escalation in a confrontation to compel submission.

**Brundtland Commission:**   the 1987 World Commission on Environment and Development that called for sustainable development.

**Bureaucratic politics model:**   an interpretation of policy making that stresses the bargaining and compromises among the contending governmental organizations that exert influence on the foreign policy choices of political leaders.

**Camp David Declaration on New Relations (1992):**   a joint statement by Russian President Boris Yeltsin and U.S. President George Bush that asserts the relationship between Russia and the United States will be characterized by friendship and partnership.

**Carrying capacity:**   the maximum biomass that can be supported by a given territory.

**Cartel:**   an organization of the producers of a commodity that seeks to regulate the pricing and production of the commodity.

**Carter Doctrine:**   a statement by President Jimmy Carter declaring U.S. willingness to use military force to protect its interests in the Persian Gulf.

**Chemical Weapons Convention (CWC):** an agreement signed by 147 states requiring the destruction of existing stocks of chemical weapons.

**Chernobyl nuclear accident:** a nuclear catastrophe that occurred at a power plant in the Ukraine during 1986.

**Classical imperialism:** the first wave of European empire building that began during the fifteenth century, as the English, French, Dutch, Portuguese, and Spanish used their military power to achieve commercial advantages overseas.

**Classical realism:** see political realism.

**Closed economic system:** a system based on a centrally planned or command economy.

**Club of Rome:** a private group that has popularized a neo-Malthusian interpretation of growth.

**Coercive diplomacy:** the use of threats or limited force to persuade an adversary to call of or undo an encroachment.

**Collective good:** goods that are jointly supplied and from which it is not possible to exclude beneficiaries.

**Collective security:** a system of world order in which aggression by any state will be met by a collective response.

**Colonialism:** the rule of a region by an external sovereign power.

**Commonwealth of Independent States (CIS):** the political entity that replaced the Soviet Union on January 1, 1992.

**Comparative advantage principle:** any two nations will benefit if each specializes in those goods it produces comparatively cheaply and acquires, through trade, goods that it can only produce at a higher cost.

**Compellence:** the use of nuclear weapons as instruments of coercive diplomacy.

**Complex interdependence:** an approach to the study of international relations that challenges the realist assumptions that nation-states are the only important actors in world politics, that national security issues dominate decision-making agendas, and that military force is the only means of exercising influence in international politics.

**Concert of Europe:** a system of great power conference diplomacy organized in Europe after the Napoleonic Wars.

**Conciliation:** a conflict resolution procedure where a third party assists both sides but offers no solution.

**Continuity:** persistence of a trend without a fundamental change.

**Conventional (liberal) theory of economic development:** a theory that emphasized indigenous impediments to Third World development. Based on the assumption that growth meant increasing increments of per-capita GNP, the task was to identify and remove obstacles to growth and supply missing components, such as investment capital.

**Cornucopians:** optimists who question limits-to-growth analyses and contend that markets effectively maintain a balance between population, resources, and the environment.

**Council for Mutual Economic Assistance (CMEA):** an international economic organization created in 1949 containing the Soviet Union and the countries of Eastern Europe.

**Counterforce targeting:** targeting an opponent's military forces and weapons.

**Counterinsurgency:** combat against revolutionary guerrillas.

**Countervalue targeting:** targeting an opponent's industrial and population centers.

**Crisis:** a situation that threatens high-priority goals, restricts the time available for response, and surprises decision makers.

**Cultural imperialism:** imposing one country's value system on another people who do not welcome such foreign influence.

**Current history:** an approach to understanding international relations that focuses on the description of events, not theoretical explanation.

**Debt decade:** a prolonged financial crisis that began in 1982 when it appeared that Third World debtor nations might default on their loans.

**Debtor's cartel:** a proposal that Third World debtor nations confront the creditor nations with a coalition when pressing for a solution to the debt crisis.

**Declaration on the Granting of Independence to Colonial Countries and Peoples (1960):** a declaration passed by the UN General Assembly that proclaimed the subjection of any people to colonial domination was a denial of human rights.

**Demographic transition theory:** an explanation of population changes over time that highlights the causes of declines in birth and death rates.

**Dependence theory:** a theory that claims the relationship between advanced capitalist societies and those at the periphery of the world economy is exploitative. According to this view, capitalism's need for external sources of demand and profitable investment outlets led to the penetration of virtually every part of the Third World and the establishment of a dominance-dependence relationship between North and South.

**Dependent development:** the industrialization of peripheral areas within the confines of the dominance-dependence relationship between North and South.

**Détente:** the relaxation of tensions between adversaries.

**Deterrence:** a preventive strategy designed to dissuade an adversary from doing what it would otherwise do.

**Disarmament:** agreements designed to reduce or eliminate weapons.

**Diversionary theory of war:** the contention that leaders initiate conflict abroad as a way of increasing national cohesion at home.

**Dollar convertibility:** a commitment by the U.S. government to exchange dollars for gold.

**Domino theory:** a metaphor that predicts the fall to communism in one country would cause the fall of its neighbors, and in turn still others.

**Dualism:** the existence of a rural, impoverished, and neglected sector of society operating alongside an urban, developing, or modernizing sector, where there is little interaction between the two sectors.

**Dual use technology:** technology that has both commercial and military uses.

**Ecological transition:** a process in situations of high population growth where human demands come to exceed sustainable yield.

**Economic sanctions:** governmental actions aimed at inflicting deprivation on a target state through the limitation or termination of economic relations.

**Elitist decision making:** a model of the policy-making process that ascribes disproportionate control over foreign policy making to a small ruling group.

**Engel's law:** poorer families spend a greater percentage of their budget on food than do higher-income groups.

**Entente Cordiale:** an alliance between Britain and France that was established in 1902.

**Environmental refugee:** a person who abandons land no longer fit for human habitation due to environmental degradation.

**Ethnic nationalism:** devotion to a cultural, ethnic, or linguistic community within an existing nation-state.

**Ethnocentrism:** the belief that one's nationality is special and superior, and that others are secondary and inferior.

**Eurocrat:** a member of the professional staff who assist the Executive Commission of the European Union.

**European Community (EC)/European Union (EU):** a regional organization created by the merger of the European Coal and Steel Community, the European Atomic Energy Community, and the European Economic Community; known as the European Union after November 1993.

**European Free Trade Association (EFTA):** an organization created in 1960 as a counterpoint to the European Economic Community.

**European Monetary System (EMS):** an arrangement designed to stabilize the currency values of EU member's against one another and against the dollar.

**Export-led industrialization:** a strategy that involves developing domestic export industries capable of competing in overseas markets.

**Export quotas:** a barrier to free trade imposed pursuant to negotiated agreements between producers and consumers.

**Extended deterrence:** a strategy that seeks to deter an adversary from attacking one's allies.

**Feminist theory:** a body of scholarship that emphasizes gender in the study of world politics.

**Fertility rate (total):** the average number of children born to a woman (or group of women) during her lifetime.

**Financial veto:** withholding payment selectively from certain UN programs as a way to register resentment of the organization's activities and to change them.

**Firebreak:** the psychological barrier between conventional and nuclear war.

**First World:** countries that share a commitment to varying forms of democratic political institutions and developed marked economies, including the United States, Japan, Canada, Australia, New Zealand, Israel, Malta, South Africa, and the countries of Western Europe.

**Fixed exchange rates:** a system under which states establish the parity of their currencies and commit themselves to keeping fluctuations in their exchange rates within very narrow limits.

**Food ladder:** a conceptualization based on the biological food chain. As personal income increases, individuals move up the ladder, consuming grains indirectly as meat rather than directly.

**Food security:** access by all people at all times to enough food for an active, healthy life.

**Fossil fuels:** fuels such as coal, petroleum, and natural gas that are formed from organic remains.

**Fourteen Points speech (1918):** a speech delivered by U.S. President Woodrow Wilson that called for open diplomacy, self-determination, free trade, freedom of the seas, disarmament, and collective security.

**Fourth World:** indigenous people that often live in poverty and deprivation within a nation-state that occupies the land from which they originate. Sometimes used to refer to the "least-developed" of the less-developed countries.

**Free-floating exchange rates:** a system in which market forces determine currency values.

**Free riders:** those who enjoy the benefits of collective goods but pay little or nothing for them.

**Functionalism:** a bottom-up approach to fostering political integration through transnational organizations that emphasize sharing sovereignty.

**General Agreement of Tariffs and Trade (GATT):** an international organization that seeks to promote and protect the most-favored-nation principle as the basis for international trade.

**General Assembly:** one of six principle organs established by the UN Charter. It is the only body representing all the member states. Decision making follows the principle of majority rule, with no state given a veto.

**Generalized System of Preferences (GSP):** a scheme that permits First World nations to grant preferences to developing nations without violating GATT's nondiscrimination principle.

**Glasnost:** the Russian word for Mikhail Gorbachev's policy of openness.

**Global warming:** a suspected consequence of greenhouse gases that trap heat remitted from earth that would otherwise escape into outer space.

**Good offices:** the third-party offering of a location for discussions among disputants.

**Green revolution:** the introduction of new high-yield grains to Third World countries.

**Group of Seven (G-7):** the United States, Britain, France, Japan, Germany, Canada, and Italy. Leaders from these industrialized nations meet in regular economic summit conferences.

**Group of 77 (G-77):** a coalition of the world's poor countries formed during the 1964 United Nations Conference on Trade and Development (UNCTAD) in Geneva. Originally composed if 77 states, the coalition now numbers over 120 developing countries and continues to press for concessions from the wealthy nations.

**Groupthink:** the propensity of cohesive, insulated groups to suffer from a deterioration of mental efficiency, reality testing, and moral judgement.

**Gunboat diplomacy:** a show of military force, historically called naval force.

**Hague Peace Conferences (1899, 1907):** international meetings that restricted the use of certain weapons and sought to promote peaceful methods of dispute resolution.

**Hard power:** the ability to exercise influence in world politics because of the user's possession of tangible military and economic resources.

**Hegemon:** a dominant military and economic state that uses its unrivaled power to create and enforce rules aimed at preserving the existing world order and its own positions in that order.

**Hegemonic stability theory:** a theory that draws attention to the impact of preeminent states (hegemons) on international cooperation.

**Helsinki Accord (1975):** an agreement signed by NATO, Warsaw Pact, and thirteen neutral and nonaligned European countries that sought to establish peace in Europe by calling for the implementation of confidence-building measures, economic, environmental, and scientific cooperation, and the free flow of people, ideas, and information.

**Hero-in-history model:** an interpretation of foreign policy behavior that equates national action with the preferences and initiatives of the highest officials in national governments.

**Hidden veto:** the ability of the United States during the formative period of the United Nations to persuade a sufficient majority of other UN Security Council members to vote negatively on an issue so as to avoid the stigma of having to cast the single blocking vote.

**Hierarchy:** a division of entities (such as nation-states) into ordered ranks.

**High politics:** geostrategic issues of national and international security that pertain to matters of war and peace.

**Horizontal nuclear proliferation:** an increase in the number of states that possess nuclear weapons.

**Horizontal system of law:** a decentralized, self-help system of law.

**Host country:** The country where a corporation headquartered in another country conducts its business activities.

**Hot line:** a teletype communications link between Moscow and Washington that would permit national leaders to communicate directly during a crisis.

**Human Development Index (HDI):** an index that uses life expectancy, literacy, the average number of years of schooling, and income to assess a country's human development performance.

**ICBM:** intercontinental ballistic missile.

**Imperial overstretch:** a condition where commitments exceed a state's ability to fulfill them.

**Import quotas:** a nontariff barrier to free trade that involves limits on the quantity of a particular product that can be imported from abroad.

**Import-substitution industrialization:** a strategy that involves encouraging domestic entrepreneurs to manufacture products otherwise imported from abroad.

**Inadvertent war:** a war that is not the result of anyone's master plan; rather it occurs due to uncertainly, confusion, and circumstances beyond the control of those involved.

**Independents (oil companies):** competitors of the major oil companies who historically stood outside of the international oil regime controlled by the majors.

**Instrumental rationality:** a conceptualization of rationality asserting that individuals have preferences, and when faced with two or more alternatives, they will choose the one that yields the preferred outcome.

**Interdependence:** a situation of mutual dependence defined as mutual sensitivity and mutual vulnerability.

**Intergovernmental international organization (IGO):** an international organization whose members are nation-states.

**Intermediate-Range Nuclear Force (INF) Treaty (1987):** an agreement between the United States and Soviet Union to remove intermediate range nuclear forces from Europe.

**International Court of Justice:** the primary judicial organ of the United Nations; also known as the World Court.

**International Labor Organization:** a UN Specialized Agency responsible for improving working conditions in member countries.

**International Monetary Fund (IMF):** a specialized agency of the United Nations that seeks to maintain monetary stability and assist member states in funding balance of payments deficits.

**International nongovernmental organization (INGO):** an international organization whose members are private individuals and groups.

**International regime:** the set of rules, norms, and decision-making procedures that coordinates state behavior within a given area of activity.

**Intervention, military:** an overt or covert use of force by one or more countries that crosses the border of another country in order to effect the authority structure of the target county.

**Irredentism:** the desire by one nation to annex territory held by another that is historically or ethically related to the first nation.

**Irreversible conservation measures:** permanent steps taken toward conserving a resource.

**Just war:** a doctrine that pertains to the moral considerations under which war may be undertaken and how it should be fought once it begins.

**Kellogg-Briand Pact (Pact of Paris, 1928):** a treaty that sought to outlaw war as an instrument of national policy.

**League of Nations mandate system:** the placement of colonies previously held by the Central Powers of World War I under the administration of certain Allied nations. Implicit in the system was the idea that colonies were a trust rather than a territory to be exploited.

**League of Nations:** a global intergovernmental organization established after World War I.

**Least developed of the less-developed countries (LLDCs):** the most impoverished members of the Third World.

**Levels of analysis:** alternative perspectives on world politics that may focus on the personal characteristics of decision makers, the attributes of states, or the structure of the international system.

**Liberal International Economic Order (LIEO):** the set of regimes created after World War II designed to promote monetary stability and reduce barriers to the free flow of trade and capital.

**Linkage theory:** a set of assertions that claims leaders should take into account another country's overall behavior when deciding whether to reach agreement on any one specific issue.

**Lomé Convention (1975):** an agreement between the European Community and the ACP nations that granted the latter trade preferences and established STABEX.

**Long cycle theory:** a theory that focuses on the rise and fall of the leading global power as the central political process of the modern world system.

**Long peace:** the period of great power relations extending from the end of the Second World War until the present. It represents the longest period of great power peace in modern history.

**Low-intensity conflict:** fighting that falls below the threshold of full-scale military combat between modern armies.

**Low politics:** socioeconomic and welfare issues that pertain to matters of material well-being.

**Maastricht summit (1991):** a meeting of European Community members in The Netherlands that set forth a framework for achieving greater European unity.

**Macropolitical perspective:** an approach to the study of international affairs that looks at world politics as a system, with general global patterns of interaction among parts.

**Majors (oil companies):** Exxon, Gulf, Mobil, Standard Oil of California, Texaco, British Petroleum, Royal Dutch Shell, and Compagnie Francaise des Petroles.

**Malthusian projection:** the prediction that population when unchecked increases in a geometric ratio, whereas subsistence increases in only an arithmetic ratio.

**Marshall Plan:** a program of grants and loans established by the United States to assist the recovery of Western Europe after World War II.

**Massive retaliation:** the strategic posture of the U.S. during the Eisenhower administration.

**Mechanical majority:** a complaint voiced by the Soviet Union during the early history of the United Nations that the United States enjoyed a commanding position in the General Assembly due to the fact that its allies constituted a majority of the United Nations membership on whose support the United States could always depend.

**Mediation:** a conflict resolution procedure where a third party offers a nonbinding solution to the disputants.

**Mercantilism:** the economic philosophy advocating government regulation of economic life to increase state power and security. Under this philosophy, state power was assumed to flow from the possession of national wealth measured in terms of gold and silver. Exporting more than is imported constitutes one way to accumulate the desired bullion.

**Mirror images:** the propensity of each member of a conflict to see the other as the other sees it.

**MIRV:** multiple independently targeted recently vehicle.

**Montevideo Convention (1933):** an agreement that summarizes the major components of statehood and the rights and duties of states.

**Mortality rate:** crude death-rate is the most common measure of mortality. The age-adjusted death rate is often used in its place because it is free of distortions due to differences in age composition.

**Most-favored-nation (MFN) principle:** tariff preferences granted to one nation must be granted to all others exporting the same product.

**Multilateral aid:** aid that is channeled through international institutions.

**Multinational corporation (MNC):** a business enterprise organized in one society with activities in another growing out of direct investment abroad.

**Multipolar:** an international system containing more than two dominant power centers.

**Munich Conference (1938):** the conference at which Britain and France accepted Adolf Hitler's demand to annex the German-populated area of the Sudetenland in Czechoslovakia.

**Mutual assured destruction (MAD):** a system of mutual deterrence where both sides possess the ability to survive a first strike and launch a devastating retaliatory attack.

**Mutual security:** a belief that a diminution the national security of one's adversary reduces one's own security.

**Mutual sensitivity:** liability of states to costs imposed by external events before policies are changed to deal with the situation.

**Mutual vulnerability:** liability of states to costs imposed by external events even after policies have been changed to deal with the situation.

**Nation:** a collection of people who, on the basis of ethnic, linguistic, or cultural affinity, perceive themselves to be members of the same group.

**National attributes:** characteristics of nation-states (such as level of economic development or extent of military capability) that may influence their foreign policy behavior.

**Nationalism:** loyalty to a nation.

**Nation-state:** a polity (system of government) controlled by members of some nationality recognizing no higher authority.

**Neocolonialism (neo-imperialism):** unequal exchanges that permit the wealthy First World countries to exploit others through the institutionalized processes of the contemporary world political economy.

**Neofunctionalism:** a reconstitution of the functionalist theory of integration that directly addresses political factors.

**Neoliberalism:** a perspective on world politics that concentrates on the ways international organizations and other non-state actors promote international cooperation.

**Neo-Malthusians:** pessimists who warn of the global ecopolitical implications of uncontrolled growth.

**Neomercantilism:** a trade policy whereby a state seeks to maintain a balance-of-trade surplus by reducing imports, stimulating domestic production, and promoting exports.

**Neorealism:** a variant of realism that emphasizes the anarchic structure of world politics rather than human nature in its explanation of foreign policy behavior.

**New Imperialism:** the second wave of European empire building that began in the 1870s and extended until the outbreak of World War I. In contrast with classical imperialism, extraordinary competition among the imperial powers marked the new imperialism as colonies became an important symbol of national power and prestige.

**New international division of labor:** a projection that developing nations will provide the First World with manufactured and processed goods, while the latter will provide developing nations with raw materials and agricultural products.

**New International Economic Order (NIEO):** a demand by the Third World to replace the U.S.-sponsored Liberal International Economic Order (LIEO) with an international economic regime that is more favorable to the interests of developing countries.

**Newly Industrialized Countries (NICs):** a group of upper-middle-income countries that have become important exporters of manufactured goods, as well as important markets for the major industrialized countries that export capital goods. Included within this group are Brazil, Hong Kong, Mexico, Singapore, South Korea, and Taiwan.

**New World Information and Communication Order (NWICO):** a demand by the Third World for new regime covering the flow of information between North and South due to dissatisfaction with the media coverage provided by news agencies from the developed countries.

**Nixon Doctrine:** the position taken by President Richard Nixon that U.S. allies should bear a greater share of the burden for their own defense.

**Nomothetic generalizations:** lawlike statements that are presumed to hold across time and space.

**Nonaligned movement (NAM):** an organization founded in Belgrade during 1961 to promote nonalignment and a reduction in East-West tension.

**Nonalignment:** a foreign policy posture in which states do not participate in military alliances with either the East or West because of a fear that one form of domination might simply be replaced by another.

**Noninterference principle:** the duty of states to refrain from uninvited involvement in another's internal affairs.

**Nontariff barriers:** an inhibition against the free flow of goods and services across national boundaries that does not involve an import tax or duty.

**North American Free Trade Agreement (NAFTA):** an agreement designed to bring Mexico into the free-trade zone that already linked Canada and the United States.

**North Atlantic Cooperation Council (NACC):** a NATO council that was proposed in 1991 to build a partnership between NATO and the countries of Central and Eastern Europe.

**North Atlantic Treaty Organization (NATO):** a military alliance created in 1949 in order to deter a Soviet attack on Western Europe.

**Nuclear Nonproliferation Treaty (1968):** an international agreement that seeks to prevent horizontal proliferation.

**Nuclear utilization theory:** a body of strategic thought that claims deterrent threats could be more credible if nuclear weapons were made more usable.

**Oil shocks:** the rapid increases in oil prices in the aftermath of Yom Kippur War, the revolution in Iran, and the invasion of Kuwait.

**OPEC:** Organization of Petroleum Exporting Countries.

**OPEC decade:** the period between October 1973 and March 1983, which saw the rise and decline of OPEC's power in the world political economy.

**Open economic system:** a system based on a market economy.

**Open skys proposal (1955):** a call for allowing aerial reconnaissance to monitor military maneuvers.

**Operations Plan 90-1002:** a plan devised in the early 1980s that called for a massive air- and sea-lift of U.S. military personnel and equipment in the event of conflict in a distant region where the U.S. had no military bases.

**Orderly Market Arrangements (OMAs):** voluntary export restriction that involve a government-to-government agreement and often specific rules of management.

**Organization for the Prevention of Chemical Weapons (OPCW):** an international organization headquartered in The Hague that is designed to control chemical weapons.

**Ozone depletion:** the thinning of the ozone layer in the upper atmosphere due to the release of chlorofluorocarbons.

**Pacta sunt servanda:** the norm that treaties are binding.

**Paradigm:** a theoretical perspective that gives direction to research by indicating what problems in a field of inquiry are more important than others and what criteria should govern their investigation.

**Parallel currency:** the universal acceptance of the dollar in the immediate postwar period as the currency against which every other country sold or redeemed its own national currency in the exchange markets.

**Pattern:** a regularized configuration of features.

**Peacekeeping:** the use of a United Nations military force to function as a buffer between disputants in order to prevent fighting.

**Perestroika:** the Russian word for Mikhail Gorbachev's policy of economic restructuring.

**Physical Quality of Life Index (PQLI):** an index that uses life expectancy, infant mortality, and literacy rates to assess progress in meeting basic human needs.

**Plaza agreement (1985):** an arrangement by the major industrialized nations to coordinate efforts at managing exchange rates internationally and interest rates domestically.

**Pluralist decision making:** a model of the policy-making process that highlights the impact of competitive domestic groups in pressuring the government for policies responsive to their interests and needs.

**Political idealism:** an approach to international relations that assumes people are not by nature sinful or wicked, and that harmful behavior is the result of structural arrangements that motivate people act selfishly.

**Political integration:** the process or the product of efforts to build new political communities and supranational institutions that transcend the nation-state.

**Political realism:** an approach to international relations that assumes people by nature are sinful or wicked, and that the purpose of statecraft is to acquire the power needed to survive in a hostile environment.

**Pooled sovereignty:** the sharing of decision-making responsibility among several governments and between them and international institutions.

**Population momentum:** the concept that population growth will continue for several decades after replacement-level fertility is achieved.

**Postbehavioralism:** an approach to the study of international relations that calls for increased attention to the policy relevance of research.

**Postmodernism:**  an approach to the study of international relations that emphasizes the study of texts, hidden meanings, and discourse in the writing and speeches of those policymakers and analysts who interpret world affairs.

**Power transition theory:**  the contention that war is most likely when the differentials between the capabilities of rival states narrow.

**Preferential trade:**  the granting of special trade treatment to certain states.

**Price inelasticity of demand:**  a condition where price increases have little impact on the amount of a commodity that is consumed.

**Price inelasticity of supply:**  a condition where new producers of a commodity cannot enter a market to take advantage of higher rates of return.

**Primary products:**  raw materials and agricultural products.

**Private international law:**  law pertaining to routinized transnational intercourse between or among nongovernmental actors.

**Procedural rationality:**  a conceptualization of rationality that is based on perfect information and a careful weighing of all possible courses of action.

**Pronatalist policy:**  a conscious governmental attempt to increase fertility.

**Protectionism:**  the use of tariff and nontariff barrier to restrict imports.

**Public international law:**  law pertaining to government-to-government relations.

**Rapacki Plan (1957):**  a call for the denuclearization of Central Europe.

**Rational decision-making model:**  an idealized portrayal of decision making according to which the individual uses the best information available to choose from the set of possible responses that alternative most likely to maximize his or her goals.

**Reagan Doctrine:**  a pledge of U.S. support for anticommunist insurgents who sought to overthrow Soviet-supported governments.

**Rebus sic stantibus:**  the norm that reserves the right of states to terminate treaties unilaterally if conditions at the time of the signing have since changed.

**Relative burden of military spending:**  the ratio of defense spending to gross national product.

**Reparations:**  compensation paid by a defeated state for damages or expenditures sustained by the victor during hostilities.

**Reprisal:**  hostile and illegal retaliatory acts.

**Retorsion:**  hostile but legal retaliatory acts.

**Reversible conservation measures:**  nonpermanent conservation measures that often derive from behavioral changes.

**SALT (Strategic Arms Limitations Talks):**  two sets of agreements reached during the 1970s between the United States and the Soviet Union that established limits on strategic nuclear delivery systems.

**Satisficing behavior:**  the propensity of decision makers to select the choice that meets minimally acceptable standards.

**Schematic reasoning:**  the processing of new information according to a memory structure that contains a network of genetic scripts, metaphors, and stereotypical characters.

**Second-strike capability:**  the capacity of a state to retaliate after absorbing a first strike attack.

**Second World:**  a group of countries that possessed centrally planned economies. It consisted of the Soviet Union and its allies in Eastern Europe during the Cold War.

**Secretary-General:**  the chief administrative officer of tne United Nations and the head of the Secretariat, one of the six principal organs established by the United Nations Charter.

**Security Council:**  one of six principle organs established by the UN Charter. Its primary responsibility is the maintenance of international peace and security.

**Security dilemma:** the propensity of armaments undertaken by one state for ostensibly defensive purposes to be perceived by others as threatening.

**Self-determination:** the doctrine that asserts nationalities have the right to determine what political authority will represent and rule them.

**SLBM:** submarine-launched ballistic missile.

**Soft power:** the ability to exercise influence in world politics due to such intangible resources as the user's culture and ideas.

**Sovereignty:** the principle that no authority is above the state.

**Special drawing rights (SDRs):** reserves created and held by the International Monetary Fund (IMF) that member states can draw upon to help manage the values of their currencies.

**Sphere of influence:** a region dominated by the power of a foreign state.

**Spillaround:** the stagnation or encapsulation of regional integration activities.

**Spillback:** the failure of regional integration.

**Spillover:** within the process of international integration, the deepening of ties among states in one sector or expansion of ties to another sector.

**Spiral model:** a metaphor used to describe the tendency of efforts to enhance defense to result in escalating arms races.

**STABEX:** a compensatory financing scheme created by the European Community for the benefit of the ACP nations.

**Standard operating procedures (SOPs):** established methods to be followed for the performance of designated tasks.

**START (Strategic Arms Reduction Talks):** a series of negotiations that led to a 1991 treaty to reduce U.S. and Soviet strategic forces.

**State:** a legal entity that possesses a permanent population, a well-defined territory, and a government capable of exercising sovereignty.

**State terrorism:** the support of terrorist groups by governmental authorities.

**Strategic Defense Initiative (SDI):** a ballistic missile defense system using space-based laser technology.

**Summit conference:** personal diplomatic negotiations between national leaders.

**Supranational authority:** the power of an international institution to make decisions binding on its national members without being subject to their individual approval.

**Sustainable development:** economic growth that does not deplete the resources needed to maintain growth.

**System transformation:** profound changes in the units that make up the international system, the predominant foreign policy goals that the units seek, or what the units can do to each other with their military and economic capabilities.

**Terms of trade:** the ratio of export prices to import prices. Developing nations believe that the prices they receive for their exports fall in the long run, while the prices of the manufactured goods they import increase steadily.

**Theory:** a set of interrelated propositions that purports to explain or predict.

**Third World:** a term commonly used to refer to the world's poorer, economically less developed countries. It includes all of Asia, the Middle East, and Oceania except Israel, Japan, Turkey, Australia, and New Zealand, all of Africa except South Africa, and all of the Western Hemisphere except Canada and the United States.

**Three Mile Island nuclear accident:** an accident in Pennsylvania during 1979 that resulted in the largest-ever level of radioactive contamination by the U.S. commercial nuclear industry.

**Tied aid:** the existence of conditions or "strings" attached to foreign aid.

**Tokyo Round of GATT:** multilateral of trade negotiations held between 1973 and 1979.

**Tragedy of the Commons:** a metaphor widely used to explain the impact of human behavior on ecological systems. Rational self-interested behavior by individuals may have a destructive collective impact.

**Transfer-pricing mechanism:** the trading of commodities between a parent company's subsidiaries in different countries in order to record profits in jurisdictions where taxes are low.

**Treaty of Rome (1957):** the agreement that created the European Economic Community, popularly known for many years as the European Common Market.

**Truman Doctrine:** the declaration by U.S. President Harry S Truman that the policy of the United States must support "free peoples who are resisting attempted subjugation by armed minorities or by outside pressures."

**Unipolar:** an international system containing a single dominant power center.

**Unitary actor:** a conceptualization based on the assumption that all states and individuals responsible for their foreign policies confront the problem of national survival in similar ways.

**United Nations Conference on Trade and Development (UNCTAD):** a special trade conference held in Geneva during 1964 that has become a regular forum for developing world trade policies.

**United Nations Educational, Scientific and Cultural Organization (UNESCO):** the UN Specialized Agency responsible for promoting cooperation in the fields of education, science, and culture.

**United Nations Emergency Force (UNEF):** authorized by the General Assembly in 1956 under the Uniting for Peace procedures to attempt to restore peace in the Middle East following the outbreak of war between Egypt and a coalition of Israel, Britain, and France.

**Uniting for Peace Resolution:** a device which empowered the United Nations General Assembly to meet in emergency sessions to deal with threats to peace and acts of aggression.

**Vertical nuclear proliferation:** an increase in the capabilities of existing nuclear powers.

**Vertical legal system of law:** a centralized, hierarchical legal system.

**Voluntary Export Restrictions (VERs):** a generic term for all bilaterally agreed restraints on trade.

**War contagion:** a metaphor that likens the diffusion of war to the spread of disease.

**War weariness hypothesis:** the contention that a nation at war will become exhausted and lose its enthusiasm for another war, but only for a time.

**Warsaw Pact:** a military alliance created by the Soviet Union in 1955 that included communist regimes in Eastern Europe; disbanded in 1991.

**Washington Naval Conferences (1921-1922):** arms control meetings that resulted in an agreement among the U.S., Britain, France, Japan, and Italy to adjust relative tonnage of their fleets.

**Weighted voting:** a system in which votes are distributed among states in proportion to their financial contribution to an organization.

**World federalism:** an approach to integration based on the merger of previously sovereign states into a single federal union.

**World-system theory:** a theory that claims there is an international division of labor in which core states specialize in the capital-intensive production of sophisticated manufactured goods and peripheral states concentrate on the labor-intensive production of raw materials and agricultural commodities.

**World Trade Organization (WTO):** a multilateral agency established as part of the trade reform pact signed by GATT negotiators in Morocco during 1994.

**Yalta Conference (1945):** a meeting of Winston Churchill, Franklin Roosevelt, and Joseph Stalin in the Russian Crimea to design a new, post-World War II order.

**Yoshida Doctrine:** a security policy proposing that Japan should avoid international disputes, keep a low profile on divisive global issues, and concentrate on economic pursuits.

**Zero-sum:** the perception that gains for one side in a rivalry are losses for the other side.

# ACKNOWLEDGMENTS

**Box 3.2:** From George F. Kennan, *American Diplomacy, 1900–1950* (1951: New American Library), p. 59. Reprinted by permission of University of Chicago Press and the author.

**Box 5.1:** From *Preparing for the Twenty-first Century* by Paul Kennedy. Copyright © 1993 by Paul Kennedy. Reprinted by permission of Random House and David Higham Associates.

**Box 5.2:** From Brian Wallace, "True Grit South of the Border," *OSCEOLA*, January 13, 1978, pp. 15–16.

**Box 6.1:** From *Preparing for the Twenty-first Century* by Paul Kennedy. Copyright © 1993 by Paul Kennedy. Reprinted by permission of Randon House and David Higham Associates.

**Table 6.2:** Source: *The Economist* (1992: 22, 53). © 1992 The Economist Newspaper Group, Inc. Reprinted with Permission. Further reproduction prohibited.

**Table 6.3:** Source: Rudolph C. Ryser, "Fourth World Wars: Indigenous Nationalism and the Emerging New International Political Order," pp. 304–315 in Menno Bolt and J. Anthony Long in association with Leroy Little Bear, eds., *The Quest for Justice* (Toronto: Univ. of Toronto Press, Inc.). Reprinted with the permission of the publisher.

**Box 7.1:** From *World Development Report 1985*, p. 15. Copyright 1985 by the International Bank for Reconstruction and Development/The World Bank. Reprinted by permission of Oxford University Press, Inc.

**Box 7.3:** From David Rosen, *The Basics of Foreign Trade and Exchange* (New York: Federal Reserve Bank of New York, 1987). Reprinted by permission.

**Box 7.4:** From *World Development Report 1987*, p. 141. Copyright 1987 by the International Bank for Reconstruction and Development/The World Bank. Reprinted by permission of Oxford University Press, Inc.

**Box 7.5:** From Paul Krugman: *The Age of Diminished Expectations: U.S. Economic Policy in the 1990s* (Cambridge, Mass.: MIT Press), p. 105.

**Box 8.1:** From *World Development Report 1991*, p. 22. (New York: Oxford University Press, 1991).

**Figure 8.5:** Source: World Bank's Debt Tables, 1991–92, from which *International Economic Diplomacy* developed these figures. Reprinted with permission from *International Economic Diplomacy*. Copyright © 1992 by the Foundation for Teaching Economics and the United Nations Association of the USA.

**Box 9.1:** "The Secret of the Persian Chessboard," Carl Sagan, *Parade*, February 14, 1989, p. 14. Reprinted by permission of the author.

**Box 11.3:** From *World Security: Trends and Challenges at Century's End* by Michael T. Klare and Daniel C. Thomas. Copyright © 1991. Reprinted with permission of St. Martin's Press, Inc.

**Box 12.1:** Sources: "A Physician's View" from International Physicians for the Prevention of Nuclear Was, Associated Press, March 8, 1980. "The View of Atmospheric Scientists" reprinted with permission from *Journal of Peace Research*, 30, November 1993, p. 369, by Carl Sagan and Richard Turco, copyright 1993, by permission of Sage Publications Ltd.

**Box 12.2:** From Deutsch, Karl W., *Politics and Government*. Copyright © 1974 by Houghton Mifflin Company. Used with permission

**Box 12.3:** From the Playboy column titled "Reporter's Notebook: Terrible Payback," by by Robert Scheer. Reproduced by special permission of *Playboy* magazine. Copyright © 1993 by Playboy.

**Box 13.1:** From Innis L. Claude, in *Review of International Studies*, Vol. 15 (January 1989). Reprinted with the permission of Cambridge University Press.

**Figure 13.1:** From NEWSWEEK, January 11, 1993, p. 17. Newsweek, Inc. All rights reserved. Reprinted by permission.

# Author Index

• • •

Abdolali, N., 444
Abrahamsson, B. J., 338
Adelman, K. L., 403
Aho, C. M., 219, 223
Akehurst, M., 508*n1*
Albright, D., 392, 394, 395
Aldrich, J. H., 487*n13*
Alger, C., 164, 530
Allison, G. T., 48, 53, 53*n4*, 54, 425
Ambrose, S. E., 211
Amin, S., 129*n8*, 137*n10*
Amuzegar, J., 284, 342, 350
Angell, N., 19*n6*
Ansari, J., 134, 135
Apter, D. E., 184
Arad, R. W., 359
Arad, U. B., 359
Arkin, W. D., 465
Arms Control Association *Fact Sheet*, 389, 391, 393, 394, 412, 492, 493, 494
Ashley, R. K., 28*n10*, 28*n11*
Aspin, L., 418
Atkinson, R., 48–49, 55

Attali, J., 73
Auerbach, S., 365, 386
Augustine, N. R., 403
Axell, K., 429, 430, 445, 455, 456
Axelrod, R., 208*n3*
Azar, E. F., 93

Babai, D., 237
Baker, J. A., 73
Baldwin, D. A., 31, 208*n3*, 360, 373, 443
Ball, G. W., 176, 391, 392
Ball, N., 144, 146, 380, 386, 432
Bandow, D., 275
Baran, P., 137*n10*
Barber, B. R., 195, 545
Barkun, M., 514
Barnaby, F., 322
Barnes, F., 309, 410
Barnet, R. J., 100, 176, 188, 189, 309, 319, 333, 455, 504, 540
Baron, S. H., 61
Baumann, R. A., 453
Beer, F. A., 437

• • •

613

# Subject Index

· · ·

foreign aid and, 276–278
foreign policy decision making and, 46
free trade and protectionism and, 238–241
leader role and, 61
migration, 309–310
multinational corporations (MNC) and, 187–188
neorealist school and, 30
population growth and, 312
refugees and, 306, 308
Soviet Union, 98, 99–100, 103, 104
warfare and, 459–460
Dominican Republic, military intervention in, 461
Domino theory, Cold War and, 89
Drought, population growth, 304
Drug trafficking, United Nations and, 163
Dualism, developing countries and, 134–135
Dubos, René, 551
Dulles, John Foster, 16n2, 89, 95, 406, 459
Dunkirk, France, 83

Eagleburger, Lawrence, 109, 413n8, 414, 484
Earth Summit (Rio de Janeiro), 328, 330, 331
East Asia, military expenditures, 383
Eastern Europe
    debt of, 282
    economic power and, 201
    environmental degradation, 327
    foreign aid, 274
    international monetary system and, 223
    migration, 308
Eban, Abba, 508
Ecological perspective. *See also* Environmental
        degradation
    cooperation and, 327–332
        freedom and, 331–332
        global warming, 330–331
        overview, 327–328
        ozone depletion, 328–330
    demography, 294–310. *See also* Demography
    described, 291
    human needs, 561–562
    population pressure and, 291–292
    tragedy of the commons, 292–293
Economic Community of West African States
        (ECOWAS), 175
Economic development. *See also* Developing countries
    civil war and, 459
    communism and, 442
    culture and, 130
    debt crisis and, 284, 285n10
    decision making and, 65–66
    democratization and, 276–278
    developing countries and, 253–254, 255–256, 260
    energy consumption and, 335, 336, 339, 343–345

human development and, 129, 131–132
international trade and, 223, 224
least developed countries, 123–126
measurement techniques and, 129, 131–133
military expenditures and, 401–405
neoliberal school and, 31
newly industrialized countries, 127–129, 139
North-South conflict, 111–112. *See also* North-South
        conflict
oil-exporting countries, 127
population growth and, 310, 314–315
post-Cold War era, foreign policy, 425
theoretical perspectives on, 136–139
    dependency theory, 38, 136–138
    liberal economic development theory, 136
    world-system theory, 38, 138–139
United Nations and, 162
warfare causes and, 439–440
Economic factors. *See also* Employment
    arms race and, 504n18
    arms trade motive, 385
    commodity exports, resource power, 357–358
    United Nations, 535
Economic growth. *See* Economic development
Economic power
    China, 421
    European Union and, 170–172
    Germany, 423
    imperialism and, 119
    international system and, 6
    Japan, 422
    multinational corporations (MNC), 177–181
    national power and, 376, 378
    national security and, 199–200
    neocolonialism and, 113
    neoliberal school and, 32
    post-Cold War era, 106, 107, 108–109, 413–414,
        555–556
        multipolarity, 484
        redefinitions required, 425–426
    realist school and, 23
Economic sanctions, 360–367
    failures in, 360–362
    future use of, 367
    generally, 360
    rationale for, 365–367
    successes in, 362–364
    warfare and, 519
Economic transnationalism, neoliberal school
        and, 32
Economic unions, increase in, 6
Ecosphere, human history and, 3–4
Education
    military expenditures and, 400, 401

Sri Lanka, population growth, 305
STABEX, 270–271
Stability, international institutions and, 208n3. *See also* Hegemonic stability theory
Stalin, Joseph, 83, 87, 95
Standard operating procedure, decision making and, 53
State Department, decision making and, 52
Statehood, international law and, 509
State system. *See* Nation-state
State terrorism, 463–464
Stealth technology, 389
Stock markets, international monetary system and, 219, 220, 222
Stockpiling
  chemical and biological weapons, 390–391
  commodity exports, resource power, 358
  nuclear weapons, 388
Stoiber, Edmund, 543
Strategic Arms Limitation Treaty (SALT), 97, 408, 503
Strategic Arms Reduction Treaty (START), 98, 411, 494, 496, 498–499, 500–502
Strategic Defense Initiative (SDI, 1983–1993), military power, 409–410
Strategic trade, described, 232, 234
Strong, Maurice, 332
Structural Impediments Initiative (SII), 245
Structuralism
  Cold War and, 88
  World War I, 76–77
Structural realism. *See* Neorealist school
Subsidies, agriculture, 241
Sudan, food production, 319
Sudetenland, World War II, 83
Sugar, commodity exports, 356
Summitry, arms control and, 491
Super 301 provision, international trade, 243, 246n12
Supranationalism, European Union and, 167, 170
Sustainable development concept. *See also* Economic development
  environmental degradation, 327
  foreign aid, 275
  post-Cold War era, 561–562
Sutherland, Peter, 199, 241
Sweden
  European Free Trade Association (EFTA), 171
  European Union, 164, 170, 171
  warfare and, 436
Switzerland
  decision making, 67
  European Free Trade Association (EFTA), 171
  European Union, 171
  geopolitics and, 63
  migration, 309

military expenditures, 396
  warfare and, 436
Syria
  arms import, 144
  chemical and biological weapons, 390–391
  League of Nations mandates, 121
  military expenditures, 382–383
  nuclear weapons, 393
System dynamics, warfare causes, 446–450
System level, level of analysis and, 40
Systems theory, neorealist school and, 29–31

Taiwan (Formosa)
  Cold War and, 94
  economic development, 127, 128, 263
  Formosa Straits crisis, 450
  imperialism, 117
  international trade, 235, 243, 248
  military expenditures, 383, 384
Tanganyika, 121
Tariffs
  General Agreement on Tariffs and Trade (GATT), 236–237
  history of, 225
  World Trade Organization (WTO), 242, 255, 265
Taxation
  European Union and, 172
  multinational corporations and, 187, 281
  war reparations as, 206
Taylor, Robert, 543
Tea, commodity exports, 356
Technology
  advantages and disadvantages of, 554
  agriculture and, 316
  arms trade and, 382
  Cold War and, 97
  dependency theory and, 137
  developing countries, 134, 146, 256
  energy consumption and, 336
  environmental degradation, 327
  human history and, 4
  imperialism, 116
  international trade and, 268
  military expenditure and, 378
  military power, 387–391
    balance of power, 474
    chemical and biological weapons, 390–391
    delivery capabilities, 388–390
    missile technology, 144, 146, 409–410, 480, 493, 500–502
    nuclear weapons, 387–388
    warfare and, 432
  multinational corporations, 177–178n8, 279